P9-BZK-733

A Bishop's Confession

JIM BISHOP

A
BISHOP'S
CONFESSION

1907-1987

LITTLE, BROWN AND COMPANY
BOSTON · TORONTO

FIRST EDITION

Lines from "At the Grave of Henry James" copyright 1941, renewed
1969 by W. H. Auden, from *Collected Shorter Poems 1927–1957* by
W. H. Auden. Reprinted with permission of Random House, Inc.,
and Faber and Faber Ltd.

Library of Congress Cataloging in Publication Data

Bishop, Jim, 1907–
  A Bishop's confession.

  1. Bishop, Jim, 1907–   2. Historians—
United States—Biography.   3. Biographers—United
States—Biography.   4. Journalists—United States—
Biography.   I. Title.
E175.5.B54A33   973'.072024   [B]   81-2570
ISBN 0-316-09669-5   AACR2

MV

Designed by Janis Capone

Published simultaneously in Canada
by Little, Brown & Company (Canada) Limited

PRINTED IN THE UNITED STATES OF AMERICA

Dedicated to
John "Jocko" McCormack,
a stand-up friend

All will be judged. Master of nuance and scruple,
Pray for me and for all writers, living or dead:
Because there are many whose works
Are in better taste than their lives, because
there is no end
To the vanity of our calling . . .

W. H. AUDEN,
"At the Grave of Henry James"

FOR THE RECORD

This is the mistake of my life. It resurrects the others. Somewhere within this massive nonsense, I looked for a triumph. What appeared to contain an essence of nobility now smells of luck and the charity of the gifted. Many held a door open for me with a foot. Until I began to write this book, I had seen myself as a sort of back-alley Irishman throwing rocks at editors. It is a lovely fiction and I should have nurtured it and taken my place in the rear bank of the great rebels.

Now, as I tread the final truths in hobnailed boots, my most acute sense is uncertainty. It is possible that the old Jim Bishop is not fit to write about the young Jim Bishop. Was he really the brash, brazen bastard I see through these bifocals? Was he the sarcastic, cocky little man who elbowed and shoved his way to positions where his most remarkable attribute was his inexperience?

He had fallen in love with words at age nine. Inside the Clinton Avenue Library in Jersey City, he found that he could be anyone he chose, go anywhere he pleased, and could, for example, share the joys of pillage and rape with Attila the Hun without understanding all the words. Among his chums, he became a storyteller. Among the nuns at Saint Patrick's School, at the same time, he became a liar who seldom had a passing grade.

Explaining him in print is not easy. He was never the great writer he wished to be, never the superb editor who won the craven adulation of his writers, never the matchless literary agent who could tell Dashiell Hammett: "You have ruined your manuscript in chapter seven, old boy. The reader already knows the butler didn't do it." As the founding editor of Gold Medal Books, he took little and created something, but then he came to despise what he had made.

As a syndicated columnist, he continues to do well after twenty-five years. There is no modesty here, because there aren't many who can tell a complete story in nine hundred words. This is the result of stealing a smidgen of style from two men who became friends — Ernest Hemingway, an author worthy of assiduous study, and Mark Hellinger, a one-time

Broadway columnist whose terse sentences and single-syllabled words came close to Indian talk.

The genesis of this book is flattery. The editors at Little, Brown thought it would be a good work. My literary agent thought it might have episodes both tragic and hilarious. I signed the contract with big flourishes, meditating on how important I am. Surely, I felt, no research would be involved. It was my life. I had lived it and could replay it in words. This, to my sorrow, is not so. An autobiography is the plundering of the human mind.

If one is not certain of his talent, one works harder. I could not write a "how-to" book, nor could I, in good conscience, locate some of the better passages of what I have written and quote them. My brother, John, asked if it would be a "warts and all" book. Yes, it would. A writer is, most of all, the nourished product of his environment. His scribblings may be full of understanding and compassion, but away from the typewriter he may be an all-purpose pain in the ass. I would have to face a portrait with a lot of shadows in the face.

As this is written — early 1980 — the book is almost complete. A last chapter is to be written. All my life, I have been a string-saver. In the adult years, I have saved calendars. All have large squares for each day's events. The dull things are perpetuated: "Sullivan's Saloon for shooting pool"; "church picnic at the grove." The important events occupy no more space than the others. I am grateful to the calendars.

My memory for precise dialogue does not match that of my sister, Adele Steencken, or my brother, John. I marveled that they could recreate family situations and speech patterns much better than I. In some cases, this led to disputes, but, when the vote was two-to-one against, they won. This was also true in conversations with old friends such as William Scanlon, Fred Grimsey, Kay Herman, Jocko McCormack, and Jerry Edelberg. The memory fonts were tapped one by one. In a utility room, all the letters, contracts, published material, and original notes are filed. My second wife, Kelly, ransacked those by month and year to fortify a misted memory.

At some point, Kelly and I tried to pinpoint the area when I became obsessed with time: (*The Day Lincoln Was Shot, The Day Christ Died,* and so on). The best we could do was to recall that, when I was doing homework as a child, my father, a police lieutenant, shared the dining room table as he wrote reports of criminal activities. His reports detailed the precise moment when he spotted a suspicious character, the time when he apprehended the person, the minute when the criminal was booked at a particular precinct. My early work on newspapers showed no special interest in time. However, in 1930, when I began to copy passages relating to the assassination of Abraham Lincoln — something I would continue until 1954 — each one was filed under the proper minute in a series of notebooks marked with each hour of the day.

The obsession led to an amusing incident. In the mid-sixties, I was at the headquarters of the Federal Bureau of Investigation as part of the research for a book called *The Day Kennedy Was Shot*. Before me were eight FBI inspectors with notebooks. I asked the questions; they tried to supply answers. I asked an inspector at what time he left the building to go to the M Street garage to vacuum the presidential limousine, which had been flown in from Dallas. He flipped his notebook. "I left here at eleven fifty-nine P.M., he said. The interview endured for hours. There was a great deal in their heads that I was trying to transfer to mine. In the afternoon, I asked another inspector: "You flew the rifle back to Washington. At what time did you reach here?"

He consulted his book. "Eleven fifty-nine P.M.," he said.

"That's funny," I said. "This inspector was leaving here at that time to go to the M Street garage." They smiled. "We know," they said. "We passed each other in the revolving door."

I would not counsel any young writer to become immersed in time. It worked for me — for a while — but it was only a distinctive format. The imaginative writer needs more room in which to paint his characters and events. It was a pleasant prison, if one enjoys constraints.

It is part of the writing of this book to acknowledge that nothing more of interest will happen in my life. No one with part of a life left to live writes an autobiography, unless, of course, he is an actor, a general, or a politician who feels that an elaborate apology is overdue. I expect to continue to tell stories, to be underpaid for them, to pen obscene poems to my wife, to play golf with ever-shortening arms, and, most of all, to do what I did at the age of nine: read.

Jim Bishop
Hallandale, Florida

CONTENTS

HO?

THE CLAY WAS HARD AND THE SKY WAS PALE AND cold. The football bounced badly on the empty lot. I stayed back as far as possible from the red-brick building which represented the goal line. Dolan was kicking good and complaining that it was suppertime. It wasn't. Everybody on Bramhall Avenue in Jersey City, New Jersey, knew when it was suppertime because dozens of windows went up and stout women called a name twice and slammed the window. The players voted Johnny Dolan down, so we played a little more. It was Gilly Newell's football. He would call the game. Dolan was bossy; he was two years older and bigger.

I made a good catch of a high hanger and ran toward the brick wall. I was small and could run, but whenever we chose players I was picked last. Two boys got to me and when I went down the clay made no dust. I slapped at the corduroy pants, but they were as tawny as the earth. Gilly took his football. The boys dogtrotted from the lot at Siedler and Bramhall in several directions. Nobody said good-bye. I stood alone in the cold, rubbing my knuckles and snuffing my nose, looking at the sky. It paled off in cold weather. There was a thin cloud torn at the edges. I could tell when it was winter even if the day was warm because when the sun went down, an edge of orange hung over Sulz's drugstore. In the summer, there was no orange — just pink ribbons or lead gray.

The sky and the sea infused me with faraway thoughts. They said so many things. I have watched the sea say five or six things in one hour. The sky, no matter what its mood, spoke slowly. I jammed my fists into my pockets and I saw her watching me. She was on the Bramhall edge of the sidewalk with a small bag of groceries. She must have thought I was weak-minded, staring up like that. I put my head down, pretending I didn't notice her. Slowly, she began walking a collision course. She wouldn't say hello. A couple of times I had said hello to Tessie McDonald, but she had shaken her head and tossed her dark hair behind her shoulders. On our block, Tessie created more hard-ons than Mae Murray, Aileen Pringle, and Nita Naldi did in hours of vamping on the silent screen. In the warm weather, when she wore a silk print dress with hibiscus flowers

[3]

on it and a tight sash, my throat slammed shut. I would not stare until she had passed, and then I would watch all the separate parts of Tessie McDonald recede like a symphony with woodwinds, brass, strings, xylophone, and drums. I could hear her.

Miss McDonald was one of the superb masturbatory fantasies. Often I bathed her slowly as she stood in the tub, torturing her with warm water and suds until a deep, almost mannish moan came from her throat. I put her to bed, tucking her in with me; I awakened her with light brushing kisses on those breasts which seemed to dangle from piano wires. This behavior, three times a day, made me the master, Tessie the slave. In real life, I had a girlfriend in Newark who wore Mary Pickford curls. She played records on an Edison talking machine and ate raw hamburger with onions. She was too pretty for fantasies; besides, when I touched her shoulder, Connie became rigid. At the age of fifteen, I was sufficiently sophisticated to know that Connie was like my mother — the kind a fellow marries. I knew why too — Chastity. But Tessie was the kind of guy could break commandments with — if she would let him.

I didn't look up as she approached because she was seventeen; she went to the movies with men of twenty and sat in the last row of the balcony. To her, I had to be Shorty, a kid. In this, Tessie was right. I was short and broad and had black shiny hair and hazel eyes with an Oriental cast. Sometime, when I was in the bathroom squeezing pimples, I tried to look at myself honestly — you know, pretend it was me (I?) — and my mind told me I had no future. I had given serious thought to two careers — a movie star or a vaudeville tap dancer — because everyone else was working in a factory. I declined to be seaweed in surf.

I was nobody among nobodies. The only important person I knew in Jersey City was my father. He was John Michael Bishop, Sr., son of Irish immigrants, a two-hundred-and-fifty-pound lieutenant of police. He was "the man" in headquarters; he had influence with Mayor Frank Hague. His notability did not penetrate my consciousness until one day when Dolan chased me and was going to punch me for breaking the stitches in his baseball. "You do," I shouted, "and I'll tell my father." It was, in retrospect, a dangerously long speech with which to stop a cocked fist. But it worked. He didn't hit me. On another occasion, a policeman caught me as I stood on Bergen Avenue where the Jersey Central Railroad passed underneath. I was trying to drop stones down the chimneys of passing locomotives. He grabbed me tightly and asked my name. Instead of giving it, I said: "I'm Lieutenant Bishop's son." He studied my face for a moment and said: "Go home before I give you a touch of the nightstick."

"Hello." I looked up from my dreaming. She stood before me, the bundle high in her arms, the collar of the coat up. The size of the smile surprised me. "I was watching you play," she said. "You know how to run."

I said: "It's cold." Tessie had a face which was almost round; it was not moonlike, but it gave the impression of broadness, as an Indian's is broad. The cold wind took the short ends of the black hair and whipped her cheeks. She was taller than I, older, perhaps wiser. Her face was frozen pink, but the smile remained constant. "Why don't you ever say hello?" she said. I couldn't think of a response. My greetings to her had been frequent. "Somebody said you're working in Wall Street," she said, I nodded.

"Lehman Brothers," I said. "They're bankers, you know."

She didn't know. It must be interesting, Tessie said. The work was dull. I was an office boy. At 16 William Street, it was my function to sit in the outer office near a bird-cage elevator and be polite to distinguished visitors — brokers, bankers, judges, millionaires. Get up from the desk, say "Good morning, sir," or "Good afternoon, sir," and point to a couch. Take the embossed calling card in to Philip, Arthur, Herbert, Allan, Harold, or Robert. That was all. They had six desks on a deep rug in a paneled office. "Show him in, Jim." "Oh, tell him I'll be with him in a minute." "Take him to the conference table and offer him a cigar."

I was accustomed to stealing a cigar. One a week. Homeward bound on the Jersey Central ferry and the train, I made one cigar last until I got to the house. When it was smoked down, dinner became tasteless. I knew that stealing was bad. Herbert H. Lehman had the best cigars. On Monday mornings, I watched him open the second drawer on the right and select a cigar from an ornate box, but he never frowned, or looked down to count. Had I outwitted a shrewd banker who would become a governor and a senator? Or, in an anginal squeeze of conscience, had I made less of a human of myself? Once, when that old dandy, Philip, departed for home early, he left an intact lunch tray in the empty board room. I turned the lock in the door, ate the cold roast beef, and drank an obnoxious substance called Fermilac Milk.

"What are you doing after supper?" I looked up. "Nothing special." This was a half-lie. I was doing something, but not special. The year before, at fourteen, I received a diploma from Father Edward Kelly, the pastor of Saint Patrick's School. Almost everyone had gone on to high school, some to Lincoln, some to Saint Peter's — but, in spite of my father's plea that I might make a good lawyer, I enrolled in Drake's School on Newark Avenue and there, close to the thunder of the Pennsylvania freight trains, I studied typing, stenography, and bookkeeping. It was a dusty room with saffron electric lights and a sweaty male teacher who explained the function of what he called "a trial balance." Few academic subjects engaged my interest. Most wars were a series of dates attached to proper names. Geography consisted of continents, products, countries, and oceans. Fundamental English, the most poorly taught of all subjects, was a mysterious maze of nouns and pronouns, adverbs, verbs, prepositions, and conjunctions.

At Saint Patrick's, there had been a Miss Alcott who sat in the fourth seat; I was in the fifth. Helen Walsh, a tiny figure who won gold medals for scholastic work, sat across from me. By raising myself slowly at the proper moment during a test, smoothing my knickerbocker trousers, and yanking my black stockings up, I developed a swift scan and a memory. They had the answers. I had the answers. In the eighth grade, an acerbic convert, Sister Maria Eustelle, more Catholic than the Pope, was pleased that I not only achieved passing grades, but seemed genuinely interested in figures of speech, such as similes, metaphors, and personification. At one point, I became so interested in etymology — truly interested — that I made a dining room table game of finding words whose definitions I did not know, and, by separating the prefix, suffix, and root, trying to define the meaning.

In Catholic schools at that time, the nuns who had pledged their lives and souls to Christ were imbued with a will to share their suffering with students. A few sisters, like Helen Dolores, would not beat a child. This was also true of the stately Sister Maria Agatha. Others, like Sister Alice Joseph, who taught the fourth grade, and Sister Maria Eustelle, the martinet of the graduating class, used ruler and pointer freely. Some used a swing which started close to the floor behind them, whistled in a perfect arc, and was stopped by welts on the hands. Once, in the graduating class, I flinched and withdrew my hand and Sister Maria Eustelle almost fell forward on her habit. "Now, Master Bishop," she said panting, "turn the hand over." She caught me on the back of the knuckles. My knees sagged. Her eyes were bright inside the white corrugation. "Once more," she said. The whole class laughed. I wept. The salt of tears hesitated on the upper lip, and curled inward. It was the last time I cried. Many years later, when I watched a mahogany lid lowered on my mother, I tried to cry and failed.

Some nuns were unfit to teach. They could neither relate to, nor capture the interest of, students and thus impart knowledge. They taught religion in a manner which inspired terror. The young mind struggled to understand that God always was, and always will be. At seven, when I received First Holy Communion, I could recite the Ten Commandments from first to last, or from last to first. No one explained adultery to us, although that was a commandment which, in violation, could condemn the guilty to eternal fires. It related, I felt, to something my mother told me: "Never touch yourself down there. It's a mortal sin." I tried urinating without hands. It was sloppy. I tried washing by dropping soapy water on it, but it felt good, so I returned to the use of two hands, which was an infantile wedding of sensory nerves. Another commandment was a rebuke about "coveting my neighbor's wife." "Covet," at age seven, was obscure, so I substituted "cover." By accident, I was on target. Later, I wondered why an eleventh commandment did not forbid coveting a neighbor's husband.

"Well, stop up and see me if you can," Tessie said. "I live over there." She pointed to an ugly two-story house on Siedler Street. I marveled at my wandering thoughts. "Sure. We can play cards or something." She started to walk away. "My father works nights," she said. I blew on my hands. I recalled that her mother was dead. If her father worked nights — well? My thought was that she would have to cook her own supper. I ran home. I always ran. I ran to the store; I ran home, to school, to church (unless my father was with us), to play street ball, ride a bicycle, whip over the uneven flagstones on roller skates, get a head start with a Flexible Flyer on a snowy hill, trot for the exuberance of endurance, to see how far I could go without stopping. I was running at top speed in many ways. I despised my neighborhood and my city with something approaching venom. If, at fifteen, a sailor had approached me and said: "Would you like to sign on for Singapore, kid?" I would have pledged my life to get aboard a rust bucket.

Nothing was right. This is an impression, not a fact. I cultivated the herd instinct of seeking friends, of learning and imitating the right and the wrong things they did. Within that small circle — Robert O'Brien, Fred Grimsey, Francis Moran, Tom Kerrigan, Arthur Taylor, Jack Aston, John Dundas, Al Porter, Bill Drummond — there was an insulation of camaraderie against the world of adults. For a few hours, in one house or another, we were the men. It was elation to mimic the old-fashioned credos of parents; to dream of a new suit of clothes with wide trousers; to betray girls with boastful lies. The sarcastic greeting of one boy to another was: "Well, did you get your end wet yet?"

Within the span of a year, between the ages of fourteen and fifteen, we had organized a counterculture. The nuns had been busy urging boys and girls toward vocations as priests and sisters; the results were negligible — two boys had "the call" and moved on to seminaries. Vincent Kane became a priest; so did Joseph Stockhammer; a third gave up the altar for the tavern. Another, who had no "call," became a flaming homosexual.

In the secretive enclave of youth, it was agreed that we should not "do it" to Catholic girls. It would be a sin, assuming that any of us understood the mechanics of "doing it." It was agreed that Protestant girls were fair game because, in our ignorance, we thought there was a chance that screwing was not forbidden in their tenets. We took turns assuring each other that the Protestants had reduced the Ten Commandments to nine, eliminating the sixth, which was driving us crazy. Black girls were also off-limits on two grounds: first, their fathers were addicted to the thoughtless use of razors; second, a fellow could catch a disease. At this time, no one had explained *what* disease, or even why Black girls monopolized it. We agreed that a disease, any disease, was something which could not be kept secret from parents — ergo, any pleasure which could not be kept from the incessant interrogation of mothers and fathers must be avoided. The sex sessions were exhilarating until the circle reached me. I told them that I dated a plump girl named Irma, a girl who attended a school in

Greenville. This was true. I spent fifty cents a ticket every Sunday to buy two box seats at the State Theatre on the Boulevard.

The reason for the box seats was that Irma and I were secluded from the orchestra and balcony seats. She allowed me to slip one hand over her shoulder and reach down and play with her right breast. I did it through six acts of vaudeville, the coming attractions, the newsreel, and a feature motion picture. I do not recall getting to the left breast because it would entail hooking my right arm around her throat and, as Irma was chewing candy all the time, and watching the show, I contented myself with one breast and consoled myself that the second must be similar to the first. On the bus homeward, Irma annoyed me with recapitulations of the show, jugglers and all. I had the barest recollection of the movie; besides, I was in abdominal pain. The third or fourth time I told the story, Bill Drummond said: "Yeah. We heard that one." This disarmed me until I could find a new and more compliant subject. Irma had been worked out. I had gone as far as she would permit. The slamming of the door, so to speak, occurred when I entreated: "Doesn't this make you hot?" She shook her head no. "It feels nice," she said.

The hallway at 573 Bramhall was always dark. The building faced on busy Jackson Avenue, a shopping area served by trolley cars. There was a fruit merchant on the ground floor. The Mansman family lived on the second floor, the Bishops on the third. I knew the flights of steps two at a time. As I opened the kitchen door, my mother stood inside. I leaned forward for the kiss. The sting of the slap was harsh. My head rocked; anger spiraled to the point where I could have strangled her. The world was bad enough without being slapped for nothing. My teeth clenched. "What was that for?" She was short and plump and pretty, a woman with long wavy hair — brown with glints of bronze — and large blue eyes. "Johnny's been playing around a bonfire again."

My cheek felt hot. "Why hit me?"

"Because you're the oldest; you're supposed to watch him." Punishment, in our family, was accepted as a concomitant to life. It had several facets: the slap; the beating with a broom; my father's predilection (rare) for taking us into the bathroom, holding us by the back of the shirt collar, and cracking his razor strop across the calves of our legs; being sent to bed without supper; denial of playtime on weekends; the threat of spiritual punishment from God, who was everywhere at all times and could see everything.

The slap, this time, was one too many. I told my mother I was going to leave. She flipped the codfish cakes over in a smoky pan. "I'll help you pack," she said.

When supper was ready, I sat with my brother, John, younger by two years, and my sister, Adele, younger by four. When my mother brought the pan to the table, she was blinking tears. My spirits fell. "I'm sorry," I said. "I didn't mean it."

"Why?" she snapped. "You think I'm crying? Ha! The smoke from fishcakes blinds me. You go. I don't need you, Lonnie."

Lonnie. Another sore spot. I had gone through school thinking my name was Alonzo James Bishop. My mother insisted that I had been named after her father, Alonzo Tier, a policeman; and James Bishop, my paternal grandfather, who worked in a Jersey City oil refinery and died before I was born. James, she told me, had died in 1904, so she had placed her father's name first. Father Scharken of Saint Paul's R.C. Church had said: "The saint's name will come first." The fiction of Alonzo and Lonnie led to fistfights in school. When it was enunciated in baby talk, it led to a challenge to meet in an empty lot at Forest Street and Ocean Avenue after school. My classmates did not know that I was addicted to nosebleeds.

The fight over the name Alonzo enjoyed its longest engagement with a classmate named Donald Gildea. He was my size and less belligerent. The bigger boys engendered the battle by telling Donald that I said he was a coward; they told me he said Alonzo was a sissy name. The first time we met in the empty lot, I sent Donald to the grass with one punch. This was a grievous error. He remained there, bleeding and crying. The bigger boys set up a return match. Gildea knocked me down four times. My face was a ruddy smear. I had nothing left except courage. Each time, I crouched on hands and knees, trying to stand. And each time, Donald sent me sprawling. The older boys stopped it, took a look at my face, and ran. I had no handkerchief; I was accustomed to wiping my nose on my sleeve.

At home, my father was unbuttoning his uniform and placing his gun, handcuffs, and police shield in a drawer, which he locked. "What happened to you?" he said. I looked up at him.

"What the hell do you think happened?" I said. My errors were never so flagrant that I couldn't compound them. His left hand whistled and caught me on the side of the head. I went under a table.

"Don't ever use those words with me again," he said, and walked into the bedroom for a nap. My mother crouched and petted me. I felt sick; sick of life, sick of living. There would be another fight with Gildea in a few days. And another. I would not win one. Sometimes Gildea would beg me not to get up again. On one occasion, tears sprang to his eyes as I set my hands on the grass and slowly stood.

When I was fourteen, my father sent me to the Bureau of Vital Statistics for working papers. I required a birth certificate. The clerk ran through the files and, with flourishing penmanship, filled out a large certificate. He tossed it at me. "No Alonzo Bishop for your date of birth," he said. "Just a James A."

BUREAU OF VITAL STATISTICS

Court House, Jersey City, N.J.

FACSIMILE OF RECORD OF BIRTH

ISSUED Aug. 2 1922....

PLACE OF BIRTH: Jersey City   ADDRESS OF MOTHER: 113 Linden Ave.

FULL NAME OF CHILD: James Alonzo Bishop

SEX: Male   DATE OF BIRTH: November 21, 1907

FATHER: John M. Bishop   White   24   Flagman

MOTHER: Jenny Tier   White   23   Is mother married to father of
    child? . . . . . Yes.

BIRTHPLACE: U.S.

I hereby certify that I attended the birth of this child, who was born alive
on the date above stated.

SIGNED: *F. E. Lambert*, M.D.

I dropped Alonzo and Lonnie. "You'll be Lonnie to me as long as you
live," my mother said. I spread the word. Nobody believed me. James,
to me, was only slightly less repugnant than Alonzo. Jim sounded natural,
unaffected. I made a point of being introduced as "Jim." Chaos developed
when friends gave my name as Jim and followed it by saying: "What's
new, Lonnie?" Michael Heir, who sold clothes on the time-payment plan,
said: "I thought you was a Spaniard. You look Spanish." Mr. Apple, the
butcher, was willing to toss a marrowbone or a pound of frankfurters into
each order of meat, but he said he couldn't think of me as Jim. "You don't
look like no Jim," he said. "Archie maybe. Algernon." Mike Ceretta, the
barber, snapped the scissors behind my head and said: "Okay. It's Jimmo.
Your father and I go back a long way. The Irish never say Jim. It's
Jimmo." Mr. David Bloom, who owned one of the first Greenville Line
buses, shrugged with Hebraic philosophy. "Your father, to me, is lieutenant. Even when we're playing pinochle he's lieutenant. You I see as
Lonnie. When I say Lonnie, if you think Jim, feel free."

Part of my work around the house was to wash the supper dishes. We
ate at five-thirty P.M. and I was washing by six. Johnny dried. My mother
was teaching Adele to sew. Dishes were drudgery. Their filth is enduring.
A clean dish in a closet has no function except to be soiled. John and I
vowed that when Adele was old enough to wash and dry, we would use
extra knives, forks, spoons, and side dishes for everything. The thought of
revenging ourselves was consolation. She was a skinny-legged, fragile mite
who faithfully carried tales of our misdeeds from teacher to parent. My
brother and I knew that Adele was good because she didn't have the nerve
to be bad. On Saturday mornings, none of us was allowed out to play. We
had to dust the furniture, wax and polish, press our trousers and jackets

under a damp cloth, shine our shoes on a toilet seat, and do the grocery shopping. At noon, Mother walked around the house rubbing a finger on the underside of tables and chairs. If she saw dust, her voice became over-calm. "This," she would say, "is still dirty. Now I don't know who did it and I don't want to hear. You must learn to do everything thoroughly. You may all start at the beginning." Pleading, begging, promising availed us nothing. We could hear the joyful shouts of the children in the streets. On the second time around, we were not allowed to finish the work quickly. "Do it again," she would say. Our wails of grief did not affect her personal weekend work, which was the baking of layer cakes and tea biscuits, the making of apple and berry pies, and, in the autumn, the stewing and canning of vegetables and fruits, the boiling of grape jelly and grape jam.

In good moods, which were frequent, she had a low soft laugh. A gold tooth showed. She told us stories of her girlhood, of how she fed two hundred chickens every morning before attending school; of jealousy of her younger sister, Henrietta, who would squirm onto their father's lap and cuddle; Jenny couldn't. Henrietta could hug their mother; Jenny couldn't. She would tell, again and again, how she was working in the cotton mill when she met my father. He was tall, thin, and ambitious. He frequently alluded to making "something" of himself. They dated steadily for six years, "not counting," as my father often interjected, "the one year we weren't speaking."

Listening, remembering, fitting separate pieces of information together, I concluded that the Bishop side of the family had been hit with considerable misfortune. Jim Bishop came to America from Lower Scoby, County Wexford, Ireland, around 1880. He gave up a fifty-acre farm which could no longer support the hungry people that worked it. He crossed the Hudson from Ellis Island to Jersey, fell in with some other Wexfordians, and got a job as a fireman in an oil refinery in Jersey City. Winter and summer, the short stocky man shoveled bituminous coal from dawn to sunset. Mary Murphy, born in 1854 on a ship passing through the Gibraltar Strait, was born to a Corkonian who was on his way to the Crimean War as a British colour sergeant. At her birth, her mother died. Mary Murphy grew up under a stepmother who, she insisted, was "kind and good." Mary came to America in the steerage of a sailing ship and got a job working as a maid for rich Jews in Washington Heights, New York. She wore a white uniform with a puffy hat. The employers were so generous when she was ill that, for the remainder of her days, she would not permit a word of anti-Semitism, even in jest. When she met and married Jim Bishop, she wore their poverty as a snapping banner of pride.

John, the firstborn, weeded a farm on Fulton Avenue, Jersey City, from dawn until the schoolbell rang at Saint Paul's. He earned two dollars a week and his mother gave him five cents for the uncertain purchase of a baseball, or to save up for a rugby ball. The gracelessness of poverty is that it is never static. It grows worse. There were five children. Jim, the father, contracted what is now called silicosis from breathing the dark diamonds of coal. The family called it "the asthma." When attacks came, the oil refinery did not pay him. The doctor said that there were but two remedies for it: either return to Ireland for a year and breathe the clear air, or get a pint of whiskey and down it at a gulp. Mary Murphy Bishop detested whiskey almost as deeply as she did the devil — and the devil, to her, was a real being with cloven hooves and a forked tail.

On subzero nights, young John was awakened gently. "Your father is having an attack. Hurry. Get into your clothes and run up to Finn's and tell him to fill this pint bottle." She knelt beside the bed on which her husband begged for breath and murmured a rosary. John ran to Jackson Avenue and got Finn out of bed and hurried home with the filled bottle. It cost twenty cents; Finn marked it in a book. Jim Bishop drank and gurgled until the whiskey slopped down his neck onto the bed. The odor, even the presence of it, sickened Mary. "That stuff has destroyed more men than the plague," she said. After a few minutes, her husband began to breathe easily. The magic of whiskey — especially as a specific for warding off sudden death — was permanently fixed in my father's mind.

In early winter, 1895, all five children had sore throats. The doctor examined them and said: "Diphtheria." Nothing, he said, could be done. Three of the five — Jim, Mary, and Margaret — died in Christmas week. The decorated spruce went into the refuse can as old man Routh arrived with three small white caskets. He closed the folding doors to the parlor. In the kitchen, Mary stirred a pot of vegetable soup simmering on a back lid of the stove as young John and Tom sat watching. They were fearful and silent. She did not cry. When Routh was ready, he opened the folding doors. Mary Murphy Bishop wiped her hands, took her apron off, and walked into the room. She looked at the small colorless imitations of faces she once knew. They were wearing better clothes than they had in life. She knelt, clasped her hands, lifted her eyes to the ceiling, and said loudly: "Thy will be done."

Later, she would give birth to two more girls, and name them Margaret and Mary, after the two who had left. She understood hardship, expected it. As the century turned, she borrowed money to send her husband back to Ireland. He remained a year with his brothers, but they treated him askance because they said he was a victim of "the trouble." It was a terrifying year for his wife, trying to find work and feed babies, but when he returned, Jim Bishop died. For an hour, perhaps more, Mary appeared to have been crushed. Then she put a shawl over her head and walked four houses to the landlord. He tried to console her. "I didn't come here for that, Mr. Mulligan," she said. "I am here to tell you that the rent is going to be a few days late this time. If Mrs. Mulligan will pass the word to the women of the neighborhood that I'll be taking in washing, I'll be grateful to her."

It was an old story; not a matter on which to dwell, but when I had to do something distasteful, such as washing dishes, the Bishop family history made me feel courageous. The old lady was heroic. She truly believed that life was a series of severe blows through which God tested faith. She had it, and she was sure that she would serve an indeterminate sentence in purgatory, and then be brought to the heavenly radiance of God's face.

When the dishes were finished, I washed, combed my hair, spread a little of my mother's powder over the acne with a small puff, and shined my best shoes.

"Where are you going?"

"I have a date."

"You have a date?"

"Sure. I'll be in by ten or a little after."

"With a girl?"

"Tessie. Lives on Siedler Street."

"Tessie? You're not going. She's too old for you."

"She's inviting a few people over, fellows and girls."

"Who?"

"People."

"That's the one whose mother died."

"Her father is home."

"Oh." (Recreating fairly accurate dialogue is akin to rebuilding a brick wall which has caved in. I consulted with my brother and sister, some relatives, and warm friends in Jersey City and other places — some of whom were reluctant to recreate scenes. Cementing the old bricks in place to restore the edifice of a life was not much of a problem, but I am certain that the bricks have not been restored to their original places. The dialogue is as close as an assortment of memories can make it.)

It was good that she did not forbid me, because I would have gone anyway. Although, of the three children, I was her "favorite," it is doubtful that her love for me matched mine for her. I could walk out — as I would on this night — and hope to achieve my first sexual adventure. The thought, which sometimes flitted across the landscape of my mind like a summer shower, was noisy and repelling. Life had wronged my mother in several ways, and I was aware of them. As a child, she needed love and received little. Her older brother, Willie, and her younger sister, Etta, won the kisses and the approval of Alonzo Tier and his severe wife, Mary McSwiggen Tier. Jenny was the drudge.

No one invited her to a ball. The young men who admired a pretty face and carriage were discouraged by her mother. Grandma Tier, a self-confident woman with a roll of hair which broke like a wave and spumed upward to a mousy brown and white bun, was God-conscious and class-conscious. She taught her daughters that sex in marriage was designed for two purposes: to be blessed with babies, and to calm the lustful ferocity of the male. It was a female duty never to participate in these acts; they should permit a husband access to their bodies on occasion, but never, never should encourage him. Jenny said that if she ever got married, she would slip into bed and pull a pillow over her face. She did.

When the tall, cavernously thin, John Bishop met her in the cotton mill, he pursued Jenny with indomitable respect. He accorded her the niceties which were alien to him: holding a door open for her; taking her to early basketball games featured by postgame dances; walking at night to outdoor nickelodeons where, for an extra five cents, he could buy two rattan mats for use on the backless benches; bringing her home no later than the stroke of ten. Inside the vestibule, John Bishop applied his ardor to Jenny, but it was futile. Her mother had been sitting behind the lace curtains since nine-thirty and she thought of herself as generous, allowing him five minutes in which to become excited. Then her finger pushed the door buzzer, and remained on it until Jenny said: "John, stop. My mother knows we're here."

There is a philosophic question whether two persons, deeply in love, are suited to each other. Is love enough? The masters of the sonnet say yes. They are in error. The love between these two would prove, in time, to be unquenchable, but it would be crippled by divergent goals. Jenny wanted a "steady" man who would work hard toward buying a home, having children, living close to God and church, and who would enjoy a small pension in age. John was aflame with desire, knowledge through study; ambition to climb all the rungs to success, to be important and command the respect of his fellows, to chase any woman who smiled at him. After working in the cotton mill, he started as a brakeman on the Pennsylvania Railroad, moved up to become the youngest conductor, dropped it to don the uniform of a policeman, and, in 1921, became the most knowledgeable lieutenant on the force.

He bought sets of encyclopedias on the time-payment plan and read all the volumes, starting with page 1, volume 1. He studied astronomy until he could tell, by looking at his watch, which star, which constellation was at the zenith in the heavens any night of the year. He bought the most advanced books on police procedure, took all tests. He never ranked below second; attended night school at Number 14 school on Union Street; and bought standing-room-only tickets for the great operas at the Metropolitan. He filled out his frame and became a dashing, proud figure, one who walked with his head thrown back. He took lessons on a B-flat cornet and was accepted by the Elks Band (Lodge 211) and the Jersey City police band, which gave concerts in Hudson County Park on Sunday afternoons.

Often, I was awakened in darkness by shouts in the next bedroom. No one explained what caused them, but I recall some expressions which were loud enough to penetrate walls and door: "You trying to get my nanny?" "You're a liar." "You're another." "That's a fine howdydo." "Nothing of the kind." They occurred mostly when my father got home late and intoxicated. Often, they stopped with the sound of two flat boards slapping together. My mother would scream, and subside in sobbing. He had hit her. I remained in the pillow and pulled the sides around my ears and told God that if He ever wanted to call her to Him, I wish He would take me instead — a cowardly cry.

Our tiny back porch adjoined another. On the far side were Warren, Donald, and Helen Capuozzo, a little younger than the Bishop children. Mrs. Capuozzo was a stout blond with beautiful features. When she laughed, the sound was silvery and hearty. She played piano in movie houses. Her husband, Ralph, was a small man with dark wavy hair who delivered Lucky Strike cigarettes in a panel truck. Clara and Jenny became close friends. Mrs. Capuozzo didn't know how to make a dress or a man's shirt, as my mother did, but she read the latest books, could discuss the librettos of operas with authority, and had an appreciation for a virile man.

She was not obsessed with religion and hellfire. At night, when the children were in bed, the two couples played cards. When I was thirteen, it seemed to me that most of my father's dissertations were directed to Mrs. Capuozzo; most of the appreciative laughter belonged to him. Our telephone was in the master bedroom. Often, my father used it before he removed his uniform. He spoke in whispers, using initials: "Are you sure R. doesn't understand? J. seems suspicious, but I don't give a damn."'

My mother often asked who it was he called. "Police business," he would say.

"You think I don't know?" she would say. "You were talking to your affinity." None of us learned the genesis of the word, but she used it when she wasn't sure which of her friends had become Dad's pets. Her love was, in a practical sense, indestructible. It was not a credo, nor even a vow; her instinct was one life given to one man. Nor can it be said that she was a suspicious wife; she seemed born to be gulled. It required time for her to recall the extraordinary attention young wives accorded to my father, or the times, bringing cakes and coffee from the kitchen, she was able to see a stockinged foot under the dining room table caressing his shoe.

One might say that John Bishop had a double defense: ladies of good repute — at least some — felt an irresistible gravitational pull toward the man in the uniform. At home, his submissive wife was willing to lend herself, but not to participate. In addition, his mental horizons had grown broader with study, with cultivation of accomplished friends, while Jenny's remained confined to God and church, husband and family. At dinner, he said he suspected that Arcturus was an old heavenly body because of its bright yellow winking. If it was young, he said, it should emit a lot of blue. Jenny nodded and said something polite. Quickly, with embarrassment, I picked up the conversation so that my father would have someone with whom to speak. I did not know Arcturus, and felt little interest, but someone had to say something.

There was a question of how much love either of them could give. My father had been brought up in a house where three deaths in one week elicited few tears. All emotions except hilarity and anger were to be suppressed. The Bishops suffered in silence, labored without complaint, and seldom embraced each other. The inferno was deep in those chests, but the fire walls were stronger. The Tiers looked upon kissing as a familial salute; they pressed cheek upon cheek and their lips made a smacking noise. The capacity to love has as many levels as gold mining, from panning in sparkling brooks to digging in the black bowels of the earth.

I always kissed my father full on the lips, even though I felt him flinch. I kissed my mother on the cheek where she smelled of face powder because, she said, with a chuckle which was designed to ameliorate the sting of disapproval, that her lips belonged to her husband. At the age of fourteen I felt that we were going to lose my father to someone else. The worry caused nightmares, and I sat up in bed in the predawn hours thinking carousel-style. I saw people creeping in windows where we didn't have windows. When my father got out of bed and held me close and soothed me, I awakened but I could still see the strange figures pausing with one foot in the window. When visitors asked about the children, they were told: "Lonnie has nosebleeds and nightmares." Then, trying to think of something favorable, one parent or the other would say: "That's the one who never lies." Johnny was called "puddin' head," a term of endearment and a pejorative. He might have failing grades in school, or lose money on the way to a store, or do his impersonations of silent motion picture stars, and my father would tousle the blond hair and say: "Ah, Johnny, you're my puddin' head." Adele, who was blond as the Tier family was blond and wore her hanging conical curls with ridiculous dignity, was thought of as "frail." Of her my mother would say: "She had the bronchitis when she was an infant; they say she'll grow out of it."

There was a muffled explosion and he left. My mother sat with her hands on her knees, rocking and sobbing. John Bishop had tried the gentle approach. The marriage wasn't working, he said. He proposed to go live with his sister Margaret for a while. The McCarthys would take him in and give him a room. He wanted no public commotion. Forty dollars would be given to my mother every week to take care of house and children. It was, for its time, generous. Nor did he wish to relinquish his hold on the family he was leaving. He wanted the rights and prerogatives of head of the group and he expected each of them to report to him when he visited, once a week. Jenny told him the game was a fake; he was going to the McCarthy household temporarily; later, he would take up residence with Mrs. Capuozzo. He said she was a liar. She said he was another. "John," she said, as though trying to awaken him to the realities: "John, John." I was allowed to listen; I could not speak: "You're a witness," my father said sternly. "I want you to remember all the things your mother says."

I could not bear to watch her sob. "For Christ sake!" I yelled. "Stop it."

"May God forgive you," she said softly, "for using His name in vain. Go to mass. Go to confession. From now on, you're the man of the house." From now on. I was fourteen, a boy immersed in Free Public Library books because he had few friends. Life — all of it — was full of fear and uncertainty. Where were the carefree days of boyhood my father mentioned? Why was I always reluctant to awaken in the morning? Why wasn't I going to high school and college instead of to work? My fears proliferated — the wild unwanted weeds of the mind — and I hid them behind a sullen expression and an insolence which invited additional fist-fights. I defied Mother, and when she tried to slap my face, I grabbed her wrist and squeezed and pushed her backward. She had traded an older John Bishop for a younger one. "I'm going out," I said, slamming the door. At fifteen, I had exchanged the short trousers for long ones. It mattered not at all whether she needed coal or wood from the cellar for the kitchen stove. I was on my way to meet a haughty girl who, until this day, had never said hello. This, I felt, was man's business and had nothing to do with my mother. I had minuscule knowledge of aggressions and instincts, but I was going to see Tessie if I had to tear the door and my mother down.

The night air was cold and still. The gas mantle lamps on Bramhall Avenue fought the darkness of night, and lost. Between them, the shadows hid trees and stiff empty hedges. I made an effort to walk like my father, to throw my head back in the darkness, to be brave. Siedler Street was darker. There were public stables and two rows of old flats facing each other in fatigue. A workman in heavy shoes walked toward me. I clenched my fists. He went by in the gloom, looking down to read a face. I could hear his footfalls long after mine had faded in his ears. I went up the stoop two steps at a time.

When I pressed the bell, the joy of adventure died in my chest. What if, as Mom warned, Tessie turned out to be "loose"? What could I do with a grown woman seventeen years old? The fellows on the corner said that you spread her legs and put your thing in her thing. But what was her thing like? Not that it mattered; nothing was going to happen. But someday it would, and a growing man ought to know something about where his thing goes, and what to do when it gets there. The buzzer sounded. I stopped worrying. Tessie wasn't loose. All the big guys on the block laughed and shook their heads and said they sure would like to screw her, so if she wouldn't do it for them she could hardly be expected to swoon over a shrimp.

Once, at the age of eleven, I stood on the sidewalk as the Lydecker girls sat open-legged on the top step and I talked frantically while peeking. They asked me what I was trying to say, but I wasn't sure. I saw the snowy insides of their thighs, but, all the way up, there were white underpants — nothing. It was this which convinced me that the older boys had been making up stories about females. Boys had something hanging which could be rubbed; girls had two legs which met at the top. Hopping the stairs in the dark hallway, smelling the rancid cooking, I felt safe. Nothing was going to happen. I knew by instinct that a real man would never admit ignorance. If Tessie had a phonograph, or a piano, we could sing and tell stories.

One thing did not occur to me. My mood had altered. The dismal thoughts had evaporated. It was, in a manner of speaking, as though I had left Lonnie Bishop home in that fractured flat, and had transmuted the sullen boy into a buoyant man named Jim Bishop. Near the top of the dark stairs, there was an infusion of confidence. Tessie might let me kiss her. I paused at the top step. How did Rudolph Valentino hold his women? I thought it was with hands around the shoulders, one palm above the other. As I recalled, it was important to bend the girl backward, not forward. I was certain that it was backward. Although no sound came from the huge silver screen, I suspected that the man must breathe deeply and swiftly. I wasn't sure whether he kept his eyes open while she closed hers, or vice versa. It didn't matter. If Tessie permitted me to kiss her, I could peek and do whatever she wasn't doing.

I had kissed girls before, but these were experimental failures. At parties, we played Spin the Bottle and sometimes it was my turn to go out into the dark hall and kiss a girl. Most of them had attended school with me and I nerved myself to find part of the face and touch it with my lips. That was it. All of it. Frequently, I returned to the well-lighted room ahead of the girl. My foot was on the top step as the kitchen door opened. Tessie was silhouetted in a sliver of saffron light and said: "Oh, it's you." Clever retorts were important in dealing with females, but I couldn't think of any except "Who did you expect? Rudolph Valentino?" I didn't say it.

Entrances to flats were by way of the kitchen. This one was familiar: a black Boynton stove with hot lids, a gas mantle hanging from the ceiling, a deep morris chair beside the stove, a white enamel-topped table with an assortment of worn chairs, an icebox with drip pan, and two curtained windows leading to clotheslines. Tessie smiled and grabbed my hand. "It's cold out," she said. Something about the grab of the hand made me feel that perhaps I would be lucky: Tessie might be loose.

There was a black hole of a doorway leading to the rest of the flat. Without seeing, I knew that behind it would be a bedroom, then another, each increasingly colder than the last, and a living room. Tessie took my coat and asked for my jacket. "Why?" I said. The kitchen was blazing hot, she said. Her father had put fresh coal in the stove before he left for work. I gave her the jacket. As she disappeared into the cold bedroom, I had my best look. She was wearing a white shirtwaist with shirring, and a woolen skirt the color of which escapes me. She wore black shoes with high heels; the slender ankles turned slightly inward with each step. The legs flourished in perfect symmetry at the calves. I watched as I warmed my hands over the hot lids and I was surprised that, due to some deformity in her stride, one cheek of her ass lifted as the other dropped. The tightened skirt made the waist look small, not more than two-and-a-half hands around, and this seemed either to increase the cheeks of the ass in size, or else the cheeks were correct but the waist was emaciated. When she returned, she stood smiling in the doorway. The skinny waist also had a deleterious effect on the breasts, making them undulate ahead of her at right angles. She insisted that I use the morris chair. This, I figured, was her father's favorite. She used a kitchen chair which she pulled to my side of the table. In this way, as we chatted, I could see all of Tessie — the shiny black hair walking on air off her shoulders; the thick curving brows; the eyes, which I had always seen as antagonistic, sparkling with amusement.

The conversation was sparring. She asked about fellows and girls we knew. We shared opinions. We disagreed politely. Some fellows were "sheiks"; one girl was acknowledged to be "the cat's meow." I had not noticed a small wicker table against the wall. On it was a portable phonograph. She picked up a cheap ukulele and tried to accompany the records which played popular songs and movie themes. The uke was off-key. When I was small, I had taken piano lessons and violin lessons. They were among my minor accomplishments, but both gave me hypersensitive ears. When she crossed her legs to rest the ukulele, I took a chance and said: "Tessie, you're sure some hot tomato." She came over and sat on the arm of the morris chair and played and hummed. Part of her leg was touching one of mine.

Without desire, I could feel a lengthening and thickening inside my shorts. I clasped my hands over it. She played the uke again, and I said: "You know what, Tessie? You have real talent." She grinned. "You think so? I mean, really?" She held the uke close to her ear to retune the strings. When she replaced the instrument on her thigh, she pulled it toward her. The dress, by dramatic accident, moved up over her knee. The stove was burning one side of my face. Tessie's breathing chest chilled the other side. My head was jammed with bad thoughts. She asked me if I would like her better in a boyish bob. I said no. "Feel," she said. "It's so thick." I felt. I felt excited. It would be easy to lay the palm of my hand on Tessie's knee, but then she would have an excuse to holler and people would come running. I could hear my father's scornful tone: "I told you he was a bum."

She asked me if I had read Warner Fabian's new book, *Flaming Youth*. I admitted I had not. "That," she said, "is real hot stuff. It explains — you know — everything."

"Everything about what?" I said. I looked up at her with what I thought would be a jaded smile. She knew I knew what; I was forcing her to say it.

"Oh," she said, "you know. Hot necking and how far you should let a fellow go." We were on track.

"When he gets that far," I said insinuatingly, "how does a girl stop him? I mean . . ."

"Suppose, mister wise guy, she doesn't want him to stop?"

That did it. Tessie was what Momma called loose. Nobody in the world needed a loose woman more than I. "All the way?" I whispered.

She shrugged. "Depends."

Around this time my boyish erection had walked across my loins with hobnailed boots, jazzed my heart action, made me breathe like a tired horse, and set me to wondering how I could take Tessie's clothes off without Tessie realizing what was happening.

In an engineering sense, there was no way I could reach up from the depths of the morris chair to place both arms behind her shoulders. I was still shielding my lap with clasped hands when she left the chair and said: "Hey, I forgot to show you my picture album." She disappeared into the dark bedroom. There was a moment for thought. Tessie and the stove were killing me. Girls had a name for boys who did not know how to proceed from a cold handshake to a hot bed: "Dumbbell." This word also applied to girls who resisted a fellow's advances. On the other hand, suppose Tessie was being friendly? Suppose she was making up for all the times she had ignored my polite salutes? Or, to allow an insidious thought, suppose she still did not like me, and was leading me on to tear her dress off and then would call the police? Why were fellows so honest and girls so devious? A boy could tell a girl, without speaking, the direction in which he was heading. He could hold her in a close embrace and she could tell. Or he could foxtrot and she could place one thigh between his and be aware, without shouting in shock. Tessie remained away for several minutes and I recalled how my mother told me that my father wanted to "have a talk" with me.

He was in the bathroom, shaving with a straight razor. "Sit on the tub," he had said. I sat. His face, except for eyes and nose, was hidden under a snowbank of lather. He squinted his eyes and pulled at his neck as the razor cut through the fluffy white. The sexual education of Lonnie, thirteen and a half, was succinct. "Your mother tells me," he said with pauses between slides of the razor, "that you are growing up." He wiped the spent lather on folded toilet tissue. Looking in the medicine chest mirror, he could see me behind him. "I assume you have heard of the word *sex?*"

"Yes, sir."

"All right, then," he said. "Don't believe a word you heard. My advice is, stay away from the goddamn women. They'll get you in nothing but trouble." I sat. "That's it," he said.

I left the room. My mother seemed surprised. "Did he have a talk with you?"

I shrugged. "I guess so," I said.

"They'll get you in nothing but trouble." Why would Tessie bother with a younger fellow like me? It was pointless. An additional warning thought intruded: if she allowed me to "go all the way," I might become a father at age sixteen and there would be hell to pay. Until this moment, I hadn't thought about babies. A guy could get a stifferino and end up in prison or at the altar. The effect of fretful thoughts had an astounding effect on that instrument. It subsided as though it sensed the danger.

Tessie was beaming and apologetic. "I couldn't find it," she said. "Here," she said happily. "Look." She plopped on my lap with the book. The wise instrument of which I speak lost its fear at once and, in a most practical manner, said, "The hell with the danger."

As she bent forward to turn the pages, I placed a barely touching arm around her back and was astounded to find that I could look down the front of her dress. I do not recall ever seeing anything as fascinating as those creamy things rising and falling, rising and falling. She was flipping pages, but my eyes, which had been 20/20 when I arrived, were 20/200. The pages were blurred, the images indecipherable. There were old snapshots and new. Tessie couldn't seem to sit still. I warned myself that one more twitch and the evening would be over. I tried to slow the process by dwelling on my mother hitting me with a broom if she found out. In Momma's eyes, it would be a mortal sin even if I went "all the way" alone, which was my imminent fate.

Sin, I had learned, was supremely fascinating. I was in a transitory period between boyhood and manhood and, although I confided my fears to no one, I suspected that my soul was already lost. Put simply, it was more gratifying to steal an apple than to buy one. In confession, the priests with their murky heads bowed kept asking: "How many times? How many times?" I overconfessed. If they asked if I disobeyed my parents, I said yes, ten times a day, even though it may have been one or none. Did I avoid receiving the sacrament? Five times. It was one, perhaps two. Did I masturbate? Yes, Father, six times a day — it may have been twice. I vowed that I would not be caught with a solitary stain which had not been conceded.

"How do you like this one?" Tessie said. My sight cleared a little. The photo was of her in a black bathing suit. "That," I said, "is something."

"Want me to model it for you?" she said happily. "I mean, put it on?" A light dawned. Tessie was going to let me do it to her. This was proof. She would not have asked about that swim suit and offered to don it in the dead of winter, unless she proposed to take it off. "Sure," I said, smiling upward at her pudding chest. "I would love to see it." Again she hurried inside. I began to wonder what secret attraction I had for older women; what was it they could divine that others did not suspect?

When she returned, I was at the point of failing to resolve who assumes the lead in these matters. It could not be the man because he might stick a cold hand inside the bathing suit and the girl would call him bad names. Females practiced shrill screams — even at football games. Also, what was permissible yesterday might be felonious today. It must be the woman who makes the aggressive moves in this complex game. It had to be, and yet I could not imagine Tessie reaching down to unbutton my trousers. She might; she must suspect that I would not call for help. In the movies, the wild-eyed Theda Bara seduced the noblest and strongest of men. It was she who initiated the several stages which led, eventually, to the dawn shot with lovers racing down the beach laughing, hand in hand.

"Like it?" She stood in the doorway of the bedroom. If everything inside that black bathing suit was Tessie, only Tessie, then she made my secret fantasies, Aileen Pringle and Norma Talmadge, look like a hundred and ten pounds of desiccated warts.

"Like it?" I said, rising from the chair. "It's beautiful, Tessie. It's the most beautiful suit I've ever seen." Slowly, she walked toward me with her arms outstretched in gratitude. Somehow, the back of my knees were against the morris chair and she pushed me down. She sat on my lap, brushing her lips against my cheek. I kissed Tessie. I kissed her again. My body, including the roots of my hair, became one huge flaming erogenous zone. Tessie was breathing loud. She locked her arms behind my neck and tried to thrust her tongue into my mouth. I clenched my teeth. "Help me," she moaned, like someone in pain; "help me." She was unbuttoning my shirt. Underneath were B.V.D.'s. I knew she would have trouble with those buttons. I kissed her again and again and, in one violent, never-ending explosion, did it to myself.

A great lassitude overcame me. I leaned back, panting. Tessie placed her head on my chest. She was, I guess, willing to give me five minutes to recover. Her black hair streamed over my face. She undid two buttons of my underwear and kissed my chest with little pecks. "Oh," she murmured, "I'm so tired, Jim. So, so tired." Her head fell on my chest and instantaneously Tessie was in deep sleep. I have never seen fatigue overcome anyone so quickly. So I sat quietly, letting her sleep, one side of my face still frying near the stove.

I lifted her head a little so that I could see down the front of the suit. The snowy white fruit, with a mask of black bathing suit halfway down, was irresistible. My fingers stuttered. The plan was to unbutton the bathing suit so gently that the sleeping girl would not awaken. There was a suspicion that she was not sleeping, but pretending. Her head had fallen so quickly after she murmured, "So, so tired" that it was akin to being hit with a flask of ether. The two shoulder buttons were undone slowly. The strap fell. I pulled the other one from the shoulder, lifting it off her skin. It came down easily. I peeled the suit down to the stomach. In all my fifteen and a quarter years, I never had been so excited. To look or to grab: a monumental question. Tessie was built like some of the African natives I had seen in the *National Geographic,* without the saucer lips.

Softly, slowly, I worked the suit down to the navel. It is my custom to ask myself ridiculous questions in moments of crisis. I asked myself how the hell I was going to get this suit off the girl if she remained on my lap. There was no way I could slide the suit off Tessie's delectable body unless, in some magical manner, I could put her on the bottom and me on top. I decided to think. While I was pondering, Tessie must have noticed the lack of action. She awakened suddenly, and asked convincingly: "Jim, whatever are you doing?" In my embarrassment, I mumbled and helped her restore the suit to the shoulders. She turned and frowned. She played two more records. I didn't notice the tunes. She was as enticing, twisting and turning in her bare feet in that furnace of a kitchen, as when the suit was half-peeled. Tessie wasn't angry with me. She smiled and made hula motions with her fingers. Then she said, "Excuse me." She was puffing a little as she disappeared into the dark cavern of the railroad rooms.

Tessie didn't come back. I returned the quavering needle to the start of the record four times without hearing or seeing anything. If she had retired, she might have said goodnight. For a while, I entertained the notion that she might have been overtaken again by sleep. I decided it would not be impolite to step slowly into the first bedroom, calling "Tessie" softly. I stepped into the darkened room. The light from the kitchen told me she was not there. "Tessie," I said softly. There was no response. I moved to the next room. It was cold, and darker. She wasn't there.

By the time I reached the living room at the front of the house I was shivering. A pale streetlamp tossed a weak echo from the ceiling. Faintly, I could see Tessie. She was flat on her back on the floor in that bathing suit. In the gloom, I could see her face turned to one side in deep sleep. That woman could sleep on nails. In what can be described as bitter cold, all the symptoms of the emerging male returned. I got on my knees beside her. This time, that bathing suit was coming off. The two buttons were undone again. My breathing created twin plumes on her chest. Tessie slept with defiance. This time, I unbuttoned my trousers and brought out the offering which, in the sudden chill, almost retreated. I stroked the bared breasts gently to persuade my parts that this time the result was guaranteed. I tried to yank the suit over the hips, but it was impossible. In her sleep, Tessie moaned restlessly and lifted her hips accidentally. The suit went all the way down to the ankles. Carefully, I lifted each foot and the suit was off.

In the freezing night, I could distinguish the great beauty — the jutting breasts, the stiff icy nipples, the slender waist, the cool pale flanks curving outward and falling into round configurations of thighs and calves. My thinking was a hoarse whisper. What if, after I put this thing where it was supposed to go, the force of it shocked Tessie awake? If she screamed, I would run from the flat, recalling the sage words of my father: "Stay away from the goddamn women. They'll get you in nothing but trouble." And yet I was on the edge of a shattering discovery. Deep inside, I felt that I was about to fire a cannon which would crack walls.

I took one ankle and moved it far right. She did not awaken. I lifted the other and placed it far left. Whatever the thing was had to be in the vicinity of where these two limbs met. I had not seen one, and knelt shivering, wondering whether it was high up in front of that mass of short hair, deep down, or possibly medium? There was but one way to make certain. I reached into my sagging trouser pockets and pulled out a kitchen match. I struck it on my shoe and, when the flame flared, I held it high up between Tessie's thighs to ascertain the what and the where. For no reason whatever, the girl popped straight up in the air screaming. Then she held her hand over her mouth. She stood nude in the dark, whispering: "Get out, you little son of a bitch! Get out, you goddamn pervert!" I ran through the rooms, tugging the trousers up. I made the hall and the stairs two at a time, I ran out and down the short steps, diagonally across the street, not feeling the intense cold, holding my coat in my fist, and getting to the house at ten minutes after ten. My mother looked at the clock and said I was a "good boy."

Two days later, in the late afternoon, I was flipping a football and running with it. I saw Tessie walking toward us from Jackson Avenue with her bag of groceries. I did not know whether to yell hello and wave. She placed the groceries between her feet and cupped her hands in front of her mouth. "Pervert!" she screamed. "Pervert!"

The office manager was a nun in spats. Mr. Bertschy seldom smiled. He was tall and slender, one who seemed to enjoy having people stare up his nostrils. He wore pince-nez and the aloof attitude of the man who, in the echelons of a banking firm such as Lehman Brothers, desired to understand that he stood on top of the bottom. When he swept off the elevator, I said: "Good morning, Mr. Bertschy." He nodded without losing stride, the furled umbrella swinging from an elbow. He said, "Good morning, John," to Mr. Courtney, a retired policeman who guarded the outer offices. He wore a gray uniform with a square-peaked cap and had fierce mustaches, a belly, and the puffed cheeks of an Irish Santa. Mr. Courtney saluted Mr. Bertschy with hand touching cap brim; the Lehmans were accorded the same respect.

He spent the rest of the day walking up and down outside the rail of the reception office, hands clasped back, harrumphing now and then as though to hear that he was alive. He carried no gun; in the two years and two months I sat at the reception desk, he protected the firm from no one. He had a broad brogue and, in benevolent moods, would assure me that someday I would find a place as a clerk with Mr. Ludy in the bond cage. He was sure of this because he found out that most of my ancestors were Irish. "Good stock," he would say. When he learned that my father was a lieutenant of police in Jersey City, he became more protective. I became a fine boy, a comer to be sure.

My father, on one of his visits to our house, advised me to stick to Lehman Brothers. "Good bankers," he said. "Fine people. I told you and your brother that, when the time comes, I will speak to the politicians if you want to get on the force — and I meant it — but you're short, and Wall Street may be just your number." What I learned at Lehmans' — if I may disregard the sporadic lectures of John Courtney regarding the evils of drink and women — was how to bend a paper clip, fashion a slingshot with a rubber band, and negotiate the difficult trajectory from my desk, over the glass partition of the bond cage, onto Mr. Ludy's bald head.

He jumped. I sometimes held my fire until Courtney was pacing with a rubber band between his fingers. Fred Ludy glared at the cop; he stared with suspicion at the clerk who worked on the canvas-bound ledgers — in time, he caught me. He trotted out in his linen jacket and said he would punch me in the nose. Mr. Bertschy joined the lynching. Courtney's loyalty dissipated and he told Bertschy: "I've been watching this lad, and I can tell you, sir, he had better watch his step." The speeches cascaded from the mouths of stone frogs in a fountain. I swam in words, hung my head, apologized, and hoped I would not be fired because, of the twelve dollars weekly, my mother got ten and I took two. Neither of us could afford for me to be fired.

The sweet days warmed the cold stone of Wall Street. Brokers walked Broad Street with jackets open. There was a subtle odor of road tar, and that signaled summer. After lunch one day, Mr. Bertschy came to my desk waving a piece of paper. "Take this to the Corn Exchange Bank," he said imperiously. It was not in an envelope, so I studied the piece of paper. It was a check for one million dollars. I counted all the zeros. It was not an unusual transaction. Often, Lehman Brothers borrowed a check from the Corn Exchange Bank (which was directly across the street at 15 William) in case unexpected fluctuations of the stock market required large amounts of ready cash. I cannot recall any time that the check was used. It was always returned, unendorsed, on the same day.

I stuffed it in my jacket and started down the steps. It was a piece of paper — nothing more. In my opinion, a Hershey bar with almonds would have been a tangible asset. When I reached the sidewalk, I sniffed the warm air. It had a slight odor of salt, as though brine was on the breeze. My mistake was in not crossing the street. I turned right, walked slowly toward Wall Street on William, then turned left past the Subtreasury, J. P. Morgan and Company, and the conical granite of the Guaranty Trust Company. I crossed Broadway and slowly walked the paths of Trinity churchyard. There I hunched on a stone slab and studied names and dates on headstones. Most of them had been staggered by time and wind. On a few, slices had fallen and only parts of names and dates could be deciphered. The etching of the handsome colonial gallant, Alexander Hamilton, had been weathered so that the name and the pale stone had melted into each other.

For a while, I meditated among the gentlemen and ladies of the colonies and I could see the brass-buckled shoes, the silk stockings, the sweeping gowns, and, if I listened hard, could hear the spinet, the flute, the cadenced obbligatos of the strings. I dreamed well and soon the skyscrapers melted and the wharves on Water Street were unloading casks of Madeira for the burghers. Nor did I forget to listen to the hooves of horses drumming the tawny clay of the Albany Post Road, nor the click and sweep of Zenger's old press and the mongers hawking fish at Castle Gardens. It was all there — and much, much more — for anyone to see. One of the gravestones told of a man who died in 1717; his wife expired in 1727. The names meant nothing, but it set me to wondering whether a decade of widowhood was not, indeed, a minuscule moment in time two hundred years later.

Ten years would, I thought, be an interminable length of days and seasons as she lived them, and yet the inexorable tick of the clock diminished the lady's grace period of living until now, as I sat thinking, I could not conjure anything of importance which occurred between the two deaths. I was aware that I had an abnormal interest in time. I was enamored and fearful of it. It was something which moved steadily, without hurry or hindrance, but it did unkind things to faces, careers, history, beating hearts — the thunder of the sea against the rocky coast would, in time, reduce the granite to damp grains of sand. My interest was abnormal because it was insatiable. When I first began to read newspapers in other people's vestibules, at the age of ten, I became intrigued. The railroad worker who sat at dinner with his family yesterday was in an obituary notice today. A cartoon depicted Kaiser Wilhelm II, wearing a spiked helmet, standing with one foot on the neck of a helpless lady called Belgium. I wondered why, if she had been small, helpless, and free such a short time ago, this powerful man was permitted to pin her today with his foot. Everything was related to time.

There was a time to be at school — a precise time. There was another for church. There was one for going to bed. A cheap alarm clock ticked louder at night than by day. Supper was five-thirty P.M. — not five P.M. There were birthdays and anniversaries to mark the motion of time; there were family deaths; there were calendars given free by merchants so that a boy with imagination could leaf through the monthly paintings from the sprig of pussy willow in spring to the stiff rusty leaves of late autumn swirling a rigadoon of the dead. Time, not destiny, was the key to life. To comprehend it, to stretch it by running, rather than walking, to stores; to execute a task, such as dusting, sweeping, or dishes, so well on the first attempt that a boy could find time to be lazy, to think, to strike the shackles of the mind, gave him extra time to wonder.

Books, I found, had the power to make time stand still, retreat, or fly into the future. At the age of nine, I got a library card at the Clinton

Avenue Branch. At first, the librarian permitted me to withdraw but two books. After she had taught me not to dogear a page, but to use a bookmark, and to protect the books from weather and household accidents, she became gracious and allowed me to take five at a time. I read Nick Carter's detective stories; the Rover Boys series of books were favorites; so was *Tom Swift and His Electric Automobile*; Horatio Alger taught me that an intelligent boy who applied himself with honor would someday marry the banker's daughter; the soft-cover Liberty Boys gave me dramatic insight into the Revolutionary War; I read books about other countries, other people, other customs; there were thousands and thousands of words which were strangers to me — my father taught me to write them on a pad and "look them up later." The Dumas series, starting with *The Three Musketeers*, was almost beyond price. I read them twice. Bram Stoker's *Dracula* had such a frightening fascination that I read it in bed until I heard my mother say: "Is that light going out or do I go in there and remove the bulb?"

Everything was in a time frame. And everything and everyone was good or evil. When Grandma Bishop gave me her copy of Butler's *Lives of the Saints*, she thought it would make a better Christian of me, but I was gratified to learn that most of the heavenly customers started life by breaking most of the commandments. It must have been fun to succumb to temptation, hoping that, in later years, time might grant a period of remorse, repentance, and redress of wrongs. I loved the saints for their sins. Only the males, it seemed to me, appreciated the secret joy of evil. The females were timid creatures who pledged their lives, their souls, to God and never changed, even when black-hooded executioners were lighting fagots around their bound feet. I would not choose to be a female saint for any reward. The proper perspective, I felt, was first to be a hearty sinner and, when the legs, heart, and brain began to falter, to fall to one's knees, beg forgiveness, and stand in line at the Pearly Gates.

I got up from the tombstone, still dreaming, and dusted the back of my trousers and returned to Lehman Brothers. Most of those people in Trinity churchyard must have been important or they would not have found places there. Who were they now? With a few historical exceptions, I knew none. They had been born, grown up, done something, and died. One thing was certain in my mind: I was not going to die. Death was unacceptable. My friend Willie Stahl died and my mother sent me to his house with some limp carnations in green wax paper. The house was dark, except for candles and a crucifix, and the people were red-eyed from weeping. I had handed over the flowers, taken a deep breath, and walked to the casket. There was Willie, holding his breath forever. His appendix had burst and he could not ride his bicycle in lazy figure eights. He could not make a circle in the earth between sidewalk and curb and place marbles inside, to knock them out with another marble. It was all so long ago, but Willie never came back and I knew he would not return.

They had imprisoned him in that walnut box and they told me that he was sleeping with the angels. He wasn't sleeping with anybody. I had run behind the last coach all the way to the cemetery and I stood panting to watch the workmen lower him with those ropes. There were no angels down there. I heard the dirt slam the box. Willie could be suffocating, so I ran away and took a trolley car home. Softly, my father said it was something that had to happen to everyone. I resolved that it would not happen to me. Sometimes, I awakened perspiring as shovels of dirt fell on my face. My thoughts spiraled downward. In my childish desperation, I reasoned that if today lived forever, there could be no tomorrow. Thus, time would stop and if that could be achieved, what happened to Willie Stahl could never happen to me. The true, the only, enemy was time.

I got off the elevator in a dream state and was surprised to see Robert Lehman, Bertschy, and Courtney leaning on the rail before my desk. The dialogue is lost. There were some questions about the check; did I or did I not deliver that million-dollar slip of paper to the Corn Exchange Bank? I reached into my jacket pocket and withdrew it. My intention was to show that I had not stolen it. The voices became shrill; Bertschy pointed at the office clock — the time was three forty-five P.M. The bank was closed. Lehman Brothers had not returned the check within the bank day, and owed interest at 4 percent. This would come to $109.59. The three men kept asking where I had been "all this time." In turn, each told me I was fired. Bertschy dogtrotted to the cashier's cage and got some small bills from Mr. Hertzberg, an old cashier. I took the money in shame. Courtney told me to clear out my desk and leave at once.

I had lost an engagement.

The most painful aspect of living was a dissertation by Big John, called "A good talking-to." These were prearranged with my father and mother sitting with me at a dining room table under a hanging lampshade which featured bits of colored glass and grapes. My father had a frightening gambit in which he talked of matters of casual interest for a time before he turned the glittering pince-nez on me and asked what the hell was the matter. It was executed softly at first, rising steadily to a crescendo of shouting and fist-pounding. Sometimes, when I tried to respond with the truth — that I felt miserable, a failure — he dismissed it as an excuse and said: "I'll break your face. That's what I'll do."

I dreaded the "good talking-to." Most of them began with my mother writing letters to my father c/o Aunt Margaret McCarthy, all of which opened with the salutation "My dear Husbent." He arrived, sometimes in uniform, sometimes in gray suit and homburg, barely concealing his irritation that, as a father, he was forced to repeat a duty over and over. My mother used these meetings to inquire how he was faring with his "affinity" — Clara Capuozzo. The lady had moved to a two-family house a few streets from Aunt Margaret's house at 631 Garfield Avenue. Before I submitted to the "good talking-to," he got one. My mother told him that her "lady friends" had seen him with Clara at the movies, or walking, or on a trolley car. In such situations, his anger was quick. "That," he would say righteously, "is a goddamn lie." She would shake her head sadly. "Go to confession, John," she would say. "Tell it to the priest."

There was never a moment that she did not want him back. Sometimes she said: "I wouldn't take you back if you were the last man on earth." Jenny Bishop lied with transparency. When the arguments began, Adele left the room weeping. Johnny would find an excuse to go out and play. When the argument subsided, heavy breathing could be heard in the silence. When he had regained his composure, it was my turn. Always it was *his* game; his gambits were executed on both sides of the board. "Sister Rose Patricia told me before you dropped out of school that you have intelligence. Now I don't want to argue with you; I just want to ask what is wrong. Why can't you keep a job? Why do you read books all day and all night? A good education leads to success. You can study law at Newark Law School at night. I think you would make a good trial lawyer. I know you have it inside. But something is wrong with your attitude. You're weak. Shallow. Tell me, do you play with your penis? If you do, it's bad. It's the worst thing a young man can do to himself, and he'll pay for it later in life.

"Lonnie — I mean, Jim — nobody is going to give you anything for nothing. When I went on the force in 1909, I bought every book I could find on police procedure. A man must know more than law enforcement; he must know law. None of it was easy. But by God I wasn't satisfied to be a flatfoot. The way you're heading, you're going to be a bum. You can't even shine your shoes. Do you realize how much appearance means? Have you ever stopped to think about it? My men pick up boys like you on street corners every night. They give them a touch of the nightstick, that's what. We get your kind off the corner at ten. Tell me — why do you wear those workmen's blue shirts with a button-down collar? Why don't you get some nice stiff Marlboro collars and wear a maroon tie? You'd be surprised what it will do for your appearance. And press your own clothes. Get a hot iron and a damp cloth. You're a holy disgrace...."

He did not understand my personal and chronic aimlessness nor, had he asked, could I have explained it to him. Puberty had banished the nightmares to the dark corners of an empty mind, replaced them with visions of myself standing beside d'Artagnan enjoying the clash of swords with the evil men sent by Cardinal Richelieu. Sometimes I was captain of an ocean liner and my mother occupied the royal suite on the sun deck, sailing to the East Indies to find my father, who was an alcoholic wreck lost in a jungle. At other times, I captured the copper market in a clever gambit in Wall Street and Mr. Bertschy begged me to come to terms with Lehman Brothers and, if I chose, become the first Christian partner. There were occasions when beautiful girls lowered their eyes beside a bed and removed the multifarious lacy things which lie between the ornate gown and the woman. All the girls were unabashed hellions who entreated me to do licentious things to them. In my dreams, I never met a homely girl. Sometimes, I was riding a fast black horse through dense forests, keeping my head low to his neck to protect my eyes from swinging branches. Now and then, I invented something which everybody in the world was impelled to buy, like a small kit, no bigger than a box of matches, which would furnish a house with all the electricity it could use at a cost of ten cents a month — five cents of which was my royalty. On a few occasions, I wrote a book explaining what was wrong with the world and how to correct it. Statesmen read it. Prime ministers, Popes, and Presidents invited me to discuss my conclusions.

My mother was distressed that I refused to awaken each morning. She called to me; she shook my shoulder; I told her, "Leave me alone." The cure for my illness was to remain unconscious. Often, when I got out of bed, she looked at me in underwear and a soiled bathrobe and sat and buried her face in her apron. Secretly, I began to go to the clinic at City Hospital for diagnosis and cure. The fee was fifty cents. The young interns with their pointed hammers tapped my knees, focused small lights at my eyes, thumped my chest and back, used tongue depressors, made blood tests, and once — just once — a mustached doctor sat on a small enamel stool and said I had tuberculosis of the lymph glands. I wallowed in self-pity because there were many in my neighborhood who died of TB. Now I knew what I had, I understood my lack of energy, and I knew that I could not live to become an adult.

I made one clinical visit too many. On a Sunday, I was climbing a cliff at Palisades, New Jersey, when I fell. The drop was backward, about seventy-five feet, passing through a stout and sturdy tree. Some campers said that I was unconscious for a while, but the only injury was a small piece of branch jammed into the left leg behind the shinbone. Strangers insisted that I lie back while they called an ambulance. I declined, stood, limped, got to a road, and hitched a ride on the tailgate of a truck. At City Hospital, I came under the professional care of a young man with reddish hair, Dr. Emmett Connell. He was studying to be a urologist and syphilologist, but, under the rules, had to work Sundays in the clinic. He was a subdued person, one who spoke in whispers as he twisted head, neck, torso, pressed the rib cage, moved the ankles, and finally got to the obvious — removal of the branch from the lower leg. "It requires a talent of sorts," he said slowly, "for a young man to kill himself. That is," he said, "properly." The leg was anesthetized and the branch came out. Dr. Connell enlarged the wound, looking for foreign matter.

I asked about his career, and how long it would require to become a doctor, and when he reached the part about syphilis and gonorrhea, I acquired both instantaneously. I told Dr. Connell that I was certain that

I had a bad disease. He held my leg and looked at me a long, long time. "Have you ever been with a girl?" he said gently.

I nodded. "Lots."

"I don't mean dates."

"No."

"You have not had sexual relations?"

"Not yet," I said, "but I went to the Central Theatre and saw a movie, *What Every Man Should Know*, and I have contracted both diseases." For a reason which escapes me, Dr. Connell decided to turn the remaining patients to another resident, and he bound my leg and sat outside on a bench with me. "Aren't you going to take a whatsis test?"

"Wasserman. No. If I do, and it is negative, you will have pneumonia next week or tuberculosis."

"I already have tuberculosis of the glands."

Connell shook his head sadly. "I can run some tests on that, but I'm afraid I'm going to disappoint you."

"A doctor said . . ."

"I don't care what he said. Tell me something about your family." I told him.

When I had a dressing changed, he asked more. And more. Always slowly, with long silences. "My father," he said, "is a physician up on the hill. He's about ready to retire, but he knows your father. Your dad is known in the Hague administration as a comer. Do you know what that is?" I said it was a man who would rise in rank. "Right," he said. "Now, this is reputed to be a pretty big city — about two hundred thousand or more people — but it is made up of families who know each other. Most people know John Bishop. And he knows a lot of people. You are going to have to understand that practically everybody heard that he has left your mother for another woman. This is not my business, young man, but you have made it yours. You are determined to be sick."

"I am sick," I said belligerently.

"I am not an alienist," he said, "but I feel that you are not sick. Now we must ask ourselves why you want to be sick. If you were not you — somebody else, say — would you feel that this young fellow was revenging himself on his father, or trying to die so that he did not have to live with his mother's sorrow?"

"Neither," I said.

"Calm yourself," he said. "If we are going to be friends, I must be able to tell you what I think."

We became friends. Often, he upset me by stating that I was falling deeper into a syndrome of hypochondria. When he went into practice on Virginia Avenue, I demanded blood tests, examinations for gonorrhea and buboes, and, when the tests were completed, I refused to believe the results. I was losing weight; I began to pray aloud at dinner, to the amusement of John and Adele. ("He's praying again." "Look at him, he's praying and blessing himself." "I saw him do it in the bathroom too.") Whatever the maelstrom, I was in it and swept downward.

Nothing was right. The masturbation became more frequent, the visions of soft lovely girls more realistic, and the sins more poignant. In the dim light of Saint Patrick's Church, I examined my conscience, staring at the red vigil light over the altar, and took my place in line at Father Hagerty's confessional booth: "Bless me Father for I have sinned. It is two weeks since my last confession."

Inside the dim screen, a hand shielded the face. "Go on, my son."

"I missed mass."

"How many times?"

"Five."

"How could you miss mass five times in two weeks?"

"I mean, once."

"Go on."

"I disobeyed my father and mother about twenty times."

"Go on."

"I touched myself."

"Where?"

"You know."

"Idle hands are the devil's toy. How many times?"

"Two weeks. Fourteen days. About fifty-six times, Father."

"How many?"

"Forty."

"Are you in trouble?"

"I have a venereal disease."

"Oh, my God. Oh, my God. Well, you're lucky. It could have been syphilis."

"It is."

"Oh my God, how old are you?"

"Seventeen, Father."

"I will pray for you. Do you understand that there is no cure for syphilis — that it will run its course and you will get paresis — "

"I saw the movie, Father. It starts off with a Hunterian sore and then goes to stage — "

"Never mind. Say five Our Fathers and five Hail Marys and make a good Act of Contrition."

"I haven't finished, Father."

"More? Go on."

"I stole money from my mother's pocketbook."

"How much?"

"I don't remember. I went to a block dance on Union Street."

"I feel very sorry for you and I will pray for you."

"There's a friend of mine who cures everything with Salvarsan, Father."

[32]

"Please leave."

"Dr. Connell says it works."

"There are other people waiting."

"First, let me say the Act of Contrition. 'O my God I am heartily sorry for having offended Thee, and I detest all my sins. . . .' "

Big John — my father — had the political power to get jobs for friends. He wrote notes to factory superintendents on police headquarters letterheads and, magically, the worthy poor found themselves earning a salary. He drew joy from helping others. In my case, he agonized because the record is incontrovertible that I seldom lasted more than three weeks. I was a "bird dog" for salesmen who sold the first electric refrigerators: Frigidaire Model 110. I rang doorbells at random and told sleazy unkempt housewives of the marvels of science, of never having to empty a drip pan again. If they seemed at all interested, the name and address was written in a notebook to be given to a qualified salesman for follow-up. The salary was twenty-five dollars a week. My interest in the electric ice box declined and I sat in bed writing names and addresses of persons whose bells I had no intention of ringing.

Fired. Always discharged. Rarely, I anticipated the boss and quit. Sitting in a panel truck with a briefcase, I tried giving away a new soap called Camay at twenty dollars a week. Other boys in the truck rocked and jostled through the early spring days. We had a speech. Ring the bell, smile engagingly, and say "Madame, I have nothing to sell; I have something free to give you. Have you tried Camay soap? It is a new product which is so gentle to face and hands that it feels like a cream. I would also like to leave a small sample of Oxydol. . . ." If, at any point, the lady interrupted the speech with a question, I found it impossible to continue.

I started over: "Madame, I have nothing to sell; I have something free. . . ." The door slammed. The boss gave me twenty dollars and told me to find my way home. Adolph Zukor built a new theater in Times Square called the Paramount. This time I was in a powder blue uniform, swallowtail, wing collar, and white bow tie. "Please remain in the lobby, ladies and gentlemen, until the orchestra is cleared. The next show starts in ten minutes." Flashlight. Find two empty seats. Together, if possible. Stand against the rear wall, watch the movie. Be in uniform at nine A.M. Parade around the outside of the theater, swinging arms and legs in cadence count. "Don't forget: A soldier never forgets his flashlight. In time of action, it's his best friend."

Fired. More letters from police headquarters. A job in Ehrhardt's butcher shop. Deliver meat orders on a bicycle with a basket. Help grind top round and pork and hold salted sheep entrails over a nozzle to make frankfurters and sausage. Chase boys away from hares and rabbits hanging by their ears from a barrel out front. Carry change of ten dollars on all deliveries. Do not forget to return it to Mr. Ehrhardt at six P.M. Fired. Clerk in Eagle Grocery at Bidwell Avenue and Ocean. If no customers —

weigh out sugar in one-pound bags, two pounds, five pounds. Tie with white string. Grind coffee. Do not smoke cigarettes in back room. Do not spend time in toilet. Do not be detected stealing chocolate cream cookies with walnut on top. Fired.

Take a bus to Kearny, New Jersey. Ford plant. Blank bodies of cars moving slowly forward. Hold mouthful of tacks. As each car approaches, pull cheap upholstery on front seat taut and wrinkle-free. Tack edges under seat. The next man in line will do the back seat. For Christ sake, stop raising your hand for relief. The bathroom is gray with cigarette smoke. Fired. Office boy at Coverdale & Colpitts, consulting engineers. It required a few days to discover why anyone should be paid for consulting. The current project was to find out why Canadian National Railways was losing money. To solve the riddle, young engineers were sent to Canada to traverse every foot of the railway, assess the economic worth of railroad engines, freight cars, passenger trains, cabooses, real estate right-of-way, railroad stations, competitive railroads, bonded indebtedness, cash flow, and many other things, including the structure and efficiency of the board of directors. After two years of work, Coverdale & Colpitts would present a bound volume full of profound observations, graphs, and charts, and, as an appendix, the recommendations of the consulting engineers depicting the distasteful steps which would have to be taken to convert the railroad from a losing proposition to one with a respectable return on investment.

I became so interested in the process that I read some of the old reports on other big losers and was dismissed for not sharpening pencils, listening to the buzzer which summoned me to the private offices of partners, and, worst of all, treating visitors with disdain. Coverdale & Colpitts was so august that, for once, I was not fired. The boss said I was "separated." I went home. Lonely thinking is meditation. What, I asked scores of times, would I like to do with my life? What day-in-day-out work would maintain sheen and joy? I felt a kinship for nailed-down facts. It occurred to me that, given four or five progressive facts, the sixth could almost be deduced. It wasn't an absolute, but it was a discovery of sorts. Bringing it to the absurd, if I arrived home and found my mother in a sullen mood, she would probably be wearing a handkerchief pinned around her head. If these two were true, I would look at the kitchen stove and find a huge pot of vegetable soup simmering. The facts could add to but one quotient: she had been scrubbing the family laundry on a washboard all day, hanging it on the line with clothespins — ergo, it was Monday. The old fascination with time had a new ally — facts. On occasions when my father spent the evening with us, I watched him pirouette the black fountain pen in fine Spencerian letters, his head cocked to the right as he wrote police reports.

Sometimes, when he felt friendly, we went for a night walk. When I was an infant, he said, he had seen Halley's Comet. Its presence had been predicted, a bright slow-moving grace with a tail thousands of miles long, and it had come into view on time. The inner magnetism I felt for time and facts as interrelating integrals went deep. I do not understand why this should have led to an interest in psychology, but I altered my taste in books at the Clinton Avenue Library. I was so ignorant that I but partly comprehended what I was reading. Freud and Jung and, most of all, the early engaging books by Adler, opened a huge double door in my mind. The authors called it psycho-analysis, a young and suspect science. Also, from observation, I felt that individuals were afflicted with instinctive habits — which shoe to put on first, cocking a head to listen, incessant moving of feet under a table, the poor often walking with grim arrogance, an animalistic attitude in sleeping, false amiability, the snobbery of young people who were insecure. Even words had a gender: "adorable, gorgeous, cute, shocked, lovely; bum, shit, balls, creep, stacked, drag, heel, loaded, mooch, pussy."

Sometimes I would read a page or less, and slam the book shut to think. My thoughts led to the conclusion that I was insane. *Fact* books, whether in psychology, history, biography, or the sciences, became the springboards from which my brain jumped too far. I landed on rocks. The great novels were abandoned for nonfiction. I was learning, not through study, but rather through a devouring interest in man, his moods, methods, goals, cruelties, and morbidity. In summer, when the sun lingered, I sat on the porch and watched people. Mrs. Kerrigan always lifted her skirt a little with the right hand when she crossed a street. Why? An old habit? An automatic action done without conscious thought? My father swung his billy club on leather thongs and it made one and a half turns before it snapped back into his hands. Where had he learned that? Was he imitating some officer whom he admired? Shorty Chapple had a chronic running ear which created a bad odor that he could not smell. Was this why he did small unasked favors for me after I chose him for my team in stickball? Why did the workmen en route home in their heavy shoes pause to urinate at street trees? Old ladies who lived alone scurried along the sidewalk under dark shawls — frightened mice hurrying to and from a nest. At the beach, what made waves when there was no wind? Why the silence of the poplar trees before a violent shower?

And why must I believe that God always was and always will be when it was impossible to digest "always was"? My tottering brain rocketed back and back in time, through the darkness of outer space, toward a time when God must have begun. The almanac told me that there were two billions of people in the world — how could He, in His omnipotence, know what was going on in every heart at every minute of every day? A book by a new author, Will Durant, was called *Transition*. I got it because he had attended Saint Peter's College in Jersey City and, although he disguised names and places, he dismissed my hometown in a sentence: "I will never forgive it for being what it was when I knew it, dirty, run-down . . ." Scores of times my mother asked me not to read. "You'll get brain fag."

But books were the key to get out of town — to go to far places and meet strange people. To know, to learn, to select such facts as I chose to remember, to forget others, to feel a welling excitement in the chest because an astronomer had discovered a dull red sun thousands of light-years away and said that it had died long ago in cold ash, but that its beams of light were still traversing space to be reflected on the retina of his eye.

I took tap-dancing lessons in Belleville so that I could go on the stage. Someday, people would pay to see me. I mastered a time step. Among the students was a sweet girl named Edna. She had a moon face and fat ankles. I had failed too many times to make an approach. She invited me to her house. Her mother and father looked up from newspapers on the dining room table to say hello. Edna and I sat on a couch in the living room, where the grown-ups could see us and we could see them. She put her tongue in my mouth. After doing this several times, Edna appeared to become as weak as Tessie. Staring anxiously at the parents in the dining room, I opened my trousers. Edna did not fall asleep. She took one look in the gloom and grabbed it. Then, hiking her dress and pulling her step-ins aside, she sat on it. I kept telling myself: "I'm getting laid." I could barely believe me. The girl didn't master the time step in class, but she perspired with energy as she squirmed. I was finished before her father reached the sports section. It was the most gigantic, surging ecstasy of an exhausted mind. When it was over, I suspect that Edna was ready to start, because her jumping became more pronounced and she pouted when the thing fell out.

All the way home, I replayed the sex scene on the trolley car. It got better. The excitement was on me again. I would tell the priest, of course — this sin, in the eyes of the Church, appeared to be more mortal than murder — but I would add a few sympathy-inducing notes about my many diseases and the short time I had to live. This might cut the penance. I chased Edna everywhere. We couldn't screw in front of her parents, so we screwed in the back room of the dance studio ("Excuse us for a moment. We have to change our dancing shoes"). I knew a harmless old fairy who had a flat at Green Gables. There we took time and clothes and flung them away. The great and awful thing about Edna was that she was always ready. I did not have to cuddle up and kiss. A solitary tap on her shoulder; her knees began to knock. She had a self-starter. She seemed to gain strength and desire as we proceeded. Her strength became my weakness. I was gasping in bed as she tried her dance steps barefooted and bare-assed. In time, I dropped her gently.

My mother was pleased that I was giving up the books for an early bed. "Get your proper sleep," she said, "and you'll be a strong man." One afternoon my father arrived in uniform, laid the nightstick on the dining room table, and, without the usual disarming preamble, said: "Do you know a Newark girl named Edna ——?" I was stunned. Yes, I said, I knew the girl. "Well," my father said with a snarl, "she's pregnant and her father told me he's coming here to blow your head off." My mind raced. If she was pregnant, I would have to marry her at age seventeen. If she wasn't, then she was angry because I had been neglecting her and she had told her father a lie to get me to the altar. "She is not pregnant," I said as nicely as I could. "The girl is lying." My father lost his temper. "I'm not accusing you; her father is. He phoned me at headquarters and I'm not fooling. He says he has a gun and he's going to kill you. And stop telling me that she isn't pregnant. The important thing is that you seduced her at a dancing school. Well, you bum, what are you going to do about this?"

My mother was horrified. There was sobbing. It was on my tongue to say: "Like father, like son. Mom tells me that I have brothers and sisters in this town that we don't know about." I didn't. "Let the man shoot me," I said. I wished hard that I could weep, but I had lost the ability. My throat constricted until I could respond to the shouts only with negative and positive shaking of the head. Even breathing was difficult. My mother, in a gentle manner, tried to explain that sex was reserved for the sacrament of marriage and that — God forbid! — if I should be in an accident I would court hellfire.

The best way to get out of this mess, I thought, would be a call to the priesthood. I told my mother I had been thinking of becoming a monk, turning away from the world to meditate, to study, to pray, to do God's work. She sobbed louder. "You're a liar!" my father shouted. He was right. But I was not lying at that moment, when all desire had fled from my loins and I could imagine a man with a revolver ringing the doorbell. It was easy to renounce women; the monastic life was safe. The Church would feed me and keep a roof over my head. My thing could repose like an anchovy under clanking rosary beads.

Edna's father did not call. Nor did she. Nor I. There were new girls and new jobs, more of the latter than the former. There was cast-iron logic in my father's appellation: "Bum!" If one is seventeen and aware that he has nothing to offer, no skill, time becomes a dragging clanking chain which hangs heavier from the leg as new links are forged. I was a time-keeper at the Eagle Oil works. I was not discharged. After a month, I quit.

My next field of endeavor was in the literary world. There was a certain pleasure in carrying a heavy case full of lending-library books at 30 Church Street in New York. Clerks and secretaries rented best-sellers. The man who owned the books had eight boys working eight office buildings from top floor to bottom. My problem — and problems represented my solitary asset — was that I was more of a critic than a salesman. Or, if the word *critic* is too strong, I was a book tout.

Some asked for copies of A. A. Milne's *When We Were Very Young*. I called it third-rate doggerel written for retarded children. A living water-fall of praise cascaded from my lips regarding Aldous Huxley's *Those Barren Leaves*, but some of the stenographers sniffed and said Huxley was "too deep." *Arrowsmith* by Sinclair Lewis was popular. Those who had read *Main Street* and *Babbitt* were willing to reserve the book weeks ahead. I pushed F. Scott Fitzgerald's *The Great Gatsby*, but the only person I recall who evinced an enthusiasm was a wheezing man who tried to pet me in aisles of tall filing cabinets. He said the book was great. With unusual kindness, he told me I was great too — I had a square build and he marveled at my muscles every other week.

There were many books. Gertrude Atherton had published *The Crystal Cup*, but I advised my clients that Willa Cather made Miss Atherton's work look pale indeed. In the same satchel I had Sherwood Anderson's *Dark Laughter*, DuBose Heyward's *Porgy*, and Mary Roberts Rinehart's *Red Lamp*. On a certain payday, the boss said that he could not understand how I managed to reduce book rentals at 30 Church Street by more than 40 percent, but he had made a few judicious phone calls and found that my real vocation was to write books and he would withhold his admiration and his money until the first one was published. We parted on bad terms because I called him "a son of a son of a bitch," which required time to decipher.

In the presence of the other boys, he asked me what great literary works I had read, so I prattled whatever surfaced: Tarkington's *Penrod*; Freud, Jung, Adler; Tom Swift; Jack London, O. Henry; Balzac; the Rover Boys, Nick Carter; Theodore Dreiser; the Liberty Boys; Dr. Warner Fabian; Dumas, Carl Sandburg; *American Mercury* magazine; and, if he was interested, a periodical from France called *La Vie Parisienne*. He tried to stop me with feeble waves of the hand, but I kept ticking off authors on my fingers, repeating some already mentioned to stop him from speaking. As I walked toward the door, he shouted, "You're a sullen bastard." I recall it well because *sullen* was not his type of epithet.

I went home and joined the National Guard field artillery. It wasn't that abrupt. First I called my friends for a secret meeting. We were all young and very wise — Alexander Porter, Arthur Taylor, Fred Grimsey, my younger brother, John — and, after much consultation in a freezing living room, we devised something called the Spur Club. We would learn to ride horses, and we would purchase swords and learn to fence like d'Artagnan. With becoming modesty, I became president and sent a publicity release to the sports editor of the Hudson *Dispatch*. There was excitement in the group when it was published. The words were mine. I read the sentences over and over and my stomach bubbled and tickled. I could not believe my words — my own thoughts — would run through a press thousands of times.

The Spur Club had no horses, and no money. We traveled to East Orange, New Jersey, and joined "A" Battery, 112th Field Artillery, National Guard of New Jersey. We received ill-fitting, itchy uniforms with campaign hats and were astounded to learn that the United States government had no intention of permitting us to ride their horses up and down

Branchbrook Park. What they had in mind was for us to get in the stalls with those dull creatures and give them a bath with currycomb and brushes. They expected us to attend drill once a week, to execute squad exercises on a tanbark floor, salute, obey orders without question, attend Pine Camp two weeks every summer, and, in time, to become cannoneers (French 75s) or drivers (these guided the six witless animals who hauled the French 75s). Al Porter, who became enamored of the military life and would one day be a major, was a lead driver. He sat on one horse, and guided the reins of the other. I was on the next two — called a swing driver. My brother was a wheel driver — third team. Officers in gleaming boots, which they tapped with riding crops, were fond of explaining how much our monumental mistakes were costing the United States government.

I served my hitch, got an honorable discharge, and went to Atlantic City with Artie Taylor to look for work. He was a sleeper. Artie could hop into bed on Friday and get up on Sunday. For a time, I worked in a boardwalk window stamping gold names in wallets. It paid twenty-five dollars a week, ten of which matched Taylor's ten to pay for a small room on South Carolina Avenue. My father wrote a friendly, almost cautious, note, asking if I had any objection to a visit from him and Clara. I admired the stout blond woman who had once lived next door. She had a beautiful face with skin a shade paler than a pink dawn. She also had intelligence, an inner motivation which is called drive, and could play the piano well. With misgivings and guilt, I wrote Big John telling him I would be happy to see him — and Clara. My manners, I think, were impeccable. The one thing I did not tell my father was that I had been fired from my wallet-stamping for spending too much time grinning out the window at people who were grinning and watching me.

For a while, Artie had to pay the bills. Later, my mother came down by train. I borrowed money to buy lunch for her. Her glasses, like my father's, were pince-nez and she kept them turned my way, smiling and hugging me and asking little questions. When she returned home, she wrote a note, which I saved:

August 23, 1928

My Dearest Son

I want to thank you and Artie for the nice time you gave me and I got home safe and it was 10–30. Adele was waiting for me, she cryed because she didn't see you but we will go down in 2-Sunday from now. She want to see you so bad. Write to Dad and ask him to come along with us it a grand trip — I enjoyed it very much and Sunday 2 is the last excursion train so trye and get him to go with us. Lonnie, get a job like a good boy and go to church as you know you promised so much when you were sick. You look offill yesterday. I don't mean in health, in your shabbiness.

Now please do that for me will you? Artie may go home and

[39]

then tell his mother if you were not there he would of saved money, which is true, so get a job and stay at it and be indipendent from everything else. Thank Artie for me as I had a grand time. Will see you very soon again.

Love and kisses from Adele and your mother

X X X X X X X X X X X

X X X X X

The two-cent stamp on the envelope was canceled upside down. It symbolized the way I felt about myself. The letter was complete and accurate. It required no divination for me to see that I was not equipped to be the person she needed — the man of the house. From the age of fourteen to twenty-one I fled that responsibility. Once, in the Florida boom, I ran away on the Clyde liner *Arapahoe,* and worked in Miami. Four months later, broke and out of work, I went home. I was running from more than an agony of spirit; I could not bear the knowledge that, no matter how callously Mother was treated by her husband, she wanted him back. The subtlety in the note, "Write to Dad and ask him to come along . . . ," made me wince. When I ran away, she didn't ask for money and I didn't send it. And yet, at each return she held me to her breast and wept. The greatest reward she could devise for my disloyalty was "I'll make something you like for supper. And, yes, I'll bake a chocolate layer cake."

At the age of sixteen, Adele found an escape. The fragile blond was about to marry Edgar Parmelee, a thin boy who was studying to be a naval draftsman. She met him on summer vacation at Highlands, New Jersey. Edgar ran Perry's carousel at night, and Adele got free rides. The proposed marriage upset my father. "She's a child," he said. "This is a disgrace."

"You are not home," my mother said, "to know what a disgrace is. I have had long talks with Adele. She's in love with this boy, John, and you and I are not going to stop them." My father agreed when Edgar, who was Protestant, assented to a ceremony in the rectory of Saint Patrick's Church.

Johnny would not work. I was unable to keep a job. The last in a long list was as milkman for Sheffield Farms Dairy Company. At midnight I harnessed a horse, drove to a railroad docking platform in Greenville, lifted twenty-two cases of "A" milk, eight cases of "B," two cases of pints, and six bottles of buttermilk. I was ordered to drive from Jersey City along Broadway in Bayonne to the far end. My route was called Bergen Point. I was armed with a lantern and a small book which showed the addresses and orders of the customers. The horse knew the route. As I was studying the book to line up the next customer, he was walking across the street to the next house. I quit the job in a month.

This forced my mother to break up what was left of the family. Dad refused to advance more money. She incurred his enmity by resorting to an attorney, who told my father he was about to be sued for separation.

[40]

This meant publicity in the *Jersey Journal*, and Big John made the mistake of threatening Jenny. He told her if she sued, she would get nothing, nothing, nothing, and she would have to go out and scrub floors. She had two worthless sons who would not support her, or even help. I listened to it. The louder he shouted, the more softly she spoke. He said that the whole idea of a public suit was the notion of her mother and sister Etta.

This was true, because I was with my mother when she visited them at 41 Randolph Avenue. Her relatives goaded her to destroy him and, in a practical sense, they were right. Grandma Tier was a wizened woman with mouse-gray hair and star-splashed wrinkles. Etta was an attractive woman with visible pride. She felt that my mother had married beneath the Tier family. On each visit, they nudged Mother, demanding that the Bishop world be set in flames. Then they would turn to me and say: "Lonnie, you wouldn't speak to him, would you? You know your mother is a good woman. She's too good for your father. Don't speak to him when you see him. He isn't worth it. He's sleeping with another woman. You know what that is, don't you? It means she's a trollop. And don't visit your Grandma Bishop and your Aunt Margaret. They're on your father's side. They're trying to hurt your mother. You wouldn't hurt your mother, would you, Lonnie?"

The story got into the newspaper once. It was enough. Mayor Frank Hague called my father to City Hall. He was abrupt. "John," he said, "get rid of that woman and get back to your family." As my father told me the story years later, he decided to face the mayor down. It was a poor tactical move. "Mayor," he said, "I don't think you know the whole story about my personal problems, and if you want me to resign..." "Hell, no," Hague said. "I'm taking you out of the Bureau of Patrol to become captain of the Fifth. John, you're on the way up. You can make chief. As soon as I get Tom Nugent out of the Fifth, you go in. Now be sensible and get rid of that woman. I don't want any scandal on my police force. One more thing, see if you can get your wife to keep this thing out of court and out of the papers. It makes us look bad."

He thanked the mayor and said he'd give it thought. Big John had a teeth-grinding dominance that brooked no ultimatums. The biggest mistake occurred immediately after. He tried to pacify Jenny by telling her that, if a temporary truce could be arranged, he would see what he could do about more money, the marriage, everything. This was designed to soothe her, to give her hope. He said that Hague told him he would be promoted to take Captain Nugent's place. This would mean more money, more prestige, more power. She would have to keep it secret, of course.

My mother confided the news to her friend, Mrs. John Peters, as they sat over tea and cake and gossiped. Jenny Bishop forgot that John Peters was a patrolman in the Fifth Precinct, a good man who had not been promoted. Mrs. Peters whispered the news to her husband. Peters whispered it to Captain Nugent. The old man with the bristling white mustaches was overdue for retirement, but he was not going to be pushed. The next time Lieutenant John Bishop stopped into the Fifth Precinct, Nugent pointed a finger at him in a dramatic manner and shouted: "Here comes the devil!" My father didn't forget those words. His career was over. Nugent wrote a note to Hague accusing him of trying to dump the old captain for Bishop. Word was sent to my father to forget the promotion. He asked why. "Ask your wife," he was told.

Jenny moved into a furnished room. Johnny and I were sent to Aunt Margaret's house. She had a husband, Eddie, eight small children, Grandma Bishop, and her younger sister, Mary — all living on one floor. Aunt Margaret McCarthy was a no-nonsense woman. She was the matriarchal martinet of the age. Her words resounded like orders on a battlefield. Eddie worked in an oil refinery in Bayonne and few appreciated how Margaret struggled to keep the healthy young stomachs filled. She never lost faith, she never lost hope, that she and she alone could do it.

Underneath, she had a sense of humor which sent her into gales of laughter until tears streamed from her eyes. She wasted no spurious sentiment on the newcomers. "You sleep in there on that cot," she said, "and you sleep in the other room. Your father asked me to take care of both of you until he can get straightened out, but I want to tell you one thing — no work, no eat. Tomorrow morning, you will both get up at seven and go out and look for jobs. On the first day, I'm going to give you lunch money. If I hear that you went to the movies, you'll pay for it. If you don't find a job in one place, go ask next door. Keep asking and don't come back until it's dark out. Understand?" We understood.

Mom wrote to me on occasion. The letters were heavy with heartache. "At ten I put out the light in my room, say my prayers, and go to bed. I feel that ants are crawling all over me. I scratch all night. As you know, I was always a light sleeper. . . ."

I decided to request a final conference with my father. He met me in a coffeehouse.

"I know what my career is going to be."

"What?"

"A writer."

"A what?"

"A newspaper reporter."

"At the age of twenty-one, you have finally decided to favor the world with your writing?" The voice dripped disappointment.

"It's writing. I don't want to be anything else."

"My boy, in all the history of the Bishop family, there was never a writer. We were farmers, peasants, day laborers — honest men who worked with their hands. For Christ sake, you couldn't get a passing grade in English."

"Remember the time I was in Miami? Well, I used to buy the Sunday edition of the New York *News*. They have a columnist, Mark Hellinger. Dad, I think I can write like that."

"You're crazy," he said. The words were not vindictive; they faltered. He reminded me that reporters spend a lifetime working hard to reach a stage where they write professionally. He seemed distressed to remind me that the job as milkman paid forty-eight dollars a week, plus four dollars in bonuses, and I had to quit it for what — to become a copyboy at ten or twelve dollars a week? At the age of forty-six, his career was over; mine was about to begin. There was something sad in his imperious attitude. The next day he asked me to meet him at an address on Wegman Parkway. There, I learned, he lived with Clara Capuozzo and her three children. The reason for the wide-open conference was that he required her opinion.

I began my plea again. She sat with her hands folded on her lap, watching me. "Bim," she said, "I think Jim has a real ambition to write. Who knows? He could surprise all of us. Certainly, he has the intelligence. If he has the proper application — well, he could go somewhere." It was the first time I heard the nickname "Bim." Her children had read it in a comic strip called *Andy Gump*, and hung it on my father. He was "Bim." He kept shaking his head no. Then he slapped his big hands on both knees. "All right," he said. "All right. I know a retired cop on the New York *News*. His name is what — it'll come to me — Dan O'Keefe. That's it. He used to get baseball passes for me. I'm not sure, but I think he's in charge of copyboys. Anyway, we'll see."

Love had come. My emotions were like bits of confetti caught in a whirlwind which spun upward. It was a first love, but I cannot denigrate it to the status of puppy love. Whatever ability I had to think, to rationalize, was lost the moment I thought of Ellen. To those who knew her, she was a beautiful girl with shoulder-length blond hair, parted on one side to hang in two soft waves. She was encased in an exciting feminine figure with legs which swelled gently at the calves, then inward to ankles too fragile to support a body. My memory is of a pale complexion and a concealed sense of amusement at the edges of the lips.

The exterior was more than attractive; it stifled my breathing. And yet she seemed not to know that she was beautiful. She accepted male compliments as examples of good manners. In high school, she led her class in four subjects. In the late evenings, I stood on her doorstep and talked of dreams, ambitions, my multitudinous shortcomings, not excluding the twittering bird of hypochondria that caused me to be beset by rare ailments which would, I was certain, kill me by age twenty-five. In Ellen, I saw a universe of goodness. There were bright stars and strange planets, areas of darkness which begged for a probing light.

To think of her while waiting for sleep in darkness insured a restless night. I was possessive, jealous, adoring, soaring in spirit so ridiculously high that, for the first time, I wanted to beat the world at its own game, to win all the treasure and all the fiery gems and place them before Ellen. I hummed. I sang. I made plans. I neglected my friends. Trousers and jackets were pressed. Scotch-grain shoes were shined until they gleamed. The winter sun seemed brighter. My reading was confined to the poetry of Edna St. Vincent Millay and Oscar Wilde and a dozen others who, in some mysterious manner, told me how I felt. Wilde's *Charmides*, a long poem about a Greek sailor boy, was studied again and again and the joy of it saddened me.

There were evenings when Ellen was busy making dresses and these, for me, were nights of emptiness. There were a thousand things I wished to confide in her, but they flashed like summer lightning only when I was home. She lived in a small house a long bus ride from Aunt Margaret's. Our expressions of love were tentative, timid. We held hands in the Stanley Theatre; we kissed goodnight at her door. Men are reluctant to touch a goddess. All of it was an unstable euphoric experience — I met her mother and father many times, but they are blank faces. I brought her to my mother, a nervous son bearing a gleaming trophy, and, after some tea and hot biscuits and woman-to-woman chatting, my mother's gold tooth gleamed in a smile of approval. After two or three visits, Mother said that Ellen might be too good for me. "First of all," she said, ticking on her fingers like a scorekeeper, "she is obviously a lady, and not all girls are ladies. Second, you have always been a dreamer and this has caused you a lot of trouble. There is no place in family life for the dreamer, son. He must work; he needs a sense of responsibility — you haven't learned these things. In the next place, you're sulky."

"What's that?" I said.

"Moody. Sometimes you don't answer when you're spoken to. When you do speak, you're blunt. You hurt people's feelings. I would say that a girl's feelings are a lot different from a boy's. Now Ellen, as I see her, is very, very feminine. She would be easily hurt. . . ."

"Oh God, can't you think of anything good to say about me?"

"Lots of things," she said. "I always said you were the only person I knew who would tell the truth no matter what. You look a lot better since you met Ellen. You're more particular about how you look. I notice things. . . ."

Truth can be unbearable. The things my mother was saying about me echoed my sentiments. And yet I felt a justification in wanting to marry Ellen precisely because she was too good for me. With her intelligent help, I could improve my life. I did not believe that marriage helped a man to "settle down," any more than I subscribed to the credo that the way to make a man of a boy was to sign him into the United States Marine Corps. But a partnership based on respect, affection, and mutual assistance could, I was certain, make for more contentment, more success, than the sum of the individual contributions. I had no faith in sustained happiness. The status seemed too lofty, too giddy, too much out of reach precisely as intense grief cannot endure for long periods.

Ellen and I whispered of love and marriage, wealth and poverty, as though we had invented them. I could not plan a wedding at a time when my father was trying to get me one more job; a position, which, if attained, would pay lunch, carfare, cigarettes, and one movie a week. Better to plan for the future; better to think of salaries in another year; to think of a small apartment, a small radio, a thrift account — most of all, better to reassure each other how deeply we understood that we belonged to each other and to no one else. Standing on that small stoop with the rail behind Ellen's hips, we had all the night stars in our hands. I told her I planned to work by day and to write a book at night. She was surprised. What would it be about? Homosexuals, I said. A small frown fretted her forehead. "Why those people?" "Because you and the whole world say 'Why those people?'" I had no training in writing, or in researching, but I was about to write a daring book. "Millions of readers," I said, "are not aware of homosexuals; those who know about them are afraid, or feel disgust. Don't you see, a first book is going to be worthless unless I can find a shocking subject. It might even be banned in Boston. Think of the publicity. I even have a title: *There Are Such People*. Like it?" She wasn't sure. It seemed wild, she thought. Such a book might bring the wrong kind of attention to my work. Ellen believed that if I said I was going to be a fine writer I would be one, but she wasn't certain she understood the ideas, the moods — especially the moods of someone who, on one evening, was exalted to the stars and, on the following night, had revised his goals downward and assured her that no editor would want him or his work.

My father advised me to take a temporary position until Mr. O'Keefe could find room for me on the *News*. I took a night job in a dye factory. The vats smelled of hot vinegar. I hated the work, the multifarious odors, and, most of all, not being able to see Ellen. We wrote to each other by day, assuring and reassuring. In the middle of one of her letters were the words: "I think you remember Harold Lynn. Anyway, he works in an engineering office in the Trust Company Building. Last night he took me to the movies. We're going to the State Friday to see John Gilbert and Greta Garbo. I wish it was you, instead of him. . . ."

My father didn't want to lend his car. I said it was important. He asked how important. "My future is part of it," I said. He gave me the keys to the Hupmobile. I phoned Ellen and took the night off from work. The rain was heavy and windless, the kind which spatters on sidewalks and windows, making momentary dimples. She wore a tan topcoat. I drove up to the North Street grounds and switched off the key. Ellen asked what was the matter. A great deal, I said. We would have to settle the matter of Lynn tonight. I was unreasonable, she thought. I edged toward the left side of the wheel, leaning against the door.

In the darkness, diluted faintly by a streetlamp which fought the heavy rain, she slouched near her door. The discussion endured for hours. I posted one ultimatum after another. I was outraged that she could have a "casual" date. He was just a family friend, she insisted. I reminded Ellen that I had not dated anyone since I had fallen in love with her, and wouldn't dream of taking even a female cousin to the movies. Did we have separate standards? Her voice remained soft, her words conciliatory. She had no engagement ring, no wedding ring — why must she stay home for weeks on end while I worked? What could be wrong with Harold Lynn? My questions became irrational: "How casual is he? Does he put his arm around you in the movies? Does he kiss you goodnight? I'm asking — what's casual? Does he like you? I mean, as a girl? Or is he taking you to the movies just to keep you warm until I get back?" When the tears came, they were silent, like the fat drops which slid down the windshield. It was not a quarrel between lovers because, in the sexual sense, we were not lovers. Paradoxically, we were more than lovers; we had pledged our lives to each other.

At last she broke a final silence. "Please take me home."

"What is that supposed to mean?"

"We're not getting anywhere, Jim."

I turned the key. The car throbbed; the wipers flicked the tears aside. "Are you going to see Lynn Friday?"

A big sigh. "Yes."

"Then we have nothing further to discuss."

"If you say so."

At Hudson Boulevard, there was a long red light. Stubbornly, I had pushed a small matter to a position where I had to surrender to Ellen or kill love in silence. We said nothing until I stopped the car in front of her door. I did not get out in the rain to open her door and walk her up that stoop where, for a year, we had planned to conquer the world. "Good-night, Jim," she said.

I did not look at her. "Good-bye, Ellen."

She closed the door and I studied her back as she walked up the few steps. I could call to her but I wouldn't.

She stepped into the little vestibule and I sat. I heard the door click. It was I who had slammed it. There was a slight chance that she might find an excuse to phone — some photos, or a book I had left with her. Very slight. Ellen knew I would see it as a bid to give our love mouth-to-mouth resuscitation. She would not call. Nor would I. Moods, high and low, are the curse of the Bishops. I never saw Ellen again.

WHAT?

"REPORT TO MR. DAN O'KEEFE, *Daily News* BUILD-
ing, Park Place, nine A.M. Wednesday, Jan. 2nd, 1929.
Second floor." The starting gun. The crack in the doorway. An opportunity
to run hard and fast until I ran out of talent. First, I had to frisk my
character to find out how much frustration I could endure. I borrowed
Big John's Number 4 Underwood, and hunted and pecked with two fingers
until the printed words and sentences and punctuation almost, not quite,
matched the speed of thought. Gone were the teachings of Drake College
in touch-typing and stenography. My father was appalled. "Are you trying
to tell me that you don't remember?" I nodded.

Three days before reporting to Mr. O'Keefe, I rode the subways. The
B.M.T., the I.R.T., the old B.R.T., double-ender Broadway trolleys —
all became my visual aids. Suppose the editor said: "Bishop, get up to a
hundred and twenty-eighth and Lenox and cover a murder" — what would
I do? All I knew of New York was Times Square, a little of Wall Street,
and Tottenville, Staten Island. Grandpa Tier had a summer bungalow in
Tottenville and sometimes, in the early days, we had spent two summer
weeks there. It was far from enough. There was much to learn and little
time in which to absorb the great city. The East River was spiderwebbed
with bridges; Manhattan was a busted comb upside down; there were
areas of affluence and poverty — Wall Street, the Jews and pushcarts on
Houston; Joralemon Street in Brooklyn, where, for a brief moment, I had
worked for the Manufacturers Trust Company as assistant teller; Harlem
with blinding bulbs and cellar gin mills; there were nightclubs and Yankee
Stadium and the Polo Grounds; Ebbets Field and Uncle Wilbur Robinson;
the Bronx; Mosholu Parkway; Chinatown; Cherry Hill; the remote
brownstone mansions on Fifth Avenue; cathedrals, synagogues, the resi-
dential aura of Queens; Washington Heights; the big liners at piers along
the North River; Brooklyn Navy Yard; police precincts scattered everywhere; Central Park; taxicabs owned by a hoodlum named Larry Fay;
the beautiful chorus girls owned by men with sagging bellies; the gangs;
night court on West Fifty-fourth Street; county courts at Foley Square;
tennis courts at Forest Hills; alimony jails; the Tombs; the Garment

District, teeming with dresses on perambulating street racks; the dismal sight from the Queensboro Bridge of Blackwell's Island below — the north end consisted of a poorhouse, the south was a collection of prison buildings. There was much, much more to New York and no neophyte copyboy would know it in three days. Or three years.

The morning was cold and clear. The sky was a watery eye. Rusty snow encrusted the curbs. Park Place, in the shadow of the Woolworth Building, staggered in its old cobblestones past dark decrepit loft buildings which, near the river, became markets and warehouses with sagging overhangs. Long ago, perhaps in another century, it had surrendered to the last living things — Norwegian rats who darted and stopped as they hugged ancient walls, and whose small feet barely raised the dust on the empty floors of the lofts. If there was a gleam of light anywhere, it came not from the *News*, a rickety building which throbbed all night with the spin of Hoe presses. It would be the place next door: Suerkin's, a saloon with star-chased windows, a free lunch of steaming sauerkraut and wurst, waiters with long aprons cinched under armpits, and bar mirrors which reflected faithfully an array of cold beers and elbows and penitents who studied the stains under the steins.

The *News* had a glass display of daily photos around the front door. Inside there was a small elevator which complained whether rising or descending. The editorial department was on the second floor; I took the steps two at a time. They were concave with wear and the boards squeaked. There was a splintered desk for a receptionist. Once, a bearded man in sandals and toga stood before that desk and asked to see the city editor. The receptionist began to fill out a visitor's sheet and asked who wanted to see him. "Jesus Christ," the visitor said. The receptionist stood and shook hands. "Glad to meet you," he said politely; "I've heard a lot about you."

It was empty now. I walked into the big room. Desks with inserted typewriters were in rows, some facing front, others facing each other the length of the building. Almost all of them wore the wound stripes of cigarettes. The floor was confettied with torn strips of newspapers. Two-thirds of the way back, there was walking space around two large facing desks. Over them hung green cones of light. There were partly empty wax containers with the sludge of yesterday's coffee. A stiff sandwich lifted its ends from the dirty floor.

Facing the open space and the coned lights was a long bench. Two boys sat on it chatting. A balding man in a green visor sat at one of the big desks. He was reading something typewritten on cheap paper; his thick pencil made paragraph marks; as I passed I saw him run the pencil through a herd of words, and stab them to death with a vertical arrow. He was Frank Carson, day city editor, a professional originally from Chicago. His form sheet showed that he had worked for Colonel Robert McCormick on the Chicago *Tribune*, been taken to a speakeasy by Hearst's editor Walter Howie, who, in uncompetitive camaraderie, got Carson blind drunk and signed him to a contract as city editor of the Chicago *Herald-Examiner*. Later, McCormick's men got Carson loaded and packed him off to New York to become day city editor of the *News*.

There was a door on the left side of the room and one on the right. The first led to part of another loft building. There, a half-dozen desks constituted the Sports Department, administered by Paul Gallico, a horn-rimmed owl with thick lips, the lower of which hung like a dangling participle. In that room were the wire machines, the noisy gossips which told everyone in the name of the Associated Press and United Press and City News what was happening, and where.

The door on the right side smelled strongly of ammonia. This was the men's room, a stifling place with three urinals, a depository for empty pint bottles. An old man with a slight limp, unkempt gray hair, and a hollow questioning expression, emerged from this room. "Who are you?"

"Jim Bishop, sir."

"Oh, Lieutenant Bishop's son." He pointed. "Sit on that bench with the other boys. I'll get to you in a minute." Carson looked up from under the green eyeshade. The face was pale, abused, and wise. "You the new boy? I'm Frank Carson."

I shook hands timidly. "Thank you," I said and forgot to give my name.

I sat, wondering where my hero, the Broadway columnist Mark Hellinger, might be. I would have to learn to write with sentimental cynicism, because that was the way his O. Henry stories read. "Do you know how to make books?" It was the limping man.

"You're Mr. O'Keefe," I said.

"Of course I am," he said. "You're working for me." "Books," it developed, were three sheets of copy paper with two sheets of double-sided carbon paper between them. My boss sat me at the copy desk, showed me how it was done, how to fold each finished product so that it would not fall apart before it was encased in the rubber roller of a typewriter. I began to make books. He gave me a cardboard carton and told me to fill it. A boy came over to help. "I'm Bill Meurer." A blond boy shook hands. "I'm Artie Siebelist. We'll give you a rundown on this place."

Reporters began to come in. Overcoats and scarves and hats were draped on clothes trees. A stocky, good-looking woman came in. She was Irene Kuhn. The identities were given by Meurer. He also gave me a friendly rundown on each one. A dignified man walked in and removed gloves, a finger at a time. "John O'Donnell," he said. "Reporter and rewrite man."

"What's a rewrite man?"

"He can take a story by telephone from a reporter on the scene and write it for the city desk."

"Oh."

"Down near the front — that's Nelson, Brooklyn editor."

"What does he do?"

"What the hell would you figure? He edits the Brooklyn edition. It gets sandwiched inside the city edition and it features Brooklyn news. It's supposed to cut into Brooklyn *Eagle* circulation. We have three Kennys."

"Three?"

"Yep. All reporters. Well, not exactly. Jack and Ed are reporters. Nick sits in for anybody who has a day off."

"Never mind the talk," a voice said. "Make them books." It was O'Keefe. Meurer and I hurried to fill the carton. Doris Fleeson — thin, with eyes as expressionless as ball bearings, sat at a desk next to O'Donnell. The newspaper at this hour was dead. Each day the resurrection began at ten A.M. and the big room filled with chatter, voices, and typewriters. "Boy!" a voice would bawl, and, whether it was a reporter who wanted a story rushed to the city desk, or an editor who wanted something taken to the copy desk, five boys edged along the bench, shining it with their pants, until each achieved the number one position. There had been a room I did not see. It was on the same side as the men's room. It was called a studio. In it, photographers edged into darkrooms holding cameras and shoulder bags full of exposed plates. This was a picture newspaper, and pictures were important. A jolly man with brown curly hair called the photographers, sent them rushing off to the ends of the city to shoot pictures, and told them to develop and print their photos when they got back to his desk. He was Ted Dalton, photo editor.

Facing him on the city desk complex was Harry Nichols, a dark, ulcerous man who spoke in spasms. All the reporters who were out on stories phoned him, told him where they were, what they had in story value, and Nichols looked up at the beaming Dalton and snapped: "We got pix?"

Dalton would nod, and Nichols would look down the line of rewrite men and call a name. "Take Feeney on four," he would say. "Give me a page and a paragraph." Sometimes he had phones hunched against each ear and one hanging loose in his hand. The slow daily crescendo of the newspaper responded to his baton. When copyboys ran out to get the first editions of the afternoon newspapers, it was Nichols whose eyes scoured page 1, then the inside pages, to see what they had that the *News* hadn't covered. He would tear part of a page, hand it to a reporter, and say: "Run out there and get me a follow-up on this. Call Charlie at police headquarters first and find out why he didn't have it. What the hell does he do — sleep on Center Street?"

A short man in glasses came in, the gait slow, the manner confident: Martin Sommers, star rewrite man. He was followed by Tom Cassidy, the only man who, drunk, could rap out an errorless newspaper story with his head riding the carriage of the typewriter back and forth. A tall redhead stood blowing on his hands. He was Red Dolan, star reporter, the only one who earned two hundred a week. A short plump girl opened her coat and sat at a desk near the front of the room dreaming at a blank "book" in her typewriter. She was Irene Thirer, motion picture critic. "See the guy coming in now?" Meurer said. "The man with the slick black hair and the puppy sticking out of his coat pocket? That's Mark Hellinger." I stood to look. He wore a snap-brim gray hat, a black Chesterfield overcoat out of which, indeed, a puppy glanced and shivered. Hellinger wore a dark blue suit and black gleaming shoes. This was his "uniform." My man. He removed the coat, hung it, stooped to kiss the pup, and sat up front facing the window.

The hair had been parted with an ax. The pale blue eyes hid from the lights behind heavy lids. I was not aware that, for years, he had been writing a "Sunday only" page. The *News* had promoted him to write a daily column about Broadway. From a distance, I liked the molasses skin, the air of fatigue which is the accoutrement of the Broadway columnist.

Bill Meurer seemed surprised that a new copyboy knew the names of so many of the reporters. "I always read the by-lines first," I said. "I know the ones who write frequently. You have a reporter named Alfred Albelli."

Meurer grinned. "He has an in with divorce lawyers. Sits over there, next to Kenny." A short chubby young man with black hair approached and asked for "books." I gave him a half-dozen. He flipped two back to me.

"That's Jimmy Cannon. He was just made cub reporter."

"He's new?"

"No, no. He was a copyboy three years. Deuell gave him a raise and put him on assignment."

"Who's Deuell?"

"City editor." Bill saw my puzzlement. "It goes like this: Captain Patterson is the publisher. He and his cousin, Colonel McCormick of the Chicago *Tribune*, own the joint. You won't see much of Patterson. He comes in like he's on parade. Under him is Colonel Frank Hause. He's the managing editor."

"Two colonels and a captain," I said.

Meurer was being extra friendly to a new boy. "I think they were all in World War One. Anyway, under Hause is Deuell. He runs the city room. Then I guess Frank Carson. Nichols works for Carson. You won't see Gene McHugh until around four o'clock. He's a tall skinny guy — night editor. McHugh is more than that. He feeds pink pills to his ulcers, but he's nice to everybody. I mean, if you ever get jammed up here, run to Gene McHugh and he'll bail you out. . . ."

O'Keefe ordered us back to the bench. We sat waiting. I could hear my heart in my ears. This was my niche, my career. Before lunchtime, I had made a decision. When the first day was over, at five-thirty, I stood leaning on lockers to watch the action. The newspaper and I were time machines. I had seen it dormant and dusty at nine A.M. and watched all day as men and women hurried out to return later yelling "Boy!" The *News* was indeed an orchestrated crescendo, but it was the clock, not the editors, which called the tune. At six P.M. the noise was deafening. The staccato clack of many typewriters, the lisp of running feet, copy flowing in sheets across Carson's desk — some to be read and impaled on a spike, others flipped into a basket marked "Copy Desk"; shouts and orders; phones ringing; night copyboys taking stories from the slot in the copy desk with accompanying headlines; the wire services calling attention to new and startling developments with a ringing bell; a makeup editor dummying each page and marking each story with a code word; hot, exciting photos being rushed upstairs to the engravers; halftone cuts coming down; louder, louder, more strident, an impatient roar, and then, as the big wall clock flipped to six-forty, the sudden silence of a well-run funeral home. Men sagging on their spines, whispers, a few running down the sagging staircase for a quick drink at Suerkin's. Norma Abrams, slender and calm, reaching for her coat. She was covering a murder trial which might go on for weeks. Hellinger had departed, his column for the day complete. I wandered to the front window to look down. He emerged to sit at the wheel of an automobile which looked like a lavender bathtub. It was a Kissel roadster with a prestige license plate: "MH-7."

Silence. The sound of dust settling. Now and then, the small shriek of a paper torn from a typewriter. A veil of blue smoke hung shoulder-high, undulating as men walked through it. Somewhere, a phone rang with predictable rhythm. At home, supper was over. I waited. It came — the dull tentative growl of presses. It was slow. It gathered confidence. The hollow sound, like a train approaching a tunnel, hit its stride, and the floor, the walls, the ceiling trembled as though in fear of the news they had spawned. The green-shaded lights, hanging on long cords, shivered. The newspaper was living, breathing, excited in its own bedlam, churning a cascade of high-speed sheets of paper which ran through rollers, funneled themselves, folded, and emerged in a proper sequence of fifty copies at a time.

I took my coat and walked downstairs. Outside, trucks had been backed up to a platform. It was cold. Hard-looking men in pea jackets carried the bundles deep into the trucks. They shouted and yelled. A foreman sent them off — east, west, north, south — to Times Square, to Jersey, to trains panting in depots, to ferries — the Pink Edition of tomorrow's newspaper was on its way. Going home, walking, meditating, I wondered if, with luck and application, I might someday leave a small scar in this feverish world where, from hour to hour, everything that happened was fresh and exciting, and nothing could ever be the same as yesterday. I wondered.

Lying was easy. To my friends, I was not a copyboy; the *News*, recognizing my qualities, had hired me as a cub reporter. I showed my police identification card, which said: *"Daily News* — Editorial Dept." I found I could flash it to policemen and it got me inside fire lines and areas of crime which had been staked off. This card was a floating carpet. Standing in line for tickets to a movie, I showed it to the manager and he whispered: "Follow me. You don't have to buy tickets." I wore the importance of the card with gentility, never with arrogance. Paradoxically, the card was unimpressive among reporters and editors, but in the great outside world, it engendered respect. Without it, I was the same human cipher I had been. With it, I was somebody in a city where my only claim to recognition had been that I was "Lieutenant Bishop's oldest boy."

My father assumed, with insight, that my self-importance would keep me working; he phoned O'Keefe and got a confidential report that I was doing all right. I responded to the calls of reporters and editors with speed and a desire to carry out orders to the letter. The only thing O'Keefe didn't like was that I had "gone over his head" to Frank Carson and had been granted permission to use a typewriter between editions, practicing the rewriting of stories published in yesterday's newspaper. O'Keefe said: "That boy is going to have to make up his mind that he's a copyboy; he's working for me. I don't want him using typewriters."

The job had an echo effect. I wanted to get my mother out of that furnished room. Somewhere, I felt, we could find a small cheap flat. Adele was married and living with Parmelee in Highlands. John was drifting, so my father seduced him to sea with a coast guard sales talk. Big John told John that life on the ocean was not only adventurous, but that the United States government would teach him a trade while he was steaming aboard a destroyer in the center of a cobalt dinner plate, never reaching the edge, always in dead center. At the time, the coast guard had an energetic interest in locating boats laden with illegal liquor. He was assigned to New London, Connecticut, and served aboard the old destroyer *Cassin*. Johnny enjoyed being in uniform. When we were in "A" Battery, he had borrowed corporal's stripes, promoted himself, and had a formal photo taken. In the coast guard, he was in blues, wearing a pea jacket in winter and a cupcake hat. Something was missing. He went to a shop in New London and had an artist tattoo, "Eternal Love to Bubbles" with overlapping hearts.

Unhappily, he learned that Bubbles, in his absence, had been laughing it up with the neighborhood boys. With his "Bubbles" tattoo, he met an attractive redhead named Anna Gryniak and fell in love. Anna was the product of an industrious Polish family; the men favored hard work and liquor. The women spent considerable time in factories and church. Mother favored this romance because Miss Gryniak was "a good girl" who, like her mother and sisters, was not averse to working with her hands. Anna's dream of a successful life was to own a cottage and collect a pension. The pretty face, the flaming hair, and a sober view of the world had a steadying effect on John. The reformation was not complete, but our family knew, without a spoken statement, that John planned to marry Anna.

He sent a small amount of money to Mother. My father continued to send "alimony"; I contributed ten of my twelve dollars. She had found a small furnished flat on Van Wagenen Avenue. This was the nadir of our existence. At the same time I began to shed the weight of hypochondria.

Tests showed that the glands thought to be tubercular were, in fact, only "palpable." I was invited more frequently to spend evenings with "Bim" and "C." The shame of this was real; my love, my loyalty, belonged to my mother. I began to assess the marital situation anew. The trouble with Jenny Tier Bishop was that she was innocent and determined to remain naive. From fragments of conversation, I understood that she had turned her mind away from two things: general knowledge and sophisticated sex. Piecing the puzzle, I learned that when John Bishop married Jenny, his mother and the Roman Catholic Church had convinced him that the pleasures of the flesh were sinful. As his sophistication increased, Mother's innocence became a shield between them.

After the honeymoon, he had broadened his horizons in two areas: women, he found, were enamored of a big "chesty" man in a uniform. They were not only willing to surrender; with becoming timidity, they taught him things he did not know. The more he tried to bring erotic notions into the bedroom, the louder my mother denounced him as a beast. Second, he spent time studying sciences and arts.

Thinking about it, I marveled that the marriage had lasted fifteen years. My mother seldom read a book. She spent her spare time at a Singer sewing machine with a foot treadle, making starchy dresses for Adele and shirts for John and for me. She crocheted ornate antimacassars and doilies; grew ferns on pedestals; and bought "cut glass" — a glass and a punchbowl at a time to fill a sideboard.

Her husband slept with other "affinities," but she was caught in a vise of love which was squeezing her to death. Her mind teetered with thoughts of "my husbent." One afternoon a neighbor found her reclining on the floor of the kitchen, the oven door open, and her head on a clean towel. The windows were smashed open, and Mother was slapped back to consciousness. She cried. I came in from work stunned. The gas jets, I was told, had been open and hissing. I found it difficult to believe that Mother wanted to die. All it brought from Big John was a visit, a stream of vituperation. He called her a goddamn fool and made it appear that she was trying to destroy him. She wanted him back home, not destroyed. Her mistake was in thinking that his "affair" with Clara was an affair. If that were true, it would have died quickly under pressure from City Hall and the impossible burden of trying to support six children in two families. It endured as love endures. In the evenings, he helped Clara with the dishes; he discussed the state of the world and the nation with an equal; he entreated her to play the piano; he got drunk with her. He respected this stout woman, and gave up the sporadic games he played with other women. She was jealous of what she had stolen from her best friend. He missed dinner one night and Clara hit him with a solid right and John slid under the piano. Years later, he referred to that solitary blow, grinning and rubbing his jaw. "I never saw it coming," he would say. "Imagine being flattened by a woman. What a woman!"

On a Saturday in September, 1929, Al Porter phoned and asked me to accompany him on a blind date. I was wary, because Al, the pale redhead, seldom did well with girls. He was an assiduous student of the piano (Liszt, Chopin, Bach) and an amateur mathematician who worked at New York Life Insurance Company and hoped someday to become an actuary. In addition to these dolorous accomplishments, Al was addicted to logic in conversation. When a date said something illogical, Porter faulted himself by laughing uproariously — sometimes bending double and holding his stomach. So I said: "What do you mean — blind date?"

"Remember that old fairy in the Green Gables Apartments? Well, he's throwing a gin party, and two girls without fellas are going to be in the lobby at eight. One is named Elinor Dunning. She's supposed to be a well-stacked brunette and she is my . . . blind . . . date. Got it? Mine.

"She refused to attend the party without a friend, so she's bringing Mathilda Schultz. What? How the hell do I know? You have to take a chance. She may be a winner. Wanna come?" I said yes. There was a suspicion within me that good old Al had devised a Beauty and the Beast combination, and I was going to get the beast.

On the evening of the date, I bathed, shaved, pomaded my hair, and arrived early to get first look. Green Gables had a spacious lobby with wingback chairs. Two girls sat facing each other near "Aunty" Elwood's apartment. The girl facing me wore a bright expectant smile as though she knew I was intended for her. She was slender and twitchy, the legs and arms crossing and uncrossing many times. I approached the other chair from the back, leaned over it, and said: "Hello." This one was a girl with black hair, a moonlike face, and big brown eyes. Turned upward, the thick pouting mouth was akin to that of a startled fish. "Are you Al Porter?"

I shook my head no. "Jim Bishop. I'm the other one. You going to the party?" The girl was defensive. "We have been invited to *some* party," she said. "My name is Elinor Dunning. My friend is Tilly Schultz." I nodded to the nervous smiler. "Where is Al Porter?" Miss Dunning said. I said he'd be around.

I was not going to be stuck with Mathilda Schultz. She was tense — the type who laughs, dances, and kisses on cue. "Let's go in," I said. The Dunning girl thought she would wait for Porter. "He knows the way," I said. "No use sitting out here." It was a furnished apartment, fairly nice, with a vagueness of green rug, sofas, burning incense, and candy-striped wallpaper. "Aunty" was short and bellied, a balding man who wanted no more from life than a boy who would be faithful to him; he was now in the desperate position of inviting *girls* and boys, in hopes of winning one boy from one girl. He wore a spurious jollity, a "one of the gang" attitude, but it was no more genuine than his gin. Elinor edged into the corner of a sofa; I found a place beside her. She was not friendly. Formally hostile.

She was pretty in a boop-a-doop way, a girl with a voluptuous figure and gorgeous legs. We exchanged careers; she was a secretary working for

Dominick & Dominick, a Wall Street firm. "Aunty" placed a bucket of ice, a bottle which proclaimed "Gilbey's," some glasses, and lemon soda on a low circular table. "Everybody help yourself," he said. Fellows and girls were coming in in singles and doubles. Some I knew; some Miss Dunning knew. A few were strangers to everyone but that sorrowful manhunter, "Aunty." He had a tall loud boy he introduced as "my nephew." Whoever he was, or whatever, he was loud and unsubtle in his grinning sweaty belief that girls had been invited so that boys could lead them by the hand into the bedroom for what he referred to as some "good old-fashhioned fucking." He gulped his gin straight and took dead aim on Mathilda Schultz as a likely subject. In the dimly lighted arena the incoherent shouting and the music of Paul Whiteman's band interlocked with bathroom sounds of retching and the flushing of water. Miss Dunning began to smile. The moonlike brown eyes were full on me and she asked: "Do you like gin, Mr. Bishop?"

"Call me Jim."

"Jim."

"Sometimes."

"You're missing something. Peps you up."

"I need pepping up." Al Porter came in, smiling, bowing, wringing the piano hands. "Aunty" offered him a drink, which he accepted with a flourish, bowed gravely when he saw me, and said: "Now, which one is Elinor Dunning?" The girl looked him up and down, and the fish pout returned. "Who is that?" she whispered.

"Your blind date."

"Not mine."

"Watch."

He approached, crouched in front and introduced himself. "This," he said, nodding toward me, "is my best friend. Pay no attention to him." "Aunty" shuffled into the kitchenette, ransacked closets, and emerged with another bottle.

Porter sat on the arm of the chair. Elinor Dunning edged away. He decided to rest a friendly arm on her shoulder. Boldly, she lifted it off. "What's the matter, kiddo?" he said. "Am I in the wrong pew?"

She looked at me: "Will you take me home, please?" I asked where she lived. "Around the corner. Wade Street near Loew's."

Al became grim, almost lipless. He set his gin down. "Come in the bathroom," he said to me. "I wanna talk to you."

"Just a minute," I said to Miss Dunning. "Before I go, do you want to party with this guy?" She used the most outrageous pejorative on command: she closed her eyes and shuddered. That did it. Porter locked the bathroom door and tried to punch me.

The room was too small. His face was livid. The pale blue eyes were venomous. I grabbed his arm. "Just a minute," I kept saying. "Now just a damn minute." We grappled and, in the grunting and swearing, we ruined two slick coffures. As the accused, I kept asking him to listen, to please listen. I admired Alexander L. Porter and I cherished his friendship. He listened when he tired, panting and glaring. "Take the girl," I said. "She's yours. So is the other one."

He sat heavily on the lavatory. "For Christ sake," he said, "don't be funny. You're in. I'm out." I felt no triumph. Elinor Dunning had made her choice. We took our time combing our hair, muttering phrases long since lost. When we returned to the group, "Aunty" was lowering a big silver tray of sandwiches, cheese, and crackers.

When "Aunty" got drunk — which was the goal of all parties — his grin was glazed, even when guests called him a dirty old fag. The girls became louder and giggly, kicking off shoes to dance. The men extinguished all the lights except the saffron shaft coming from the kitchen. Each one selected a girl, squeezed down beside her and, in the charcoal fog, began the serious business which was called necking. This amounted to kissing and fondling.

At any stage, from arm-around-neck to hand-on-thigh, the girl could stop the play. The difficulty lay in trying to differentiate between "stop" and "I-am-saying-stop-but-expect-you-to-persist." Porter had a girl, and was breathing heavily when I stumbled over a three-legged stool and found Elinor Dunning. I squeezed beside her and put a loose arm around her neck. "Did you fight with him?" she said. I shrugged and the loose fingers found the swelling breast. "We argued," I said. "You don't need him." She lifted the hand. Somehow, she was more amenable to kisses. The hostility began to dissipate. "You going steady?" she said. I shook my head. "I heard you were."

I smiled. "You never heard of me before tonight." This too was a game.

We played that game. Her head rested on the back of the sofa and the kissing became good. She knew how to play. The teeth were clenched; when I probed too hard she bit the end of my tongue. I stood. "That," I said, "will be enough of that. I'm leaving." This blocked her queen's bishop gambit because it ended the play at stalemate.

"Aren't you going to take me home?"

I stood looking down. "You found your way here."

"Okay," she said. "Get me a drink." I got it. "Don't go," she said softly. I thought about it. "My tongue hurts."

"I'm sorry," she said. She took my hands and pulled my head down so that she could whisper. "If you want an easy girl, I'm not your type. I like kissing. But most of the fellows get fresh. . . ."

I took her home. The party was working toward a grappling climax. This was "flaming youth": the Lost Generation which followed the exhaustion of World War I. In the twilight of the room, a girl in a corner sat on a boy's lap, the back of her dress over her hips, bouncing with both hands on the arms of the chair. The odor of gin and cigarettes was strong. A man, probably Arthur Taylor, watched me depart with Elinor. "Somebody is going to make it big tonight!" he said.

It was a soft September night. The poplars spun their leaves slowly, dark-side, light-side, in the hot breeze. We talked little. Her father, she said, was a steward at Elks Lodge 211. He was Frank Dunning, a gray-haired bartender with ulcers. The Dunnings lived on the ground floor of a two-family wooden house. The gray paint was similar to that of thousands of houses in Jersey City. We talked on the porch. It is impossible to recall the topics, or even the opinions. What I know is that we became friendly, and we confided more in each other than I had planned. We bubbled. There were more kisses. I backed her close to a screened window, out of the rays of a streetlamp. Somewhere inside, I heard a growl, then a snapping bark. "We have a poodle," she said, yielding those cushioned lips. I grabbed hard and felt the length of her against the length of me. "This," a sharp voice said from behind the screen, "is a nice time to be bringing a decent girl home."

Emotionally, I died. I stepped away. "See you," I said.

Glancing at the screen she said: "Give me a buzz."

"Sure," I said.

The matronly voice said: "You get in here...." I walked home. The time was near two A.M. It couldn't be; it was. Elinor Dunning — who or what was that? I didn't want a love affair; one mortal wound was enough. Nor did I need a sexpot.

The lust for paradise and the paradise of lust clashed and I hid inside a flawed conscience. The self-administered flogging began anew. At the Public Library, I located two stout volumes on comparative religions and studied them slowly, with long periods of assessment. The problem was not to find a *better* religion, but to strike a truce with the one I had.

At twenty-one, conclusions can be reached before the problem is propounded. Within thirty days I decided: (1) the Roman Catholic Church was best suited to me because it nourished my roots; (2) the Pontiff could not be "all wise, all knowing" because, in the main, he was a political being elevated by confreres to a position of moral despotism; (3) if Jesus assumed the form of man, then it was quite possible that God the Father, the Son, and the Holy Ghost had no physical resemblance to either men or doves, and both Christians and Jews were guilty of inventing a Supreme Being in their image; (4) it is impossible to conceive of a Supreme Being looking down on an established religion with disfavor and contempt; (5) this being so, no church or temple had a copyright on God; (6) priests were sinners and required the absolution they were imparting to me.

The solution to the problem was to accept my imperfections. I decided the best way to lift the weight of guilt from my shoulders would be to allow myself to crack a couple of commandments. As Ambrose Bierce wrote long ago, if temptation was not devised for man to succumb to it, then it has no function. In furtherance of making peace with myself, I would discontinue going to confession because the repetitive aspect of the commission of sin must constitute hypocrisy — the worst crime of all.

There was an additional, almost subtle, concomitant of adulthood. At times I doubted there was a God. He could have been invented by the ancients who, like the men of today, wail at the harshness of life but dread to depart from it. The Old Ones had devised gods of clay and stone and gold and, having molded them, built ornate temples and knelt as supplicants and begged favors. In a more enlightened civilization, men of wisdom grouped constellations of stars and drew up majestic and complex interpretations of rewards and warnings of the luminaries of the night. As recently as the Roman Empire, Caesars became "immortal gods" though none could start a warm summer shower or stop one. Perhaps it was man's id which tortured his mind to fever when he dwelt upon death as an eternal silent darkness, a dreamless decay.

And so, at what I regarded as the peak of my wisdom, I whirled between believing and not believing; sometimes, when I dismissed God as a fake, I forced myself to dwell upon the vastness of space and to ask who invented it. There was no point in moving on to the complexities of matter — solar systems and their billions of bodies hot and bright, dark and cold. It was simpler to start with antimatter, billions of light-years of emptiness, and wonder how it started, who or what started it, and ask if it had outer edges. If there was no rationale to space, no beginning, no end, no length, no width, then whatever slender talent I had for thinking must, of necessity, be shattered. The boy's mind was the man's ruin. As an owl is reduced to "Who?" I was confined to "Why?" The word would plague me forever.

In church there were no doubts. I could feel a *presence*. The ballet of lighted candles, the faint odor of incense, the huge pillars and the lofty vault of the roof, the altar with vested priests bending forward, swaying and tapping their chests, the brittle innocuous white wafer which, once blessed, became the real body of Our Lord and Saviour Jesus Christ — "Do this in commemoration of Me." The commemorators seldom looked happy. They returned to their pews, hands clasped, heads down, trying to get the wafer of Holy Communion off the roof of the mouth. My doubt, I finally decided, was not of God; my quarrel was with the Church. As God had ordered the faithful to accept His dominance without seeing Him, I was willing to abide by it because His Supremacy would be meaningless if He was challenged to appear in city streets to cure lepers, extinguish the sun, and turn the evil into stone. One would have to begin by acknowledging that the earth did not fashion itself with its tides and land masses and air ocean at a distance uniquely perfect from the sun to maintain a temperature and a weather spectrum sufficient to sustain thousands of life forms from the fragile fern of the forest to the daily needs of a ninety-foot air-breathing whale.

My doubts centered on that humble imitator of Christ, Benedict XV, who wore a triple crown and was carried on a sella gestatoria at functions. It was he, the Pope of my boyhood, who was proclaimed to be as infallible in matters of faith and morals as God Himself. The Church had had about two hundred and sixty Popes since the time of Peter, and anyone with a modicum of interest in Church history had only to glance through the list to discern that some Popes broke commandments; others were wily politicians; there were saintly men and chronic sinners; diplomats who traded quid pro quo; self-aggrandizement ad absurdum; and then, after the Middle Ages, a succession of timid Popes who, with their Colleges of Cardinals, seemed pleased to maintain the Holy Roman Catholic Church a century behind the events of the world.

I did not divorce myself from the Church. I felt that it was bigger, stronger than the sum of its parts, and I felt free to disagree, or even to disavow, any part of it. It was not the only path to God and paradise; it was one. Lack of faith in Church and God became sporadic; at the age of twenty-one, I had it and it fled and then I had it again. Reason amounted to no more than a conversation with a mirror.

The New York Times gave the people what was good for them. The *News* gave them what they wanted. The swaying subway riders demanded what the editors referred to as "C and C" (Cunt and Crime) and that's what they got. It was a five-column tabloid jammed with comic strips, vice, gossip, four pages of photos, columnists, conversational prose, sports, pictures of leggy show girls, facetious captions, prize contests, a subliminal keyhole. "Kiddie," Hellinger said, "if you want to write you are going to have to learn to pound out terse sentences composed of small words."

Hellinger was a professional cynic. He was generous, helpful, and believed in no one. Life was a double-cross and he had a compulsion to find it in almost everything he wrote. Birth was treachery because it was the sole avenue to death. It surprised no one when he selected Jimmy Burbridge, a humorless alcoholic, as his secretary. When he married, in 1929, he selected a statuesque blond from the Bronx, Miss Gladys Glad, whom Florenz Ziegfeld would bill as "the most beautiful woman in the world." She had two paramount emotions — pity and hostility. The first was reserved for the helpless; the second for men, including husbands. In the *Follies*, she walked slowly down a rhinestone stairway at stage center, a waterfall of plumes behind her head, the body as lean, leggy, and languorous as any work of Botticelli or Degas. Offstage, Miss Glad could, at times, pour the vitriol of the Bronx from the side of her mouth. When she was angry or suspicious, her words cascaded like stones from the back of a dump truck. Her bridegroom, when stripped of his trappings, was a famous columnist who earned five hundred a week, spent six hundred, drank a fifth of brandy each day, and, at the age of twenty-seven, was obsessed with a fear that he was impotent. The overtures of chorus girls were often declined with "Never mind the bed, kiddie. I'd rather hear about your poor sick old mother who needs four hundred for an operation." His credo — he had one — was "Unless you can love whole hosts of people you have never met, you will never become a writer. The only way to write a sob story is for the author to be callous, pitiless. This makes it more poignant. Go out and find the guy who won the Irish Sweepstakes ten years ago, and I'll bet he's in hock to a loan company. Tight declarative sentences using small words constitute the most difficult form of writing. A ten-year-old child has it. By the time he gets to college, he's lost it in what I call the hedges — the interjectory clauses. So, whatever you think you know, unlearn it and start over."

He was up at noon, in the office at two-thirty, maintained a camaraderie with reporters and sports writers. Often, when the daily column was finished by four P.M., the dancing, pirouetting figure of Walter Winchell arrived from the *Evening Graphic*. As Hellinger's "new boy" I was permitted to hear some of the conversation. None of it was happy. Both were insecure, both feared their editors. Winchell worried because his managing editor, a short dark man, Emile Gauvreau, didn't like him and wanted to fire him. WW (as he signed himself) was a short blondish vaudevillian from East Harlem, who began his career as a child dancer in the Gus Edwards troupe. Hellinger confessed that he worried about receiving memos from "Col. Frank Hause" stating that publisher "Captain Patterson" did not like Hellinger's Broadway stories and demanded that he purvey terse gossip in the manner of Winchell.

On the surface, the two columnists were the weightiest figures on Broadway; the best tables and the finest prohibition liquor were thrust at them in all nightclubs from Texas Guinan's place down to an offbeat boozery run by Barney Gallant in Greenwich Village. An item in Winchell's column, a mention in Hellinger's, was, to an actor, worth more than a second curtain call. The mood of the era was sensual and materialistic; gangsters such as Owney Madden, Dutch Schultz, and Johnny Torrio were given more space in the New York tabloids — the *News*, the *Evening Graphic*, and the *Daily Mirror* — than a speech by President Hoover announcing a treaty between the United States, Great Britain, and Japan to reduce the size and number of warships. The amount of space to be given to a murder, for example, was hefted by the editors for its ingredients. If two barflies shot it out in a drunken brawl at a neighborhood tavern, the rewrite man was told, "Give us a couple of paragraphs."

If one of the drunks was well known, the order was: "Give us a page of copy — no more." If one of the two was a woman, preferably attractive, the dictum became: "Keep it under two pages of copy. We have pix." Should a husband find his wife in bed with another man, and kill her or the "other man," a photo of the sheet-clad body with disordered bed-clothes became a two-day wonder; in the parlance of the trade an "overnight." If any of the parties to a homicide was listed in the *Social Register*, the story could be serialized for several successive days. Any male member of "Society" caught in flagrante delicto was called a "Society playboy" throughout the story, even though he might never have played before.

To the tabloid editor, the best murders were those involving beautiful women (either as victims or avengers), in which there was a lubricious gloss of sex, and, best of all, a diary which could be stolen by a reporter and published in installments with pietistic editorial tongues clucking and a suitable quotation from the Bible about the wages of sin. Gang murders were always page-1 stories and, although most were not solved, there was an unspoken agreement among tabloid editors to attribute the crime to the Detroit Purple Gang. They were in no position to sue.

In sum, I was working in an editorial whorehouse, but it was an edifying whorehouse and there was much to learn besides carrying towels from room to room. The struggle among three tabloid newspapers to gain circulation first, to be followed by respectability and the advertising dollar, quickly involved the better newspapers. William Randolph Hearst owned the *Daily Mirror*, the New York *American*, and the New York *Journal*. The *American* was an eight-column morning newspaper designed to strangle Joseph Pulitzer's *World*. The fight had started before the turn of the century and, though Mr. Hearst laved his paper with good comic strips, first-rate features, and such daily writers as Arthur Brisbane, O. O. McIntyre, and Damon Runyon, it lost slowly and steadily to Pulitzer's paper and his editor, Herbert Bayard Swope, the pedant of Park Row. Mr. Swope wore glittering pince-nez to enhance his icy eyes, and, when he met Presidents or Popes, he bowed curtly and said "Swope of the *World*," words intended to impress.

The *Journal* was an afternoon newspaper, housed in the same red-brick building as its sister *American*. Mr. Hearst would lose millions of dollars with equanimity, but he could not bear to close his newspapers. From the late 1920s onward, he supported losing papers with profits from winners — if the *Journal* was earning money, it went to the *American* or the *Daily Mirror*. It was his custom, at the San Simeon mansion in California, to wait until his secretary, Colonel Joseph Willecombe, Sr., had placed all of the papers on a large rug with spaces between. Then, with Willecombe behind him, he would step gingerly from the San Francisco *Examiner* to the Boston *American* to the Los Angeles *Herald-Express* to the *Daily Mirror* to the Chicago *Herald-Examiner* crouching, examining each front page, making comments of a critical nature or congratulatory, all of which Mr. Willecombe copied in a notebook. Around noon California time, the Hearst wire service, INS, began to chatter and all the messages began the same way: "The Chief Says . . ." Editors from coast to coast waited fearfully. The "suggestions" were mandatory and inarguable.

Hearst could have had the edge in the tabloid field when he visited England in 1918 and saw one. The magnetizing effect on the readers of news photos, as opposed to pedestrian one-column cuts of faces, impressed him deeply. He determined to start such a paper in New York City, even though he was struggling to keep the *Journal* and the *American* afloat. He waited a day too long. McCormick and Patterson started the *Daily News* in 1919, and had a flying start. Five years later, Hearst started the *Daily Mirror*. It was a fight, perhaps, that he could not win, but he worsened his chances by using cheaper paper than the *News*, so that identical photos in both newspapers looked much better in the *News*; he made the additional mistake of urging his succession of editors to use larger and ever-larger headlines, make bigger stories of average ones by spiking them with innuendo, and, in a moment of pique, hiring Emile Gauvreau from the *Graphic* to jazz the *Mirror* to a million circulation.

Exposé followed exposé; the phrases "Love Nest," "Vice Raid," "Gangland Slays," and the single-quote: "Beauty Queen Confesses She Slew 'Because I Love Him'" went from seventy-two-point caps (one inch tall) to hundred-and-forty-four-point. Circulation hoodlums hopped from trucks to grab a pile of opposition newspapers and scatter them in the gutter. The *News* sent a photographer to Sing Sing with a concealed camera strapped to his ankle under his trousers. He sat in the front row of the Death House to snap a shot of Ruth Snyder squirming and burning in the electric chair for plotting with a lover the murder of her husband. At one A.M. the shocking photograph was all over page 1. By two A.M. the *Mirror* had brazenly photographed the shot from its rival paper and placed it on the back page, where sports pictures were used.

At the time of which I speak — 1929 — there were fourteen papers in the city, not counting local sheets such as the Brooklyn *Eagle*, the Bronx *Home News*, and other editorial pilot fish which nibbled the edges of profits. The New York *Sun*, emerging with honor from a dusty office on lower Broadway, saw Scripps-Howard's New York *Telegram* as its competition. The *Evening Mail* had fine writers, but readers were slipping away. *The New York Times*, cultivating a hauteur, did not deign to acknowledge that the frenzied tabloids were, in fact, newspapers. *The Times* and Ogden Reid's New York *Herald* could get more advertising at a higher rate per line with but 300,000 circulation than the *News* could with 1,200,000.

The New York *Post*, founded by Alexander Hamilton, decided to join the tabloid battle and cut its format from eight columns to five. Circulation sagged to 108,000. The *Tribune*, staid and aloof, decided to merge with the *Herald*. At no time in the history of American journalism were so many newspapers, with circulation areas in a radius of sixty miles from Times Square, so deeply involved in a ceaseless fight to remain alive, to romance readers with cash-prize puzzles, dance contests, newsphotographs, fitting pictures of famous people together, amateur boxing matches, beauty contests, and the incessant search for the exclusive story. The latter was usually a brittle victory because competitive newspaper editors read it, gave it to a rewrite man, and said: "Gimme as much as you got, and attribute it to a high police source..." or "the mayor's office." The so-called exclusive story, even though it sometimes carried a copyright under the by-line, seldom lasted more than ninety minutes. Once, in pique, Gauvreau of the *Mirror* published a fake exclusive and, as the *News* stole it, Gauvreau published a retraction the next day, acknowledging that it had no basis in fact.

There was trouble with Dan O'Keefe. The retired policeman, the thin gray face creased with contempt, ordered me to keep away from reporters' typewriters. "Mr. Carson said it's okay if I practice," I said. It was not defiance; I thought O'Keefe would abide by the will of the day city editor.

"You're a copyboy, Bishop. You get twelve a week to sit on that bench and answer calls. Now get this straight. It usually takes three years of hard work for a boy to become a cub reporter or get a job in the picture studio. If Carson says — "

I amended the permission. Mr. Carson said I could practice when the city room was not busy.

"Makes no difference," O'Keefe said, and he was right. "You were hired as a boy. I want you on that bench."

I was discouraged. If Dan O'Keefe fired me from this job, it would represent one more defeat. I warmed the bench apprehensively. My eyes were on O'Keefe. Whatever the old man wanted, I ran to get it. I tried harder to please him than the editors because O'Keefe was my roadblock. I would not appeal to Hellinger or Carson. The cop would not forgive it. I was on the *News* six weeks when Carson, with a phone cradled on his shoulder, looked up for a rewrite man and found the city room empty. "Hey, kid," he said, "go in the phone booth and take a paragraph from Benny." The man was a district reporter at the Marriage License Bureau.

"Who's this?" he shouted on the phone. I had pencil and paper ready. "And who the hell are you?" he said when I gave my name. I told him. "Okay, boy," he said. "The police of the Elizabeth Street precinct — got that? — found the body of an old man in a furnished room on Mott Street this morning. Number fifteen. Am I going too fast? Do you know where Mott Street is? Jesus Christ! Chinatown. His name — the dead man — is Rafael Anders. One *f* in that. Right. The police say he was once an actor. Cause of death is believed to be starvation. He was about sixty-five, white hair, apparently used a busted fruit crate as a chair. At least they found one next to the body. There was a soggy mattress soaked with urine, but you don't need that, kid. He had a nickel and two pennies in his pockets. The Chinks in the neighborhood say they haven't seen the old guy in a week. Look him up in the clips. Now switch me back to the city desk."

I hurried back to Carson. "Do you want me to write this?"

He squinted from under the eyeshade. "Give me a little bit," he said. "You need the practice."

I rolled a book into the typewriter, thought, and hurried up to the morgue where all the old clippings and photos were filed. There was a slender folder on Anders, Rafael. The clippings were yellowed reviews of plays in which he had starred in the 1890–1902 era. Also, there were two faded photos of him, one in tights with a long aigrette in his hat.

O'Keefe watched me at the typewriter. I felt that he would be infuriated by the final insubordination from me, and would do something about it. I wrote: "The road to success is long, steep and hazardous, but the road back down to poverty and death is swift and shattering. Mr. Rafael Anders, who won the applause of New York as an actor, was found dead of starvation yesterday in a room in Chinatown. . . ."

The story was worthless to the *News*. Nobody would remember Rafael Anders. But I wrote on and on, giving it a page and a paragraph. Then I edged it onto the desk next to Frank Carson and sat on the bench watching. Twice he looked up at me. Then he arose, and walked to the drama department. Burns Mantle was not in. His assistant, the warty-skinned John Chapman, was. They talked. Chapman called me. "Nice work," he said. "I'd like to give you a by-line, but Burns has a rule — nobody but the two of us."

I was gushing. "Oh, that's all right." Carson pinned a carbon of it on the bulletin board. In red crayon he wrote over the top: "This is the way to dramatize a story." I felt anesthetized.

That evening I didn't get home on time. The first edition seemed slow; I taxed my patience in the manner of Columbus shading his eyes against the setting sun looking for land. Editorial "cubs" had waited as eagerly, as hopefully, as I. None, I was certain, ever waited in the shadows of the pressroom with pounding heart waiting for a Klaxon to signal the first feeble turn of the press. Somewhere in those big rolls of paper was my future — if I had a future. When the papers gushed off the presses, I took three and read the story over and over in the Jersey tube train. At the least, it was dumbfounding that John Chapman had not altered the sentence structure. I had managed to "think" a story through my fingers.

My family was pleased because I was pleased. Mother thought it was sad that the actor had died in a furnished room. John and Adele read it and I stood near the wall, modestly waiting. "You wrote this?" they said. I nodded. "How come your name isn't on it like the others?" I folded a copy and took it to Elinor Dunning. The boop-a-doop girl was surprised, perhaps slightly offended, that I had not phoned for an appointment. The *News* was sticking out of my pocket, but it had to wait until I was introduced to her parents. Her mother had been the voice behind the screen. She was five feet tall, a hundred and ninety pounds, a wheezing woman with a stout Irish face and prognathous jaw. Her name was Maggy. When she smiled she had four top teeth which slid downward and returned to their proper position when she slammed her mouth shut. She was gracious and ignorant, a woman, I would learn, who was laden with fears about doctors, hospitals, thunderstorms, and boats; she enjoyed the company of women, gossip columns, frizzing her hair with a hot iron. She used an antediluvian tranquilizer called Tom Collins, sneaked coins to children for candy, listened to an unending number of daytime radio dramas without ever confusing the plots, and enjoyed a cease-fire relationship with her husband.

Frank Dunning was having his supper. He came into the living room, a thin ulcerous man with graying hair which appeared to be uncombed. He shook hands without smiling, said he knew my father, and returned to the kitchen. With him went a fat white poodle who turned to growl in a whisper. Mrs. Dunning said she was sorry she had berated me the other night, but Elinor was her only child and "I brought her up right." This was a quasi apology and a warning. When she left, I sat on the couch and told the girl about my first story. She read it with interest. "You wrote this?" she said. She returned to it a I studied the gorgeous legs which crossed at the ankles. Elinor read parts of it aloud. This indeed was the balm I sought. I asked for a date — movies. She kept on reading, then looked up. "When?"

"Tomorrow night at eight."

"I'll be waiting."

It wasn't a movie. She lived less than one street from Journal Square, which was the center of action in Jersey City. She suggested a cellar speakeasy managed by a flat-footed man who wore a permanently pressed-on smile even when he was tossing drunks up the stairs and out into the gutter. I said no. "Oh, come on," she said. "How can we get to know each other in a movie?"

I drew in a long embarrassed breath. "I don't have enough money," I said. The salary of the great writer was twelve dollars.

"I have it," she said, tapping her black purse. "I just got a raise from twenty-five dollars a week to thirty-one."

"Why the odd figure?" I said.

She shrugged. "Dominick and Dominick are Wall Street brokers. When we work late, they don't pay overtime — they give you supper money. At Christmas, we get a bonus. Sometimes a hundred; sometimes two hundred. Anyway, let me treat."

I declined, It was a bad start. "Okay," she said. "I'll *lend* it to you." The point had been delicately drawn; she wanted to talk and drink, or drink and talk, and it was obvious that she didn't want to appear to be stubborn the first time around.

The waiter said: "Good evening, Miss Dunning." The thick pouting lips parted in a smile. "Gin buck," she said. I leaned across the small table. "What's that?" "Gin and ginger ale," the waiter said. "The same," I said.

We spun the cold drinks in slow circles. She was nineteen; I was twenty-one. We exchanged simple statistics but, by the time the third gin buck arrived, we were on a deeper, more personal level. Her father had told her that Big John had left my mother for another woman. It was, Elinor said, "the talk of the town." I said it had happened a long time ago. We ran down a list of names, to ascertain whether we knew the same people. We knew Bill Drummond. I liked him; she thought he was "shallow." She had attended Saint Dominic Academy, a private school for Catholic girls which must have strained the family purse. Her father, she said, worked behind the bar but was not a bartender. At the Elks Club, he was called a "steward." Once he had owned a saloon of his own called "The Spot," but something — perhaps the onset of the Volstead Act — put him out of business. The Dunnings, as well as the Bishops, had no money.

She was obvious about liking me. And yet, Elinor gave the impression that, sexually, she would be a stone wall. Her remarks about her parents gave me the impression that she felt more pity than love for her father. He had a duodenal ulcer. She knew when he came home drunk because he sat in the kitchen talking softly to the poodle. Elinor's world, I would guess, was her mother. Several times she said: "My mother thinks," "My mother says," "I give my paycheck to my mother and she gives me ten dollars and then spends the rest on hats and dresses for me. I love hats. Big ones. Do you like big hats?" There was an aura of ultrafemininity about her which was so deeply etched in her character that she seemed almost proud to know little about matters which might be termed masculine. This included all sports, politics, international affairs, science, nonfiction books, and sexual aggression. Once, she said, she had worked as a stocking model in the Garment District, but her mother had ordered her to quit. Recently, there had been a boy living near Paterson, New Jersey, in whom she had become interested. His people had money. Twice Maggy had given her permission to spend a weekend at his house, as long as his mother was home. Her interest in him — or his in her — had died suddenly, and Elinor didn't want to discuss it. She explained that she had mentioned it only to show that she was "free." Was I? Yes I was. I had been through a serious love affair, I said, but the girl was interested in another man.

I was light-headed. We walked to her gray frame house and stood on the porch. There was the black window screen; I felt inhibited. Maggy must be behind it, I felt, breathing softly, squinting. The gin created the matador. I kissed her hard and jammed her against the glass door. She was exciting, alluring. "Oh boy," I whispered, "are you nice!" It was a stupid remark; it sounded wrong as I heard the words. "I must go," she said. We made a date — which surprised me — for the following night. "If Momma asks where we went," she whispered, "the movies."

"The movies," I said. I held her at arm's length. "You're one hell of a movie."

We met three to four times a week, sometimes to hold hands in the balcony of the Stanley Theatre, sometimes to attend parties, sometimes to go to the Irish cellar for drinks, a few times to walk Hudson County Boulevard, talking seriously about the future. No counseling was required to warn me that I was sinking swiftly into love, but I had a low opinion of a man who could fall out of love and back into it so quickly. Was there a "bounce" to this romance? Could I be revenging myself for a failure? How about Elinor and that two-weekend guy near Paterson? Had he seduced and dumped her? Was I her "rebound"? Impossible. Within three months we were planning marriage for June 14, 1930. There was no money for an engagement ring. I kept explaining that marriage on twelve dollars a week was impossible, but Elinor was sure that Mr. Carson would give me a raise. Besides, twelve plus thirty-one adds up to forty-three, and her father was getting by on forty-five.

Her mother became interested in whether I attended mass and went to confession; what my mother really thought of her daughter; "My Frank told me that reporters drink a lot"; could a writer support a family; was my father still living with "you-know"; her Frank knew Walter Dear, publisher of the *Jersey Journal* and could put in a good word, et cetera, et cetera. I worked up a contempt for Maggy. Day by day I appreciated her abysmal ignorance more and more. There were good people, and very, very bad people. Sometimes, when I watched the four top teeth slide and lift, I got the impression that she was trying to be diplomatic because she did not want to reveal too much of herself too early. Sometimes, after a visit next door with her friends Mr. and Mrs. Spatz, Maggy would appear to be flushed, with the forehead hair plastered wet with sweat. "I really enjoy a highball," she said.

I began to enjoy them too. On some mornings, I had no recollection of saying goodnight to Elinor, nor of how I boarded a bus — or if I walked. Our friends knew the affair was serious before we did. Drummond was the only friend who said: "Take a tip. Stay away from her." I demanded to know why. He shrugged. "Just a suggestion." My mother liked Elinor. When my girl stopped at our furnished apartment, she hugged my mother and kissed her. "That," my mother said, "is a nice girl. Treat her nice."

Hellinger shook his head when I asked how to get a raise in salary. "Kid," he said, "you can't get a raise. You might get fired. O'Keefe has been talking to Harvey about you." I didn't believe it. I had worked hard to imitate Mark's style of writing and, finding it easy, had devised a few stories for his column. With exceptions, they were published as written. Somewhere in the third or fourth paragraph, he would give me a "credit line": "As Jim Bishop can tell you, our friend Sammy was on the level. When he told his wife he was going to the movies, he actually went to the movies. If he picked up a glass eye from the sidewalk, Sammy would put an ad in the Lost and Found column. . . ."

Mr. Deuell asked me to come into his office. A tremor shook me. The city editor was about to fire me. I had written a second news story about a Negro boy in a track and field meet who had been warned by Whites not to win a sixty-yard dash. The boy won and, when he changed back into his street clothes, the White boys were waiting behind the 168th Street armory with stones. The Black boy bled the same as the Whites — red. He died in fifteen minutes. Carson sent me on the story. I tracked the facts, and got to the Harlem apartment of the parents. Tears on black cheeks glisten like lightning.

I had the story, but I wrote it poorly. Deuell read it, looked up dispassionately at Nick Kenny, and said: "Here, Nick. Give me a quick rewrite on this, will you? Cut it in half." Now I followed Harvey Deuell to his small office. He sat behind the desk. I stood. He seemed to have trouble starting. I do not recall the precise phrasing, but I can never forget the sense of what he said:

"Bishop, they tell me you have a little talent for writing. Now I am not opposed to ambition in a boy; it's a good thing and today too many kids are lazy. They don't want to learn. But Mr. O'Keefe has been complaining about your behavior. He says he hired you as a copyboy. You're paid to be a copyboy. You take boys like Siebelist and Meurer. Siebelist wants to work on the city desk some day. Meurer wants to be a photographer. Both have been here much longer than you, and they are satisfied to sit on that bench and do as they're told.

"O'Keefe has a point. He needs the services of every boy on that bench. You're the newest. How long have you been with us?"

"I think nine months, sir."

"Brand new. O'Keefe tells me that you connive with Mr. Carson and Mr. Hellinger to write little stories. This may be your idea of being clever, but it isn't mine. I've been thinking it over, and I feel — from what I've seen of your work — that you stand a chance of being a big pebble on a small beach, such as a Jersey newspaper, or a small pebble on a big beach — right here. My advice is that you quit and get a job in Jersey."

My throat slammed shut. I could barely speak. "Do you want to think about it?" he said softly.

I shook my head no. "I would rather stay here," I said. "If Mr. O'Keefe wants me to sit on the bench. I'll stay there."

He sighed. The disappointment was obvious. "You may stay," he said, standing. "But I'm warning you. If I see you at a typewriter, you're through. This also applies to any further complaints from O'Keefe. Do we understand each other?"

"Yes, sir." I followed him from his office and found O'Keefe on the far side of the copy desk. "Mr. O'Keefe," I said humbly, "Mr. Deuell was talking to me and he said I should sit on the bench — "

"Don't start an argument with me!" O'Keefe shouted. "You belong on that bench. Now git or git out."

In less than a year, a career had opened and closed. I realized that, no matter how many years I sat on that bench, Harvey Deuell would not promote me because I had rejected his suggestion. O'Keefe was angry because, after he had testified against me, I was still sitting before him. The word reached Carson too. I delivered copy to him and, under his breath, he muttered: "Stick with it. I can't help you now, but you'll make it." Hellinger warned me not to stop at his desk except on business. As always, I had a facility for slamming doors in my own face. The word got around the office. I had hoped it wouldn't. A few reporters told O'Keefe that he should encourage his boys to write. The old man became aroused. "He was hired to sit on that bench," he said. "He's paid to sit on it, and, as long as I'm around here, he'll do as he's told."

Irene Kuhn slid a gift-wrapped package across her desk to me. "Stay with it, Jim," she said. "You'll be all right." I opened it on the way home. It was a book called *The Fundamentals of Good Writing*. At home, I borrowed Big John's Number 4 Underwood and pecked stories on the kitchen table. The *News* was the first newspaper to buy Ford automobiles for reporters and photographers. I became a driver for my betters. This brought me to the scene of "hot news," but I was not permitted to ask questions. I watched reporters work, kept extra pencils and copy paper in my jacket pocket for them, drove photographers to the Polo Grounds, Yankee Stadium, and Ebbets Field. I stood by as they operated huge long-lens cameras from the second tier. I took the plates back to the office after the first inning, so that the picture department would have photos on the back page of the early edition.

One afternoon, Hellinger departed without his mail. O'Keefe ordered me to take it to Suerkin's and look for him. He was standing at the bar with Red Dolan, who was actually referred to by Deuell as "star reporter." I had assumed that the phrase was used only in motion pictures, where drunks with police cards stuck in their hatbands yelled, "Stop the presses!"

Hellinger pocketed the mail and said: "Have a drink, kiddo." I said no thank you because I didn't want him to know I drank. "Have a beer, then," he said. I took it. His remarks were addressed to Dolan. "Winchell," he said, "is in a jam. Gauvreau wants to fire him. Why the *Graphic* would want to can their only card, I don't understand. Walter has a big mouth and Gauvreau said he expected Winchell to bring in some theatrical advertising." Dolan studied his ruddy face in the bar mirror. "Walter told him what to do with his advertising."

My interest centered on the fact that the personnel turnover on newspapers was high. "Harvey is trying to make me quit," Red Dolan said. "Says I'm late in the office every morning, late with my stories — late, late, late. So, beginning Monday, I'm on ship news." This assignment was about the lowest on the reportorial ladder. It required arriving at the Battery promptly at five A.M. to board a coast guard cutter, and then to go to the Narrows to meet incoming ocean liners and interview celebrities. The assignment paid thirty-five dollars a week; Dolan was reputed to be earning two hundred. "What did you say?" Mark said. Dolan shook his head at the apparition in the bar mirror. "First I thought he was kidding. When I saw he was serious, I said, 'Okay, Harvey. I'm gonna have to sit up all night to make it.' "

There was insecurity on newspapers. Gil Parker, tall reporter and drinker, a man with one eye which looked toward his ear, had worked on the *News,* married a sob sister, Hettie Cattell, lost his job, got a position on another paper, and returned to the *News* just as Hettie got a job as rewrite on the *Mirror.* A second-string movie critic quit for first string somewhere else. Paul Gallico's sports department used Jackie Farrell as a boxing writer although his expertise was in baseball. Hellinger was frightened because he was getting messages from managing editor Hause to write dot-dot-dot gossip items about Broadway in imitation of his friend Winchell. Walter was about to be canned by Gauvreau, but Hellinger said he thought he could save the former hoofer's ass. As he told it to Dolan in my presence, it involved getting a letter from Herbert Bayard Swope, editor of the *Morning World,* offering Winchell five hundred a week to leave the *Evening Graphic.* Hellinger said that Swope refused, unless Mark wrote a separate letter proclaiming the offer to be a fake. "I don't want Winchell on my paper at any price," Swope said. "If I do this, it will be as a favor to you."

Hellinger proposed to give the letter to Winchell, who would then take it to A. J. Kobler, publisher of Hearst's *Daily Mirror,* and use it to prod him for a job. "It won't work," Dolan said. It did. When Kobler saw the Swope note, he offered Winchell five hundred dollars a week to do a daily gossip column for the *Mirror,* plus five hundred more if the column was syndicated by King Features. For Hellinger, this act wasn't motivated by friendship. Mark was afraid that Hause would find out that Winchell was out of work, and hire him to do the gossip column for which the *News* hungered, and fire Hellinger.

In the autumn of 1929, the *Mirror* bought Winchell and promoted his name and face on the delivery trucks and gave him space on page 10. Winchell was such a big draw that advertisers had to pay extra to get their material on the same page. WW bounded from hysterical fear to the status of a star earning a thousand dollars a week. He had his own office and an attractive secretary named Ruth Cambridge. King Features Syndicate sold the column to hundreds of newspapers. From black pit to sunny summit required ten days of plotting. Kobler, pleased with what he had done for William Randolph Hearst, hired Emile Gauvreau as his new managing editor. Overnight, Winchell was again working for the dark limping man who despised him. In November, Kobler learned that Hellinger, the storyteller, had a lot of readers at the *News,* but was unhappy with his bosses. He signed Mark to a five-year contract at seven hundred fifty dollars a week. Ironically, the stout and arbitrary publisher of the *Mirror* had stolen the best "yellow journalism" editor and the two best columnists from his rivals, the *Graphic* and the *News*. Whatever madness possessed readers and editors at that time, it paid off. The *Mirror* jumped in circulation from 550,000 to 800,000. The investment did not pay off. Kobler expected more advertising linage from Macy's, Gimbels, Bloomingdale's, and the theaters, but he didn't get it. They looked upon the tabloids as caricatures of newspapers. Gauvreau consoled Kobler. "In a year we'll have a million readers," he said. "Watch me." Kobler shook his jowls. "I will," he said. "I will."

In late October, there had been a big story in the collapse of the stock market. Brokers were jumping out of windows. Bucket shops filed for bankruptcy. President Hoover reassured the people that America was as sound as its dollar. At first, the three tabloids paid little more than lip service to the story because it failed the test of Cunt and Crime. The gangland killings, such as Frankie Uale's in Brooklyn, graft in the police department, love-nest raids, suicides of lovesick girls who had been betrayed were still the breakfast dish for millions of New Yorkers. A flagging beauty named Peggy Hopkins Joyce found it unnecessary to marry for the third or fourth time to make page 1; all she had to do was to have a press agent start a rumor that she was about to wed another millionaire.

Hellinger asked me to meet him on the second floor of the *Mirror* building at 235 East Forty-fifth Street on my day off. My best apparel consisted of a black Chesterfield overcoat with velvet collar, a dark gray suit with pinstripes, a pearl-gray double-breasted vest, gray spats, and a black derby hat. Hellinger's lavender Kissel was in the "No Parking" zone at the *Mirror*. On the third floor, directly over the editorial office, there was a huge newspaper morgue with rows and rows of metal files holding old and new folders of hundreds of thousands of photographs, and a section with back issues of the *Mirror*, the *News*, *The Times*, the *Journal*, and the New York *American*. A sepulchral man with a Brooklyn accent, Harry Adams, presided over the department. He also had hundreds of thousands of folders with clippings trimmed and stamped with dates concerning almost every well-known person or event of the past thirty years. He said that if I was looking for Hellinger, I was on the right floor but in the wrong pew. He pointed to a minuscule corridor near the elevators. "Try the first door," he said.

There were two doors on the same side of the wall. No names adorned them. Both offices were slender, deep to a back window, and were separated by squares of cardboard lath nailed to two-by-four uprights. The first was occupied by Hellinger; the other belonged to Winchell. Anyone whose voice rose a decibel above quiet conversation was addressing both offices. Mark fashioned a five-by-five reception hall, hung a mirror with a filigreed frame, jammed two backless benches with plush upholstery against each of the walls, and had an inner door erected. A blond girl answered the knock. She was not pretty, but she wore the tight smile of tension. Mark emerged, pumping my hand, and brought me to the back window where his desk reposed, covered with yellowed slabs of paper. "How do you like it?" he said expansively. I said hello to Jimmy Burbridge. His handshake recoiled from contamination. "Beats the *News*," I said.

Photos of Mayor Jimmy Walker, Texas Guinan, Judge Frank Murphy of Detroit, and Mae West shielded some of the broad cracks in the cardboard wall. "Got some great plans for you, Jim," Mark said in his hoarse voice. "First of all, I got a good contract — all aces. From time to time, I'll give you some story ideas. You write them in my style and give them to Jimmy. He'll give you ten out of petty cash. Okay?"

"Okay."

"Second, Glad and I have moved into an apartment on East Seventy-eighth, and I want you to know how to get there in a hurry if I need you. She's going to write a beauty hints column —"

"What?"

"Who better? Ziegfeld bills her as the most beautiful woman in the world. Oh, excuse me." He stood and walked back toward the reception office. "Sonny," he said to the blond, "this is Jim Bishop. You'll see a lot of him around here. Jim, this is Sonny Fohrenbach. She's Glad's secretary, but she will also help —" I knew. Miss Fohrenbach would write the beauty hints column under the name of Gladys Glad.

He led me out of the office. In the hall, Hellinger whispered in the manner of a conspirator. "We're going downstairs to meet Emile Gauvreau. Know who he is? Good. I'm going to con him into giving you a better job than you have. When we get into his office, listen, and don't say anything." We used the stairs. The second floor had a reception hall flanking the elevators. An elderly man sat behind a badly chipped desk.

From my knowledge of the *News*, I knew the *Mirror*. It was the last of the extravagantly wild sheets, if one discounts the *Graphic*, which was dying. Knowing the *Mirror* was like understanding a third-rate tap dancer. Both were jazzily frenetic, a pleasant sensation of swift motion without going anywhere. The *News* had money and spittoons. This one had sawdust on the floor, no spittoons.

"Come on," Hellinger said. We went into a private office. A secretary with big bosoms sheltered her typewriter. "Winny Rollins," Hellinger rasped. "Jim Bishop." "The chief is waiting," she said without looking up. We were in a square office. There was a large window facing Forty-fifth Street, a catercornered desk loaded with busts of Napoleon, and a small intelligent-looking man who had cajoled a lock of dark hair to form a question mark on his forehead. I was mannerly, obsequious. Hellinger said that he had worked with me on the *News*. I was, he said, the brightest writing talent they had, and he thought he should bring Jim Bishop over to the *Mirror*. "What do you do at the *News*?" Gauvreau asked. My mouth opened and Hellinger said: "Reporter. He's getting fifty, Emile, but he'll come over with us for less."

Mr. Gauvreau frisked me with his eyes. "Mark," he said, "you're a pretty good judge of writing talent. If you say — what's your name, kid?" I told him. "If you say he can write, we need a reporter who can shake his ass out of here, dig up a story, and come back and write it. We have a hundred characters who can get a story, but they can't write. I'll tell you what, Jim Bishop. You start Monday morning at twenty-five a week." I thanked him and, with Hellinger, fled. My lungs hungered for cold air. I had made it. I was a reporter, a real reporter. My salary had been doubled. The postoperative thought was wondering who had screwed whom. Had Gauvreau suspected that I was a copyboy? Obviously, he didn't believe the fifty a week because, as he offered me twenty-five, he picked up a pen and began to sign mail. He had not waited for an acceptance.

There might be greater honors ahead, more money, but nothing would match that status of reporter and twenty-five dollars. I left Hellinger welling with gratitude. I walked across the street and looked up at the windows where huge gold letters proclaimed "The Daily Mirror." For the first time, I had held onto a job, faced the threats, and emerged a winner. It was still my day off, but I took the subway downtown, scrutinizing passengers as possible news stories, nodding to policemen as though we were parties to a fraternity of law and order, and went upstairs to O'Keefe.

He frowned at the spats and derby. "What do you want?" he said.

"Mr. O'Keefe," I said, "I'm quitting."

He smiled. "Today?"

"Today."

"Kinda short notice," he said. "I'll get a voucher from Mr. Carson for your pay." The word spun over the desks like a sullen breeze. Everybody wanted to know why I quit — why I didn't fight the system. Where was I going? Times were hard. Better stick around. I was afraid to confide to anyone that I was a reporter on the Mirror. If anyone phoned Emile Gauvreau and told him I was a twelve-dollar copyboy, an editorial troublemaker, he would have second thoughts. And third. So I told everyone I was tired of sitting around.

Jimmy Cannon, round as Humpty Dumpty, called me nuts. "How long you here?" he said. "Almost a year. Listen, I was on that bench three years before I wrote my first story, and I still hold the record." Carson was nice. "I'm not asking you anything," he said, "but I hope Mark gave you a lift." We shook hands. I said good-bye to Irene Kuhn and Alfred Albelli and Meurer and Siebelist, and yes — I shook hands with Dan O'Keefe and thanked him for giving me a job. He softened. "I got just so many boys," he said, "and I need them all on that bench. If Deuell wanted you to be a reporter, why didn't he give me another boy?" No harm done, I said, and left.

Humility — or perhaps dispensability — was a form of brain reconditioning on the Mirror. I was given a desk and a typewriter and no assignment. The gathering speed and fever of a morning newspaper in midafternoon swirled around me, but neither the city editor, George Clarke, a short, sleek charmer, nor his competent assistant, Selig Adler, called my name. I decided to fill in the time writing, as tersely as possibly, the things I could recall of my life. I called, "Boy!" loudly, and demanded books. The boys obeyed. Hellinger walked through the office, heard me call, and stopped.

"How is it going?"

"I have nothing to do."

"Don't worry. They'll work your ass off. You're pretty bossy with the copyboys."

"I am?"

"I could hear you halfway up the stairs."

I shrugged. "I'm not a copyboy any longer. It's their turn to take it."

Mark smiled and wagged his head from side to side. "You must be rich," he said. I looked up from the paper in the typewriter. "I mean," he said, "only the very rich can afford bad manners. Who knows? Someday one of those boys may own this paper and you'll need a job." The situation, in the retelling, appears to be minuscule. The effect was titanic. There was no lesson in manners or consideration taught by my parents or my teachers which cut deeper than that short speech. I did not know that most of the editors and rewrite men had been watching and listening to the new man, and had stamped "insolent, egotistical" on his report card.

"Gauvreau wants to see you." It was Mr. Clarke. I was conditioned to sense that when a boss wanted to see me, it would be bad news. Gauvreau was looking out his window. He limped toward me. "Jim," he said, "I don't know anything about your work, but Mark says you're okay and I believe him. For a while, I'm going to try you at various positions — a sort of troubleshooter." I nodded; the term was unknown to me. "We're having a little problem with the Readers column. Selig tells me we average four to eight letters a day. That column runs on the editorial page. I want you to build it up."

"When shall I start?"

He chuckled. "When? When? Right now. Today. On a newspaper, everything is today. I want more readers sending mail. I don't care whether they like us or hate us as long as Mr. Hearst gets a good mail count. Go." Mr. Selig Adler gave me the day's mail. There were five letters. Two criticized President Herbert Hoover for the Wall Street crash and the closing of banks. One complained that the Patent Office had stolen an invention to make safe planes of hard rubber. The others are forgotten. I sat, boiled them to the essentials, and devised a fake letter. The Atlantic fleet was at anchor in the Hudson River. Times Square was heavy with sailors in blue pea jackets. I do not have a copy of the letter, but it went like this:

Dear Editor:
    A neighbor told me that the United States Navy is in harbor.

This means that thousands of uniformed rapists are roaming our streets. Until the fleet leaves, I will keep my young daughter indoors.

I think I would kill her before allowing her to go out with a sailor.

Frightened Brooklyn Mother

Within forty-eight hours, big gray mail sacks were hauled into the editorial office. They were jammed with outraged pros and cons — mostly cons. The sailors wrote. Their parents wrote. Relatives of navy men wrote. Girls wrote. Later, we began to hear from the Far Eastern Squadron. Mr. Gauvreau called me in. "What the hell did you do?" It was apparent that he did not scan the Readers column. I told him. He laughed uproariously, which, in his case, consisted of throwing his head back and making his Adam's apple bob like a yo-yo. "Good work," he said. "Good work. Run through some of the pile and find some sharp-tongued responses in both directions. Publish them. Keep the ball rolling. When the mail declines, think of something else that will make everybody mad."

Good work. On Tuesday — payday — I found an extra ten dollars in my envelope. I asked the cashier, old man Cobby, if there was a mistake. "Nope," he said, "you got a quick raise." George Clarke ordered me to go to the Parc Vendome and join a nudist colony.

"A what?"

"Nudist colony. There's a reverend divine running a free-for-all whorehouse, I think. Put your identification in a desk drawer, take fifty dollars expense money, and join up. I want a series of three articles on sin, wanton lust, the defilement of innocent girls — you know, fucking."

I told him I didn't think I could do it. Clarke looked up from the city desk with chill in his eyes "Three things I never want to hear around this office: one, I don't think I can do it; two, how do I get there from here; three, I didn't read this morning's paper. Be a good boy and do as you're told."

I joined. At the Parc Vendome, the Reverend Insley Boone had a license for a health club. A man showed me a locker room and said: "Everything off, including the socks." The first thing I saw in the gymnasium was a gray-haired woman pumping on a stationary bicycle. The young man who told me to undress said: "This is the gym, if you want a workout. The swimming pool is over there. The only rules we have are that we never shake hands, or touch, and no dates after meetings with members. Understood?" I understood. There was a beautiful bronzed girl with perpendicular breasts on the wrestling mat with a muscular Adonis. I watched. There was a lot of nude grunting, flipping, and extremely suggestive positions, but she finally pinned him and jumped up and clapped her hands over her head.

At the pool, I sat on the steps, hands clasped over crotch, and watched fellows and girls dive and swim. Some came over, aware that I was new, and introduced themselves. The Reverend Mr. Boone, a man with white hair and gray skin, introduced himself and said: "See, there's no false modesty here. Clothes are seductive because they hide things. You want to try our sunlamps?" I declined. "Up the corner is a cafeteria. Afterward, some of our people will stop in and have a piece of Danish. They can explain everything you want to know." I wondered if he guessed who I was. The old man appeared to be innocent.

After a week, during which I made the error of telling Elinor the nature of the assignment, I quit. At the city desk, I told Clarke: "No screwing."

"No screwing where?" he said.

"At the nudist colony," I said.

"You're kidding. Are the girls young?"

"Some are."

"Write it."

"Okay," I said, remembering his three admonitions, "but the Reverend is running a puritanical meeting." When I finished part one, he sent Frank Doyle and me out as a team to take private lessons at the small dance studios to ascertain how much sex was going on there. Doyle was a frustrated police sergeant; he talked and thought like one. We made a poor team. Night after night, we went to the dime-a-dance places, with their slowly revolving mirrored chandeliers, selected girls from a small stockade, and peeled off a green ticket for a new dance every time the orchestra concluded sixteen bars and stopped. I propositioned mine, told them I was rich, offered to find hotel rooms, and was spurned by twenty-year-old blonds with eighty-year-old eyes. We moved on to the private studios, private apartments with bare living rooms and a Victrola. Doyle and I consulted advertising lists and split them. Doyle lost because he wasn't trying. I lost because I tried. The best I could do was an offer from a neat Latin girl with long straight hair who wanted to rent her hand for five dollars.

Clarke was unhappy. He had given me two story ideas and I had failed on both. What is more, we bought some drinks for the dance girls and I cheated on my expense account and bought a new suit. The city editor put me at a desk between Arthur James Pegler, seventy-two years old and the father of Westbrook, and Jimmy Whittaker, probably the fastest and best rewrite man in New York. Pegler, who had been a top-flight reporter in Chicago before I was born, used an Oliver typewriter. There were three things wrong with it: it wrote on the bottom side of the roller so that "Peg" had to lift it up to see what he was doing, it did not use the standard keyboard, and the *Mirror* had to pay for repairs done by hand.

Whittaker was a pianist married to an actress, Ina Claire. He was a benevolent pixie who did not believe in the *Mirror* or anything he was doing for it. Albert Kobler, as a publisher, had become alarmed when the *News* successfully published a serial by Katharine Brush called *Ex-*

Wife. The best he could do was to ask Whittaker how long it would require to write a book called *Ex-Husband*. Jimmy, who had a face and head like a peeled egg, said six weeks. He could do it, he told Kobler, but he would want to write at home and he would need three thousand dollars in addition to his regular salary. The publisher agreed with reluctance. Whittaker, as he explained it to me, went home to Washington Square and played the piano and drank for six weeks.

Not a word, not even the title page, had been written when Kobler dashed down from his office to look at chapter one. Whittaker finally wrote the book, day by day, between rewrite assignments. He did some sweating and told me he had no idea how it would come out, but he would keep going with salacious scenes until the original couple reunited, or the ex-husband crashed in a plane trying to fly the Atlantic.

It was that kind of newspaper. I was a rewrite man, a Readers column man, a caption writer, a reporter on the street, and coeditor of the Sunday bulldog edition. I worked hard to learn, to succeed in each position. Whenever I was transferred, I asked older confreres who was the best man at that particular work, then emulated him. Good captions, for example, do not tell the reader what he can see in a picture; they sell it, enhance its value by the use of wit or intrigue, to stop a million eyes from moving on to something else. I started in January, 1930, at twenty-five dollars a week. Gauvreau and Clarke were pleased. By May 15, I was earning sixty dollars a week.

In a city of stone, a tree in leaf is a delight. Jersey City was Brooklyn on the wrong side of the river. Poplars crouched warily between sidewalk and curb. It was June. Women snipped roses from backyard vines and arranged them in brass vases on church altars. On West Side Avenue, Colacurcio's Jerseys battled Buffalo for a place in the first division of the International Baseball League. Boy Scouts laden with rucksacks marched off on weekend hikes. The Catholic Columbus Cadets, wearing overseas caps and puttees, were ready for two weeks' encampment. Girls with ropes skipped double-dutch. Boys with rubber balls played stickball or, if there weren't sufficient players, bounced the ball off front steps and called it "points."

It was one of the smokiest cities in the country and some feared, as the depression deepened, that the smoke would stop. The city and its disreputable sister, Hoboken, were America's gateway to New York. Food, merchandise, oil, and coal thundered in from west and south on the Pennsylvania Railroad, the Jersey Central, the Lehigh Valley, the Lackawanna, the Erie. The cracking plants at Standard Oil, Eagle Oil Works, and, in Bayonne, Constable Hook, drenched Hudson County in a film of dark sludge. The smoking factories were everywhere — sugar plants, Colgate's, Butler Brothers, smelting plants, saltpeter, Ryerson Steel Works, Mallinckrodt's chemical plant, the cotton mill, wire works, pipe and foundry works, tugs, barges, ferries, ocean liners, and burning garbage dumps.

There seemed to be unwritten laws that scores of streets should be arrayed with two-family houses which, except for the freshness or age of the paint, looked alike; in addition, houses were designed without garages, so that when the age of automobiles came to Jersey City, cars were parked on both sides of narrow streets. The small affluent class of families lived on Bentley or Gifford Avenue, or on the Boulevard near Hudson County Park. The city of factory workers told strangers that the 325,000 people were divided into four main geographical groups: Downtown, the Hill, Greenville, and Bergen. Actually, among themselves, most people spoke in terms of political wards because politics, in Jersey City, was the one, the only, game to play.

It was in this humid atmosphere of beer and sweat that Elinor and I had a premarital talk. It was a litaneutical conversation, one that I had touched again and again. It concerned my mother. I would not desert her again; I could not. Jenny told me that no house is big enough for two women, that it was right that, at a certain age, children should fly from the family nest. She had good judgment, but I knew that I could not lie peacefully at Elinor's side while my mother was alone again. Jenny would have to come with us even if she slept on a couch. In January, 1930, I had announced my intention to marry in June. Within a few weeks, my brother said he would marry Anna Gryniak in August.

There was family growling about two brothers marrying in the same year; or two sisters. It was, the seers said, a bad omen. John was not a good provider and knew it; I begged him to hold off a year and live with Mom until I could earn sufficient money to help her. His rebuttal was: "If you can get married, I don't see why I can't." Adele had two daughters and a brilliant husband who was sick with alcohol; he drafted the designs for turbines in the hulls of navy destroyers. Sometimes, in a hangover, he made a slight error and once, at Gibbs & Cox, ranking naval officers questioned him about political affiliations. He was in the unhappy position of living in a body composed of taut piano wires, a man who dared not take a drink and could not refuse one.

Adele could not take care of Mother. John could not. It was up to me. So I protested my love for Elinor, pledged my life to her, and asked her to allow my mother to live with us. It amounted to shameless begging, but she said she understood. "She can keep the house clean for you," I said. "You'll be working in Wall Street. She can scrub and cook and she'll keep out of our way. She has a couple of old biddy girlfriends she'll be visiting in the evenings."

The large brown eyes were full upon me. Tears were close. "I wish," she said, "that you'd stop bringing this up." I said okay. "It isn't the best arrangement, but I get along with your mother. She even hinted that you should propose to me."

"True," I said. "I told you how I felt when the three of us deserted her — not counting Dad. I just couldn't bear it one more time."

"Could she hang onto the flat on Van Wagenen for a couple of weeks after we get married?"

"Easy. A cinch."

"Tell her not to give notice until we come back from our honeymoon."

I breathed again. After years of darkness, the future looked blindingly bright. I was willing to abase myself to make sure that Mom was not to be dropped into a cockroach-infested furnished room. "I won't mention it again," I promised.

Elinor touched a finger lightly to a big firm breast and made a cross. "Your mother can stay with us. Maybe you can talk your father into coming back."

"Jim Bishop marries a broker's sec on June 14th (Flag Day to you!)," Winchell wrote in his column. The important day was almost sunny. I paid for a morning shave and hot towel. There was no doubt in my mind, no subliminal fear that I might be revenging myself on one girl by marrying another. The love was real and I was confident that a life of contentment lay ahead. The moon face, the black shoulder-length hair, the large serious eyes, the buxom figure, the faith she expressed in my future, her rocklike faith in God — Elinor was so good in so many ways that I wondered how she could have fallen in love with me. Within me there was a euphoria which brooked no contrary emotion except jealousy. Suspicion is a merciless master. It creeps with timidity into the mind, and soon dominates all it beholds. I was jealous of every lingering glance Elinor bestowed on another man, young or old, handsome or ugly.

I began to dislike the Irish speakeasy and the friendly attitude of the waiters. When I walked with Elinor, and a man passed, I looked back to see if he was taking a second look. There was a "boss" at Dominick & Dominick who devised spurious excuses for her to work late with him; a man who asked to take her to dinner and the theater. I ordered her to quit the job. She said I was insane; we needed all the money we could earn. She and her mother selected a fourth-floor-front apartment at 145 Kensington Avenue at seventy dollars a month. It had a canopy and an elevator.

"We don't have to live that rich," I said.

She cried. "I thought you'd be pleased."

"Okay, okay."

"We can buy furniture on time."

"I forgot furniture."

"Momma is helping me. We looked at some stuff at Ludwig Baumann in New York."

On my day off, we went to look. The furniture, as well as the apartment, were Momma's notions. There was a modern console radio; a three-piece living room set (the couch was not convertible); a robin's-egg blue Chinese rug with flame edging; a bedroom set with vanity mirror; towels, kitchen utensils, end tables, dishes, fancy ashtrays, table lamps — $1,879. I was frightened. The floor manager squeaked amiability in his shoes. "You're just starting out?" he said, pulling his nostrils downward. "I thought so. Our firm thinks it is a mark of responsibility for a couple to worry about the size of a bill.

"Mr. Bishop, you have no established credit, so when the young lady and her mother selected this stuff, we took the liberty of checking your job status at the *Daily Mirror*, and I would say, sir, that your position is pretty secure."

"You checked my what?"

He shrugged. "No offense, sir, but we also checked Miss Dunning's. The total amount comes to a little over two thousand and you will have two years —"

"Two thousand?" I glanced at my bride-to-be. "I thought you said eighteen hundred."

"Well, when you add the interest — the carrying charges — it comes to, let me see" (he consulted a book) "two thousand twenty-nine dollars and thirty-two cents, which amounts to only eighty-four dollars and fifty-five cents a month."

I excused myself for a conference. "Are you crazy?" I said. She turned her head away to use a handkerchief. "We do want a nice apartment," she said.

I was angry. "Listen," I said. "Neither of us has ever lived in an elevator apartment. We don't need it, for openers, but Momma likes it."

"That's untrue. I like it. So do you."

"I like the Taj Mahal too, but that's out. We're paying seventy a month for a middle-class neighborhood, and we're moving in with Chinese rugs and console radios at eighty-four fifty-five a month. Honey, we haven't got it."

Tears. I felt strongly about indebtedness. The disagreement was not casual. My voice was loud and abrasive. I knew lots of two-family houses where the rent was thirty-five dollars. Who needed a Chinese rug? It was a scene, and it closed with my signing for everything. "Get it in the apartment before June fourteenth," I said to the floor manager, "or cancel the order."

I felt an uneasiness. Elinor hugged my arm all the way home, but I began to wonder if the combination of mother and only child was too strong for me. It was like staring clear-eyed at a distant beautiful scene and noticing a floating black spot in one eyeball. "We need knives and forks and spoons," I said. She smiled upward and shook her head. "The office is giving us a set of hammered silver as a wedding present." The black spot disappeared on the periphery of my vision. At home, my mother heard the story. "Isn't that a little steep for newlyweds?" she said softly. I said I thought so. She said, "Oh."

It was a four o'clock wedding at Saint John's Church on the Boulevard. My relatives, my friends, were on one side of the church. Elinor's, of course, were on the other. An organist played the "Wedding March" from *Lohengrin* twice. As Frank Dunning held his daughter's arm, genuflected, and couldn't seem to get back up, I helped him and took her arm. In flowing white, my bride looked more voluptuous than beautiful. The priest mumbled over a book. A voice in the choir sang "Oh, Promise Me." I was nervous. Her bouquet was shaking. It crossed my mind that families divide themselves on opposite sides of a church at weddings and at funerals.

Outside in the sun there were shouts and rice. My best man, John Dundas, hopped into a limousine with us and so did the bridesmaid, Grace Corrigan. It was over. For better, for worse, richer, poorer — I was a king or a slave. My mother-in-law had told me that the reception on the roof of the Elks Club would be held to the immediate families and the wedding party. I was not allowed to invite Grandma Bishop or Grandma Tier. Nor, for that matter, my mother's considerable family and my father's. The limousine made a few circumnavigations of the block to permit everyone to be seated. We went up to the roof.

The place was jammed. I knew a few of the people. Anger began to rise again. At the wedding table, after the watery Manhattan toast, I whispered to Elinor about it. "I'm sorry," she whispered back, "really I am. Momma said she couldn't afford a big reception, and yet she had to invite her side of the family, the Lanigans, and Daddy's. They went into debt for this, Jim. Honest." I believed her. Later, I excused myself and went to the men's room. My father was there, radiant in a navy blue suit, a red carnation, and the ruddy complexion that comes with highballs. He fixed his tie as I stood at the urinal. "Two things I have to tell you," he said portentously. "One, give up all your old friends and start fresh. Make her give up her old friends, too. Neither of you can inflict old personal memories on the other. Two, if you get caught with the wrong woman at any time — deny, deny deny. I have nothing else to say."

An hour later, we drove off in a Chrysler owned by an old friend, Fred Grimsey. The "Just Married" signs were on it; the tin cans dragged. I parked the car around the corner and ripped them off She had changed into what the women called her "going-away outfit," and she looked attractive. We drove in silence awhile, headed for Washington. At Trenton we turned, for no reason, toward Atlantic City. I found myself singing: "Three O'Clock in the Morning," although I cannot sing. Elinor sat close. There was a lot of agreeable dialogue, but it has sifted through the bottom of what is left of my memory.

A honeymoon is when masks begin to chip. The belief that true happiness begins and ends in the bedroom is a canard. It is a time — in and

[82]

out of the bedroom — of accommodation, consideration, a sometimes desperate effort to understand each other. The mutual love and concomitant happiness of this marriage were solid. There were no second thoughts, no regrets. It was, if one may judge by the evidence, an ideal relationship with a little time spent surrendering to the whims of each other.

She was averse to putting the caps on toothpaste or beauty-cream jars. Shoes were pigeon-toed in the middle of the rug. Elinor slept with full makeup, including slashes of lipstick. I was a slave to time; she believed that a table reserved for eight P.M. meant eight twenty-five. Frequently, she looked out a window and said: "I feel nervous." She never knew why. On my side, she objected to my habit of reading nude. Nor could she understand why I refused to wash my hair two or three times a week. She objected to my desire to dominate. My tactlessness in responding to an ignorant statement with sarcasm was not endearing. My monologues about a future as an author were, she thought, outrageous dreams. "I love you as you are," she said. "You're a reporter. But for God's sake, Jim, you never even went to high school."

The personality differences — somewhat minuscule — were to be expected. If I was serious about the tomorrows, she was flamboyant about the todays. Our late evenings were spent in a speakeasy. A few drinks dissolved the shadows on the brown eyes. She became bright, witty, a more than engaging conversationalist. She liked hats, and wore a big white silk one with a broad, sagging brim. The blue silk dress had a square neck; a slash of red hung loose from waist to hemline.

The effect of the gin on me was the opposite. I talked more and said less. After two or three, my mind was in a swimming mist of optimism. My credo was that if three made me articulate, six would make me a pundit. I dragged her, half reluctantly, into fields where no flowers bloomed — politics, authors, artists, science, the economic depression, newspaper work, baseball, flight, astronomy — matters about which I had a superficial knowledge, but which excited my interest. To Elinor, education meant a proper school. It was a series of semesters, nothing more. It is overstating the matter crudely, but Elinor's world was peopled with "us" and "them." There were the right people and the wrong people. Sometimes I heard the soft insistent ring of alarm bells. Perhaps she heard them too, listening to me. But each was sure he could remold the other. That was a monumental mistake.

The apartment was beautiful. It had too many coffee percolators and silver-plated trays. Elinor said some could be exchanged. The telephone is a great and necessary instrument, but it became a source of caustic comment. My bride phoned her mother every day. Sometimes twice a day. On our honeymoon, she made the daily report while I was under a shower. At home, it was done in the bedroom in whispers. "What the hell are the secrets?" I shouted.

She smiled. "It's all in your head, Jim. There are no secrets."

[83]

"Then tell me what takes forty minutes to say?"

"Nothing. Momma has nobody to talk to anymore."

"How about my mother?"

"She still has your brother, John." Sometimes, when these small stones were underfoot, she would run to me, hug and kiss, and beg me not to be demanding.

"That damned phone," I would say softly. "Honest, baby. I hate it." Baby. A ridiculous appellation. Baby. And yet, though she sometimes displayed flashes of shrieking anger, I felt that my woman was not quite grown. She was my baby. And her mother's.

I did not know enough about my craft to write a book, but I wanted to spend quiet evenings pounding a secondhand typewriter. It was not to be. Married life, to Elinor, was socializing. She said she worked hard all day and she had no desire to sit reading at night while I typed. She wanted guests. She would make up a platter of ham and liverwurst and some homemade potato salad. I would walk down to Lexington Avenue and West Side and buy a half-gallon of alcohol, essence of juniper, and glycerine. This would make a gallon of gin and, with ginger ale and ice, transmuted our lives. Within a few months, the Bishops became the fulcrum of an ever-growing list of everlasting friends.

The mornings were dismal. It was difficult to remember when the guests departed, and in what temper. If I awakened shivering and nude on the couch, it was safe to assume that we had had a dispute after everyone left. If she was across the bed in a slip, the breathing lips bubbling saliva, my flapper had imbibed too many gin bucks. If there was a black apostrophe in the Chinese rug, a guest had dropped a cigarette. Scraps of stale food were on end tables, a lighted lamp fought the sunlight, the radio hummed all night, someone had been sick in the bathroom. My head pulsed like a heart. I squinted against light. The clock whipped us. The coffeepot was on; the shower was boiling or freezing; two aspirin locked themselves on the back of the tongue and refused to budge. Elinor said she shouldn't speak to me; I had accused her of dancing too close to John Dundas — pressing against him — and had threatened to punch him. On another night, I kissed her bridesmaid, and Elinor closed the book on an old friendship. On other nights, she was too tired for lovemaking.

We had talks about our differences of opinion, our separate schemes of life. I may have been the persuader, because she said often: "I never thought of it that way. I think you're right." There were but two items which sent shivers of fear through my body. One was when she would say, post-contretemps, "I'll change. I'll be different." The other was when she would stare moodily down into the street, rub her arm steadily, and say: "I feel nervous, Jim. I don't understand it, but I feel as though something is going to happen."

I asked if my mother could move in after August. "Why after August?" she said, and the tone was challenging.

"Because my brother is going to marry Anna Gryniak at the end of August."

"Tell him it's bad luck to get married in the same year. Hell, he can't even keep a job."

Softly: "The wedding is in August."

"That's not our hard luck. Let Momma go live with him."

"You promised."

"Let's get one thing straight, Jim. No house is big enough for two women."

"You didn't say that."

"Okay, so I was stupid. You always tell me how stupid I am. Now I realize that it could never be. Let your father take care of her. I didn't marry your mother."

It is possible that I never believed the promise, but accepted it as an excuse to marry Elinor without pangs of conscience. It's possible. But that evening, the words began to pour loudly from two mouths at the same time. They were loud and obscene, the outfall of a rusty sewer.

I could leave her. I could stay. Communications were cut so that we addressed each other only when it was necessary. There were no parties. I made the acquaintance of Dr. Arthur Trewhella, a short blond general practitioner who lived at the other end of the street. He was a congenial, no-nonsense physician. One evening, as Elinor sat home reading, I was at Trewhella's house and asked him what items families should carry in their medicine chests. He gave it thought, and ticked them off. I went home, rapped out a short article, and sent it to a medical magazine. They bought it for fifty dollars. I couldn't believe my good luck. It was, to me, a step up from newspaper work. And yet, what I had peddled was no more than sensible information.

Elinor and I became husband and wife again. She could weep; I could not. She begged me to understand her position. I said, "Sure," but I didn't. It was my function to visit my mother alone, sip tea and eat hot biscuits with slabs of yellow butter, and explain the situation. "Oh," she said brightly, "I understand. You're young people. You should have privacy. The two times I've been to your apartment I saw that there isn't enough closet space, and anyway, how could I go to bed early when you have friends in the house? I'll get along somehow, but I do wish your father would come to his senses." She knew that, with the sums my father sent, with no additional money from me or from Johnny, she must return to a cheap furnished room. Her generosity, or perhaps her understanding of newlyweds, pressed the weight of guilt on me.

John would not entertain the thought of Mother living with him after his marriage to Anna. He seldom thought beyond the pending joys and trials of the day. His blond wavy hair, his amiable good-looking face, his philosophy of never seeming to aspire to more than the price of a movie and money for cigarettes brought him an enviable contentment. Mother didn't entertain the possibility of living with him, because she knew that, after marriage, Anna would have problems trying to get him out of bed for work.

The problems of the family — rather than its virtues — are important because it is the problem situations rather than the pleasant which, occurring in the young years, explain the attitudes of the mature and the old. The clawing, fingernail-breaking climb to success is conditioned, not by sunshine, but by storms of discontent. Often, it approaches rage to get out of the pit, to run breathless and with burning lungs to an unknown place where reason prevails. The supreme irony, I suppose, is that I maintained an affection for everyone, from my father to the edges of the family and beyond. It is as though I divined, without rationalization, that almost everyone was trapped in a cul-de-sac which was beyond his will to alter. I knew that Big John wanted his Jenny to be happy, but, as it involved his presence at her side, he could not help her. My brother was generous to a fault; if he had had a million dollars he would have divided it evenly among the members of the family, but he was broke. Adele was a one-man woman who suffered the neurotic agonies of her husband because she was powerless to leave him. Edgar could not live with the runaway carousel inside his head, and sought solace in the drug he could not assimilate — alcohol. My mother was that most reprehensible of all women — the good wife, the good mother, the perpetual lady — and she lost her man to her best friend.

We struggled to approach mediocrity. No one was free of debt. Daily life consisted of drudgery; an evening assault on crowds determined to share the same subway car; supper; reading; radio; sometimes a bottle or two of "near beer" and a phone call. The phone calls had an importance because the best one could expect was to hear a relative say: "Nothing new here. What's new on your end?" The bad news, which was common, was illness or loss of job or both. The great granite strength of the United States had cracked, and people were running to avoid being hit by falling stone.

Elinor lost her job as secretary within ninety days of the marriage. In offices and industry, the junior 10 percent were "laid off" in 1930; in 1931, men and women with seniority and skills were cut loose. The starchy, almost humorless man in the White House, Herbert Hoover, explained the economic facts of life to the nation. At the time, few regarded the depression as worldwide; Americans wondered what had happened to us. The muted hysteria became a plague. Families weren't buying houses; they were trying to sell and rent.

Automobile sales fell off; families decided to use the car "one more year." Dealers went into receivership; Detroit laid off thousands and scores of thousands; orders for steel and tires were canceled, inducing more lay-offs, less purchasing power; pay cuts became common and this led to strikes; the strikes were followed by strikebreakers armed with clubs and pistols; beggars in flapping shoes and old army overcoats walked the streets of New York whispering: "Buddy, can you spare a dime?" Men deserted their families to ride the rocking freight trains, there to join the local un-employed in shacks of peach and orange crates in garbage dumps and tawny glades. The fourth decade of the twentieth century would demon-strate that even the most impregnable nation in history could be brought to its knees.

Somerset Maugham said that he regretted never having had newspaper experience. From a successful author, it sounds condescending. The soar-ing eagle is pained that he was not once a caged canary. Perhaps. The nov-elist writes what he pleases when he pleases. If the mood is not on him — which occurs frequently with indulgence — he may romance it by walking a floor or repairing to a café. The reporter is the daily prisoner of clocked facts. He must hunt the sources, ask the questions, and hurry to the news-paper to write the story on deadline.

It does not matter whether he has a headache, a poignant personal prob-lem, or a hangover. On all working days, he is expected to do his best in one swift swipe at each story. He is given no second chance, no opportunity to polish and revise, and God help him if a competitive newspaper pub-lishes a better version of the same assignment. Mr. Maugham may have realized that there is no training, no tutelage, no school which can match the discipline of a daily newspaper. When I became a reporter on the *Daily Mirror*, an evolution of philosophies presented themselves in the first six months: (1) I was being paid by William Randolph Hearst to learn how to write; (2) the only way to improve my work would be to read and re-read the best writers and to bear in mind that I was the eyes, the ears, the nose, and sometimes the mind of the reader; (3) I could aspire to be worthy someday to write for magazines and, in time, for book publishers.

My goals not only were out of reach, but they carried an unremitting fever which would not be cured by age or disappointment. I *had* to have these things. I studied, I worried, I daydreamed. I reread Theodore Dreiser, the early Hemingway material, and sometimes dared the insanity of re-writing scenes from books. I chewed and masticated the poetry of Poe, Millay, Frost, Wilde over and over, to try to fathom metaphors, personifi-cations, and similes. Humor, on first reading, might be funny. On second and succeeding readings, it became a quest to decipher why the minor cru-elties and exaggerations of daily life are amusing. One more thing: I wanted to know a little bit about every subject — a surface knowledge — and I found that the public library would permit me to borrow each vol-ume of *Encyclopaedia Britannica* long enough to remember some of what I read. Sometimes, as in the case of medicine and military and naval tactics, I became sufficiently intrigued to dig deeper by borrowing or buying other books.

What I lacked in formal education was so enormous that I was compelled, so to speak, to dig for gold with bare hands. It was never a chore; my tastes were cosmopolitan and few subjects, from aviation to zoology, dulled my eyes. Some of the studies were beyond my comprehension at the age of twenty-two; the attempts to filter neutrons in atomic structure, for example, or the differences between fission and fusion as expatiated on in 1930 left me senseless, empty of understanding. Nor could I understand why tides rose and fell more than fifty feet in the Bay of Fundy, but only two feet off Palm Beach. Studies of the criminal mind, written mostly by psychiatrists, taught me that scientists frequently disagree — some said that the recidivist was a product of his environment; a few maintained that the criminal mind is congenital; others claimed that too much male aggression led to acts of violence. My pursuit of college curricula in reading led to despair — the noble professors seemed to inflict dull literary tripe on students who could not escape.

Clarke told me to go to Avenue U in Brooklyn. "Go to the B.M.T. station. A collector has been killed." Manny Elkins, picture assignment editor, had a photographer on his way. I wished that Clarke had told me what he meant by a "collector," and something about the manner of death. It was not considered good form to ask questions. Forty-five minutes later, I was at Avenue U. It was an elevated station on a subway, which seems like a contradiction in terms.

There were more police than passengers. Reporters from the *News*, the New York *Journal*, *The New York Times*, even the *Post*, were with a police inspector who was giving a statement. The station stood on steel stilts above the street. It consisted of concave creaky boards, a roundish change booth, a smelly men's room, and one marked "Women." Between the turnstiles was a lumpy blanket.

I showed my police card (without which all reporters are helpless) and lifted the cloth. The man underneath stared up at me with dark eyes. The top of his head had been blown off. The change booth was empty, except for a weak saffron light. The woman who worked there had been whisked to Brooklyn police headquarters. A lieutenant from homicide was willing to reconstruct the murder. The Brooklyn-Manhattan Transit Company sent an empty train to all stations once a week. The men who worked the train emptied the turnstiles of nickels. They had the proper keys and the wide-mouthed canvas bags.

Someone must have learned what day and what time the train would arrive at Avenue U. Six young men loped up the long staircase. The woman in the change booth noticed them only because they allowed two trains to pass without boarding or asking for change. She was reading an early edition of the *News*. A few minutes later, she saw five of the boys go into the men's room. When the empty train squealed to a stop, a dark sturdy young man got off, swinging a chain full of keys and carrying a canvas bag. He dropped to his knees at the first turnstile. He yanked a bag of nickels from it, sealed the top, and replaced it with the empty.

The fellows in the men's room poured out. The man who had been behind the cashier's cage produced a gun. He leaned over the turnstile and aimed it at the kneeling man's head. The subway collector seemed calm. The cashier could hear him plainly. "You guys crazy?" he said. He shook the sealed bag. "There ain't enough nickels in here to get you to Jersey." The man with the gun said: "Wise-ass." Two others shouted: "Give it to him, Vinnie!" Vinnie gave it to him. Someone grabbed the bag of change. The six men ran past the booth, and hopped down the steps two and three at a time and got into a car.

The dead man was a student at the Delehanty Institute and had planned to become a policeman. It is one of the small ironies that the first cop to respond to the cashier's hysterical phone call was the dead man's brother-in-law-to-be. The stolen cash, according to the tabulator on the turnstile, was $5.95, ninety-nine cents per man. So far as I was concerned the story ended there. By four P.M. it had been written and I was at the Commodore Hotel trying to interview Father Coughlin, the radio personality who endeared himself to reactionary Roman Catholics with undocumented charges which, beneath the unctuous tone, were anti-British, anti–White House, and anti-Semitic.

When he came to the door of his small room, he adjusted glittering pince-nez and was more interested in how I had found him than why. He was in New York trying to negotiate with additional radio stations for his network of vilification. He asked if I was Catholic. I nodded. He did not invite me inside the room. "Then I beg of you, in the name of whatever respect you have for the priesthood, not to mention that I am in New York. If my presence gets into the press, the deal will be off. Do you carry anything holy?" I yanked a small crucifix from an inside pocket. "Let me bless it for you and for the welfare of those you love," he said. He blessed it.

I didn't have the nerve to tell Father Coughlin that it had already been blessed. His earnest entreaty that I not mention his presence so impressed me that I went back to the *Mirror* and lied for the first and last time of my career. "You got a bad tip," I told the editor, Selig Adler.

He shook his head. "The bell captain called us and told us he was there. You sure?"

"I'm sure."

He looked up at the wall clock. "You can go home." I carried feelings of guilt. They diminished and returned many times. Was I more Catholic than reporter? Did a priest have the right to ask me to lie? The guilt remained as a scar and I vowed that I would never do it again.

Ray Doyle, one of the best bird dogs, drew the "Folo Up" on the B.M.T. murder assignment. No matter where a story broke, from Providence to

Paterson, he seemed always to know a chief of police or a commissioner he could call on a first-name basis. A Folo Up may last but two days, and, sporadically, it may go on for years.

The only clue was a size-seven-and-a-quarter brown fedora made by the Adams Hat Company. It was found in the washroom. At Brooklyn police headquarters, chief inspectors and deputy chiefs from Brooklyn homicide sat around a chipped and cigarette-scarred table discussing the case and sliding the hat back and forth. Someone said: "A half a million men wear this size, this color in Adams hats. We ain't got a goddamn thing."

At headquarters was a fat cop who was assigned as custodian. The desk sergeants called him "Woodenshoes" after a character in the Hecht-MacArthur play *The Front Page*. Most precincts have a Woodenshoes. He is usually an ignorant man of amiable disposition who, by some mischance, was appointed to the department but could not be trusted to pound a beat. In most cases, he worked the eight-to-four shift, cleaning cuspidors, scrubbing toilet bowls, flushing urine off the men's room floor with an odoriferous product called C.N. He also emptied wastebaskets and got sandwiches and coffee for the captain and superior officers.

This Woodenshoes made a predictable mistake. He was washing windows in the conference room as the hat was reexamined and shoved across the table. He opened his mouth. "Chief," he said, "if you don't mind, I figure that all you gotta do is to find the kid that owns that hat." It was an amusing observation to a few. To one — the inspector in charge of the district — it was an absurd challenge.

"Come here," he said sternly. Woodenshoes dropped his rags and window scraper, and wiped his hands. "Yes, sir." The brown hat was handed to him. "You are temporarily detached from duty as custodian of headquarters," the inspector said. "From now on, you will go an eight-to-four tour every day until you find the owner of this hat. Is that understood?" Woodenshoes appeared to be dumbstruck. "You mean I take this hat — " "And find the owner," snapped the inspector. "And try, please, not to lose the hat." Most of the beefy men chuckled. The consensus was that the ninety-nine-cent murder was not perpetrated by any of the known gangs in New York. Most likely, it was a neighborhood group, six boys who lived within a block or two of each other and were accustomed to stealing fruit and running, or gang-banging a girl on a tenement roof, or rifling a church poor box. The city had hundreds of such groups. Unless one of the six, overcome by conscience, told it to a parent, or a girlfriend, or someone who might tip the police anonymously, the chances of solving the crime were small.

I worked many diverse assignments day after day and week after week as Woodenshoes walked the streets of Brooklyn with the brown fedora. He accosted pedestrians and block dancers, trudged the boardwalk at Coney Island, tried all the parks, asking plaintively: "Hey, know anybody missing a brown hat like this?" His feet hurt, his mood was plaintive, and there were times when he begged the desk lieutenant to get him off the hat. The inspector was remorseless: "That man walks the streets until he finds the owner or until he retires — whichever comes first."

In a remote section of Prospect Park, there were little signs stating: "Don't Walk on the Grass." Woodenshoes walked on it. It comprised the shortest distance between benches where idlers sat all day in the pale sun. He walked up behind a bench and saw a hatless head of dark glistening hair. Almost playfully, he dropped it on the head. The sitter seemed to stiffen. Then, without turning, he said: "Okay. Okay. Please don't shoot." Woodenshoes laughed heartily. "I'm not going to shoot you, son," he said. "I'm a police officer." The young man stood slowly and turned, the hat cocked crazily. "Okay," he said again. "It's mine. Mine. I'm the guy left it in the terlet. But I didn't shoot nobody and I didn't have no gun." It required a moment or two for Woodenshoes to understand that he had made a highly improbable collar. Either he had a nut or he had one of the boys who participated in the ninety-nine-cent murder.

He had one of the boys. Within the first hour of interrogation, detectives armed with names and addresses picked up five more prisoners. Remorse? Shame? Fear? Interrogation was individual. Confessions were signed and, in time, all six were tried, found guilty, and sentenced to die in the electric chair.

Murder is the unquenchable thirst of the reader. It pours from vessels of sex, money, injustice, challenge. In newspapers, the abused phrases are *crime of passion, armed robbery, revenge, jealousy, family quarrel, love, perversion, insanity.* The most common form of challenge is when the wife (or husband) laughs at a revolver and says: "You wouldn't dare!"

I learned more of murder than of typefaces because my editors thought I was good at murders. Not good at solving them, but at unbraiding truth from evasion between prosecution and defense. Truth, at best, is an assortment of facts reduced to an approximation.

The day of the execution, editor Jack Lait said: "You go, Jim. File a good story and you can take off tomorrow. This is the first time six will go at one shot."

I arrived at Sing Sing early. It was a hot evening. The Hudson River was flat and gray. Heat caromed off the high concrete walls. Outside, a group of Italian women were on their knees, mumbling rosaries and kissing the concrete. Photographers made a few shots. I was inside at eight-thirty. The electrocutions, as usual, were scheduled for eleven P.M. The warden's office held a dozen reporters and a state trooper. They drank whiskey from paper cups. The warden tried to make a few preexecution announcements. One was the last-meal menus. Two ate; four gave dinners to men in nearby cells. All had ice cream. The warden had a hot line open to the governor's office in Albany. Only the neophyte reporters took notes.

At nine-thirty, the executioner arrived. We didn't see him. He was escorted directly to the Death House. As always, he tested the equipment.

He had previously told me that it is not the volts which kill; it's the amperes. His juice was separate from the rest of the prison, so that the lights never dimmed, nor did prisoners in other blocks shout or beat their bars with tin cups. Most were too self-centered to care what happened to others, or when.

We knew that the prayers of the sobbing mothers would not be answered. We knew that the governor would not respond to appeals for mercy. And we were wrong. At ten P.M., when most of the six had died an assortment of fantasy deaths, he phoned the warden and commuted the sentences of four to life imprisonment. Two would have to die — the one who had purchased the revolver, and the one who had fired it.

At ten forty-five we walked down the concrete path to the Death House, were frisked by guards looking for cameras, and went inside to sit in the small walnut pews which made the place look like a sanitized chapel. As always, I made notes on my knee. Others did not. The chair, strong and ugly, was alone on a dark rubber mat. It sat on what appeared, under the fluorescent lights, to be a low stage. I could see the executioner in his alcove at the left. On the right, a door opened and a priest in cassock and surplice backed in, holding a large goldish cross. He was followed by two guards. Behind them was a skinny kid with mussed hair, a white shirt open at the collar, brown slacks, and carpet slippers. His hands were clasped. His head was down. His lips were moving.

Behind him were two more guards. One closed the door. The prison physician stood against a wall twirling a stethoscope. The prisoner looked up and saw us in what must have appeared to be the gloom outside the fluorescent lights. If big eyes are frightened eyes, he was scared. If not, he was numb and curious. He stared out as though looking for a face, but he didn't find it. The principal keeper, a no-nonsense man with a bellyful of whiskey, stared at the boy and nodded at the chair.

We waited for last words. None came. The young man was almost polite. He nodded and sat. Three guards set the straps whirling. Those around each leg, the chest, and the head must be cinched tight to keep the body from jumping. The principal keeper could not abide fumblers. When the work was complete (in a trice), the guards stepped away. They glanced at each other to make sure that nobody was near that chair. The executioner looked out of the arch of the alcove. The principal keeper nodded. It was not enough. The electrician came out and walked around the chair, to make certain that all straps were in place. He crouched in front of the chair. The condemned had his head back. His fingers gripped the armrests tightly. He stopped whatever he was mumbling to take a deep breath and sigh.

The executioner hurried back inside, and threw the switch. The body jumped straight forward, the mouth opened, the part of the face which could be seen was contorted and purplish. The black straps cracked and snapped with the pressure of an unconscious body surging. One of the hands grasping the chair arm emitted pale blue smoke. Once, perhaps a long time before, the executioner must have been caught with a prisoner who, unstrapped, was not quite dead. It was his current custom to start his voltage at 1600 and 10 amperes, jump it to 2500 and 18 amperes, then bring it back down, and bring it up sharply. He did this three times. Although the young man was dead, he leaped forward at each command of the electrician.

He was pronounced dead and taken on a hospital cart from the room. The second one was brought in. The priest murmured the prayers. This time there was no response. The prisoner looked out at us and kept swallowing. He too had no last words. Twenty-four witnesses sat and watched him die, saw him unstrapped as limp and tender as a puppy, and carried away. I hurried out and down to Ossining to the Western Union office. The story was filed and I went home. In the morning, I was surprised to find that I had fallen asleep almost immediately.

A killer walked into the city room of the *Daily Mirror*. He wanted to confess to a newspaper. Tabloids exercised a magnetic effect on those afflicted with massive ignorance. We were random hosts to old ladies who could hear secret broadcasts from Tokyo through their bridgework; the divers who desired to leap from oblivion to fame to oblivion by jumping off the torch of the Statue of Liberty; the nubile nymphets who waited demurely to put their names in the paper. We had prophets, men armed with elaborate calendars predicting the exact day on which the world would end, the fading chorus girls willing to sell their confessions for five hundred dollars, the unknown song writers, the shabby men with sure-thing devices and inventions for making millions of dollars, mothers carrying faded snapshots of missing daughters, habitual losers.

Between two desks, Pete DuBerg and I had pulled out a table leaf and played chess between editions. The big room was quiet, almost empty. Big green shaded lights hung from the ceiling. The short man had reddish, wet-looking hair. He wore a tan overcoat with a knotted belt. We looked up only because he was a stranger to the city room, and strangers were usually escorted by the receptionist. The man had fresh furrows on both cheeks with drops of blood hanging to the edges. We forgot our chess game.

The night editor, bald Charles Barth, a plodding type, sat with his back to the wall. To the reporters, photographers, and rewrite men, Barth was known as a "nice man." The phrase is a pejorative — everyone liked him because he was innocuous. Facing him was the assistant night editor, Frank McMahon, one with black, close-cut hair, ruddy cheeks, and an assortment of tensions which he bottled.

McMahon wrote everything on legal-sized paper. If I passed him and exchanged the most casual of greetings, he would write, "Hello, Frank — Bishop." Every hour on the hour, McMahon lectured copyboys on a grave subject called "more respect to the editors around here." On the half-hour, he got up from the desk, walked all the way to the Forty-fifth Street windows, opened one, and stuck his hand out to see if it was raining.

For a reason no one divined, Barth and McMahon, facing each other, had not spoken to each other, except on business, for years. Like old lovers, they lived but a pillow apart and never kissed. The stranger asked McMahon for the fish and game editor. Before responding, Frank wrote, "Wants Fish & Game Ed," and pointed toward the back of the building. Sports departments are darkened early. The writers have written their morning stories and have gone home or on night assignments at fights, hockey games, or basketball matches. Most of them are unamused critics who reassemble five hundred clichés accompanied by digits indicating won or lost and commit it to paper.

It is a monumental coincidence that the only light in the sports department at this time was on the desk of James Hurley, fish and game editor. Mr. Hurley was a handsome, burly, graying man who, in World War I, had been a captain in the United States Marines. He was pecking out a column for the day after the morrow. The Stranger with the bloody face looked almost saddened as he stood beside Hurley, who did not look up. "Well?" the fish and game editor said, without moving.

The Stranger tried a small smile. "Are you really the fish and game editor?"

Hurley was annoyed. "That's me," he said. "Now I'm busy — "

"Tonight," the Stranger said, "when I killed my wife, Ronnie, I said to myself, 'Why not give the scoop to the fish and game editor?' " Hurley glanced up sideways. "Sir, you see I never had any real fun out of life. I'm a night watchman in a garage and I have time on my hands. I sit and read your column over and over. Hell, I been blue-fishing with you off Fire Island, I been hunting deer in the Adirondacks, I even went to the Bahamas with you when you caught that blue marlin." Hurley began to frown. The Stranger smiled broadly for the first time. "Oh, you think I'm a nut or something." He put his hand into the overcoat pocket and a warm shiny revolver emerged.

Mr. Hurley began to smile, feeling that this was no time to be abrasive. "This," he said tapping his desk, "is the outdoor sports department. The indoor sports are over there." He pointed to Barth and McMahon. DuBerg and I had risen from our desks, hearing parts of the dialogue, and we walked, shuffling slowly, toward the Stranger. He went back to McMahon. Before he could open his mouth, Barth flipped a piece of wire copy. "Get me all the one-column stock cuts on Mary Pickford," he said. "She just married some horn-tooter named Buddy Rogers." He turned to the makeup man. "Drop the transit story off the bottom of page three and put Pickford across with a three-column twenty-four-point head."

"I just killed my wife," the Stranger said to McMahon.

Frank wrote, "Killed his wife." "Just a minute," he said to the Stranger.

[94]

"Boy! Get me all the one-column stock cuts on Mary Pickford. Now come on. Snap to it."

Pete DuBerg wanted to bet a dime that Barth would select a photo of Mary Pickford with curls. I declined. DuBerg grinned. "Barth told me the last time he saw a movie was in 1917. Went once and never again. Honest. He said it was a Pickford thing — you know, America's Sweetheart stuff."

"Now," Frank said, looking up at the Stranger, "you say you killed your wife. What about it?" Barth was busy redesigning page 3. He heard McMahon and stopped to look at the man. He adjusted his glasses downward. The study of the Stranger resulted in a frown of disapproval. "See what he's got," he said to McMahon.

This was a poor decision. DuBerg or Bishop could have taken the assignment and made a report within minutes. McMahon assumed his desk sergeant voice and scribbled both questions and answers. If the Stranger had indeed killed someone, McMahon would have to complete the interrogation, report to Barth, who would then call a rewrite man to take the story from the beginning. The following, without McMahon's questions, is an approximation of what the Stranger said. (In instances such as this, where correct names and addresses will not add to the story, they have been changed.)

"My name is Timothy Duff. I am thirty-three and I live in a flat at Three eighty-four West Fifty-fourth Street. I am married, have no children, and have never been arrested for anything. I work as a night watchman at the Quik-Trip Parking Center, Four-oh-two West Fifty-eighth. I report at eight — I usually get there a few minutes ahead — and knock off at four in the morning. I am married to Veronica Duff, twenty-six, three years. She works days as a waitress in Sam's Luncheonette, Ninth and Fifty-third. Ronnie works days.

"She has to work because my forty a week won't carry the rent. But I got tired of me working nights, her working days. So I asked my boss, Mr. Michael, to give me a shot on the dayside and he said it pay thirty-seven dollars. I can't figure why days pays less than nights, but I tell Ronnie and she calls me a nut for taking three bucks less. This makes me sore so we start a fight.

"Anyway, I tell Mr. Michael I'll stay on the night trick. It makes me mad, mister. I got a head full of ideas, all of them bad. So tonight Ronnie makes my two sandwiches and the thermos of coffee and I'm gone at a little after seven. Only, instead of going to work, I hit a bar. I'm not much for drinking, but this idea of her not wanting me home when she's home is driving me crazy. So I do some serious drinking. At eight-thirty or so, I'm tiptoeing up the stairs with my shoes in my hand. On duty, we have a license to carry a gun. I have it in the other hand.

"Honest, I don't know what I'm going to find, but I know it can't be too good, if you know what I mean. I open the kitchen door and the light is on, but Ronnie isn't there. Just an ironing board and some clothes in a basket. So I sneak in the doorway of the bedroom." The Stranger stopped speaking and he looked dreamily toward Barth. "The light from the kitchen isn't much, but it's enough. Ronnie is in bed balls-naked with some fat guy on top. The guy must have seen me as a shadow or something 'cause he stops. Ronnie is moaning and crying and she says, 'What's the matter?' The guys gets off slowly and backs up against the far wall.

"Then she sees me, and boy, did she scream. The neighbors must have thought I was giving her the trouncing of her life. She came out of bed flying right at me. She looked like she was gonna take me on. Like wild crazy eyes. I just pulled the trigger and Ronnie kept coming. She grabbed my face; I think she was after my eyes. I pulled the trigger again and I started to cry. The guy against the wall kept clasping his hands and saying, 'Please! Please!' but I pulled the trigger again and Ronnie fell on the bed. Like backwards."

He began to take long deep breaths. Control returned, and he said: "We have a hoop trunk. You know, a round top. My old man gave it to us. I tossed all the junk out and found some twine in the kitchen. Maybe my mind went blank. All I know is I wanted to get Ronnie in that trunk so I couldn't see her anymore. It ain't easy, mister. I got some twine from the kitchen and tied her wrists behind her." He fished in his overcoat and brought out part of a ball of twine and placed it on McMahon's blotter. As an afterthought, he placed the .38 revolver on the desk. "All this stuff about putting people in trunks is the shit, mister. That fat slob never moved from the far wall; he was mumbling or praying — I don't know. But Ronnie was a job.

"In case you wanna know, I found out how to do it right. Tie the wrists together behind the back, then run the twine double down to the ankles and pull up as hard as you can. With the feet against the small of the back, she fits. Now I'm getting sick and I need the slob as a witness. So I wave the gun and order him into the kitchen. Honest, I'm not mad at him because I don't know who in Christ he is. I never saw him before. But believe me, when the clutch is in, he's a ton of jelly. I sit him on a kitchen chair and tell him to shut up. I tied that guy so many different ways he'll never get out of that flat unless he can walk with the chair on his bare ass."

Barth studied an envelope of one-column cuts of Mary Pickford and selected one with curls. DuBerg grinned at me. Then Charlie looked at the scratched face of the Stranger, the revolver with the three spent bullets, and the twine. "What do you say, Frank?" he said. "Think there's anything to this?"

The story had the elements of a *Daily Mirror* story — sex and murder. I could visualize it written as it happened, with the Stranger walking into the office to surrender to a sports editor. The night editor nodded to me. "Jim, take the story and give me about three paragraphs." I was stunned. It was obvious that he chose Pickford's marriage to a trumpet player as the story of the night, so I took the Stranger by the arm and gave him a chair next to my battered desk and began at the beginning. The story was purposefully lifeless and three paragraphs long.

The difference between the world of reality and the printed word was often a matter of maddening images. Research, depending upon the lateness of the hour, was superficial. In political and ideological stories, we were bound to adhere to Hearst policy. In 1931, this policy was swinging from Herbert Hoover and his conservative Republicanism toward the adventurous optimism of the governor of New York State, Franklin D. Roosevelt. Labor unions were led by men who were at least pink, if not red. Communism was evil incarnate. Intellectuals were double-domed woolly-heads. Tammany Hall, a potent New York Democratic organization, was repeatedly exposed in the *American, Journal,* and *Mirror* as the iron-fisted handmaiden of Sachem John F. Curry, "Tin Box" Farley, and Alfred E. Smith. Somehow New York's dandy, James J. Walker, a Tammany product, escaped much of the editorial invective. Addicted to rakish snap-brim fedoras, pearl-gray spats, and double-breasted suits, Walker was a wit, a raconteur, a habitué of the Broadway night spots, and, beyond dispute, the most admired mayor in New York's history.

Politics was chess to William Randolph Hearst. He was a tall, horse-faced man with keen eyes and a quick mind. Economically, he was fearless. If his newspapers, in any given year, were losing or earning money, it was of passing interest. The focus of all his energies was power. Ironically, his political endorsement had less value than his condemnation. When he advocated a national candidate, it did not seem to move his millions of readers to follow his superpatriotic stance. However, when he sent word to his editors to condemn, to excoriate, to exterminate — his battalions of reporters and photographers became indefatigable in their efforts to bring a man down.

When the Republican legislature in Albany, New York, created and subsidized a humorless judge named Samuel Seabury to convene a committee of prosecutors and investigators with subpoena powers, the Democratic governor, Franklin D. Roosevelt, was embarrassed. He knew that the Seabury Committee would move into New York City to destroy Tammany Hall, its mayor and minions. Roosevelt expected, in 1932, to fight his mentor, Alfred E. Smith, for the Democratic nomination for President. He knew that he would need the New York Democratic delegates to achieve his goal. With obvious regret, FDR approved the Seabury Committee and unsnapped the Republican leash. Hearst felt no such qualms. He ordered his editors to back Seabury all the way. We were to paint Tammany Hall as an octopus with its tentacles embracing the skyscrapers. It came in chattering on the Hearst wire late one afternoon, beginning: "The Chief says..."

Within a year, Tammany Hall was in shattered disrepute. "Tin Box"

Farley and the police department had been exposed as corrupt; the personable mayor admitted that some of his friends had enriched themselves throughout his administration. Walker had trouble explaining how he'd managed to buy stocks in Wall Street at bargain rates, and sell at a profit. Seabury was merciless and so was Hearst. Within eight months, Jimmy Walker was in Albany pleading with the governor. FDR sat back, pince-nez glittering, the cigarette holder jaunty, murmuring between his teeth: "Resign. Resign, Jim. Resign." Walker resigned, became a traveler, divorced his stout wife, married a showgirl, and, when she left him, the dandy moved into a room at his sister's house, wore a faded bathrobe all day, and said the rosary until he was rescued by death.

Such continuing stories were not assigned to me. I was still on Sing Sing executions and feature material. On a snowy winter day, for example, I was assigned to a small story in Brooklyn. A nine-year-old girl took her little sister to school for the first time. Both heads were lowered against the flurries of stinging snow. In the middle of Flatbush Avenue, the older sister heard the muffled roar of the trolley. She yanked the little one's hand too late. The child skidded and fell under the wheels. Both legs were severed at mid-thigh. The little girl had a few minutes to live. The older sister screamed as though her breath was inexhaustible.

Men stopped. They saw the trolley and the child lying between the tracks. They did nothing. The youngster wasn't crying. The accident seemed to have affected her sight. She was staring up into the falling snow whimpering, almost in a restrained demand. "I want my mommy. I want my mommy." A big automobile stopped. A lady in a fur coat got out and shoved her way through the circle of men. She looked at the mashed legs on the tracks and heard the whimper. She removed her fur coat, lifted the child's head, and rolled the coat under it. Then she stroked the little one's face: "Here's your mommy," she said. "Here's your mommy."

It was a small thing, lost inside the newspaper. It was the only story I couldn't write. It was turned over to rewrite man Hettie Cattell.

The news that "we" were pregnant gave me no pleasure. It was an interruption, a roadblock. I adorned my face with my most ecstatic smile, and made the spurious speeches about "Don't lift anything heavy"; "Sleep late"; "I'll do the dishes. You sit and read," but I felt none of it. I knew nothing about infants, their care and feeding, and did not want to learn. A baby was women's business and I could not imagine myself staring down into a beribboned bassinette murmuring: "This is mine."

The examination was done by Dr. Arthur Trewhella, who emerged from his office to say: "Yep. She's caught all right. Full term — let me see — a little short of Christmas. Nothing to worry about, Jim." Nothing. My wife was an only child. She — not the fetus — was the baby. Elinor, I had learned, could lend herself to lightning anger and sullen silences. There were more good days than bad, but the bad ones were often vengeful and vicious. In retaliation, I pursued a collision course, stubbornly determined that I would not be dominated by the whims of a woman.

But this was a time of surrender. The slightest disagreement on my part over dinner, a movie, or attending a party brought instantaneous hurt. Symbolically, I fell to my knees. It was my fault. I knew the words which would arouse her and I said them.

And yet, in spite of unpredictable heights and depths of emotionalism, it was a good, loving marriage. The test, I suppose, occurred when, with shiny bolts of tears still on her cheeks, she would murmur: "I know I couldn't love anybody else. I couldn't live with anybody else. It's you or nobody, and sometimes being with you is sheer hell." The best I could do was to hold Elinor in my arms and mumble: "I know. I know." She was a voluptuous girl physically, a puritan emotionally, a backwoods wife intellectually. The pregnancy kept us back-to-back.

It was a sunny day in October when Adler said there was a personal call for me on an extension. It was Trewhella. "Can you come home?" he said. "Elinor is in labor and asking for you." Within an hour, I was walking down Kensington Avenue wondering what it would be like to be a father. Did I hope for a son? A daughter? I wasn't sure. "Make it a healthy baby," I begged in a silent prayer.

With a baby, Elinor could not return to work. Besides, there was no work anywhere. In New York, the soup-kitchen lines were longer; panhandlers in flapping shoes begged for a dime; on the docks, big men armed with baling hooks clustered around one man who said: "I'll take you, and you, and you" for a day's work. The unpicked sometimes wept. On the East Side, Jews with peddler's carts couldn't afford to eat the fruit they were selling. We would have to find a cheaper place.

Trewhella's car was in front of the canopy. I started toward the lobby. The horn honked. The doctor waved to me. "Come on," he said, "we're going to take a ride first." Why? I wanted to hurry upstairs and see my wife. "Doctor's orders," he said.

I got in the car. "Anything wrong?"

He put the car into gear, turned left on West Side, and drifted out toward Bayonne. "Not a thing. Elinor is doing fine."

"Then why I am on this ride?"

"Because there are a few things I have to tell you man-to-man."

"Like?"

"Take it easy. I have to get my thoughts together."

We were in Bayonne before he got to the point. Elinor had given birth to a girl. The onset of labor had been so fast that there had been no time to get her to a hospital or even to find a nurse. The baby had been born dead. "Dead?"

"Dead. May have been dead several days inside."

"You mean dead like stillborn?"

"Exactly."

"Why is that?"

"I wish I knew. She's premature by about seven weeks. That's part of it. She was resting about noon when amniotic fluid spilled all over the bed."

"What's that?"

"The thing you people call water. Listen to me. These things happen. It doesn't mean anything. The reason I'm driving around is to explain that both of you are normal and should have as many babies as you want."

"The hell with that shit."

"Don't talk tough to me."

"You want to let me out? I can find my own way home."

"I knew you wouldn't listen. That's why I wanted you away from her. She blames herself."

Shock and anger melted to contrition. "Bring me back, Art. Nothing is her fault. Lots of couples have stillbirths."

"Now you're talking." He turned the car and brought me home. A stillbirth had not entered my thinking. The dumbest peasant could have a healthy baby. Fifteen-year-old girls were in Florence Crittenden homes having them. People who had six or seven or eight were having them. Couples who hated children were having babies. Except us. All except us.

The result of the stillbirth was humiliation. I walked to Lawrence Quinn's funeral home and paid fifteen dollars to bury the remains. The affair was an assault on my ego. I had the right woman, the right career, health, and confidence. This blood-smeared wrinkled crouching thing which had not lived managed to kill something inside me.

In the bed Elinor looked pale, fatigued. Her black straight hair was parted and combed. As soon as she felt strong, she became amorous. Elinor had been denied a baby. She seemed determined to become pregnant at once. But nature too can be devious.

It represented a change in attitude. Her girlfriends were spreading a story that Elinor could not have a baby. It was more than an assault on her pride; she was a willful, stubborn young woman who had casually decided to have a baby and could not brook an affront. Soon, it was I who begged off as "too tired"; "I have a headache"; "I must get up early." Her response was dangerous and challenging: "I heard all about you and your women before we were married. Now, Jim, if you really love me . . ."

I would not play the game. We were not going to have a baby for a while. I wanted to wait. Passion and pregnancy are individual states. This led to threats of a separation. Neither of us wanted to break the marriage. Still, when Elinor said she might go home to Momma, she left me but one heartbreaking option: "Go." She didn't, but she declined all affection, including good-bye kisses. Three weeks later, I asked if it was her plan to have us live together as brother and sister. "If that's what you call it," she said. I told her that the arrangement was her device, not mine. I told her I could find affection in New York. "Do it," she snapped.

The marriage was two years old when I stayed out all night with a brassiere model. I think of her as the brassiere model because her picture was
in the windows of lingerie shops. She was small in height only. Her name
was Frances and her interests were cosmopolitan. The eyes were small and
blue, the lips thin, the mouth seemed set in a wise grin. Her wit was sharp,
her laughter explosive, her politics left. Frances, who was feminine, was
also a libertine. She was sweet, a conversationalist who spoke in whispered
bursts, but in the boudoir she was an innovator. Whatever Thomas A.
Edison forgot to invent, Frances forgot to patent.

The dark corners of conscience brighten with dawn. It doesn't matter
whether the man desires to acknowledge guilt; it is there when he says
good morning. He assures himself that his stony wife has forced him to be
unfaithful; delusionary absolution. The suds of an alien shower will not
wash it away. Frances liked a spritz of milk in her coffee, and she stirred
slowly and steadily. "Now," she said softly, "you will go back to your dear
Elinor." I looked at her in the oversize blue velvet robe, something man-
ufactured for a big man. "Not necessarily," I said. The small smile. "Necessarily," she said. The stirring continued. "You love her, you know."

I was wearing a T-shirt and socks. "It must be great to know everything about everybody," I said. The shrug was perceptible. "I will not
play coy," she said. "I am not going to tell you about a woman's intuition
and I will not try to take you away from her. On the other hand" — she
stopped stirring and sipped — "I am not going to be your revenge."

"What is that?"

"Why discuss it? You know what I'm talking about. You are desperately unhappy about something, and in one night I have evened your
score."

"Crazy. What time is it?"

"Early for you. I loved last night and I like you, Jim. I don't say I
love you because I tried it twice; I don't think I know how to be in love."

It was an old form of morning fencing. There are rubber tips on the
foils and they may bruise, but they leave no blood. What troubled me was
that I admired Frances. Her conversation was brighter than Elinor's; her
field of vision was broad; she could challenge a man without demeaning
his manhood. I left her in Greenwich Village and walked to Washington
Arch and took a double-decker bus uptown. A husband who cheats should
find a laughing girl, a superficial girl. My eyes were on the Fifth Avenue
windows, but I saw none of them. I could not be one of those whimpering
husbands who hurry home to Momma to tell her how bad they have been.
The truth would enrage Elinor. Better to lie. Better to look her in the eye
and say I worked late and holed up in a second-rate hotel. I had covered
the New Year story in Chinatown, with the long wriggling papier-mâché
dragon and the firecrackers and the laughter of children. Frances had been
a spectator on another curb. I wrote my notes quickly and, when I looked

up, the faint sly smile was what I saw. It was necessary to break the ranks of the parade to reach her, but I raised my hat and said, "Hello." She nodded. We talked about the Chinese.

"You a cop?"

"A reporter. *Daily Mirror.* Whatever happened to those tong wars — you know, they used to chop people's heads off?"

"The Hip Sings and the On Leongs have a pact. Like a union. They got together and elected their own mayor."

"No more killing?"

"No more." I took her for coffee and doughnuts. Now and then, when I got a dinner break, Frances would come up to Forty-fifth Street and we would talk and eat. The day before, I had phoned and said: "How about me staying over at your place tonight?" The laugh was loud. "How about that?" she had said. My heart pounded. Little strings of diamonds scored the creases of my hands. I got off the bus and walked east. The evil was in what I had done, but I feared the notion of liking Frances. How many more steps were required for me to become my father?

The *Mirror* would not be my career. I absorbed everything I could. I found excuses to spend an hour or two in the composing room, learning about printing, page makeup, stereotyping. The foreman, Mike Hodgins, reminded me that, at his whim, anybody including the editor could be ruled out of the composing room. "Should I leave?" "No, son. But stay out of our way." I watched printers set eight-point body type; I learned to handset and lead the spaces in large handset type; I counted out headlines that would fit. I learned how to trim a story which wouldn't fit in a given column by studying the galley sheets and cutting waste paragraphs from the middle of the story rather than lopping off the overset.

The foreman adopted me. He taught me printing tricks such as reading type backward quickly, and reading it upside down and backward. "I ruled Winchell off the floor," he said.

I was startled to know that a thousand-dollar-a-week columnist could be isolated. "Why?"

"His stuff is always on page ten. He came in last week after it was locked up and he wanted to replace some type, and kill other stuff. The printer told him the page had been locked up. 'Screw that,' he said. 'Bring it back and run that column the way I tell you.'" The printer had complained to Hodgins. The foreman asked the dapper columnist if he had said "Screw that." Winchell, who was sure he was indispensable to the *Mirror,* shouted: "You bet your ass I did." Gauvreau had been told that Winchell had been ruled out of the composing room indefinitely, and if he showed his face inside the revolving door, all the printers would walk out.

Gauvreau was happy. The boss had disliked WW when they were on the *Graphic*; he despised him on the *Mirror.* "How will he correct his column?"

"Tell that little man to have a secretary come in and pick up a galley of the column, make his changes, and have her bring it to any printer." His secretary was an attractive showgirl, Ruth Cambridge. The printers enjoyed watching her comings and goings so much that Winchell's penance was extended.

One of the ironies concomitant with time is that I began to see the *Daily Mirror* for what it was — a mismanaged circus. It was hilarious, the illegitimate journalistic child of the slightly mad newspapers of Chicago when Ben Hecht and Charles MacArthur were writing *The Front Page*. The circulation was steady at 800,000 and Emile Gauvreau, the limping Punchinello, sat at his desk dreaming up mad schemes for reaching the magic figure of 1,000,000.

When the Lindbergh baby was kidnapped, the nation fell into sorrow for the hero of the first solo flight from New York to Paris. Gauvreau was in the composing room, ordering a printer to put a three-line filler at the bottom of every other page. It read:

> COME ON IN X-2;
> COME ON IN.
> WAITING WITH MONEY

Excitement surged within me. If the boss had a feeler out to the kidnapper, or kidnappers, the story would be the scoop of the century. "How did you do it, Chief?" I said. Gauvreau frowned. "I have no contact with anybody, Jim," he said. "I'm just trying to excite the readers." He was in the business, not so much of reporting news as of making it. Some of our exposés backfired and exposed us. If, hypothetically, we could locate and photograph a Jewish senator in bed with a Negro stripper, it would be worth a double-bank 144-point head on page 1 and the "Folo," consisting of senatorial denials, probes, investigations, even a presentation to a grand jury, would be engineered with a sure touch. Beyond doubt, the *Mirror* would have offered the stripper five thousand for her life story in installments.

The only bed photos on hand were not to be printed. They were the private property of Mr. Hinson Stiles, assistant managing editor. He was a handsome man with graying wavy hair, a Barrymore profile, a priceless product of the Peter Principle. "Hinss" had vanity rather than intelligence. The Hearst hierarchy at 859 Eighth Avenue selected Stiles — as it did all editors, and mailed them to the proper papers. Some said he had been a caption writer in Boston. As assistant managing editor, he was working for Gauvreau, before whom he truckled daily. The city editors and all lesser folk were working for Hinson, to whom they learned to bend the knee. At its most serene, the *Mirror* was mass confusion. When the managing editor made a decision, and forgot to tell Stiles, Hinss often made another, and contrary, ruling, so that in our daily communion reporters and photographers often met at the elevators and learned that they were off on assignments which had been canceled.

One of the news tips that he received was that his wife was sleeping with a B-flat cornet player who worked in the Rudy Vallee band. Stiles was so handsome that he was certain that any wife of his was beyond temptation. The tip was phoned in twice. Those who made a living exposing wives and husbands in mundane and boring peccadillos froze in a frieze. They spoke not nor did they nod. I was reading at my desk when Mr. Stiles read the second tip and he burst into laughter. I was alarmed because he never laughed and often questioned the point of a joke. A third tip, as I recall, said that he could find his wife in bed with the B-flat cornet player at the Roosevelt Hotel.

Stiles laughed until he had to wipe his eyes. "This is funny," he said. "Truly funny. Naturally, you do not know my wife as I know her. If she won't go to bed with me, what chance has a cornet player?" A poor question. A city desk man said it could be that someone was passing herself off as Mrs. Hinson Stiles. He was lying, but it was the right kind of lie. "Get me Dick Sarno," Hinss said.

Those of us who could hear the dialogue could not believe it. Sarno was the *Mirror*'s boss photographer. Who, faced with a cuckolding, would use an employee to expose a wife? Sarno and Stiles hurried off to the Roosevelt. They were back in the office in an hour. The handsome Stiles sat at his desk barking commands. On the floor above, Sarno turned his plates over to the studio manager for developing and printing. It is one of the absurdities of journalistic history that complete sets of photos of Mrs. Stiles in bed with a musician were sent to the picture desk, the city desk, and one or two favored reporters.

By accident, Stiles saw a cluster of men and leaned over to see. "Wait a minute," he said. "Just a moment. How come these men have copies of the raid and I haven't got mine?" The error was corrected. After the divorce, he married again and enjoyed the union.

The personnel of the *Mirror* seemed, in the main, to be normal until they reported for duty. Frank McMahon had once seen a vaudevillian shatter goblets with sound, and he warned me that the roaring of the presses below was permeating the steel girders of the building and would someday disintegrate all the molecules and the edifice would crash and kill all of us. An art department employee searched scores of photographs to find a nearly nude girl and repair to the men's room to masturbate.

A middle-aged reporter, fairly corpulent, boasted of his religious merit badges. He attended church every Sunday and on every holy day. He gave small amounts to worthy charities. Tuesday was payday and he boasted that, on the way home, he always stopped at the home of a Negro girl. She performed fellatio. The charge, he said, was one dollar, "but if she does a good job I always give her a dime tip." Foolishly, I asked if this was not indeed a sin. "How can it be a sin," he shouted, "if it isn't sex?

Are you trying to tell me that I'm unfaithful to a good wife?" There was the customary assortment of drinkers; it seemed, at that time, to be related to the tension of the work. Some, like art director Jack Governale, drank a little all day. He would scale photos for two-column cuts or whatever, working on a tilted drawing board, and he would pick up a phone, call Sam's next door, say: "Get a double ready," and hang up. A few minutes later, humming a Neapolitan love song off-key, he would walk through the revolving door into the composing room, dogtrot to the back, use the fire door, and run the steps two at a time. He slapped a pocketful of change on the bar, gulped the drink, and was running upstairs before Stiles could ask "Where is Governale?" As the afternoon lengthened, the odor of Sen-Sen in the art department became overpowering.

Emil Herman, a perfectionist of a photographer and my lifelong friend, had a mistaken belief that the press was above everyone, including the law. "Intelligence," he said, "is the hallmark of the good newspaperman. If he cannot think better than the herd outside, he should be outside with the witless. That goes double for my boss, Manny Elkins, who not only looks like a moose; he is a moose." Herman thought that all newsmen should be on the free list. Merchants should not charge for liquor, airlines should not expect tickets, police should be careful about the manner in which they addressed the gentlemen of the press.

He lived in New Jersey and used the Holland Tunnel homeward bound. Unfortunately, an editor with bladder trouble lived in the same county and was too drunk to drive. Mr. Herman drove him home as a courtesy and as a means of insuring his job. Somehow, in the windy tunnel, the man was impelled to urinate in a rubber bag. Herman, who was terrified of germs and often circled pigeon droppings, chided the editor about "dirtying my car with diseased pee." Obligingly, the editor emptied the bag out the window. The wind in the tunnel sometimes blew it back, and Herman called the editor foul names. "I hope you break a leg, you dirty bastard" was the mildest.

God may have been listening, because one night the editor, intoxicated but ambulatory, walked through a stained glass window at a party and fell three stories to the stone alley. He not only broke a leg; he broke every third bone in his body. I stress the point that the *Mirror* was different. One of the photographers won four thousand dollars on horseraces in a week and bought himself a stable consisting of one horse. The cameraman, realizing the high percentage of bettors in the office, begged everyone not to bet on his Fair Wind, Jr., until he was pronounced ready. When the nag was in shape, almost everyone borrowed five, ten, or twenty from the loan shark, a pale individual who affected a topcoat in summer.

The horse lost. The next time he was entered at Jamaica, everyone doubled the bet. He lost. The photographer was losing his mind because he was besieged by helpless confreres who were in the grip of the loan shark. When the horse was again ready, he said "Bet the rent money."

Some of the reporters and editors hocked watches and rings. Fair Wind, Jr., finished eighth. Henry LaChoissie, the most dignified man on the copy desk, said the horse might have been named after a gastric problem. The next day, everybody in the office assembled at the picture windows fronting on East Forty-fifth Street. Below, they watched the photographer lead a racehorse, with silks and racing saddle, to a hydrant. He tied the horse's bridle, pointed up at the windows, and yelled "Yours!"

The nutty syndrome affected the publisher. Albert J. Kobler was a fat Austrian who was addicted to gold-headed canes and winter coats with sable collars. It was said that William Randolph Hearst had employed him as an advertising executive on his *American Weekly* and that Kobler said he knew a way to make a million in advertising. Hearst is said to have asked how it could be done. "Straw hat day is June first," Kobler said. "We move it up to May fifteenth." *Simplicissimus ad absurdum.* It worked. Kobler was promoted to publisher of the *Mirror* and, as befitted his concept of a publisher, was insulated from the editors.

Winchell, a chronically inflamed ego, often sat on the edge of my desk to chat. It was an awkward situation. He said he liked my "phrasing." I didn't like his. The American Tobacco Company was about to give him a contract for a network radio show. The terms and the format were agreed on. He would open the show with the chatter of a telegraph "bug" clicking, followed by a breathless "Good-evening-Mr.-and-Mrs.-America-and-all-the-ships-at-sea, let's go to press." This would be followed by breathless gossip. The show, on the air each Sunday evening, would last fifteen minutes. Walter was afraid that the gossip might not last the thirteen minutes he would be speaking at speed, so he asked me to provide one-paragraph human-interest stories to fill out his time. "Tell you what," he said. "I will give you five dollars for every item I use."

"Suppose you don't need any?"

"No deal, of course. Most likely, I will need one or two. It's an extra ten for you — okay?"

"Okay."

He showed his bankbook to me. "You know my motto," he said. "Get it while you're hot, kid. You'll be cold a long, long time. How much do you send your mother?"

"Nothing."

"Ha. I send fifty clammeroos a week to mine."

Between Hellinger and Winchell, I was taking home about twenty dollars over my sixty-dollar salary. It wasn't enough. We moved out of the Kensington Avenue apartment and took a small apartment near Journal Square. The rent was fifty-five dollars a month. Elinor liked it because it was within walking distance of her mother's place. The deadly dispute about babies was resolved in a compromise. We would wait a year or two. The nation was in ruins. The huge spires of New York were as awesome as ever, but few people were in the elevators. Older people spoke of the "hard times" of 1907. The elders outdid each other painting portraits of dismal days. Grandpa Tier earned, at best, two dollars a day on the police department, and managed to put a down payment on a flouncy house with a porch and a half-acre of land on Cator Avenue below a red-brick edifice he called "The Rooster Church." That was long ago. In each age, all the bright and good things occurred long ago. The eternal now is fretful only to the very young and the very old. Both are recompensed by a strong faith in God and the hereafter. This is often denied to the successful and mature.

It was a source of elation, and worriment too, to know that my personal tide was running high as the nation's was ebbing. Gauvreau told me, "We're putting out our first Sunday edition. It will have a good magazine section and Mr. Hearst is calling Jack Lait in to run all the color stories. You know what a bulldog edition is? It's a fake news section we run off the Wednesday before the Sunday the paper goes on sale outside the metropolitan area. How would you like to be editor of the bulldog section?"

Another promotion. I gave it thought. "Frankly, I don't know how to select news stories which will keep from Wednesday until Sunday."

"Forget it. I'm putting a man in with you named Al Daniels. He has experience. In fact, you will both be coeditors." I took the job and ten dollars more. The move was fatal. Daniels and I were given a roomy office on the fourth floor — away from the exciting action. We had desks back to back. Mr. Daniels was edging forty, and wore carrot-colored hair in tight waves. He accorded to me the honor of doing the work. His swivel chair had a rhythmic squeak and, although his conversation was minimal, it was seldom cordial. He wanted me to understand at once that I did not have an equal voice in the fake black-and-white news section we conjured each week. He would be the boss; he would make the decisions; I would rewrite stories from *The Times*, the *Tribune*, the St. Louis *Post-Dispatch*, and the Chicago *Tribune* — stories, which, predictably, would remain credible until Sunday. In addition to the rewriting, under a variety of by-lines, it was up to me to locate, research, and write two full-page "feature" stories to publish on facing pages — called a double truck.

Al Daniels smoked and cogitated. I wrote the captions under the photos. "Here's a safe one for page one," he said before the first Sunday. The photo depicted two ladies holding the propeller of a Stinson monoplane. They were about to take off from Lambert Field, in St. Louis, for Rio de Janeiro. By Sunday they would be in Rio, so the caption had to say that wildly enthusiastic crowds had greeted them in Brazil, although the photo showed them in St. Louis. It was done. Late Wednesday night Daniels and I went over the twenty-four-page section and it looked all right.

On Sunday we learned that the women had not left St. Louis. At the last moment, they had detected a dangerous cough in the engine. It was a bad gaffe. Daniels told me that, as the superior of the coeditors, he would explain it to Gauvreau and take the blame. The next day the chief passed me in the composing room without saying hello. His head was down and he wore a frown. Four months later, I returned from lunch and stared at my typewriter. There was a pink slip of paper in the roller. I had heard of these things, but didn't realize that they were truly pink. It said:

Hearst Newspapers Inc. has ordered me to cut the staff ten percent in the current crisis. It was decided to lay off the juniors in each department and, as you are the junior in yours, I am sorry to say that we cannot use your services for the time being. You will be paid up to and including Tuesday. Naturally, we feel that the depression cannot last long and we plan to rehire you as soon as advertising income permits it. Meanwhile, if a recommendation from me will help, please see my secretary, Miss Rollins.

Emile Gauvreau

As my father might say: "From bum to bum in thirty months." The reaction was fury. There was a forge fire in my brain with a blowing bellows under it. I despised the *Mirror*, Gauvreau, Hinson Stiles, and, most of all, the newly hired *senior*, Al Daniels. I had an attractive wife, a good apartment, a spike full of debts, no career, no job, no future. Call it an unfortunate roll of the dice; whatever, the situation was catastrophic. Neither my wife nor my mother was sympathetic to writing as a career, and I knew when they heard the news, they would ask if I wouldn't be better off trying to "get a job." This could be translated as going back to the milk wagon, learning to be a junior salesman, or swinging a pick and shovel.

Hellinger was the first to hear. He was sympathetic. There was nothing he could do. He was a generous check-grabber with a private payroll of unemployed actors and alcoholic newspapermen to whom he sent twenty and twenty-five dollars a week, but I did not expect to get on that payroll and would have refused if he had suggested it. He did the only thing he could. "Let me give you fifteen a column instead of ten, and I'll try to find two for you to write every week. Will that help?" It would. I didn't ask Winchell, or even tell him what happened because once I had asked him to lend me ten until payday and he had said, "Nothing doing." It was an easy phrase to remember.

Gauvreau was apologetic. He was obeying orders. Yes, he knew that I'd been there longer than Daniels, but management had picked Daniels to stay. The first opening, however, if a reporter died or got drunk or moved on, was mine. He was sure of that. For a while, there was no me on the *Mirror*. A few years later, there was no more Gauvreau. He accepted the invitation of a New York congressman to make a trip to the Soviet Union — one-sixth of the globe which was left blank in many American school geographies. When he returned, he wrote a book, *What So Proudly We*

Hailed, which, depending upon the readers' point of view, either exalted the Spartan work ethic of Russia and deplored the economic depression, drunken binges, and gang shootings of America, or gave a kindly face to the Russians and made Americans look like rich brats. Whichever, William Randolph Hearst received a copy from the publisher, Macaulay. Within forty-eight hours, the telex was chattering from California "The Chief Says...";, Emile Gauvreau was to be discharged at once.

The newspaper business was precarious. The news moved through the editorial department like odorless gas. Editors and reporters were shocked, not so much on the grounds of unfairness as by the lively knowledge that Hearst could dump anybody, no matter how highly placed, without compunction. A wind of fright permeated 235 East Forty-fifth Street. Some were so discreet that they didn't want to be seen shaking hands good-bye. Only one rushed into his office and pounded his chest and shouted: "If they fire you, they've gotta fire me too." This was Hinson Stiles. It brought a wry smile to the face of Gauvreau because he appreciated the ambitions of Brutus. Hinss would stay to see if he could get the appointment. A side effect of the debacle was that a hunt for communists within the Hearst organization began. Another was that the few communists within the ranks began to win converts to their notion that reporters and photographers should organize a Newspaper Guild, which would give protection against arbitrary firing, suspensions, and favoritism in the granting of pay increases.

WHEN?

AT HOME, I WORKED DESPERATELY ON AN OLD NUMBER 4 Underwood. The place was quiet and clean, and the rent clicked like a taxi meter. The gin parties were aborted. Elinor was stunned to learn that those we had invited to our place so many times did not invite us to theirs. This gave me time in which to work. There were columns for Hellinger, bits and pieces of "fillers" for Winchell. I tried two short magazine articles. They were returned fourteen times with thanks.

The quality of writing, I felt, was better. The struggle toward more meticulous work had been accomplished, but Elinor and I could not live on my conceited opinion. The owner of the apartment house lived on the top floor. He was one of those aging Jews who is predisposed to a warm smile before he learns the nature of the problem. I said we could not afford to pay him, and would move. The man surprised me; "Listen, young fella. I got more empties than full. Stay awhile. Pay when you can. Take a tip from an old man. Vote for Franklin Roosevelt. With God's help, we'll all come out of this alive."

In succession, I found two jobs. A Broadway press agent named Jay Faggen needed a writer. He had a small office with splintered furniture and a typewriter. Some of his clients gave him fifty dollars a week to get their names in the newspapers. A few gave more. Phil Spitalny had an all-girl band and paid well. A comic paid one hundred fifty. Three dance halls paid fifty dollars each. My salary was thirty-five. "They tell me," the stout Mr. Faggen said, "that when you write, you make the words sing. All I want from you is to hear the music. There's the typewriter."

That job lasted three weeks. In a manner of speaking, Mr. Faggen worked me as his clients worked him. It was the fashion on Broadway to hire a press agent, squeeze him for whatever publicity he could get from columnists and city desks and theatrical reviewers, then fire him and work a new one with other connections. Jay squeezed my brain for publicity ideas. Beyond the work, I was expected to sit with one or another of his clients late in the evenings while they played gin rummy and told and re-told stories which they thought would be good for Winchell, or Heywood Broun, or Hellinger, Karl Kitchen, Don Marquis, or Franklin P. Adams.

Jack Romer, an acerbic art director, got a job as caption writer for me on the Newark *Ledger*. It paid thirty-five dollars. The editorial department was on a creaky floor at Bank Street. Carfare and lunch, getting from Jersey City to Newark, ate into net earnings, but I was glad to get the job. The campaign between Roosevelt and Herbert Hoover was a rising tide of vituperation and exalted promises. Romer was leaning over a drawing board with an airbrush and said, "Jesus Christ." I asked what was wrong. "Take a look at this picture." I studied an eight-by-ten he had pinned to the board. It was of Eleanor Roosevelt smiling. "Do you realize," he said solemnly, "that if Roosevelt wins I'm going to be retouching that fuckin' mouth for four long years?"

The *Ledger* was more of a character than a newspaper. The editors practically owned a bar around the corner named White's. It was good for a midnight glass of beer and a sandwich. Mr. White, who was Italian, recommended the services of a plump brunette who sat at the elbow of the bar smiling vacantly. "Ten bucks," he told me. "It's worth it, kid. No V.D. I try out all these dames myself." I became friendly with the woman. There had to be a story. Even if half of what she said were lies, it would be colorful copy.

Her faith in me went in another direction. When I tried to talk to her about growing up, parents, school, and things like that, she whispered in my ear: "When you quit work, meet me downstairs. I'll take you to my flat and give you one on the house." I said I was married. "So?" she said. "What does your sweet little wife know about these things? Meet me and I'll give you the ride of your life." I didn't get the story.

The *Ledger* used its columns to reward friends and punish enemies. One editor owned a window-cleaning business and he had the contract for all municipal buildings. Some editors had ne'er-do-well relatives on the public payroll. When a friend of the paper, such as Mayor Breidenbach, said something, I was told to write the caption under his photo as though he had uttered a profundity. The same words, enunciated by an enemy, were "sneered," "snarled," or uttered with his back to some unidentified wall. Whatever schemes were hatched to endear our friends to the electorate and damn our enemies were concocted in the exclusive Newark Athletic Club. There, as attendants molded pale and flabby muscles, editors and politicians on adjoining tables breathed steam and worked out deals. I was invited once because my boss wanted me to take a leave of absence and publicize a mayoral candidate named Vincent Kane.

I had not met Kane, felt no rush of enthusiasm for the work, but he had me whether he liked it or not. The pay was sixty dollars a week for six weeks. A plea to the city editor that I knew nothing about Newark drew a smile of pity. "I'll have a policeman drive you around. There isn't much to know. The poor and the Negroes are down in the Ironbound section; Broad and Market is big business; you go up to Roseville and Branchbrook Park and find substantial citizens. Any questions?"

"Yes. Am I Kane's publicity man or what?"

"For sixty a week we expect you to be his de facto campaign manager and P.A." Mr. Kane was a short, pleasant man who, in my estimation, appeared to be honest. He was doomed. He had rented a store on Broad Street with a big sign: "Headquarters — Vincent Kane."

If he understood the issues of the campaign, he was unable to explain them to me. A trip to the library required an entire day for reading politics in the Newark *Evening News*. If the State of New Jersey had a thundering *Times* of London, this was it. I surmised that the kidnapping of Colonel and Mrs. Charles Lindbergh's infant, at Hopewell, had probably gotten a one-column head. I made notes of the contentions of the political parties and it became clear to me, having grown up under the benevolent despot Frank Hague, that Newark was controlled by the Republican party, which, in turn, was amenable to the aspirations of the Public Service Corporation, a gas and electric company, and other giants such as the Prudential Insurance Company.

Vincent Kane couldn't get into City Hall with police protection. We sat in the office and talked like winners. Issue by issue, I wrote speeches for him and he read them to reporters or had them hand-delivered to the newspapers. The editors gave him good space, but all he got from the campaign was to become known. My recollection is that out of thirty-two political aspirants, he polled enough votes to finish in the bottom third.

When I moved my effects back to the *Ledger*, city editor Jerry Nussbaum said he didn't "have a spot" for me at the moment. As soon as he had an opening, et cetera, et cetera, ad nauseam. Nineteen thirty-two was not my year. Bonus Marchers in Washington were shamelessly dispersed from their shacks by the same army they had served so well in World War I. The pyramid utilities millionaire Samuel Insull placed one too many cards on his cardboard skyscraper and it fell into the dust. A German scientist, Albert Einstein, visited America as a possible refuge assuming the whirlwind storm of the Nazi party attained power in Germany. Twelve million persons were unemployed in the United States, and President Herbert Hoover promised crooner Rudy Vallee: "If you can sing a song that will make people forget their troubles and the depression, I will give you a medal."

The Women's National League for Law Enforcement told Hoover that the country was dry, but not dry enough. The ladies demanded that the President order U.S. ambassadors abroad to stop drinking. The President's spirits lifted a little in July when the Democrats nominated Governor Franklin D. Roosevelt of New York to oppose him. Hoover's cabinet had advised him that FDR would be the easiest opponent to defeat. Carolina farmers who could not afford twenty-three cents a gallon for gasoline sawed off the backs of their trucks and built harness traces for mules. Cotton was selling at seven cents a pound; tobacco eleven cents.

It was a time of emotional depression too. The riches of the earth turned to brown talcum in the farmer's hands. The man who had a job labored in fear. Middle-aged citizens lost their stake in the future: sheriffs sold big gingerbread houses for the taxes owed, often two thousand dollars. The Franklin Roosevelt political team invented phrases and music to transmute despondency to euphoria: "A New Deal"; "The Forgotten Man"; "Happy Days Are Here Again." The people saw it for what it was, a promissory note. It seemed almost asinine to grieve when a canine movie star, Rin Tin Tin, age fourteen, died. He had earned three hundred thousand dollars. An enterprising photographer shot men standing in soup-kitchen lines wiping their eyes. America was no longer logical or practical. Neither was the world.

France, surfeited with good wine but short of wheat, supported the son of a butcher of Auvergne as premier, Pierre Laval. In the Soviet Union, where starvation is endured with grace, Premier Josef Stalin discovered the rabbit. He ordered the press to announce that a rabbit-breeding trust had been organized. Russia would start with 1,500,000 rabbits on farms and, within a year, would have 7,000,000, which, it was hoped, would number 25,000,000 in two years. *Izvestia* wrote: "Eschew those who under-estimate the rabbit."

Week after week, Imperial Japan arranged insults to occur in China from Mukden in Manchuria southward to Tsingtao, Shanghai, and Nanking. By fortuitous circumstance, Japanese task forces were lying over the edge of the horizon escorting troopships laden with Japanese marines. For the honor of the emperor, and the nation, it became necessary to move inshore, bombard the nationalist cities governed by Chiang Kai-shek and his Kuomintang, and land Japanese marines to restore order by fire, pillage, and rape. The Japanese government, through its representatives at the League of Nations, in convention at Geneva, insisted that His Imperial Majesty had no ambitions in China and ordered the coastal occupations to protect its nationals. It went a step farther. Japan said that if any of the other fifty-six nations in the League drew sinister interpretations from her action, she would leave the League of Nations.

The gentlemen at Geneva were not quite prepared for the speech which followed. Up stood France's tall André Tardieu and, in exquisite French, a delicate symphony of harmonic words, told the League that it was not a League and couldn't be one unless it had the power to impose its collective will on recalcitrant nations. Glancing over the tops of his spectacles, he said that this also applied to the World Court, which was not a court in any sense because it had no means of enforcing its decisions.

Briefly, with the percussive effect of a naval rifle, Tardieu suggested that all fifty-seven member nations make available to the League (1) all their long-range artillery; (2) all warships exceeding cruiser size; (3) all long-range submarines; (4) all civil airplanes capable of military con-version, in addition to a per capita donation of all heavy bombers; (5) an international police force, one not to be referred to as an army, with tanks, artillery, and infantry capable of imposing "international decency" on any member nation.

No one laughed. The French plan could win no vote but its own. The Italians created an understanding smile when their spokesman suggested that Tardieu, trying to reconcile fifty-seven nations, was attempting to create a fifty-eighth. Smiles everywhere were nearer to being wry and wistful than amused. In India, Mohandas Gandhi, sleeping in a tent atop a Bombay tenement house, was arrested by the British for civil disobedience. Lord Willingdon, the viceroy, was aware that the detention in Yerovda prison would spread a stain of disobedience and boycott of British goods across the face of the subcontinent, but like his subordinates, Willingdon was afflicted with inflexibility.

He stiffened the jail sentences and made it a heinous crime to picket a British shop. Police picked up a nine-year-old boy shouting anti-British slogans in front of a dry-goods shop. His name was Krishna Kant. A British judge, a portrait of rage in a periwig, sentenced the boy to four years in prison and said: "If you disobey orders in the reformatory, you will be whipped." The youngster bowed courteously. "I am ready to die for Gandhi," he said. Within two days, the story had been told in every province in India. The Hindus found that the little boy was a more potent martyr than the Mahatma.

In Rome, the former newspaperman Benito Mussolini sat at a typewriter in the Palazzo Venezia and spelled these words for his countrymen: "Above all, Fascism does not believe in the possibility or advisability of perpetual peace. It therefore rejects pacifism. Only war leads to the maximum tension of all human energies and sets the seal of nobility on people who have the virtue to face it."

The United States, sick and hungry, insisted on the trappings of normality. It had become a land of paradox. Close to 3,000 banks had locked their doors, but 42,500 baseball fans paid to see Babe Ruth power a 436-foot home run off Chicago pitcher Charlie Root in the third game of the World Series between the Yankees and the Cubs. In Washington, the Senate Committee on Banking and Currency spent enormous sums investigating the New York Stock Exchange and its snobbish president, Richard Whitney, but had no money to solicit counsel from economists on measures to get the richest nation off its knees and onto its feet.

It was becoming difficult to tell the heroes from the villains. The head of the government-owned Reconstruction Finance Corporation, Charles G. Dawes, resigned to hurry to Chicago, where his Central Republic Bank & Trust Company was in financial trouble. Within a week, it was out of trouble: Dawes had borrowed millions from the Reconstruction Finance Corporation, and was called a savior. In New York, brokerage clerk George D. Phelan confessed that he had stolen six hundred ninety-five thousand dollars from the petty cash of J. S. Bache & Company over a span of thirteen years. "I can't continue these thefts forever," he said. Phelan was a loser.

On Broadway, crooner Rudy Vallee was earning a fortune singing nasally into a miniature megaphone. The star of *Kid Boots*, Eddie Cantor, was impelled to generate more and more laughs to repay the two million dollars he had lost in stock trading. The poor escaped reality by attending motion picture theaters and, in cold weather, remaining longer. Films which critics called notable in 1932 would be called notorious later. Clara Bow punched a horse in the stomach in *Call Her Savage*. Rough-tough James Cagney kicked his girl, Virginia Bruce, in a script sardonically entitled *Winner Take All*. Ernest Hemingway's *Farewell to Arms* was rendered almost mute by the restrained speaking-with-eyes of Gary Cooper and Helen Hayes.

Perhaps the strangest of the ebbs and flows of confusion was that more Americans were buying books than before. The novel was king. Christopher Morley wrote *Swiss Family Manhattan*; Aldous Huxley created a stir, and more than a stir, peeking into a computerized future with *Brave New World*. John Dos Passos wrote *1919*, an equally dismal look into the past. Hemingway titillated and shocked readers with ugly words in *Death in the Afternoon*. Books based on fact, fleshed out with the imaginings of authors, began to emerge as literary trial balloons. Although *The New York Times* hammered the word *fiction* on it, *Mutiny on the Bounty* by Charles Nordhoff and James Norman Hall became a runaway best-seller as history. Carl Sandburg wrote a short biography called *Mary Lincoln*. *Time* magazine, deftly avoiding an opinion, said "A later day will probably rate [Sandburg's] biographical work on the Lincolns." Winston Churchill, who agreed with critics that, at age fifty-eight, he was growing old, finished an assortment of eloquent cast-iron opinions called *Amid These Storms* and said of his life, "I have no doubt that I do not wish to live it over again."

If the mood of the world was confusion compounded, then it is equally true that this mood funneled downward to the minuscule existences of Elinor and Jim Bishop. When the sun was bright and warm, and lacy forsythia had surrendered its yellow for drab green, we surrendered our independence. We moved out owing one hundred eighty dollars to the landlord, placed the furniture in storage, and lodged with my in-laws, Frank and Maggy Dunning. He was gray and ulcerous; she was stout and fearful. They had an empty back bedroom at 80 Wade Street. It was an act of generosity to take us in, but with it came the unforgiving attitude of the Irish toward the unemployed — silence. Beyond greetings of hello and farewell, it was impossible to engage the Dunnings in a meaningful conversation. It was obvious that their only child had made a monumental mistake in marrying a slick, black-haired boy who wore the attitudes of success without a dime in his pocket. He spent the evening hours reading books aloud to his wife in his bedroom, trying to explain craftsmanship and inspiration, but he seldom looked for a job. Any job. Indeed, he had the colossal conceit of narrowing his goals to a newspaper job or nothing.

"Your father ought to be able to get something for you in a factory," Maggy said, "even though it's beneath you."

Frank returned from his bartender's job at about five P.M. Maggy sat in the enclosed front porch, looking up the street toward Jackson Avenue for a southbound trolley to stop. "Here he is," she would say. A moment later, she would squint and say: "No, Elinor, it's not him." When, finally, he was seen walking slowly, heavy-footed, toward the house, my mother-in-law squirmed out of a wicker chair as fast as she could, and shouted: "Elinor, turn the gas up." She had generated a contest to have dinner ready when her husband climbed the steps. In the house, he nodded, went to the bathroom to wash, and retired to his bedroom with the *Jersey Journal.*

I never saw him kiss Maggy. He put his feet on a hassock, and read. Within three to five minutes, dinner was ready and Maggy said to Elinor: "Go call your father." He would emerge slowly, an old and sick man at the age of fifty-two, and sit. It was difficult, at dinner, to share food at the kitchen table because sound was taboo. Meat and potatoes and carrots were passed perfunctorily. If anything was said, it was his option. On those occasions, the rest of us tried to crowd in with agreeable responses. The news usually concerned something about the stewards of Lodge 211, Elks Club, or a political supposition concerning a forthcoming appointment by starchy Frank Hague.

Dunning's world was encompassed by Jersey City, except for his Sunday afternoon recreation, which was to tune a small cathedral radio to the unctuous words of Father Coughlin. On weekdays, after supper, Dunning walked back up the block slowly, waited for a trolley, and returned to bartending. The club closed at two A.M. with a final crash of bowling pins and a raid on brown crocks of cheddar cheese and Saltines by survivors. Afterward, he removed the trappings of office — a white apron — added up the cash receipts, and sat to play poker and drink with his cronies.

Sometimes he won; sometimes he lost. Sometimes he wandered in noisily drunk; sometimes he was ill. Maggy kept to her side of the bed and pretended sleep. If he was intoxicated, Frank Dunning fell to his knees beside the bed with a great cracking of joints, and his prayers to Saint Joseph were a little louder and less intelligible. In the morning, when he spat blood in the bathroom, Maggy begged him to stop drinking and to give up Bickford's Cafeteria at Journal Square, where he indulged stomach ulcers with baked beans, frankfurters, and coffee. It was common for the Dunnings to postpone their disputes until we were off the premises. Maggy feared Frank's wrath, but when he challenged her, she fought with eye-bulging shouting. Once committed, she rebutted his charge that she was spending too many afternoons drinking with her "lady friends" with a valid accusation that he was killing himself with late drinking. When Dunning ran out of ammunition, he would retire to the bedroom, slamming the door. Mrs. Dunning, aroused and indignant, fell into silence, combing her memory for past crimes, then approached the door to shout sporadically.

This method-madness, I was surprised to learn, would be used by my wife. After the first two years of marriage, our lives vacillated between passionate embrace and the buckshot of old indictments. Whatever the disagreement — it could be as academic as Alfred E. Smith's chances of being nominated one more time — if it endured more than a few minutes I found myself defending my father as a bum who had deserted a wife and children for another woman. Or my mother was stupid for not suing him in court. "Everybody knows your father is a public disgrace anyway." There were variables. Another ploy was that if I was one-tenth the writer I thought I was, then why was I the first to be fired? Or: "You think I don't know anything about your past with women, but I have friends. Everybody is wise to you and your perversions. Just don't try them on me." Or: "If you had any ambition, you wouldn't be living off my sick father. You'd go back to the milk company and work nights." Or: "Someday I'll tell you what your friends are saying behind your back."

If I was responsible for half the happiness in the marriage, I was also the cause of half the disagreements. Jealousy of Elinor was easily fired. She enjoyed dancing. I didn't. If she danced with someone else, I accused her of trying to arouse the man. If she fell into sullen moods, a fairly frequent occurrence, I tossed oratorical knives designed to infuriate her. Our deepest recurring problem was Maggy. Elinor's love of and loyalty to her mother were irrational. I was slow to realize that the only child and the only mother represented a combination of mutual exclusivity which placed Frank Dunning and me at the periphery of their love. Time after time I tried to bend the link between mother and daughter. If I suggested taking my wife to a movie, and Maggy said, ever so casually: "Oh, I thought Elinor would help me hang the curtains tonight," I could take my wife into our bedroom, shut the door, and beg her on the grounds of marriage, love, and logic to please grant me the favor of a movie, and the mildest response would be tears. The wildest would be roars of rage and recrimination. If I had any pocket money, I would go out and meet the handsome William Scanlon and the tall, fashionable John Dundas, and get drunk.

Alcohol is the eraser of the immature. Dundas was the dry wit with the pencil mustache; Scanlon was a laugher, a young man of intelligent curiosity. Sometimes we borrowed his father's car by jumping the cables and drove around town feeling the night wind against hot ginned-up cheeks. It was a time of life when, in the morning, a warm shower, two aspirins, and two cups of black coffee slowed the spinning world and brought friendly faces into focus.

As loyal friends, they wished me well in my aspiration to someday become the most knowledgeable writer — not the greatest — in the country. There was no competition between us, and we shared deep secrets which would never be heard beyond the sound of clinking ice. Sometimes, when funds were low, we counted our quarters and dimes and bought a fifth of Dixie Belle gin for a dollar forty-nine and sat in the car drinking, telling stories, and laughing.

One night we were pulled to the curb by a police car. It was a bad situation. I was behind the wheel. I couldn't find my driver's license, so I gave the officer my wallet. Fear of arrest, fear of my father's fury, sobered me to dismal depression. The policeman took his time examining the contents.

"You a son of Lieutenant Bishop?"

"Uh — no, sir."

"Then what's this Police Benevolent Association card doing in the wallet? And where did you find this snapshot of him?"

In the darkness of four A.M. I tried to look, but my eyes saw two wallets. "He's my father."

"Get in the police car." I got. Dundas said he would walk home. Bill tried to blend with the upholstery.

We drove the block and a half to 80 Wade Street. Scanlon would have to hide in the hedges until the police left before he could reclaim his father's car and get it into the garage. The only reason this episode is chronicled is to show that the police, sparing me on the one hand, were determined to deliver me, sodden drunk, into the hands of my in-laws on the other. The policeman rang the side doorbell and punched the door several times. A yellow light flickered inside. Frank Dunning, the white hair hanging like a dollop of dirty whipped cream on his forehead, came to the door in his robe.

"He belong to you?"

"Yes, officer. It's my son-in-law."

"When he straightens out tell him to keep off the road or we'll run him in."

"Yes, officer." Dunning looked at me. I looked up at him. "Go to bed," he said. I did, my remorse almost smothered by elation that he had chosen not to make a scene. I sneaked into the back bedroom, wriggled out of clothes and shoes, and slid slowly between the sheets. When I got out of bed in the morning, three stony faces were at the kitchen table. No good mornings — silence.

My head, and my marriage, were skidding imperceptibly. The fault lay mainly in Elinor's ambivalence toward her mother and me; or, put another way, her emotional compartmentalization with her mother traveling first class and me lost in the back of the bus. It is important to point out — then and now — that my wife loved me, admired me, as much as she could any man. Although I was an admitted failure who could not hang onto a job, she did not love me less. She was a plump young religious brunette whose life, whose security, even her ineradicable fears, swung silently around the approval of Maggy. The contention for the young lady's love became, in time, strife acknowledged by both protagonists.

We endured a two-day battle over whether it was right to pray to a church statue. My laughter was a tactical error. "I know," Maggy said, "you're saying I'm dumb." She was equipped, I found after many pleasant and a few sarcastic conversations, with monumental ignorance. If the world was round, she said, the oceans would fall off. She knew nothing of other nations, and discouraged discussions about them. She did not believe that ocean liners had "rooms inside." She *did* believe that heaven was equipped with pearly gates, that God had a big ledger with all the rights and wrongs of individuals written therein, that because her older sister Bridget had died on an operating table we must promise her never to permit anyone to operate on her; hospitals were "butcher shops"; if it is not right to pray to statues, why do the churches have them?

Maggy bought her spectacles from the counter of a five-and-ten-cent store. When she read the gossip columns in the *News* and the New York *Journal,* she squinted; one eye wept. She was inordinately interested, it seemed to me, in the downfall of men. If a woman was adjudged guilty of murder, Maggy would not introduce it for discussion. If a man was found guilty, or if a married man was rumored to be unfaithful to his wife, she clucked her tongue and talked and talked. Sometimes, when she was drunk, she would lean on her elbows and smile: "Listen, listen a minute. I tell you that when Frank and me was young we had our fun. Don't ever forget it. We had our fun." Elinor would blush. The thought which occurred to me was that she was only just over fifty. Obviously, the fires were banked and cold. Once, in a burst of candor, she told me that she had no notion of how Elinor was born. The doctor told her that she would have to endure pain. In labor, she had become hysterical and, at times, comatose. "It was the worst day of my life, I tell you. Once is enough. Then my cousin walked in and said: 'Let me see the little monkey.' Can you imagine — monkey? I haven't spoken to her to this day."

She had heard the word *vagina,* but didn't know what it was; *clitoris* was a new word; she understood *womb* only because her prayer included ". . . blessed is the fruit of thy womb, Jesus."

Mark Hellinger phoned. The deep jaded voice said: "Hello, kiddie. Are you working?" It was the summer of 1934. I said no. "Come in tomorrow morning around ten. I have a job for you."

Hellinger and his secretary, Jimmy Burbridge, were drinkers. Gladys Glad, author of the syndicated beauty column, was a drinker and so was her secretary, Sonny Fohrenbach. The Broadway columnist felt that four imbibers in the same office was two too many. He asked Burbridge and Sonny to quit. They promised. What they promised was that they would be more careful. It was an uneasy situation. All four tried to set an example for the others.

The result was disaster. Mark Hellinger drank a fifth of brandy a day and did it before or after office hours, or both. Glad, a sipper, drank Canadian Club at their fashionable East Side apartment as a stout German maid helped the beauty to find her shoes, purse, and makeup at noon. Burbridge, dark and taciturn, had a double whiskey before arriving at the office to dim the memories of the previous night. Sonny was the mystery drinker. She was small, a blond with wispy hair and a bright face. On the dot of ten, she hung up her coat, sent a copyboy for a breakfast of bacon and eggs and orange juice and coffee and toast, then began to open the beauty questions sent by readers. She read bales of mail every week, many enclosing ten or twenty-five cents for a Gladys Glad beauty booklet.

At eleven A.M. Sonny fell unconscious on her desk blotter. This did not happen every day, just frequently enough to mystify Hellinger, who engineered a heroic sacrifice by arriving at nine-thirty A.M. to see how it was done. Desk drawers, filing cabinets, even waste-paper baskets were searched. Hellinger, pretending to write a column, would watch the ten A.M. arrival, growl the friendly "Good morning, kiddie," and await the eleven A.M. collapse.

He told me that he had fired Burbridge for drinking. I was to be Hellinger's secretary at forty-five dollars a week, in addition to five dollars for every column I wrote on his time. Part of my job was espionage. I was charged with finding out how Sonny got loaded without leaving the room. I wasn't happy with a position as secretary to a writer, but I had a sense of gratitude for having regular work at a time when twelve million men were still unemployed. Besides, I knew that Burbridge would not stay fired. He and Hellinger went together like a ball and a beer. Jimmy was being taught an expensive lesson. Miss Fohrenbach, on the other hand, could not be fired because she wrote a pretty good beauty column, appreciated the stacks of mail, and could not be replaced.

It required a week to find out how Sonny got drunk. Each morning when she phoned for a copyboy to bring breakfast, I noticed that when she asked for Ben, and Ben was not available, she hung up, saying: "Ask him to call Sonny." Next, I located Benny working on the floor below, and told him that Hellinger was about to ask Hinson Stiles to discharge him for bringing intoxicants to Sonny. The effect was miraculous: "Now listen. I didn't do a damned thing. Sonny made a cash arrangement with me a long time ago that I was to buy a pint of gin every morning on my way to work. When I go down to the restaurant on the ground floor, I order a large orange juice and dump almost all of it in the sink. I fill it with the gin — it still looks like orange juice — and bring the breakfast up. What happens after that is none of my business."

I told it to Hellinger. He beamed with amazement at the ingenuity of drinkers. Then he told Sonny that the game was over. No more orange juice. No more gin. Miss Fohrenbach was frightened. Mark made it appear that it was he who had deciphered the breakfast dodge. Two weeks after we began to work in the same office, Sonny and I became friends. We trusted each other. There was a plum plush bench in the reception room. Under it Sonny kept a brightly colored umbrella and overshoes. The gin was now inside the overshoes. Each day, as Hellinger and his wife left the office, the outer door was locked and Sonny and I shared a few drinks. It brightened her dull day and dimmed the vision of thousands of ugly women asking for beauty hints. I found that I could not afford the treat because, after two drinks, my fingers fell between typewriter keys.

Hellinger's office was a panhandler's paradise. When he left each day, he had at least a dozen bills folded small and placed in his coat pocket. As he and Glad walked across town to dine at Dinty Moore's, cold-looking men in threadbare suits stepped out of doorways to say: "Well, whaddya know. My old buddy Mark Hellinger." He was seldom a buddy, and he knew he was being stalked for handouts, but he considered this part of being a Broadway columnist. Others, mostly old actors out of work, came to the office once a week for twenty or twenty-five dollars. Mark ordered me to take the money from the petty-cash tin and give it to them with his compliments. One man with unshaven face and ruddy eyes said he was tired of walking from his furnished room on the West Side to the *Daily Mirror* office every Friday for twenty-five dollars. Would I please mail it? I asked Hellinger. His uproarious laughter was a delight.

"The guy's got a lot of nerve," I said.

Mark nodded. "Mail it. Isn't he something? Mail it."

In the late summer, the same man asked me to stop mailing the money to his room and gave me an address near the Saratoga racetrack. "I love the old bastard," Mark said. "I only saw him once in a play, but I love him. Send it."

If there was anything remarkable about Mark, it was that he fashioned his own world, then stepped into it and lived. He regarded Texas Guinan, Larry Fay, Owney Madden, George Raft, Evelyn Nesbitt Thaw, and an unknown character whom he referred to as "Roscoe" as special people. He was as sophisticated as a madam and, in the same breath, as naive as a three-year-old regarding the glittering lights on a Christmas tree.

Beautiful women, in his eyes, were to be treated gallantly and, in time, taken to bed. He told me that he was having a problem with his wife. In this, he misjudged Glad. She was tall and blond and as beautiful as Florenz Ziegfeld said she was, but, as she told me, she had a low opinion of men because when she was twelve, a butcher had chased her around his shop trying to get her into the walk-in freezer. To coin a cliché, the more she was chased the more chaste she became. By the time she married, she was prepared for a convent life. Her great joy seemed to be jewelry; it might have been her sex life too. Ziegfeld sent two dozen long-stemmed American beauties to her dressing room, and Glad knew, from the gossip of other girls, that among the flowers would be a gift. In her case it turned out to be a large sapphire.

A jealous husband-to-be sees many things — all bad — in expensive gifts from other men. Gladys wore the ring, but hid it when Hellinger took her on a date. One day she forgot. Men, customarily blind to new gowns, to fresh coiffures, are prone to see things they shouldn't. Mark saw the ring. "Where did you get this, honey?"

"Oh, that. Some of the girls went shopping and I saw it in a hock shop window for sixty dollars."

"Take it off," he said, "let me have a look at it."

"What for? I'll probably throw it away when you buy my engagement ring."

His voice, always deep, dropped to a growl. "Let . . . me . . . see . . . it."

The columnist examined the ring. "It isn't a bad buy for sixty bucks," he said, "but the setting is loose. The stone is practically falling out of the prongs." He slipped it into his jacket pocket. "I have a pal who does this work for practically nothing." Glad was helpless. She could — and did — say it wasn't worth the trouble, but Mark insisted. The ring was gone three weeks. Each time they met, she demanded to know where it was. "Getting fixed," he said coldly. When it was returned, a glance told her that the expensive stone had been exchanged for a cheap one. "This isn't the right sapphire," she protested. "I know, doll, I know," he said putting his arms around her. "My jeweler said you bought a piece of blue glass. So, being the generous guy I am, I shelled out a hundred bucks for this one. Wear it in health," he said.

One morning, Hellinger's father died. Death, to Hellinger, was an unwelcome apparition. In spite of his jaded attitude, it was common for him to half-finish a column and stare off at a blank wall. When I asked if I could help, he shook his head no and asked: "Do you really think there's anything on the other side? After we die, what happens?" The best I could do was to relate the teachings of my Church, that there is a soul, that it shall be judged, and that it shall live on forever in paradise or in flames. Did I believe it? Sometimes yes; sometimes no; mostly yes. He asked what he would have to "go through" to become a Catholic. I suggested that his interest was founded on the promise of eternal reward, ignoring possible eternal damnation. He nodded, smiled vacantly, and returned to the one-fingered violence to a typewriter. I suspected that Mark had placed a lid on his fears. The dark, handsome face, the pale eyes, the slickly parted black hair seemed almost cultivated — just as he had made a "uniform" of his many deep blue suits, blue shirts, and white-on-white ties.

He did not propose to strip to give me a look at the real Mark Hellinger. His mother died of heart disease. So did his father. His younger brother, Monroe, was in the Far West trying to improve a cardiovascular condition. The columnist lived at top speed — brandy, late hours, poor appetite, and attractive women. His wife loved him, but didn't trust him. When we talked sex, which wasn't often, he sometimes said: "Kiddie [or Pappy], you're the one who studies everything. How come I can perform until the moment I have to? Then I can't do anything."

No response. "How old is old?" he asked many times. He was thirty-one.

Six years after I had started as a copyboy, the new editor of the *Mirror*, Jack Lait, offered me a job as caption writer for fifty dollars a week. It was not exciting, but it was a fresh start. Hellinger advised me to accept it; he missed the services of Jimmy Burbridge. I was back studying eight-by-ten glossies, and counting words to fit the spaces underneath. My Napoleonic friend, Emile Gauvreau, had divorced his wife, married his secretary, Winny Rollins, and was writing thinly disguised novels about tabloid newspapers for Macauley — *The Scandal Monger*, a merciless portrait of Walter Winchell; *Hot News*, an elastic lesson in methods of creating news; *My Last Million Readers*, a book about gangsters and editors, and how to tell them apart.

The unionization of newspapermen, which had been proposed many times, had become fact. A rumpled scholar of the press, Heywood Broun, lent his energies and the prestige of a respected columnist to the new organization. Managing editor Hinson Stiles passed the word that the Hearst organization would not recognize a union. I joined and drew card number 18. It had to remain a secret. A guild, I felt, would protect a man's job if he did his work well. The Hearst attitude was that, excepting Broun, the moving force behind the Newspaper Guild was communism. It was such an obvious defense that I did not believe it. Wrong again. Secretly, I was selected to the Grievance Committee and the House of Delegates. At a meeting of the latter group, I had a chance to look at live warm faces from the *Mirror*, *The Times*, the *Herald Tribune*, the *World Telegram*, the New York *Post*, and other papers.

One could not be positive, because communists at that time denied they were communists. President Franklin D. Roosevelt had recognized the Soviet Union in 1933 and the two nations enjoyed a diplomatic hostility. Within the United States, the Red witch-hunt which had been spawned by Attorney General Mitchell Palmer in 1919 was still vigorous. Anyone who was more liberal in his politics than the President was a "Red."

Thus, domestic communism was a political subtlety. I looked around at the Guild and saw reporters and sportswriters whom I knew to be to the right of the administration. There were others, few in number, who were young and bright, persons I remembered who talked "left" in office discourse. Almost all the motions offered were presented by this group. The others, including me, literally sat on their hands. One young reporter read a *Daily Mirror* editorial which referred to a construction union as "Red dominated." He asked us to vote public condemnation of the editorial.

It was the first time I got to my feet, waving an arm to be recognized. Narcissus could have ruined his image by dropping a small stone into the pool. I wrecked mine. Mr. Hearst, I said, owned the newspaper, presses and all. I didn't have to agree with his editorials. His policies were his business. Our business, I said, was to entice more than fifty percent of the editorial department into the Newspaper Guild, then request an election. We were few in numbers, loud in condemnation. I joined, I said, because I had learned that a craftsman could be furloughed for over two years and be grateful to return at a lower salary.

The motion for condemnation of William Randolph Hearst failed to carry. So did my usefulness. At the next election, I lost my seat among the delegates, although I was still a member of the Grievance Committee. This too led to problems. When the Guild attained sufficient power to become the sole bargaining agent for all editorial employees, one of the first grievances was brought up by an old reporter who sat on the edge of my desk and told me he had been fired. The man had sufficient seniority to get Saturdays and Sundays as days off, but his habit was to have his wife report him ill on Monday.

The situation wasn't new. Frequently, young reporters are part-time drunks; old ones are sots. The man said that I would have "Mr. Johnson" (Hearst management representative) cringing to take him back. I told him I was well acquainted with the case, and would tell Mr. Johnson that, as I saw it, the reporter had been discharged for "cause." My whispering friend became a shouting enemy. He told the city room that I was in the pay of management, that I was sucking asses to hang onto my own job, that I had no character. That night, I went into a conference with the other two members of the Grievance Committee. They supported my stand. The reporter disappeared into the mists outside and I felt depressed. He would have little chance of getting a job on another newspaper. Someday — who knows? — I might be an old sot.

All changes at the *Mirror*, good or bad, occurred without warning. A memorandum from Hinson Stiles stated that I was to become promotion editor at once. This took me away from the despised captions, but placed me in a gray area of promoting giveaway contests. In one, pasting thirds of faces together, the *Mirror* gave away $40,000. It was a stunt designed to take circulation from the *News*. We picked up 78,000 fresh readers while pushing the contest, and dropped 60,000 afterward. I promoted the first Night of Stars, at Yankee Stadium, for United Jewish Appeal. My job was to phone the Milton Berles, the Jack Bennys, the George M. Cohans, the Belle Bakers, the Sophie Tuckers, and others and get them to agree to perform free for a worthy cause. In return, I guaranteed that the *Mirror* would publish a one-column cut of each of them, plus a story praising their accomplishments.

The *News* and its big brother, the Chicago *Tribune*, had organized a late-spring event called the Golden Gloves. It was open to youngsters who fancied that they might become boxing champions. It worked so well that it was a sellout all over the metropolitan area and took circulation away from the *Mirror*. The papers had another successful promotion — an autumn event called the Harvest Moon Ball. Couples, young and old, who felt they could waltz, foxtrot, tango, or Lindy Hop got into the elimination contest. We countered with photo contests and beauty contests. It was fake and unrewarding.

Elinor was pregnant. I did the things she expected — helped her on and off buses, pandered to her craving for pepper steak in the late hours, placed cold cloths on her forehead when the headaches arrived, gave up a one-sided sex life, took her to Dr. Trewhella's office for examinations and admonitions, and hoped for the best. The doctor said that she would have a normal pregnancy. The womb was tilted. "Elinor cannot hold the weight of the baby full term," Art said. "I want her in bed at the end of the seventh month." And so it was. She spent the days saying: "Don't worry about me. I'll be all right," but she lived in a quilted robe, the dark hair spiked wildly at the sides of the head, a lack of makeup adding to a gray, ghastly appearance. All I felt was guilt. The marriage was not unhappy; it was predictable. It was a game of checkers on a slow train.

The summer of 1935 had barely begun when Elinor felt rhythmic abdominal pain. I phoned Trewhella, who said he would meet me at the Margaret Hague Maternity Center. An examination indicated that much time would elapse before she had her baby, so I went home. My mother-in-law was happy. She broke out a fifth of Four Roses. We waited. I knew that the chance of successive stillbirths was remote. Worry is interior sweat. A shaded light over the kitchen table caused the ice in the glasses to sparkle in red and yellow flashes. We talked aimlessly.

The phone rang and we knocked chairs over to get to it. It was Trewhella. "A little baby girl," he said. "No use coming up. I'm putting Elinor to sleep for the night. She had a tough time." Again the sensation of fear overcame me. Maggy was ecstatic. "I'm a grandmother! An honest to God grandmother! Thanks be to God almighty!" I was ready for bed when the phone rang again. It was Trewhella. "Take it easy," he said. "The baby was too small to live."

"To live?"

"I called the hospital chaplain and had her christened Mary Bishop. Is that all right?"

"How is Elinor? And no bull, Art."

"Fine. Fine. It's a difficult thing, worse for her than for you, but you're both young. See you."

In the morning, Elinor was under control in the hospital bed until she saw me. The round face twisted into a comical expression and the tears seemed to squirt out. "What did we do wrong? What are we being punished for?" Maggy was with me. She cried. The flowers I had sent were in a big vase. Their death seemed prettier, more leisurely, than the other one. I asked Trewhella about burial. "I'll take care of it. We have a special plot in Holy Name Cemetery for little angels."

Little angels. That baby was no angel. She was a mass of puckered redness unable to face the struggle. Angels are bodiless spirits. Within ninety minutes, Mary Bishop had come into the world, wept, and died. Calling a baby an angel was, to me, as fallacious as pet lovers explaining that a faithful old dog "had to be put to sleep." I tried to be manly, kissing Elinor's tears and telling her that babies were a mathematical uncertainty. She wasn't mollified. So many of her girlfriends from Saint Dominic Academy had married and had children. Her maternal instinct had become undeniably frustrated. She looked inside perambulators, cooing and stroking the chins of infants.

I suggested that we adopt a baby girl. We could have our own later. It started a dispute which was now firmly etched across the face of the marriage. She said she couldn't love someone else's baby. We would have our own someday, sometime. She accused me of giving up on her. Who, she asked, endured the pregnancy, the nausea, the endless nights on the pillow wondering whether the next one would live or die? Who underwent the unspoken fears twice without blaming anyone except herself? What kind of man, what kind of coward, refused to volunteer his small part in such a momentous matter?

The little tragedy was followed by little personality changes. My wife appeared to be close to an explosion. Anything less than hearty applause for everything she did, every meal she cooked, her cast-iron opinions, was sufficient to start a shouting match which died off in sporadic and distant gunfire. The bulging of her eyes, the saliva which bubbled on her lips, the accusations which always receded from the point of the argument to my father's abandonment of his family, my mother's mispelled notes, the "thick Irish" attitudes of my cousins, my inability to further my career, the never-ending array of women with whom I was reputed to have slept, her girlfriend's early advice not to marry me because "everybody knows you're a sex maniac," my brother, John, who was lazy, my sister, Adele, who married an alcoholic — culminated in "the whole Bishop family should hang its head in shame; even you will agree that you're not on the same level as the Dunnings."

Frank Dunning died. He had had a bleeding ulcer for a number of years. Maggy discovered him in bed, too weak to be aroused. Elinor phoned me at the *Mirror*. Could I come at once? Her father was in Jersey

City Medical Center. She and Maggy were out in the corridor, weeping. In the disgusting antisepsis of the hospital corridor, I paused to kiss both women. The head nurse was Miss Quinn. She had nursed Frank Dunning to health before. This time his clock had run out. "You can stay at the bedside," she said coldly, "if that's what you want to do. Keep those women in the hall." I sat on the edge of the bed with its frayed bedspread and wrinkled sheets. Frank Dunning's hand was cold and snowy. I held it. This would not have pleased the old bartender. I was not his favorite person.

The quiet man was slipping away. It might be in a few minutes; it might not come until night. A priest bent over the bed and anointed the unconscious man. The patient stopped breathing for a moment; something which looked like soft black tar began to slide over the edges of his mouth. I asked for a towel and wiped it away. Then I reached in and took more of the old blood out. He breathed again, but I had done no favor. I had postponed something. A half-hour later, I walked out as Miss Quinn lifted the spread and placed it over Frank Dunning's head.

In the corridor, the shrieks and moans were unpleasant. I escorted the ladies out. Funerals — most especially Roman Catholic ones — bear an aura of show biz. Each person has a role. The flickering candles, the gold-plated crucifix which allies the deceased with Jesus, the overwhelming scent of mixed flowers, the widow seated with a black rosary dangling from the fingers of the left hand, the multitudinous mourners who walk into the house without knocking, the eternal sound of whispering, the saffron skin of the dead man pressed firmly toward the neck to restore a youth he no longer needs, the penitents on the prie-dieu trying to utter a meaningful prayer while fascinated by the face of the dead, the priest on his knees loudly reciting the rosary and a litany, the unctuous morti-cian, the sobbing when the casket is closed, the calling of names in order of rank to help each other into sleek limousines, the long slow ride to the cemetery, the last intercession to God at the graveside to take our dearly beloved Frank to heaven, the black-edged handkerchiefs, and the swift ride home for liquor and a meal prepared by neighbors.

Funerals are designed to inflict pain on the living. The irony which never seems to be apparent to the mourners is that grief is as difficult to sustain over a period of time as ecstasy. The next of kin return home to salads and hot coffee, a boiled ham and bottles of rye, reminiscences and recollections which induce hearty laughter, and in the late afternoon, a debris of dishes and a silent house. I wondered if anyone really cared about Frank Dunning.

It was a crisp autumn day; the broom of the gusts swept the factory smoke from Jersey City and made the town appear to be clear and close to the spires of New York, across the Hudson. My father selected that day to put on his uniform and visit John Beggans, director of public safety, at City Hall. A uniformed policeman escorted him into the dim, high-ceilinged office. Beggans was an old-time cop who had gone to the top. "What can I do for you, John?" he said.

Big John sat, the nightstick across his thighs. "Today," he said, "is my fiftieth birthday. I also have twenty-five years in. I want to retire."

Beggans threw up both hands in mock protest. "Come on, Johnny," he said. "I'm not going to let you get away. You're still a young fella."

The lieutenant admired Beggans. It didn't matter. The city was paying salaries half in cash, the other half in scrip. If he retired, he'd get the same amount of U.S. currency. Besides, Hague never had forgiven him for not giving up Clara and not returning to Jenny Bishop. "I'm getting out, John," he said, reverting to the familiar name. "I went on the force with men like John Underwood and Johnny English and Harry Walsh. Underwood and Walsh are deputy chiefs. I'm not going to be the brains for the chief anymore." Beggans pressed a button. A policeman came in. They whispered. The cop left. When he came back, Beggans said firmly: "Johnny, I just checked your record. You're forty-nine years old today. You'll have to stay one more year, and I can guarantee that —"

"That's plain shit," the lieutenant said. "Will you take the word of a priest?" Beggans nodded dumbly. "Okay, I'll be back in an hour."

He went to Saint Patrick's rectory for his birth certificate. He was surprised to find that his mother had him christened the day after he was born because she didn't expect him to live. He returned to City Hall and dropped the certificate on Beggans's desk. The director of public safety barely glanced at it. He sighed. "Okay, Johnny."

When the children were in bed that night, Big John and Clara sat and drank and reminisced and drank. "Don't feel bad," she said. "You should never have been a cop. What the hell is a policeman? He's a mug in uniform at the mercy of the politicians, taking all they can hand out while he bucks for a pension."

"I'm going to miss it," he said. "I went back to headquarters and put my gun and shield on the chief's desk. Know what he did?"

"Yeah. He made a loud noise."

"No. He knew what they meant. He shoved them off onto the floor. 'You're not putting in for a pension,' he yelled. 'Not until I say so.' I told him I was sick and tired of wiping his ass and writing his general orders. Finally he picked up the shield and handed it to me. 'Okay,' he said. 'Okay. Keep the shield as a memento. I could lock that door and we could have this out man to man —'

" 'Lock it,' I said, and he smiled. He really smiled. I would have mopped up the floor with him."

They drank to celebrate Big John's freedom. They were wrong. It was a time of mourning. Twenty-five of the good years had been wasted. His hair was white. Then he laughed. He remembered the time he went back to Saint Paul's to arrange a police escort for a parade. He told Father Pfister that, in the long ago, he had attended that school. There was a nun, Sister Josephine, who had written a note to his mother: "Your son John is a bright and apt student," or words to that effect. "I predict great things for him in later life."

The priest, as Big John recalled the story, said, "Sister Josephine is still here."

"It can't be the same one. She'd have to be ninety or more by now."

"Close to it," the priest had said. "She hasn't taught school in years. Want to say hello to her? She's in a wheelchair in the convent." The two men trod old snow to cross the street. In the back, next to a hot stove, a nun sat in a wheelchair with her head down. "Sister," the priest shouted, "I have an old student of yours." She did not lift her head. "Man name of John Bishop."

Big John, in his resplendent uniform, pushed the priest aside. The nun nodded her head. "Now that's a long time ago," she lisped through a toothless mouth. "His mother was a widow woman on Fulton Avenue. I once wrote a note to her — or was it somebody else? — saying the boy was bright and would make something of himself."

My father thrust his chest out. "Sister," he shouted, "I'm a police lieutenant."

She shook her head from side to side. "What a pity," she murmured. "What a pity."

My work at the *Daily Mirror* was not improving. I felt that I had learned all that could be absorbed on a tabloid. As a rewrite man, I could put headphones on, listen to a reporter assemble the facts of a news story, ask questions, run sheets of yellow copy paper in a typewriter, and, after a moment of hesitation, rap out a story in four paragraphs, one page, two pages, or "let it run." I could write swiftly and superficially and could do my best on the first try.

William Randolph Hearst was dissatisfied with the *Mirror*. Circulation was at 900,000, but its pictures were thin and watery. The *Daily News* was at 1,500,000 and had enough advertising to make it seem healthy. Hearst had promoted Jack Lait to run the editorial department. He was a thick-lipped, dowdy man who spent his days trying to divine what William Randolph Hearst would do in any situation. He sent Ray Doyle and other reporters to Flemington to cover the trial of Bruno Richard Hauptmann in the kidnapping-murder of the Lindbergh baby and, even then, he wondered what "slant" the paper should take. We were opposed to the Roosevelt administration, Great Britain, the Soviet Union, and the Yellow Peril of the Far East. Benevolent Benito Mussolini was flogging the Italians into a nation of warriors. Adolf Hitler, who had assumed power as chancellor, was a "strong man" with a potential for lifting the German nation into the company of first-class powers.

Lait's brand of journalism wasn't as yellow as Emile Gauvreau's, but it was saffron. As editor, he tried to work with Hinson Stiles. Between them, they divided the whole world into compartments of good and bad guys. This also applied to everybody in the editorial department. I was a bad guy; a revolutionary; a member of the Newspaper Guild.

I was summoned to the editor's office. His thick spectacles were close to what he was writing. Without looking up, he said: "Why don't you stop being a troublemaker?"

A sliver of fear stiffened me. "What troublemaker, Mr. Lait?"

"Oh, joining the Guild and things like that." He looked up. "We ran a check on you and you come from nice people. Our kind of people. Your salary has been raised to seventy dollars. It can't be more money. What's the matter, Jim?"

I shrugged. "We need job protection, not more money. Hines can fire anybody whenever he's in a bad mood."

"Stiles is not going to fire you. Take my word." He chuckled. "I had to explain to him that you're a pretty fair country writer. He didn't know." I grinned. He ran his lower lip across the upper. "We know you're asking reporters and photographers to join the Newspaper Guild. We also know that you have been elected to the Representative Assembly or whatever they call it. Now stop it or I'll can you."

I would lie in bed and squirm over that scene. Lait brought out the coward in me and I was ashamed of myself. After that, I was careful. When reporters asked me what the Guild would do for them, I turned away. Lait had his informants and no one knew who they were. I worried because, although I was no longer excited about the job, I needed it. Editors of other newspapers who scanned the *Mirror* saw nothing noteworthy under the by-line "Jim Bishop." Few newspapers were viable. The *Morning World* died. So did the *Evening World*. The staid *Sun* expired. The Brooklyn *Eagle* was gone. The *Herald Tribune* was seeping money. So was the New York *American*. I quailed in the presence of Jack Lait, knowing he had me in the palm of his hand and could squeeze at his whim.

A few weeks later, I had a visit from Hinson Stiles. He held an armful of photos. "I want you to write good captions for these," he said. "Good selling captions. Every year the Hearst newspapers send their best photos to Mr. Hearst at San Simeon. He looks them over in leather-bound volumes and awards prizes. Now, Jim, we want the *Mirror* to win all the prizes and you're going to help us, my boy."

"Do you want me to start now?" I said.

He shook his head. "No, no. You have work to do. I want you to do these at night. On your own time."

"Oh, do I get something extra?"

The good-looking face frowned and purpled. "This," he said softly, "is an order. Are you going to obey me?"

I shook my head no. "I am not," I said. "I work an eight-hour day,

Mr. Stiles. When I finish, I think I should be allowed to go home." He glared and carried the pictures back to his desk.

Stiles dictated a memo which was before me in five minutes.

> To: Jim Bishop
> From: Hinson Stiles
> You have seen fit to disobey a direct order from your managing editor. You are hereby suspended from the *Daily Mirror* indefinitely; this to take effect at once.

I bent over his desk. "Get away from me," he shouted. I didn't. "Listen," I said, "why don't you ask Aaron Altman to write those captions? He's been head caption writer for years. Nobody wants to work day and night for a week. Even if you paid me —"

"Get away from this desk."

"Mr. Stiles, you know I need the job. You know I need the salary every week. I can't afford a suspension."

"Don't you whimper to me," he said. "Take your beating like a man. You rate it."

I was angry at myself; I had walked boldly into the trap. After six days, I took a long chance. I phoned Robert Johnson, assistant publisher. He was a short, gray-haired man with a sharp sense of justice and a liking for some of the stories I wrote. He said he had "heard about it."

"Look," I said. "I still don't see how anybody can be ordered to work extra duty for nothing."

"Hinss says you disobeyed a direct order."

"For Christ sake, we're not West Point cadets. We're a newspaper. Anyway, there is no such thing as an indefinite suspension. Indefinite could be forever. If I haven't been fired, how long is indefinite?"

"How long you been out?"

"Six days."

"Let me speak to Stiles. I don't promise anything, but if I can get him to call you back to duty, will you apologize?"

"For what?"

"Will you?"

"Yes, sir."

"Okay, don't leave the house."

A call came from the city desk in late afternoon. "Get your ass in here at seven P.M."

"P.M.?"

"You got it."

When I arrived, my confreres on the dayside had left. The night desk was on duty. Hinson Stiles was direct. "You had a lot of nerve calling Bob Johnson for help," he said.

I nodded. "I was desperate."

"Well, that's a good state for you to be in. Now get this straight. You're starting work tonight. No more dayside for you. You will report in at seven P.M. and work until the four-star is in bed at three A.M. You will do rewrite for Charlie Barth. He will assign a couple of days off — I think it's going to be Monday and Friday. I also reminded Charlie that Lait thinks you're the best writer on the paper. He has been ordered never to give you a by-line under any circumstances. Jim, I am going to jam your stubbornness up your ass so far that you'll never forget it. Now, get to work."

I was becoming proficient in fashioning formidable enemies. Stiles had the trappings of a Hollywood actor. He dressed well, exuded confidence, and was more than considerate of those who acknowledged his rank. And yet, Stiles had to please Lait, Johnson, the new publisher, Charles McCabe, and the nebulous Hearst hierarchy at 859 Eighth Avenue. He could not be as windy, empty, and pompous as I saw him. The Hearst crowd had a short attention span for inefficiency. Stiles was, at the least, a survivor. I had a sickening sensation that someday the *Mirror*, in spite of my conceit, would let me go and would promote Hinss to editor.

On this summer Sunday we left church — each with a different sense of buoyancy — and walked to Kensington Avenue, where our car was parked. It was a racy-looking Graham-Paige with slanted silvery grillwork, a pale coupé with a rumble seat. This was a special day, the start of a two-week vacation. Two valises were full of summer dresses and suits and sneakers, a tennis racket, underwear, bathing suits, and two books for rainy days. For obvious reasons, I suggested that we take Maggy with us. She was waiting on a curb on Summit Avenue, fanning her face with a newspaper.

Sea Bright was unpretentious. It was a village of seventeen saloons and one church on the second knuckle of a tan, six-mile finger called Sandy Hook. The permanent population consisted of second-generation Swedish fishermen who worked two-man dories at sea. Sometimes a small boat would come in with two thousand pounds of blues. A bather could buy one, still flopping, for fifty cents. Ocean Avenue ran through Sea Bright like a frightened streaker. A half-dozen side streets broke off Ocean Avenue, hiding cheap bungalows, neglected lawns, and broken screen doors from tourists. Pud Anderson, over three hundred pounds, was the police department. He spent his days in Charlotte's beanery, sipping coffee and munching Danish. There was a drugstore; the pharmacist sold bathing caps, combs, and suntan lotion. Fowler had a hardware store. A frosty man named Hemple had a delicatessen with strings of rock candy hanging from the ceiling, pickles in brine barrels, homemade salads in iced trays, cold cuts of all kinds, and real sour rye bread.

The village had two elderly hotels. The Peninsula House was reserved for the affluent who indulged overage memories of an era when the Sea Bright Lawn Tennis Association was important. The other was a sagging fleabag on the beach called Ryan's. The rooms seemed to be encased in cardboard; a man, wife, and three children would get a double bed and three army cots in one room and enjoy all the noise they could stand. Ryan's was made for a drinking Irish clientele. There was a dark, cool bar on the ground floor where a tourist could run up an imposing bill. Rooms went for fifteen dollars a week and, if sufficient whiskey was consumed, there was no rent.

We stayed at Ryan's. I engaged a separate room for Maggy, but Elinor said we would save money if she stayed with us. A considerable amount of romance was strangled.

This vacation consisted of long alcoholic fogs and short clear areas. Maggy did not want to swim. "I burn," she said, rubbing her shoulders. She did not want to walk. She did not want to drive slowly up beautiful Rumson Road. She did not want to go to bed. Mrs. Dunning had a stool at the bar. She was the first one up with a five-dollar bill. As the day wore on, the round face became bright red, the poached eyes sparkled, the tongue was in amiable conversation with strangers, who, after one or two treats, became buddies.

It required no effort on her part to get me to the bar. I drank gin and tonic until I could no longer decipher whether I was becoming euphoric or depressed. Elinor drank tall Tom Collinses with tart slices of lemon swimming among icebergs. Foamy beers were drawn to slide down the dark oak surface. In conversation, anything under the decibel level of a shout was unintelligible. There was the insistent ring of a pinball machine; the cries over a shuffleboard game; the hawking of little boys who came in selling huge baskets of fresh clams; the buzz of barflies.

The days became ritualistic. We were out of bed by ten. We walked across the street to Charlotte's for bacon and eggs at ten-thirty — plus a newspaper for me. At eleven-twenty we were in the bar, starting slowly, shaking last night's pain from our eyes. For every two we bought, Joe came back with one. When Maggy bought two rounds and I bought two, we had six. The sun was still high at five P.M., but we were in bed. At seven-thirty we dressed for the evening and had dinner at the Lobster House. Nor did we skip drinks there.

As drunks, we were different. Maggy approached a state of affable apoplexy; I fogged out and went for walks I remembered not; Elinor remained at her mother's side and pouted. Alcohol, for her, was a dangerous trigger. One night in the Lobster House she stood, grabbed a side dish of coleslaw, and shoved it in a woman's face. "Fat!" she roared. "Who are you calling fat? I heard you." The salad dripped from the woman's eyes onto her dress. The lady's companion demanded that a cop be called. Maggy and I got Elinor under the arms and propelled her to the safety of Ryan's Hotel. "She called my mother fat," she whimpered. I nodded. "Doll," I said, "your mother is fat, but I think you misunderstood what the woman said."

From eight-thirty P.M. until eleven we were back at Ryan's sipping booze. We helped each other up to the room. I swam in the ocean three times, alone. I dug my feet into the warm dampness of the sand and wondered what was becoming of me. Somewhere along the line Elinor and I had stopped confiding in each other. We were suspicious aliens. Slowly, inexorably, she had reduced our communication. We became civil in conversation. Manifestations of affection were looked upon as marital due bills. "It's legal if we're making babies, but we aren't."

Meditation made it worse. I suspected things which weren't true. Elinor didn't love me. An old date of hers had called her twice since our marriage. She was probably seeing him as I worked nights. She was attached by a steel umbilical cord to her mother. She was no longer reading the stories I wrote. After an argument, she enjoyed three or four days of silence. If she was jolly, it was because she was drinking. Sometimes her anger took the form of incoherent rages, with shouting and waving of fists. Marriage can be a mine field.

Dolorous thoughts are the enemy of sleep. One morning I arose at dawn, slipped on a bathing suit and slacks and sneakers, and went outdoors. On the west side of Ryan's was an overhanging porch, and below it, round summer tables and chairs. I counted seven alcoholics. Most of them sat staring high, the fingers drumming the tables in vague rhythm. Four were vacationers; three were locals. They were waiting for Joe to open the bar at six. The sky radiated with bands of pink and yellow and green.

These men were hung over. They were in pain. They would be in the same condition tomorrow and next week and next year. They barely spoke. No matter how deep the hurt, each would hurt himself again and again. Whenever they heard a bus sigh, they looked up, sad-eyed hounds, hoping that it was Joe. It was not. Some rubbed the sides of their faces. Some did some leg scratching. Everyone seemed to know when the minute of six arrived. They could forgive Joe for keeping them waiting until the precise moment, but he would be a no-good Hungarian bastard if he arrived at 6:03.

I tried to watch without being caught. Most had unwashed, uncombed, tan faces, were heavy breathers. There was no camaraderie, no exchange of symptoms. A big clock over Fowler's Hardware snapped to six A.M. They didn't look. They knew. At one minute past, Joe swung off a shore bus and walked leisurely toward Ryan's. Two men stood, stretching and yawning with disinterest. Joe held a heavy bunch of keys and a newspaper. He did not say good morning. The double door was unlocked and he went inside to snap the night-light off.

No one was in a hurry to follow. The intolerable tension died. The seven men exchanged pleasantries. Inside, they negotiated the bar stools. Joe was hurrying up and back on the slippery boards behind the bar. He punched No Sale on the register. It was empty. He started to dial a small safe. Then he looked up and grinned. "What'll it be?" he said. "I have some work to do." They ordered double vodkas on ice; a scotch in a large glass; a ball and a beer; and so forth. The bartender delivered with speed.

At once the area sounded like an aviary. It was full of happy sounds. Not one man reached for a drink. They knew it was there, and the presence of drinks struck the terror from their heads. Someone asked how the Yankees were doing, and someone else said that Miller Huggins was going to pitch old Waite Hoyt in the first of a doubleheader. A few skidded their glasses, widening the wet stain. After a while, each man bent forward to sip a little. They were at ease. Was that the life that lay ahead? Would I, by stages, become one of them? It was worth thought. Editorial work survived on tension. Newspaper offices suffered a percentage of alcoholics. It would be easy to stop at Sam's before reporting for duty at seven P.M., have a few, and then catch Sam before closing at three A.M., when the presses ground their noisy gears to a stop.

When we left, Jack Ryan shook hands. "No charge for the room," he said. We had done an enormous amount of drinking.

Those who were part of the mass madness of 1930–1935 could not detect madness. The nation had been teetering on the edge of bankruptcy for a number of years and would not recover until, in 1939 and 1940, the United States girded itself for one more massive war. In addition to unemployment lines, there was a shortage of cash, even among the affluent. The situation induced little panic. The mood was malaise; we were sick of being sick.

And yet, the people knew that the United States was gravely ill. Will Rogers tried to put a funny face on it when he said: "This will be the only country in history to go to the poorhouse in an automobile." In Detroit a man paid an employment agency ten dollars to get thirteen dollars and fifty cents' worth of work. The unemployed shouted that they didn't want a government dole. They did. Chambers of Commerce announced that it would be a shame if the government fed the poor.

In the Middle West, ignorant farmers had stripped the soil of its nourishment. The land too was poor. Raging winds lifted billions of tons of topsoil from the ragged face of the West. It flew like black talcum to far-off windowsills and seas and dining room tables. A Texas farmer squinted against a dark sky at noon and spoke the melancholy of all: "Here in the Texas Panhandle we are hit harder than most anywhere else. If the wind blows one way, here comes the dark dust from Oklahoma. Another way and it's the gray dust from Kansas. Still another way, the brown dirt of Colorado and New Mexico. I tell you, farms are buried. The towns are black."

There was one soothing voice in the wilderness. It belonged to President

Franklin D. Roosevelt. His Fireside Chats were spangles of light. He just knew that everything was going to turn out fine. All America had to do was turn its back on fear and begin to hope. He closed the banks. He repealed Prohibition. He organized the National Recovery Administration and the Civilian Conservation Corps and a span of agencies with suitable initials. The Tennessee Valley Authority began to build. So did the Lincoln Tunnel, the Triborough Bridge, new post offices in dozens of cities. He was creating jobs and priming an economic pump.

One night a telex chattered in the *Daily Mirror* wire room. The phrase "Soak the Successful" was to be used instead of "Soak the Thrifty" in all references to the administration's tax program, and "Raw Deal" used instead of "New Deal."

Like God, William Randolph Hearst was out there somewhere. No one I knew had met him. Lightning flashes came across the telegraph machine to apostles in many cities. Temporarily blinded, we fell in abasement on our typewriters. A sinner is without redemption unless he sustains relapses. Now and then we sneaked in a kindly quote about FDR and his multifarious works.

This was minuscule sneaky vengeance. My world was a disappointment; I was disenchanted with it; it could not abide me. I ransacked United States history for a couple of years and felt that I should have flourished from 1890 to 1920. There was a World War in there, and a money panic in 1907, but it was an inventive and gullible world — my kind. I felt that I was cursed, struggling in an economy where power bankrupted power; where the rewards to the suppliant ass-kisser might be a home in the country, a car, and healthy babies.

This was a dishonest appraisal. The perusal of letters of famous men and women of the eighteenth and nineteenth centuries showed that they too lamented their time and station. The mature always deplored the attitudes of the immature. It seemed natural that the strong would oppress the weak. I searched hard for a biography of a very rich man who, at some stage, decided that he had had enough money. And surely there must have been a nation which had never threatened a weak neighbor. At no time did I look for a chimerical state called happiness. I had settled for contentment before my twenty-first birthday. This could be achieved for one evening with a six-pack of beer. Or inventive sex that lived more than thirty minutes to be punctuated by glowing cigarettes in the dark. Or a note from Hellinger stating: "Your story on the decline and fall of Mayor Jimmy Walker was a gem, unmistakably you without a by-line."

It required a lot of thought for me to concede that man's miserable state was historically and emotionally permanent. The thing that most people referred to as happiness was a momentary remission from hardship and insoluble problems. To me, rancor and controlled fury are not hidden assets. They are but two of the forces a man fights all his life — himself.

I had traits which belonged inside a baser skull. And yet, there is an aura of the shivering mutt in a man who concedes weaknesses which are not as obvious as the color of his eyes.

"Why?" That word caused more discord in our home than any acts of commission or omission. Elinor and I continued our roller-coaster ride of accord and discord. "Why?" We argued, suffered silences, protested our love for each other, vowed to change our ways, watched each other being oversolicitous, went to movies, held hands, played word games with our friends, drank only at Saturday night parties, fell asleep with entwined limbs until one or the other said: "Why?"

I wanted to move out of Jersey City. She didn't. "Why?" The word had the impact of the opening fusillade in the war, a weak crackling followed by thunder. Because, she said, our roots were in Jersey City. We were born there; we went to school there; our relatives and friends lived there. What did I have in mind, moving out to a forest? I tried to hold it down. No, I said, I would like to move into the suburbs to rent a house. A whole house with grass around it; a house with a fireplace and a dog; a place, let us say, not more than a half-hour from all our relatives. A spot where I could have a workbench in the cellar and buy one tool a week. There might even be a room for a typewriter and the beginnings of a researcher's library.

"Why?" she said. That did it. "You will go with me," I shouted, "or I will go alone." She tried to laugh. "You? A big house? Cooking? Dusting? Laundry? When was the last time you changed a fuse?" I fell back to square one, accusing her of being afraid to be more than a ten-minute bus ride from Momma. "Keep my mother out of this," she warned. "Everybody knows you dislike her." Sometimes the word *why* prodded one or both of us into untenable positions. "And don't say," she said, "that you were true to our marriage vows. Some of your friends aren't your friends. They talk." "Were you true all the way?" Elinor became indignant. "Of course." "Tell me, were you ever tempted by a man to be untrue?" "Never." "Then what are you boasting about?"

All along, I knew the terms under which she would agree to move into the suburbs. Forget the typewriter; the research library. Give that room to Momma. Take Maggy Dunning with us. The marriage was infirm, rocky. I knew that my mother-in-law would not consciously lend herself to a dissolution, but I feared that as in other situations, she would ally herself with her only child. This could lead to ultimatums beyond redemption. I knew it and yet I proposed it. Elinor burst into tears of gratitude.

We drove through the towns of Bergen County for three weeks. We found a house with an orange-tiled roof at 145 Overlook Avenue, in Leonia, New Jersey. It was on the side of a hill overlooking the marshes and a somnolent creek to the west. A few blocks to the north was a wooded area with oaks and maples and an autumnal orgy of russets and reds and yellows, a clutch of shops on the Englewood side of the line, an aura of living out in the country.

It was a bonus, a Christmas toy, a promotion. There was a clean concrete cellar, an oil burner, a living room fireplace, a stairway up to the bedrooms, a big kitchen with a recessed breakfast area and high-backed benches. The house was elevated on a lawn of grass running down to a sidewalk. In the rear was a grassy yard. I bought one of those free-spinning inverted-umbrella clothes driers and set it in cement. The women seemed pleased and more than pleased. We shopped for additional furniture, an ocher Chinese rug with robin's-egg blue designs and borders. The rent was sixty dollars a month.

When I was home — from about four-thirty A.M. until five forty-five P.M. — Maggy spent considerable time in her room. She slept, or sat on the side of her bed looking out the window at traffic on Grand Avenue, saying her rosary. There were certain times for listening to the afternoon domestic dramas on her radio. To my knowledge, she could recite the current and past status of at least eight ongoing plots. It occurred to me that she was discreet, trying to give me time with Elinor. On days off, I chopped thick branches in the woods, stacked them on the side of the house, and reveled in blue and ruddy tongues curling and snapping around pine and spruce.

The new honeymoon lasted only from October until December of 1936. It was time, and beyond time, to end the marriage. There was sufficient error on both sides to place it beyond endurance. We had reached the stage where, if I arrived home with a cheery hello, Elinor said I was being sarcastic. The disputes were endless. They rose in pitch until the collision of shouting was indecipherable. No other man, no other woman, was involved. Frequently, Maggy jammed both hands over her ears and fled to her room. No matter what the original thought was, my wife backtracked to earlier offenses — my mother had said something or failed to say something; my sister was married to a drunkard; my brother was no good. When she didn't condemn my father as the "laughingstock" of the city for leaving my mother, she tried the opposite tack: "He was the only intelligent one in the family; he walked out on all of you."

The ripostes were just as pointless. Her old man had been nothing more than a bartender. He used to come home so drunk he would get on his knees to pray and couldn't get back up. Maggy was by far the most stupid mother-in-law in the world. "I wish, before we married, that I had borne in mind that you are an only child. By Christ, I'm now living with a corporation — you and your mother. I have to please two morning, noon, and night to get affection from one. This is no marriage. It's a goddamn duel. And why must I humiliate myself night after night trying to make love to you, and you whispering, 'No. No, Jim. Momma's a light sleeper.' Who the hell cares? What are you, the Blessed Virgin Elinor? She's deaf

[138]

as a bat all day, but at night she wears some kind of a sonar set. The hell with her. If my mother has to live in a furnished room, why can't yours?"

Many of the arguments are blanked. I know they occurred, but I cannot recall the reasons. Almost subliminally, I realized that most of my anger was sexual. The more my wife declined, the more I wanted her. The pleading, the coaxing, the abasement, were destructive. I begged her to tell me the truth — if I didn't please her in bed I would try hard to do better. She burst into tears. The large brown eyes blinked. She hung her head and the tears fell on her skirt. No, she said, that wasn't it. She was in love with me. Whichever way we did it was close to ecstasy. She could tick off on her fingers the number of orgasms and it was not a matter of being a great lover or a poor one — it was love's response to love.

The more I listened, the more bewildered I became. If it was so terrific, why did she turn from me? Elinor became timid, hesitant. Her voice became soft, almost ashamed. Really, she said, it was a combination of things. She reverted to the use of nicknames we applied to genitals. "Angie just doesn't need it as often as Zeke."

I burst into laughter. "So? How much will it hurt Angie to indulge Zeke?" There was more to it than that. She had been raised to think that carnality in any form was sinful. I tried to indulge childishness. "Tell me what that has to do with the sacrament of marriage?"

She shrugged. "Nothing. I didn't say it did. It's just a feeling. Some girls can shake it."

I pulled a long breath. "Isn't it obvious to you that you would rather be Momma's little girl than my wife?"

The hackles began to rise. "Who cooks your meals? Who keeps your house spotless? Who is true to you while you're out playing around? Who do you think you're kidding, Jim? I know you like a book." The tone was rising. Then it descended. "Maybe you're oversexed. Have you ever thought it out? Any man who wants a party every night in the week — there's something wrong."

I was losing aplomb. "Oversexed? You were terrific on the honeymoon and for a long time afterward. Terrific. My nonstop bride. How about those mornings when I didn't think I could get out of bed? No, dear, I'm not oversexed. I'm not over anything except dumb. You're a pretty good fake, you know. How do I know if all those comings were true? How about you trying to convince me that I was too big for you? The medical books say that if a baby can come through there, no man is too big. For a long time, I had to be content with a half-screwing. Half."

"Now you're vulgar."

"You bet your ass I am. And how about all the times you didn't want to get pregnant and I had to pull out? That's a lot of fun for a man. We might as well go to church and tell the priest we're going to live as brother and sister."

"Suits me." I was silent. In all disputes, Elinor always held the last trump — denial, abstinence. She reached across the table and patted my hand. I withdrew it. Somehow, someway, I had to reach a moment where I could say, with no asperity: "I'm leaving. There must be a better life for both of us. I do not blame you, and I hope you won't blame me for what is about to happen. This is March 1937 and we have had almost seven years of it. I'm earning seventy-five a week; I'll send forty. We don't believe in divorce, so we'll separate. I'll get a room in New York and be in touch."

"I'm pregnant," she said.

I looked up from the table. "This a joke?"

She raised her hand as though being sworn in. "I missed periods in December, January, February, and now this month."

I could feel viscera falling to the pelvis. "Have you been to see Trewhella?"

She shook her head. "We've been through that before," she said (again the timid tone). "It didn't work. This time I'm going to carry my baby my way. Oh, I'll go to him all right." She stood and turned sideways. "Noticeable?" I shook my head no. "That's funny," she said. "Momma noticed. She knows."

I felt weary. Exhausted. My speech died in a dry mouth. "Are you sure?" I said once more.

She rapped the table twice. "No morning sickness yet, thank God." She glanced at me with what seemed to be hope. "Maybe this is it," she said. "Maybe this is what's missing. Maybe" — the tears started to well again — "maybe I can try harder to please you."

I did the thing I was certain never to do again. I reached across the table and kissed her. The salt was sharp. "When?" I said.

"August, I think. Maybe the first or second week. Trewhella will know."

The news did not make me happy. It was not honor that kept me in that house in Leonia. Nor duty. The pregnancy was a cruelty. I was aware of what it was like to be without a father. I would stay — but in protest. I donned a woolly jacket and slammed the door. Walking the woods alone calms some men, gives them perspective. Last autumn's leaves were a cold cereal underfoot. The tall trees were lifeless against the sky. I was angry at myself. It was wrong — and I knew it was wrong — to weigh the viability of a marriage on sexual compatibility. Like pearls on a necklace, it weighed no more, no less, than any of the other factors.

The blunt truth was that Elinor and I did not get along. We were in love, yes. If one can judge by depth of sentiment, by caring, by jealousy, by each wishing the best for the other — yes. What did we lack? What was missing? I knew. It was mutuality of interests. I was reading Carl Sandburg and Ernest Hemingway. She devoured trash. I wanted to invite my father and "C" to the house, also my mother, Al Porter, John Dundas, and Bill and Helen Scanlon. She would be satisfied with her cousin Agnes Stone and her three children, Raymond, Margie, and Billie.

I wrote for the *Mirror*. She bought the *Journal-American* to read Dorothy Kilgallen, Louis Sobol, and Cholly Knickerbocker. I liked to go to the movies. She said: "You go." I wanted to listen to sports events on the radio. Elinor listened to soap operas and, on Sunday afternoons, to the pietistic vitriol of Father Coughlin. Now and then, Broadway press agents invited us to see a show. "Baby," she said, "you know crowds make me nervous." One year, when I phoned my father to invite him for Christmas dinner, he snarled: "Once a year you invite the field hands to the main house for dinner? The hell with it. I have other plans."

I kicked a tree. There were periods when Elinor and I moved out of our natural elements to be agreeable to each other. We were overdoing it. We were trying so hard to avoid confrontations that sometimes we acted like smiling strangers who had just been introduced. If she did something I didn't like, I would say, "Oh, that's all right." If I did something to arouse her, she would murmur: "I understand. Forget it." The surface was false and brittle. It could be cracked with a harsh phrase. It was not just Jim who was stuck with wasted years. She was too.

Early in July, Elinor and I were at Dr. Trewhella's house. Ostensibly, we were to have dinner with Art and Ruth, play silly parlor games, and enunciate a few pleasant lies. In truth, we were present so that Art could convince Elinor to go on an early July vacation and have her baby in August.

The mother-to-be appeared to be at her finest. All the tests were within normal range. The brown eyes sparkled with amusement. The belly was far enough out to hold an etui without its falling off. One more time she was joyful; I was apprehensive. The doctor subscribed to her attitude. He insisted that this time it was going to be all right. He reminded us that, in prior pregnancies, he had tried long-term bed rest and it had not worked. I told him that we were thinking of driving south to Washington, then on to the Civil War battlefields of Virginia. Go, he exhorted. Go, Jim. She is practically eight months pregnant. When will you be back? I said the sixteenth or seventeenth. "Go. Go."

We went. Maggy took care of the house. The Gordian knot would not be snipped. We would phone every evening to see if she was all right. I was solicitous, protective. She became a mirror of the girl I married, newly resurfaced. I drove at a reasonable rate of speed and, God help me, I sang. Her favorite was "Ain't Misbehavin'." I had memorized almost one-half of the lyrics and hummed the rest. We stopped at a waterfront bar in Baltimore and ate oysters off the shell and drank the briny juice. We almost finished broiled bluefish, and washed it down with tall, frosty Tom

Collinses. The dock area was old and odoriferous. We thought it was quaint.

There were hours of intimate exchanges. Once or twice, Elinor tried to revise history. She wanted me to know that, although she loved Maggy to distraction, she now realized that this could hurt a husband who wouldn't settle for second place. All that would be changed because I had been so generous in inviting Momma to live with us. Each time, I stopped the monologue with an observation of scenery on the road. The topic, even in renunciation, was dangerous. I patted her hand and drew her attention to the Washington railroad yards, shimmering in July heat, and the capitol beyond. We drove around the city slowly, like provincials staring at majesty. The pristine walls, the fluted columns, the quiet of the Potomac creeping to the sea, the awesome stone hand of Abraham Lincoln, the incalculable riches of the Library of Congress, the Smithsonian looking older than its exhibits, Ford's Theatre and the Peterson House, even the homeliness of the old Washington Hotel.

It was dinnertime. Elinor was tired. Not sleepy-tired, pleasantly sagging. We had dinner on the roof garden — her notion of makeup was to plaster the heavy lips with vermilion, feather a bit of rouge on the cheeks, and streak a bit of blue-green on the upper lids. In twilight, she approached in neon. The maitre d' was a finger-snapper. We sat at a window and didn't feel hungry. To avoid contempt, we ordered and didn't eat. Except, of course, for more oysters. Elinor asked the waiter to grate fresh horse-radish. My sinuses went up in flames. We doodled; we chatted; we stared at a great city.

She thought we shouldn't mix drinks. We had more Tom Collinses. I began to feel a resurgence of sentiment. How could I dream of leaving this lovely, helpless creature? Why was anger so witless and pervasive? How could a man who thought of himself as mature walk to the edge of a precipice and say "Farewell"? I shuddered. We returned to our room — a double with a huge bed — and undressed. It was early in the evening. Neither of us wanted to retire. How about a little more gin? The bellboy brought a dollar-forty-nine fifth of Gilbey's for five dollars. It also included a bucket of ice and a plateful of sliced lemons and limes. We drank each other toward coma reciting clichés about love and marriage and birth and life and all the mysteries. As each spoke, the other nodded.

There was brazen sunlight when I lifted my head off the pillow. My trousers were on the floor. The leather belt was still in the loops. The shorts were limp at the bottom of a wall. One shoe was under a chair. I was nude. Elinor was on her side, still in a slip. We sat up ashamed. In the bathroom, I studied the desiccated remains of my tongue and the small bird-wings of gray at the temples. I was older, but not wiser. Elinor staggered out of bed, not intoxicated, but sick. Her head ached; her stomach hurt. The eyes were dimmed in red. We agreed that it was one hell of a start to a vacation. "Do we have to drive today?" she said. Yes, I said.

I wanted to visit the Lee mansion up on the hill, and then go on slowly over the roads of Virginia. "Can't it wait until tomorrow?" It can, but we won't.

We had survived temporary deaths before. The breeze in the car would be good for both of us. At eleven A.M. we had checked out. The joy of yesterday was replaced by mutual mourning. There was no singing. At the Lee mansion, Elinor sat in the car. The lower lip was out and up. "I don't feel good."

"Neither do I. We emptied that bottle."

We crossed over to Route 9 and drove slowly northwest. I wanted to see Winchester and part of the Shenandoah Valley. The farms, the trees, the sleek horses staring from behind white fences, the innate richness of land which refused to bend to time, even the pale sky helped to heal bleeding eyes.

There was a side road pointing to a village called Ashburn. I remember it because she said she had a pain. A different pain. I said something thoughtless, like "Please. Not in the middle of nowhere." She was pouting again. We drove in silence. She stirred. Another pain. I cut the speed of the car, hoping it would subside. It didn't. After the fourth pain, I began to clock them. We were two stupid people in a Ford. I asked if she had noticed the name of the next big town. We could stop and see a doctor. She didn't notice any signs. The town of Leesburg came up over the hill. It wasn't much, but an elderly woman said it had a hospital, as I recall, on our right.

Hospitals do not comprehend panic. The nurses exude calm. A corridor floor gleamed with wax. A doctor filled out a brief medical history and asked me to wait. He was back in ten minutes. "She's about to have her baby," he said. The words were familiar. Once they had been exhilarating; now they were depressing. She was about to give birth to another premature infant, one who might be born dead or live a few hours. "Is she all right? Can I see her?" The doctor said she would get good care; she appeared to be overly sensitive to pain. His advice to me was to drive down the road to a small motel and return later.

These were not good hours. Nor minutes. *Mea culpa* was not involved, but I reflected that it was I who insisted on the July vacation. Trewhella's role was minimal.

I unpacked her things and mine, and looked for a dressy nightie, a robe, slippers, and cigarettes. Those, and nothing more. I was back with a small suitcase quickly. The nurse at the desk didn't know who I was or what I was talking about. In addition, I could not recollect the name of the tall, thin doctor. She found him. He came out peeling rubber gloves off his hands. "Miz Bishop tells me you folks been having trouble having babies," he said. Then he smiled and held his hand out. "Congratulations. You have a fine baby girl. Seven and a half pounds." I am speechless only when I want silence. My wife was fine, he said. No problem. Tired, perhaps.

Fatigued. He wished I wouldn't bother her right now. Later. The baby? He said he had told me. Healthy, hungry, complaining.

"My God," I shouted. "How fast did she have this baby?"

He studied a card. "'Bout thirty, thirty-one minutes."

It was, for both of us, a new, shiny universe.

Toward the close of the 1930s, apple sellers disappeared from street corners. If this was an index that the United States was improving its economic fortunes, it was a rare one. Few corporations were hiring. Newspapers had lost millions of lines of advertising and, frequently, a big city newspaper appeared in twenty-four pages. Blood had been spilled at the Ford Dearborn plant, at steel mills, and mines. The nation, childishly ebullient and robust in the early part of the century, had become cynical and fearful in one decade.

Millions of sufferers turned to God because there was no one else who could be trusted. He was the ultimate employment office, the money machine, the forgotten joy of the world. Church was free — or almost so. Paranoid preachers referred to America as a godless country. We were punished for crimes of commission and omission. White paint on big rocks proclaimed, "Jesus Is Coming." Anti-Semitism enjoyed a resurrection. Money was scarce because the Jews had it. The word was that the Jews controlled the government, the banks, Hollywood, radio, and communism. People read with interest of the ascendency of Adolf Hitler, who was lifting Germany out of despair by expelling Jews and expropriating their property. He was seen as a bold, imaginative man who promised work to all Germans. His Brownshirt cadres had restored law and order by pummeling Jews. In a spirit of brotherhood, German-Americans organized brown-shirt Bunds, which marched with truncheons, proclaiming that they were for America first and anti-Jewish second. This bred a surface wave of revulsion followed by secret contributions to the Bunds.

I met Fanny Schulein. She had a warty, homely face with lenses which magnified her eyes. She was older than I, a tense woman caught squarely between tears and laughter. My editor had transferred me back to day work as promotion editor. This involved base prostitution, involving benefit shows and contests. Hinson Stiles said I could take it or quit. I took it.

A boy named Bermudez ran back into a tenement fire to rescue his pet cat and was burned to death. The *Mirror* promoted a pet ambulance with his name on it in bronze. We staged forty-thousand-dollar beauty contests in which I was the sole and frightened judge. We published a bathing-suit snapshot of a "finalist" each day.

My name was over all this trash. Miss Schulein, a German screen writer, tried to win a photo contest of scenic shots snapped from the Chrysler Tower. Our readers paid fifty cents to get into that lofty cubicle and, at the same time, the paper began to get some advertising linage from

Chrysler Motors. I did not like Miss Schulein because she appeared at the *Mirror* to explain how to take a prizewinning picture.

Nor was I interested in her forlorn life, but I listened to it in the reception office. She was a stout spinster who had been raised in Nuremberg. Her father was a prosperous Jew who had owned a chain of dry-goods stores featuring fine linens. He was dead. Her mother, Mathilde, was the focus of sentiment and attention. She was seventy-eight, a small woman with a tidy white bun on top of her head. There was an older sister, Berta, who lived with her mother in a small upstairs apartment with an iron-railed porch.

Fanny had been a screen writer in Berlin. She worked for Max Reinhardt. When Hitler came to power, his propaganda minister, Dr. Joseph Goebbels, had ordered all forms of communication — movies, radio, newspapers, magazines, and book publishers — to denounce Jewish employees. Miss Schulein had rushed back to Nuremberg, made a secret agreement with her mother and sister, and hurried to America. No one seemed to appreciate that Hitler meant to be rid of all Jews — deport them or kill them.

Her accent was heavy, almost incomprehensible at speed, and I asked her to wait until quitting time. I took her home for dinner. Elinor liked the lady at once. She saw no competitive spirit, just a middle-aged woman who was half-scared to death of Nazis. She spoke explosively, bugging her eyes and waving her arms. The Jews in Germany did not understand that Adolf Hitler was Satan personified. Few of them had ever read his *Mein Kampf* because they had heard it was anti-Semitic. I pointed out that the chancellor's primary goal was *Lebensraum*. Was he not busy building an empire, annexing Austria, part of Czechoslovakia, demanding a corridor through Poland to East Prussia? He was defying the Versailles Treaty, rebuilding a mighty army, a navy, and a brand-new Luftwaffe. Surely Jews must be low on the list of priorities.

Fanny burst into tears. The problem, she said, was not which way he would face for more living space. It wasn't even important whether he got it or not. The great towering truth, she said, was that he sincerely hated all Jews and blamed them for the sickness of the world. It would require time and propaganda to bring the German people to his level of venom. She had read the Nuremberg Laws of 1935. Hitler was not devious; he was blunt when he said that no Jew may own property in Germany or hold public office. The problem, she said, was with the Jews. They did not believe that the Jewish issue was any more than domestic propaganda. Hitler would use it to attain power; when he achieved the status of dictator, he would change his attitude.

She insisted that she was not easily frightened. "I have lived with anti-Semitism before. This man will be rid of all Jews one way or another!" If he deports Jews without compensation, I said, he will alienate the sympathy of the world. He can't afford it. She laughed. She said I sounded like the Jews in Germany. I asked her what secret agreement she had reached with her mother and sister.

This induced a rare smile. The Nazis were beginning to censor all Jewish mail inbound and outbound. Once a month, her mother said, she would send a photo of herself and Berta sitting on their little porch. On the table would be a small bouquet of flowers. This would mean that all was going well with them. If, at any time, Mother felt that time and circumstances were closing in on them, she would send a photo without the bouquet.

Fanny Schulein became a close friend of the family. She stayed at our house; she phoned at any and all hours. I tried to get work worthy of her skill. In time, she became a grandmotherly baby-sitter. The monthly letters arrived promptly with the accompanying snapshot. Tearing the envelope became a frightening experience. It was followed by something approaching a momentary nervous breakdown. "See?" I said. "You are far away from Adolf Hitler but, inch by inch, he is killing you."

A day came when she opened a letter. There was no bouquet. At the time, Elinor and I were her oldest friends in America. She turned away from us. Fanny booked a room on the fourteenth floor of the Edison Hotel and crept out of the bathroom window. She fainted and fell in on the tile floor. One shoe was embedded in the metal sill. The call I got was from Doctor Baumann, chief of Bellevue Hospital's psychiatric division. I told him her story and he marked her chart: "Allowed to go home in custody of Jim Bishop, c/o Daily Mirror, 235 E. 45th Street, N.Y.C."

She was neither remorseful nor apologetic. She promised not to try suicide again. There was a serenity in the way she waited for the tragic news. On November 18, 1938, a cable arrived. It consisted of four words: MUTTER UND BERTA GESTORBEN. The German fascination with thoroughness brought a reward. Mrs. Schulein and her daughter had spent two days tidying their apartment. It was immaculate. They placed all papers of consequence, birth certificates and deeds, bank accounts and business addresses over a lace counterpane on the bed. Newspapers were taped to all the windows and doors. They turned on the kitchen gas range and dressed their best. They were found lying across the bed.

An Obersturmführer of the SS was so pleased with the way it was done that he granted special permission to a downstairs neighbor to send the details to Fanny Schulein in New York. After that, she lost all interest and traveled to Windsor, Ontario, and reentered the United States as an immigrant. Fanny moved to Hollywood to be near movie stars. She lived meanly in a small room. Her biggest thrill was to stand, a gushing old lady, behind wooden horses at premieres. She saw the movie stars close up and applauded. One day I received a formal little letter stating that she had died, and had left word that Elinor and I were to be informed.

The new baby became a love, a world, a humbling experience. The upstairs bedroom was large and square and bright. It had a polished floor and flowered blue wallpaper. There was a big bed in it, but it no longer mattered. One-third of the room was occupied by a wicker bassinette threaded with pink ribbons and with a half-canopy. Inside, four tiny appendages moved constantly. There was a round head with little yellow wisps standing. The blue eyes, the beatific face, the deep bare chest, the tiny white diaper, the up-looking gummy grin were designed to render a man defenseless.

I knew nothing of infants. Inwardly, I had been bragging about my cosmopolitan spectrum, but nowhere had I read anything about the care, feeding, and love of a newborn, a firstborn. It was a she, weighing seven and a half pounds. We brought her home in a washbasket on the back seat of the car. As the automobile bumped along mile after mile from Leesburg, Virginia, she was quiet. When I stopped for a red light, she wailed.

Elinor wanted to call her Margaret or Peggy. We settled on reversing town and state. She became Virginia Lee, often called Missy. Elinor was pleased, delighted, somewhat triumphant. She couldn't contain herself. My sentiments went to her because I knew the jarring disappointment of the first two pregnancies. She now knew that she could give birth to a normal baby — more than that, a beautiful youngster who dredged superlatives from friends. I learned to make formulas, to warm them, to test the thermal values on the inside of an elbow, to lift the child without breaking her into halves, to whisper to her, to smell the fresh-bread odor of her skin, and to adore (which is dangerous).

When we went to the movies, Maggy became the baby-sitter. She was the best because she worked by instinct. When the baby cried, Maggy sang "Easter Bonnet" and "Alice Blue Gown." To Missy, it was as good as listening to Madame Schumann-Heink. The soothing voice, the intimate presence of her grandmother, made her content.

This was the glory day. This was the time when we wanted to start all over. It was a sublime honeymoon. I became conscious of Elinor's smallest wishes. She urged me to try to write magazine articles at night. Her attitude toward her mother became diffident — not less loving, but conscious of the truth that there is room in the human heart to feel affection for many, not just one.

I was a husband and father, and felt like one. On warm nights I placed the typewriter on a table in the breakfast nook and pounded prose. This was for magazines — *American, Collier's, The Saturday Evening Post, Esquire* — and for extra money. The rejection slips were in colors; the words aloofly polite. "Someday," I said, "we'll make a big Japanese screen of these things." It was a brazen expression, designed to convince my wife that someday these magazines would be buying articles from me and that we would treasure the early failures. *American* magazine bought a short piece (I cannot recall the subject), inserted it in a box, and paid fifty dollars. We kept the rejected articles. These were exposed once a year to a rereading. If they seemed weak and disjointed in structure, I felt elated. It meant that I had learned a little in the past year. If they read well, I worried.

Often there were no ideas for writing. Rarely, I would take volume four of Carl Sandburg's *Abraham Lincoln: The War Years* and turn to the chapter heading "The Calendar Says Good Friday." I would copy a few pages on the typewriter, hoping to infuse my head and hands with a flow of solemn prose. Afterward, I would write a confidential letter to Virginia Lee possibly to be read when she grew up. The comparison was so sickening that my emotions constricted my throat. There seemed to be no way up, and surely there was no way back. I had to keep trying.

The extra twenty or thirty a week I earned writing Hellinger's columns stopped. The urbane columnist and his beautiful wife were going to California. He would write his columns from there. "How much do you owe me?" he said. It was forty or fifty dollars. "Okay, kid," he said. "Forget it. We're even. When I get back, we'll start all over again."

He had been to Hollywood on his honeymoon. Few of the producers knew him then and he had been invited to few parties. This time, he was a syndicated columnist. He had several hundred newspapers. This, to some, is power. The word permeated Warner's, Columbia, Fox, Metro, Universal that the Hellingers were coming. They would not only be invited to important events; studio heads would be honored to stage a party for the Hellingers.

Mark wanted revenge. His attitude was smooth and smiling, but his columns whipped the movie capital raw. He made sport of what producers told him; he urged his readers not to bother attending certain motion pictures now in the making. He poked fun at famous stars who had to be in bed at ten P.M. as the Hellingers were looking around for an open club with cases of Three-Star Hennessy. He spoke loudly and went to press often. In some instances, his criticism was well founded. The New York offices of the studios were reading this material with dismay; the phone lines from coast to coast were busy.

Toward the end of a month-long visit, some timid producers were asking Hellinger for story suggestions. In that gravelly voice, he assured them: "If you don't have it in the story, pal, you don't have it anywhere else." He may not have realized it, but he was quoting the philosophy of studio managers from the days of the original two-reelers. It was easy to tell, reading the columns, which Hollywood luminaries had expressed respect for Mark's approach to the making of movies. They were mentioned with kindness with a garnish of flattery. He was partial to the Broadway crowd: Jay C. Flippen, George Raft, Nunnally Johnson, Mae West, Bing Crosby, W. C. Fields, John Barrymore, Fredric March, and others who had once been part of his cynical world.

He sent an expensive baby carriage with a card: "Happy riding, pal.

Uncle Mark." When he returned, he asked for my opinion and I gave it: he was a nut. Mark turned on his forgiving smile. The people who matter, he said, do not respond to anything but the whip. Within a year, he said, they will be offering me a job as a producer. "I have William Morris as my agent." He was right. Warner Brothers asked him to move west to start as associate producer. He dropped the column — except for a big page in the Sunday "March of Events" section of the Hearst newspapers. I thought he might now confide to King Features that I had been writing a great deal of his stuff for eight years and could continue. He didn't. I didn't ask.

My father moved with Clara and her children to a little house in Cliffside Park, New Jersey. We visited frequently. There was an odor of guilt to this, but I consoled myself that anything which can endure for sixteen years is love. He was fat and sparkling, as much a friend as a father. There was pride in the way he addressed "C." She was stout too, but the pale skin, the blue eyes, the pinned-up blond hair made her attractive. Her facial expressions were so viable that, in conversation, it wasn't necessary to wait for her response. Her frowns, smiles, nods, and perplexities were as audible as tempered words.

Sometimes, my father was unintentionally repetitious. "Jim, there is so much out there to learn. I've had five jobs since I retired." He had been a clerk at a chemical plant, an industrial refrigeration salesman. At the moment, he was head of security at a plastics plant. They were doing secret work for the government. Big John's job was to investigate each of three hundred employees to locate aliens, radicals, fascists, and antigovernment personnel. He said that the general manager wanted to promote him to become personnel manager. It would be a big step up, and more money.

He decided to resign. "C" entreated him to accept the promotion. He was adamant. "I spent twenty-five years in the police department" was one of his favorite quotes, "and I didn't learn a damned thing. I'll bet none of you understand plastics. It's new. It's going to be a big thing in time. But I know all I want to know. I'm moving on to learn how to sell real estate."

He phoned me at the office. The date, like so many others, is lost, It was in the late autumn of 1937. The voice was subdued. He said he was a few blocks away from the *Mirror*. He would appreciate it if I could get the rest of the day off. I asked why. "I'll tell you," he said, and didn't. "Pick me up downstairs," I said. It had to be important. Hinson Stiles asked why I wanted the hours off. "Something at home," I said. He shrugged.

My father stood outside the parked car. His arm rested heavily on the roof. "Thanks," he said. "Thanks, Jim."

There was a slow-motion knot in my stomach. I stared at him.

"It's 'C'" he said. "She's dying." The big ruddy face contorted. He sobbed.

"Let me drive," I said.

He felt his way around the automobile. I had never seen him like this. Big John was beaten, defeated, out of control. The tears wouldn't stop. The sobs were like spasms for air.

"Where to?" I whispered. He pointed uptown. I drove north on Third Avenue until he composed himself. "C" dying? She seemed hearty a week or so ago.

The story came, a clause at a time. Several days earlier, Cliffside Park had been inundated with a severe storm. The cellar was flooded. In the morning, Dad had had breakfast and hurried to work. "C" waited until the children had left for school. She put on Big John's carpet slippers to go to the cellar and find out how much water there was. The big loose slipper had caught on the top step. "C" fell to the bottom. When she recovered consciousness, her face was in the brackish water. There was an inch-and-a-half gash in her forehead. Dad found her in the kitchen with a squarish bandage and strips of adhesive on her head. She was giggling. "Your big feet, and my clumsiness . . ."

Big John phoned a doctor. It was a nasty cut, he said, but not dangerous. "C" had pain tolerance, but she flinched and shouted when the doctor peeled the wound open to cleanse it. Antibiotics were not yet in use. He douched it clean. Then he tucked the ragged edges together with three stitches. A small wet dressing covered it. A nurse made out a card to "Mrs. Bishop" to return in six days. On the fourth day "C" had headaches. They were neither mild nor ordinary. She shielded her eyes from light. The pain frightened her. He phoned for an appointment. The doctor was "out of town." She protested, but he drove her to Englewood Hospital.

In the emergency room, a resident examined her and pulled Big John aside. "Without tests," he said, "I don't know what we're dealing with. If she sustained a hairline fracture — the worst it could be would be septicemia." "C" was given a quarter grain of morphine and admitted. She felt better within an hour. She wanted to go home.

Dad was worried. He could not share this. He did not call me. A long time before, they had chosen an isolated life. They had no friends. The following afternoon he was at the hospital, carrying mixed flowers in green waxed paper and breathing hard. "C" was propped up, smiling but fatigued. A doctor said they had taken a spinal tap the previous evening. The result was not good. Dirt or poison had lodged inside the skull somehow. The hospital would do its best, but he mustn't expect miracles.

He became the outraged lieutenant of police. "I want her out of here." He was snarling. Columbia-Presbyterian Hospital in New York said they would take the patient. He ordered a private ambulance and rode with her. He would not believe that his Clara was about to leave. The symptom wasn't sorrow; it was rage. He demanded the best doctors; the best surgeons. This morning they told him she was slipping away. He needed me to help him hold up. We drove north and parked at 168th Street off Broad-

[150]

way. His stride was brisk. I barely made it into the elevator behind him.

At first glance, "C" looked good. Her pale skin was slightly flushed, barely pink. The lips were red. The swirls of yellow hair were in seductive disorder. She was sleeping. He shook his head no. "Jim," his voice cracked, "Jim, she is in a coma." I edged onto the side of the bed. Lightly, I stroked her cheek with the back of a finger. The blue eyes opened briefly. She smiled. Abruptly, she was back to sleep, the big bosom rising and falling slowly.

She died in the morning. I phoned the *Mirror* and asked for two days off and borrowed two more from another reporter. Elinor said I should stay with Dad. I begged her not to tell anyone. By afternoon, the word was all over Jersey City that "Lieutenant Bishop's woman died." The word reached my mother before sundown. Her mother said it was God's vengeance on sinners. Her sister told her to be glad. No, she said, she wasn't glad. She felt sorry for both of them. She didn't want it to end with death. She had hoped, as always, that my father would "come to his senses." She said she would go to church and pray for Clara's soul. One of her friends said she was a hypocrite.

The three days and nights in Dad's house were interminable. The body was in a walnut casket in the living room. Big John seemed to wrest control of himself, then lose it at unexpected times. In the sun room, we chatted in whispers. "C's" mother, a small lively woman, took charge of the house and the children. Her grief was masked by composure. Through the hours, Dad remembered and remembered how much he loved her — "worshipped her" — and the memories kept his emotions above the line of hysteria. When he fell below, he ran to the casket and called to her, the tears falling on the gray lace gown she wore. Sometimes I got him outside for a walk.

On the last night, Elinor arrived. She burst into tears. Dad grabbed her and shouted: "She's gone, Elinor. She left me. Oh, my God." The roars could be heard on the sidewalk.

On the morning of the funeral, I spoke to the mortician. "When the time comes, just slam that box shut and carry it out quickly. Otherwise, we're going to have a scene." He didn't do it. At the final moment, he moved among mourners in the rooms murmuring: "Anyone who would like to say good-bye. If you would like to have a memento of Mrs. Bishop, please take a flower from the casket."

Big John heard it. In the deep blue suit, the gleaming black shoes, he hurried to the casket saying: "No, no." In the presence of all, he reached in and lifted the body up. He hugged her. Meaningless sounds came from his chest. He talked to her. A young undertaker tried to pry him from the body. One hard shove send him reeling among the folding chairs.

Twice in the years that followed — and by accident — I met him at Christmas at the cemetery gates. A man was selling Christmas wreaths with holly for the graves. Big John bought slender branches of evergreen and knelt on Clara's grave. Clumsily, he wove the wreath and laid the circle of green on the clean snow. He would not, could not, forget her.

Elinor was not born to compromise. Her instincts were charmingly feminine, but in a conflict between those and intelligence, instinct would win. I begged her to allow me to buy a house. The first response was laughter. "With what?" Her second, third, and twentieth were no, no, and no. She would like to return to Jersey City. Momma would like to get back to the old neighborhood. To which Maggy responded by fluttering both hands and begging "Leave me out of this."

One layer below Elinor's adamant attitude lay a slab of vanity. Her house had to be better than those of our friends. Her furnishings had to be richer, the rugs deeper.

I asked her to look at some new houses. Brand new. Never lived in. Four walls and a roof which, with time and indebtedness, could be molded into something befitting her personality. She said she'd think about it. I dropped the subject. One sunny Sunday she asked me to take her, the baby, and her mother for a drive "up Teaneck way." I phoned Dad. He said he would have nothing to do with it. "You looking for new houses?" he said. "Take her up to West Englewood. There's a whole development near the armory."

West Englewood is not a part of Englewood. It's part of Teaneck. The town had nine thousand people, a movie house, a golf course called Phelps Manor, Holy Name Hospital, and a big sign which stated: "Teaneck — a Restricted Community." Maggy asked what it meant. I explained that it proclaimed that no one would be permitted to build a house under a certain figure — say $4,000. All real estate was restricted to a higher figure. The old lady thought that was interesting. So did I, sometime later, when I had the sign explained to me.

The new houses were on Longview Court. The street was unpaved. The houses were Cape Cods, each a variant of the others. The one at 1827 had a lot of good-looking fieldstone in front. The sign said, "Open for Inspection." There were a dozen cars parked and a dozen gaping couples leading adenoidal children through the rooms.

Elinor toured the rooms with her index finger against her lips, a sign that she was thinking seriously about something. The cellar was concrete and spotless, with an oil burner in one corner. On the ground floor the kitchen was spacious and sunny with plenty of closet space. There was a gas range, an oven, a hot water heater. The living room was sixteen by eighteen with a little porch looking off big windows. The dining room was behind it, with an excellent view of some empty lots, tin cans, and broken bottles. Upstairs were two large bedrooms, a modern bathroom, and walk-in closet space. The attic had been insulated.

"How much?" I said to the salesman. He was a hearty man who wore a stump of a cigar and chuckled, even when saying "Howdy do." He took me aside in the manner of a conspirator. "These are models," he whispered. "My company put them up just to see how they go. If they sell, we'll build ten thousand of them all over the East. We're giving these away — fifty-nine ninety, five hundred ninety-nine cash down." I made a face. "Look," he said, "we have a deal with the West Englewood Bank. You pay thirty-eight forty a month for twenty years. Christ, it's cheaper than rent."

"Christ, yes," Elinor said, "but my husband is trying to find out where he's going to get the down payment."

We talked about it. "You're trying to get me out farther in the woods" became the next hurdle. She liked the house. She admired the gleaming hardwood floors. The back bedroom would be nice for Momma. There was a clean, suburban air about the neighborhood. She had noticed that some of the occupied houses had young children, which translated into young parents. She wasn't sure about shopping. How long would it require to drive to Jersey City to see Cousin Agnes? A half-hour? Incredible. And yet. And yet there was a translucent film of fear. Elinor's enemy was the unknown, the unexpected.

I bought the house. The Morris Plan lent three hundred dollars on my signature; I had two hundred saved, and I told the salesman that I would owe him the ninety-nine dollars. I promised him 4 percent interest. He hesitated, and shook hands. There was an enormous amount of paperwork done by the West Englewood Bank. So much, in fact, that the president, Frank Weber, and I became friends. There was a title search and insurance and taxes and a lawyer with an office over the bank who could speed matters for me, et cetera, et cetera.

This made me a responsible citizen. Teaneck was Republican, so I enrolled in the Democratic party. Couples on the block baby-sat for each other. Each payday, I bought a tool to go with my workbench in the cellar. I dug fenceposts, jammed them with rocks and cement. I stole small trees from the woods and replanted them in the yard. A weeping willow spread its wings on the front lawn. I hunted huge rocks for the driveway and painted them white. Overnight I became a fixer, hanging pictures, drilling holes, resurfacing end tables, even shutting off the water to replace a leaky washer in the bathroom. I mixed my own oil paints.

It was a milestone: Jim Bishop, home owner. To Elinor, it was a showplace where old friends showed up to ooh and ahh. To Virginia Lee, it was a neighborhood of little boys and girls who invented games and inflicted cruelties on each other. To Maggy Dunning, it was a lovely refuge, a roomy hideaway for listening to the radio dramas all afternoon with a cold rosary between her fingers. It was also being invited to game-room cellars to drink, to brag, to play dart-board games, to discuss the antics of the town council as though we of Longview Court were the only watchdogs in town.

It was a time of well-being, with war approaching as insidiously as a midnight shower. Everyone talked of war and everyone agreed America should keep out of it. We analyzed Neville Chamberlain's flying visit to Adolf Hitler in Munich as though we were privy to the conversations. Great Britain would not allow a war to start. She had guaranteed Poland's borders. On the other hand, if the Germans raced through Poland, how could the British — or the French — come to the rescue? The geography of war, we all agreed, was bad. We also agreed to discuss it again — the men, that is — while the ladies made the coffee and the ham sandwiches in the kitchen and gabbled four at a time with everyone nodding in assent.

Elinor had a superficial interest in international politics. She was certain that Hitler was bad for Germany, but she didn't know why. Just a feeling. Like a chill on the shoulders. She studied his face in the newsreels at the movie and said his eyes were maniacal. "He shouts," she said, "but he won't look anyone in the eye." I told her that if war came to America, I would have to go. I was thirty-two. "You won't go," she said, "because first, we're not going to get in it this time. Second, you're a family man. I do wish you'd stop scaring me."

The editor left for Philadelphia to make sure that the Republican party kept its senses and nominated Robert A. Taft of Ohio. Jack Lait was small, balding, homely, a man whose lips executed figure eights without sound. Everyone at the *Daily Mirror* believed that Lait's mind was hooked into that of William Randolph Hearst at San Simeon in California. Anyone could ask Jack a question involving editorial policy and, without moving anything but his lips, Lait gave us the morning line.

He left the department in the hands of the handsome Hinson Stiles, something akin to leaving Little Red Riding Hood in charge of the wolf. As the dayside staff dragged through the greasy portals, Hinss shouted that big news was coming up out of Philadelphia. I was to write a short biography of Senator Taft marked "Lead to Come." Arthur James Pegler would, at press-time, rap out the lead unless we had early wire copy from Lait. The art director, Jack Governale, was busy laying out a double truck of Taft and some also-rans: Alfred Landon, Senator Bricker, Wendell Willkie, Taft's father, President William Howard Taft.

We were expectant. At two P.M. three men in coveralls arrived and began to remove the typewriters. Stiles stopped them. They shrugged. "Mr. Lait told us to take them down the hall and clean them," one said. Hinss asked how long it would take. "Aw, we just rub cleaning fluid on the keys. A half-hour." Okay. A half-hour. They were gone an hour before Stiles realized that the *Daily Mirror* had been the victim of a massive burglary. Three men had walked off with almost all the editorial department typewriters. Police from the East Fifty-first Street precinct stomped all over the place, asking questions. There was no way to get out a morning newspaper unless we could borrow typewriters from the sports department and the business office upstairs.

Stiles was furious and searched faces for cynical smiles. At five o'clock, Lait's lead began to chatter on the machines. It said:

"Philadelphia. — On a hot summer evening the Republican party buckled to the business of nominating a winner for the Big Prize. As the last windy speeches echoed across the iron rafters, the tabulators estimated that Robert A. Taft of Ohio, with 400 votes, would be nominated on the second ballot. It was still a wide-open convention, but the men behind the big cigars in the back rooms said that the only sure loser is Wendell Willkie, the flamboyant businessman. . . ."

Our page-1 headline, double-banked in 96-point caps, stated:

G.O.P. TO NAME
SENATOR TAFT

Wendell Willkie, of course, was nominated. The police traced the typewriters to a pickup truck with New Jersey plates. We were out of our milieu, picking political winners and preventing robberies. Circulation edged a little over 900,000, but their purchasing power approximated that of Black All-American polo players. If it was true that the readers of the *Daily News* were 2,000,000 gum-chewers, then ours were people who kicked the machines until they vomited gum.

Adolf Hitler was news, but not for us. The *Mirror* published a daily war map on page 2, with a digest of bulletins from London, Paris, and Berlin. Air raids, whether they were over London or Kiel, were banner headlines. When the first British pilot fell in flames over German territory, Hitler had ordered a state funeral with flowers and the snap of rifle fire over the grave. In time, this extraordinary respect would degenerate to where Allied pilots, hanging by chutes in trees, would be shot by German farmers and policemen. In any case, we saw through the whole war — it was spurious and barely harmful to the health of the combatants. The German army couldn't get through the Maginot Line, the French and British couldn't get through the Siegfried Line, and nobody was going to violate the neutrality of Holland and Belgium. In any case, as soon as Hitler secured Poland, there would be peace talks. As a source of editorial matter, World War II was a whimpering fizzle.

Still, we had to sell papers. There had been a surfeit of love-nest raids. We required hyperexcitement, and it was becoming difficult to find. Without it, circulation sagged and the word was passed that heads would roll.

For a while, the *Daily Mirror* maintained its pulse with murders. The importance of these is that they were "nine-day wonders," crimes which kept unfolding day by day. The first concerned an innocuous old man named Albert Fish. He lived alone in Manhattan in a small apartment featuring a brine barrel in the kitchen. He had white wavy hair, subservient manners, and a whispery voice. He had an enormous affinity for little girls. On trolleys and in schoolyards, he lured them with candy, took them for a ride, and brought them, protesting feebly, to his apartment.

Mr. Fish cupped his hand over the mouths and dragged the little girls to the bathroom. They were placed in a tub of water and their throats were slit. He undressed them carefully, hacked off limbs and parts, and placed them with some tenderness in the brine barrel. As he explained it to the police he ate the parts only when he wanted to achieve an orgasm. Albert Fish had never found another way of easing sexual tension. He had, according to his admission, never tried a full-sized girl, in or out of the barrel. Nor, it seems had the little man ever heard of foreplay. Police officers sat fascinated as he explained his bite-and-fire system.

Two of the detectives were quoted as saying: "This is a certified nut." The law forbids capital trials for psychotics who cannot determine the difference between right and wrong. Fish, who was so mannerly that he was given to holding a cell door open for a keeper before entering, had no notion of right or wrong. He babbled on and on about his sexual finesse and signed confession after confession. If he wasn't certain about killing a little girl, he denied it and rubbed his watery eyes.

The *Mirror*, which understood the limits of its license, could find no way of explaining that an orgasm was involved. It said he cut little girls up and chewed on the parts, which made Mr. Fish seem animalistic and, to a grave degree, cannibalistic. The prisoner looked for no sympathy and there was none. Never, in the modern history of New York State, was a nut tried so quickly, condemned, and sentenced. Short and old, he stood blinking before a county judge and heard the date of his death. Appeal is automatic, but the old man didn't want it.

In the death house at Sing Sing, he seemed lonely. Three others who were to die refused to play checkers with him or converse. They called him "Scum." Apparently, he began to dream of the good old orgasms. Mr. Fish took his bed apart one night and swallowed a bedspring. He fired a shot heard around the prison. New York State was placed in the awkward position of having to save his life so it could kill him. X-rays showed the open-ended bedspring between the stomach and the small intestine.

Good surgeons were employed. Mr. Fish survived. He convalesced in the prison infirmary. Guards watched him day and night. When he was returned to his cell, weak and tottering, he was overcome by the old mating call and swallowed a handful of tacks. This started a scandal with charges and countercharges. A sensational Sunday newspaper suggested that Fish be castrated because a guest psychiatrist wrote that this might chill his ardent desires. The state postponed the electrocution and brought Fish back to surgery. He apologized for being such a bother, but reminded everyone that the bedspring and tacks were a substitute forced on him by an unfeeling bureaucracy.

When he recovered, the old man was placed in a compartment which tabloid writers called the Dance Hall. This is an assortment of three cells close to the execution room. Spotlights were placed high in the corridor, beaming brightly on Fish at all times. The bed was removed. The cinder blocks were sanded smooth. Fish slept on an assortment of blankets. On the morning of the day he was to die, the prisoner asked the principal keeper: "Will I feel the first jolt?" He was told: "No. It hits you so fast you're unconscious before you feel anything." The old man shook his head sadly. "Too bad," he murmured. "Too bad."

There were two other unusual crimes which the faded file cards of memory insist occurred close to each other. One was the rape and murder of Ana Almodor in Central Park. The other was the shooting of a policeman in Queens. Mrs. Almodor, a small person with huge, wondrous brown eyes, was found strangled to death at the bottom of a granite ravine. Her clothing had been shredded. The cop was found in front of a hardware store with five pounds of grass seed in the crook of his arm.

They were separate crimes, but it was the habit of sensational newspapers to stake a claim to one, to play it up, to assign more than one reporter to it and to keep it alive, if necessary, with artificial revelations and interviews. The most archaic of all devices is to prod a detective into stating "We expect an arrest within twenty-four hours." Another is "We have a prime suspect, but we cannot reveal anything at this time because he is still at large."

An editorial conference in Lait's office selected the wrong murder. The gentlemen decided that rape murders are common. Cops never quit when one of their own is killed. They will literally hang onto the hot hinges of hell to bag their man. I was told that our Brooklyn man, Harry, would cover the day-to-day events of the police murder, and that I would take the story every day at five P.M., finish writing it by five forty-five, and make the first edition with ease. The Almodor murder would be covered by Jerry Edelberg, Walter Marshall, Ray Doyle — anyone who wasn't assigned to something more important.

The *Journal-American* decided to feature the Almodor murder. This was Hearst's afternoon newspaper in New York, a bookkeeping sister of the *Mirror*, as much of a competitor for news as any other paper. Of all the periodicals in New York, the *Journal-American* carried a sense of excitement. It was closest to Hollywood's notion of newspapers, with reporters sticking press cards in their hatbands, and shouting "Stop the presses." The editors could turn the carrying of penicillin from a pharmaceutical laboratory in New Jersey to a sick little girl in Brooklyn into a Pulitzer prize. The editors — Eddie Mahar, Paul Schoenstein, Guy Richardson — had a greater comprehension of the use of type, stunning photos, charts, and sidebar stories than any group of editors. In a sense, they made news. On the second day of the Almodor murder they had a story by Dr. Richard Hoffman, Park Avenue psychiatrist, with descriptions for the police on precisely what kind of fiend they were looking for.

We had hoped for some mileage on the police killing, but it was solved within a few days. The cop was on his way home from night duty with grass seed when he passed a hardware store at six A.M. He thought it was unusual that the night-light was out, so he peered through the glass doors. Inside were two average burglars. The cop drew a gun. The burglars had one. The policeman fired twice into the air. The robbers ran around inside, up and down aisles, looking for another way out. In panic, they couldn't find one. Around the corner, a police squad car was parked. Two patrolmen heard the shots, drew their guns, and came around the corner. As the burglars decided to brave their way through the front door, guns were firing from three directions.

The cop with the grass seed went down. The two men fled in an old car. As it passed over a canal bridge, one of them tossed the gun into the water. An informant snitched on the burglars. They were arrested, the gun was retrieved, and they denied that they shot the policeman. The only way in which we could work reader sympathy was to use large photos of four small children in nighties waiting for Daddy and the grass seed.

The Almodor murder appeared, on the other hand, to work its way up to a sensational story. Cops were all over Central Park interrogating wayward males. The mayor issued a warning to women not to walk in Central Park at night. A civic group demanded to know why the police made it safe for muggers and rapists to use the greenery. The police of the Arsenal precinct, some of whom still used horses, were pictured doing a cowboy act as they chased boys off baseball diamonds and routed whimpering lovers out of the glens.

The mortuary at Bellevue Hospital was a dismal red-brick structure. It seemed proper that, entering it from the street, one had to walk *down* stairs to get into the antiseptically tiled room where autopsies take place. A German martinet, Dr. Alexander O. Gettler, was the city toxicologist. He was addicted to blue serge suits, maroon ties, high laced black shoes, and a crew cut. He wore glittering pince-nez, sat at a rolltop desk, and insisted that his laboratory assistants ask permission before using any of the instruments. They had also to return them at day's end and acknowledge that the instruments had been "put back."

Gettler had an extraordinary interest in the Almodor murder. Had it been done with poisons rather than by strangulation, the case would have been within his purview. Something about it engaged his interest. He went to the mortuary to witness the autopsy. He stood apart from the green-gowned doctors who spoke into a microphone as they opened Mrs. Almodor from sternum to pelvis. The pathologists were curious. What brought Gettler to the autopsy of a young Puerto Rican woman? The case did not involve his department.

At the point when vaginal smears were made, Gettler asked for a slide. "Are you checking our work?" a doctor said. Gettler shook his head. "No," he said. "I have read about this woman and — oh, it's just an unsubstantiated feeling — I think she may have been eager to comply with her killer."

The pathologists stopped work. "Help yourself to a smear, doctor," one said. "You suspect what?"

"That she didn't resist. That she was eager to have sex with the murderer."

Most doctors respected Gettler, but looked upon him as eccentric. He had helped to solve several garish murders. His whim was to have a slide. He got it. His findings were surprising. The vaginal swab revealed a high sperm count, but it also yielded a rich female secretion, an indication that Mrs. Almodor drew considerable joy from the final act of her life. Back at his office, Gettler phoned the chief inspector. "If you can," he said, "I would like your men to get for me the trousers, shirt, jacket, shoes, and socks worn by Almodor the night his wife was killed." Headquarters too looked upon Gettler as an intellectual loon. No one quarreled with him.

Two detectives found Mr. Almodor sobbing with his mother-in-law. His grief was almost incoherent. He was a wire of a man, babbling in Spanish. The mother-in-law told the police they could not have the man's clothing; he had but one suit, one pair of shoes. One cop went out and, on 110th Street, bought brown slacks and a jacket in a used clothing store. He also returned with sneakers in the wrong size. Almodor was stripped to his underwear, a semicomic weeping figure. "Don't worry," they said, "we'll find the guy who did it."

Dr. Gettler, in the presence of assistants, turned down the trouser cuffs and vacuumed the jacket. The result was a very small pile of lint, grains of sand, dead leaves, and bits of grass. The old man seemed elated. He filed the components in separate folders. He asked the police department to pay for the services of a half-dozen qualified botanists for a month. The department refused. Gettler went to the mayor. The cops were ordered to comply. The toxicologist hired six professors from nearby colleges.

He told them nothing about the Almodor case. His dicta were always austere. All he said was, "I want some samples of sand, small leaves, and grass. The area will be, in general, all of New York City, northern New Jersey, and southern Connecticut. Wherever you go, take all three samples." He gave them the proper scientific terms for the type of sand, leaves, and grass. "If you can find all three in one place, come to me at once. If you can't, keep a precise record of every sample, the place where you got it, and its proper identification."

Gettler was into something not properly his business. After a month, he called the scientists in and reviewed their reports. Some of the samples were the right silicone, but the wrong grass or leaves. Others had the proper grass and, in two areas, the proper leaves. In no place did any of the men match all three samples. Gettler smiled. He was going to let them in on a secret. He ordered two big police cars and drove them to Central Park. He pointed to a rocky ravine. "Any of you try here?" No one had.

"I want each of you to take samples of soil, leaves, and grass." All three matched. It was, as Gettler pointed out at the Almodor trial, one chance in many thousands to make a perfect three-way match. It also answered the question why the young woman cooperated so heartily with her murderer.

The *Mirror* played the story, but the *Journal-American* fashioned it into a page-1 mystery which kept its readers in suspense. Almodor was convicted of first-degree murder.

It was not my story. I was still working the trial of the two burglars who shot the policeman. The defense was concluding its case. Harry was on the phone from Queens.

"What does ballistics show?" I said absently.

"What does what show?" he said.

"Ballistics," I said. "They recovered the bullet that killed the cop. Right?"

"Right. What does that have to do with it?"

"The shot, Harry, could have been fired by the two cops coming around the corner."

"What are you," Harry said, "a communist?"

"It seems strange to me," I said, "that if the shot came from the burglar's gun, which was found in a canal, that the prosecution would not present it as evidence. It also seems strange that two court-appointed attorneys who work with the police department are about to wrap up their case without discussing ballistics."

"Jim, gimme the city desk."

"Sure." I told the assistant city editor that I had asked Harry a proper question and he didn't want to answer. Selig Adler heard me out, and said: "Keep out of it. Give Harry to Pete DuBerg." The burglars were convicted of killing a policeman.

Reporters who spend more than two years covering a police department — or any civic or federal agency — find themselves working for the cops, or bureaucrats. Newspaper loyalty lapses into lassitude. Such reporters are seen in newsrooms only on payday. They not only appreciate the problems of officials, they adopt them. Some of our reporters began to speak like cops, out of the sides of their mouths, as their eyes roamed the city room and they clenched their hands under the tails of their overcoats. They knew policemen who accepted bribes, but they would not report them. They became accustomed to doing favors for lawyers and assistant district attorneys and, when they wanted a favor, they called in such "due bills." One installed a wall phone in the cellar of Bellevue Hospital and, whenever an accident case checked in, got the name and home address, ran to the cellar, and phoned a lawyer. He took his kickback until an acidulous young district attorney, Thomas E. Dewey, said: "You use that phone one more time and I'll indict you."

There was a radio columnist who would publish your name in 5½-point type on your birthday for five dollars. Even on *The New York Times* there were reporters who would accept a free meal, a free nightclub dinner-show, or a couple of tickets to the Garden fights in the right kind of situation. Columnists expected everything to be free. It was abhorrent, after an evening out, to get a check. One tabloid gossip columnist accepted payoffs in Chinese girls.

A contributing factor to venality was salary structure. In the late 1930s, I was the best-paid rewrite man on the *Mirror*; my paycheck was eighty-one dollars and fifty cents a week. A feature writer, Jimmy Whittaker, got a hundred, but only because Lait said that Whittaker could do anything, including rewriting the Bible in a page and a paragraph. Some reporters were earning forty dollars and glad to be working. Others, who had seniority, were getting sixty-five dollars. The scale was the same for most newspapers.

In the early days, there was no Newspaper Guild to protect the working stiff, who was fired at the whim of the editor. Frank Farley, an old man who wrote an innocuous political column, was fired by Arthur Brisbane for offending Tammany Hall in print. Farley said: "Do you realize that this is Christmas Eve, sir?"

Brisbane chuckled and held his belly. "By God," he said. "It *is* Christmas Eve. Farley, you're fired."

The baby became important to me. Virginia Lee, as a first child, had my affection. That is not what I intend to convey. Stated another way, I am not a man who will sit on the floor and romp with a little girl. But I became a man who sat on the floor with a little girl and her dolls. This had nothing to do with her beauty, which was remarkably blond, with curly hair and a candlelit smile. Her early overbite had charm. In sum, my love for Missy was effortless magnetism. It was also a diversion of dammed affection.

When she became two, I found that I was possessive. In the hours at home, I took her driving to the stores, staged adult conversations, took her to the cellar, where I had a workbench, and helped her to identify all the tools by name and use, discussed New York and journalism with her; in sum, I was desperately busy trying to evict Elinor and Maggy from the baby's heart. I wanted to be there first and alone. When I felt depressed, there was a feeling that the marriage would terminate abruptly. Bad dreams pursued me. The thought of ending the marriage was repugnant, repulsive, frightening. It was easy to make love to other women; it was impossible to love any of them. Elinor ... moon-face, brown eyes, jet straight Indian hair, a figure of a thousand roundnesses. Elinor ... small-town snob, Mommy's only girl, hiding the little demons which danced in her mind. Elinor ... smart dresser, jolly party girl, compulsive housekeeper, fearful Roman Catholic. Elinor... who selected friends as some people pick flowers... and who could snip them dead for a fancied effrontery... whose face I traced in the dark with brutal fingers.... Mine.

And so, more and more, I sought the love of Virginia Lee. It was a refuge, a solace, a wonderful world of wet kisses. It was at that time that I started to write letters to her, notes which would be read when she grew up and — who knows? — have a family of her own. All of them were written at the *Mirror* between editions; all weathered Elinor's scrutiny. They were too sugary, but they tried to convey a capsule of family life and world events.

November the 23rd

1 9 3 9

Dear Virginia Lee:

This is the first of a series of letters designed to reacquaint you, when you are fully grown, with assorted facts about yourself, our relatives and the news of these days. I had intended to start writing these letters a few months ago. But the new war brought so many writing duties that I felt that one extra effort would be too much.

And so I begin now, on a historic day. Normally, the last Thursday of each November is Thanksgiving Day. This year, it would normally fall on November 30th. But President Roosevelt seemed to feel that the 30th is too close to Christmas for business to get the full benefit of both holidays, and moved Thanksgiving up one full week.

We had dinner about 11:30 A.M. Nanny cooked it and it was delicious. As always, your mother fed you first, then ate with us. Afterward, she put a peasant dress on you, and sent you out front to play with your dolls (Hilda and Gretchen) and your baby carriage.

Earlier, I took some pictures of you in your nighties by the fireplace. I hung one of your stockings with walnuts in it. You are a good model. You posed willingly, cheerfully. Tonight at the office I developed the negatives. This year you will be our Christmas card.

Two days ago I had my thirty-second birthday and, with little gray hairs studding the sides of my head, I'm beginning to feel old. My ambition is to remain Dorian Gray young until you grow up and marry. If I can achieve that, I'll be happy. If not, do not feel sorry because I have had a great deal of happiness.

You talk, talk, talk, noting everything, even commenting when I put on a new tie. You stand on a toilet seat when I shave. Sitting in the window box, you mentioned that a lady across the street was cleaning her living room with a carpet sweeper. When Grandma and Grandpa Bishop arrived for a visit, you made a complete inspection of his new Nash car.

You are now two years and four months of age, a bit tall (38 inches) for your age. Your hair is a shade deeper than gold and it is your mother's delight that it is naturally curly so that she can "do anything" with it. When she twists a lock of hair around her finger, the curl remains long after the finger has been withdrawn. This pleases her. Me too.

I am at the office now. It is 8:06 P.M. and I'll probably leave here for Teaneck at 9:30, a half hour earlier than usual. I brought the car, which is good, because your father doesn't like the long subway ride to 167th Street and a long wait for the bus to New Jersey.

I'll write more soon. Love. Dad.

Two weeks later:

Dear Virginia Lee:

This has been a most discouraging week for the world. Finland, a nation of 3,000,000, was invaded by Soviet Russia in the air, by sea and on land. Tonight the Finns' lovely capital, Helsinki, casts a red glow over the northern sky. Demolition bombs have wrecked old buildings and have killed men and women and little girls like you.

I despair of mankind as I despair of myself. The great governments who aspire to manage the world are incompetent. Bullies prey on little boys. Often, they do not bother to invent an historic excuse. The phrase in use at the moment is "power politics."

Treachery is not new to history. Since 1938, at Munich, it has become popular, almost legitimate. The authoritarian figures — Hitler, Mussolini, Stalin and Tojo — take what they dare to take. The land mass of the Soviet Union at this time occupies one-sixth of our planet. Why it must subdue a small neighbor is beyond me.

It started when Russia asked for military and naval bases on Finnish soil. It would have been impossible for the Finns to agree without surrendering their sovereignty. The Finns declined. The conference, staged in Moscow, ended two weeks ago with the departure of the Finnish delegation. The Russians started mobilization of a massive and untried army, a small naval squadron in the Baltic, and an obsolete bomber fleet at Murmansk and Leningrad.

At the same time (typical of Soviet superiority in the field of propaganda) the Russian newspapers cried that Finland was threatening the Soviets. Helsinki wanted war. Finland was about to march on Leningrad. Above all, the Finns refused to reason. This, dear child, is like Mickey Mouse threatening King Kong.

Your dad has lots of time to read the Associated Press and United Press dispatches coming into the wire room. My newspaper doesn't use much of this copy, but there is no penalty attached to reading it. The Soviets massed on the Finnish border. The Russians demanded that the Finnish government resign. The Finns refused. The next demand was that the Finnish army retreat fifteen miles behind its own borders. This too was declined. Moscow announced that it wanted the world to know that it seeks nothing but peace. Russia abrogated its non-aggression pact with Finland, and handed the Finnish ambassador and his staff their passports.

This morning, Soviet planes bombed Helsinki. At dawn, Soviet brigades moved into Finland at three points. This evening, the Russian Baltic fleet is cruising the Gulf of Finland trying to find the small Finnish coastal gunboats.

All of which is a facet of the main theater of war. The German Army has destroyed Poland and rests on the Vistula. Britain and France have declared war on Germany, but their forces rest behind the Maginot Line and the Dutch and Belgian borders. A little girl has no interest in these matters, I know. When you grow up, you may want to know what the world of nations was like when you were chewing on a teething ring. The situation was bad, which is the common state.

More later, my love.   Dad.

December the 7th
1   9   3   9.

We had the accouterments of American middle life: house, car, mother-in-law, baby, debts. Something was missing. We needed a dog. The *Mirror*, in its warmer moments, ran a pet column. Not quite a column. It was a series of letters from readers responded to by a veterinarian named Dr. Irving Cohen. He was a small stout man guilty of nothing more reprehensible than noisy breathing. I asked him for a dog. The doc said he had one, but it was a hunting dog and required lots of space. I said I had lots of space.

He gave Duke of Amherst to me. This was a forty-five-pound springer spaniel. He was liver and white in irregular color and had long, floppy ears and dolorous eyes. Duke of Amherst appeared to be on the verge of tears even when his stubby tail was wagging. He was young, almost full-grown, and had been given to Doc Cohen by a trumpet player who was addicted to one-night stands of all kinds.

Elinor didn't like him. Maggy did. Virginia Lee exchanged kisses with him. My wife said he would track up her kitchen. I insisted that he was a good watchdog. We waited two weeks for the first woof. The hardware store sold me an unknottable chain fifteen feet long with a metal stake. Duke of Amherst spent considerable time in the yard woofing at the kitchen door. Missy and I taught him tricks. How to sit, how to speak, how to pee on a Chinese rug. Elinor's attack was sporadic. At times Duke won her favor. At others, she would say: "He's your dog, not mine. You want a dog — you take care of him." When times were stormy, Maggy hid the dog in her room.

One Saturday a new friend gave me an old rifle and I took Duke to the woods near the Englewood golf course. He was a hunting dog and all his instincts were for the hunt. I was not a hunting man. No matter what moved in the woods, I could not nerve myself to aim at it. However, they say it is important to get a springer spaniel acclimated to the sharp report of a gun. We traipsed the woods, I with the rifle under one arm, he trotting and pausing to sniff, or point, cocking his head. I aimed the gun at the sky and pulled the trigger. That dog had reflexes. Nothing has ever moved that fast from a standing start. He was about two-thirds his natural length as the strong rear half caught up with the front. Duke crashed into an elm, and paused only to shake his head. He didn't stop to save me from whatever caused the loud noise. He was rescuing number one.

He was exhausted on the front steps, six inches of tongue salivating on his front paw when I arrived. When he saw me, Duke cringed. I was the betrayer who tried to bust his eardrums. He frowned, turned away from petting and soothing words, and acted the sensible coward. There was no more hunting. My affinity for dogs was irreversible. Dr. Bernard Krull, my first friend in Teaneck, said that it was based on my desire to be obeyed. He liked Siamese cats. They were lazy and haughty and used expensive drapes for stretching and yawning. I enjoyed training dogs — not so much to teach tricks — but to help them to know the limits of the corral. No jumping up on beds or chairs, no animosity once guests were admitted to the house, no witless barking, no chewing of objects found on the floor, no conversion of premises to a bathroom. In only one instance was Duke allowed license. We had an old kitchen chair. He made it his. His frame was too large for the seat, but he fashioned himself in the style of a coffee ring and managed to stay up.

To Elinor, the dog was on probation. He remained in the house only because Maggy, Virginia Lee, and I loved him. One night when I came in, I was hanging my coat in the center hall closet and she said: "Your dog drinks, you know." I was accustomed to foul blows. It is difficult for me to replay this conversation correctly, but I know I didn't laugh. I said something indefensible, like: Dogs do not drink. She pressed the point. She had noticed that Duke slipped his collar now and then and disappeared. In spite of the weather (it was February), he always returned wet and shivering and, let it be said, red-eyed. At first, to hear her tell it, she paid little attention because, frankly, she didn't care if my dog caught pneumonia and dropped dead. However, she became curious.

She had smelled his breath and he had puffed his cheeks and burped in her face. A few days later, he had gone away. When he returned, she found that he couldn't get up on his kitchen chair. Duke had hiked three legs up, but when he tried, with monumental effort, to spring the fourth one up, he had gone over the other side and had skidded on his face on the floor. The thought of an alcoholic dog amused me. Still, I argued for sobriety.

She would not be persuaded. I promised that, on Saturday, I would sit in our car at the curb, she would release Duke in the backyard, I would watch him hop the fence, and follow. It was a waste of time, but it had to be done. On Saturday, I followed a half-block behind. He moved off in low gear, trotting on a bias, tongue lolling, paying no attention to the children who called his name. He moved easily through the shopping center on Cedar Lane and turned down a side street. He sat in front of Matt Moran's saloon. He woofed once. The door opened and he disappeared. It could not have been more incredible if the dog had produced an I.D. and a wallet.

I knew Matt. He was an aging ruddy face behind gold-rimmed spectacles, a man with three fingers and a missing sense of humor. The dog was standing at the bar; that is, his front paws were curled over the rim. He looked around at me and wagged his tail. "Your dog?" Moran said. I nodded. "Then you and him get the hell out of here." He filled a drink order for two barflies whose faces seemed to melt into the afternoon gloom. "Matt," I said, "the animal society could bust you for this." He turned to me slowly, and spread what was left of his fingers on the bar. "Jim," he said in the manner of a teacher running out of patience, "that dog has been blackmailing me for two months. If I had known he was yours, I'd have called you. He's a mean bastard, that mutt, and I'd appreciate it if you got out of here."

I ordered a beer. It required time to get the story. The barflies bought a couple of vodkas for the dog. I ordered a third, and Matt came back with one on the house. Originally, Duke of Amherst had found the saloon without help. As a hunting dog, he knew what he was hunting and, in wandering, had sniffed out Moran's place. When a customer opened the door, the dog had slipped in with him. As Moran recreated it, Duke had sniffed around the perimeter of the big room, under the shuffleboard game and along the edges of the jukebox. Then, as though he understood the ultimate quarry, he had bounded to the bar.

Standing with his forepaws on the rim, he must have been worth a chuckle to the customers. Matt said he paid no attention, until someone said: "I'll have a scotch and see what my friend with the long ears will have." The bartender cleaned out a glass ashtray and poured a drink. Duke sniffed, lapped it up straight, nosed the ashtray aside, and licked the ring underneath. This created great jollity for the afternoon trade. All of them learned a great deal about Duke within an hour. He could stand at the bar as long as anyone else. He would drink any alcoholic beverage straight, but would growl if it were diluted with soda. He was also fond of beer served in soup plates. When he departed, Matt recalled, the dog was considerably sloshed. No one knew who he was. He wore a leather collar and a license. Moran considered it a small one-day joke.

At noon the following day, Moran was tapping a fresh keg of beer when he heard barking. It had not occurred to him that a dog might have a hangover. The barking became monotonous. Duke could be seen sitting on the sidewalk, turning his throat to the sky and emitting lonesome sounds. Matt drew a pail of hot water. This is not recommended as a means of ridding oneself of hungover animals, but Matt opened the door, yelled "Scat!" and tossed the pail of water.

The dog was nimble. And irritated. He scurried to the opposite side of the street and barked in earnest. Moran was not a worrier, but he could become light-headed if anyone mentioned the state liquor authority. He was certain that some official was trying to revoke his license. So he tried the opposite tack. In apron, he went out on the sidewalk and tried to coax the dog indoors. He found it impossible to snap his fingers, so he made small cooing sounds. Duke of Amherst was suspicious. He cocked his head to listen.

Gingerly, he traversed the street, edging sideways toward Moran. The bartender drew him inside, slammed the door, called the animal ugly names, and drew a belt of gin. The stubby tail began to wag. This was followed by a second and a third. Fresh customers arrived, and Moran, as though divulging a state secret, told everybody about the drinking dog. In a moment, they were buying the drinks. Duke wasn't particular. When he could hardly hold his position at the bar, he left, trotting back home with, I would guess, a head full of strange images and noises.

Moran admitted the dog did not return every day. He was back often enough so that practically all of the customers were suckered into buying drinks. He was always homeward bound before dark, and he never arrived before noon. I explained the situation to Elinor, and she said the dog would have to go. I didn't think so. Drinking made him more endearing. The trumpeter on his one-night stands had found a way of keeping a puppy quiet in all those hotels. If man had made an alcoholic of the dog, I reasoned, then man should stand by him. She said no. The drinking we did was sinful enough, but we would not share with a neurotic dog. I told the story to my father. He was entranced. He had a solicitous attitude toward people who drank too much. Drinking in a dog was, in his ken, an almost human attribute. My mother sided with Elinor. "I wouldn't give him house room," she said.

I lost that fight. There was a farmer in Pike's County, Pennsylvania, who had four children. He would love to have a blooded hunting dog. The night before Duke left, I sat up with him before a fireplace, reading something into the blue and yellow flames, filling dessert dishes of Laird's Apple-jack for him and having a small one for myself. We had a long one-sided dialogue. I loved him; I would miss him; I betrayed him by not telling the farmer that he was a drinker.

The farmer's children met him and made a big fuss. As we got in the car to drive away, Duke of Amherst made hard lunges to return to us. The farmer held on to the leash. The dog tried to shake himself out of the collar. As the automobile turned away, he wasn't barking. It was a pitched shriek.

A few days later, I stopped in Moran's for a beer. "How come that dog always came home so wet?" I said.

He smiled. "I watched him. That mutt may have been timid on his way here, but he was a brave bull on the way home. A block up is Overpeck Creek. It's winter, Jim, but on the way back, he wouldn't use the bridge. He swam the ice floes."

There was a letter to Virginia Lee on January 18, 1941. It rambled through the usual family remembrances, then moved to a larger canvas:

If war is coming this way, there are few signs of it. President Roosevelt is building aircraft carriers, cruisers and heavy bombers. The size of our "defense forces" is augmented, but the president insists that we want peace. We are friendly, and more than friendly, to Great Britain and France. We keep a chip on our shoulder for Germany and our attitude toward the Soviet Union is sullen. If war is coming, I cannot see it. The Axis would have to draw us into a conflict. Strategically, this would be bad for Hitler and Mussolini.

The Teaneck Draft Board has reached my number, 601. On Monday I will file an eight-page questionnaire. If Dr. Krull is right, I will pass my physical without a problem. For the moment, they want to move me to Class III, able-bodied men with dependents. In a way, I am elated that my country is preparing for the worst while hoping for the best. A casual study of American history shows that, when war is imminent and inescapable, the United States usually needs about a year to put soldiers in the field.

Studying these yellowed letters, I learned with dismay that I did not write one about the attack on Pearl Harbor. One was dated December 28, 1941, and spoke of Christmas and the family.

Throughout the continental United States, aliens are being rounded up, patriotic songs are being written, dances and shows are being given for "Our Boys," marriage license bureaus are playing to standing room, mothers are weeping, pink-cheeked kids sheepishly stand inspection of the family in military uniforms, food profiteering has commenced, tires will be rationed, automobile production is down to a trickle, Wall Street appears to be hysterical, newspapers run scare headlines on poorly researched "higher authorities," factories are advertising Help Wanted, anyone who hints that we could lose this war is called a spy, military censorship is just beginning to assume power, the price of sugar is high, New York speaks of an impending air raid, blackout curtains are advertised by department stores, Japan is denounced as treacherous, reservists are being called up, World War I soldiers are learning to become plane spotters, harbor entrances have been mined, anti-aircraft guns are in New York City parks, housewives complain that the enemy is behind a counter at the corner grocery store.

Meditation is a special thing. I needed a place, a locked bedroom would do, and no sound more pressing than the indecipherable buzz of conversation in other rooms or the whine of the street. Usually, I sat on the side of a bed and studied my hands. Meditation is not daydreaming nor an assortment of random thoughts. In my case, it had to involve a decision of consequence. To reach it, I had to discipline myself to dwell on the several sides of whatever was involved, reflect, decide, and not be dissuaded from the decision.

I meditated about breaking the marriage. It was a cold afternoon in the first week of March, 1943. This was not done in anger. Elinor and I were in agreeable moods. This made it a better time for me to decide. The door was locked; I sat on the side of the bed; the hands twisted and clasped. For a moment I dwelled on suicide. This is easily translated into self-pity. There were ways, in the medicine chest. The thought was weighed, and discarded. I was interested in the future — mine.

The economics were bad. A separation might be possible if I could sell the house at a profit and get the three of them into a small apartment. Still, in my thoughts, I knew that none of this represented the ancillary problem. I could not live alone. I would not return to my parents (I could endure the questions, but not the silences). An empty room would depress me. On the other hand, it would not do to threaten Elinor with a separation. Her response would be to burst into tears and say: "Go. Who needs you?" Before I left the bedroom, I had memorized the structure of my hands and had come to the conclusion that I might depart, but I did not know when, or whether I had the courage.

By the time I got down to the living room, there was considerable excitement. Some neighborhood women were there, all able to function simultaneously as speakers and listeners. Missy, aged five, had engineered a burglary. She persuaded Barbara Ward and Billy House — larcenous chums — to rob the Meyer house. The Meyers were in New England visiting relatives. It was Virginia Lee who broke a cellar window with a rock. Risking shards, she had lowered herself into the cellar and unlocked the door for Billy and Barbara. Tiptoeing upstairs, they found a jar of pennies.

Missy and Barbara agreed to give these to Billy "because he can count." Outside, Billy refused to divide them and had run off to some Fagin at a corner store, who cashed them for candy.

Elinor was having a fit. "Your father," she intoned, "is going to beat the daylights out of you, you little vixen." It was astonishing how quickly I could be elected executioner. Some of the ladies remained, hoping to watch. I said no. Missy was fond of her coin savings, fond of counting and never spending any. I called a glazier to fix the cellar window, made Missy pay, and had her go to the Meyers when they returned and tell them how bad she was.

Within a few days, Elinor and I drove to Jersey City to see the Trewhellas. Doc had kept reassuring Elinor that she could become a mother as many times as she chose. We munched on cold cuts, drank wine, and played word games. In the middle of the game Art smiled at Elinor and said: "Who talks? You or me?"

She leaned over and kissed me on the cheek. "We're going to have a baby," she said.

I could feel my spirits sag. "When?"

"Oh, sometime in November." The meditation had been a waste.

The days were becoming spring-scented when the desk told me to take a story from Walter Marshall. He was a chubby, competent reporter who, for a reason no one understood, wrote under the name of Tony Mayfair. He was at the Waldorf-Astoria covering a press reception for Madame Chiang Kai-shek. The story was that her husband, the generalissimo, wanted one hundred and eighty million dollars more as a loan or grant. He and an American general, Joseph Stilwell, were fighting the Japanese on mainland China. Behind the story, the Pentagon was disappointed in Chiang because he was spending hundreds of millions in cash and weaponry to fight Chinese communist armies. He had sent his attractive, diminutive wife for more. It had become a successful ploy for distinguished foreigners to reach over the heads of Presidents and the Congress to win the sympathy of the people. This was especially apt if the borrowers detected diminished enthusiasm on the part of the American government.

I told Marshall that I would mention the hundred and eighty million, but, rather than write a straight news story, I hoped he would give me a word image of Madame, her entourage, and the setting in the Waldorf. The result was hardly a spot news story. I allowed it to run with color. It was atypical of *Daily Mirror* political stories, which would have preferred to publish this one briefly, with a charming photo of Madame. The lead:

"Madame Chiang Kai-Shek held her first New York press conference yesterday with 80 of our most callous inquisitors. The Madame kept them waiting twenty minutes. The Madame garroted their dancing pencils by asking not to be quoted directly. The Madame juggled prickly political questions without pricking her tiny fingers. In thirty minutes, the Madame had added eighty slaves to her American collection. . . ."

It was one of a half-dozen stories I wrote that day. Like the others, it was easily forgotten. Late the following morning, Frank Braucher, vice-president of Crowell-Collier, was riffling through the morning newspapers piled on his desk like a shuffled deck. Somehow his eye was drawn to the *Times* coverage of Madame Chiang Kai-shek. He read similar stories in the *Herald Tribune* and the *News*. By the time he reached the *Mirror*, which Braucher regarded as a rag with few pretensions to journalism, he was surprised at the amount of space given the story. It ran all the way down the side of page 3 and jumped to page 14.

He settled back and read it. He read it again. He called William Chenery, who had just retired as editor of *Collier's* and was now in a front office. Chenery was a graying man who maintained that the writing must be superior to the story. "Pick up a *Mirror*, Bill. Read a story on page three by a James A. Bishop and call me back." Braucher took shears and cut the story and folded it in his wallet. He phoned the new editor, a short Scot, Charles Colebaugh.

At lunch the clipping went to Colebaugh. The Scot liked the story. He was not overwhelmed. "A nice piece of writing," he said. He wanted to get to more important subjects: an editorial budget. *Collier's* had Quentin Reynolds in Great Britain, Martha Gellhorn with the Fifth Army, Ernest Hemingway about to leave Finca Vigia in Havana and join Eisenhower's forward elements when they invaded Europe, Frank Morris at Pearl Harbor, Frank Gervasi in the Middle East, William Hillman in Washington — the most aggressive group of spellbinders since the days of *Harper's* and the Civil War.

Braucher kept talking about the Bishop article. "When I was a young editor," he said, "we used to write little mash notes to kids like this to see if they were a flash in the pan."

Colebaugh nodded at the bar. "There's Charley McCabe. Why not ask him?"

McCabe was publisher of the *Mirror*. He was tall and slender, a pleasant fop seldom seen in the editorial department.

"Charley," said Braucher, "you have a reporter named James A. Bishop. Can you tell me anything about him?"

McCabe shook his head. "Bishop?" he said. "Never heard the name. You sure he's with us?"

"He wrote a story about Madame Chiang Kai-shek this morning."

"What's the matter with it?"

Braucher patted McCabe on the shoulder. "Nothing. Nothing," he said.

The two men — Colebaugh and Braucher — had an opportunity to discuss budget. The payment per article was liberal: four hundred dollars for one page, five hundred for a longer article. After acceptance of four articles, the price was hiked two hundred and fifty dollars. The top price was a thousand dollars per article plus expenses. The magazine had a steady circulation of 3,100,000. Its rival was *The Saturday Evening Post*, edited by Ben Hibbs. It too had a family of writers who kept returning to the readers once every six or eight weeks. The difference between them was twofold: the *Post* was a thicker magazine (heft is important to the reader), and *Collier's* had dropped from the use of forty-five-pound coated stock to thirty. Some of the fine color paintings bled through from one page to the next. *Collier's* maintained a higher standard of writing and a more liberal political attitude. The third weekly, *Liberty*, had been cheapened by editors who were more interested in how long it took to read an article

(3 min. 42 sec.) than in the quality of work. Bernarr Macfadden bought it from Joseph Medill Patterson, and, as Macfadden's editorial sights were no higher than his successful *True Story*, *Liberty* lost its dream, shortened its format, and bought a lot of material from Hollywood about movie stars.

A letter came to me from Colebaugh. It said something like: "I read your story on Madame Chiang Kai-shek. I thought it was well done. If you are in the neighborhood of 250 Park Avenue, please stop in. Sincerely . . ." I didn't go.

Bob Considine came in late. It was the middle of the afternoon. He had a desk in the sports department where he crossed his ant-eater legs sideways and rapped out a column called "On The Line." He was a magnificent mistake. We had a sports columnist, Dan Parker, who was competent, painfully honest, and amusing. The Hearst hierarchy recognized the talent of Considine, but didn't know where to put him. He was assigned to the *Mirror* sports department until someone could decide whether he was another all-purpose writer like Damon Runyon, or just a clever sportswriter like Jimmy Cannon.

He skidded around the corner, stared at me, and shouted: "You get in touch with Colebaugh? No? Why the hell not, you nut?" He leaned across my desk and whispered: "I think he wants to hire you." He fled to his desk. The words had the effect of cocaine. They lofted me off the seat, dizzied the head, and paralyzed concentration. Was he mistaken? Was this a loud joke? And what would *Collier's* want of me — a tabloid reporter?

An hour later Considine was back. He read his copy and gave it to a boy. "Listen," he said, "come next door with me. I'll buy you a drink." Selig Adler said okay. We went to Sam's. Considine was buying so I had scotch. He asked if an editor had written to me. I said yes. Why hadn't I got in touch? I saw no need for it. What, I asked, did he know about it? He had written a book about the Doolittle raid over Tokyo with a Captain Lawson. The book would be published in three months and he wanted to sell first serial rights. The story represented America's first, somewhat puny, victory over the Japanese and was called *Thirty Seconds over Tokyo*. Specially rigged B-25 twin-engine bombers had taken off from an aircraft carrier near Japan, had flown over Tokyo and Magoya, and dropped their explosives, to the astonishment of the Japanese Imperial Command. They had — some of them — continued west to mainland China. Lawson made it. Some were killed. Some were captured. President Roosevelt said the bombers had come from Shangri-La.

Colebaugh had offered Considine seventy-five hundred dollars for a condensation of three parts. In the conversation which followed, Charles Colebaugh said he had been impressed by a story written by Bishop — had written a note to him, in fact — but had had no response. One of the virtues of Considine (fortunately unknown to Colebaugh) was that his response would have been the same no matter what writer was mentioned.

"Bishop?" he said. "You're only talking about the best writer we have on the paper."

I phoned Colebaugh. The voice on the phone was that of Miss Weed, his secretary. I would be welcome to stop over any morning for a cup of coffee. An appointment would not be necessary. I was afraid to go. Always I was conscious of the fact that I was independent in the wrong way, and stubborn in opinions. Elinor advised against it: "You have a good job. Why take a chance?" She had no notion that, in my eyes, if I moved to *Collier's* magazine, the jump would represent the difference between drifting on a raft and sailing in a suite on the *Queen Mary*.

I pressed a gray herringbone suit, polished my black shoes, wore a subdued tie, and went. The lobby directory carried the names of editors. I was impressed. A receptionist showed me to Miss Weed, a handsome, tall young woman who wore a two-piece tawny suit with pleated skirt and gleaming shoes the color of baked beans. She showed me to an office with a deep pile rug and a short man with a friendly grin. He ordered coffee. I realized that, if I played the conversation safe, I would respond to questions with brief sentences. In effect, it would not be a chat; rather, more like an interrogation. So, with trepidation, I played alert. Mr. Colebaugh had a lot of questions. My parents, church, our lineage, my favorite writers and why, my knowledge of the war, the Congress, new weapons, and American history.

I hit a rock when he asked: "What do you think of H.R. 1135?" (Or some such number.) I gulped. "Mr Colebaugh," I said, "I haven't the remotest . . ." He made a mark on a foolscap pad. "Ah," I said, " a minus for that." The grin turned up. "To the contrary. You get a plus for honesty, Mr. Bishop. The bill is for additional lend-lease for Great Britain and the Soviet Union." We spoke some more. He touched on so many diversified targets that, when I left, I could not remember them. He was reaching inside my head. He wanted to know how long I had been on the *Mirror*. Thirteen years. Was I happy? Not quite. My primary interest was studying writing. He had no room for a writer, but he might find space for an editor. Did I think I could edit copy without bruising it? Yes, I did.

He asked me to return. I did. Three times. At last came the word: "Mr. Bishop. I think that, with patience, you will make a good associate editor. We need an articles man, one with a special knowledge of war, strategy, weapons, tactics. You understand cablese?" I nodded. It was a lie. My tongue went to the roof. It stuck dry. "Yes sir," I managed to say. "I would like to give the *Mirror* two weeks' —"

"Of course. The position pays seven thousand five hundred to start. Is that agreeable?"

I thought he might be joking. "Mr. Colebaugh," I said. "It's — it sure is fine."

"In two weeks?" He stood with hand extended.

The distance between Second Avenue and Park Avenue is small. The difference in work was enormous. *Collier's* was dignified, urbane, unhurried, eclectic. I was in a small, half-glassed office with Herbert Asbury, an old-time writer. He was grumpy, aloof, a man inclined to exhibit his past books like a string of credit cards. It was not that he didn't like me, or wasn't willing to help a neophyte. He seemed fearful that I wouldn't remember that he had written *The Barbary Coast* and other books. He was short and pudgy, a well-dressed man with dark wavy hair and an appreciation of dry martinis. His mood, after lunch, was more amiable than in the morning.

On the first day, Frank Braucher introduced himself. I had no idea who he was, or what he had done for me. "When I like a guy," he said, looking around, "I like to put him in a fishbowl." He sat and chatted for a half-hour. When he left, Asbury growled: "He's vice-president of Crowell-Collier. If I were you, I wouldn't get too friendly."

Walter Davenport, a pixie, stopped by. He had once been a rewrite man on the *American*. He and I had many whistle stops to cover and a great deal of laughter. A gray-skinned, serious man introduced himself as Joe Alex Morris, managing editor. His wife, I learned, was dying of cancer. Over his office door was a sign: "Please don't mention it." A tall, clever man, William O. Chessman, was art director. I visited his office because I was interested in layouts. We became understanding friends. A tiny roly-poly, Ulrich Calvosa, was picture editor. He and our star writer, Quentin Reynolds, had attended college together.

I was in over my head. Editors spent considerable time chatting with each other. Denver Lindley, the fiction editor, looked like Abraham Lincoln. His assistant, Allen Marple, wrote books about writing. The absence of noise stunned me. I shared a secretary with Asbury. She was short, married to a cop on horseback. Somehow, she found that my father was a retired policeman. Without condescension, she spent time explaining how to do things the *Collier's* way.

On the second morning, Chessman brought a two-page layout into my office. It showed closeups of Pius XII trying to calm hysterical crowds of Italians as the Americans bombed Rome's railroad yards. Chessman placed the big bristol boards on my desk. He said I would write a master caption, which would explain the bombing, the targets, and the fact that the Pope seldom leaves the Vatican. Then, under each photo, I was expected to explain it, using every bit of space so that the type, in all cases, fit snugly.

I was careful. I was precise. I tried to think of sentences — not gratuitous ones — which would fill out the spaces exactly. I perspired over that first assignment. Chessman told me that when it was finished, it should go directly to Colebaugh. At three P.M. it was on his desk. He adjusted his glasses. "Mr. Bishop," he said, "is this the layout I gave to Mr. Chessman this morning?" I said yes. "Then what is the problem?" I pointed to the sheets of copy. "Those are the captions," I said.

At four he called me into his office. It was the first time he laughed. "I wish I could find fault with it," he said. "It's good work. Mr. Bishop, we average a minimum of three to four days of work for a layout like this. I am not going to pay you for speed."

For years I had been working on deadlines in which the average elapsed time was ninety minutes. I was geared for ninety minutes. All of us, on newspapers, had long ago learned to do our best in that span. It was as though, with baseball players, one strike were out. We took a sharp swing at the pitch and hoped to hit. There was nothing superficial about our work. We were trained to think our best and write our best in the tick of a clock. Slowing the process would not bring better work. Additional thought might induce wordy, specious copy. "I'll do my best," I said, and left. At the bottom of the main caption, Colebaugh wrote: "by James A. Bishop."

It was witless to have so much fresh money and not incur debt. We sold our $5,990 house in Teaneck for $7,000 and bought a big one in Haworth for $10,000 on an acre of woodland. Those who seldom knew where the next bottle of gin was coming from now had a checkbook in pages of three with their names printed on each one. Elinor, whose mathematical skills were slender, kept writing checks until Frank Weber phoned to ask if we knew how many times we had been overdrawn. "I'm sure," he said, "that writers are dumb about money, but why do they have to marry Zeldas?"

The house was white, a porchy, roomy place with starchy pin oaks as sentinels. Behind the house was a brook and, farther back, a toolshed. Haworth had a population of a few thousand, spaced far enough apart so that citizens barely nodded at each other. Elinor was in advanced pregnancy as the summer of 1943 faded. She was given to flights of industry — whirling mops and dustpans, curtain rods and drapes — and tears. She would cry without sound. Sparkling tears stood on the lower lids, the lip trembled, a lightning bolt of wetness stained her face. She seldom knew why she cried. She had been enthusiastic about the new house. The mood changed: "Look around. You've got me out in the woods."

Our little girl was six, spindly, pretty, one who fell off bicycles, roller skated, punched a boy, tried hard to win the approval of her mother, and settled for the bosom of Maggy. Elinor would not use a Haworth doctor, or even one from Teaneck. At each examination time, we traveled to Dr. Trewhella in Jersey City. In a way, Elinor was almost instinctive; if she felt at ease with someone or something, she could not be dissuaded or persuaded. Conversely, the merits of another doctor, or another banker, or butcher, were given a blank stare. At this time, her contempt for my mother began to flower again. "She's cold," Elinor said. The word, to the Irish, meant unfeeling, callous. "How is she cold?" I said. Elinor said my mother spoke loosely of death, that she was prone to say that when God was ready to call her, she would be ready. I couldn't see why sublime faith would classify anyone as cold. I said I wished I had it. Decent people, Elinor said, didn't discuss death. She and Maggy were abnormally fearful of illness and death. Hospitals were not places where people went to get well. Funeral services were the painful penance of the living. Doctors always found that the patient was far worse than expected.

Our circle of friends became smaller. We were in a house big enough to invite guests for a weekend. "Not in my condition," Elinor said, and it was a valid point. We visited her cousin Agnes and the three growing children in a small, hot flat on West Side Avenue in Jersey City. That summer, Agnes married Frank Westphal, an electrician, a burly, quiet man who had approached his middle years as a bachelor. He was what they referred to as a "steady" man. Westphal was more than that. He was the scion of an old-fashioned German family, the kind who save small sums, paint the porch, and knotty-pine the cellar. Agnes, approaching middle age, said she was going to try to have his baby because he deserved to have one of his own.

Cousin Agnes was important to Elinor and Maggy. She was Bridget's daughter, a part of the Y-shaped umbilical cord emanating from Maggy. She was older than Elinor, a skinny, energetic, loud-talking, excitable woman. She had been adolescent when she met and married a good-looking gum-chewing cynic whose best moments were spent at a saloon piano singing "That Old Gang of Mine." They were content until after the children began to grow. Whatever the strains, I did not ask, but Agnes left him and worked hard in spice factories to keep the children fed. It seemed good that she had met a "steady" man and had remarried.

Came a gorgeous day in November, a remission of a forgotten summer. After lunch I asked a secretary to place some manuscripts in my briefcase. There was no work on my desk. Editors were expected, now and then, to take manuscripts home, read them, tap out opinions, and, if they held promise, forward them to Miss Weed. If they were to be rejected, they were returned to the "slush-pile editor."

Coming up Maple Drive in Haworth, I had the feeling that Maggy was in a window waving hello. She wasn't waving hello. She was there, but the expression was frantic. Elinor must have fallen. Inside, it was as though my wife expected me to be home early. She was in sporadic pain. I asked how frequently. She thought about every four minutes. That indeed was a drive. The police of half a dozen Jersey towns should have targeted my car. I asked Maggy, as we rushed out of the house, to please have Dr. Trewhella at Margaret Hague Maternity Hospital. If he was not there, my wife would make a scene; she would not accept the ministrations of anyone else.

Prayer has always been more important to me than attendance at church. I prayed hard. Between spasms, Elinor asked me not to drive so fast. Tonnelle Avenue is a long, dismal road flanking a swamp between

Bergen County and Hudson. It is used by slow, heavily-laden trucks snorting black smoke through vertical pipes. I managed to run between those going in my direction and those blinking their lights and tapping their Klaxons coming the other way. I parked at the hospital where it says "No Parking." Magically, Trewhella was waiting, his stethoscope loose around his neck. As a nurse assisted Elinor, I tried to explain pains, type, duration, frequency. He burst into laughter. "Who's having this baby?" It was typical of me, trying to explain someone else to a third party.

In the solarium, I grabbed a handful of magazines, braced for the long siege. Three men sat about, crossing and uncrossing their legs. There was a scimitar of rouge from a late sun over the rooftops. I had the impression that the eyes of the others were open and unseeing. I ran down the table of contents of the first magazine without understanding anything. A nurse appeared in the doorway. "Mr. Bishop?" Everybody looked up. She said that I was the father of a baby girl. I told her she had the wrong man, that we had arrived only a half-hour ago. "I know," she said, wrinkling the nose. "Close. Very close. It's a healthy little premie, about six pounds. Mrs. Bishop is doing fine. If you wish, you may see her sometime tonight."

"Both healthy?" I said. She nodded. I departed, wondering why I had not wished for a boy.

I walked down the hill of Montgomery Street slowly. There was no ecstasy; it was a sudden lifting of depression. I phoned Maggy ("Oh, thanks be to God! Thanks be to God!") and Virginia Lee ("I know, I know. It's a baby sister. What's her name? When she gets home, can I hold her?") and my father ("Now that's good news indeed. You say both are okay? Very good. Now don't stop anywhere on your way home — know what I mean?").

The slow aimless walk was good. My head was sorting its notions. The door had just slammed on a separation. As I would not leave her with one child, never, never with two. There was an additional point. I did not trust Elinor as a mother. She had strong maternal instincts, and she kept Missy immaculate. She felt that love and proper care were sufficient. But, in the presence of the child she revealed her abnormal fear of death, her distrust of doctors ("expensive butchers"), her belief in omens and signs, her dread of thunder and lightning, her quick and complete condemnation of those who affronted her, her backbiting before the lavish welcome to the house, her certainty that it was more important for girls to be pretty than to be intelligent, her whispered "Now don't tell Daddy," her portrait of God as an omniscient being of wrath and vengeance, her fear of a knock on the front door, her obvious lies to friends on the phone.

The girl I married, the one I loved above all, was backpedaling furiously. That, or I had an illusion that I was pedaling forward too fast. It was more than looks that drew me to Elinor. She had a bright, alert mind and, in the nine months we had dated, I felt that I got to know her better than if we had shared a bed. Her interest had encompassed a broad spectrum, and, most certainly, she was anxious to understand the work of a cub reporter. Was being a reporter the end of a career, or the beginning? If he was "ambitious," where could he go? What made me think I could write professionally and, even if I could, what would I write about?

What had happened? The spate of disagreements was a symptom, not a disease. Were we, after thirteen years, mismatched? At one time I suggested that we try the services of a psychiatrist. The result was fury. "You may be nuts, Jim. But not me. There is something definitely wrong with you. But if you think, for one minute, that you're going to take me to one of those crackpots to tell him about my dreams and my sex life, you're crazier than I think you are. You may be surprised to find out that some of your dearest friends think you're a little off the beam."

I walked and walked. It was dark. A cold breeze flicked the face. I loved this city. Jersey City and Hoboken had been vaudeville jokes. Turning right on Jersey Avenue, past the huge library which looked like a stone fortress, I walked up Grand Street. Every street had a sharp boyhood memory. Here, I had hitched rides on the backs of trucks. There, I had stolen metal and sold it for three cents a pound. Once, at a turn in the tracks, I had placed a big bolt on the inner track and stood a half-block away to watch a trolley derail and go halfway across the street toward some shops.

I swam nude off rocks at the foot of Cummunipaw, recited doggerel in the Tivoli Theatre on amateur night, played kissing games at house parties on Clerk Street, rode a bicycle to the Bond Baking Company to buy cheap, day-old bread, lugged big cardboard boxes onto tube trains, boxes full of arm garters on which my mother sewed fake rosettes at a penny apiece, discussed the politics of Frank Hague with other boys because politics was to boys here what baseball was in other towns, masturbated in the matinees at movies featuring Aileen Pringle and Mae Murray and Constance Bennett and Mae Marsh and Mabel Normand and Pola Negri.

Walking, I knew the men with their heavy shoes and the jackets pinned at the throat, homeward bound, head down. I knew the women with their dark shawls and milk cans on their arms. I knew the girls who skipped because their legs were cold. And the growing boys, jogging in sweatshirts, as sure of themselves as their kin were unsure. I knew the smooth faces of the Belgian cobblestones, the sighing overworked buses, the streetlamps where once there had been mantles and a lamplighter.

Somewhere, I had a cup of coffee and a doughnut. In the evening, I returned to the hospital. Elinor was fatigued, a pale face without makeup on a pillow, but in good spirits. Had I seen the baby? Not yet. Out in the corridor, the nurses displayed them behind glass, precious hairy prunes. Ours had black hair. She was small, but had electrifying legs. I could not hear the protest, but the distortion of the gummy mouth was eloquent. I asked Elinor how we would name her. Well, she said, after her mother.

I said no. Margaret was not what I had in mind. She agreed. "I'd like to please Momma, but Margaret is not it."

"Neither is Jenny," I said. She had no idea of naming her baby after my mother. She thought Gay would be a lovely name. "These are modern times," she said. "Let's have a modern name." We were killing time in the hospital. "How about Gail?" she said brightly. "Gail with a *y* and an *e*." I agreed. "Let's get Momma in there. "Gayle Margaret."

I countered with "How about Gayle Peggy?" It was agreed.

Incredibly bright describes the world at *Collier's* magazine. Every aspect of it was beyond my imagining. I had lunch with the best bookish and frumpy literary agents. Authors whose work I had admired now sat in my office discussing articles to be written. I bought a piece from a blind writer who had written poignantly about his Seeing Eye dog: "My Eyes Have a Cold Nose." Colebaugh expected me to be an editor-writer. Other editors would sit in judgment on each article. If it was accepted, I got five hundred dollars extra. If not, I received two hundred and fifty. After four acceptances, Colebaugh said, I should remind Miss Weed to jack my price to seven hundred and fifty. It was a heady, dizzying world in which integrity was important.

The first test occurred when a cabled article arrived from Quentin Reynolds about PT boats. These were small swift craft, armed with machine guns and torpedo tubes. Whatever their tactical value, they were a disappointment in some theaters of war. Navy Lieutenant Roger Straus, Jr., told me that *The Saturday Evening Post* was planning an article about PT boats from a correspondent in the Far Pacific. Straus and Lieutenant Alan Jackson were in charge of navy public relations at 90 Church Street. Jackson, a former editor at *The Saturday Evening Post*, pushed navy material toward all magazine editors. He assigned Straus to keep a special eye on *Collier's*. He felt that we were giving too much prominence to the air force and the army. Whatever the scheme, Straus and I became friends.

I read the Reynolds article with dismay. As it was the first one about PT boats, I expected that it would technically describe these feathery splinters, and detail some battle action. It consisted of a first-person story about Reynolds, how he got into a PT boat in Africa and became seasick on the way to Gela, Sicily. Declining it, I was on dangerous ground. Reynolds was the *star* writer; whenever he wrote an article, it was featured on the cover. Besides, Colebaugh read articles by the house writers before they came to me. This meant that he approved.

I did considerable thinking and heavy breathing. Herb Asbury was dreaming over some copy. I asked what an editor should do. "Kill it," he said, without looking up. No, that wouldn't do. The article looked like elephant toilet tissue as I took the long sheets of cablese to Colebaugh's office. I asked him if he had read it, which was foolish. "Yes, Mr. Bishop," he said. "A pretty good article. Is there something you want to say?" I said yes, sir, indeed there was. I had gone over the copy and it was not, properly, a magazine article about PT boats. It was an account of Reynolds's becoming seasick. The *Post*, I told him, had an article from Guadalcanal about PT's. There was silence and I died. Colebaugh looked up, placed his glasses on properly, and looked up at me. "Bad?" he said. "Give it to Miss Weed and tell her to put it in the dead file."

"Sir," I said, "Wouldn't you like to read it again — ?" The eyes fell away toward the desk. "The dead file," he said. "I assumed when I hired you that you were literate." It was not a feather of victory, but rather a lesson in fundamental ethics. Months later, when Reynolds returned, he charged into my office, a big, jowly, usually jolly person, demanding to know why I had killed his article. "Do you know," he said, "that as long as I've been here, that's the first piece killed?" He had an engaging baritone voice and it could be heard over the glass partitions. "Who the hell do you think you are?"

There was a similar scene with Martha Gellhorn. The biggest problem for our war correspondents was to fashion an article that would "keep" a month. In an emergency situation, we could edit an article and see it published within three weeks, but this would entail killing something ready for the presses and filling that space precisely. I sympathized with the writers, but I could not abide windy copy.

Miss Gellhorn, who was married to Ernest Hemingway, sent a story from somewhere near Foggia, Italy. Her lead spoke of nude Poles bathing in the Adriatic. I killed the lead and picked up the copy where it spoke vividly of war and battle. To me, it seemed that, when she returned to New York, she tried to intimidate me. She shouted that nobody was going to kill her leads. She worked hard to get one, and how dare I lop it off. I had little patience with her. "Sorry," I said. "It was done with your interest at heart as well as the magazine's. Tell it to Mr. Colebaugh."

"Don't worry," she shouted. "I'm going there now."

The third undiplomatic move occurred with Ernest Hemingway. He was in France with a forward unit, but I suspect that he was drunk when he rapped out four thousand words for us. The sentences wandered, almost singsong, about censors and censorship, became coherent in places, and then fell apart again. This man was my early hero. I tried to rehook the sections which regaled readers with his machismo; how he slept on a stony cot with a .45 under the mattress; how he warned American units to stick to the road, that the Krauts had mined the fields; how he drank wine with the Free French and told them he would meet them at the George V in Paris. It wouldn't hook. I was becoming a dangerous editor in my estimation as I took that one to Colebaugh. He glanced up briefly, smiled, and said: "Miss Weed. Dead file."

It was with a degree of shame that I realized I had never traveled. Once, I had been to Miami. From New York, I had gone to Washington a couple of times. That was it. Now, depending upon the urgency, I could travel anywhere at company expense. The air force flew me to Dayton, Ohio, to write an article called "D-Day's Back Room." Lieutenant Straus thought that I should go to Bermuda to do an article on our new naval base. The Churchill government had leased several bases to the United States in exchange for fifty old destroyers. Now, Straus pointed out, some writers were claiming America had been swindled. The Bermuda base was under water.

The island is a nineteen-mile fishhook of coral. A tomato-faced sundowner, Admiral Souell, ran the base. Seeing me made him miserable. A small task force in the eastern Atlantic had captured the first German U-boat and was towing it to Bermuda at two knots. Code books and gear were intact. Also, a squadron of destroyers was due in the morning. A commander of one was Franklin D. Roosevelt, Jr., and Souell had been telling his staff that if Roosevelt so much as touched a reef on the way into port, he would be drawn, quartered, and beached, no matter who his old man was. The admiral did not want the press present for either event.

The destroyers arrived slowly, like proud gray ducks. Roosevelt was third in line and didn't scrape a barnacle. Two days later, tugs warped a half-awash U-boat into Hamilton harbor and Souell leaned across his desk and shouted: "Mistuh Bishop, you don't see nothin'; you never saw nuthin' here, and if you so much as even tell Mrs. Bishop you did, I'm gonna make a special trip to New York to take you apart." Ironically, until I was warned, I had not noticed the familiar conning tower of a U-boat. It was a great story, but not the one I wanted.

Bermuda was administered by bankers and landed gentry called "The Forty Thieves." They granted spot mortgages to the poor. Such debts may be called in overnight, and in full. They were called only when the poor and Blacks refused to vote for one of the Forty Thieves for public office. The colony was a semiprivate fief, with plenty of warm sun, private coves for beach parties under black cliffs, and lovely restaurants where the young naval officers chased war widows.

In the evening, we sat on cool verandas sipping stingers and telling the Black servants to make the steaks medium and go lightly on the garlic in the salad. Souell invited us over to his place one night and I learned the excellent military posture of his aides: every one of them could cook. They looked strange, in tropical whites, whirling in and out of the dining room with steaming platters and iced drinks. Once, we stopped off at bachelor officers' quarters — a lovely hotel at bayside — in time to see the pilot of a patrol bomber tell an American submarine crew how he "almost" got a U-boat. He caught the enemy on the surface and straddled the craft with bombs before the submarine disappeared under the sea. The pilot was a tall man, fond of executing graceful sweeps and dives with his hands. The submarine commander was interested. He asked what day, what hour, what position. Then he hauled off, almost to the floor, and caught the pilot under the chin.

Glasses and bottles skidded drunkenly. The submarine officers pitched into the air officers. It was their goddamn submarine, they shouted. Didn't the bombers have charts showing the precise channel for American submarines? Didn't the flyboys know a friendly when they saw one? The submarine skipper said the aerial nuts almost sank his craft, jarred the batteries off their housing, doused the lights, and made an emergency crash dive necessary. The executive officer of B.O.Q. pulled the combatants apart. Fortunately, everyone later agreed that the scene did not take place. The pilot and crew chipped in to replace the broken glasses and bottles, at twenty-five cents a drink.

The material in the article depicted the Forty Thieves as greedy and unpatriotic. I asked them to have someone in New York in a week to study the article. If there were provable errors, I would correct them. They sent a nervous Briton to my office two days before deadline. He read the article and appeared to be perspiring and dizzy. He would not correct anything — all of it, he said, was too horrible to contemplate. When it was published, the island parliament staged an angry row, members blaming each other for not shepherding the American properly. Bermuda became the first of several colonies and nations to which I would be invited not to return.

The Easter-egg figure of Francis Cardinal Spellman appeared in the office. As chief of chaplains, he had spent several Christmases abroad with "the boys." Colebaugh bought the serial rights to a book written by His Eminence. My function was to cut it into three parts. Spellman was a gentle pusher. He pushed himself into prominence in the College of Cardinals in Rome by sending more money than the others. His "in" with Pius XII was deep and personal. When Spellman had been consecrated a bishop, Eugenio Cardinal Pacelli had insisted that the young American wear his robes. There was no one, not even a member of the Vatican secretariat, who could reach into the innermost chamber as quickly, as deftly, and get as many favors.

Spellman fancied himself as an American Richelieu. He had avenues to Franklin Roosevelt, got himself invited to dinner at the White House frequently, and could ask favors there too. The manuscript he had written was hardly professional, but Colebaugh, an Epicopalian, bought it. The money — all of it — was to go to the Foundling Hospital, less 10 percent for Gertrude Algase, a literary agent. Miss Algase ordered me not to cut the imperishable prose of His Eminence. In that case, I said, she might take it to another editor. She got a ruling from Colebaugh, who said lamely: "Bishop is Catholic. He's the editor. Whatever he does will be with deference to the cardinal."

Whenever I cut a section, I sent it by hand to the "powerhouse," which is what we called the archiepiscopal residence on Madison Avenue. No protest came from the cardinal. Miss Algase, however, gave an imitation of a maiden on the verge of rape. At one point she shouted and slammed her little fist on my desk. "The cardinal," I said, "has not written the

Bible. Reading it, I doubt that he was inspired by the Holy Spirit, and that's whose help I'm getting in tearing it down."

My life was a succession of rhapsodic dreams. I was doing more important work than I thought would ever become my lot. Frank Braucher told me that Colebaugh said I was the best young editor he knew, and that he appreciated the way in which I researched material before I wrote articles. No one had ever told me that I was good at anything. A few authors who were selling books to *Collier's* asked if I could be assigned to the projects. One flattered me by inscribing his book: "What do you say to a guy who cuts your book — your baby — so that you don't know where the cuts were? . . ." Now and then, to balance the act, I would stub my editorial toe.

I found an illiterate Italian painter who was given a one-man show on Madison Avenue. He lived with his mother in a ratty flat in the Village. Joe Gatto was very short and had black hair. He painted lions and tigers. A few interviews showed that all his life Joe Gatto had been a plumber's assistant. He had never married, never dated a girl, never spent more than the thirty-five cents it cost to attend an afternoon movie. Mother was all. In the cold weather, he had few pipes to sweat or seal. He bought canvases and some pigments.

His jungle scenes seemed to me the product of a nine-year-old mind. He squeezed paint on a brush, then slapped it on the canvas without stroking. His lions and tigers were out of perspective, his jungle grasses could be read in Braille. A press agent found Gatto and promoted him as "America's Number One Primitive." On Madison Avenue, the rich were buying his junk for fifteen hundred and three thousand dollars. I wrote an article for *Collier's* entitled: "This Painter Says Pitcha." It was bad, neither funny nor edifying. It made Gatto look like an aborigine, and it painted the agent as a sleek character who could promote vasectomies in monasteries.

Somewhere in that first year, I changed my by-line from "James A. Bishop" to "Jim Bishop." The change is obvious in the clippings. It is a small matter. I never liked James. I heard it only from teachers and persons in authority. Usually, the Christian name was a preliminary punctuation mark, the opening of a critique. On the other hand, whenever I was in Charles Colebaugh's office, no matter how well we got to know each other, I was "Mr. Bishop."

To me, Lieutenant Straus was Rog. The navy articles and article ideas he brought to me required clearance of copy at the Pentagon. They red-penciled some material which I thought picayune. At other times, the censor, a four-striper who lived on dry martinis, would pass material which I would have guessed should remain secret.

New York City was in a deep dimout as I worked over an article about the Battle of Midway. How Admirals Jack Fletcher and Raymond Spruance managed to find the four Japanese carriers was still a secret, but the heroism of Torpedo Squadron Eight was not. The art department had beautiful color paintings of the carrier action. It constituted an extensive story of the greatest naval battle in the Pacific and, as America was short of decisive victories, we were anxious to go to press with it. The article was published on a Friday. On Monday morning, Joe Alex Morris peeked into my office and said: "Brace yourself."

There were two admirals, four captains, and a commander. In cold, unfriendly terms they asked who had censored the paintings. I looked at the magazine held before me. I had forgotten to have the painting — or copies — sent to Washington. Being dressed down was not new to me. It had happened before. These men acted as though I might be a spy. Herbert Asbury picked up his spectacles and left the office. I asked what was wrong. A captain pointed to a carrier being refueled at sea. "Where," he said, "did you learn about these new rotating valves?" I looked. I didn't know what he was talking about. He kept pointing to the couplings. "We didn't know about them," he said archly, "until we got a call from Admiral Morreell in BuShips Friday."

I apologized. Through the glass, I could see Colebaugh, grinning. I was sorry. The paintings had slipped my mind. "How did you find out about the valves?" That was different. We had an English artist, a timid man who wore a black derby winter and summer, who lived on Staten Island. He had executed the paintings. They insisted that I phone him at once. Bring him to the office. They would return in an hour.

There is no doubt that I was frightened. They hadn't even called Straus to find out where I got the article. It was the paintings. The artist arrived, saw the group, and seemed to totter. They hit him hard and rapidly. When the air cleared, it seemed that the artist lived on a promontory over the Narrows. All the great ships passed under his nose on their way to and from the Brooklyn Navy Yard. He studied all of them with binoculars, to make certain that details on carriers, cruisers, battleships, and destroyers were exact. He had seen the swivel couplings and, not realizing that they were secret and currently being used for high-speed refueling, had sketched them.

The navy brass ordered him to go home and copy no more. They ordered him never to look at the Narrows. One more violation of the secrecy act and he would be jailed. Me too. Toward noon, they let up a little and said they wouldn't have been so harsh except that the Bureau of Ships was in a frenzy over the paintings.

Straus was glad I hadn't mentioned his name. He had not made the mistake, and played no part in it except to get an excellent article for us. Still, he told me how easy it would have been for those men to have transferred him out of 90 Church Street to the damp edges of the Aleutians. He said he had a book for me. Had I thought of writing a book? I had, many times. Would I? Sure I would. He had a publisher, and the publisher had a character in search of an author. I wasn't an author, but I could pretend to be one. Or sound like one.

The editor was LeBaron Barker, a tall man with gray hair and skin to match. He wore a studied elegance. He was editor at Doubleday and he had a man named William Wynne Wister, of the Philadelphia Main Line Wisters, who had been an alcoholic for nineteen years. He had tried every so-called cure, every sanatorium, and had finally been sobered by psychotherapy. He had been upright five years, had studied abnormal psychology at Columbia University, and was now a therapist in alcoholism. In sum, the bum had become a doc.

We had lunch. Did I know anything about drinking? Only from the neck of a bottle. Well, chronic overindulgence involved shyness, parents, childhood trauma, and so forth. Would I be interested in writing Wister's biography? I would. It was difficult to contain enthusiasm. After all, Wister lived in Tudor City, which was on the other side of town from *Collier's*. After work, I could go there and interview the man about his life, say, four nights a week. At my age, I could bear the extra work without sacrificing whatever I could offer in quality.

Wister was short, red-haired, handsome, a collar ad. He was a ready smiler, self-contained, and was glad to find out that I knew nothing about the subject. "You won't have to unlearn a thing," he said. My indebtedness to Straus was lopsided. He could have taken that book to any of his writing friends.

Wister and I signed a contract with Doubleday. I got fifteen hundred; Wister got fifteen hundred. The royalties would be mostly 10 percent and 12½ percent, but it didn't matter. I was about to see a book with my name on it. Well, not quite. The smiler turned out to be strange. Four nights a week I went to his apartment. He had a beautiful wife, an articulate, intelligent woman, and two growing boys. His practice, straightening out drunks, was a good one. Underneath the smooth bedside manner was an inner irritation. He seemed convinced that I was a stenographer, taking down his recollections word by word. I tried to disabuse him. He would smile and say: "Jim, you're right." He would rub a delicate hand over his brow. "Absolutely right. I give the material to you, and you fashion it in your words. Now, where were we?"

In the morning there would be a hand-delivered note in my mail at the office, saying something to the effect that he, Wister, was the only one who understood the psychology. We must do it his way or drop the project. . . .

I appealed to LeBaron Barker. He wouldn't confront Wister. Sometimes I bent, other times I bristled. Always Wister came back and asked that we pick up the work. We started again and again. Sometimes Mrs. Wister would intervene. Sometimes he would listen. When I left Tudor City at ten P.M., I began to stop at a nearby tavern. I needed drinking.

At one point, I said: "Why did you want a book written?"

He had elegant hands. "That's easy. I straightened a patient out and he tells me he's writing a book about alcoholism." I felt an icicle under the heart. "You mean, we might come in second?"

"Forget it," he said. "Charlie Jackson is very slow. Besides, he's writing a novel called *The Lost Weekend*. We're writing the facts."

Mr. Jackson won easily. His book became famous. Ours was called *The Glass Crutch*. It hit *The New York Times* best-seller list within three weeks and died within three more. Therapeutically, *The Glass Crutch* was a great thing for me. It proved that I could tell a long story and tell it professionally. Like swimming, book authoring cannot be taught in a classroom. The neophyte should be immersed alone. I had also proved to myself that I could be disciplined; that I knew how to draw significant truth from a living subject, how to be patient in the face of ultimatums, how to write my best the first time around, not tapping a scene or sentence until I could "hear and see" it.

None of these virtues is cashable or bankable. The reviews were mixed, as they usually are. A few psychiatrists said *The Glass Crutch* was the definitive work on alcoholism (which it wasn't); Wolcott Gibbs, an alcoholic critic, wrote a meandering assortment of jokes about Alcoholics Anonymous in *The Sunday Times* (which was not a part of recommended therapy in the book); and some county judges cashed in on the publicity by sending drunks to read the book and report back to the court.

Twenty-two thousand trade books were published in that year, 1945. It seemed unlikely that *The Glass Crutch* would be one of the few to pop to the surface, however briefly. *Collier's* magazine became enthusiastic and published a house advertisement. It showed the book open, face down. The last of the copy read: "Jim has not only written a good, controversial book, but he's written a successful one as well. All that surprises us is how he ever managed to find the time." They got their daily pound of flesh, and more. They had no appreciation for how far and how fast the student wants to fly from the eighth grade of a strict parochial school.

The editors at *Collier's* were outside Joe Alex Morris's office. His wife had died. There is a gloom which cannot be assessed at a distance. It makes the bones ache, the eyes blink; questions are answered with "Excuse me?" It becomes pervasive, something almost comedic in its fumbling. I sat at my desk and didn't know it. Walter Davenport, the one-time *American* rewrite man, came in, sat down, spoke to me, and gave it up. A short while later, I came in after a late lunch with an author. Ulrich Calvosa, the tiny picture editor, stopped me. "You hear the news? Colebaugh dropped dead on his office rug."

My greedy world broke. The editor had not been sick. He had been to the office every morning at ten, had made his decisions firmly and without strain and, in a moment of rare confidence, had told me that he and Mrs. Colebaugh (I wasn't aware that there was a Mrs. Colebaugh) had bought a small house near St. Petersburg, Florida. "Someday, Mr. Bishop," he had said, "I will leave this office and go off to study the Gulf of Mexico and palm trees. I might even subscribe to *Collier's.*"

He had not died on his office floor. He had fallen. Someone found him and called an ambulance. On the way to the hospital, Colebaugh became irrational. He had waved a small key and said: "Tell Calvosa to get to my apartment and lock the liquor cabinet." At the hospital, his neck and face had blown up and purpled. Then Colebaugh relaxed and took my peace of mind with him. In a few short months he had taught me more about good editing than I had learned in the previous fourteen years; he had taught me how to achieve judgment without rancor; how to relinquish a project which cannot be saved; how integrity will save a mediocre editor's ass if he has it.

I didn't go to the funeral. I was not invited. He was my hero, although I would not acknowledge this. Tom Beck, a fat man with a tough speaking voice, ran Crowell-Collier. He, William Chenery, and Frank Braucher moved the pawns. Beck selected Henry La Cossitt, a tall man with big square teeth who was equipped with a real har-de-har laugh. It was a time when magazines cost more to print than subscriptions brought in. The weekly magazines were in a struggle to survive. *Collier's* needed a new look. La Cossitt worked in his shirt. He said: "Call me Henry." He felt that he had a mandate to make the magazine livelier. I was deferential and he said he didn't want that. "Speak up," he said, laughing heartily. "I'm the new boy. I've got a lot to learn." I began to think that a magazine is its editor. *Collier's* became livelier. I wrote an article on "Dolls for Men." They were small sexy things to be sent to men overseas. We began to prowl, not into national politics, but into the whispering voices under the capitol dome. We wanted to know, not so much what happened, but who made it happen.

One afternoon Henry called me in and pointed to an article I had written. "Jim," he said seriously, "are you stuck with this style of writing?" I asked what style. "Oh, you know," he said, "those lean little sentences. Now it may go well with the readers, Jim. I don't deny that. It rubs me the wrong way, my friend. Sounds as though you're writing on stilts." He and I knew that there was no way I could devise a new style, any more than I could alter my handwriting. He and I also knew that I was finished at *Collier's*. We would be polite to each other. Henry La Cossitt would not fire me. Fewer articles would come to my desk to be edited, and fewer would be written by me.

I went home searching for other editorial avenues. The first was to resume an old hobby. Since 1930, I had been collecting notes on the assassination of Abraham Lincoln. It was not to be a book — too many had been written. My original interest was predicated on the variances in the accounts of what happened on that cool damp day in April, 1865. My notebooks, black leather and gleaming with age, numbered twenty-six.

There was one for each hour of the day, from seven A.M. to the following seven A.M. There was one which was a cross-section of quotations from the various characters and gave the volume and page of reference. A final one listed all the sources I had read.

I thought of writing a magazine article about the assassination, reconciling all the little mismatches of time and personalities. Then I asked myself who would publish it, and the answer was nobody. The only interest in Lincoln among my fellow editors was a forlorn thought that maybe the deed had been perpetrated by Secretary of War Edwin Stanton.

I would have to look for a job. I asked Roger Straus to send out feelers. I got timid responses. Stuart Rose of *The Saturday Evening Post* thought I might do well there, but the editor, Ben Hibbs, sniffed at the notion. One of the primary factors against getting a job was my feeling that *Collier's* was the best weekly, and, if I went elsewhere I would be working with less enthusiasm. I knew the mastheads of all other magazines — in many cases, I knew the editors too — but it didn't help. On some occasions, I saw published articles which I had declined. This in no way meant that I was right and they were wrong, but when I saw material which I knew had been contrived, and abused by poor craftsmanship, the magazine became shoddy in my eyes. This was a weakness, and an expensive one.

All of it was grief over the loss of Colebaugh. La Cossitt did not threaten to fire me. Straus didn't relish the notion of asking people for a job for me. I thought I had been pulling my weight at *Collier's*. The death of a patronizing editor was frightening. Maybe — just maybe — Colebaugh had been carrying me. If this were not so, why was I so unsure of myself? Was La Cossitt ignoring my work — ignoring me — or was I waiting to be patted on the shoulder, reassured that I was still the fairest of them all? I wanted to write an article, anything at all, to prove to myself that I could still do it. All my life there had been an inner boldness, a mannered confidence. This had been challenged.

There is an inflection in the word *metamorphosis* which makes change sound glacial. In my case, this wasn't so.

Fresh news came from Europe that Hitler had killed all the Jews. It seemed absurd; no person in power, no matter how mad, eliminates a people. We had heard rumors of Jewish persecution at *Collier's* in the summer of 1943. It was on a parallel with stories that the Germans had a secret weapon which split atoms and would devastate entire cities. Or that the Japanese had twenty divisions of soldiers who had sworn to kill two Americans apiece before dying for the emperor. Or that the Russians had a fleet of bombers which operated without a crew; they would fly to Berlin and back to Minsk on radio signals.

Then the photographs arrived, thick sets of them. They were of poor quality, gray with grain, but the German photographers shot endless lines of emaciated Jews at concentration camps. They were en route to poison showers, to ovens; they stood pitifully naked before long rectangular graves facing a young man behind a machine gun on the opposite side. They were jammed into trucks, peeking out of cattle cars; the children had big docile eyes. The Germans appeared in the pictures to be solicitous as they ushered the unarmed to their deaths. The final total was 5,933,900 dead. The Jewish population of Europe had been 8,861,800 before the war. Sixty-seven percent had been slaughtered. It was a story so vast in scope, so horrifying in its implications of guilt, that no magazine editor thought it could be handled — or even understood — in one article, or one book. In America, which has always had a viable and articulate Jewish community, the shock waves ricocheted without diminishing. At first, the outspoken anti-Semites saw it as propaganda. The photographs brought a deadly silence. It was not the numbers, which were beyond comprehension; it was the pictures of gaunt faces pleading silently to a camera. It was a story which would continue for decades. At *Collier's* it was an odor which would not leave the nostrils. We smelled it every day and we knew that the wire services had sent back pictures of hills made entirely of bones, of black ovens with double doors where Jews were reduced to malleable chemistry. The first, halting survivor stories began to trickle into newsrooms and then a few began to understand that Hitler's hatred and fear of Jews was so psychotic that in the final year of the war he had kept entire divisions of SS troops working at the herculean task of genocide rather than use them in the front lines where, for a time, they might have delayed defeat.

Had President Roosevelt known — really known — about genocide? In February, 1945, he conferred aboard a cruiser in Great Bitter Lake with King Ibn Saud of Saudi Arabia. Cordially, the President asked what America could do for the king. "Send no more Joosh," the Arab said. This amused FDR. He rocked with laughter and told the story all over Washington. "From Ibn Saud of Arabia I learned more of the whole problem of the Moslems and the Jewish problem in five minutes than I could have learned by the exchange of a dozen letters." He would hardly have been amused had he suspected a holocaust. OSS reports told him that European Jews were mistreated and imprisoned. In any case, the American government could do nothing to stop it.

Earlier, at a recess of the Casablanca Conference with Winston Churchill, the leader of the free world had dinner with the Sultan of Morocco. As usual when Roosevelt felt well, he gave freely of his counsel. After the war, he said, "the number of Jews engaged in the practice of the professions should be definitely limited to the percentage that the Jewish population in North Africa bears to the whole of the North African population. . . . The plan would further eliminate the specific and understandable complaints which the Germans bore toward the Jews in Germany. . . ."

History has not uncovered the precise date when Roosevelt and Churchill first heard of the fate of European Jews. In January, 1943, both statesmen heard "rumors" that unarmed Jews were being killed. The frequent correspondence between the two shows that the extinction of Jews was low in credibility for both men. The collective shrug indicated that they did not want to be concerned about matters which, in the broad strategic concept of war, could not be helped. Without collusion, both men decided to say nothing about it.

In the White House, Roosevelt had a meeting with Anthony Eden, Secretary of State Cordell Hull, and others on March 27, 1943. Hull said he had word that sixty or seventy thousand Bulgarian Jews were threatened with "extermination unless we could get them out." Eden hastened to respond that the British were ready to take sixty thousand more Jews to Palestine. Harry Hopkins, who sat listening, paraphrased Eden's remarks: "the whole problem of the Jews in Europe is very difficult. . . . We should move very cautiously about offering to take all Jews out of a country like Bulgaria. If we do that, then the Jews of the world will be wanting us to make similar offers in Poland and Germany. Hitler might well take us up on any such offer and there simply are not enough ships and means of transportation in the world to handle them." Cordell Hull dropped the subject.

Four months later, President Roosevelt directed Generals Eisenhower and Giraud to set up a refugee camp at Mogador in Morocco for six thousand stateless persons, "largely of the Jewish race," who had fled from Germany and France and were unwanted in Spain. He ordered medical care, food, and "something more than tents as temporary housing." From North Africa, Roosevelt thought ahead to permanent Jewish exile in Madagascar or Cyrenaica and Tripolitania in Libya. None of the allied leaders saw the problem as salvaging a race until the Russians moved deep into western Poland and Stalin sent word to London and Washington that mass extermination of Jews was not only possible, but had been accomplished. This would be in the latter part of 1944.

In most of this I was a reader, not an editor. Then I was no longer a war editor at all because there was no war. The fire and smoke which had been at stage center for so long had dissipated. Ernest Hemingway stopped filing articles; Quentin Reynolds had left London when the noiseless V-2 rockets began to fall on the city. He had witnessed a great deal of war and said his nervous system was no longer reliable. He came home. So did Frank Gervasi, who was filing material on Jewish immigration to Palestine. The great naval task forces of the Far East were riding at anchor.

It was a time for Roosevelt's dream of a United Nations. The Russian delegation in San Francisco seemed more interested in how its veto would work in the Security Council than in how the many small nations would vote in the General Assembly. It was a dream, as Woodrow Wilson had dreamed of a League of Nations in 1918. But the dreamer, the one who had phoned us long distance with his Fireside Chats, had always told us not to be afraid, that everything would be all right — that dreamer was dead.

Margaret McCarthy had moral fiber matching the tensility of high-grade steel. There was a little bit of right and a great deal of wrong in the world, and Aunt Margaret could detect one from the other. It was she who, the night her mother died, called a priest, not a doctor. She was a strong, affirmative person, one who dominated her husband, Eddie, and her eight children. In this, her personality was akin to that of my father. She loved her brother in spite of the wrongs he had inflicted on his family, and she begged him loudly to return to "Jenny and give yourself peace of mind."

He had remained at Clara's side for sixteen years and brought up another man's three children with devotion and grace. In that span, his children — Adele first, then Jim, then John — had married. Jenny had gravitated downward to a furnished room. She had a bed, two chairs, a table, and a combination kitchen and lavatory. Her children obfuscated their guilt by inviting her to their homes once a month rather than visiting her. Now and then, Jenny wrote notes to each of them: "When you see your father, ask if he wouldn't like to spend the evening with us — all of us — and we could have a nice time. The room is driving me crazy. I mean crazy. I have no place to go, no money to go anywhere. I visit my sister Etta, and sometimes a friend will invite me to dinner. There is no radio here, nothing to do in this room. At night, when I go to bed, I itch terribly. I feel that ants are crawling all over me. . . . Above all, be a good boy. Your baby Gayle Peggy is so cute I could eat her . . ."

When Clara died, Big John bounced around like a colored sphere in a pinball machine. He hit all the bumpers; rang all the bells. After the funeral, he went to live with his sister Margaret. The McCarthys were in a two-family house on Garfield Avenue, in Jersey City. They were healthy and noisy. My father occupied his mother's room. He whiled away the long evenings playing penny poker with Aunt Margaret and some of the children. He needed massive doses of laughter and that's what he got. Sometimes he walked Uncle Eddie up to Ocean Avenue, where they got drunk. This infuriated Aunt Margaret, who, years before, would not even tolerate liquor at her wedding reception. At the bar, my father reminded his brother-in-law that if a man gets drunk enough, he may awaken hung over but he will have no recollection of reprimands.

Inch by subtle inch, he romanced Momma. He was fifty-nine; she was fifty-eight. He was a stout noisy-breather in gold-rimmed spectacles, a fop in attire who was in icy loneliness. She was in advanced diabetes, a small woman grown smaller. Her sight was so poor that she incurred a venetian-blind vision. She was so eager for him that she forgot to be accusatory;

she failed to revile him for ruining her life. No matter what he said, she turned that one-gold-tooth smile up at him and murmured: "Yes, John. Of course. Whatever you say, John."

It required an assortment of dates for him to ask the question the entire family knew would be asked. No one dared suggest it. It would happen, and everybody was betting Momma would say yes. She had died of loneliness years before, berated by her mother, her sister, her friends for being "spineless," for not suing him for a legal separation and exposing him to newspaper stories, for not demanding a small piece of the good life he was leading.

It was pointless to flog him with guilt. Dad had a honed conscience. He was aware. The time came to ask the question and, as he told it to me later, he fumbled a little. "The reason I stuttered," he said, "is because I knew that if I were your mother I would say no." She didn't. At first she didn't respond. Her head went down and tears came. She didn't want him to see her cry, because, as she said, she had no reason to weep. He put an arm around her shoulders and she shrugged him away. Then she composed herself and said: "I think we should try again." That was all. There were no grandiose speeches, no bitter statements, nothing memorable. He told me he kissed her. Dad might have covered sixteen years with "I'm sorry," but he couldn't wrench the words from his throat. The best he could do was pat her shoulder and murmur: "I'll make it up to you, Jenny."

They found a small second-floor apartment in Bogota, New Jersey. Here, the long penance period began. She could no longer see to cook. He made the breakfast, sat her in an easy chair near a radio, and took the urine tests daily and administered the insulin needle in her thigh. He worked as credit manager for a local group of weekly papers, and enjoyed the work. In the evening, he returned fatigued. Dad was losing the bull-like bounce he had had. He made the evening meal, which seemed to consist of the same dishes: a leafy salad, a baked potato, and porterhouse steak. I asked why and he said: "I never learned to cook anything else." He also washed the dishes. Jokingly, he said: "Did you know that Joy makes dishwashing almost a pleasure?"

Sometimes he read aloud to her from the newspaper. They subscribed to the *Jersey Journal*. Jenny asked him to read the obituary page to her. He read the sports section to himself, literally grinding his teeth when the New York Yankees lost a game. She managed to return to an old hobby, crocheting antimacassars, this time for granddaughters. She squinted and used higher wattage lights, and sometimes, when she missed an eyelet, she would toss the work and the hook down and sigh. Now and then, when I visited, I sneaked a container of rice pudding to her, because this was her favorite. My father begged me not to do this, and I promised, but a big smile came to her face when I opened the door because she knew I had it behind me. Before he could get out of the kitchen, it was on the cushion behind her, with a spoon deep inside. All that was needed was for me to suggest a rousing game of pinochle on the kitchen table.

They had good times together. She went to the movies to please him. He led her to seats away from other moviegoers. Under his breath, he whispered the action. He whispered a long time before he realized that Jenny was sleeping. Sometimes he drove her for weekends to the Catskills, through Saugerties to Tannersville and other places. She enjoyed the mountain air and the good food and the lovely little one-room bungalows. In time, he stopped. These were the places he and Clara had been; the mountains were dredging memories he tried to erase.

In both sides of the family — the Tiers as well as the Bishops — death was not much more than an event. It was as though each of us was a book on a shelf. Now and then, one of them slammed shut. Some of the books were exciting; others were dull; but, no matter what, one day a book slammed and you could almost hear the small slap as it shut and you would not read that one anymore. The families held their wakes, sat on camp chairs around the gleaming caskets, and were hypnotized by the flickering candles and the faint gold on the crucifix. Some wept. The men wore ties and jackets and stood in remote corners whispering, with hands clasped before them. The ladies wore dark modest dresses and carried handkerchiefs with lace on the edges, the glistening eyes on the door to see who was coming in and who was leaving. They stood when the priest came in, and they knelt when he knelt, looking at the off-white ceiling and roaring the prayers and the antiphons to the litany. It didn't matter whether the deceased was a scoundrel. The prayers were bound to lift him out of the fires of purgatory toward quick redemption. If he died with the proper disposition, that is. Disposition is important. One must feel a true contrition for wrongs in the final hours. Without the proper disposition, everybody knew that the old son of a bitch would burn forever in hell.

Grandma Tier's death is a good example of how the family departed. She was Mary McSwiggen Tier, a proper Christian who enjoyed sentiment for her husband, Alonzo, but had little for anyone else. When her time came, she was in bed at home on Randolph Avenue. She summoned her daughters, Jenny and Etta, and said: "I want you to go downtown to Bernstein's and buy a nice funeral dress for me." They began to blubber. "Stop that!" she said. "I'm seventy-eight years old and I'm going to die. Now try to find something in a deep lavender, not a light one, fairly deep but not purple. I want a nice lace yoke and long sleeves with maybe a little lace at the cuffs. If you can't get lace at the cuffs, try to get something with tiny lavender buttons."

She gave them the money from her small purse, and they took it as once they took her money to get a loaf of bread or a quart of milk. They wept all the way downtown and all the way back. They took the dress out of its tissue and dressed it on a hanger and hung it on the bedroom door. Mary Tier clutched her spectacles and studied it for a moment. She smiled.

"You girls did good," she said. "Now make sure that when Routh gets here he puts me in that dress. I hope you had sense enough to get a slip to go with it." She lived about a week, and when she was in the box I saw Grandma in that dress. She still looked proud and forbidding, with her wrinkles pressed back against her neck and her mousy hair piled in an oval crown on her head. One of the men at the wake couldn't cry, and he must have tried hard because he began to choke and people punched him on the back to help him get his breath. Other than that, she went casually.

I felt sorry for Grandpa Tier because, like most old men, he was not equipped to live alone. He, to a certainty, did not feel sorry for himself. There was his widowed daughter, Etta, upstairs who could fry eggs, make a bed, do errands. Physically, he had once been handsome, with a smooth, pale face foliaged by yellow pompadoured hair and a mustache to match which swept wide and turned upward. His mother was disappointed when, in 1883, he became a policeman. Tier wore a high, fawn-colored helmet, a blue uniform, a black patent-leather belt, and a nightstick. He earned two dollars a day.

The remarkable feature of his life with Mary McSwiggen was that they were frugal. They rented a gingerbready house with a half-acre behind it. They had two hundred chickens. The number may have dwindled now and then through sales of fryers and broilers, but the hatching was on schedule to build the population, and fresh eggs were sold at less than the price at the grocery store. Alonzo Tier also managed to buy a lot here and there and hold it long enough for accretion. By the time Mary died, it is said that he had ten thousand dollars in the Greenville Bank and owned the house outright. This, according to my mother, led to strife within the family.

She accused her sister Etta of being a signatory to the bank account. The implication was that Etta could make withdrawals of her own. Etta announced that when her father died, the house would go to her because she had rented the upper floor for many years. This produced a familial chill. No one dared to mention the subject to Grandpa, but the disputes broadened to include a niece. Marie had been orphaned while young, and had been brought up by her grandparents.

In the thrust and counterthrust, Marie induced Grandpa to come live with her. He made some arrangement with Etta to own his house. Marie was getting the once-handsome man, who now was bald and smooth-shaven. He was also partly deaf, which he referred to as "deef," and, as he approached his eighties, the trying years were ahead. Marie needed money. Her husband was an ox of a man who devoted his life to hard work. No matter how much he brought home, it was not quite enough.

Marie took excellent care of Grandpa, but he began to assume a senile attitude that she wanted his money. In the next breath, he said he planned to leave it to her anyway. The family schism broadened.

Alonzo Tier endured deep into his eighties, waving people away from his presence and saying that he wanted only to rejoin his Mary. It was not until he was actually dying that the family advised him that, as a communicant of the Dutch Reformed Church, he could not rejoin Mary in consecrated ground. This upset him and he raged about the iron rules of the Catholic Church. He was in his bed, breathing in labor, when surrender occurred. "Go," he said to Marie, "get the priest." He wrenched the words from deep inside because his family had been Protestant since, in the seventeenth century, they had come from Holland with their cousins, the Astor family.

It was enough, he felt, that he encouraged Mary to follow her faith. It was more than enough that, on Sunday mornings, he rapped the nightstick against the bedroom doors of his daughters and shouted: "Up! Out of bed! Time for mass." He had made the contribution of a generous man; now they expected him to lie. On his deathbed, he did. A priest came in and asked the reason for the sudden conversion and Alonzo Tier told him. It was not enough. The priest explained that, to convert, one must believe that the Holy Roman Catholic Church was the one Church, the true Church. Grandpa turned his face into a pillow. It was too late for proper instructions, but the priest seemed to comprehend the enormous devotion this wreck had for a dead woman. He was baptized and received his first communion and he died. When the box was lowered into the moist soil with Mary, I grinned. It was an archaic love story, and it was also proof that the family slides toward eternity without struggle, without whimpering.

Elinor wanted to tear up my draft card. I kept it. Some squirrellike attitude inside me made me save old photos, love letters, clippings, rubber bands — not string. The card stated that I was "1-A." In a few months, I would be thirty-eight, a man with shafts of white hair like bow waves. In the field of letters, I was a shade mediocre to be called second rank. It was an arena for young men, for fellows of twenty-five and thirty who, at first try, could write a smashingly successful book.

The word was all over Park and Madison avenues that I wanted to leave *Collier's*. The phone was silent. The word was everywhere that I wanted to write another book. The only acknowledgment came from Bennett Cerf of Random House. "Jim, baby. We like you at Random. We will publish *anything* you write. But for God's sake, write something." Anything. I could not write anything. What I needed, more than skill, was an idea. The war was as dead as the depression. No one wanted to read about it. Now the great stories of battle were available. The Pentagon was prepared to forget all about military security. But no editor would touch it. The readers, they said, were sick of war. The subject would remain somnolent for three or four, maybe five, years. Then nostalgia would assert itself. Fourteen million persons who had served, and the millions who had built the bombs, the great fighting ships, the tanks would want to read about it.

There was a new book publisher. The name was Farrar, Straus. Roger Straus organized it and attended all the local literary teas. He was greeting literary agents and young writers. I saw him. He had an idea for me. Build a house. Write a book about it. I signed a contract and got a five-thousand-dollar advance. It was an exciting venture for me, not only because it gave me a second book but the royalties might pay off most of the house. It was ideal for my kind of wallet.

I hired my old friend from the *Daily Mirror*, Emil Herman, to do the photography. "All you have to do," I said, "is photograph the lot that I buy, and then shoot pictures as the building goes up. We'll put the children in some."

Elinor said it was crazy. We returned to Teaneck and bought a lot on Fayette Street on the side of a hill overlooking the Hackensack River. It was a grassy, quiet place, polka-dotted with red beeches, elms, and oaks. The morning mists hung in a film below the lot and the exploding sunsets were behind it. We had six thousand dollars in the bank. That and the five thousand advance gave us a good start. I conferred at the West Englewood Bank with Frank Weber about it. He thought it was a great idea. The only shadow, he pointed out, would be in getting material. The government restricted the purchase of I-beams, steel casements, even some types of lumber.

It was a shadow, but shadows have no substance. I moved ahead. There were builders everywhere, but there was a small meticulous man whose habit was to put up one house at a time. He was mine. The contract stated that he would build this house for "cost plus 15 percent." I engaged a local architect. This man had my sympathy because I saw at once that the vision of a new home is a malleable thing. It moves. It stretches. Two of the bedrooms were too small, but if he made them larger, something else must be smaller. The kitchen, it seems, was never big enough. The living room projected as ornate, but it squeezed the lavatory behind it into a hall closet.

The thing we agreed on was that it should look modern — a two-story brick structure, painted white. In the back, down the slope, there would be a large second-floor porch and, beneath it, the game room and fireplace would be above ground. The kitchen would have a garbage disposal and an electric dishwasher. When Elinor placed her hand upon the plans — a whole sheaf of stiff blue ones — and agreed that she was satisfied with the house, the builder started work. He said the edifice, with his 15 percent, might come to twenty-three thousand dollars.

This was a considerable amount of money. Frank Weber said that if I put my six thousand in, and the publisher's five thousand, he would give us a mortgage for the rest. We computed the monthly payments and everything became possible. It was going well. The pictures of a steam shovel gouging the earth, the precision of the concrete forms, the raising of wooden skeletons with arches and doorways were thrilling.

The builder was patient. He answered questions, spoke of prices, gave decisions to a foreman, watched bricklayers place bubble levels on the first courses, watched a truck disgorge huge steel I-beams, and said he was having trouble with window casements. All the steel casements were off the market. The last ones made in Pittsburgh could now be purchased in Antwerp, Belgium. Of course, the Belgians would hold us up for higher prices, and then he would have to wait for a ship to bring them back to New York — so what did I say? I said okay. As time went on, his problems seemed staggering. He could not buy bathroom fixtures; they could be had on the black market — what did I say? I said okay. Then there was the marble trim in the bathrooms. Before the war, he said, they practically gave that stuff away, but now — what did I say? I said okay.

A little mist was gathering on my forehead. We had some war bonds. These were sold. A friend, Sidney Goldberg, lent five thousand. It was fiscal quicksand. I begged the builder to give me an overall figure. He scratched the back of his head. "I'd say forty-two thousand ought to do it." I went to Frank Weber and said: "Take the house." He refused. He said I give up too easily. We were playing roles opposite to the customary ones. The banker was begging me to stand by an expensive lemon. I begged the bank to take it and let bygones be bygones. "Stay with it a year," he said. "The bank will take care of the builder. We'll give you twenty years to take care of us." I had sixteen thousand in it. I would owe twenty-six thousand, more than the original estimate.

We needed rugs and a lot of new furniture. For this we had no funds. We ordered gray broadloom and hall carpeting; we ordered new bedroom suites and wing chairs and a gray couch for the living room. There were smart-looking lamps and, good God, I forgot drapes. There were drapes everywhere. The upper porch in the back required some furniture and a lounge. The basement needed a game table, andirons, and black leather couches. The deepest, most unremitting pain of all was that every bit of this would have to go in the book. It was nonfiction, a horror story. I warned the builder that he had signed and agreed to allow his name to be used in the book and that he wasn't going to look good. He smiled and said: "I'll get by, Mr. Bishop."

I remained after hours at *Collier's* to write a running account. The book was lagging behind the structure. A lot of zest and ebullience died in the copy. I was bankrupt and deeply in debt when Roger Straus called me in. He was sorry — and I knew it was so — but he had to tell me to stop writing the book. "In six weeks," he said, "someone is going to publish a similar book, called *Mr. Blandings Builds His Dream House.*" I went back to the contract. He had a legal right to cancel. It was the first and only time I sat alone in the kitchen of a brand-new beautiful house and drank half a bottle of scotch and felt sorry for myself. I mean, sorry. I sat there, drunk, and said: "Your poor benighted son of a bitch." Somewhere there were more eloquent words. I wouldn't hunt for them.

It was indeed a beautiful home, a blinding white diamond in a setting of cabochon emeralds. I understood Straus's reasoning; I agreed with it. *Mr. Blandings* had beaten me fairly. Then too, my book would have been the story of a disaster. I got some money for Emil Herman from the publisher. The interior looked like a Rockefeller cottage. Visitors marveled. I flinched at each superlative. I was bleeding to death and they were telling me that *House and Garden* should photograph the interior. Frank Weber and his wife stopped by, and he said: "Walls one foot thick of solid masonry. You got a Japanese pillbox." Frank and Agnes Westphal and their children showed up for a housewarming. Frank admired the big game room in the cellar with the picture windows above ground. We built a crackling fire in the fieldstone fireplace. I owed for the cord of wood.

At Christmas, 1944, the editors had seen that there was something wrong with *Collier's* magazine. It was something you could put your finger on — advertising. Advertisers were hedging. The excuse was that continuing war allocations did not give them enough raw material for products. This amounted to polite fiction. *The Saturday Evening Post* was fat. It could not have been our circulation, which hung around 3,100,000. Demographics depicted our subscribers as young couples moving upward. It could not have been our editorial content, which featured the good name writers who had stayed with the magazine. It could not have been Henry La Cossitt, who was enthusiastic about most of what his editors suggested.

It had to be a simple physical thing: the paper. It was lightweight glossy. The art director tired of showing that a hundred-and-fifty-page edition of *Collier's* felt far lighter in the newsstand buyer's hands than a one-hundred-and-fifty-page copy of *The Saturday Evening Post*. Even worse, our color paintings bled through to the art on the next page. We looked cheap. Now, with fewer full pages coming in from national advertisers, the magazine felt skimpier. The company was rich; at any time, it could have ordered more expensive paper and published "loss" editions with more editorial content than advertising.

They didn't. Suddenly, it was not I waiting for an ax; it was La Cossitt. The word was out that he was through. He sat in Colebaugh's office flashing the square-toothed smile, buying fiction and articles, initialing art layouts, and enjoying the camaraderie of a couple of martinis at lunch with editors. It seemed to the rest of us that blame had to be assigned and Henry was a victim. On a Friday, he was out. On Monday morning, a rousing Chicago editor named Louis Ruppel was in. This man seemed to have more energy than intelligence. He was the new boss and he swirled around the editorial department in the manner of Hinson Stiles trying to get out the first edition of a tabloid.

He called us in and said he wanted "excitement" in *Collier's*. This translated as old-fashioned scoops, news beats. To do this, we would have to buy material which would not only reveal something new, but would have to "keep" about a month until we could get it into the magazine. He worked in shirtsleeves; everybody was Herb, Jim, Quent, or "you." He almost asked — not quite — for exclusive headlines on the cover of the magazine.

It did not matter that he seemed to like me and my work. I had to leave. Once more the word went out. This time there was an echo. Edward Maher of *Liberty* magazine asked if he could have lunch with me. Mr. Maher was a peculiar magazine personality. He wore the slouchy, petulant manner of one whose great desire is to debunk literary figures. We had a pleasant lunch and he said he had heard a lot of nice things about me. Would I meet with him in the office of Paul Hunter, publisher of *Liberty* magazine? I was glad to.

Hunter had all the polish that Maher didn't. He said that *Liberty* was tired of being plain old *Liberty*. It aspired to a little class; it wanted to be *Collier's* magazine. Edward Maher, he said, was editor of the magazine, but was essentially an advertising man. He could not edit *Liberty* properly and was willing to surrender the editorial department to me. Did I think I could improve the content? To be sure. *Liberty*, among magazines, reposed in a warm gutter. It had the cheapest covers, the cheapest and most superficial content (many of its articles were "written" by Hollywood movie stars who revealed the revealable); its fiction content was good because someone had the sense to retain the services of Kathryn Bourne, an old war-horse of an editor who had the confidence of many of the better short-story writers. The layouts were superficial. David Brown, the articles editor, had just returned from war to sit at his old desk and wasn't sure what Maher wanted to buy.

Maher cut in to state that, although he was unhappy as editor, he would hang onto the title for a while until I became accustomed to running the shop as executive editor. The job would pay twelve thousand a year; no extra money for articles written. I accepted. One of the vilest canards is that men like a challenge. *Liberty*, as a weekly, was so far down that, as the aphorism goes, it had nowhere to go but up. I would have liked to have expanded the format and made the magazine larger, and thus be in sharp competition with the *Post* and *Collier's*. Paul Hunter, an inoffensive man who seemed to wander in deep pile rugs which left nap on his shoes, said we had a printing contract with a Chicago organization which prohibited changing the size. I was given a beautiful office with a view of East Fifty-seventh Street, a couple of couches, and some art on the wall. I asked my secretary to call as many literary agents as she could and advise them that I was in the market for top-flight fiction; good articles; even cartoons. The response was fretful: "Are you sure you can pay enough for good stuff? Has Maher changed his policy?"

This led to a conference with Eddie. He didn't want to throw money away. Everything I asked bounced against a wall of negatives. If the *Post* was crazy enough to pay a thousand or more for a piece of work, *Liberty* was not. If he wanted to, he could scrounge around New York and come up with great material for four hundred bucks. Maybe five. Wasting money would not improve content. Besides, what reader could detect the difference between a great piece of work and an average one? When I complained that our covers were cheap, he said that we couldn't afford Norman Rockwell. I had a suspicion that this man, admired by the staff, wanted to continue to play editor while deploring it; that he wanted a *Collier's* touch only so long as it reposed under his thumb; that he was going to get the message across to the editors that they were not to think they were working for me.

The first test occurred when I called all editors and art directors to my office. I told them that my first assumption was that they were competent. I had noticed that they were in my office almost every day asking for okays on stories bought, on photo layouts, on articles — some even asked me to initial material. I wanted no more of that. "Assuming that all of us in this room know what we are doing," I said, "then I don't want to see any of you unless you have a problem. Buy what you think is good. Pay the best price *Liberty* will allow. Try to find new, young writers. Do not be afraid of me second-guessing you. Or Eddie either. If you are not sure whether to buy or reject, let me see you and the piece."

They were encouraged. They said they hadn't been allowed to buy anything without filtering it through Maher's spectacles. I had seen this man as a debunker, but it was deeper than I thought. He held Monday morning meetings in his office. Behind his desk (we sat out front) he held up an anemic *Liberty*, displaying the cover, then he showed a *Post*, then a *Collier's*, and whined: "I think anybody with sense can see that *Liberty* is the best buy. It's alive; it's moving. The others are surviving on the same old stuff." He looked up. "How about you, Mr. Bishop? Would you buy *Liberty* over the other two?"

"No," I said, shaking my head.

He laughed. "Everything is a matter of taste. Some guys have highfalutin ideas which don't mean a damn." He spoke on. I watched the editors. They nodded affirmatively to the things he said.

There was an odor of fear in the office. Nobody acknowledged it, but, although Maher appeared to be amiable, jingling coins or keys in his pockets as he urged the staff on to greater glory, nobody was prepared to tell him that he was wrong when he was wrong. At lunch, editors gleefully ticked off the faults of *Liberty*, but no one wanted to correct them. The most costly fault was that the color printing was off-register. Portraits of women had the red lips somewhere between the left nostril and the cheekbone. The hair color was partly off the head.

I asked Maher to have it corrected. He suggested that I speak to Hunter about it. The publisher paced his office. I opened copy after copy of different issues. "The printer," I said, "is screwing you. The readers will fear they have double vision." Hunter replied by saying that he was with me all the way. In the next breath, he doubted that anything could be done about the printing. In several hundred halting phrases, he appeared to be saying that Cuneo Press of Chicago owned *Liberty*, that there had been a transfer of stock because of a large overdue printing bill. My naiveté stunned him. I argued that if the printer owned the magazine, he would be interested in turning out a superior product. Otherwise, he could not sell at a profit. This induced laughter. Paul Hunter's feeling was that the printer didn't care about saving *Liberty*. What, I asked timidly, am I doing here? Why hire me?

I wondered what might be rock-bottom for this magazine. At what point do fewer pedestrians — habit buyers all — stop picking it off the news-stands? I found out. One week the bulk of annual subscriptions expired. The cover looked watery. The material was unexciting. That issue sold 540,000 copies. If *Liberty* published nothing more than a cover, and sand-wiched a hundred and fifty blank pages inside, I believe that 540,000 persons would buy it.

Nineteen forty-five will go down in history as the year a world war ended. For me, 1945 went down.

Sometime in the spring of 1946 I reached out and found Mickey Ma-guire's hand. From the days of the *Daily Mirror*, the tiny redhead seemed always to be standing offstage waiting. It was an affair which burned brightly, died as suddenly as though smothered by a rug, then was fanned into instant life years later. Mickey never said she loved me. I never said I loved her. She was a potent political animal, preaching the virtues of the Soviet Union, criticizing our government, speaking of freedom as though it was something passed out like food stamps everywhere else except here.

We argued. We made love. I phoned Elinor that I would be staying in New York overnight. She sounded relieved. It was a crude game played without raucous laughter. Maguire was so, so alive. We ate out, we went to nightclubs. Sometimes we sat around her damp little flat in Greenwich Village speaking of things about which we knew little. Many, many times she asked me about Elinor. She would run her hands tight up the sides of her flaming hair and shriek: "Why do you put up with it?" And I would say: "How do you know I'm not lying? Maybe I'm the one at fault." She would shake her head. "I don't want to be your pen pal, Bish, but it seems to me that any psychiatrist would say that neither of you is any good for the other. Hell, the nicest time of your lives is when neither of you is communicating."

I accused Mickey of being a communist. Perhaps *accused* is the wrong word. I said she was. She said no; she had thought of joining the party, but it entailed too much discipline. She was not carved for carrying picket signs and passing out tracts. I asked her if she had ever been in love. She mentioned a jazz bandleader. She said she was not sure what love meant, but if it was devised for total commitment, maybe she was in love with him. At that point I said something stupid: "He's a heroin addict."

She nodded. "I know. What has that got to do with anything?" He had a well-known band, but he had run out of agents. The man was unreliable. He and his combo played weekend stands at resorts. He earned enough, and more than enough, for the six fixes a day an affluent addict needs. If he was not in love with Mickey, he was as close to it as his jarred mind would allow. She said he knew about me. Did he mind? No. He wanted her to go with him on a band date to Hazleton, Pennsylvania. Would I mind? No. She broke into wrinkled-faced laughter. "Know what? I don't think that either of you gives a shit about me."

For a time, she was secretary to a Sunday columnist. She executed her chores without spirit, doing precisely as she was told, laughing perfunctorily at his jokes, reading galleys for errors, deploring the blind items he got away with (e.g., "What beauty is about to be shelved by what scion who has eyes for an elevator girl?" . . . "Washington biggie says he must leave Truman's yes-men or go crazy" . . . "Word from London is that the British may do something about Jewish immigration to Palestine"), phoning for freebie tables for the boss at nightclubs and hit shows, making excuses to his wife for disappearances which went on for days.

Mickey, I thought, was unhappy. It was not a surface situation. She had a fine sense of humor. I had a feeling that she had been reaching for a place in life — not a man — something that would tax her talent and enthusiasm, and she never found it. She was far younger than I — at least a decade — and I told her that if she got out and met some well-muscled radicals, it might change her life. She said I was about as efficient in solving her problems as I was in straightening out my own. Sometimes, when the dialogue slowed, we would sit at her kitchen table under an exposed forty-watt bulb drinking. She would smile over her glass — maybe she was laughing — and say: "How is it that in all the years we've been drinking together we never had an argument?" I asked why. Because, she said, almost everything I told her about Elinor started with two people drinking. I thought it over. That could be the nub. I had tilted glasses with lots of men and women and I could recall but two disputes. And those were low on substance, high on volume.

I sat dwelling on women. (This may not have been the same night.) We drank in silence. I ransacked the files for women who could be referred to as affairs. My ruminations surprised, rather than shamed, me. From the beginning, I never enjoyed going with a woman one time. Or two. I enjoyed a semipermanence. There was nothing attractive about going with a girl in a violent fever of panting, and then trying to find a glib reason for running home. Sex, I found, was much more enjoyable if I got to know the girl.

The blond on the bus was the dramatic exception. She sat. I stood. I tilted my head to read her newspaper. She smiled and handed it to me. I declined. She asked where I lived. I gave her the neighborhood. She said she lived farther on; would I like to have a drink? Sure I would. We got off the bus, walked into the ground floor of a two-story building which was dark. The blackness was dissipated by a streetlight. I stood waiting for her to say something. "Help me," she said. She was trying to unhook a dress and a brassiere. I helped. We made love on a living room sofa and I recall, when I dressed, she spoke shyly. "My parents will be home soon." Twice after that I saw her on the bus. Each time she turned away. It would have been nice to know her first name.

There was a friend of my sister Adele's. I might have fallen in love. She was dark, a girl with an attractive figure, but I was very young and more than a little afraid of love. The affairs ran across my memory with the concomitant question: "Her? Would it have worked out?" This is fair musing when drunk, because the brain drifts in unhurried fashion revising and editing the history of lovemaking as it goes. They were all great, polished until they gleamed. They were intelligent — oh God, how intelligent! — even the dullest of them. I could have. I might have. I would have. But I didn't. Pouring one more drink didn't answer one question. How did each of them end? Did we execute courtly bows and murmur: "It's been so nice ..."? Did we quarrel? Did we miss one appointment? Did she find another man? Maybe, as I left, I forgot to say: "I'll call you Tuesday." Could that be it? The end of each affair was of no consequence. I was annoyed that I could not recollect what had happened.

Love was not only different, it was self-perpetuating. Turning away from love will not stop it. Stomping on it may bruise, but will not kill it. I had been in love twice in my life — once with the studious blond from Sparrow Hill when I was eighteen, and once with Elinor. Love, it seemed to me, is a magnetic force which drags victims. No will is required, and a disinclination toward this most arrogant of sentiments will not help. Her voice on the phone elevates the pulse, flushes the face, scrambles the mind, and induces a mortal to mumble. It was pointless to pledge one's life to a diffused image who, until a short time before, was a stranger. There is something illogical about wanting to hold a girl close for all time, telling yourself that it is she or nobody, that life will not go on without her, that the proper setting for the two of you is a remote tropical beach alone as you grow old and die. Nonsense.

Oh, no. This is the stuff of cheap fiction. It is this kind of ignorant aspiration which keeps all those old crones at the ironing board, and all those limping men liftin' them bales one more day. It could not be my lot because it was a confidence game, a delightful delusion indulged by romantics who tease and toy with the word *love* until they think they understand it. It was in full knowledge of this fakery that I fell in love twice. Now, like a jade, I was sitting at a kitchen table racking up memories of affairs as though no one could tell the players without a score card. Why wasn't I ashamed? Because my love wasn't available to me, not even for hand-holding. Oh, sometimes she became the electrified sport. When the whim was upon her, all that was expected of me was to be ready. And appreciative. That can be fatiguing.

And so, when I was home, we slipped into our neat little beds and kissed goodnight and she smiled and turned her back and pulled the bedclothes over her head and I shaded the light on the night table and reached for a book. I was a left-elbow reader, sticking one foot out to catch coolness, and I became immersed in books. I read as much as a well-versed librarian. I had devised a neat schizophrenic method of doing this — part of the mind enjoying the story, the other part dissecting the scenes and learning how the author did it — and sometimes I would go back a couple of pages to find out truly how he (or she) had managed to do it.

I read some of Willa Cather. For a while, Theodore Dreiser was a favorite. His *American Tragedy* did not impress me as much as *Sister Carrie* and *The Genius*. Faulkner's *Light in August* found me applauding with one hand. I liked the work of Philip Gibbs and Margaret Leech, but I returned again and again to Carl Sandburg's four-volume *Abraham Lincoln: The War Years*. Nothing written in English could arouse me as Sandburg did. Nothing could make me choke with sorrow as easily as his solemn, almost lugubrious, portrait of Abraham Lincoln.

So I read. And in the morning we chatted over coffee. Elinor was not interested in what was going on at *Liberty*. She tried to understand, and she tried valiantly to give me time to vent my feelings, but her compass needle wavered between her mother and Gayle Peggy. She turned farther and farther away from Virginia Lee without, I am sure, intending to. By the time the little one was two, Virginia Lee and I occupied the same space in Elinor's heart. She loved us but she was too busy for us. The shrieks were now directed against Missy almost as often as me. An excellent report card from school elicited a "That's nice, honey." If Gayle made a mud pie and displayed it, motherly hands were clapped; the child was sure to become a sculptor. Elinor not only spoon-fed her, with the mother opening her own mouth with each bite, but she bathed the little girl in the kitchen sink every evening, brought her along on shopping trips, and told Missy to remain at home and try to finish her homework.

The marriage was mended so often it began to take on the appearance of a shoe cobbled too many times. The stitches were breaking. It required no meditation to know that I was now looking for points of dispute. As Elinor's targets shifted from me to Missy, mine alternated between Elinor and Maggy. Could love survive an atmosphere of chronic bickering, something which, in an old two-reel comedy, might have been hilarious? Indeed yes. An unseen plasma cement bound us in a slippery but tight molecular adhesion which permitted us to teeter on the brink and shout "I quit. I'm leaving," without doing it. For the second time, I dwelled on suicide. I was not sorry for myself. I was not sorry for her. It could be a perfect escape from pain.

I closed a book and gave it time. For me, of course, suicide was a mortal sin. My soul would be condemned eternally. Father Quigley might forgive me conditionally on the grounds that I was psychotic. I tried to think of suicide stories I had covered. What had those men and ladies used? Uniformly, they looked peaceful, pink of cheek with calm expression. Whatever was used, I would have to find some way of getting a prescription from Dr. Bernard Krull.

I had seen what rat poison and its arsenical components do to humans in the old Creighton-Applegate murder case. Ada Applegate, fat unwanted wife, was convulsive for days, begging, "Don't touch my feet!" It was a cruel death. If I was going, it must be a pleasant way; a substance that would make me feel drowsy. There were ways of identifying such a chemical. When I got it, I would write a "Dearest Elinor" note, explain that this had nothing to do with her, that I was discouraged because my beneficent protector, Charlie Colebaugh, had died, setting me adrift; my book on alcoholism lacked greatness and came in second to a fine novel; my book on building a house had to be aborted; I was in debt to my brows; I was an executive editor in an organization where bankruptcy was the ultimate goal. These were the reasons. It seemed like good thinking. I slept well. In the morning I thought of the word *suicide* while brushing my teeth and retched. Sunlight nourished the coward in me.

After that, I took Elinor to The Brass Rail and we had a private talk. What we achieved was an armistice. We agreed that we could not live together and we could not live apart. The problem in this situation was that, sooner or later in the conversation, she resorted to tears; Elinor said it was all her fault; she was an only child and owed all to her mother. I pitched in with a recital of my crimes and, in a burst of stupidity cum arrogance, I confessed the story of Mickey Maguire, admitted that I was jealous of Maggy, promised to mend my ways, attend mass and receive the sacraments, take Momma with us wherever we went and stop making a babysitter of her — in short, we were babbling boobs swearing instant rehabilitation.

It worked. In the manner of all other heart-to-heart chats, this one gave the house an aura of peace. More than that, we became overly considerate. The children were told to obey both of us and to stop pitting one parent against the other. The honeymoon was renewed. We crowded into a single bed and I fell out. I phoned from the office at midday. Flowers were delivered with messages in cipher. We held hands in the movies. We made weekend trips to the shore alone. I felt like a tightrope walker carrying an attractive parasol.

There was time for the sights and sounds around us. The radio featured such gems as "Juke Box Saturday Night," "Green Eyes," "Mairzy Doats,"

"Elmer's Tune." People spoke with reverence of a panacea called penicillin. A modest non-author named Betty MacDonald became rich with a book called *The Egg and I*. Americans were mailing dollar "chain letters." The greatest salesman on radio was an ex-sailor named Arthur Godfrey. Senator Theodore Bilbo thought that the American Negro was the enemy and that "all niggers should be deported to Liberia." Slender John F. Kennedy, with campaign posters proclaiming "The New Generation Offers a Leader," was elected to the House of Representatives by 78,000 votes.

Few things in life seemed to arouse more interest in women than the opportunity to be fashionable. They bought *Vogue* and *Harper's Bazaar* to ascertain how outlandish the styles might be. The war was over; limited fabric was available; floor-length dresses, with a slit to the calf and tight wrap-around neck, became evening wear. Beauty marks were pasted on chins and bare shoulders. Eisenhower jackets with pearl buttons were made of crepe. Shoes became open-toed; toenails would be lacquered; the first strapless brassiere was devised with wires; women who could not buy nylon stockings painted their legs. Hats became puffy creations of material and feathers, making some look like dessert. Women shrugged at criticism. The Reverend A. Powell Davies thundered: "If American women humiliate themselves by following these imbecilic fashion changes like a herd of ludicrous cattle, their twentieth-century emancipation is just an empty boast."

Liberty neither led nor followed the shifts of public opinion. The most dangerous posture for any magazine is to assume no posture. We cared not what was going on in that great big postwar world. The editors felt that our niche was entertainment. *Liberty* was drifting. At age thirty-nine, I was hardly a boy wonder. It was not a time to be allied with a loser. It was like trying to run through an acre of molasses. Week after week after week, I studied the pre-production copies and felt sick. The editorial department seemed to be more interested in honoring deadlines than in searching for material. Maher did not block my work; he persuaded me that the easy way was the better course.

We were paying a lot of money to photo agencies for exclusive photos. I suggested to Maher that I hire Emil Herman of the *Mirror* as our staff photographer and get Allan Witwer to be picture editor.

It was three against the rest of *Liberty* and that too was witless. I devised ideas for magazine articles; Witwer invented the types of photos to illuminate it and Emil Herman made the pictures. The best we could do was one article every two issues. It was not enough. The magazine was anoxic in its senescence, and dying was so slow that, from time to time, it appeared to sit up and take nourishment. Witwer worked hard because he was beset by a loser's syndrome that it was *Liberty* or nothing. Herman did not know how to do less than his best. My fear was that the inertia would overcome them and me.

An article was published in *The Saturday Evening Post* which seemed to me to have minimum reader interest. It was entitled "The Star Spangled Octopus." The subject was the Music Corporation of America, a booking agency for entertainers. The author traced the origins of MCA to a diminutive Chicago optometrist who started by booking bands in night clubs and at resorts. He took 10 percent of the proceeds for himself — which was reasonable — and established phone contacts with theater owners, motion picture producers, and club owners all over the United States. Orchestras signed exclusive contracts with MCA and the little 10 percent became a fortune.

The article indicted MCA for growing too big. The subliminal indictment was that MCA was a proper subject for the antitrust department of the Justice Department. They booked more than bands. They had comedians under contracts; also motion picture directors; actors such as Fredric March; playwrights; and now they had bought the Leland Hayward Literary Agency so that MCA could scan the products of a hundred and eighty authors and get them under contract too. Bigness seemed to wound the *Post,* which pointed out when a hit play, *The State of the Union,* reached Broadway, the Music Corporation of America owned a bit of everything. It had 10 percent of the stars, Ralph Bellamy and Ruth Hussey; it had 10 percent of the playwrights, Lindsay and Crouse; it had also cast some of the lesser players and, to top it off, had invested MCA money in the production. Who, the press demanded, owned the ushers?

The article would have been of little interest except that I got a call from Charles Miller, vice-president of MCA. Would I please stop in and see Frances Pindyck, head of the literary department of Leland Hayward? I had respect for Miss Pindyck, attributable to the fear in which all book publishers held her. She was a homely, fortyish woman whose disposition seemed to be chronic irritation. She did not seek authors; she fired them. Now and then her judgment was faulty, as when she told the author of *A Tree Grows in Brooklyn* that it was the most sickeningly saccharine subject she had ever read and that it would never be published.

We met in her office at 444 Madison Avenue. She had a corner overlooking the roof of Saint Patrick's Cathedral. She was leaving the Leland Hayward office, she said. No, it was not because of the merger with MCA. She was getting married and would live in California. The new president of MCA, a buck-toothed man named Lew Wasserman, had asked Miss Pindyck to select a successor. She picked me. I reminded her that I had no experience as a literary agent. It didn't matter, she said. Of course I would have to study dozens of book contracts before I would know what to ask for an experienced writer, as opposed, say, to a first novelist. I would also have to learn a lot about the trends in fiction and nonfiction. I would be expected to attend the literary cocktail parties where the agent meets new authors and reacquaints himself with old publishers. Also, I would have to learn to handhold some of our clients, who were addicted to fancied terrors called "writer's block" and personal indulgences of self-pity. "If you are interested," she said, "you are going to have to learn to drop good writers who will not write. New York is full of talking writers. You'll find them at Toots Shor's and 'Twenty-One.' They will enchant you with great story plots. Do not — repeat do not — sign them to agency contracts. Better to spend your time with a dozen mediocre authors than one great talking one."

Two years had been spent at *Liberty*. It and I were going nowhere. I asked Miss Pindyck what had brought my name to the surface. She said that she had heard a lot of good things about me as a magazine editor. Mainly, writers seemed to enjoy working with me. MCA told her they wanted someone with magazine or book experience. They wanted to spread the word that they had an editor in charge of their literary department, and I was a reasonable facsimile. The job paid twelve thousand dollars a year and unlimited expenses.

It was a way out as well as a way in. Maher said he was genuinely sorry that it hadn't worked out for me. David Brown thought I'd be happier in literary affairs. Emil Herman was frightened. So was Allan Witwer. They felt insecure without me to protect them, although both were doing good work at lower cost to the editorial budget. Elinor, of course, thought I was crazy to leave any job. My father couldn't understand the function of a literary agent. Mickey Maguire hoped that, while coaching authors toward success, I would not neglect my own writing. Within a month, I had signed as a writer with Ingersoll and Brennan, agents. I was the only literary agent in New York who had a literary agent.

I became a professional listener. With one hundred eighty authors on our list, I learned to keep an updated series of file cards in my top desk drawer. When I asked my secretary to go out in the reception hall and fetch a writer, I opened the drawer and glanced at his card. It might read like this:

> SMITH, John . . . middle-aged, divorced . . . wrote "The Bee Rebellion" in 1935, has done nothing since. Drinks some . . . no alcoholic . . . needs encouragement large doses . . . been working on modern history of China 4 yrs. . . . has minimum contract Appleton-Century-Crofts . . . weak on research . . . give him fresh avenues . . . always needs money . . .

Under "Hammett, Dashiell," I had written: "Seldom comes into office. Phones when he needs agency. Don't bug him with friendliness. He deals directly with publisher. Popular craftsman who works less and less . . ."

My department, I learned, was a pipeline to Hollywood. MCA was not interested in writers or the contracts I hammered out with publishers. Completed manuscripts were sent down the hall to Miss Kay Brown, a strident, friendly woman whose favorite position was standing with feet apart, knuckles on hips, laughing. It was she who took the manuscripts home, devoured them, and told the Hollywood office that she had another movie, or returned it to me without comment. If she thought it could become a motion picture, Kay Brown would set a figure for selling it to producers. If, for example, she hefted it and said: "Two hundred thousand and this is a natural for Ingrid Bergman," no one disputed her judgment. I saw her persuade actors such as Florence Eldridge and Fredric March to accept roles they didn't want.

A good literary agent is a nurse, a mother, a lawyer, a pleasant liar, a baby-sitter, an ear, a magician. I applied myself to learn as much about this oblique salesmanship as quickly as possible. I debated contracts with publishers, percentages, clauses, serial rights, how much to whom, picture rights, radio rights, the definition of proceeds, copyright, the elasticity of dates of delivery and publication, the quantity of first editions, percentages of book clubs, and dozens of little goodies which were buried under the fourth "Whereas."

I was intrigued by the departure of Frances Pindyck. The true story — if indeed it was the true story — surfaced in isolated bits, like life jackets from a submarine. Somehow, romance had never touched Pindyck's hem. She was busy fighting the world of the written word. An author had come in from California with a good manuscript. Pindyck, who was cautious, had several chats with the man before agreeing to represent him. He took her to dinner twice, and may be the only author whose invitation was not declined.

When the contract was signed, he told her he was returning to a small town in northern California. Frances Pindyck made her adieu, but the writer seemed to have something further on his mind. As it was repeated to me, he was blunt. He was forty-eight years old and had never been in love. He was, now. He wanted to marry Pindyck. No response was expected from her, at the moment, he said. She would need time. He wrote the name of a town on a slip of paper. He named a date. "The morning train gets in at seven-oh-three," he said. "I'll be waiting on the platform on that day. If your answer is yes, you will be getting off that train. If no — well, I'll stick around until the train pulls out."

After he left, Frances Pindyck, the regal, the efficient, the cautious, the homely, lost her head. She had an appreciation of the ridiculous, and took the story to Kay Brown. Miss Brown didn't think it was mad, or funny. Pindyck would have to decide whether she would travel across an entire continent, risking job and career, on the chance that a stranger would be waiting to marry her. No, Miss Pindyck said, she would not demean herself by taking a chance. Even if the man were serious, she hardly knew him. What ever happened to love, dewy roses, and stereotyped moonlight? She begged Brown not to mention the subject.

And yet, each day Pindyck found something to discuss alone with Brown. Always, the conversation got around to the mysterious stranger. The nut, the bug, who had given her exactly sixty days in which to torture herself. It developed into an affliction because, as the days went by,

Frances Pindyck altered her attitude from a discussion of madness to "How do I know I would be happy with him?" And from there to "Suppose I took a chance and he wasn't waiting?" And from there to "I wouldn't want a leave of absence, because this is bound to get out and if he's not waiting for me, I don't want to come back to New York." And from there to a note to vice-president Miller, resigning and proffering help to find a successor.

Frances Pindyck took the Twentieth Century Limited, then the Super-Chief to California. From there she boarded another train to northern California. A week later, she phoned Kay Brown. "The train was on time. When I got off, it was very early. There wasn't even a town in sight. The train left. I looked around. The station platform was empty. I knew that the whole thing had been a joke. I sat on my suitcase and cried. When I looked up, he was peeking around the corner of the station like a little boy." They were married a couple of days later. From what I heard, it was a reasonably happy union, a swallow of good wine a little bit late. The toughest, most respected literary agent confined herself to a small apartment, helping her husband with his next book. Two years later, he died.

When she took that train, Pindyck left the agency in good running order. Two books come to mind. I had little to do with either. One was *The Young Lions* by Irwin Shaw. All it required were a few contract changes by Random House. The other was *Our Plundered Planet*, to be published by Little, Brown. This, in substance was the first popular book on ecology. It was written by Fairfield Osborn, president of the New York Zoological Society, a proper and prissy man whose most excitable gesture was to raise one brow. The book was an experience for me. It detailed how humans were rifling the bank of nature, taking without replenishing, scarring and destroying what could not be used.

When it was published, I put Dr. Osborn on as many radio talk shows as I could. He sounded like a Vermont Yankee, and some of the knowledgeable hosts drew startling facts from him. The critical reviews were good, but it is a cliché to state that the people didn't buy the book. At that time — 1948 — very few used the word *ecology* or worried about "our plundered planet." I was moved when Osborn handed a copy of the book to me inscribed "With appreciation . . ."

It was possible to learn something of Hollywood without indenturing oneself. I was fourth on a list of persons who received carbons of office memoranda. Many were dull, involving sums of money with four and five zeros. Others involved suggestions for casting certain of our clients in motion picture properties. A few defined certain Hollywood executives as alcoholics, homosexuals, narcotics addicts, sadists, and a special pejorative was reserved for the owner of Columbia studios, who was referred to as a "prick."

One of our clients was a chubby producer named Jerry Wald. A decade earlier, he had been fired from a sixty-dollar-a-week post as radio columnist for the *Graphic*. Seldom in the history of journalism was the importance of being canned depicted in a sharper light. Mr. Wald was a two-thousand-dollar-a-week producer hammering out problem pictures for women, firing Pulitzer Prize writers for not following his orders, switching his allegiance from Warner Brothers to Twentieth Century–Fox and back again, always surfacing like a rubber duck.

Within a few months, Charles Miller, vice-president of the agency, asked if I would like some time off. I said no. Miller was a prissy fop, a man who might decline to give you the right time on the grounds that he would then be liable to be at the mercy of anyone who asked the right time. He said that Jerry Wald wanted me to write a movie. I told Mr. Miller that my kind of writing didn't match up with play-writing, that they were as different as the skills of an orthopedist were from those of an orthodontist. He told me that Wald was a good client, a special client, and Jerry thought of me as a gutter Hemingway.

I phoned the great producer. On the phone he sounded just like the insolent kid who had been fired by the *Graphic*. He had negotiated an expensive contract with the University of Notre Dame. Within its terms, he would be allowed to make a movie about the university, so long as it did not involve football. This seemed as clever as buying a book about the navy without mentioning water. He insisted there must be a "good story" at the university, and he hoped that I would go to South Bend and find it. How long did I think it would take to find it? If there is a story, I said, a week. He asked if I would spend seven days there, at six thousand plus expenses. I began to brighten.

The man at Notre Dame was Father John Cavanaugh. He was short and gray, a priest addicted to pale trench coats and understated anecdotes. He was president of Notre Dame, but not too busy to say mass alone. We shared breakfast, to dredge his memory of all the good stories about the university. The yarns were good indeed, but not enough to sustain a hundred minutes of running celluloid. Nor could any six or eight of them be hooked into a loose continuity. The moment we departed from football, the priest and I fell into the *Reader's Digest* pit; poignant stories with a homely philosophy.

We tired of talking about the college, its great science programs and hellion juniors who placed the statue of the founder adrift in a rowboat. We wore out the story of the Irishman who, on his way from Cork to a sister in the Far West, got as far as South Bend, saw the gilded statue of the Blessed Mother atop the university, and paused forever. As janitor, he lived a long life. When he died, the glee club stood beneath the windows of the infirmary and sang the Alma Mater. I choked my nausea.

Little by little, Father told me something of himself. He had arrived at the university late in years (twenty-two, I think it was) to trade a Michigan farm horse for a year's tuition. He had toured South Bend, the townies, and the town girls, and had fallen in love. She was, I understand, a sweet girl who believed that her John Cavanaugh would someday become an automobile manufacturer. He had an afternoon job at the Studebaker plant. Cavanaugh worked in the advertising department. Somehow, the young man drew the attention of John Studebaker. The old character was, in a manner of speaking, a one-man General Motors. He asked Cavanaugh when he would get his bachelor's degree and John said, "Next June." Studebaker was given to concrete whims. "You come to work for me, young man, and I will make you vice-president in charge of advertising." The automobile industry, John Studebaker said, had fallen into cliché selling, promising low prices and high performance. He wanted a person whose mind was not overrun with tire tracks.

The news was so stunning to John that he proposed marriage to his girl and they set off among the shops of South Bend selecting furniture. They preferred a small house rather than an apartment and, on weekends, toured the edges of town. It was more than a happy era for Cavanaugh; the days of study and the evenings with his girl bordered on ecstasy. He had not quite finished school and he was already a vice-president–designate.

Then the dark question intruded on a bright mind: would you like to be an executive or would you prefer to be a priest? This one-man dispute has afflicted many young men in many ages. It seldom carries with it an outright response. It is a burdensome, troublesome, sleep-robbing question. John did not know where the question came from. It was there, and sometimes it faded, leaving time for other concentrations and then it was back, sharp, steady, persistent. The young man was reasonably certain that he did not want to become a priest. So he asked a university professor: "How do you know when you should become a priest?" The older man was expansive: "Sometimes we know. If there is a question, young man, go to confession. Go to a strange church, a strange priest. Confess your sins. When Father is giving you absolution, he is at his most priestly. Ask him then and abide by what he says."

John Cavanaugh went to confession. At the conclusion, the penitent began the Act of Contrition. The priest began to absolve him in Latin. The student said: "Father, how do I know whether I should become a priest?" The confessor halted a moment, then continued. When he finished, he said softly: "That's easy. All you have to do is pick your funeral." There was a moment of silence. "You see," the priest said, "if you continue whatever work you have chosen in the outside world, you could become successful. With application, very successful. In time, let us say, you might own a big something somewhere. You will, with luck, have a lovely family. Let us make one more assumption — you have been generous and encouraging to your employees. Now, the day comes when you must die. It's a common event.

"You die and a great part of the town mourns your passing, because you were a good man. Your widow sobs. Your children weep. The undertaker will go to great lengths to make you look lifelike. The casket will be composed of rare woods or metals. The handles will be solid silver. The plant foreman will declare a holiday to mourn your passing. The local newspaper will feature your picture on the front page.

"That is a death, my son, which can be yours for the choosing. On the other hand, suppose you decide to become a priest. At a certain stage, you will become prey to the infirmities of age and somewhat crotchety in manner. Priests and laymen alike will tire of your admonitions, your homely homilies, your creaking pains. Dying will be a relief both to you and to your confreres. The moment you die, the priests will strip you of your vestments because it is poor thinking to bury good garments. Whatever is old and patched up, they will put on you. A pine box will be good enough as a resting place. The services will be brief. Few will be cynical enough to pray for you, because, if you were a good priest, you won't need the prayers. If you weren't, all the prayers in the world mouthed by the College of Cardinals in concert will not save your immortal soul. So," he murmured, as he closed the confessional slide, "all you have to do is pick your funeral."

It was twilight when John Cavanaugh walked to his fiancée's house. He had no appointment, but she was waiting for him. Hoarse in voice, phrases staggered, he told her that he had decided on the priesthood. He was stunned when she accepted this as though, with sure-footed instinct, she had divined it before he arrived at the gate. There were no tears, no recriminations, not even a smidge of persuasion. He held her hand, he said good-bye. In the seminary, some tried to dissuade John because he was older than the others. He hung on.

After class, when the weather was kind, they got their exercise by marching in twos. They marched away from the university, across Dixie Highway, and around the smaller Saint Mary's College for girls. One evening, as they marched, Cavanaugh saw a file of novice nuns marching in the opposite direction. There was no reason for him to search those faces. But he did. And there she was, his beloved. After that one encounter of the eyes, he did not see her again.

Cavanaugh became a Father of the Holy Cross. His girl became a nun and was stationed for years in India. He was graying a bit when he was restationed at the University of Notre Dame as president. The kid who had traded the farm horse for tuition had made it to the top. Each year, in September, Father Cavanaugh addressed a letter (almost like this) to the president of Saint Mary's College across the highway:

Dear Sister:
We have registered 485 freshmen at Notre Dame this week. In their honor, the university is staging a dance next Friday on campus. If you will permit your freshmen to join, we will send

buses and chaperones. I promise to see that the young ladies are returned at a proper time.

Please let me hear from you. . . .

His once-intended bride, now president of Saint Mary's, would respond in kind. I asked Father Cavanaugh if he ever saw her again. He shook his head no. Then he grinned. "But there's a funny thought in it. Each September, she and I arrange to bring all these young people together. Most of it is meaningless, but, now and then — perhaps rarely — two of those young people fall in love. I mean, they get married in time. In a way, we two who didn't get married are spawning love affairs in September." He sat back. "But all that was years ago. I picked my funeral."

The motion picture story was written succinctly. It went to Jerry Wald. I was back at Music Corporation of America when he phoned. "Terrific," he said because, in Jerry's lexicon, the comparative of terrific is lousy. "I like it. Of course we'll have to do some rewriting. Would you be interested?" I would not.

The reading of "almost" manuscripts is dull and debilitating. They consist of unsolicited material which has passed the screening of subordinates who think it is too good to be rejected out of hand, and not quite good enough to warrant huzzahs. There is a great body of manuscripts which are "almost." In most cases, passing it on to me did not help. The story line, let us say, is fresh and exciting, but the task has been executed with a highly predictable series of clichés. It cannot be returned with a note stating: "Good story. Write it better." The worst thing that happens to "almost" authors is that they reread the polite rejections. This leads them to interpret the agent or editor to mean that if you will rewrite it a bit more carefully, we'll be happy to publish. The polite editor seems not to be aware that the sucker has done his best the first time around. That's it. Unless he is young and innocent, his work will not improve. Applause deafens him to all legitimate criticism.

It was Wednesday, a week before Christmas. Teaneck was clear and cold. For Virginia Lee, it was the last day of school before the holiday break. Gayle Peggy was following a paper pinwheel at top speed. Maggy was checking off a list of Christmas-card recipients. Elinor was polishing mirrors. My "almost authors" were piled on the kitchen table. The "almosts" were never quite professional. Now and then we had an "almost" whose pure writing sang poetically, except that the story line was hackneyed. I read swiftly, flipping pages, looking for something exciting, watching the pile grow smaller, and wishing it would disappear.

The phone rang. It was Mark Hellinger. I was kiddie or pappy. The falsely deep growl was confident. Whatever I was doing, I should quit it by January 2 (two weeks) and prepare to join him in Hollywood. It was a lengthy conversation, which was surprising. The Hellinger I knew could get on and off with "Hello, kiddie. . . . Yep. . . . Nope. . . . See you. . . . Bye." This one was happy. He had produced several good pictures — translate to profitable — within the past few years. Among these were Ernest Hemingway's *The Killers, Brute Force* with a new star, a circus acrobat named Burt Lancaster, and he had just completed his personal salute to New York called *The Naked City*.

Hollywood had been good to him, and vice versa. He was earning thirty-five hundred dollars a week plus another thousand from William Randolph Hearst for the syndication of Hellinger's Sunday page. He was up. Starting in a few weeks, he would become an independent producer with David O. Selznick. This would mean his own company, his own cameramen, directors, writers, his own bungalow on the lot. He would be given his own front money for a picture, his own budget, and he could spend it as he saw fit.

It was, as they say, a juicy portrait. He had been out there ten years, had fought every studio boss with tigerish tenacity, and was ready to fight himself. Did I want to join him? Yes, I did. It would be like old times, I said. No, it wouldn't, he said. He said that he had always been aware that I was an Irish revolutionary and, if I thought I was going to bring democracy to Hollywood, to stay where I was. He explained that the so-called moguls of the cinema capital had long ago established some sort of caste system. I would start work at seven hundred fifty a week, and it would not be good if I socialized with the five-hundred-dollar writers, or if the thousand-and-up writers invited me to dinner. "Do I wear a sign with my salary on it?" I said. I could hear the sigh. "See? There you go. Don't come out here if you think you're going to change things. You won't." I agreed to abide by the strictures.

Leave Elinor and the kids home, he said. Get yourself established first. "I'm not sure you can write for the ear and eye and I don't think you are." I agreed. He went into a discussion of Ernest Hemingway. There, he struck a gold mine. Hellinger had a press agent, Al Horwits, who was ideal. Mr. Horwits had been a baseball writer in Philadelphia. In the manner of some good reporters with bad legs he had gravitated to press agentry and Los Angeles.

It was known that Hemingway refused to sell any of his works to motion pictures. His reason was valid; he said he could not bear to look at what they had done to it after they did it. Horwits knew that Mark admired Hemingway. He urged the producer to take him on a flight to Havana, hang out in the Floridita Bar, and wait for the great American novelist. It sounds witless in the telling, but it worked. Hellinger was at his most unctuous. Over drinks, he began to tell stories. Over drinks, Hemingway began to like the slick-haired one-time Broadway columnist.

It is doubtful that either of them realized what they saw in each other, or, if they did, would admit it. Both were cynical sentimentalists, with a fascination-repulsion of death that was more than casual. The third-rate reporter and the first-rate novelist fell in love. Horwits, who didn't drink, was bored guffawing at stories he had heard many times. After two days of drinking, Hellinger said he would give his buddy Ernest fifty thousand dollars for the movie rights to all the Hemingway short stories. The author extended his ponderous paw. It was a deal. It seems obvious that Hellinger didn't know what he was buying, and Hemingway had no idea what he was selling.

The producer sobered on the plane back to the United States. He became even more sober when Horwits said: "Where are you going to get the fifty thousand?" Hellinger had nothing. To be more accurate, he had about four hundred dollars in the bank. Among Hellinger's monumental virtues was an incessant devaluation of the dollar. He spent and spent with very little knowledge of how much was left. He would not enter a barbershop unless he could pay the check of every stranger. He would not buy a drink at a bar unless the bartender agreed to give him all the tabs. On Broadway, the only person ever to muscle Hellinger out of a dinner check was Sime Silverman, editor of *Variety*, who grabbed it and growled at Hellinger: "Who the hell do you think you are?"

He placed large bets on every race at Hollywood and Santa Anita. He had large sums bet on football games. He attended fights every Friday at the American Legion Hall and always bet on the underdog. To be brief, he didn't have the fifty thousand. "Screw it," he said to Horwits. "I'll get the money." And he did. When they reached Los Angeles they found executive producers willing to pay the entire fifty thousand and a percentage of the profits for one of Hemingway's stories.

Mark selected "The Killers." It was, at best, a fragment of a story. It concerned a character called The Swede, who loafed on a couch in a cheap Jersey rooming house. A small boy listens to two obvious hoodlums in a diner badgering the cook and asking where The Swede lives. They will kill him for some great wrong which is not explained in the story. The little boy hops fences, runs frightened to The Swede, bursts in, and tells him that two men are coming to kill him. The story ends with The Swede telling the little boy that there is no use running, he is going to stay right there and wait for them to burst into the room. That is it. That is all of it. It was not in the plot mode of the American movie, which embraces adventure, mystery, and romance in a neat braid.

Hollywood had many men who carried the title "producer." A song plugger was a producer at Columbia Pictures. Mark Hellinger drew attention to himself when he produced *The Killers*. He followed Hemingway's terse line about the murder of The Swede, then hired two inventive writers to decipher why they had to kill The Swede; in effect a five-minute movie with an hour-and-a-half flashback. Al Horwits carried the finished print to Sun Valley to show it to the author. Hellinger was too nervous to bring it himself, and Hemingway was almost too nervous to look at it. Al showed it in a freezing-cold hall near a hunting lodge. When the writer emerged, he emptied his jacket pockets. In one was a full pint of gin. In the other a pint of water. "See?" he said. "I didn't need them." When Horwits phoned the producer, Mark was so enthusiastic he yelled: "Hemingway is me if I could write."

Now, in late 1947, he was indeed one of a handful of independent producers. He owned a five-acre mansion up in the Hollywood hills with electric gates, nine servants, and a lodge across from the main house which he used as a projection room. The money would be good for me. Everything had been poured into the house Elinor and I built, and a lot more was overdue. I realized, when Mark was telling me about the caste system among writers, that he was warning me about our relationship. It would not be as it once was. I would not have access to him and to the beautiful Gladys Glad. There would be no invitations to dinner at his mansion. Nor would I be allowed to barge in on him on the studio lot with a problem.

I understood it. I thanked him and said good-bye. Elinor was still polishing mirrors when I gave her the news. She was happy for us, but concerned about Maggy. Momma's roots were in Jersey City. My thought was that we could afford to support her no matter where she wanted to live. I studied the saddened face, and realized the problem was Maggy and Elinor; there was no way of disengaging them. There was an additional factor; she was beginning to change moods with the rhythm of thirty-five-millimeter pictures being displayed on a screen. She was happy; she was stark; she was conversational; she didn't speak to me for three days; she was enthusiastic about something I had written; she had no time to read; she was too tired to dress and go out; she couldn't stand the four walls one minute longer; she would like to do charity work for her church; she was too sick to attend mass.

Let's think about Hollywood, I said. Whatever you do, she said, don't tell MCA you're quitting. Not yet. I tried computing what seven-fifty a week would do for our family if we managed to live on three hundred. The mathematics had the appearance of a sunset behind a tropical island. It was beautiful. I checked the maps of Los Angeles. I saw Brentwood and Bel Air and Beverly Hills and East Los Angeles and West Los Angeles and Pacific Palisades and Long Beach, Malibu, Van Nuys, and Burbank.

At the time, I was forty, old for new mountains. It would be worth the customary two years of my life to work in a studio, learn a little about how plays are written and put on the screen. My entire knowledge of Hollywood was contained in such hieroglyphs as "Ext. Night," "Ext. Day," "Dissolve," "Cut to," and "The End." It wasn't worth seven-fifty. I hadn't asked how long the contract would run, nor when I would have to sweat those fabled options.

Sunday morning I stopped thinking about it. Maggy was halfway down the stairwell, shouting. I was in the kitchen, dressed for church, waiting for steamy coffee to cool. "Mark Hellinger died!" she shouted. "It's on the radio upstairs. Mark died last night." It was true. The kitchen radio gave the news in antiseptic tones: "The Hollywoood producer, Mark Hellinger, died last night of a heart attack at Cedars of Lebanon Hospital. Three weeks ago, the famed producer Ernst Lubitsch died in the same hospital. . . ." A lot of dreams closed out in wakefulness. Not just the new job. Not the seven-fifty. This man had been my editorial father. He had taught me the first few words on a typewriter. He had imparted an excellent acuity for the story. Understanding the story, being aware of its muscled frame and its bones were vital. It had cost that man a lot of time explaining. He had been the master of the sob story and he taught me how to write one. "Be callous when you write a sob story. Be unfeeling. The reader will do the crying."

Now he was gone, snatched off in mid-flight, a man who, with little talent and enormous understanding, would have liked to stay on for one or two more acts of the cosmic vaudeville show. On Monday, I read all the obituary notices. Only one captured my attention. It appeared on the back page of the New York *Evening Post*. It was written by my old associate — not friend — and it had one sentence which, I thought, captured the pseudo-hardboiled attitude of Hellinger: "Always he would frisk a stranger for a trait he could admire." That said it well.

As a literary agent I learned and was paid to learn. Agents pander to authors. It involved cash, courage, critiques, and counsel. It was not my style. As one who had done some writing, I understood the vacuum in which authors work. No matter how good or how bad the work, the author is the last to know. He feels that he does his best and that the quality remains the same. Reading manuscripts at home, I could detect the assuredness, the confidence, and the depressed cycles. When an author stopped by, I did not listen and hurry him off. It was exciting to me to discuss the scenes remaining to be done and to give the writer the best of my thinking.

My best wasn't good enough, but all of the writers seemed grateful that I made suggestions. There were six people working in the department, and all were competent. I used two of my assistants to read material from young writers who were looking for literary agents. A small percentage of this was good and we would ask the writer to come in and discuss the work. It was important to know whether we had a new, serious writer or a bright young housewife who wanted to put the neighborhood gossip to music. A few were natural magazine writers who wrote short stories or nonfiction profiles, but who were overwhelmed at the thought of writing a book. Others wanted to write nothing but novels. All of them insisted they had "an ear for good dialogue." I had little time for one-book authors such as Dr. Fairfield Osborn. What he had to say was both beautiful and frightening, but having said it, he was finished. This was true of senators and statesmen, each of whom was willing to canonize himself at 10 percent of the retail price of the book on the first five thousand copies, 12½ percent on the next five thousand copies, and a straight 15 percent beyond that.

Insecure writers drink and talk loud. These are the executors of imperishable prose who would rather not be published than have a comma straightened. Some fine writers are timid and self-effacing. Their eyes beg a kind word. Many of my novelists lived Walter Mitty lives through their works. Those who could not bear rebuff wrote the sexiest material, featuring heroes who left swaths of fallen virgins all over the continent. The nonfiction writers worked harder for fewer rewards. Most of them fell into what I called the three-to-one category: they required three times the energy and time for research as they did to write the book. The most difficult of all authors was the one who was coming off as a resounding success. He had money, book clubs, and adulation. This one was certain that he had discovered the "formula" for writing great books. He wanted no advice, no disagreements, and he did not want to deliver his manuscript on time. Sometimes he joined a lecture bureau and went off to places like Provo, Utah, to settle the affairs of the world in thirty-five minutes. A few were unique inasmuch as they did not know how good they were and didn't want to hear about it.

Two years of a learning process is enough. As the best-educated man-of-letters-to-be in America, I needed to move on. I had learned how to counsel writers and how to draw up a publishing contract, got to know which areas were negotiable, and, best of all, left the agency without making enemies. I followed Hellinger's credo: "If you think he dislikes you, do him a favor." Most of the people at the better-known publishers, from Knopf to Signet, were now friends. It was, for me, a gigantic leap from working for four thousand dollars a year at the *Mirror* to six thousand for a week's work pleasing Jerry Wald. The difference was that the four thousand was steady money.

After leaving MCA I lived on writing a dozen magazine articles a year. In the late summer, I was introduced to another man who had a bearing on the set of my sails and the course I chose. It happened at a literary cocktail party. These events were uniformly dull unless you were the guest of honor or drunk. In those days these parties were held in someone's apartment with a window on Central Park. There was a piano, permanent or rented. Someone played; someone listened. People stood on gleaming floors in little grape clusters, gabbling about this author or that writer. They drank cocktails and ate warm mouse-bait.

Someone said: "Say hello to Ralph Gorman." I looked at a tall handsome man — a truly handsome man — wearing a Roman collar. "Oh," he said, smiling, "we are aware of Jim Bishop but he is not aware of us." I didn't know who Ralph Gorman was, but I deciphered the remark. He represented some Catholic publication and, although I was a writer of that faith, I wouldn't write for them. Father Gorman was eminently correct.

To get away from Father Gorman's little cluster, I said: "You wouldn't publish what I might write."

He was smiling. "Like what?" he said.

I ran through my mental files; a group was listening. "Oh," I said, "like what does a priest do all day long."

He was interested. "I'm the editor of *The Sign*," he said. "It's published by the Passionists in Union City. Why don't you write that article?"

I was irritated with myself because Gorman had mousetrapped me. "Suppose I find out that all he does is sit around in carpet slippers reading or looking at one of those big Dumont television sets?"

"If you say that's what he does, we'll publish it."

"Do you want to pick a priest?"

"Oh, no. You do that."

"All right, Father," I said. "I'll pick one and we'll call it 'A Day in the Life of a Priest.'"

Worse, I found that the top "honorarium" would be a hundred and seventy-five dollars. I went home angry. I phoned a monsignor and asked for a candidate: "Have you got an Irish priest, a sort of Barry Fitzgerald type, who runs a parish, has a school, and is in debt up to his ears?"

The silence didn't last. "There's a pastor at Saint Michael's in Jersey City. Name is LeRoy McWilliams."

I said: "Lee Roy?"

"That's it. What do you have in mind?" I told him. "McWilliams might be ideal. At one time, Saint Michael's was an affluent parish — Frank Hague and Johnny Kenny grew up there — but they built the Holland Tunnel right through Saint Michael's backyard and a lot of the swells have moved out. Anyway, give it a try."

McWilliams was perfect. He was five feet tall, master of the neighborhood. He had a Great Dane called "Himself" who screened rectory visitors. There was a big school, a convent full of teaching nuns (Will Durant's sister was one), and snotty schoolboys who enjoyed punching each other except on Sundays, when they donned long black cassocks and white surplices and were angelic. I gave McWilliams one glance and I knew him.

He once had refused to speak to the mayor because His Honor forgot to remove his hat. For a week, I was all over Saint Michael's. I was in the convent, the school, Saint Francis Hospital across the street. I saw Father McWilliams in his white helmet and boots as fire chaplain; I listened to him counsel married couples who had jarred their marriage to complete disarray (no couple in Saint Michael's ever went to a lawyer); I watched him watching the nuns eat to see if any was concealing an indisposition; I heard him threaten big awkward boys with a punch "all the way from the floor."

There were two remarkable features about this priest. The first is that he cared. If any boy of Saint Michael's served time, the moment he emerged into sunlight he was ordered to see Father McWilliams, who implored shop owners and fruit peddlers to employ the jailbird and give him a chance. If, in its indebtedness, the parish was too poor to help the poor, he phoned the mayor and wheedled a ton of coal and a big basket of meats and vegetables "for the good of the Democratic party." He visited the sick, shamelessly ordered two collections to be taken up at each mass, read the *Jersey Journal* assiduously looking for attacks or slights on the Holy Roman Catholic Church or its teachings. He not only wrote indicting letters to the editor, he called press conferences.

I wrote "A Day in the Life of a Priest." It was a good article because Father McWilliams was pure color copy. I stepped into a small office building in Union City, New Jersey, for my hundred and seventy-five dollars. Father Gorman was pleased. "It's a beauty," he said.

I shook my head. "I looked you up," I said. "Your circulation is around three hundred thousand. Don't you ever feel ashamed handing out a hundred and seventy-five bucks?"

He shook his head sadly. "All the time," he said. "But that's the going rate here. I don't suppose you would consider —"

"I have. I'll write another article for you as an act of Christian charity."

He grinned. "I'll take it any way I can get it," he said.

Gorman became my friend, and I his. Against my better judgment, he became my good-luck charm. I seldom sought him unless I was troubled. I told him I did not mind being a writer who happened to be Roman Catholic, but I was not going to be a Catholic writer. He would turn on the gleaming toothpaste smile and lean away from the punch. I got to know him in fragments. He was, at that time, the only priest-editor who, if he were not a priest, could have graced the mastheads of such publications as *Life* and *Look*. The Passionists did not allow any of their numbers to remain long in one job; the provincial and his counsel kept renewing Gorman at *The Sign* because they knew that no one else could command the type of broad-spectrum articles he was publishing at such an insulting honorarium.

He asked me to call him Ralph and I refused. Gorman wasn't just any priest; he had studied in Jerusalem at the Ecole Pratique d'Etudes Bibliques in the last class taught by the great theologian Père Lagrange. "The trouble with the Catholic Church," he said one day, "is that they are now down to one commandment — violation of chastity." He was a sturdy specimen, but I had a feeling that, without its being mentioned, the pump inside his chest was unreliable.

In the years ahead, when I was broke, he sent a check each month for one hundred and seventy-five dollars. He *smelled* that I had no money. When I phoned to ask what the checks were for, I heard the sound of that chuckle deep in the throat, then: "Oh, they're for articles I want you to write when you have the time." Years later, when the accounts were tidy, I heard that he was dying in Saint Mary's Hospital in Hoboken. I didn't go to see him. I couldn't.

A long time ago, in a sober moment at the Floridita, Ernest Hemingway said that it is bad for a writer to attempt to describe something which he has not witnessed, or in which he has not participated. So, when a political messenger came to the house bearing a gift, I held the door wide. He came from Frank Hague, and asked if I would like to help in a gubernatorial campaign at three hundred a week and expenses.

The fedoraed tyrant was in trouble. One of his loyal lieutenants, John V. Kenny of the Second Ward in Jersey City, had dared to lead the palace guard in revolt. Let it not be said that Kenny was a better crook than Hague. The revolutionary was a small man, given to standing on street corners palming two dollars in clinking quarters. He lifted his hat to priests and old ladies and sent baskets of food and coal to the same tenements where Democrats had once prayed for the continued health of Frank Hague. The boss, who had been in office in Jersey since 1917, had lost touch with the people. A revolt was not only in order; anyone with the credentials of being ward leader, Democrat, and Catholic could have stolen the election from Hague.

Now it was 1949 and a gubernatorial race was on. Hague reasoned that he had lost the city, but, if he could put his man in the state house, he would control patronage. It seemed strange to me that the old man would want a resurgence of power, because Frank Hague had invented the legal steal. In the early 1920s, he had passed the word that, in Jersey City and Hudson County, nobody could look with hope for promotion unless he was prepared to hand over, surreptitiously, 3 percent of his annual salary for "campaign purposes." If, at campaign time, it came hard on some to dredge the 3 percent, Hague was prepared to help. Across the street from City Hall was the Majestic Theatre, which wasn't either of those things. In an office over the lobby, he opened his own personal loan office. A cop or a street cleaner, a commissioner or a county judge, could apply at the Majestic and, at a reasonable rate of interest, be given the money so that he could hand it over to a bag man.

The chief bag man was a semiliterate named Johnny Malone. He was also deputy mayor. It was considered good form to get Malone's ear if a favor was desired. Hudson County was the most thickly populated of the twenty-one in New Jersey, and Malone had big ears. He also carried a large bag because 3 percent of the city and county payroll amounted to millions of dollars. Hague had resisted all efforts to raise his salary as mayor above eight thousand dollars a year. This was seemly because Jersey City's 325,000 persons were, with some exceptions, blue-collar workers. Those who didn't live in paint-flecked cold-water flats lived in peculiar two-family houses built shortly after the turn of the century. They were made of lapstraked wood with peaked roofs, a deadly similarity in block after block for mile after mile. The space between them consisted of a narrow alley and no garage. The city was the terminus of six trunk railroads coming out of the west and south to the edge of the Hudson River and New York City.

Hague called me to his office at 921 Bergen Avenue. The day was a sunny Sunday. He wore his stiff, old-fashioned collar, the pink wattles hanging over the top. He wore his pearl-gray fedora indoors as well as out, brim up. Hague's method of domination was to fix the victim with his unblinking blue eyes and assume a deferential attitude. "Now, Mr. Bishop, they tell me that you're quite a man with words." He held up a full-page glossy proof of a political advertisement. "I have written an ad which I propose to bring to the attention of the people. . . ." I looked behind. His nephew, Frank Eggers, sat on a leather couch. So did a state senator. Two tame county commissioners stood near a wall, holding their hats over their crotches. ". . . And I think you should read this before I okay it."

I glanced at it. He was off on the wrong foot. I was eager to learn something about the inside of machine politics, but if total agreement was the price, it was too high. "May I say something?" I said. He nodded. I handed the proof back to him. It had a small cartoon and about four thousand words of copy. "You're a voter on a bus," I said. "You open the paper. You see this ad. Now, mayor, I would like you to sit and read this." Heads behind me and to the side were wagging no.

The mayor studied his advertisement, then me. He nodded. "This man has a point," he said. "If I was coming home from work, I wouldn't read all of this." He didn't crumple the page. He handed it to me. "Cut the hell out of it," he said. "But leave full employment in there and leave in our fight to make the railroads pay their share of taxes. The rest of it — well, you're the expert."

It was, for me, an exciting campaign. The Republican party had nominated a cool, efficient man named Alfred E. Driscoll. Hague had combed the ranks of the Democrats and come up with a pompous chicken farmer named Elmer Wene. This man had served a term as state senator, was addicted to fawn-colored suits and cowboy hats. He was stout to the point of blubber and drank milk continually. Each glass was laced with three ounces of scotch; this was no one's business but mine. Wene was given to accepting sizable donations to the campaign and depositing them in his personal account in Vineland. In his blustery manner, he found it impossible to speak a passable sentence. His best effort, delivered before four hundred lady Democrats, came up: "The people are the kind of folks we need, and if we're not fair to our humans then we're being unfair to the voters as well."

After the first week, I drank with him. Hague provided me with three sparkling Packard automobiles. Inside these, I husbanded carloads of reporters from Newark, Trenton, Camden, Hackensack, New York, and Jersey City. We raced Wene from town to town, followed by a dismal black Cadillac with the Wene Quartet. They sang ninety-proof barbershop.

The people liked their music. I tried to persuade the senator to address himself to the issues, but he saw it as a dangerous tactic. Once, in a western county, a reporter asked if Wene had a farm program. Wene said: "I'll be back in half an hour." He went to his hotel room and returned in time to read a windy — and, within my ken, incomprehensible — diatribe on tomatoes, corn, milk, chickens, eggs. He was partway through when the reporters, one by one, began to cap their pens. Later, I asked why. "Why?" one of them said. "That bum was reading Driscoll's farm program, that's why."

At night, I had adjoining rooms for the reporters. We had dinners and drinks sent up. I remained astonished at how drunk reporters can get. They were supine on beds and under beds. For those errant brothers, I wrote their stories. It was not a task. I jiggled the sleeper, asked what paper he worked for, asked whether the paper was Republican or Democrat. Each evening, Frank Hague or his nephew, Eggers, would phone. They knew what had gone on throughout the day, but they wanted to hear it from me. My version was always less enthusiastic than what they got from their county chairmen. "Jim," Hague would boom over the phone, "I believe you. I think you give me an honest count."

Every Friday, a black car pulled up to our house in Teaneck. Two men got out. One had the three hundred. The other watched him give it to Elinor. They tipped their hats and fled. Toward the end of the campaign, two truths became apparent: the first was that I could not vote for Elmer Wene. He was insufferably ignorant. Not to know is not a crime, but not to know and to insist that you do is unforgivable. Wene told me in confidence that he had Hague and Kenny "over a barrel." I asked how. "Okay," he said as though he was reading to a dyslexic, "Kenny now owns Jersey City and Hudson County — right?" I nodded. "Hague needs me to get back in power — right?" Agreed. "The only way they can save the Democratic party is for both of them to fight like hell to get me elected — right?"

"Wrong." He was affronted. "Look at it this way," I said. "Hague has lost the county. If he loses the state, he'll be through. Done. Finished. Isn't it worthwhile for Kenny to pass the word to all those happy Democrats to vote Republican this one time?"

The senator sucked his whole belly up. "I'm going to speak to Hague about you," he shouted. "You don't know beans about politics and you're a smartass."

The weekend before the election, John V. Kenny staged a rally for Elmer Wene. The candidate and I met him beforehand in police headquarters. The senator said: "Well, Johnny, how much plurality ah'm gonna leave Hudson with?" Kenny had happy teeth and sad eyes. "Senator," he said, jiggling the quarters, "you'll get out of Jersey City with one hundred and twenty-five thousand."

The senator's face purpled with pleasure. "Well," he said slyly, "you won't regret it, little fella."

I held my tongue, waiting for the night rally. Jersey City stages only one kind of political rally. The ward leaders order everyone on the public payroll to get in the parade and cheer hard. Bands are leased. Patriotic airs are blared. The Roman candles and rockets begin to arc and hiss in the night sky. The police chief was ordered to give a heavy crowd estimate.

Tonight the figure was one hundred thousand. Hague could see some of the parade and crowd from his nephew's office. An old reporter's trick in estimating a crowd is to draw an imaginary square and count the persons inside. Then multiply it by the number of squares encompassing the width and breadth of the mob. I came up with eighteen thousand. Hague phoned me later. "How many?"

"Eighteen."

"The papers are going to say a hundred."

"Let them say it. It was eighteen. Maybe twenty, tops."

"If you're right, I'm through."

"I've been wrong many times."

The game was over. My quest was to learn something about politics, and I did. When the election returns were counted, Elmer Wene won in sixteen counties, broke even in four, and lost one — Hudson. He also lost the election. The following morning, the reporters asked me to be their guest at breakfast. I stopped in a hardware store and bought a beautiful carving knife in a lavender plush case. I got a bottle of ketchup in a grocery store and poured some of it on the blade. At breakfast I showed it to the reporters. "This," I said, "is being sent to John V. Kenny. The card says: 'Dear Mayor, I took this out of Wene's back this morning; you might need it in the next election.' "

A job was waiting for me: to become the founding editor of Gold Medal Books. Fawcett Publications had been printing Signet Books at their Greenwich plant and realized that, while the United States of America could hardly be called a book-reading country, there appeared to be a mass trend toward twenty-five-cent books with lurid covers. The Fawcetts counted the Signet press runs and learned that a print order seldom ran below 200,000 copies. Sometimes it was a million; in rare cases, more.

The Fawcetts examined their contract to print Signet's reprints, and learned that they were forbidden to get into the reprint business. Ralph Daigh, the editorial director, thought that the contract left one door ajar — to publish original manuscripts. Bill Lengel, Fawcett's best editor, who had an appreciation of writers, was afraid that Gold Medal would get only the losers, those whose books had been rejected by a half-dozen or more hardcover publishers. On the other hand, it could bring to Gold Medal successful authors who had an old manuscript in an attic trunk.

He asked me to run it. Ralph Daigh wanted me to run it under Lengel's editorship. I said no. Fawcett, to me, was a cheap publishing house which spawned magazines and comic books in stunning arrays, killing those which did not get public approval. After two chats with Ralph Daigh, I was convinced that, although his notions turned a profit for his employers, his taste was superficial. He told me that he was addicted to westerns, and hoped I would find some good ones for Gold Medal. I recalled that, at a previous luncheon, his attitude toward the so-called good writers of the time was less than respectful. I got the feeling that Daigh (pronounced Day) felt that a good rousing plot with lots of unexpected twists and turns was all that was required to sell a book.

I took the job. I had been selling manuscripts. Let me, for a time, buy them. On Forty-fourth Street off Sixth Avenue, two doors and a saloon away from the old Algonquin, I was given a suite of offices and told to hire some editors. My salary was a hundred and seventy-five a week, so I had to find competent people who would work for less. Each morning, Lengel came in, eyes smiling, scraggly mustache sniffing, urging me to all the great deeds he saw inside my head. One of the first things he said was: "Listen to Ralph Daigh and pay no attention to him. If Gold Medal fails, he'll hang it on you, so be your own man."

This has a ring of practicality, but doesn't work. Daigh was vitally interested in Gold Medal, above and beyond all the other publications at hand. This was a good attitude because it was a newborn baby and, when we wrote publicity releases to agents, authors, and editors that we were in business to publish "brand-new, unpublished" books, "originals," it stirred New York all the way down to the New York *Enquirer*. Daigh sent a woman to me, a pretty one who wore filmy dresses and no slip. The ploy he used pushing her into my office was the one he would use with manuscripts I didn't like: "You don't have to. You're the editor and you must make the decision. However, if you want my opinion . . ."

He asked me to write a standard book contract. Gold Medal would advance two thousand dollars on a manuscript and a penny apiece on the first two hundred thousand copies. The minimum first printing was to be two hundred thousand, so, if we sold out, the author broke even and had sold his precious baby for two thousand dollars. If it went into a second printing, or a third, he could earn a considerable amount.

I sent out word that I wanted a managing editor with book experience. Also I wanted two good readers and a secretary. Among those who applied for the position of managing editor — we didn't attract more than five — was a short man in a neat brown suit. Long before, I had learned that the easy way to dispel tension is to tell a few stories on oneself, yarns in which I am the ultimate boob. I was attracted to the man in the neat brown suit. He not only understood the word *economy*, he had a taste for good books. This being so, why would a qualified sailor, so to speak, desert an ocean liner for the Fawcett raft?

He said he was an alcoholic. I asked if he thought he could remain sober as managing editor. He said he was sure he could, because it was his last chance. He had worked for fine book houses and they had passed the word that he lived inside a bottle. I said: "You're hired." He would start at one hundred and fifty dollars a week and, as he became acclimated to the position, I would ask Daigh to jack his salary. He didn't burst into tears; he didn't wring his hands with gratitude. He said: "You're getting a good man," and I said: "I know it." When the word "got upstairs," the two men began to worry. Lengel, who had trouble fighting the demise of his wife and the nightly situation of living at The Lambs listening to hilarious anecdotes, was fearful of his drinking. Daigh donned his dangerous smile and hoped I knew what I was doing. Although I hadn't asked, he said he had had a lot of experience with heavy drinkers. They were unreliable. I said that the brown suit was my managing editor and I hoped people would stop looking over my shoulder.

The man was a gem. He was quiet, efficient, an excellent assessor of manuscripts, one of those bookish types who leave the office with three manuscripts under an arm and return in the morning with a detailed review of why they should be rejected out of hand, or bought. The woman who wouldn't wear a slip spent a lot of time gazing out on Forty-fourth Street at the stone facings of a parking building across the street. It was not that she neglected her work, which was to supervise our two readers and find out if, by chance, they had discovered a nugget in the conical pile of unsolicited *merde*. She spent time leaning low on her elbows over my desk.

Daigh asked me, after three days, where the standard contract was. I began to believe that it was my rotten luck to be compelled to deal with people who "knew better." On every trail, from my father onward, there was always someone who "knew better." Long ago, Hinson Stiles had warned me to write for twelve-year-olds or quit. Louis Ruppel had been determined to make a high-class scandal sheet of a good middle-class magazine — *Collier's*. Eddie Maher was certain that *Liberty*'s glassy little articles about how Clark Gable mulched his roses, or how Joan Blondell dealt with spiritual fears, made it a finer magazine than *The Saturday Evening Post*. I was not working for Ralph Daigh; I was confronting him. In retrospect, I marvel at his patience.

I explained that a book contract requires time. There is nothing to a book contract, he assured me. I told him that I had a working knowledge of contracts, but, to make sure, I had taken copies of standard contracts from Doubleday, from Harper, from Little, Brown, and from Random House. Through amalgamation and condensation, I would have a proper Gold Medal contract within ten days. He said he would write one. If he didn't mind, I said, I would continue with my laborious project at home.

He wrote one of a few paragraphs. I wrote one consisting of four tightly spaced pages. He felt sorry for me. I asked him to please submit both to the Fawcett attorneys. They accepted mine, which was basically nothing more than a rewrite of others. It did not make me a hero in the eyes of the boss. It required little divination on my part to acknowledge that he had hired me because he was aware that I knew a lot of authors and might draw some to the new publishing house.

I did. A polite letter went to many writers asking if they had an old, scented book in a trunk. Some yellowing manuscripts arrived. They confirmed the judgment of earlier editors that they weren't worth publishing. Still, Gold Medal had to get a start. A few good names on bad work would help. Bill Lengel picked up some unpublished Fu Manchu stories by Saxe Rohmer. He fine-combed the hair of forgotten writers and resurrected some. Daigh found a brace of competent western writers. These and the third-rate mystery writers were good for three books or more apiece each year. These were bread-and-butter accounts for Gold Medal.

We moved off into the skies of American letters on leaden wings. Daigh began to concern himself with covers. He was closeted with the Italian art director almost every day. Gold Medal wanted tits. Lots of tits. In conference, we talked tits. Lengel agreed that tits sell. Daigh was afraid that too much tit might hurt Gold Medal. The question resolved itself into a small nipple with proper areola — not whether to tit or not to tit, but how much. At one point I was sure that if he managed to get a manuscript from Bishop Fulton Sheen, the cover would feature some benighted saint in leering agony with filmily draped breasts.

The sale of books should have been a concern, but I was too busy trying to find anyone who could write eighty thousand or more words without fracturing his syntax. A tall man with an engaging smile walked into the office. He said he was Ed Lewis, a Fawcett salesman of magazines, comics, and books. Mr. Lewis, I am convinced, had more to do with the success of Gold Medal Books than the editors or publishers. He was far from young, but he made all the one-night stands from coast to coast, persuading druggists and candy-store proprietors to find space for our line.

He was late; they were inundated with soft-cover stuff from Pocket Books, Signet, Dell, and a host of others trying to cash in on the American desire to buy something long and racy for a quarter. Lewis practically invented the rotary rack. He also had suggestions for displaying books without screening shoppers' eyes from aspirin tablets and Baby Ruth candy bars. When, after six months, I looked over our assortment of books, I realized that they were selling not because they were good books, or because they had been written by name writers; it was a combination of the sexy covers and Ed Lewis which made Gold Medal a profitable venture.

Within a year, we had authors who didn't do very well under one name writing under three. The book business prospered. Some hardcover editors, who did not look upon Gold Medal as competition, rejected "almost" manuscripts and urged the authors to bring the book to me. The business became so profitable that Roger Fawcett, a jolly dumpling, took to the road with Ed Lewis to promote sales. We stepped deeper into the literary waters and contracted to publish a few long-winded novels called "Gothic" in the trade, but which we referred to as "blockbusters." These sold for thirty-five cents, a sum which, in later years, seemed quaint. We also capitalized on the more asinine aspects of the Unidentified Flying Object craze by printing books which, while proclaiming the author's scientific objectivity, in reality gave credence to the madness.

With few exceptions, it was a friendly place in which to work. Lengel supported my department all the way, and even managed to browbeat Daigh to give me a raise in salary. Toward the end of the second year, Ralph began to read the books I decided to publish. Onto each manuscript was clipped a terse critique by editors of what the book was about, how credible the story, how well written, and why we should publish. For a long time, I was the last man on that page.

Casually, Ralph Daigh asked if he could read some of those fit for publication. "I could take one home, like tonight, and have it on your desk in the morning. Or, at worst, the morning after." Well, sure. Our business was not secretive, and certainly the top editorial man was entitled to see where we proposed to risk Fawcett money. That was not a problem. I was beset by an inner voice which told me that, somewhere, Daigh was going to challenge my judgment and I was going to publish anyway.

It didn't happen at once, but it came to pass. The brown-suit had passed along a manuscript called "The Brass Cupcake." It was, as I understood it, a first novel by a nobody named John D. MacDonald. The first reader liked the book; Brown-suit thought we should publish; I was enthusiastic about it on paper because the characters and story epitomized the superficial, racy kind of writing which sold in the millions around the racks. If I were to select one book which had all the qualities that millions of two-bit book buyers enjoyed, it would be "The Brass Cupcake."

I wrote a hymn as my opinion. Daigh asked if he could read it at home. He took it. When it was returned, he told me that it wouldn't sell. I shrugged. "You're the editor," he said, smiling. "I don't want it said that I'm second-guessing you. And I won't. If you insist, Jim, it's at your peril. If I thought it would stand a chance" (or words to this effect) "I'd let it go. However, I feel so strongly that I have typed my opinion under yours. That's so that we can always refer back to our written opinions."

He had the right, as editorial director, to forbid me to publish "The Brass Cupcake." He didn't. Lengel was told how he felt, and Bill came to me and said: "One book doesn't matter. Send it back." I refused. The book, I said, would be published. The moment the author signed the contract, I would quit as editor. My friend Bill called me a fool and asked where I would go. I told him I had an offer to write a book. It occurred to me that, while I was keeping the family fed as an editor, a lot of people were out in the jungles writing books and getting rich. I told Lengel that it would be impossible to be a full-time editor and a full-time writer. I had decided to write books. I might turn my thousands of notes on the assassination of President Lincoln into a book. He said I was crazy; every schoolboy knew about the assassination.

I went home and did two important chores: one, I told the West Englewood National Bank to foreclose on the house. I could no longer keep it. The Bishops would buy another one, a cheaper one in a cheaper neighborhood. The second was to write a letter resigning as editor of Gold Medal Books. In spite of my promise to stick around until John D. MacDonald and I signed a contract for "The Brass Cupcake," I quit. It was a Friday. I brought Virginia Lee to New York with me, bought some drinks at the Algonquin bar, got pleasantly drunk, and said farewell to the Fawcett editors. Ralph Daigh told me that "The Brass Cupcake" would be published as soon as he hired a new editor. I begged him to promote Brownsuit to my job, but he said no. I never met young John D. MacDonald, and haven't read any of the many books he published thereafter, but I knew all along that he was the right man for the right crowd.

The customary curriculum of two years was up. Had it not been "The Brass Cupcake" acting as the cocking of a pistol between Mr. Daigh and me, it would have been something equally inconsequential — I was thinking of asking Daigh to transfer the slipless lady from the department. There is an additional facet to Fawcett. The jobholder should feel a respect for the organization and its product. Fawcett was to the written word what Heinrich Himmler was to the Humane Society. We were, in relation to original ideas, what an impersonator is to the person he impersonates. The marvel of the impersonator is that, without great talent of his own, he can create an illusion in words and mannerisms approximating someone generally known and admired.

We were second or third rank in most of our aspirations and happy to be there. At Fawcett, our magazine and book people studied publishing for the phenomenal successes, and sometimes we would find a writer who, on order, could tailor-devise such a book within ninety days. An aura of apologetic prostitution permeated the ranks. The editors were aware that we inspired little respect among the literary agents and ambitious authors. On the other hand, they were pleased that the work was secure because Fawcett was profitable. It was Daigh, not the Fawcetts, who made the decisions which earned the money. It mattered not to him that the three brothers hurried to Africa to fell helpless game with elephant guns, or that they embarked on world cruises, or merely thought up elaborate practical jokes, like the time one of them poured five tons of lime Jell-O in an adjacent swimming pool because the neighbor sang off-key at dawn. If the Fawcetts did not invent the original hotfoot, that cruelty of lighted match and shoe, then it must be assumed that they remained in character and imitated the inventor.

There was a house on Garrison Avenue, a block and a half from the shopping district, which was for sale for thirteen thousand dollars. It was an old wooden place, two stories, with a mangy hedge across the front, a cracked concrete driveway to the back of the house, and a separate structure, which leaned perilously to the right, called a one-car garage. Elinor and I bought it.

Economically, I feared my wife. This fear was enhanced when I learned that she looked upon me as a financial wizard. We made our down payment to a stern German type who kept repeating "as is." He knew me before we met. The town had a weekly newspaper called the *Sunday Sun*. I wrote a column for it without fee. The paper tried hard to be unexciting, headlining that the Teaneck Council had spurned Miss Norton's public library plea for more books. Or that a Negro family had moved into a decaying house on the border between Teaneck and Englewood and both towns were prepared to go to court to find out which one would refuse his taxes.

The closest the paper came to something controversial was the time, in 1947, when I organized the Christians for Zionism. It was one year before the organization of the State of Israel and the effect was magical: Jewish merchants suddenly saw me as a prop for fair play in the municipality; the anti-Semites wanted to contribute small sums if the Jews would accept one-way tickets to Israel. The little column kept me in the forefront of local affairs and the Bishops were invited to cellar parties. In middle-class Teaneck, most cellars were elegantly furnished and, because they were almost hermetically sealed, clung to the cologne of booze winter and summer. Children were on the second floor in bed at nine, as the couples far below played games, shouted joyfully at each other, drank, and flirted. Ogling and the surreptitious squeezing of hands between disparate spouses were as important as the drinking. The drinking not only loosened inhibitions, it did as much for girdles.

The first payment on the mortgage was a check which bounced. Elinor wrote it and mailed it, even though I had reminded her that a check for five hundred dollars was due from *Business Week* for writing about how easy it is for middle-aged executives to go to Arthur Murray's and learn to dance. The German mortgage holder was angry. On the phone he blistered me and my reliability. When he had concluded demeaning me, I assured him that a fresh (and valid) check would go out at once, that I was sorry, that it would not happen again. He was not mollified. His voice moved up to a shout, calling me more names. I told him to go fuck himself and hung up. Within me, I resolved that if ever I earned a lot of money, I would pay this man off first and tell him, in infinite detail, how little I thought of him and his race, his forebears, and most especially his adoration of Adolf Hitler.

Always I have been a political animal, conscious of the community and the world, always fearful that, if there is one misstep to be made in the next twenty, the most prestigious statesman will make it with the best of intentions. As an example, when the United States formed an alliance with European nations and called it NATO I felt that it would not prevent a war or start one, but would drain American resources. I felt also that a heroic incompetent, Dwight D. Eisenhower, would someday be rewarded with the presidency as the citizens had once done with Ulysses S. Grant. My political views were not cynical; *critical* and *fretful* are more appropriate words. In August, 1949, four years almost to the day after an atomic bomb was exploded over the Japanese city of Hiroshima, President Harry Truman was told that a B-29 reconnaissance plane had returned to base with radioactive proof that a similar device had been detonated in the Soviet Union. Events, with few exceptions, fell into classifications such as sad, bad, and cataclysmic.

The Russians, in peace, would cost the Americans more than all the wars combined. Weaponry made quantum leaps, not only in sophistication, but in destructive power. The national agony over losing its copyright on atomic weapons to the Soviets led to a general suspicion that there was a communist conspiracy inside the nation. President Truman issued Executive Order 9835 creating a Federal Employee Loyalty Program. This encouraged young congressmen, who, with impunity and immunity, thrive on innuendo. Nixon of California charged that the Democratic party was responsible for the "unimpeded growth of the communist conspiracy." His confrere John F. Kennedy of Massachusetts blamed President Roosevelt, "a sick executive," for giving the Kurile Islands and Poland to the Soviets at Yalta. Congressman Robert Rich of Pennsylvania said that Dean Acheson was on Joseph Stalin's payroll. Unthinking America, which constitutes a great body of the electorate, believed almost everything it read.

The fever was general and chronic. Whatever was wrong was the fault of the communists — not the Russian communists, where socialism is practiced, but the Americans who, in more pacific times, might be called liberals. David Lilienthal, chairman of the Atomic Energy Commission, was accused by Senator Kenneth McKellar of Tennessee of hiding and harboring communists in the vast Tennessee Valley Authority. Denials had no coinage. In fact, they were expected of the most reprehensible of public figures. It was a time of righteous joy and anger not to be a communist, to be known as a rightist reactionary. I gave a short talk at a Teaneck restaurant to a Chamber of Commerce group and, as I left the lectern, a man grabbed my sleeve and said: "Jim, I know you'll be glad to know we just cleared you." I yanked and shouted: "Let go of my arm." Congressional committees held hearings, cleared some, destroyed others. They were exultant in Hollywood because some of the script writers and directors were, in fact, members of the American communist party. The thrill came in exposing them one at a time and watching them grovel in public.

It seemed inevitable that the nation would invent a Joseph R. McCarthy. It is not my intention to recapitulate what happened; merely to divulge what I know. In January, 1950, the press corps voted him to be the worst senator. He had taken twenty thousand dollars as an unsecured loan from Pepsi-Cola. In Wisconsin he had been reprimanded for running for elective office while holding a judgeship. He drank too much too frequently.

McCarthy was nervous, prone to panic, and feared that when he ran for reelection in 1952, he would lose. The story which has been published is that he encountered a priest from Georgetown who started him on a hunt for ghostly communists in high places. I doubt it. He stopped in to see Richard Berlin, president of the Hearst Corporation. (Berlin told this story to me in his office six years later.) Berlin was an autocrat who, with the assent of William Randolph Hearst, ran the newspaper and magazine empire. He was a stern, unforgiving type who had arrogated to himself the right to decide that the real enemy, the true enemy, was communism. He made the decision in 1934, when Franklin D. Roosevelt exchanged ambassadors with the Soviet Union.

Berlin was rich in stock and real estate. He had a duplex apartment on Fifth Avenue with its own canopied entrance. No cardinal ever held court with more majesty than Dick Berlin. If, in truth, he did not wear a ring to kiss, he permitted his subjects to do it with their eyes. For years he had a man in his office whose sole function was to card-index all communists. Many years before, this man and I had worked at adjacent typewriters, so I will veil him with the name Max. Berlin paid for Max to locate and track communists. There were weeks and months when no new ones could be found. So Max put names in the active file whose crimes may have been that they espoused Franklin Roosevelt and Social Security. Berlin and Max had a key to that file. In time, it became four feet of tin casing.

Senator McCarthy paid a visit (I do not know the date). As is proper when a senator is in the presence of a powerful personage, he slobbered over his chances of being beaten for reelection. "What you need, Joe," said Berlin softly, "is an issue. I have one — communism." Berlin raised his eyes ceilingward. "They are everywhere. This great country is being defeated by a fifth column — an army within." He pressed a buzzer. "Send Max in here."

That is how McCarthy was ignited. That was the flaming issue. That is why he flaunted blank sheets of paper swearing he had hundreds of names of members of the communist party who worked in the State Department. When he was pressed, he pleaded with Berlin for more names, more lambs for the feast. Day after day he demeaned and vilified witnesses; in session after session he moved farther and farther into fields of speculation, knowing always that Max's files were self-replenishing. Richard Nixon, at the same time, was trying to pin perjury on Alger Hiss, the man who wrote the bylaws of the United Nations. Senator Karl Mundt was blustering against all "pinkos" on two committees. For Joseph McCarthy, it was a game of survival achieved by shooting the helpless. For Richard Berlin it was a precious public forum for his coveted files. For Max it was a well-paying job.

Politicians are the only craftsmen who must enhance their reputations for integrity while stealing. Street reporters get to know thieves who are losers. They are in jail, on bail, on probation, or "trying" to go straight. The good politician must steal cleverly. He attends church and prayer breakfasts, he expresses horror in the presence of bribery, and knows before anyone else where the new highway will go through the swamp and dragoons his wife's cousin to buy the swamp. His priorities are fairly firm: himself, his family, enrichment, quasi legalities, his constituency. The exception, I found, scared the regular politicians.

Once, in Newark, a city commissioner approached me and said that three hundred thousand would be given to "the governor" if "we" were permitted to name his attorney general. The candidate was at breakfast when I brought the news. The eggs almost slopped off onto the fawn jacket. "No, no," he said. "Tell him no, Jim. Keep away from those people." I confess that I was delighted to see how upset he was. I couldn't fathom whether it was the bribe itself or his knowledge of who "we" were.

It was said that the city of Newark was owned by a hoodlum named Abner "Longie" Zwillman. I never met him, nor could I tie the commissioner to him. A few years after, when a Senate committee was investigating gang control of municipalities, I wrote to the Senate and offered to testify. The chairman said: "Now, Mr. Bishop, tell us in your own words . . ." and I did. My mistake was in thinking the story of the commissioner would create an explosion. When I completed the yarn, there was an embarrassed silence. The chairman said: "Thank you very much." There was not one question from the senators. My story was a dud. After it appeared in the newspapers, the Newark commissioner issued an outraged statement, denying everything and asserting that he would sue me. He didn't.

WHERE?

IT WAS A HOT AND BREEZY SUMMER. IN JUNE I wrote two articles for magazines and took the family to Highlands, New Jersey. It is a village which gives the appearance of having slid off the hill to the edge of the Shrewsbury River. Several of my growing summers had been spent there and across the river on that finger of land called Sandy Hook and Sea Bright. I knew the pebbled streets, the green flat river which flowed at three knots, the brownstone salt and pepper shakers called the Twinlights; the clam bars; Bahr's Landing, where the goodness of a bowl of chowder and a cold beer could make your throat ache. I had known the town when the rum-runners sped in with a couple of hundred cases of scotch, pursued by coast-guard cutters firing machine guns. On the ocean side, I had climbed that seawall, a skinny kid, fighting those eight-foot green combers which came in swelling with pride to crash in thunder on scoured sand.

Within me there was something almost atavistic in my appreciation of Sea Bright and Highlands. It was a privilege to lie face-down in hot sand and dream through the ugly cries of gulls standing high in the wind. It was an unremarkable resort patronized by cops and firemen and whining children, all of them holed up in small hot bungalows for two weeks. Side-wheelers came down from New York — the *Mary Patton*, the *Little Silver*, the *Sea Bird*, and the *Albertina* — leaving white bridal trains in the smooth river as they churned at eight knots, the piping whistles echoing off the hills.

Elinor didn't want to sleep with me. I was sure the reason was my failure, but, in solemn and private conversation, she assured me that it wasn't so. She loved me, she said. On the second and third mornings at the shore, I noticed that, as she left her bed, she drew the bedclothes over it. When she was in the kitchen, I pulled them away. She had wet the bed. I said nothing. In later days, I found that she had become incontinent. That is why she slept alone.

She feared the world of medicine as her mother did. If I suggested that she might be suffering from a prolapsed bladder, I would be accused of spying. At this time she and Maggy began to drink by day. Their tolerance decreased. After, for example, three drinks, they wanted an afternoon nap "so that we'll feel fresh tonight." Some nights, at the shore, they went off by themselves to drink. Finding them was a task. I had a drink in every tavern.

One morning they awakened not knowing where they had been, or how they got home. My esteem was at an all-time low. Maggy, it seemed, had stood on a curb waiting for a taxi to pick them up and fallen backward. She had a lump on the back of her head. The drinking, I felt, had gone far enough for all of us. I shouted at Elinor that I knew she wet the bed, that her mother was a lush. Virginia Lee, my favorite, shouted at me to shut up; that if there was a problem I ought to study my own behavior. My left hand, coming hard, caught her open-palmed on the side of the face and her features seemed to shatter into a grotesque mask. She sobbed. "All my life," she said, holding her face, "I have known nothing but drinking in my house and parents screaming and arguing. I just can't stand it."

I had hurt the child I loved and made a vow to stop drinking. The long war to win Elinor to me was over. Whatever her feelings in the matter, it was obvious that she was helpless to alter them. She lived in a ghostly edifice of fears, wandering from room to room looking for moving shadows. The more I shouted, the more I begged, the quicker she sought refuge in three-day silences. At times, the sparkle of the gum-chewing, Melachrino-smoking flapper enjoyed a resurgence, and she would bend and sway to the music of a kitchen radio, smiling at the small secret fantasies of her mind. Sometimes, she would be cuddly, almost loving. I could no longer respond. It was like hugging something well remembered.

The deeper hurt was losing the affection and approval of Virginia Lee. She was thirteen, tall, blondish with long wavy hair, an excellent high-school student who for the first time could look upon her parents objectively. The child loved me, but was disappointed. I suggested that "Mommy is beset by fears. Maybe a psychiatrist..."

"You're the one who should see a psychiatrist," she said. It didn't matter because such a suggestion in our house would have spawned prolonged fury. Gayle Peggy, short and plump with hair of black ringlets, was seven — too young to engage in family councils, a child born with running feet and an inordinate desire to win approval. Gayle not only ran to the store for her mother; she ran a second time when her mother said she had forgotten an item. She would run upstairs to get "Nanny's" glasses, help with the dishes, and hunt for whatever had been misplaced.

Long ago, I had rationalized the Saturday Night Drunk as an Irish characteristic. It was fun. We would invite couples similarly addicted, those who could devise amusing memories, drink and talk, eat cold cuts from a platter, and, if we were broke, buy the second bottle. We suffered our Sunday morning hangovers; we bathed and dressed for church; we passed the bottle of aspirin silently. Drinking had never cost a day of work or one moment of recrimination. Now it emerged as the symbol of disintegration. It wasn't the cause; it was the snapping banner of failure.

I told Elinor that I would not drink again. She burst into laughter. "Two weeks," she said. "Jim, I'll give you two weeks." I reminded her that we had "gone on the wagon" for a year and it had been a reasonable, sweet time. She said something about wishing me good luck, but not to count her in. This would make it difficult. If she and Maggy continued to drink, and I remained sober, the question narrowed itself to abuse and patience — how much of each.

Among the automatic depressants in my life are visits to hospitals, weddings, funeral services, graduations, and medical examinations. We attended a wedding. These events are formalized rituals, predictable occasions with built-in smiles and sobs, or both. Raymond Stone, cousin Agnes's son, married Elizabeth Jane Kelly. He was tall and handsome, with dark wavy hair. She was blond and beautiful — an ugly word, beautiful, but appropriate here — with blue eyes cast modestly down. My glance lingered on the bride, because her expression was solemn. Brides, I had heard, radiate. This one appeared to be in meditation, except when someone spoke to her. The smile had the aura of a formal salute.

Everyone hurried from church to Meyer's Hotel in Hoboken. This was an old beer and potato salad establishment; a place where, in other days, affluent drunks dried out, where petty political deals were offered and consummated; a landmark in a city of rotting piers, tired tenements, clam bars, sailors, and hoodlums who loaded and unloaded ships. There is a cool mustiness in the odor of Hoboken. I sat at the bar with the bride's mother. She was small, a woman with a piquant face and black bangs. She wore a smart brown suit with fur collar and cuffs. She was Mrs. James Kelly, wife of a physician who died early and left her with four small children. It had been a cruel blow, and she seemed to have made peace with herself by deciding to be slightly sick the rest of her life.

She joked about the colas I drank. I made a point of watching her sip whiskey slowly, in ladylike fashion, pushing the empty glass toward the perspiring bartender. Maggy, a few stools down, was puffing and laughing, Elinor at her side. A small musical combination played old-time sing-along tunes. The Stone family had a monopoly on good voices. With applause, the bridegroom harmonized with his sister Margie and brother Bill.

It was depressing. I had felt this way at my wedding, at my brother John's marriage to Anna Gryniak, at dozens of these ritualistic hymeneal sales. The bride, I heard, was a secretary at a New York bank.

The bridal couple departed in a flurry of raw rice, and the party got down to serious drinking. There were no disputes, although this is prescribed in many Irish weddings and wakes. Everyone had switched the joy button on. Those who couldn't dance, did. When the whiskey bottles were corked, the guests took turns buying beers. Some of the older ladies on both sides of the families were over the edge — boisterous, back-slapping, singing, promising to visit, and winding down toward over-affectionate farewells. It was a big day for Maggy. Forever after, when Elinor mentioned a name to her mother, Maggy would frown, until her daughter said: "You know, the one with the pink dress and the square neck" and Maggy would light up and say: "Oh, her!" and the conversation would proceed.

Ecstasy, like grief, is difficult to sustain. The Stones had been married a few weeks when the bridegroom was recalled to active service in the Marine Corps. International effronteries had occurred in Korea, and President Harry S. Truman responded with the U.S. Army, the Navy, the Air Force, the Marine Corps, and the commanding figure of General Douglas MacArthur. Ray was away from his bride. The corps reminded him that he had served in World War II, had landed at Iwo Jima on D-Day plus six, and owed his country another tour of duty. They sent him to Cherry Point in North Carolina. If Betty Jane could save enough from her earnings and his allotment, and could get to a motel near the base, he could get a liberty pass for a long weekend. It was a sorrow to both, one shared by hundreds of thousands of young couples. He was a bona fide hero in his dress blues, and she was the kind of rock about which no bridegroom dare have doubts. For them, it was an unbridgeable cruelty, but the government was short of sympathy. As Maggy said so sagaciously: "I don't think there was ever a time in the history of man when times weren't tough."

Gladys Glad phoned. She was at the Warwick Hotel with her new husband. Would I stop by? I knew, without knowing, that she wanted me to write a biography of Mark Hellinger. The grand lady was in a theatrical suite of rooms full of white shag rugs which had a snow-blinding effect. Beautiful women grow old more quickly and more irrevocably than average women. She was tall, stately; a tired, lined face hiding behind green sunglasses. The voice was the same: brittle baritone.

I knew her, I think, better than she knew me. She grew up in the Bronx in a cold-water flat. Her father, Nick, was an inventive man who could armor-plate gangsters' limousines. He died early and naturally. Her mother, Henrietta, was an old-fashioned person who, after a visit, opened a paper bag and cleaned out the candy and nut dishes in the suite. Henrietta lived alone, treated herself to a pint of gin, and used a broom handle to invite company from downstairs or upstairs.

Gladys Glad was hostile to men. Neither fame nor riches impressed her. She had a middle-aged German maid named Vera Winkler, a woman Glad regarded as her friend. Mrs. Winkler once told me that Glad had bragged that she had not slept with Hellinger for six months. The columnist-producer said he was worried about his sexual potency. What he didn't say, and what I understood, was that he spent considerable time with beautiful showgirls engaged in what later came to be called kinky sex.

It was ironic that the woman Florenz Ziegfeld billed as the most beautiful in the world was married to the handsomest, most affluent columnist and the best they could generate was incessant quarrels. They divorced once and, a year later, remarried, which, in the gossip columns, gave the impression that love still flourished. In its way, it did. Both were daily drinkers. Hellinger admitted to a fifth of Hennessy a day. At noon, Glad left the darkened bedroom with a tumbler wrapped in a napkin. At two the next morning, she would be talking, carrying a tumbler wrapped in a napkin.

Two of her lawyers were present on the day of my visit. She gave me her cheek to kiss and spoke of Hellinger's death. He had sustained a few secret heart attacks before the final one. He begged her to conspire with him to hide these events because, as he pointed out, "nobody is going to advance front money to a dying producer." There was a cruel rip in that veil, she said. He had an attack in the Sherry-Netherland Hotel and refused to go to a hospital. His physician ordered tanks of oxygen. As they were wheeled off an elevator, a Twentieth Century–Fox producer stared at them and at the white-suited medical aides and said: "For Christ sake, where are they going?" An attendant looked at a slip of paper. "The Hellinger suite," he said.

On the last day of Mark's life, he sat across the street from his mansion studying the final print of *The Naked City*. He didn't like the music. It was, he said, "both loud and wrong." The gray eyes snapped with fury. The picture, he said, would not be released with that music. The score would have to be done again. He returned to the mansion and blistered some people on the phone. Few sensed that this was not one more motion picture to repose on a list of credits. It was Hellinger's love letter to the City of New York. It was his somewhat cynical, at times bitter, exposition of the towers and canyons as he once knew them.

He had done something rare: had taken an entire production crew to the metropolis to film *The Naked City*. He had shot street scenes from a tarpaulin-covered truck with the camera lens poking out through a small slit in the canvas. He had hoked an average murder story into a monument for a great city. The music would not spoil this effort.

The rib-cracking weight hit his chest and he slumped. Glad called the doctor. The hairless, molasses-colored chest was exposed. The doctor called for an emergency run from Cedars of Lebanon Hospital. He found a decanter and poured a stiff brandy. "Here," he said. Mark shook his head. The man who drank a fifth every day refused the last one on the house. Glad begged him to take it. He declined. He cursed the ambulance, his fate, and the musical score. Against his better judgment, he was off to a hospital which could not keep secrets. Mark Hellinger was news. He knew he would make the newspapers and he feared what it would do to his career.

Death, sometimes, is unhurried. Three doctors and a clutch of nurses ran in and out of the immaculate little room. There were hours in which to stabilize a fibrillation. It resisted each medical ploy. That night, in restlessness, he tore up the bed. Glad stood inside the room, leaning against the wall. She, who had great practical sense, was helpless. He reared himself up, glared at the doctors, and shouted: "I hope you guys know what you are doing" and fell dead. He was forty-four years and nine months of age, one of the few of whom it might be said he was truly burned out.

Glad spent the rest of the night phoning family and friends. She had a low-key speech: "Our boy has left us." The widow of a famous man might enjoy the shock waves. The cliché states that life must go on. And it did. For me, the greater shock occurred later, when I read that Gladys Glad had married Arthur Gottlieb of Toronto, Canada. My masculine judgment was that she had betrayed a great man. It was a childish assumption. And yet, knowing her old distrust of men, it seemed incongruous that she would try marriage one more time.

I met the bridegroom at the Warwick. He was short, mid-fiftyish, a rich drunk. He had a busted nose, which made him pugnacious. Mr. Gottlieb and I got along well — in truth, he was a generous friend — but he had an affliction — doing the right things for the wrong reasons. Once, he had been a poor Jewish taxi driver. He rattled that crate over the stones of the Bronx down through Harlem clattering to the bright lights of Times Square. In his poverty, he hoped some day to become a movie producer.

The odds were phenomenal, but Arthur Gottlieb worked hard for every dollar, and spent his evenings at premieres, standing on the sidewalk nodding appreciatively at the famous as they swaggered from their curbed limousines into the lobby. At night, he worked for a cousin who, according to Gottlieb, "squeezed me for every buck." The cousin ran a studio on West Fifty-fourth Street and made additional prints from master prints of movies. One evening Gottlieb was asked to make sixteen prints of a movie. "Where are these going?" he asked his cousin.

"What's it to you?" his relative said. "I want those prints before you go home. They're all going to Canada."

"Why sixteen?" Arthur asked.

His cousin became tolerant. "No film can get into Canada without paying a duty on every one. This picture will open in sixteen first-run theaters from Ottawa to Vancouver at the same time."

Gottlieb told me he thought about this, thought about his cheap cousin and all the money paid in duty. He borrowed money and moved to Toronto. He opened a small studio. Then he sent word to Hollywood that if they sent one print to him, he could make sixteen or six hundred without paying any duty. It was a simple scheme. Arthur Gottlieb became a millionaire and bought a huge estate on a green hill. His ornate home had a solid slate roof, a beautiful drawing room, a swimming pool and bath houses, and a small motion picture theater.

One of the reasons he drank so much is that he was snubbed. When he visited Hollywood to find additional business, no one introduced him as the rich Canadian producer. Everybody called him the New York cab driver who struck it rich. It is possible that he saw Gladys Glad as a ray of authenticity. She was show business; she had a certain standing on Broadway and in the film capital. Executive producers deferred to Gladys Glad. She was also the widow of a legitimate producer. Gottlieb swept her off those skinny shanks and married her. This is the way he told it to me.

He sat there, that first day, glaring as the lawyers talked. As he said later, he couldn't trust a man who could spell. Gladys walked the floor, glass in hand, Vera Winkler nodding from the door in memory of days when, as Hellinger employees, we traded confidences. The proposition was bad: Gladys Glad would find an office in the Warwick where I could work. She would take all of Hellinger's scrapbooks and personal memoranda — even his racetrack accounts with bookies — and stack them in the office. I would research and write the book and get 30 percent of the proceeds. She would get 70 percent. She would even write a foreword to the book, which I could do for her. This would make it an authentic biography.

I tried to act insulted, but the lawyers were adamant. If I didn't like it, they would take the property somewhere else. It was a thought I could not abide. I said I would need two hundred a week every week as an advance against my 30 percent. This dismayed everyone. Two hundred? Who did I think I was? I got to my feet. "Give it to him," Glad said. "Jimmy, how long will it take?"

I sat. "Who knows? I enjoy working, enjoy doing my best, but a year? A year and a half? If you think I'm going to sit in an office taking two hundred a week —"

"Give it to him."

The Warwick was not the Plaza or the Sherry. It was a home away from home for second-rank stars. My office was on the mezzanine, over the hotel marquee. Hellinger maintained a mountain of files. It had to be organized. As I worked, I realized that the book had two problems. The first was that I admired Hellinger. It would be defeatist if the book did not reek of objectivity and warranted criticism. Second — and on this point Glad and the lawyers disagreed with me — it would not be a best-seller. Hellinger had sufficient color and substance, but he had been dead four years. His fans were gum-chewers, people by the millions who would pay five cents to read a Hellinger column but would blanch at laying out several dollars to learn one more time that he had been one hell of a guy.

Glad knew better than to editorialize, but the snapping eyes behind the sunglasses were firm on two points: one was that Hellinger left her a note in a desk advising her that, if he died, she should remarry at once. She insisted that she had lost the note. The second was that Hellinger — over Glad's objections — had adopted a boy and a girl in California. They were supposed to pacify Glad, convert her to old-fashioned motherhood, and slow her drinking. She thought the adoptions should be mentioned in the book, but was opposed to any long-winded dissertations on the pitter-pat of little feet around the Hollywood mansion.

When the research was complete, I flew to California for interviews to support or deny what I had. The occupants of the mansion with the electric gates showed me around. Hellinger's lawyer said: "You want the truth? Mark died at precisely the right time." I was introduced to an attractive dancer. Hellinger had bought her a cottage in the Valley. She was cordial and more than cordial. Directors, producers, writers had uniform words for Hellinger: they loved him. The press agent, Al Horwits, was gifted with anecdotes.

Appleton-Century-Crofts published the result. The reviews were better than expected. Harry Cohn of Columbia Pictures bought the film rights for fifty thousand dollars, which helped to reduce the indebtedness incurred by my 30 percent. The publisher gave me an early copy. It was a dread winter day. In late afternoon, I drove to Tarrytown, where Mark reposed inside a vault with his signature inscribed in granite. The gatekeeper did not want to let me inside. He thought I was a shivering nut. "Why must you go inside the mausoleum?" he asked with suspicion.

"Because," I said, "I brought him a book." It required ten minutes more, beseeching and threatening, to get inside.

He insisted on joining me.

I inscribed it: "To Mark — Take this off what I owe you. Jim."

Winter and summer, Barney Finn wore a straw hat. He was an elite butcher. Finn had that deep ineradicable Irishness that comes, peculiarly, from being born in the United States of parents raised in Ireland. His shop on Cedar Lane was classy. In the front window, his loin lamb chops were displayed like rubies. If a customer wished to purchase something and, simultaneously, desired close-order conversation, Finn was prepared. His contentions were strong and he never truckled to a customer. He would not boast that he had a bachelor's degree from Saint Peter's College because Barney thought it was unseemly to concede that he had a Jesuit education and had chosen to seek his fortune among standing ribs, pigs' knuckles, and tripe.

Those customers who were trusted, no matter how early the hour, were invited to the back room for a drink. Among fat-encrusted saws and nicked knives, he kept good whiskey. And so, having weighed and wrapped the bacon with the fish, he would tip the straw hat and murmur: "After you." Mr. Finn was not a romantic type. There was no dalliance in the back room. It was a quick tilt of the head and a purification of the throat followed by a brief expression of pain.

We bought our meat at Finn's. He was contemptuous at first, maintaining that it was a disgrace for anyone with Wexford and Corkonian blood to be writing for a living. In the first place, he said, writing is not a profession or a craft. "It is truly an imposition of your poorly developed opinions thrust upon defenseless peasants who move their lips when they read."

There was a time when I had to have a talk with Barney. As bluntly as possible, I told him that I was broke and had no prospects. There were no phone calls from magazine editors asking that I earn a quick five hundred dollars; no book publishers demanded an encore to *The Mark Hellinger Story*. The store was empty, the time for such talks. Finn flicked the straw hat back off his forehead. "May I ask a favor?" he said. I nodded. "Don't go anywhere else for your meat. Tell Mrs. Bishop that your credit is good here until kingdom come. Promise you won't go somewhere else."

I promised. I was touched. He explained that what he said had nothing to do with my sterling character. You people eat well, he said. You are the kind of customer I want. I know that when you sell something, you'll pay. If you don't, you only live a few blocks away and you can't run. "If the bill runs real high," he said, "there is no use of both of us going sleepless. Let it be me. Now, my friend, what'll it be?"

These were the dog days. Elinor and I had no savings. The few editors who phoned wanted something for nothing. "Hey, Jim," it went. "I find I have an open page in the next issue and I thought you'd sit down and rap out something quick. Give me something on a new discovery in medicine, or maybe how the new hydrogen bomb will differ from the atom bomb. Or why Eisenhower thinks that two little islands, Matsu and Quemoy, have strategic importance. You know, pal, something. What? Well, it's just a page and I'm thinking three hundred." I said no. No to all of them. They knew I was broke and they wanted cut rates. It was pride and a bit more. If I wrote a magazine page for three hundred instead of five, the news would be in every editorial office by Monday.

A big box held my twenty-two years of notes on the assassination of Abraham Lincoln, but, even if I wrote it, the book would be a long-term project and the Bishop children would starve before it was published. Father Gorman kept sending the hundred and seventy-five, and I kept owing articles to *The Sign*. At one point, when all editors were out or in conference when I phoned, I took time out to write a series of articles on American defense for Gorman. I was aboard the carrier *Midway* for a week and flown off the deck to go to the Pentagon for additional briefing. For a while, I was almost even with the priest. I could have tried some form of unemployment relief or welfare payments, but I regarded those things as a little white handkerchief on a stick.

Now and then, I met Barney Finn on the street or in his shop. He would blow his cheeks out and murmur: "God, you've been in the desert a long time." Going to New York to look for assignments cost a dollar in fares, and we didn't have that. My father sometimes pressed twenties into my hand at farewell time and said: "Keep your chin up." On the good days, I got on a ladder and cleaned out the roof drains and painted them and built a trench with tile piping to take rainwater away from the house.

Bill Lengel asked if I would do a "quickie" book for Gold Medal. This did not indicate that the world of letters had rethought its posture and felt that it needed my work. I had a loyal friend at court, one who may have had to arm-wrestle Ralph Daigh to win an approving nod. He invited me to lunch at The Lambs. The book was a true murder story — the Creighton-Applegate poisoning. It had occurred before my editorial time, but, as with the Bobby Franks murder in Chicago and the antics of the James boys, my memory had a nodding acquaintance with it.

It would be a collaboration with a psychiatrist. This broke one of my commandments, but my morale was so low that I told Bill that I was eager to write anything for any amount. Lengel said I should have stuck it out a little longer with Ralph Daigh, that the editorial director was just beginning to approve of me. The brothers Fawcett liked me, he said. Ed Lewis saw me as the greatest thing since vitamins. It would do no good, I reminded Bill, to tell me what I should have done. I was wrong; I was stubborn.

The psychiatrist was Dr. Richard Hoffmann of Park Avenue. I knew him. Hoffmann was about sixty, tall, handsome, a womanizer, a seeker of ethical publicity. Hoffmann's father had been an East Side doctor among poor Jews around 1910. The old man had affected the swallowtail coat, the high silk hat, and a polished black bag which he carried from tenement to tenement. He had taken his fee in cheese and bread from iceboxes. East of the Bowery, pedestrians raised their hats when they saw him. A Jew, old man Hoffmann was a charitable man.

He had sent his son to Vienna to study psychiatry. Young Dick, who was no longer young, was a psychiatrist when most were still called alienists. Dick had moved uptown, bought a small chalet on Park Avenue, festooned the corridors with good art, and catered to stage and movie stars who were afflicted with bad dreams, rotten desires, a garden of fears, twitches, itches, impotence, and something called malaise. Readers of newspapers became aware of Hoffmann in the twenties and thirties. District attorneys called him to depict defendants as sane; defense attorneys paid good fees for an opposite opinion. Newspapers began to use Dr. Hoffmann to write special articles describing fiends who were sought for vile crimes. The doctor, who saw himself as a writer, penned sidebar articles describing the ages, weights, appearances, and dispositions of mad bombers and murderers.

Lengel said the advance would be two thousand, plus the usual royalty.

The doctor had already agreed to give me the advance, provided that he could take all of the royalties until we were even. I agreed. Dick Hoffmann turned out to be one of the all-time charmers. He was a member of the Players Club and we dined at Gramercy Park night after night. Dick was also a raconteur. He had what must be close to a poetic appreciation for description, for setting the stage, so to speak, before attacking the main body of the story. I began to make notes of punch lines, so that, at a future date, I could steal the stories.

The book, in my opinion, was a disaster. Hoffmann had been the state psychiatrist on the Creighton-Applegate case and kept not only a good transcript of the trial, but notes on his long interviews with the principals. The disaster was my fault. I was going to research and write it as quickly as possible, certainly before the two thousand was dissipated. At this time, I had three personal loans of three hundred dollars apiece. A rich lady in Fairlawn lent five hundred dollars twice.

The story, briefly, was that Frances Creighton, a dark buxom woman with brooding eyes, had a taut nervous system. When she lived in New Jersey, and certain female relatives made accusations that she had stolen a silver spoon, or was a poor housekeeper, Frances Creighton found that her nervousness could be assuaged by administering rat poison in soup, in dessert, mashed potatoes, or even in fresh lemonade. It required four or five days of sick calls for death to ensue, but, once it was achieved, a lovely peace descended over the family. Frances kept a black hat with a veil and she wore it to all the funerals. Sometimes, when the stress was upon her, Frances could take care of two relatives in one year, sending them off to their eternal reward with tears and prayers.

She had a husband who seldom made her feel nervous. He worked from nine to five at anything he could get. He would not permit himself to disagree with his beloved spouse and, if he uttered an opinion, it might be that Wally Pipp was the best first baseman in either league. They had a fifteen-year-old daughter who was charitably described as precocious. Frances Creighton, a neighborly person, hung washing on the line and said hello to Ada Applegate in the next yard.

Mrs. Applegate was five feet tall and two hundred ten pounds of ardent love. Her husband, Joe, was a movie projectionist, a busy squirrel of a man whose hands ran up curvaceous legs as though they were trees. Joe Applegate may have been — in the absence of proof to the contrary — the most finely tuned sex machine on Long Island. He made love to girls whose names he never asked. It didn't matter what they looked like. Applegate took a look at Frances Creighton and he was ready. He arranged matinees day after day. Frances and Joseph tried it in the projection booth, on floors, beds, standing in hallways, in his car, and at a late-night bus stop.

He assured her that Ada was sleeping in an alcove by herself, but Frances figured that sex fiends with endurance are hard to find in the best of times, so she made some pudding for Ada. Within a few hours, Mrs. Applegate was thrashing on a bed, screaming: "Don't touch my toes! Don't touch my toes!" The pubescent daughter phoned Joe, who hurried home. Unable to pacify Ada, he assisted her to his car and took her to a local hospital. Physicians were mystified. They agreed that she might be suffering an acute gastrointestinal attack, but no one could understand why she implored one and all not to touch her toes.

Within two days, stout Ada was sitting up in a pink peignoir devouring double portions of antiseptic hospital food. Whatever it was, one doctor told Joe Applegate, it had passed "You should talk to Mrs. Applegate about losing fifty or sixty pounds. It might have been a gallbladder attack, although tests are negative." Ada was brought home in triumph. To celebrate, her dear friend Frances made a huge rice pudding with lots of eggs and nutmeg, and spoon-fed Ada. This time it required two days for Ada to start shrieking about her feet. Off she went to the hospital. This time, Frances visited and brought some homemade food, but the doctors forbade it.

Rest in bed restored Ada so much that she invited visitors to play with her feet. Again, she went home. Applegate was so distraught that he stopped thinking of fornication for days on end. Mrs. Creighton made an apple cobbler so good that, to coin a phrase, it would kill you. That's what it did to Ada. By the time she got to the hospital, she was uninterested in her toes. The physicians thought they should perform an autopsy. Joe growled: "Hasn't this woman suffered enough?" so it wasn't done. The district attorney sent a representative to ask permission for the postmortem. Joe declined. The D.A. got a court order. The lady was disinterred and, although the arsenic was not sufficient to kill a horse, it was enough to do Ada in.

The case against Frances Creighton was circumstantial until the authorities retained Dr. Hoffmann to interview the interested parties. He sat in the kitchen listening to Frances deny lacing desserts with arsenic. The thought of being suspected of such unfriendly conduct toward Ada reduced Mrs. Creighton to tears. Her daughter walked by. Dr. Hoffmann, glancing at the girl, said: "Did Uncle Joe give you the ankle bracelet?" The child nodded. The effect on Frances was explosive. Either she had not noticed the thin gold chain, or, having noticed it, thought her daughter had purchased it. She grabbed the child and demanded the truth.

The girl wept. She was no longer a virgin, she said, because Uncle Joe had been very nice to her. He was nice to her when Momma was out shopping; he was nice to her after school; he was extra nice to her up high in the projection booth. Frances Creighton broke. Yes, she said, she had fed arsenic to her dear departed friend, but only because Joe had demanded that she do this terrible thing. She said it; she wrote it; she signed it. The police yanked Applegate out of his busy booth and tossed him into jail.

The trial had edges of French farce, but neither the judge nor the jury saw it. Applegate pleaded that he did not conspire to kill Ada; he had no reason to kill Twinkletoes; he was exhausted from trying to service all the females in the neighborhood. The jury saw Joe as a human rat getting away with secret pleasures denied to them. Besides, they asked, if he did not conspire with Frances, why had he refused an autopsy? The jury decided that it would help to restore the county to respectability if they sent both parties to the electric chair.

Applegate died whispering his innocence. Mrs. Creighton was strapped into the chair asking that the keepers please be gentle. The book, as far as I was concerned, hinged on the delicate issue of whether a woman scorned can carry her lover to the chair without substantive evidence. The answer was yes. Whatever my best is, I gave it to the book because I thought a bit of color, a smidgen of word economy, might carry it. When it was published, I learned that Gold Medal indeed had the last word in our chronic contretemps. They had rewritten the first few chapters to the level of pulp detective magazines. They called it *The Girl in Poison Cottage* and I spent a good deal of the rest of my life trying to disinherit that book.

The New Year of 1953 came up cold and friendless. I sat around the house watching the girls grow. The mortgage payments had lapsed for two months. The managers of personal loan offices were kind: "The only thing we can do is to renew the loan for the unpaid balance plus all the interest you owe." Barney Finn had four hundred dollars from the proceeds of the paperback and was ready to roll the dice one more time. A crochety old monsignor in Bayonne, New Jersey, offered me five hundred dollars to satiate his vanity by writing an overnight biography and I accepted.

I explained that publishers would not want the book. It didn't matter, he said; he would have it published by the diocese.

I researched and wrote the book, *The Making of a Priest*, in three weeks. When it came from the printer, I was surprised at the large format, the photos of his family, the large type size, and a color photo of the arch-bishop discreetly in front. The old priest was near the end of the road, and he wasn't going to be kept wondering what kind of a headstone the church would fashion for him. He had chiseled his own.

The big, brassy agency, Music Corporation of America, underwent a metamorphosis which included disintegration. The law said MCA could not produce films, and, at the same time, represent actors as a 10 percent agent, and writers too. The old Leland Hayward office, where once I had labored, broke away and moved farther up on Madison Avenue. The silk-suited crowd moved to Hollywood, bought a small piece of property from comedian Bob Hope, and built the "MCA Building" on it.

I visited the new agency — now called ICM — with the old faces on Madison Avenue. The woman who had my job was Phyllis Jackson. I needed an agent. She was the best. Miss Jackson called herself "Miss." She was married to Alan Jackson, associate editor of *The Saturday Evening Post*. In addition to the written word, they shared one more interest: the New York Giants baseball team. They could move from a dissertation on Proust to Leo Durocher and why he triumphed. Phyllis had a faint birthmark on the right side of her face, a large molasses stamp which she refused to hide under her coiffure. She was close to her venomous mood when she addressed me as "Jim dear ..." She wore hats in the office and kept a pale phone in her ear. At times, she was known to cast a well-known author loose because he drank too much, or because, in spite of capability, he wrote a superficial book for "a quick buck." Her husband, having once worked in the Navy Branch Book Section with Roger Straus, recalled me with kindness and urged Phyllis to accept me as a client.

I do not pretend to recall the first speech, but I remember sitting in her small book-lined office. "At one time you held this job. You don't now. If you think you're going to play agent, I don't want you. Last week I checked the records; you haven't written anything in a long time. You require promotion. I asked Appleton for a copy of your *Mark Hellinger Story*. The writing shows some good flashes. The subject, Jim dear, is dreadful. Whatever possessed you to think that your Hellinger was worth a biography?"

I took the drubbing. As a client, I was a gamble. I leaned on my crutch, that I had been keeping notes on the Lincoln assassination for twenty-three years. Her lower lids had a rim of pink. They widened. "Then write it. Go home and write it. Don't be Carl Sandburg. Be Jim Bishop. Give me a two- or three-page outline. Random House says they will publish anything you write. Give me an outline of the sound and feeling of the book. Then write it."

The outline, consisting of two typewritten pages and one paragraph, stated that each chapter of the book would be an hour in the final day of the President's life. I proposed to write it in such a way that the reader would feel that he was present; he would see and hear the streets and sounds of Washington; the cries of hawkers and beggars; the price of apple butter and ducklings; he would walk each step with the President until, at 7:22 the following morning, the Surgeon General placed two silver dollars on Abraham Lincoln's eyelids.

I went home. The time was September, 1953. I sat in the cellar, rolled a sheet of paper with carbons into the typewriter, and looked at the dustbeams slanting from the window. Then I wrote:

> The polished rosewood door swung back and the President of the United States came from his bedroom. He nodded to the nightman in the hall and said "Good morning." He fingered his big gold watch, anchored to the chain across his vest, but he did not look at it. The hour of seven was late for Lincoln. Many a time, the guard remembered, the President was downstairs working at six.

The big man started down the hall slowly, like a person older in years, the legs perpetually bent at the knees, the black suit flapping about the frame. He looked like a man who did not feel well. The circles under his tired eyes were pouched; the skin of his face was almost saffron; the scraggly black beard thinned and died as it approached the hairline; the hair itself was almost combed; the feet moved with conscious effort, barely lifting off the red pile rug before being set down again; the thick lips, more brown than red, were pulled back in a semi-smile. . . .

Suddenly, I could *feel* this book. It was not something proffered by generous hands, as *The Glass Crutch* had been handed to me by Roger Straus, as the Hellinger book had been offered by Gladys Glad, as Bill Lengel tendered *The Girl in Poison Cottage*. This was mine. It was as though someone had been saving bits of foil for a long time and found he could hardly lift the ball. My habit remained — as newspaper editors taught me — to do my best the first time and not to rewrite or "polish" or revise. Only the laziest or most confident of writers can afford to stare at a wall and dwell on a scene over and over until the characters come alive on wallpaper and move and speak amid the weather and smells of their lives. It is self-induced insanity, but for me it works.

Once a week — no more — I phoned Phyllis Jackson for news. It was bad. Random House didn't want it. Viking didn't want it. Doubleday thought it was a trite story whose nuances were known to schoolchildren. "Jim dear," Phyllis said, "keep writing. If you need money badly, I'll get you a magazine piece to do. But keep writing Lincoln." It got cold early that year. The typewriter was set near the oil burner. It was silent for long periods, then would stir itself in a whoosh like a jet engine. The beast would throb through my thoughts for twenty minutes or so, and then fall into a silence as sudden as the sound.

Five publishers declined. The arguments of Phyllis Jackson that the book represented a new you-are-there format were discounted as salesmanship. It went to a sixth publisher, Harper. There the little outline came to the attention of Evan Thomas, a tall, professorial type. He liked it. More than that, he predicted that it would be a best-seller. A contract was signed, a good advance check arrived, and I wrote that book as though there was nothing I knew so intimately as what happened in the city of Washington in those twenty-four hours and twenty-two minutes. My notebooks had long since been in chronological order. Where authorities disagreed about what the principal characters were doing or saying, I had my "anchor" points marked. These were the indisputables, the items about which the majority of biographers and historians agreed.

The scenes ran themselves through the cellar typewriter so fast that I feared I was not giving it my best. Gestation had been so protracted that I wanted the baby birthed full-grown. At the kitchen table, I ransacked the copy for typographical errors. Whatever quality it had, it was my best.

My mother, who regarded writing as the ultimate retreat of the dilettante, kissed me and said: "If this one doesn't sell, son, do you think you'll go out and look for a job?"

My father, the authority in the family, said: "Of course you realize that John Wilkes Booth was not killed in a barn by Boston Corbett?" I shook my head. "For your information," he said, "Booth escaped and lived out a normal life in the Territory of Oklahoma."

"Where," I murmured, "did you get that?"

"From my father," he snapped.

Elinor said she was in "no mood" to read the manuscript. "I'll wait for the book," she said. The children, as an act of love, were sympathetic to the book. They had heard me say that there were about fifty-odd coincidences of that fateful day, which, if they had not occurred in precise order, would have prevented the assassination of the President. Virginia Lee was sixteen, a book reader. At the age of ten, Gayle was a running tomboy, climbing, falling, entering herself in track meets which she lost by looking over her shoulder at the competition.

The book was at the halfway point in the late autumn. Several events, each unexpected — almost painfully acceptable — occurred. An editor at McGraw-Hill had read an old copy of *The Sign* and wanted a biography of Father McWilliams. Two priests of St. Paul, Minnesota, had founded a highly successful little magazine called *Catholic Digest*. They wanted an executive editor in their New York office who could manage to buy homely, *Reader's Digest*–type articles which carried a *slight* tinge of Catholicity. The job would pay twelve thousand dollars a year. Virginia Lee, coming out of high school, wanted to write a biography of Father Francis P. Duffy of World War I's Fighting Sixty-Ninth.

The proper response might have been no, no, and no. Virginia Lee had no writing experience. Her grades in grammar were good, but writing isn't grammar. I didn't mock the child as novice writers are mocked. I reminded her that a couple of biographies had been written about the chaplain after World War I. She nodded. She had read them. They created the urge to write another. I reminded her that the research would crush her spirit; that no biographer or historian is ever sure that, before starting to write, he has turned over a sufficient number of damp rocks. I didn't want to discourage my daughter, but I wanted to test her motivation. Even after all the research and writing was done, I told her, it is possible that no publisher will want it.

She was firm. If it was not published, she'd keep the manuscript. You will do your own research, I said. I will lay out a few rules for interviewing people who knew this priest, people who might have special information, but you will conduct those interviews. Much of it will take place in the Bronx, I said, and I cannot take time off to sit and listen. On the other hand, I cannot allow you to go alone. If you are willing to make all your appointments at night, after dinner, I will go with you and I will bring you home. And let us get one thing straight: you will write it. I don't mind going over your copy and straightening a few misplaced phrases, or even doctoring a few figures of speech, but I will not write it. She said she meant no disrespect, but it had never been a part of her plan to have me write it.

Missy wrote her outline and sent it to Phyllis Jackson. I apologized. My agent said: "It's a charming idea. Let us see...." Farrar, Straus & Cudahy gave her a contract. There was a little hook in it. The by-line would have to read: "by Virginia Lee Bishop and Jim Bishop." It was, I thought, humiliating for Virginia Lee, but she accepted it with grace. The work was formidable and I typed single sheets of paper enunciating the fundamentals of background reading, personal research, and what to keep in mind before writing a scene: the characters, the action, the weather, the attitudes of each personage, the point to be established within the scene, the smells, et cetera, et cetera.

In the manner of a mad sailor who discovers that the boat is not sinking, only leaking dangerously, I hurried into Jersey City for dinner and a long talk with Father LeRoy McWilliams. Most priests hope to be remembered as builders. They drive the parish into debt erecting marble altars, schools, convents, and acquiring adjoining property. This one radiated joy at the thought of being remembered in a biography.

I leveled with him. Father, I said, I have no time to sit with you for a few thousand hours trying to find out where you came from, what horrible crimes you may have committed in your youth, and where you are headed. If you agree to sit and write the book plainly, bluntly, not sparing yourself or those around you, I will put the finishing touches on it. If you are about to canonize yourself, get another writer. What I need is a human story of a priest. McGraw-Hill sees you as possibly the last of a breed of Irish priests who not only save souls, but meddle in the temporal affairs of your parishioners, saving them from divorce, jail, factional fights, and steering them politically toward John V. Kenny and against the Hague machine. If I were you, I wouldn't touch it.

He said yes. He would do it. Where I had hungered for a cheap magazine article to write and perhaps catch up to Barney Finn and his butcher shop, I now had two books under contract and was expected to be a watchdog over my daughter's work. Elinor saw it all as solvency and urged me to take the job at *Catholic Digest*. I was opposed — somewhat feebly, I admit — because I was fearful, actually frightened, of being labeled "that Catholic writer." And yet, a thousand dollars a month seemed so rocklike. I hurried to New York to have a talk with Father Paul Bussard, the co-publisher. He was positive, at once, that he wanted me. He was a tall man with a strong face and flecks of gray in his hair. He traced my past in the gracious Braille that one from another world would use feeling toward another. The circulation of his little magazine was incredible: nine hundred thousand. Somebody was getting rich.

The office was on East Fifty-third Street. It was a small white building off Madison Avenue. Before I entered, I knew what I would find. Little ladies of indeterminate age would be poring over manuscripts, consulting library and reference files, genuflecting every time they saw a priest. They would be working, not for money, but for the love of God, a noble element nonnegotiable at Barney Finn's shop. They would not speak; they would whisper. No matter what stand they assumed on any matter, if they were contravened, they would nod mute assent and return chastened to their warrens.

I found them. The best and worst thing the place had was a telex hooked to the main office in St. Paul. This would be my tether. Whatever I proposed to do would run through this chattering machine, followed by a silence, followed by a message starting: "Jim, of course you may go ahead and buy it, but don't you think the subject is a bit hackneyed? Give it an additional thought and let us know. Father Paul." Knowing these things, I took the job. The naive idealist had given way to the caustic cynic. One of the bonuses was the acquisition of a small, hyperefficient secretary. She understood the heartbeat of the magazine. The girl was ardent in her religion, knew (so to speak) where the bodies were buried, was single, and lived with her parents in Yonkers. She was my glittering, platinum assistant.

Catholic Digest, like the old priest who ran off with the mother superior, was full of surprises. The first occurred when I visited Francis Cardinal Spellman. He saw me in his reception room on the main floor of "the powerhouse," rather than in his private quarters on the second floor. He said he had heard about my new position and wondered if I liked it. Why not? I said. It's a job and I know I can carry it off. Well, he said, that was nice. The face radiated cherubic coolness. I said that, well, working within the archdiocese of New York, if he could help in any way ... "You don't need any help," he said.

Bussard failed to tell me that *Catholic Digest* had opened its New York office without paying the customary courtesy call on the archbishop. It is not a written rule; good manners make it *de rigueur* that, in crossing diocesan lines on public business (to make a speech, appear on television, preach, publish, and so on) the ordained make it known to each other, not so much to get permission as to obviate surprises. The New York "powerhouse" persuaded Father Paul to remain in Minnesota, where, to the dismay of many bishops, he was safe under the protection of Archbishop Mooney. *Catholic Digest* had sneaked into New York without endorsement. In effect, it made a little sneak of me.

Another surprise was my inability to find out who owned the magazine. It had been founded by Paul Bussard and Louis Gales, Minnesota priests. Father Gales lived in a bungalow with busted screens near a hospital. He was retiring, self-effacing, a man who accepted his Christian burden to live in near-poverty and to console the sick. Bussard was the near-extrovert who owned a house near a lake and who invited couples for weekends.

He was confident, outgoing, a man who seemed determined to enjoy a bit of this life before experimenting with the next. It was possible that the diocese of St. Paul took some of the magazine profits. A visit to the home office depicted a modest office, something I would call a cellar operation. Physically, *Catholic Digest* was cheap, a small format printed on paper so poor that while it would accept line cuts well, it fogged halftones. The contributors, with few exceptions, were paid little more than what *The Sign* offered for original material. In the case of reprints, our attitude was that the authors had already been paid. We filled page on page with stories which cost a hundred dollars, sometimes less.

Our slush pile — unsolicited manuscripts — was small. Most of what I bought came through literary agents who had despaired of selling a story and, assuming that the message carried the bright optimism of *Reader's Digest* content, sent it finally to us. Our slush-pile girl quit. God knows how long she had been reading this stuff, reheating pots of tea and lighting fresh cigarettes, but there came a day when she felt demeaned, degraded, and defiled and walked out.

I telexed St. Paul (the city) and said that, unless they had someone who could fly in and start reading the accumulation of trash, I would suggest my daughter Virginia Lee for the work. Nepotism never bothered the Bishops. Bussard wired okay. Missy arrived in lipstick and heels and a coiffure executed with a hot iron. She liked the work; the staff liked her. I advised her to take her salary home each week and hand it to her mother. Elinor returned enough for dresses, shoes, hats, cosmetics, and such other editorial necessities as the child might require. The baby was a grown-up.

At Christmastime in 1953, an insidiously slow alteration in my relationship with Elinor became apparent. I state it thus because, in retrospect, the change had been under way for a considerable time. Little by little, she felt the need of a friend — a loyal friend — and I was the man. Not a husband, a friend. She appeared to be breaking. The nose-to-nose arguments stopped. The tears, the long chats of reconciliation, ceased. She was older, thinner; the once full figure collapsed inside the dress. Brushing her hair made her arms ache. Dressing was a chore. Sometimes the face appeared to be unwashed, the lips cracking under yesterday's lipstick.

Her personality, at Christmastime, 1953, was craven. She represented the ashes of a one-time flapper. We sat and chatted. She begged: "Don't fight with me." I said I hadn't. Whatever rancor I felt dissolved in pity. I did not think the time would come when I would prefer a strong, arrogant Elinor to a hand-wringer who slept too long and too many times, who wrung her hands, who ordered the children not to respond to the doorbell when "Aunt" Kay Herman and other friends called, one who dreaded to hear the phone ring, or to open mail. The time came.

I had immersed myself in a rickety career so that I would not have to look into those big brown eyes and study the unattainable. The immersion had been good for me because, in the long hours, when I wasn't writing, I was reading. She was forty-three. She took triple doses of tranquilizers, followed by gin on ice. She sat pertly in a wing chair, an open magazine on her lap, not reading, just smiling faintly. Getting her attention became a problem. When I asked how she felt, the thick red lips curled slowly around the word *fine*.

Maggy was seventy-three. Her long brown hair was intact, with little edges of gray on the bottom. She got up tired; she went to bed tired. She spoke endlessly about everybody she knew dying in their forties. Her interests had never been broad; now they were confined to Elinor, her grandchildren, and her niece, Agnes. The eyes were heavy-lidded, rheumy. Most of her teeth were gone. She helped with the cooking; spaghetti and tomato sauce were her specialties. If she heard the doorbell, she lifted her skirt and hurried upstairs to her room. A few drinks in the evening caused her skin to flush, and she would ramble about "My Frank. My Frank. I tell you, we had our fun when we was young."

I asked Elinor to go with me to a woman psychiatrist. She demurred, then said yes. It was a measure of how far gone she was that she would entertain such a thought. On the drive to the office in New York, I kissed her, held her hand, and told her that it would be good for both of us. "Can this woman tell me what I'm afraid of?" Sure, I said. She's an expert. The analyst had Elinor in her office for fifteen minutes, then asked me questions for fifteen minutes. It was a waste. The lady sat behind steel-framed glasses, unblinking as she asked Elinor questions about her sex life. They were, within Elinor's ken, insulting questions. When we were back in the car, my wife said: "Is she crazy or am I?"

I said: "She is. Forget it."

It was easy to get along with this woman, except that this was not the one I married. This was a glassy-eyed smiler. Our daughters helped with the housework. They vacuumed rugs and washed dishes and placed things in the spin-dryer and hugged and kissed their mother more than usual.

It was early December and the book would be finished in a week or two. Most of the manuscript had gone to Phyllis and then to Evan Thomas. Miss Jackson said she thought I had a talent for writing suspense. "Jim dear, it is almost unbearable. When Mrs. Lincoln was pulling those white gloves on and said to the President: 'Would you have us be late for the theater?' I felt like a giddy child. I wanted to scream: 'Don't go.'" These were important words to me because no writer, no matter how great nor how weak, knows for sure whether his words have come close to the target he has in mind until he hears an echo from a competent source. Even Thomas said: "Beautiful. Keep going." With every book there is a terrible period between finishing the manuscript and publication day. Daily life has to go on, but it does in a suspended state, awaiting the public's reaction.

It is beyond understanding how Father McWilliams organized his life

[254]

into sentences and paragraphs, had them typed, and sent them so quickly to my home. It came to close to four hundred pages, a chore which brought little joy. The final scenes of the Lincoln book went to Harper before Christmas, 1953; by February 15, I had edited, revised, and condensed the priestly life so that, I hoped, it would be professional.

Father Bussard sent me to Mexico City. I wondered if St. Paul wanted me out of the New York office. And yet, this was an article I wanted to do. It concerned Our Lady of Guadalupe. Almost every city and town between Tia Juana and Tierra del Fuego has a church in that name. Whoever she was, she had enormous appeal to Latins. Someone wrote to the sacristan of the basilica before my arrival.

Bussard, I thought, made a poor choice when he picked me for the assignment. There were journalists in Mexico who wrote book English. I cannot force myself to believe in miracles. The burning bush, the parting of the Red Sea, and kindred writings strain my credulousness. I can force myself to believe in Jonah, but not the whale. It would be elevating indeed to look upon this as the product of a logical mind, but it is downright cynicism. I found it easier to concede that of course there were miracles, many of them, but all were beyond my credence.

On the telex, I asked Father Bussard what would happen if I did not believe in Our Lady of Guadalupe. "Write it whatever way you see it, Thomas," he wired back. It was my first time out of the United States, first time with a passport, first time to wander through an airport, wading in a pudding of impassive Indian faces. It is my habit, on the scene, to start work at once. This was born in the days on the *Daily Mirror*.

The priests at the old basilica treated me as though I were a real bishop. There was a Spanish edition of *Catholic Digest* and it had circulation in Mexico. None of them pressed me to believe anything. They gave the historical facts, and allowed me to work outward from them. As I recall, Cortez and the Spaniards had swept upland from the coast and defeated Montezuma. In the name of Spain, they converted the Indians, cured the maidens of their virginity, stole all the gold, and built a church in what would become the central square of Mexico City. The miracle they worked was impressing on the Indians how well the Spanish blunderbusses worked on Indians armed with arrows.

There was a place called Tepeyacac Hill. It was about eighty feet high, composed entirely of alkali. Nothing grew on it. Beyond and behind it there were some Indian lodges. Juan Diego was a baptized Indian. He was also ignorant. In the area of his life with which I was concerned — December, 1531 — Diego appeared to be more worried about a sick uncle than about food or work. He took his conversion to Catholicism seriously, and donned a *tilma* — an Indian garment woven of white fiber, like twine, with front and back panels which hung to the knees; straps held the panels together down the sides of the body — and walked down Tepeyacac Hill and into the city to attend mass daily. His uncle's health did not improve.

One day, on the hill, Juan Diego saw a "lady." She represented no threat to him, so he was not alarmed. He noticed that she was attired in an expensive-looking blue cape with gold stars. Juan Diego also noticed a radiance emanating from the cape outward, almost akin to golden beams. Somehow, he didn't think this was remarkable.

She spoke to him. The lady asked him to call on the local bishop and ask him to build a church in her name. She said that this indeed was a New World and it would need a patron. The Indian, pained and patient, lifted his sombrero to the lady and departed. Then, as now, speaking to a bishop was not a simple assignment. It would have been easier, two thousand years ago, to speak to Jesus on the streets of Jerusalem. A few priests listened to Juan Diego's request and tossed him out of the episcopal residence. There were some crude jokes about drunken Indians.

Señor Diego saw the "lady" again. And again. Her presence depressed him. She intruded on his daily pilgrimage to the church, to offer up a mass for his uncle's health, and the return back up Tepeyacac Hill to the sickbed. Her message became monotonous: in effect, that all of the New World — North and Central and South Americas — would be under her protection. At one point, Juan Diego whined: "They asked me to bring a sign from you." She pointed behind him. There, in astonishment, he saw a flowerbed of growing roses. Flowers, then and now, do not grow on Tepeyacac. She advised him to pick a bouquet and bring it to the bishop. Juan Diego was a stupid Indian, but he knew that roses do not grow in Mexico in December. He lifted the front panel of his *tilma* and filled it with dewy roses. He bowed again and departed for church.

This time, the priests admitted him to the marble reception room. They whirled about in their black cassocks, busy with whatever young and ambitious priests do to please a bishop. The notion seemed to be that this time they would wear the Indian down with waiting. He sat. History does not record how long he sat, but it states that some priests paused and teased at the way he held his *tilma* up. What was he hiding? One grabbed at it and danced away. In the afternoon, the bishop came through the reception room. He saw Juan Diego and frowned. This one was indeed a pest. Standing off, he demanded to know what the man wanted. The tone frightened Juan Diego. He stood, mumbling that the "lady" had sent a sign. The *tilma* fell, the roses cascaded to the floor. Bishop Zumárraga gasped. He fell to his knees. This so frightened Diego that he burst into tears. He saw priests and parishioners drop to their knees. They must see something that he didn't. He looked down. There, on the front of the *tilma*, was a likeness of the "lady" — blue cape, small gold stars, even the radiant bands he had seen.

Of course Bishop Zumárraga built the church the "lady" requested. In my opinion, he made two grievous errors: first, he refused to see the Indian without a sign; second, the church might have been called "The Lady of Tepeyacac," but, as a mortal, the bishop decided to name it after his favorite town in Spain: "Our Lady of Guadalupe." Around the church was a stone courtyard four hundred feet deep. Through the next four and a half centuries, pilgrims walked those four hundred feet of hot stones on their bloody knees. They believed.

The *tilma* was preserved in a glass case. In a case next to it was another *tilma*. With time, most of its fibers rotted, but the one with the image remained as it was in 1531. Early in the twentieth century, the archbishop of Mexico invited scientists to come from Europe and examine the garment. They were polite; they didn't believe a word that they heard. Proof, they said, must be objective. If they could have tiny snippets of the *tilma*, and little flecks of the original paint depicting the face of the "lady," they would be pleased to examine both in Europe, and make a judgment. The report required time. It came from several nations, but was uniform in its scientific evaluation. The *tilma*, hung carefully in a glass case, might last forty or fifty years before the natural disintegration of the fiber would cause it to fall apart. So far as the image was concerned, there was no paint known which contained the properties of this one, and experiments proved that there was no way to paint an image on rough twine.

I asked the Mexican pastor for permission to mount a ladder and open the glass cases. He gave it. The skeptic examined both, and noted the mark on the back of the original *tilma* made by Bishop Zumárraga and stamped "1531." It is difficult for the cynic to confess that he began to believe, but it is true. I worked hard to create a doubt, because miracles are simplistic only to simpletons. Outside the church, I bought an eight-inch bronze statue of Our Lady of Guadalupe and put it in my briefcase. If she pledged to help citizens of all the Americas — not just Mexicans and Argentinians and Peruvians and Guatemalans — then I knew a wretched writer who needed help.

Lunch at a restaurant called Toots Shor's was a sporadic pilgrimage. In its way, it was ninety-proof Lourdes. It was a brickish place on Fifty-first Street between Fifth and Sixth avenues, through whose revolving doors passed such successful writers, editors, actors, and gangsters as could afford two hours for lunch. The entrepreneur could not pronounce "entrepreneur." He was a fat, rude man from South Philadelphia who was afraid of dark hallways. Bernard Shor may have invented the callous sentimentalist. Once, when an official of the Bureau of Internal Revenue was sent to prison for taking instead of giving, Shor rented a Carey Cadillac every Saturday, loaded it with flowers, smoked turkeys, hams, nuts salted and unsalted, and drove one hundred and eighty miles to Lewisburg Federal Prison to assure the man that he had not been forgotten.

Shor was a terminal gossip, a man whose heavy feet threaded between the white-clothed tables, shouting insults which translated into affection, whispering the latest about Walter Winchell, Frank Costello, Jimmy Cannon, Bill Corum, Joe DiMaggio, Harry Truman, Lucky Luciano, Dorothy

Kilgallen, Bill Hearst, Bob Wagner, Francis Cardinal Spellman, Whitey Ford, and such others as might be considered important enough to warrant oratorical tidbits. Shor did not dispense his goodies to everyone; at lunch the casual patron could detect important patrons in two ways: by how close they were seated to the archway at the front of the restaurant, and by Toots's stopping to lean forward for a chat.

It is a blessing that Shor did not mature. He was fifteen years old forever. He could ably dispute old baseball averages, the appalling inflation in the price of hookers, his bleeding-into-the-wrist friendships for Hellinger, Corum, and Costello; his contempt for money; his predilection for drinking contests in the late hours, and his memorable devotion to his wife, "Baby," and their children. It was he who first said: "I don't want to be a millionaire; I just want to live like one." Shor never spent a dollar advertising his restaurant, because newspaper writers featured him and his restaurant in their columns. The sight of the fat restaurateur walking away once excited Jimmy Cannon to write: "It looked like two little boys fighting under a blanket." Once, to the dismay of prissy readers, he became the subject of an interminable profile in *The New Yorker*.

Customers were "in" or "out." I was "in" because I had written the Hellinger book. The columnist-producer was Shor's hero. When he first read the book, he confronted me at the cloakroom, made a fist, and said: "You dumb Irish bastard. How could you write those things about Mark? You told me you loved the guy." Later, Mr. Shor would get lonesome drunk at four A.M. and reread the book, sometimes bursting into tears.

Each year at Christmas, I took Virginia Lee to Shor's for her favorite, scallops, and then on to Rockefeller Plaza to view the huge lighted Christmas tree. Later, I also took Gayle, who seldom ordered anything but spaghetti in its virulent forms. Between times, I lunched alone or with an author perhaps once a month. Toots had left word with the captains that I was to have a table in the second echelon from the arch. This made me "in," but not all the way. I usually met Jackie Gleason, the fat comic who was all the way "in" with the fat restaurateur. He sat adjacent to the arch and was known to order twice. With the additional tonnage of drinks, he also threw up twice.

Gleason was starring in a one-hour variety show on the Dumont Network, a patchquilt of desperate television stations which waited nervously every Friday night to see what the Great One had to offer. Gleason had a manager who can be described as well over four feet tall. His official name was Bullets Durgom. In the early days, when Gleason was living on a top floor of the Edison Hotel, Durgom looked upon Jackie as one more second-rate comic. This is remarkable because Gleason was a runaway genius. I did not know him then, but I never missed a performance. He was comedian, tragedian, actor. His needs, as he saw them, were a pool table, a girl, and five hundred a week.

One lunch Durgom came to my table. "Jackie would like to say hello," he said.

I glanced over his shoulder. "Then tell him come over."

"No. He wants to talk." I got up. The actor didn't need much time to get to the point. Would I write his biography? My respect slammed the door on a flat no. I would think about it. What made him think that people would pay several dollars to read in detail what they were getting in the gossip columns in bits? He was hurt, but patient. He held out those cocktail-frankfurter fingers and began to tick off the current biographies of actors and comedians. Besides, he said, he was leaving Dumont for a super-network show on the Columbia Broadcasting System. Couldn't I see that he would have millions of fans? I wondered how many of them had four ninety-five to throw away.

Harper had an option on the next book. I sent the Gleason idea through Phyllis. When I heard the "Jim dear" on the phone, I knew it was trouble. "Have you lost your mind? You are on your way to becoming a well-known biographer and historian. At this stage, you don't need Jackie Gleason. That stuff is Broadway trash. Please." The word from Evan Thomas was, in its way, infinitely worse. "The board of editors at Harper have considered your Gleason idea. I'm afraid they're fairly unanimous in a negative vote. Eleven of our editors asked who Jackie Gleason is." I found out later that those editors did not have television sets. Harper thought of TV as a fad, like coonskin caps.

The thing that troubled me about Gleason was that the man was what writers call pure color copy. Everything he did or said was funny or forlorn. A full-length character study, rather than the straight biographical form, could be an intriguing piece of writing. The only votes I got in favor of the book came from Elinor and Maggy. They, who could not seem to get through the other books I had written, saw this book as one long laugh. The next time I saw Jackie, he said: "I don't want none of the royalties."

I smiled. "I should hope not," I said.

Virginia Lee's manuscript was complete. Elinor saw this work as additional evidence that Missy and I were a team. She had, unwittingly, I'm sure, punished the child since the birth of Gayle. There was a space of six years between them. When infant Gayle was sleeping in her bassinette, Missy, sniffing her nose with the excitement of street play, had hurried in for a drink of water. She was noisy. Her mother frowned and snapped: "Shh! The baby's sleeping." The words meant little to Elinor. The child was going to hear them for a few years. She would, in the growing time, court her mother's love, and not attain it. Missy romanced her mother for affection. And got little. Later, she would settle for friendly approval. And barely achieve that.

The book should have won hugs and kisses. What it got was: "Are you and your father still working on that book?" The suggestion was collusion in some esoteric scheme. The effect was to make the child feel isolated; she was aware that her mother's opinions would be reflected in her grandmother. And yet she often sought refuge in her Nanny's arms. Ginny was called "lovey," a misnomer. She felt proud of her book. I was flabbergasted that she had finished it.

One of the truisms of newspaper work is that former Hearstlings remain attuned to what is going on in the "Empire." William Randolph Hearst, Sr., had died at age eighty-eight. He enjoyed a long power reign. It had always been a feudal lord operation; one man with a fistful of strings. No matter how august the positions of the Damon Runyons, the Bill Curleys, the Dick Berlins, the Gortatowskys and Brisbanes, the most trivial decisions could be negated by that leonine old man treading a Persian rug in his marble castle, looking down at the newspapers and magazines which were his to have, to hold, if necessary, to squeeze to death.

In August, 1951, the mantle fell to William Randolph Hearst, Jr. He was the perennial cub reporter. He had what the politicians call "no power base." The vast properties belonged to him and to his brothers. But, with the exception of Bill, they were not reporters. Nothing excites a dictator more than weakness. Richard E. Berlin, president of the Hearst organization, thought he detected it in young Bill. (Some of what is written here was learned later, when I signed contracts with the Hearst organization. My informants were Hap Kern and "Gorty" Gortatowsky.)

Berlin could grunt more power than most men can enunciate. In the Hearst Building at Eighth Avenue and Fifty-seventh Street, the editors and account executives assumed that the direction of all Hearst enterprises would be taken over by Dick. He would give to the Hearst sons whatever their hearts desired, but would not tolerate a challenge. To reinforce this notion, he sent memoranda everywhere advising that business would go on as usual, even suggesting what kind of obituary notice would be adequate for the old man.

It is one of the ironies of publishing that few appreciated the tensile strength of Bill Hearst's character. He had worked all the menial jobs, and some of the better ones, coast-to-coast. He had a greater appreciation for the story — getting it and writing it — than for publishing. I feel that he drew a bigger thrill from seeing his by-line on a story than his name on a masthead. When his father died, he turned to two men for support. One was Frank Conniff, a blond, wavy-haired tough-guy columnist. The other was Burris Jenkins, a fine newspaper artist. They reminded nobody — not even themselves — of the Three Musketeers, but they stormed Eighth Avenue and took it.

Dick Berlin decided that the best way of dispensing with young Hearst would be to make decisions, and wait for Bill to protest. As expected, the young heir did not. He spent his time locating office space in the Eighth Avenue building, conferring with Conniff and Jenkins, and waiting for a moment. It came at the first meeting of the board of directors. Hearst was entitled to sit at the head of the long, polished table. When he arrived, Berlin was in the chair. The vice-presidents and publishers sat down the sides of the table. Bill found a chair in the middle.

Berlin opened the meeting with a pontifical speech about William Randolph Hearst, *Senior*. How much Dick owed, how much they all owed. How the old man had built a gigantic and flourishing empire from a single newspaper — the old San Francisco *Examiner*. And how he, Dick Berlin, proposed to carry on the tradition and policies of the old man. The speech grumbled onward, a tank in a forest. He hoped that if any executive had an idea which might further the fortunes of the organization, he would send it on — to Berlin. Some of the gray ones in attendance glanced at Bill furtively. They had Ticonderoga pencils and foolscap pads to keep them busy.

When he finished, Berlin looked around archly, as though expecting questions. There was none. "I want to say something," young Hearst said quietly. Berlin sat back, trying to be patient. Bill spoke a moment about his father, about treasured memories, about his own work on many publications. Out of the periphery of his vision, he saw Berlin rolling a pencil back and forth on the gleaming tabletop. He paused. "Stop doing that!" he roared. "When I speak, Dick, pay attention." The power struggle ended. As the pencil stopped and the manicured fingers lifted from it, the gentlemen assumed that Bill Hearst was the new boss. He was.

In reality, Hearst, Conniff, and Jenkins were like three Katzenjammer Kids. At the start, they weren't sure how to run things, or even what they were running. Still, if excitement is talent, they were geniuses. Hearst conferred with the other two on almost all major decisions, and one of the first was that they needed a fourth man, a top-flight writer. They enlisted Bob Considine, the man who never learned how to make an enemy. He became the new Damon Runyon. To seal it in blood, the four went out and got drunk.

Autumn arrived early in Teaneck in 1954. Behind the house, the gray bonneted wasps' nests, half under the eaves of the garage, were closed. The climbing roses shivered on a rusty wire fence. The lawn, at dawn, was an old man's beard. The girls were up before daylight, arguing about bathroom privileges. Nanny took her long hair, twirled it twice at the back of her head, and stapled it with three hairpins. The perfume of coffee and the complaint of frying tongues of bacon stifled the baritone burp of thick oatmeal.

As always, I required two hours to rediscover my identity and to be responsible for whatever tripped from my tongue. I departed at nine to drive to the office, so I was up at seven, an unconscionable hour.

On this chilly morning, we had a moment to ourselves over the second cup of coffee. "Do you think the Lincoln book will sell?" she asked.

I had been daydreaming. I looked up, startled. Sell? I didn't know. She asked, somewhat innocently, if the assassination wasn't a sort of worn-out story. Yes, I said. Had she read any of the manuscript? No, she said, I had whisked it away too fast. Chapters had been all over the house for months. Had she read any of Ginny's book? Some of it. It's a sort of war book, she said, and not quite her dish. I picked up my trench coat and gray fedora. "I'll be home for dinner," I said. "To answer your question about the Lincoln book, I regard myself as a pretty fair judge of books. This one will sell reasonably well. It's no blockbuster. I hope it sells well enough to pay off our debts." So do I, she murmured. So do I.

I had company driving to the office: Ginny. She was bright and neutral We spoke of her new gentleman friend. He was a big, almost shy, redhead, Charles Frechette. His father came of a French Canadian family in Massachusetts. Dave was an official with the Teamsters Union. There was a second wife, Adele, petite and energetic, and a second group of children. I was ashamed to tell Virginia Lee that, having divined that Charles was not just another series of dates with another boy, I had checked him with a jury of merchants on Cedar Lane. The verdict was not in yeas and nays. The shopkeepers said "Mannerly." "You got something to deliver? Give it to Frechette and he'll deliver it." "You got trouble with kids at the soda fountain? Get Frechette to cool the kids." "Your daughter going out with the Frechette boy? Take my word, she could do a lot worse."

On the way in, I asked Ginny if she thought she loved Charley. She thought so. She wasn't sure. She wasn't in any hurry to make up her mind.

In love, I said, you are never given an opportunity to make up your mind. It comes unbidden, sometimes unwelcome. To be silly, I said, it's like a sneeze. Tapping your nose will not stop it. If she didn't know whether she was in love, then she wasn't. We talked about the office and the work at *Catholic Digest*. She enjoyed it and wondered if she had inherited anything from me. I doubted it. The males in my family were policemen. She thought I did a good job organizing the *Catholic Digest* Book Club. In this, I was pleased with myself. I had written all of the promotional copy, devised the test patterns of books to give readers a broader choice than simply religious tracts. In sum, we were buying books declined by the big book clubs.

To be practical, I said, what really gave the club a boost was when Father Bussard rented the stenciled names and addresses of sucker lists. He had paid four cents a name — four dollars a hundred. If we got two subscribers out of each hundred names, we'd be out of the red. In addition, we had taken full-page ads in our own magazine with coupons. This would be a built-in audience. She hoped I was happy in the work. Well, no. I wasn't happy; I wasn't unhappy. After exactly twenty-five years, I wasn't certain yet whether I should be an editor or a writer. It's like having a foot in each of two small boats, I said, and watching them drift apart. She hoped I would be a top-flight editor because she wanted to remain in her job. As we turned for a parking lot, I reminded her that she was on her own. She was a good slush-pile editor, and didn't throw abysmal manuscripts at the senior editors. Besides, in a few months, she would be an author.

"Oh, come on," she said. "Daddy, you know everybody is going to say you wrote the book."

"You and I know I didn't. We also know that a hundred percent of all royalties go to you."

She got out of the car. "That's the nice part," she said.

The work that day was humdrum. I carried a highly polished briefcase which looked like an adjunct to the busy editor's fingers. It wasn't. In it were two liverwurst sandwiches and a thermos of coffee and a book. The briefcase took better care of me than Toots Shor. Looking out the front window from the fifth floor, I could see pedestrians hurrying, the coat collars up, the hands in pockets. I looked at the calendar. It was Thursday, October 14, 1954 — too early for chapped lips and blue knuckles.

At three P.M. I took a phone call from Phyllis Jackson. I do not recall what I said to her. Numbly, I moved to the telex machine and signaled St. Paul. I typed:

```
CATH DGST STP 303      OK
FLASH BULLETIN....
    A FEW MINUTES AGO THE BOARD OF EDITORS OF
BOOK OF THE MONTH CLUB SELECTED THE DAY
LINCOLN WAS SHOT AS FEBRUARY'S SINGLE CHOICE
PAREN NO DUAL SELECTION CLOSE PAREN SO ALL
HANDS WILL PLEASE GO OUT AND GET SODDEN
DRUNK AND SEND BILL TO ME          JIM
```

There was five minutes of silence as the entire office crowded around to read over my shoulder. Then the machine spoke:

```
GA CONGRATULATIONS NOW YOURE A RICH MAN
I MUST SAY I TOLD YOU SO  PB  THANKS JIM END
ENDV
```

It was incredible, preposterous, impossible. People were babbling and I didn't know what they were saying. My eyes ached. I kept rubbing my hand across my mouth and staring at walls. I had to remind myself that no one had told me the book was being submitted to book clubs. I walked swiftly to the men's room. I soaked a paper towel and held it to my head. The pictures in the brain spun so swiftly that I couldn't find a rational thought. Main selection: February, 1955. It had taken a damned long time. I was forty-seven years old. I hurried back to the office to hug Ginny. She was crying. The world was full of eager, grinning faces shouting congratulations and grabbing my hand. The phone began to ring. Some people heard the news on WNYC. Others said they were book editors, and could I be interviewed in columns and on radio programs. Did I have any philosophy about writing? Who were my literary heroes? How much money had Book-of-the-Month Club guaranteed?

I phoned Phyllis. "What you told me is on the level?"

She seemed impatient. "Jim dear, I do my joking in the evening."

"How much money do you think it will mean?"

"I do not know. Nobody knows. If the book has average sales, you should get about seventy thousand as a first payment from Book-of-the-Month and from Harper —. "

"Seventy thousand?"

"About that. It may go higher."

"That's seventy thousand and then the agency's ten percent."

"Please, Jim. I have people in the office. Seventy thousand to you. At least."

The numbness ran down the arms. The fingers tingled. I glanced at Ginny. "Get your coat," I said. "We're going home." I wondered if a double scotch would drench the nervous system. I declined that notion, recalling that whatever talent I had was reasonable when sober, not so good drunk. If the child and I spoke on the way home, it must have been in succinct growls on my end. Never, never had my head spun with so many ideas as on that afternoon. Nothing in my work, triumph or failure, would touch me like that again. I may have sped homeward; I may have drifted. If a policeman had stopped me, I might have held out both wrists for the handcuffs.

To analyze ecstasy, one invites depression. The giddy thoughts of fame and riches tumbled end over end over end to a cellar. The news meant that one book met popular demand one time. Nowhere did the news flash proclaim Jim Bishop as a slightly overage, newly discovered, first-class writer. It was even possible that the other submissions to Book-of-the-Month Club in that thirty-day span were weak. *The Day Lincoln Was Shot* could have been the best of what I, deep inside, referred to as a pile of shit. I wanted to think that any scribbler who could take a threadbare yarn such as the assassination, and make it sing a fresh melody for a group of editors must have a degree of talent. My small depression must have sprung from a quarter of a century of disappointments. I no longer trusted *them*, or *me*.

Missy and I stood in the kitchen yelling for Gayle and Maggy and Elinor to get dressed. We would go to the damnedest, most extravagant restaurant and celebrate the solvency of the Bishops. Maggy could drink as many Tom Collinses as the bar could mix. Gayle could knock over three or four Shirley Temples and Ginny (cries of "Author! Author!") would be allowed a preprandial white wine.

Elinor seemed dumbstruck. She pinched her skirt at the side, in the manner of a little girl about to start a waltz clog, and then she smiled and cried. "Seventy thousand dollars?" she said over and over, ending in a diminutive whisper. "Seventy?" The girls seemed to be running at top speed. Upstairs. Down. Not complaining about how many trips they made to fetch oddments for the ladies. "First things first," I said." We will pay off this house — at once, completely. Some people celebrate with a burning of the mortgage. I'm going to shove the mortgage up that German's ass."

"Seventy thousand?" she murmured. "Jim, don't you think we ought to pay the Book-of-the-Month Club the nine dollars and forty cents we owe them?"

Fame, I would surmise, is public acknowledgment. This was not anticipated. Harper published the book in February, 1955. Whatever applause I might hear, whatever number of pseudomodest bows I might be permitted would, I was certain, occur within the community of letters. This was enough. This is the approval I had sought. I was unprepared for lavish reviews, the invitations to speak at universities, the bids to go to Hollywood and write screenplays, the translation of the book into fourteen languages (all of which were incomprehensible to me), the reporters who were assigned to write feature stories of what I was like at home, what I ate, what I thought of the administration, the vigil-lighted sanctum where I pondered great thoughts (the oil burner?), the voting of the book as required reading in colleges, the award of a national high-school teachers' association as "The Book of the Year," the phone ringing all day at the office, all evening at home, the pleas for money from the dying, the disabled, and disenfranchised, and the pressing offers of three thousand and more to write magazine articles which, a few months earlier, I was desperate to do for five hundred.

It was impossible for me to appreciate how much one book could do for one writer. Paul Gregory bought the television rights for "Ford Star Jubilee Theatre" and signed a young and *funny* actor named Jack Lemmon to play Wilkes Booth. Sums of money were arriving so fast that I do not recall what Gregory paid for it. I had passed a supercilious stage where I asked Phyllis: "Should we do it?" If she said "Yes," I said "Do it." I was signing contracts I had no time to read; I was depositing sums of money, not in the West Englewood Bank, but in the vaults of a competitor. I told Elinor and Maggy to go out and buy anything they chose. Barney Finn didn't want to write a "Paid in Full" bill. "Jim," he said, "it was such a joy to have you broke and scrambling — now I need an appointment to get past your front door." Our dear friends, the Emil Hermans, the Bill Scanlons, the Bernard Krulls, seemed more mystified than elated by sudden success. All of them "knew" it would come. I subscribed to a clipping service and dropped it. The head of the White House Secret Service detail, James Rowley, ordered his men to read the book and analyze the causes of a presidential assassination.

Phyllis Jackson waited until exactly seventy thousand dollars net was due from club and publisher. Then she sent it. I handed it to Elinor and said I was resigning from *Catholic Digest*. The cushion of money would give me time to end the editor/author debate and become a full-time author. She held the check; her lower lip quivered. I accused her of being saddened by the whole thing. In a way, yes, she said. What way? "I just wish you were poor again." I had no time for jokes. I left. And yet I felt that I understood the remark. When we were poor, we had no choice but to cling to each other. As she drifted off into silent depressions these days, I stopped imploring her to love me as I loved her. There was a new, sparkling life out there. I did not need the applause of the skinny, flat-chested woman who padded about the kitchen in carpet slippers with an edge of lacy slip hanging. There had always been plenty of other women out there; now there were more, and this time, they were the aggressors.

Evan Thomas was a smiling persuader. We had lunch. He said someone suggested that I write *The Day Christ Died*. No, I said. No and no. If I wrote another "day" book, publishers would think I couldn't do anything else. Biography and history were my natural leanings, because the author learned so many fascinating things in the research. The board of editors, he said, felt that the Christ book would sell better than the Lincoln. Besides, wasn't I the father of the "day" format? Yes, but that was not the best part, that was the worst. I would not define days minute by minute for the rest of my life.

Besides, I said, I am also typecast as a holy Joe. It would be hypo-critical of me to pursue pietistic material. I was, sadly, more devil than saint; some letter-writers were assuming that I was a real bishop. I hoped Evan would not regard me as a difficult author — God knows there were enough of them complaining of how editors were bruising their art form — I wanted him to think of me as a practical man who wrenched himself into frenzies trying to write simply, succinctly, with a confetti of metaphors. You're better than your self-portrait, he said, but let's drop the Christ idea for a while, and we'd try to think of a worthwhile subject.

I found it at a urinal in the men's room at Shor's. In the adjacent one was Jackie Gleason. "Well, pal," he said, "have you been thinking about our book?"

I had. My publishers wanted me to write *The Day Christ Died*, I said. Perhaps I should write another one between those two.

Gleason was flamboyant. "Isn't it proper," he roared, "to place Gleason between Lincoln and Christ? Isn't that where I belong?" The Black man holding the towels began to laugh.

I told Gleason it would take a year of research to adduce the facts. I refused to pay for that time. He would have to give me a hundred a week for expenses and a room at his hotel on his floor. He extended his hand. "You got it, pal. Deal?" I extended the unengaged hand. "Deal," I said.

For a moment, I stopped racing, skidding, doing. Virginia Lee became engaged to Charles Frechette. The big redhead had won her. This was not easy because Missy was too logical and practical to be swept off her feet. She had been raised in a marriage atmosphere which was so boisterously bad that it should persuade a young lady to ponder the excitement of life in a convent. She was eighteen, had an attractive occlusion, and no braces. Then too, she was more than my daughter; she was a cherished friend. I loved Gayle, but, for her at twelve, racing at top speed through the world, I was her first aid kit. She was a toy requiring no batteries.

My reaction to the news was to ask myself what had happened to time. All my life I had been obsessively conscious of time; my work encompassed time; somewhere between one piece of work and another, the child had grown. Elinor was excited. Maggy purred. There would be a big wedding, of course. The date was in the spring of 1956 — May 5. "That's a long time," I said. To the contrary. Time was short. Things to be arranged. Girlfriends would have to be "hustled" to stage showers for the bride. We would have to confer with Mr. and Mrs. David Frechette. Restaurants and armories would have to be priced. An engagement party, shortly after Christmas, 1955, would be arranged. The prattling sounded like stream-of-consciousness. I asked one question: "Does Charley have a job?" From the stunned expressions, I assumed that this was extraneous and immaterial.

He had a job. The boy wasn't quite twenty but he bossed his own loading platform for the United States Trucking Company. He stood inside a big aperture on Varick Street in New York. Trucks arrived southbound out of Boston for the West. Charley helped unload merchandise bound for Baltimore and the South. Other trucks, northbound, dropped off packing crates destined for ports around the world. Backtracking a bit, I learned that they had met in Teaneck High School. Frechette had been on the football team.

It had been three years since Virginia Lee's first matinee date. The boy had been polite. He stood, hat in hand, at the front door. His name, as I recall, was Tom. He had acne. Tom was gifted with feet. He had size tens on a size four body. It was obvious that he was beyond nourishment, so none was offered. Virginia Lee was vaguely blondish in one of those hats which are tied under the chin. She wore a dress to match the hat, the faintest touch of lipstick — something I assured Elinor would excite that boy to a tigerish rapacity which would rock the town.

As they left, we peered between the drapes. He had a car. The movie was a block and a half away. He took her elbow to help her in, slammed the door, and wrapped clothesline around the automobile twice. Elinor said: "What's that for?"

"So she can't get out," I said.

"Stop it," she said.

As a reporter, I said, I had considerable experience with sex fiends and that boy, who was moving off in a cloud of blue smoke, fitted what Dr. Hoffmann would call the classic mold. At four P.M. I phoned the movie. What time, I asked the cashier, does the matinee get out? Right now, she said. Elinor and I read the Sunday newspaper and waited.

At four-thirty there was no car out front. I pointed out that Tom had a whole half-hour in which to move that sagging crate away from the movie. Elinor began to wring her hands. The date had been her idea; it was she who had granted permission. She said she knew more about when the fledgling was ready to circle the nest than I. "Don't worry," I said in a manner to increase her trepidation, "what's Tom's last name? I'll call his parents."

Elinor wept into her hands. "I . . . don't . . . know."

"You allowed our baby girl to go off, tied in a car, with a sex fiend whose last name we do not know?" It was true. At four-forty P.M. I said it would be strange when I phoned the police and they — knowing us as a religious family and all that blarney — asked the name and address of the boy. I would have to tell them that I had not the remotest idea.

It was twilight when the smoke pot rolled up the street. Maggy, busy petitioning God on her rosary, stuffed the beads in an apron pocket and murmured: "Thanks be to God. Oh, thanks be to God." Through the drapes, they appeared to be jolly as he unwrapped the clothesline and helped our daughter set her dainty feet on the pavement. As they reached the porch, Elinor burst out the front door. She yelled at that youngster so loudly it was difficult to decipher words. If he, in his flight, assumed that he was no longer welcome at the Bishop house, it was an acute display of intelligence. Elinor grabbed Missy by the arm and yanked her indoors. The girl cried. They had stopped for an ice cream sundae on Cedar Lane. Was that too against the law?

That was three years before the engagement. It seemed a short time in which a father must learn to say adieu to his daughter, and mean it.

In the mid-1950s I was beset by an uneasy sensation that something was wrong with my country. Or the world. There were no specifics. It was as though a man returned to his old neighborhood and found a parking lot. The people I met in my social life had lacquered personalities; they said what they thought were the right things; they did the right things; they served the right drinks. My friends were ball bearings, each fitted in a machine to reduce friction. They told the same jokes, laughed the same laughs. They referred to me as blunt, boring, candid. This was not off target because, when I proposed to discuss signs of revolt in Hungary and Poland, they told one another to buy International Business Machines stock.

America had always been an I-want culture. Greed inspired the building of swift clipper ships and continental railroads and the steam engine. The cellar-parties-and-children-in-bed-at-nine were a depressing evolution. Everyone wanted to sell his house for an inflated price and buy a bigger one "farther out." The parties degenerated into two herds — females in one corner, males in another. Everybody knew who would get drunk and funny, and who would get drunk and obstreperous. The men knew which wives would be overly made up and underdressed and flirtatious. It was difficult to comprehend why the most ignorant man always had the most of the world's goods.

They said they were "hip." I believed them. The dance was the mambo. At the movies, they wore white-rimmed sunglasses and saw the picture in a third dimension. They agreed that the new automobile, Edsel, would not "get off the ground." President Dwight D. Eisenhower asked for municipal bomb shelters and some of my friends were on committees, but none was built. For a reason which still escapes me, they didn't think it was wise to admit Alaska and Hawaii as the forty-ninth and fiftieth states. The Supreme Court, they argued, violated the Constitution when it demanded desegregation of schools and public facilities. It would not work because the people were anti-Negro. They were aware that Mao Tse-tung had enslaved China with communism, but they laughed at his Great Leap Forward.

In the manner of most parents in all times, they did not pretend to understand their children. They ridiculed them and prayed they would "wake up." College boys made sorority panty raids. Teenagers adopted a dead actor, James Dean, as an idol. The children's taste in music dropped to a loud, incessant beat called Rock. They scorned records by Bing Crosby, Patti Page, and Frank Sinatra. The youngsters popped bubble gum listening to Elvis Presley, Frankie Avalon, and Bobby Darin.

There had been a bus boycott by Blacks in Montgomery, Alabama, but our set saw no significance except free publicity given to it by television. They understood the value of chlorophyll. They were irritated by sons who returned from barbershops with apache haircuts. Any of them could tell you what you missed on Lucille Ball's show, Jack Webb's, Jack Paar's, Jackie Gleason's. There was a sameness to these people. They took Friday nights off to go to New York to see *My Fair Lady*, or *The Sound of Music*, or *West Side Story*. They touted each other on things to see, things to read. Even the men who assured me that they were too busy to read made certain to peruse Herman Wouk's *Caine Mutiny*; J. D. Salinger's *Catcher in the Rye*; and James Jones's *From Here to Eternity*. These were read in self-defense, in case an outsider asked questions. I think that what depressed me was that all of these people had the same goals: a house, two cars, a television set, a hundred shares of AT&T, and backyard barbecues.

[269]

They vacationed in Bermuda, or they warmed a slice of winter at Miami Beach. It annoyed me to be afraid to admit that I did not understand tax shelters. They hoped I had a good accountant, one who could earn his fee and more by letting me pay less to the Internal Revenue Service than the IRS deserved. My irritation was not based on any fallacy that I was less of a crook than they were; it was that they felt no enthusiasm for topics beyond the realm of materialism. They denounced the dribble of Jews coming to Teaneck as money-hungry. A dentist told me that he was moving out to Saddle River. He had sold his house to a Jew for 40 percent more than it was worth. Some spoke of the Jewish vote as though it were a solid, secretive bloc. Another one, president of a country club, asked me if I could find a "white Jew" he might accept as a member.

It was a symphony consisting of one dreary note. I began to beg off the cellar parties. An Italian in West Englewood phoned to say that he didn't need my presence to stage a party. A writer, he said, was not much more than a grown man who was paid for scribbling. As far as my books were concerned, he said, I could ring him up as a no-sale. He got them from Miss Agnes Norton at the library for nothing.

In anger, I ran for town council. I was still writing a column, free, in the *Sunday Sun*. The young editor, a mover and shaker named Edward Flynn, asked me if I was sure I knew what I was doing. I reminded him that I was better known around town, and in better odor, than any of the candidates. He and Andrew Stasiuk, the star reporter, wore an aura of sadness when we met. "Bet on me," I said. "Andy, all I need is four thousand votes to get in office and I can get those standing on my head." When the votes were tabulated, I had 2,405. My name was on the bottom of the list.

The research on the Gleason book entailed an estrangement from Elinor. The distance from the penthouse where Jackie lived to Teaneck was fifteen miles. I used every excuse to remain overnight in New York. She seemed not to mind. She could do without accusatory stares from me. No matter how much she drugged herself, even if she drank herself into a stupor, Elinor knew that the girls would not tell me. For years, they had listened to little matronly sermonettes which, reduced to the irreducible, said: "Don't tell Daddy." The women in my house began, in 1955, to enjoy the togetherness they had missed since the wedding in 1930.

There was an editorial conference at Simon and Schuster. Jack Goodman, a jazzy editor, said the book was bound to be a blockbuster. Jackie Gleason was a favorite in millions of homes. As the author, I was now a name. The combination, Goodman said, would be irresistible to readers. All it would require would be a couple of mentions on the Gleason show and I could start pricing country homes.

The cooperation from the comedian was ideal. Whatever leads I asked — bartenders, schoolteachers, childhood chums, janitors, people in tenement houses where he grew up in Brooklyn — long personal interviews were granted at once. His penthouse was open to me. So was his mind. Getting to know the man was as easy as opening a can of tuna with a key. The odor may bother you for a moment, but you know tuna is what you want. I found eight Jackie Gleasons among my notes — each a separate person from the others. Above all, he was more human than most beings, bouncing quickly to euphoric heights and tumbling downward into enormous depressions. It was as though he had a greater capacity for joy and grief than anyone in the world.

His father ran away from home when Jackie was a little boy and was not seen again. His mother, May, was a hard-working drudge, turning to gin and a pillow on a windowsill. She was a subway cashier, and borrowed Jackie's Boy Scout leggings on winter days. She was his world. He was not hers. May's joy was having girlfriends over to drink and chat. She took her chubby youngster and moved from cold-water flat to cold-water flat, perhaps a week or two ahead of the rent. To Jackie, the cruelty of deprivation was real. He was intelligent and obstreperous in school. He ate more than he should because the promise of food at home was seldom sincere. May sent him to confession, to Holy Communion; she warned him about lying to the priest.

He was caught in a Roman Catholic syndrome which, for some, is permanent. God was behind every door, every cloud, under every bed, watching Jackie. Sin followed by remorse was automatic. As a teenager, he seldom enjoyed a sin. With the gang in front of the candy store, it was Gleason who made the wisecracks, who parodied the girls walking by, who reduced his fellows to tears of laughter. Comedy is an amiable weapon. It clubs the risibilities. He had an additional talent. He was a consummate actor.

Most of the characters he would use in his public life were drawn from the bartenders, janitors, poor souls, kitchen debaters, and "wisenheimers" he knew. One character would be drawn from imagination: Reggie Van Gleason, the top-hatted rich drunk with the walking stick. He was deft in his divination of what would capture and hold public interest. In a real sense, Jack Hurdle, his producer, was not the producer, and Jack Philbin was not the associate producer. They could suggest, and Gleason honored their suggestions when he agreed with them, but he was adamant when he disagreed. When he fluttered his arm outward, palm down, roaring, "Now look, pal," any one of a number of things might be beyond appeal — the skit could be revised, eliminated; the camera angles would be altered; the writers might be ordered to submit an original skit; even the musical score was at the mercy of the star.

Gleason was star, producer, director, and bandleader. The tenement-house kid, who had been at the mercy of a world contemptuous of genius, had a one-hour world at his mercy. He may have been the only star who insisted on having his agent in his office during office hours in case Jackie thought of something. Columbia Broadcasting System recognized that the comedian "owned" the show, and would pay himself ten thousand dollars a week out of what it earned. He was generous to his "second banana," Art Carney, paying him thirty-five hundred a week and allowing many of the laugh lines to go to the nervous wretch who worked in a sewer. He allowed considerable latitude to June Taylor, a dancer and choreographer, so long as she brought her attractive girls on stage to a fast jazz beat, kicking their legs in unison.

At a benefit show, I walked into a roomful of comics with Jackie. They were all gabbling, honing jokes on each other. When they saw the fat man in the dark blue suit with the red gardenia in his lapel, they fell silent. They too referred to him as "The Great One." At another time, I sat in a darkened theater with Phil Silvers. He slouched; he was bored. The set depicted a pet shop. Art Carney came onstage, murmuring little hellos to the animals in the cages. When he approached the rabbits, he said: "Well, aren't you the busy ones?" Gleason came onstage to say that the line was no good. He suggested that Carney say to the rabbits: "Boy, have you made a sucker out of Kinsey." Gleason moved offstage. When he came back on, silently, Phil Silvers began to laugh. He fell between the rows of seats and lost his breath. I yanked him up by the armpits. "What's so amusing?" I said crossly. "Gleason hasn't said anything."

He gasped for breath. "You don't understand," he said. "He thinks funny."

It sounded asinine. The more I dwelled on it, the more I understood. Comedy is a malleable substance, bendable, breakable, warped, hilarious, dull. I recalled a time, driving, when I saw a billboard of W. C. Fields. I glanced at the B.B. eyes, the warty nose, and I had burst into laughter. Fields had said nothing. *He thinks funny.* And that was a part of Jackie Gleason's magic. People broke into laughter when he appeared onstage. They associated his ruddy face and shiny jet hair with a promise of amusement. I saw my character as more than a top-flight comedian. He was also a dramatic actor, one who required no teaching to respond to a line of dialogue. I saw him do a one-hour show in which he played a small-town politician who, without urging, would steal the pennies from the lids of a corpse. I was aware that he had not rehearsed, that he had been drinking and shooting pool all week, and yet, as the story unfolded, he was no longer Gleason; he became a politician of lofty promises who would not demean himself by keeping one.

He was terrified of flying. When we went anywhere, it was by car or by train. He feared the wrath of God and the Holy Roman Catholic Church, and so his affairs with women were not fulfilling. He had no intention of divorcing his wife, Genevieve, who, of course, had no intention of divorcing Jackie. He didn't even separate from Gen without consulting a friendly bishop. He was afraid of the stories in the columns about other women in his life; he feared stories about his prodigious drinking too. He could not stand away from himself for a moment and see that these too were part of the psyche called Jackie Gleason. Without them he might have been a ribbon clerk.

No matter where the research led me, I fell into gold mines of stories. Two, I thought, were pure Gleason. One summer he played a resort at Deal Lake, New Jersey. It was a romantic spot for lovers who enjoyed old music and young ideas. Some danced; some hired a canoe and paddled in the moonlight, listening to the band. Jackie got five hundred dollars a week for being funny in the band breaks. He roomed farther down the beach in an Italian boardinghouse at thirty-five dollars a week. It was customary for the big sport to spend all his salary before he got it. When he left Deal Lake, he didn't have the thirty-five for the room.

The place was run by an aged lady who sat, seemingly without sleep, behind a desk at the foot of the stairs. Her accent was Neapolitan, but her acuity was for dollars. Nobody got out of a room without paying. Jackie phoned a couple of friends in New York to drive down and help him to get away. He used clothesline to lower two suitcases out the back window. He wormed his fat into an outrageously striped bathing suit and started down the staircase. The Italian lady nodded. Gleason gave her one of his hurrah smiles. "Nice day for a dip," he said.

He got into the car and changed into street clothes as he headed for New York. Two weeks later, he was working at the Club 18 with Pat Harrington and Jack White. He was earning money. When he thought of money, he thought of the old Italian lady. He owed thirty-five dollars. His conscience refused to shrug. It was like stealing. Gleason hired a Carey Cadillac and, with a couple of friends, drove to the Jersey shore. With thirty-five dollars in hand, he strode into the boardinghouse. The lady was behind the desk. He gave her the money and she burst into tears. "We thought you drownded," she said.

When Gleason was doing the hour show for the Dumont Network, the show had good ratings, but executives thought that Jackie needed the services of an expensive scriptwriter. They hired one for a thousand a week. He arrived at Jackie's apartment late at night. Late is when six of Jackie's friends lift the pool table out of the way for dancing and stomping. The writer rapped on the door, but all he got from the other side was raucous noise. He pushed the door open. Dozens of men and women seemed to have been frozen into attitudes of hilarity. He found Jackie and said he was the new writer. The man from Hollywood was told that this was no time for business, to stake a claim to "booze and a broad" and relax. "This," the writer shouted, "is Sunday. Your show goes on Friday." Gleason nodded. "See me in the morning," he said.

The man was back at noon. This time the door was ajar and there was silence on the other side. He pushed in. Chairlegs had either been broken or chewed off. Spaghetti hung like lace from end tables. A record player was on its side, spinning silently. Glasses littered the rug. The writer pushed on. He came to a bedroom. He peeked. The Great One was on his back, breathing heroically under a sheet and blowing imaginary bubbles to the ceiling. Beside him was his now-and-then girl. The writer coughed. Jackie sat up. "Who the hell are you?"

"I'm the writer from the coast. You said to show up this morning."

"Pal," Gleason said, "you know this is no time for business."

"The show goes on Friday."

"I know when the show goes on."

"It's a full hour show."

"I happen to have a hangover. This is no time for debates."

"When?"

"Tomorrow at two. I'll be right here."

The man was back Tuesday. Also Wednesday. At this time, Jackie was asking: "What are you worried about, pal? We'll do the show." Thursday, the man sat at a typewriter, perspiring, while Gleason emerged from a shower like a sunburned grapefruit. "Write number one," he commanded.

The writer looked up. "What's that mean?"

"Never mind what it means. Just write number one, and then next to it write 'Fast music, dancing girls.'" The writer wrote. "Underneath, write number two. Next to it write 'Hat trick.'"

"Hat trick?"

"That's it."

"What is the hat trick?"

"Why do you have to know? You're not going to do it. Just write 'Hat trick.'"

"Okay."

"Underneath that, write number three, and next to it 'The Kramdens.'"

"I think I may have a little dialogue for that."

"You don't need it. We know what to do. And underneath that . . ."

At two P.M. Friday, Gleason arrived for his noon appointment at the Adelphi Theatre. The stage was full of actors, grips, horn players, directors, dancers. The Great One found a barrel and stood on it. In his hand was the solitary sheet of paper which encompassed the entire show. He read it. An old-time actor lifted his cane. "Your director hired me, Mr. Gleason," he said. "But I don't know for what." Jackie was scornful. "You're a pro, ain'tcha, pal? Get on when you can." The writer left the scene, shaken. He was not a drinking man, but even sobriety earns a remission. He went to a tavern and drank. At the appointed hour, drinkers fell silent and looked up at a TV set. There was a burst of sound, Roman candles bursting, fireworks arcing, and a shrieking voice proclaimed, "The Jackie Gleason Show!" With the customers, the writer watched. He shook his head sadly. A barfly said: "Pretty good, hah?" The writer said: "You'd swear they had rehearsed for four years."

The Golden Ham was completed on time. To my way of thinking, it held an ideal balance of all the great and awful things which are common to the lives of all of us. I had promised Jackie a quick look, and he got it. He phoned the following morning at eight. I was sleeping. "Well," I said, "what do you think?" "It doesn't make a big boy out of me," he said. I tried to explain that it wasn't supposed to do that; it was not a publicity release. He felt badly. I felt sorry for him, because I admired him and his work. However, I wasn't writing to win popularity contests.

The reviewers were kind to the book. Some thought it was the best exposition of a star in years. David Susskind used it for a two-hour television show. *Look* magazine bought the serial rights and promoted it all over the country. But Gleason made sure *The Golden Ham* was not mentioned on his show. Sales were disappointing. Jack Goodman could not explain to me how he could sell the first printing and not go into a second. Toots Shor told me to be of good cheer. "Somebody at Simon and Schuster has a girlfriend," he said softly. "He wanted that girl to get a job as a Glea Girl. Someone made a trade-off: the girl could have the job, provided that the publisher buried the book. You understand, pal?"

I didn't believe it.

In the late spring, Sea Bright called to me. Things, places do not stand still — and more's the pity. Sea Bright did. It was still a broken pencil of sand, a three-mile street with the ocean on one side and the Shrewsbury River on the other. There were no new houses. They were paint-faded, with wind-slapping shutters. The Atlantic Ocean was barely contained by a twelve-foot seawall, an endless series of fitted stones, each the size of a pickup truck. At high tide, there was no beach. The big green combers loafed in, cresting a little, and then crashed against the wall, the white spume floating high, the offshore wind dropping it on Ocean Avenue. In January and February the northeasters came. The sea had no combers. It was in white fury, slamming the wall and jarring some stones loose, cresting over the top until the houses on the river side were lacquered with salt. When one faced it, the wind would tear one's lips apart in a frightened grin.

The village of Sea Bright was at the south end, a first-class delicatessen, a hardware store, a novelty shop, a pharmacy, a filling station, an inoffensive stucco building that was a combination of town hall and first-aid station, two dying hotels, and seventeen saloons. The year-round population was static at 1,031. There were Swedish fishermen who manned dories in the summer and hooked the big blues and sold them to a truck, which took them to Fulton Fish Market in New York.

The people were friendly. A man in a yachting cap, who called himself Commodore, was the village drunk. There were others, but he was the town drunk solely because he had been arrested more times than anyone else. There were old estate houses which once had played host to the summer dreams of the rich. They were boardinghouses now. The deep porches had white rockers which rocked empty in the ocean breeze. On the far side of the river were the truly rich of Rumson; some had maids in white aprons and tiny lacy hats. The hedges were scalloped in fanciful waves and curlicues. In other days, matched grays and blacks left the crunchy driveways to meet the master at the Red Bank station when the Bankers' Special pulled in. Later, it was done in big, quiet automobiles. And still later in Volkswagens.

Elinor and I sat in the car thinking of Sea Bright. She knew I would buy a house. It was nice, she said, to have all this money, but she hoped I would not ask her to live in Sea Bright. It had been discussed with Maggy. They would come down in the summer. This was the true separation — not saying it, not mentioning it by name, just the de facto living of one part of a family in Teaneck and one member in Sea Bright. We assured each other that we would be no farther apart than the telephone. An hour's drive. We talked about it in the car. The children could join me on weekends. Sure. Well, not children — the child. Virginia Lee would marry in May — forty days. Gayle might enjoy the cold clear air, the extra license she always achieved being with Daddy, being taken to fancy restaurants and shore movies, and trips to taverns where there was a pool table and a man could play nine-ball at a dollar a rack.

It was quick shopping. The third house shown by the lady real estate dealer was the one. It was an old house of seven gables built with its back on the edge of the Shrewsbury. It had a lawn a hundred and seventy-five feet deep toward the seawall. A German carpenter owned it. He wanted sixteen thousand five hundred dollars, and, when the title was searched, I gave it to him. It was the only house with a concrete cellar. This is rare when you consider that the ground floor was barely above sea level and, in a flooding storm, the house should have lifted out of its anchorage and popped straight up.

It didn't. The interior walls were a foot thick. Someone had built walls on tops of walls and then had to fashion doors a foot thick. The old garage in back once held two cars. This would soon be book-lined with shelves and have typewriters, desks, and research materials. The cellar had an oil burner, but it also had windows. When the heavy storms arrived, the sea would filter through those windows. I arranged for a plumber to sink a concrete well and put an automatic pump in it.

Elinor laughed when I bought black leather furniture. "Your house," she said, "*your* house is going to look like a dentist's waiting room." I found a Polish carpenter and had him rip out old sections and redesign rooms. I bought a twenty-five-inch television set and beds for downstairs and up. The upstairs rooms were small under a peaked roof, but serviceable. I found a small pedestal, placed it at the top of the stairs, and set the bronze statue of Our Lady of Guadalupe on it. I told the carpenter to find some more carpenters, and an architect, and to build a twenty-four-by-thirty-foot living room in the back of the house. It would have a cork floor, a small modern stairway leading from the dining room in the main house, a black fourteen-foot couch before a stone fireplace, and a curved Formica bar in a corner of the room.

Dreams. Outrageous dreams. No one in the world was anxious to spend money to move to the clam and booze stench of Sea Bright. Had the target been Asbury Park, Atlantic City, Long Beach, or Fire Island, my friends might have been sympathetic. Some had not heard of Sea Bright. Others saw it as a nineteenth-century sandspit where once the rich repaired for salt breezes and shore dinners. They saw the peeled paint, the dangerously rotten porches, the Peninsula House, and Panacci's Hotel with no living thing inside except plants hanging by piano wire from the lobby ceilings.

When the carpenters and movers were finished, I moved in with a Negro cook. She was small and old, a woman with a face as cracked as the top of a good chocolate pudding. She wore a uniform and a nice white apron and sneakers. She refused shoes. After a week, she told me I mustn't mind if she refused my wishes; she was a paid-up member of the communist party and I was a capitalist. Gayle said the woman would plant a bomb in the cellar. We called her Tick-tick.

My new secretary was Mrs. Ralph Walter of Rumson. Floranna was a big, good-looking woman with a husband and two growing sons. She was capable and more than capable. Flo and her Ralph knew just about every family in Rumson and Sea Bright and could brief me. When the place was organized, I drove to New York to a jewelry store, made a purchase, and returned. I phoned my parents and asked them to come down for a few days.

My mother did not recall a sunny summer day we had had on Sea Bright beach. I was ten; she was thirty-four. We dug our toes in damp sand and dreamed against the backdrop of the thundering breakers. I dreamed that I would own a house here someday. Mom dreamed that my father would buy diamond earrings for her. We exchanged dreams as we watched my younger brother, John, and my sister, Adele, chase each other along the edge of the sea.

She was a short, plump woman with a calm, exquisite face and a straight nose with the hint of a tilt on the end. There was a lot of bronze in her hair. There was a little pale down near her ears. I loved this woman more than I would tell anyone. Whatever was good and noble and charitable in life, Jenny Tier Bishop had it. She thought my dream was childish. I said that someday I would buy a big beautiful house here. I would sit on my imaginary porch and watch the big ocean liners — the *Berengaria*, the *Olympic*, the *Mauretania* — as they left New York Harbor full of rich people who were always happy and gay. In my house, I said, servants would walk around holding big silver trays loaded with chocolate bars and jelly beans and ice cream. Behind my house there would be a yacht so big that my captain would not be able to turn it around on the tide, and would have to depart backward.

My mother achieved her dream quickly. My father bought diamond earrings for her the next year. She looked at them and looked up at my father and she cried. It was, I thought, an embarrassing reaction. He was trying to make her happy. Those earrings were worn on state occasions. When she dressed to visit relatives, she wore ninety-eight-cent clip-ons. Now and then, I caught her with the dresser drawer open, the earrings on fire in a black plush box. She was only looking.

My father's weakness was borrowing money for things he didn't need. When he was in debt, we did without. My mother said she could do without a new dress — even shoes and a hat — but she would not part with those earrings. The great depression was not my father's fault. The mayor chopped salaries in half, and paid one half in scrip. The merchants wouldn't accept scrip. For a long while, I didn't miss the diamond earrings.

They were in a hockshop. My mother kept the ticket. She said not to worry. They wouldn't be sold as long as my father paid the interest each year. It was done. I grew up fingering that bent pawn ticket. And then there was a time when that too was gone. She said she forgot. The truth was that, to recoin a witless phrase, we were down and out. I didn't cry, sob, or hug her. The situation made me angry. Don't worry, I said, someday I will buy diamond earrings for you. Sure, she said. Sure.

Before they arrived in Sea Bright, I thought about the original dreams. Thirty-nine years had passed. She wasn't young and plump and ladylike. She was old and skinny, a diabetic who conspired with grandchildren to sneak a portion of cold rice pudding with raisins. I was forty-nine. She felt with her cane for a chair and we helped her sit. I asked Tick-tick to bring some tea and cookies.

I got the black box and pressed it into my mother's hands. "Here," I said, "this is for you." The blue eyes turned upward, puzzled. "For me?" I felt ashamed of my affection. "For you," I said. She glanced toward my father and said coyly: "I wonder what it is." I asked her if she remembered two dreamers on the beach: the boy who wanted a seashore house and the woman who wanted diamond earrings. No, she said gravely, not quite. She opened the box and laughed nervously. "John," she said, "help me with this. " He looked at the diamond earrings and said: "They're beautiful, Jenny. Real beautiful."

He was clumsy finding the tiny hole in each ear. She felt them. She didn't cry. She reached up and mussed my hair. "How do I look?" she said grandly. Fine, we said together. She would never see those earrings. She was blind.

In February the new Hearst team was in conference discussing ideas and talent. One of them mentioned my name and the Lincoln book. Frank Conniff had read it. It seemed to him, he said, that Bishop had once worked for a Hearst newspaper. Once a Hearstling always a Hearstling — right? Wrong. Bill Hearst and Conniff were trying to find someone who would write a series of articles about desegregation in the South. After discussion, it was agreed that Conniff would phone Bishop and ask if he would tour the South with Burris Jenkins and write a series of page-1 stories for the Hearst chain of newspapers.

My impulse, at the other end of the phone, was to ask "Where did you get this private phone number?" It was a rude thought. I listened. The proposition was that Hearst would pay me thirty-five hundred dollars for two weeks' work, plus expenses. Conniff was in a persuasive mood. I felt chilled. For years, I said, I had been trying to forget the *Mirror* and, in particular, a managing editor named Hinson Stiles. "Aw," he said, "the hell with those things. All of us can match your problems. You can write this thing any way you choose. Nobody is going to edit your copy. We'll give you a big by-line out front and do a lot of promotion about you being the author of *The Day Lincoln Was Shot.*"

There was an odor of the asinine in this. For thirteen years, I had struggled to free myself of newspapers. I told him I would soon be going to the Holy Land. "It'll still be there," he said. I told him I was overworked. A good writer is never overworked, he said. Well, I said, I would like to talk to him and to Bill Hearst about it. Turning away from their enthusiasm was like a little boy bracing himself against a high-powered summer fire hydrant. I said yes.

Burris Jenkins brought his wife, Georgia, along. She was tall and slender, a southern lady who was a fine portrait painter. We rented a car and drove down through Mississippi and into Louisiana and swung over to Alabama, Georgia, the Carolinas, and Virginia. I interviewed poor Whites and Blacks at crossroads, in shacks, at filling stations, on hayricks, and had to surmount their suspicions with windy stories about what a fumbler and a boob I am. Burris made rough sketches on the spot. Sometimes he shot little Polaroid pictures to help him to remember shadowing. The Jenkinses were a joy. Every night we rented adjoining rooms and hoped the White Supremacists and the Ku Klux Klan wouldn't burst in with rope and torches.

Everyone, it seemed, had heard about the *Brown* v. *Board of Education* decision of the United States Supreme Court. And most citizens disagreed with it on one level or another. Black mothers of schoolchildren were the most vehement. To synthesize: "Mister, the White folks just built a colored school. If my little girls have to go to that White school, they ain't gonna be dressed near as good as those other children. Ain't nobody gonna talk to my children. How much you think my husband and me gonna stand for that? You go home and tell that court to leave us alone — hear?"

The articles got a big play from coast to coast, although, to my way of thinking, they consisted of no more than a series of character studies of rural people of two complexions. It stated no message, had no point of view. And yet, when I saw my name and face on the sides of newspaper trucks, I could feel the downy feathers stroking my ego. I had — for the moment — returned to the newspapers in style. The headlines in San Francisco and Los Angeles stated:

Jim Bishop Says:
THE SOUTH CONCEDES DESEGREGATION
CAN BE SLOWED, BUT NOT STOPPED

There was but one true stinger in the series. At the last stop in Virginia, I sat next to an old desk in the office of the Richmond *News Leader*. The editor, James Kilpatrick, thirty-five and partly bald, gave me a lesson in indictment. His friends called him Jack. For openers, he said that the Supreme Court tried to amend the Constitution. "I've known colored people all my life," he said, "and it is hard to generalize about a whole race of people, but it is still almost impossible to know when a colored man is telling the truth and when he isn't. That's one difference."

Kilpatrick was a practicing Roman Catholic, father of three boys. He spoke of children playing, of emotionalism and schoolyard fights; he was blisteringly sincere. "If the Negroes were more responsible, more mature, the bulk of my objections to their admittance in our schools would be removed. I can't imagine this happening, but, even if it did, many would still object on the ground that our cultures are different."

Burris Jenkins and I were impressed with this man's candor. He said what was in the hearts of many others. Distrust and bigotry were common to Whites and Blacks. Even the most unctuous, when pressed, emitted a bouquet of scented lies. Uneducated Negroes told me that they remained in the South because they "understood" the hatred of the Whites, and they could live with it because it was reciprocated. Uneducated Whites squirmed when they related stories of the sexual prowess of "bucks," and it was obvious that they favored lynching Blacks who got close to their women.

Prejudice starts with teething. The little one listens to the gospel as preached by the father and mother. Later in life, a broad education may bleach the stain, but seldom, if ever, erases it. The truth did not hurt the series of articles. I was happy with it, because each one painted accurate images of average citizens squeezed in the vise of a Supreme Court decision. Jenkins and I were in agreement that the Court had corrected surface inequities, but it didn't change human nature. Small people think small; big people think small.

My prejudice showed when educators proclaimed that integrated schools would suffer a lapse of eighteen months in curricula to enable Black students to "catch up." I couldn't tolerate the notion that Gayle, an average student, would be marking time as ill-educated Black boys sat in class asking "Teach" what she was talking about.

It was a personal shame, but it was there. Nor was it solely predicated around Gayle. Scores of interviews convinced me that 11 percent of our population was about to humiliate 89 percent for wrongs none of them had experienced on slave plantations. A bus driver in Atlanta added a seriocomic touch when he pointed to Negro passengers and said to me: "Mister, you don't have no civil rights. They do."

When the phone rang, it was an editor from *Cosmopolitan* magazine. He asked if I would do a "longish piece" about a day in the life of President Eisenhower. When I was assured that it was not a joke, I said that it could not be done without the cooperation of the President. That part was okay, I was told. His press secretary, Jim Hagerty, had cleared me with the President. I asked the editor (I cannot recall his name) to have Hagerty phone me in Teaneck. I also asked him to phone Phyllis Jackson, who tired of saying "Jim dear, stop playing literary agent."

The White House call came so quickly that I suspected that, in some undecipherable manner, I was being used. Hagerty and his father had been *New York Times* reporters. Jim was, in some instances, a brutally candid man who saw himself more as the great protector of the President than the White House press liaison. He wore a dour, ulcerous expression, which, now and then, cracked into a raucous laugh. I was being invited by the President to spend as much time as I needed in the White House to write an article about Mr. Eisenhower. Hagerty assured me that all the doors would be opened to me. No strings? No strings. I asked if early March would be good for the President and Jim said yes. He said it too quickly. There must be a lengthy court calendar in the White House and he had not consulted it.

Off the phone I sat dreaming. The general was not my ideal of a President, but he had the majesty and the power of the office. To be a relatively unknown writer and be invited to the American shrine was heady, dizzying. Euphoric thought, in my head, is always followed by cynical depression. For a half-hour, I was an important man, someone of consequence. There would be a one-column head on an inside page of *The Times*:

AUTHOR IS GUEST
AT WHITE HOUSE

The President might even ask what I thought of his chances of renomination by the Republican party. And that, precisely, is when the cynical depression asserted itself. Of course, Ike had sustained a heart attack in Denver. A strong infarction. For weeks, the Executive Department had been run by Jim Hagerty and presidential assistant Sherman Adams. They needed me, right now, to paint a portrait of glowing health. The man would have to appear stronger, more assertive, than before. But why me? Who would suggest the name of a registered Democrat to a Republican President?

That required time. And why *Cosmopolitan*? The proper instrument would have been *Life* magazine. It had greater circulation and more credibility. Why? Why? Suddenly, I knew. It was Richard E. Berlin, that master strategist who tried to run the Hearst empire from behind a locked door. Ike was Dick's man. Berlin wanted Eisenhower for a second term. Desperately. He had — if he was smart — checked with the Federal Bureau of Investigation to see if they had run a detailed check on me. They had, in the middle of the war. He would then have phoned the President and said that he could arrange to have a "nice" article written by a "nice" writer in a "nice" magazine, which he happened to control. It had to be that way. Assuming that this was the original posture, then it would follow that Dick Berlin would say that he would see that every Republican delegate to the convention, and every congressman and G.O.P. wheelhorse, would get a copy of the article before the first gavel fell at the convention.

In March, I was in the West Wing. There was a large reception office, which held a tawny table on which an Indian treaty had once been signed. All visitors came through this room. It was full of reporters, who lounged on leather sofas. They may have been the last of the gentlemen journalists, men who saw all and knew all but wrote only what they thought was proper. They tipped me to run a check on Mrs. Eisenhower's drinking. It was a topic in Georgetown dining rooms, but I found not a shred of evidence to support it. The lady with the little-girl black bangs spent her waking hours with her mother, Mrs. Doud.

Hagerty was a first-class reporter. He had the power to give a quick yes or no to almost any suggestion. He asked what appointments he could set up. I had a list. On it was everyone who had anything to do with the President's daily life, including White House ushers and his valet. If all went well, I told Jim, I would be out of the White House in a week. What I needed was one average day. I would need about six to find it.

At two thirty-five P.M. Hagerty and I walked into the Oval Office. It was impossible not to be impressed: the immaculate white curving corridors, the silent, appraising Secret Service agents, the big oval rug in military gray with the embossed seal of the President of the United States, the dark rosewood desk, the furled flags on stanchions behind it, the french windows with an exquisite view of the south grounds, the fireplace and flanking couches, and, behind the desk, the blue-eyed, pink-cheeked bald man with the engaging grin.

He spoke in short bursts. The voice was throaty, gruff. It was obvious that, inside his head, he had never taken the uniform off. He was a five-star general in mufti. The one thing I did not ask him was how he felt. Whatever the state of his health in Denver, he was now an animated advertisement for insurance. Between 2:35 and 3:11, I knew that he saw himself as a pacifying influence on the United States and the world. He had fought a war. He was a hero. He was alarmed by people — like Senator Joseph McCarthy — who rocked the boat. Through the first interview, I felt that my role was to listen.

Hagerty stood leaning on the back of my chair. From that position he could, if he chose, wag his head no without my seeing it. I don't think he did, because, in the first five minutes, President Eisenhower stunned me. Three mornings a week, he said, Professor Feldman arrived to teach fundamental economics. Fundamental? The President began to twirl his thumbs against each other. Yes, he said, clearing his throat, fundamental. He had spent his career in the army, he reminded me, and he had never learned how to requisition a hundred planes by awarding the contract to the lowest bidder. When he wanted thousands of men, or tanks, he wrote out an order. I reminded myself that this man, each year, must submit a detailed national budget to the Congress. He had advisers. It seemed dangerous to realize that the man elected to the highest office in the land was totally blind in at least one of the requisites of the office. He smiled. "Mr. Bishop," he said blandly ,"I must learn the value of a dollar." In his candor, the President was disarming. It was not my function to expose him as a President with a sedentary mind. He was folksy without intending to be. Dinner, he said, was eaten "in the upstairs hall." He dined with Mrs. Eisenhower and Mrs. Doud in the sitting room–corridor of the family quarters. If there was conversation, it was between Mamie and her mother. An usher wheeled a portable television set in for the President; it was to the right of his dinner plate. His favorites were Western movies.

Ike seldom listened to television news, although he created a lot of it. He had an instinctive distrust of the media — written and camera — which was based on his knowledge that he was not quick-witted. This, in turn, led to a crashing of syntax and unparsable sentences at his press conferences. It was bravery on his part to hold a press conference at all; his personal paranoia was that they were out to get him — and, of course, they were. I attended one such conference in the Executive Office Building across the alley from the West Wing. I waited behind a drape as he approached. The President placed a friendly hand between my shoulders and edged me into a front-row seat.

Hagerty stood a bit apart from the President and his lectern, glaring at reporters he knew and admired. It was he who had primed the President for forty-five minutes on the curves most likely to be pitched and the responses most likely to be palatable. Watching the President, I felt that he was not hoping for victory, merely for survival. In World War II, he had controlled the press, telling as little as he pleased and slanting the victories and stalemates at his whim. He was now in the highest office in the free world and had lost control. In some cases, the reporters had more accurate information about the actions of the House and the Senate than he. They could, if they chose, make him appear to be a boob.

Jim Hagerty could sense when the President's patience was running thin. He stopped glaring and turned on his help me, fellas, expression. It was indeed a precious moment when the senior of the White House correspondents stood and said: "Thank you, Mr. President." Ike grinned for the cameras — he insisted that they be positioned at the rear of the room —

and walked offstage, timing his exit so that none of the reporters could intercept his flight with an additional question.

My work was around the President. His personal secretary, Mrs. Ann Whitman, was a good source. When he dictated a letter, she bit her lip to keep from laughing. He would stand and pace, and hem and haw, and dictate in this manner: "Dear John J period McCloy colon you have the address. I have been thinking about your idea comma, that the executive department should define the parameters of the responsibilities of the Atomic Energy Commission, caps on those comma, and comma while it has merit, comma, I must say, John cap on the John, that it will have to wait until the next cabinet meeting period. It is going to require discussion comma because we are not dealing solely with weaponry comma, but with also with utilities which are deeply engaged in the relationship between nuclear power and the private sector period new paragraph."

I interviewed the ushers one by one. Then I got to assistants such as Sherman Adams and Colonel Andrew Goodpaster, Major General Wilton Persons, the kitchen cooks, and, last, Sergeant Moaney. The sergeant was Black, had service hash marks up both sleeves, and refused to answer questions.

Hagerty came in. "Answer the questions," he said sharply. "The President wants you to cooperate with Mr. Bishop."

The sergeant was reluctant. For a moment, he resisted Hagerty. "All right, sir," he said to me. "Start over."

All I wanted from Moaney was the final ten minutes of the President's day. For three years, Hagerty had been standing outside the President's bedroom at precisely ten-forty P.M. to say "Goodnight, Mr. President." Sick or well, Jim Hagerty had not missed a night.

"Sergeant," I said, "you have served the general for many years. You know him when he's alone. He closes the bedroom door — then what? Since he had the heart attack, do you help him to undress?"

He nodded. "He sits on the side of the bed —"

"That's the one where the Truman balcony is?"

"Yes. I help him off with his shoes and socks. That's all. Then I draw a bath for him. He hangs his clothes up."

"Does he say anything?"

"No, sir. Oh, maybe that he's tired or something like that. Or he asks what kind of a day I had. Then he takes a bath towel and a robe and goes inside. When he comes out, he doesn't sleep there."

Jim Hagerty, squeaking on a swivel chair, stopped. "The hell he doesn't," he said. "I've been saying goodnight —"

"He doesn't sleep there. He goes into Mrs. Eisenhower's room."

Hagerty scratched his head. "I'll be a son of a bitch," he said.

"Does he have little white pills for his heart?" I asked.

Moaney nodded. "When he gets in his pajamas, he puts one of the pills on his tongue and he takes the pill bottle and a glass of water and he sort of sneaks into the other room."

"Sneaks?" said Jim.

"Yes, sir, he had the White House carpenter take out the back wall of his closet. You see, he says goodnight where you said. But then he takes his pills and goes through his own closet —"

"I understand," I said.

Hagerty asked the President if he should ask me to delete the sneaky closet. "No," Eisenhower said. "Leave it in. It's a good family touch."

When the story was published, there was a little burst of luncheon applause along Literary Row. Editors and writers had been trying — unknown to me — to get an exclusive story from the President. Hagerty ran interference for Ike, and declined the aspirants on the grounds that it would not be proper to invite a writer without asking the representatives of the Associated Press and United Press International to share. I should have felt some elation, but I couldn't summon it.

The reason was, and would be, a chronic one. No matter how exalted the subject, I soon discovered that he was less of a personage than I had expected. I looked for gigantic heroes and unearthed defensive pygmies. Ike never knew a rich man until the war was won. After that, he knew no poor ones. The gifts of cattle and farm machinery to his estate at Gettysburg were tendered by men who could afford a favor in hopes of getting one. He took considerable pride in his peacetime pursuit of painting in oils and watercolors, but he told no one about the talented army sergeant who traced the outlines of his paintings and taught the President how to flesh in the colors. He was a clone of Ulysses S. Grant, who was gallant in war but didn't know how to fight a peace.

To the Senate and House, he was remote and august. My impression was that he proposed to wear the presidency as a mantle he had earned overseas. And yet, I had not contracted to write a political piece which would dissect his inadequacies; the editors paid for an intimate closeup of Dwight D. Eisenhower, and that's what they got. I suspected that his resignation as a five-star general of the armies was a fake to attain high office. When he left the Oval Office, he rose to my expectations when Congress proffered the return of his five-star rank and all the emoluments, and he accepted modestly.

It was a good assignment for me, not for him. But what the hell — disillusionment was my gruel. It got to a point where I dreaded to swallow my own research. The immortal Mr. Lincoln fell off my pedestal when I found that he flipped a Bible open every morning and dropped a bony finger onto a page to read what the omen might be for today. My mentor, Mark Hellinger, was no longer the debonair, sophisticated Broadwayite when research disclosed him as one who, married to the "most beautiful woman in the world," fought vainly against sexual impotence by browsing in the boudoirs of girls who aspired to a screen test. Nor did it help to learn that, in Hollywood, when his work as producer did not please executives at Warner Brothers and Twentieth Century–Fox, he ambushed them with snide accusations before they made up their minds to discharge him.

I did not propose to sit in final judgment on anyone, least of all on myself. I picked my spots. Rule One was never to accept an assignment to write unless I first assured myself that I could do it better and more brightly than anyone else in the field. If, as was true, it was impossible for me to be a hero in my house, I was duty-bound to bend the halos of my subjects.

It was Virginia Lee's wedding. I wore a black and gray cravat, a rented suit, and my best smile. Saint Anastasia's was fairly crowded. The bride looked radiant in white veiling with her retinue of bridesmaids and attendants. I glanced at Charley; he took a deep breath and folded his hands before him. Weddings are feminine events, originally designed to legitimize and ennoble the surrender of the female to the male. One thinks of rustling skirts, brilliant color, waterfalls of flowers, a prescribed minuet inside a church, masses of smiles and tears, and the assumed endorsement of God. It is also a one-day drunk, an afternoon of envy, a moment of reconciliation among embittered relatives, trembling hands, outrageous toasts, and the early departure of the bridal couple.

My mother felt contempt for those who drink. At a wedding, however, she felt that it was "hard luck" not to drink to a lifetime of happiness for the bride. She sipped the watery Manhattan, trying valiantly to swallow. The effect, in about twelve minutes, was magical. A mist of perspiration appeared on her upper lip. She smiled until the gold tooth showed. "Would you care to dance with me?" she said. I said it wasn't nice for women to ask men to dance. She shoved my shoulder. The blind woman was asking the clumsy man to execute something with grace. We danced. Some people applauded. She felt small and bony in my arms. I whispered that she got a lot of mileage out of one cocktail. She said, "Shhh."

We danced close to the bridal table. I felt happy for Missy. She was in conversation with Charley. He was strong, sturdy, controlled. She was pretty, born with one of the most animated faces I have seen. I was happy for her on two levels: she had the man she loved; she was leaving a house in which strife and intoxication were common. In the same thought, I felt sorry for Gayle, the willing slave. She was now one crutch for two. They would use her to the ends of her strength, physical and emotional, because they could not help themselves. She was midway between twelve and thirteen, a time when sensibilities become tightened strings. It would be my pleasant duty to drive up to Teaneck on Fridays and bring her to Sea Bright for a weekend of laughter and movies and restaurants and pool-shooting. She had strong motivation to be of service to Nanny and

Mommy, but I questioned how long those skinny legs could hold up, how quietly she could sit and listen to two women retill the same conversational soil in the same theme: how rotten life can be.

After the wedding, I returned with Elinor and some of her family to Teaneck. She was mellow. "I wanted to tell you —" she said, and faltered. She wanted to tell me that, at last, she had opened a copy of *The Day Lincoln Was Shot*. She hoped I wouldn't be angry, but she had mastered forty pages of it and quit. I told her I didn't mind. She was candid. I wasn't. She had asked for three hundred dollars a month. I was sending six hundred — all of it from a book she couldn't read.

Father Ralph Gorman walked around his small office as he talked. He was in black slacks, black shoes, and a white undershirt. He lifted a book from one shelf and found a place for it on another. I had decided, I told him, to write *The Day Christ Died*. As an author of nonfiction, I didn't feel ecstatic because so much truth had been lost in antiquity. I reminded him that, for years, I had been trying to shed the cloak of Catholicism. "Don't write it as a Catholic," he said. "Do it as objective history." He asked how the Gleason book was doing.

The reviews were good, but reviewers don't buy books. The promotion I had banked on for a year — a favorable mention of the book on the Gleason show — did not materialize. For a few years after, Gleason and I passed each other at functions without nodding. With time, the book seemed to improve in his eyes. In later years, I heard that he cheerfully autographed copies of *The Golden Ham*. I don't think that anything I wrote ever pleased the person about whom I was writing.

Ralph Gorman said that there were three or four thousand biographies of Jesus. Of these, about forty were acceptable to most Christian faiths. He would save me a lot of time in the New York Public Library by buying the forty and mailing them to Sea Bright with a bill. I would not be using the words of Jesus if I persisted with "Thee," "Thou," and "Ye." He said I was placing blocks against the book. A book came off a shelf and he tossed it at me. Take this with you, he said. Two priests named Kleist and Lilly have just reduced all the original words and sermons of Jesus to the American vernacular. The book has been approved by the authorities.

I asked if I could write a check for the several checks of one hundred seventy-five dollars he had sent in the past. Gorman had a throat chuckle. No way, he said. He now had a famous author in his grasp at a hundred seventy-five a shot and he wanted written articles, not money. The sum of an hour chat was that he convinced me that *The Day Christ Died* could be a great book if I maintained my instinct for research. This work would be a joy because it would be a learning process, an unraveling of threads from rich tapestries, an amateur detective searching for the unknown. The weakness in the book would be that I would be learning a story nineteen hundred years old, one which had been analyzed by first-rank theologians. My best hope, a forlorn one, was that the Lincoln book, with its hourly chapters, had persuaded a good number of readers that it was an intriguing format and the next book, as a result, could get off to a good start.

At home I asked Elinor if she would like to go to Jerusalem. I knew the answer; she was surprised at the question. To Elinor God was a wrathful being who glared at His creatures and visited mysterious pain upon their lives. No, she would not like to go. It was too far away; Momma was getting old. Elinor said that religion and death were vaguely related. She said she had nervous premonitions about her death. I should not have laughed. What, I said, a husky, healthy woman like you? It was silly, she said, and sometimes it went away for a day or two. Then it came back strong and, sometimes in dreams, she saw herself in a casket suffocating in flowers. I suggested that if she slowed the doses of tranquilizers and liquor, her outlook would improve. The combination was depressing. No, she said, it was the other way around. In the morning, with no tranquilizers and no rye or gin, her hands trembled beyond control and her thoughts of death were sharp and terrifying. When she took the pills and the drinks, the visions faded, the hands stopped shuddering, and she felt "under control."

I asked Gayle if she wanted to travel with me. The eyes brightened; she shouted; she danced a rigadoon — sure, sure. When? As soon as I completed my notes. Of course I would have to speak to the teacher and ask whether a trip to the Holy Land would match what she was bound to lose in mathematics and geography and English. "Oh, that," she said, subdued, "what a drag."

Before I started work, Phyllis and I had lunch with Evan Thomas. As editor at Harper, he was pleased. In the contained attitude he wore, Thomas said I could have any kind of a contract I wished. This reminded me of how recently I had begged to do a book. Any book. Phyllis worked out the deal.

That week, I wrote a note to each of the editors who had declined to publish the Lincoln book. They were identical: "Dear Joe [or whatever]: Matthew 16, verse 8. Sincerely, Jim." The vengeful aspect was that each one had to locate a Bible to find out what I was saying. The applicable section stated: "Oh ye of little faith . . ." Four of the editors did not respond. The fifth wrote: "Dear Jim: Matthew 5, verse 4. Sincerely. . . ." I looked it up. The Bible said: "Blessed are they that mourn: for they shall be comforted."

I began to enjoy the research. The last full day of the life of Jesus had more substance than was to be found in the writings of Matthew, Mark, Luke, and John. Each of the forty biographies contributed to my notes. A translation from the Hebrew gave precise expositions about how a trial for blasphemy would be conducted. He had proclaimed himself God and the Son of God, and the Jews had frequent, and bad, experiences with messiahs. Among the seven thousand Levitical priests who worked in the great Temple, the fakers were known as "Egyptian magicians." These messiahs were aware that the Jews had been waiting for a savior — impatiently among the poor — and anyone who, with the assistance of a confederate or two, could devise a few miracles was accepted and given alms by those who could least afford it. Usually, they were warned by the high priests to be gone, and they departed at once. A few who were deluded would not leave. These were tried and condemned to death by stoning. Of course, since the advent of the Roman legions, the land of Israel had become a province of Caesar. Pontius Pilate, the Procurator, had but two solemn duties: the first was to dedicate places, such as the seaside resort of Caesarea, to Augustus, rather than statues, which would be destroyed by fanatical Jews as torments to their faith. The second was to appoint renegade Jews as tax collectors, assuring each one a small percentage of what he collected. Other than that, Pilate cared nothing about the Jews, so long as they did not riot near the Temple grounds.

My interest was piqued, and more than piqued. My mother saw it as a good, holy work. To ward off a charge of hypocrisy, I told her that I was writing it for the money. She stopped her ears with her hands. She had always known, she said, that of the three children I was the one who had a "calling." She had wondered why I had been spared sudden death in childhood diseases — now she knew. My father, who kept saying that there "never was a writer on my side of the family," chewed on the end of a cold cigar and hoped I knew what I was doing.

The research became a fury of delight. As each note was copied into the correct quarter-hour of time, it became the fitting together of a nearly perfect puzzle. The best of all the books was a two-volume set written by a pedantic German named Alfred Edersheim, who signed himself "M.A. Oxon, D.D., Ph.D." He wrote *The Life and Times of Jesus the Messiah*, and completed it in 1883. This man had me propped in bed reading and rereading, questioning and solving the great "why." He was consumed by his knowledge and reveled in it, but he had it. Somewhere in 1881 (as an example), he was writing a section about Jesus' thrusting his hand into the branches of a fig tree and, withdrawing it without fruit, warning his following apostles that, if they did not bear fruit, so too they would be condemned to be barren as this tree.

It occurred to Dr. Edersheim that Jesus was tried and crucified in the spring, and that fig trees do not bear fruit until the early days of summer. Edersheim was certain that he had caught the messiah in a poorly devised example. He put his pen away, packed his bags, and took a steamer from Liverpool to the Holy Land. The time was spring. He would not write another line until he learned what Jesus had in mind. After an exhausting journey, he rode an animal from Haifa to Jerusalem, dismounted, and looked for a fig tree. He reached in, drew his hand out, and found he had a few crisp leaves from the previous autumn, and some small round grayish objects. They looked like rubber lozenges. Edersheim addressed himself to several pedestrians until he found one who could speak German. The man said that the little gray substances were edible. Travelers used them to postpone hunger until they reached an inn. The stranger gave Edersheim the local name for them. "Unless you find these things on the branches in the spring," the pedestrian said, "the tree will bear no figs in summer." So, for the overly thorough German, the perfect life remained momentarily perfect.

The *Constitution* was a big, sleek liner. As the sailors hauled in the heavy lines at Pier 84, Gayle stood on tiptoe and threw rolls of colored paper down to the dock at her mother and grandmother. Elinor looked small in a print dress and a black hat. She waved mightily. It was another parting of the ways, no easier than the others but more symbolic. She was finding it difficult to leave the house. Often, when the phone rang, she and Maggy pressed fingers to their lips and waited. The doorbell got the same treatment. Kay Herman feared that they were not eating properly, and brought covered dishes of lasagna and hot bread. She knew they were in, but no one answered the door.

I understood Elinor without analyzing. The world was slowly closing in on her, but I didn't know why. As mine opened into broader and more luxuriant fields, she was disappearing. There was nothing I could do to reverse it; in 1956, she wouldn't even go to a movie. Maggy was gasping for breath at age seventy-six. Whatever else was wrong, she was overage and overweight. Both practically gave up cooking. Except for breakfast, wearing a wraparound housedress, a hanging slip, carpet slippers, and unkempt hair, Elinor seldom appeared in the kitchen. Virginia Lee and Charley drove over from their house in Washington Township, but filial devotion was not enough. Elinor would submit to a kiss on the cheek, but she kept the conversation at a distance. Quite often, she phoned Hong Kong Gardens for a takeout order of chow mein and soup. At other times, Maggy would peel vegetables and they would simmer soup all day long. Both placed their trust in God, but neither attended church services.

For me, Gayle was effervescent company. She ran the decks of the *Constitution*, made friends with the stewards, ate sumptuously, donned funny paper hats, whispered sage advice to old ladies playing Bingo, studied her school lessons in the stateroom, checked her dresses, slips, panties, and her coat, and wore them as her mother told her to, laughed hysterically as she mimicked passengers, saw the same movie twice, and seldom looked at the sea.

I tried to explain the Azores and Gibraltar, but I knew by the rapid nodding that she wasn't listening. The ship made a stop at Cannes and she seemed to be excited at the water-bug activity of the speedboats and the water skiers, but the magnificent hotels, the pale beaches, and the Corniche left her with cheek on fist. At the Excelsior Hotel in Rome, I was surprised to find that a formal card was waiting at the desk of the concierge. It stated that I was invited, with my daughter, to a special audience with Pius XII at a certain time. My interest in this man was neither religious nor journalistic. He had been born a prince. Unarmed, he and his predecessor had squeezed a militaristic fascist government into signing a concordat granting the Vatican extraterritorial rights in the middle of Rome. I had to see what he looked like.

Gayle wore a little black hat, a yellow peek-a-boo dress, white socks, and Mary Janes, and nearly froze to death. The audience was at Castel Gandolfo, eighteen miles out of town. There is something unique about my "wrong" days. They begin wrong, like barking a shin in the bathroom, and they are wrong all day. His Holiness wore a white cassock with white zucchetto; he looked like an upside-down exclamation point. He had some pilgrims in the room. His secretaries had apprised him of each one, so that all he had to do was remember. He said some kind words about the book to be written; his English sounded like that of an iceman for whom I had once worked. Then he patted Gayle on the head — mistake number one. She whipped her hands from behind her back and displayed a large paper bag. It was full of rosaries and medals. "Will you bless them?" she said. He glanced reprovingly at me. It looked as though the kid was going into business. They were blessed. It was his turn to make a mistake — the infallible one. He smiled at a lady standing next to me and murmured: "You must be very proud of him." We shook our heads no and the Pope said: "Ah, excuse!" and hurried on to the other pilgrims. On the way back to the hotel, I reprimanded Gayle. That is no way to treat a Pope, was the essence of the preachment. "He's a priest, isn't he?" was her rebuttal.

The flight from Rome to Jerusalem, in 1956, amounted to torture. The first leg, by Constellation to Cairo, was noisy and choppy. We stayed at the Hilton. Three of the great pyramids were twelve miles from our room. I was impressed. Gayle said she wasn't because she had seen them built in a movie. Her opinions had acerbic shades of Brooklyn, although we have not lived there.

History of any kind has always compelled my attention. I marveled at the Sphinx, a sort of sitting lion with a broken face. It had been excavated almost by accident. The Egyptologists had no idea what it represented, or what it was doing near the pyramids. Adjacent to it was the shell of a mourning room where kin and friends might repair to weep. We took a camel ride — snarling, odoriferous beasts — to please the Cairo cowboy who served as our guide and called himself Canada Dry. Later, we crawled up the "true" entrance to a pyramid to find ourselves, at the top of a forty-degree blind alley, in the queen's burial room. It was empty, as was the pharaoh's above it. The colossus in the desert, designed to protect the desiccated remains of royalty from thieves, had been a waste of time. All of them had been pillaged a long time ago. The size, the splendor of these tombs aroused avarice everywhere. Had the pharaoh been buried in ten feet of Sahara sand, unmarked, the fury of the wind would have saved his remains.

The Egyptians explained that they did not recognize Israel. In rusty-toothed triumph, one displayed maps which depicted Israel as "Jewish-occupied Palestine." I was barely listening to the speech until he got to the part that said: "Approaching the airport on our side of Jerusalem, we are in range of Jewish antiaircraft. Sometimes they shoot if we make a mistake in navigation." I asked if there was any other way of getting to old Jerusalem — train, perhaps. He laughed.

Middle East Airways used an assortment of DC-4s. Properly used and maintained, they are good for a steady, ear-splitting two hundred knots. MEA was busy, at the Cairo airport, cannibalizing two DC-4s in order to get a third one to fly. I saw mechanics take an engine from one, and try to bolt and wire it to *our* plane. The airport was a hive of men in long white gowns, women who crouched against walls with children, and hawkers whose black fingernails dipped into a thick muddy substance they called coffee.

The flight was exciting if the word translates to trepidation. At twenty-four hundred rpm, that aircraft did a lot of coughing, momentary dying, flying crabwise, flying low over the Nile and the desert, climbing asthmatically to a snowy cumulus, there to fight valiantly with thermal currents and almost lose, and then circle Jerusalem twice before coming in. I asked the stewardess, through sweaty lips, why it took so long to land. "Must first ask the tower to get goats off the runway," she said. I said, "Jee-zus!" and realized that this was blasphemy in the worst place.

I walked the Old City all day every day trying to fit pieces together. The Franciscans were good archaeologists. I showed my notes and they took me to the places I wanted to see. Calvary was a sore disappointment. The ancients had built an ugly temple over the hill of Golgotha. It was dim and divided. The Orthodox Church owned one part, up to a certain line in the floor. The Methodists had another; the Roman Catholics a third portion. The Roman soldiers had fought over His garments, but the enlightened ones fought over the geography of His death. The Episcopal Church, with the assistance of a British general, had found a tomb with a rolling stone outside the walls of Jerusalem, and they proclaimed that this was where He had been buried.

The Jerusalem of Jesus is about twenty feet below the roads of today. An order of nuns, digging out a cistern cellar near where Pontius Pilate had his palace, excavated flagstones about eight feet by eight feet on which were the scars of games of tick-tack-toe and another game involving the crowning of a king. It is hardly speculative to say that here the centurions rolled dice and played games in the off-duty hours. It is probable that here Jesus was flogged "halfway to death" with a rope of chain and nails. From this point, according to my figuring, He carried His crosstree of cedar (there were no other trees nearby) exactly one-half mile to His crucifixion.

The crosstree (I had one cut and measured) weighed thirty-one pounds.

My first setback occurred at the Garden of Gethsemane. It was nine hundred feet east of the Golden Gate, through which Judas and the Romans emerged with torches to arrest Him. The Garden was in a valley and, as Jesus prayed, it was easy to see them coming through the wall of the city. The Catholics had staked a claim to Gethsemane, and had built an ornate church adjacent to it. They made a mistake in appointing an Irish pastor to oversee the Garden. He locked it when he went to lunch. I asked him if the Garden belonged to Jesus or to him. "It's mine," he said between clenched teeth.

The Garden was important to me because studies indicated that it was at this point, praying to His Father, that Jesus began to feel frightened. Had He retained the prerogatives of God-man, He could have made Himself immune to suffering. To die as an act of love for all man, it would have to be endured with all the pain, mental as well as physical, which would accrue to an ordinary mortal. That is why He had a bloody sweat; that is why He begged His Father to "let this cup pass from me." He was afraid of what He knew was coming.

The Irish priest locked Gethsemane whenever he drove off in his car. This was done so that, each day, armed with research, I had to ask permission again. So did all pilgrims. Later, he shifted into a benevolent mood and drew a twenty-four-hour clock of the last day of the life of Jesus. It wasn't precise, but it was pretty good. "You will excuse me for thinking," he said, "that you aren't qualified to be writing this." Then, hastily: "But you will do it anyway. That's the way of Americans. Do it anyway. I hope it's not going to be anti-Semitic." If it was, I said, I wouldn't write it. He decided to try cunning: "Then how do you explain that it was the Jews who killed him?" He assumed that my research was superficial, trifling. He came here, I said, to be born among the Chosen People, to live among them, to die among them. He would have missed the grand design entirely if He had been killed by gentiles. "Ah," he said, touching his stubby fingers together, "you have been reading some history. Who do you read?" I said I couldn't remember. Well, he said, how about a copy when it is published. I pointed with a pen. You'll be able to buy one, I said, right in the Garden of Gethsemane. Not, he said, if he had breath of life to stop it.

The Protestant sanctuary on Nablus Road was a bus stop for pilgrims. It was made of rough stone with an interior courtyard. The hosts were pleasant and accommodating, always adding an extra piece of mutton to our plates, or a spare boiled potato. They could do nothing to slow the Arab holy man next door who, at every dawn, climbed a tower and sang his doleful call to prayer. He fractured sleep as one would snap a bone. As he prayed, I cursed him.

Bethlehem was another disappointment. It was five miles south of Jerusalem, a small town on a hill. Here too the church was divided in a three-way fight among organized religions. When we arrived, the Orthodox priests were in a fury because an ornate altar rail someone had donated had been smashed in the night. The Catholics, who owned part of the cellar, pleaded innocent. The town mayor said that an investigation was under way. His fear was that the vandalism might be solved. In Jerusalem, there was a disputed section of wall believed by Jews to be a remnant of the Temple of Solomon. Jews aspired to pray there. The Arabs refused. The Moslems worshipped under the gold dome of the Temple of the Rock. This is the second most holy place in the world to their way of thinking. Here, Mohammed began his journey to paradise. Soldiers of King Hussein's Jordanian army patrolled the steps.

There was but one Temple. To worship properly, a Jew had to make a pilgrimage to Solomon's Temple in Jerusalem. By law, no Jew was permitted to live more than ninety days' travel from the Temple. To continue to call himself a Jew, he must return at least at Passover. Then, the hills around the old walled city were tented with three hundred thousand pilgrims, not counting the people inside the walls. To a religious person, it must have excited something close to ecstasy to see the high Temple walls on the east side with a huge cluster of gold grapes, whose function was to capture and reflect the first rays of dawn over the rim of the mountains of Moab. The cellars on the east side alone — on the edge of Cedron — could house over two thousand animals. The magnificence was greater than anything Rome built.

The Democratic party is the easier about which to write. There is a charged atmosphere which most describe as "color," a poor word. The Republican party had Calvin Coolidge and Herbert Hoover and Dwight D. Eisenhower, three dim lights. To my confreres, Republican conventions were as exciting as free lemonade at a bank. But Democrats hollered. Their neck veins stood out. There were fist fights and outrageous speeches and asinine statements. (Frank Hague, sensing that his man, Alfred E. Smith, was losing, issued a publicity release at the 1932 convention which appealed to the delegates: "If you cannot nominate a whole man, for God's sake don't nominate a cripple.") The Dems smoked black cigars and drank too much and slept through the nominating speeches. When they were told to stand in a moment of prayer for a departed notable, they peeked.

Bill Hearst asked me to cover the Democratic convention in Chicago. The money was good, the assignment exciting. The Republicans, as I recall, renominated Eisenhower at the Cow Palace in San Francisco. In their platform, they might at least have made a few promises they knew they couldn't keep. They left that to the Democrats. For me, it was titillating. Adlai Stevenson had the blessing of Eleanor Roosevelt, who sat in a front row of the gallery. The Dems staged their customary seating fights, two sets of delegates showing up from one state. They also fought over rules and platform. The little giant from Texas, Sam Rayburn, swung a gavel used for poleaxing steers. He wore a shaved head and a dour expression. He was one of the few men who enjoyed displaying a bad temper. He was not above bawling for the sergeant-at-arms to throw a would-be protester off the speaker's platform. Also, when he wanted a "yea" vote, he slammed the gavel after calling for the "nays" and pretended not to hear the storm of sound.

Television, which had about the same relationship to journalism that newsreel cameras had to history, began to cover the conventions in earnest. They had booths up in the girders and men on the floor with walkie-talkies who buttonholed senators and aspirants for office to fill in the tedium of long and meaningless speeches. The print press had desks and chairs around the speaker's platform, and handouts which explained what everybody was going to say and do in each session.

Hearst had a suite of rooms at the Blackstone. The chain of newspapers was diminishing as Knight and Newhouse and Gannett, for example, were expanding, but the endearing aspect of Hearst coverage of a big story was that they not only brought their big guns, they brought them all. Vincent Flaherty of the Los Angeles *Express,* the man who brought the Dodgers to California, was shuffling around, stuttering whatever he was trying to say. Milton Kaplan, editor of King Features, whispered and frisked everybody with his eyes. Bill Hearst, trying to think of an idea for a Sunday editorial, tried to hide in different rooms, and found them all occupied. Frank Conniff raced around in an undershirt with a pencil on his ear. Bob Considine sipped something on ice and looked out a window. "Funny," he murmured, "Toots said he'd be here." Burris Jenkins sat next to a bed with a large bristol board on a flowered bed cover, sketching and chuckling. Al Armitage asked writers if they needed paper, or carbons, or a machine, or a drink. Two or three publishers wandered in to pick up promised press passes, which would guarantee seats up front. Phones in three rooms were on hold, except that no one could recall who the calls were for. Newspapers from San Francisco and San Antonio and Boston and New York were on the rug, kicked by the slovenly.

Bill Hearst put an arm around me. He said: "Now you wouldn't want to write a newspaper column, would you?" Witlessly, without thinking, I said: "Sure." Hearst turned to Conniff. "Hey," he said. "Jim is going to write a column for King Features." "That's nice," Conniff said, and disappeared in his undershirt. Saying yes like that is like agreeing to go to bed with a pretty girl. You have no notion of how much it means to her, or why she asked, or what her name is.

My interest in the convention was not Adlai Stevenson, a modest intellectual who captured the convention and press. The word spread that he would not endorse anyone for the vice-presidency. It was an open ticket. I followed Senator Estes Kefauver, because he wanted it and he had the votes. Overnight, I was derailed by the forces of John F. Kennedy of

Massachusetts, who believed that the opportunity was truly open and that he stood a chance. Quickly, I met some of his people — Lawrence O'Brien, amiable saloonkeeper; David Powers, Boston ward heeler; Robert Kennedy, who could speak faster than he could think; Kenneth O'Donnell, a thin-lipped man whose speech was reminiscent of a prisoner in a lockstep, and an assorted group of school chums. These people went to work in a shark-feeding frenzy. They buttonholed every delegate, on the floor or in hotels, drunk or sleeping, and asked for votes for Kennedy of Massachusetts. They left no turn unstoned, even though, from a practical standpoint, they stood no chance of stealing the vice-presidential nomination from Estes Kefauver. They lost, but overnight they had picked up six hundred votes. This impressed the politicians.

If the Kennedys could not win, why the all-night charge to get any votes? I wrote that I thought that old Joseph Kennedy had ordered his son's forces to charge because he was saving the kid for something in 1960. There were few who knew much about him, except that, in Washington, he was a Georgetown charmer of women. He had done something magnificent in World War II, but no one at the press table could remember what. His opposition came from his own area — the John McCormack group of Massachusetts. Skinny John was as Catholic as the Kennedys, and he controlled a much older, and firmer, political *apparat* in the Bay State. The McCormacks had expected the Kennedys to take their place in line, but Joseph Kennedy had decided to start a one-family party in Boston and to buy what he could not otherwise win. To do this, he would have to beat the Yankees, who were all Republicans, and the McCormacks, who were all Democrats.

At the press table, we were agreed that it couldn't be done.

There were second thoughts, and third too, about writing a newspaper column. I had seduced myself. To one who had groveled for years in the press pit, leaping for scraps of meat and bones, the casual offer to dine gluttonously at the head table was irresistible. Inside the author, a cub reporter crouched bug-eyed with fascination about the world, and events, and men. Bill Hearst said: "Have you thought of what you want to call it?" I nodded. *"Jim Bishop: Reporter."* To those who were interested enough to ask, I said I could not fill a space with items. I would write a story three times a week. None of it could constitute spot news. If I had a talent, I felt it would be in low-key storytelling.

After the Democratic convention, I was asked to have lunch with Richard Berlin in his private dining room. He was pompous; meeting the man, I was sure he wore a stiff collar to bed. When Berlin smiled, it was because his mind ordered his face to do it. His secretaries were male. Their function was to impress me with him before I was escorted to the inner office. We talked of books and the Hearst chain of newspapers and magazines, and of King Features Syndicate, the emerald in the Hearst diadem.

In the late 1920s, Joe Connolly organized it at the direction of William Randolph Hearst. Connolly was a hearty, jolly, sweaty man who took the many comic strips, household features, medical columns, gossipmongers, and sports writers and reground their material to newspapers in "noncompetitive areas." The Atlanta *Constitution,* for example, could buy Walter Winchell and "Li'l Abner" because Hearst didn't have a newspaper in that city. The Chicago *Tribune* could not, because Hearst owned the Chicago *Herald Examiner.*

Economically, King Features was a simple operation. They sold syndication rights to papers all over the nation, keeping 50 percent of the revenues, and giving the other half to the writer or artist. In this manner Walter Winchell could be earning five hundred dollars a week for his work on the *Daily Mirror* and earn another five hundred a week from syndication. I was offered a three-year contract for writing three columns a week, with a minimum guarantee of twenty-five thousand dollars a year. If KFS sold me for less than fifty thousand dollars, they would lose money.

Berlin was pleasant. He said he was glad I was "coming aboard." Lunch was served in a small dining room. I told him I was impressed. The only reason he had his own table, he said, was because the food-testing kitchens for *Good Housekeeping* magazine were on the floor above. His secretary phoned the ladies and asked what they were cooking and testing. Whatever it was, they were told to send a couple of portions, including dessert, to the "chief." As lunch was ending, I was eating a good custardy bread pudding with raisins. A secretary whispered to Berlin.

I was reading the clauses of the contract. Berlin said: "Guess who's waiting outside?" I didn't guess. It was the publisher of the *Daily Mirror.* I recalled that when Frank Braucher of Crowell-Collier, displaying a clipping of a story about Madame Chiang Kai-shek, asked if he knew a reporter named Jim Bishop, Charles McCabe had shaken his head. Never heard of him. I shoved the contract and its three copies aside. "You want me to sign this?" I said to Berlin. He nodded. "Okay. Keep that son of a bitch waiting in the hall. May I have some more bread pudding?" I took my time. Eventually, I signed it; he signed; I kept one copy.

Berlin showed me out. At the elevator the publisher sat waiting. The "chief" said: "You know Jim Bishop?" McCabe extended his hand. "Everybody knows Jim," he said. I had worked for this man, but this was the first time we had met.

The signing of the contract created an editorial stir. I thought of the column as a tryout. Frank Conniff saw it as a triumph in picking columnists. *Editor and Publisher* ran an article about it. Feature writers of local newspapers came to my house to interview me. *Time* magazine sent a writer to Sea Bright who hovered for three days, listening and taking notes. I told him I had been reading *Time* since 1928, and if this wasn't a hatchet job, he would have nothing to write about. The article referred to me as "The hottest writer in America," "The Golden Hack." "Bishop . . .

talks in terse, side-of-the-mouth sentences that often sound as if he read Hemingway before writing. . . . He is a tenacious reporter, with a disarming manner and a glib way of dramatizing. . . . Next week Bishop's biography of sorrowful Funnyman Jackie Gleason will get a Benjamin Franklin Prize from the University of Illinois. . . . Bishop will have earned $550,000 in royalties by year's end. . . . He divides his time between writing and research, . . . his power cruiser and the local bar, where he drinks endless pots of tea and gets many of his story ideas from chatting with clam diggers and fishermen. . . ."

My understated response was "Fuck *Time.*" It was a cool, dispassionate expletive. If a news magazine could devote that much space to me, the "Golden Hack" could afford a two-word response. Deep down, I was thrilled to be published in newspapers again. Hellinger had done well as a syndicated columnist. Now it was my turn. Moving from the world of books back to newspapers is akin to wearing an overcoat inside out because you admire the lining. Most reporters try hard to run in the opposite direction. I had a score to settle. Newspaper editors had, for thirteen years, compressed me into the image and likeness of the anonymous writer who must encapsulate the whole story in the first paragraph and then repeat it in detail through the next twenty.

It wasn't the money which attracted me. Twenty-five thousand a year for three human-interest stories a week is a reasonable sum, but, if I could attract some of the column readers to buy some of my books, I would attain a crossover pattern which would enhance sales. My contract stated that I would be one of four "general columnists" in the United States, which, translated, meant that I could write about crime, sports, politics, or pedantic opinion.

My ability to tell a story in nine hundred words was no better than it had been on the *Mirror.* I had a glassy, superficial style and a seasoned touch for saying a lot in a few words. The risk, if there was one, would be in fobbing off worthless stories on millions of readers. I worked hard — and still do — to find a character and a series of events with a built-in philosophical point. Most important, I had to impress two hundred feature editors with what schools of journalism refer to as a "style." If I couldn't impress them, my unnewsworthy column could be dropped on any day the editors needed more space.

The first thrill occurred when I saw the speeding news trucks adorned with flashy billboards stating: "Read *Jim Bishop: Reporter.*" My face on those panels was bigger, if possible, than my head. The second thrill came when mail came in from readers in cities I had never visited. There is something almost profound in pecking alone at a typewriter and, ten days later, hearing echoes from places such as Salem, San Antonio, Seattle, and St. Louis.

It was extra work, but there was a satisfaction in returning to a grave eight inches by four and resurrecting myself. I reassigned my waking hours so that I would answer mail and write a column in the morning, reserve the middle of the day to myself, and work on the next book at night. For a long time, I was so pleased with myself that I could hardly wait to find out what I was going to do next. No, that's childish. And yet, I must confess that there was something pleasantly vengeful in going back to something as fundamental, as basic, as newspapers and pressing the wrinkles out of cordial notes from appreciative editors.

The apartment was small and scrupulously clean. Momma sat in a wing chair, the bamboo cane between her knees. Someone had waved the sparse bronze hair. The dress, to my ignorant eyes, was too dressy. It was lavender lace over a lavender slip. In her blindness she wore a permanent smile because she wasn't sure who was saying hello. Dad wore his blue serge suit and a garnet tie. An unlit cigar was in his face, his elbows were on his knees as he watched a rerun of an earlier World Series. As a fan, he never conceded that the Yankees could lose a ball game. "They fired it away."

The apartment was crowded with four generations. This was the fiftieth wedding anniversary for the John M. Bishops. It had been a cold January day in 1907 when the young railroad brakeman hired a funeral coach and two black horses to pick up the bride as he waited in the sacristy of Saint Paul's Church in Jersey City. The seasons had been stormy and serene, heart-wrenching and loving, times with laughter and torture, and decades when the plain, round five-dollar gold band endured the worst of everything merely to glisten today.

Jenny had said, many times, that she would not live to see it. The children reminded her of the prognostication, and she said: "I still can't believe it." When I kissed her on the cheek, she said: "Oh, I know who this is. May I tell you something? Dad told me you are dedicating *The Day Christ Died* to me. I'm going to make him read ten pages to me every night. It'll do the old devil good."

It was a duty date. I feel an uneasiness at these events. All milestones are bad ones. Whatever the event, we are assured that it will not happen to the same people again. Nor is it a triumph. Rather, it is a breasting of the tape — a strong finish. There was an opportunity for Elinor and my family to become reacquainted with my sister, Adele, my brother, John, the children and grandchildren. It's an amiable melee, a time to watch little ones chase each other around end tables and lamps, to disappear into other rooms, from whence one expects screams and sobs. It is also a time for a generous ham and homemade potato salad and coleslaw and warm seeded rolls and Dad's idea of a good potable — cheap rye.

I wondered if my father knew how important he was to me. I loved that man in the worst of times. His eyes were on the television screen, the cigar rolling sideways across his lips, his mouth curled in a sneer as the shortstop allowed a fast-hopping ball to get through to center field. Maggy sat in a chair, pumping a younger generation for information punctuated with "Is that so?" Elinor wore a lovely print silk with shoulders which seemed to jut outward. She was at ease leaning against a doorjamb, trading the latest news with Adele. The cold sun retired early; so did Mom. "I think," she said, "I will take a little nap." She had unwrapped the gifts; the lovely paper was lying with discarded ribbon at her feet.

Quickly, I reached to take her elbow. She pulled away. "No," she said, "let my boyfriend escort me to the bedroom." Dad looked up, vaguely irritated at the description. "I ought to be your boyfriend, Jenny," he said with no humor in the speech. "We've been married fifty years, and we kept company for six years before that, not counting the year we didn't speak to each other." There was a surf of laughter. He glared at everybody. Then he took Mom by the arm, helped her up, and steered her toward the bedroom. I followed discreetly. She whispered that she didn't want to lie down in her good dress. Her gallant knew that he was missing the bottom of the eighth inning. The back of the dress had a multitude of tiny cloth buttons secured by tiny looped threads.

He jammed the glasses to the bottom of his nose, crouched behind her, and began a labor of love. I stood outside the doorway, not close enough to be ordered away, and far enough so that I could not be impressed to service. He made grimaces before he undid that first button. On the second one, his tongue came out, pinned to the side of his mouth with his teeth. She was patient. At last, the second button came loose and he paused to examine his fingers. "Would you believe," he said to me over his shoulder, "that fifty years ago I was pretty good at this?"

Before I left, I had a chance to chat with him in the bathroom. "I'm going to buy you and Mom a house." He was quick. "No, you're not. We want no charity." I put my hand on his arm. I asked permission to speak without interruption. It isn't charity. It doesn't even resemble charity. Besides, I'm not going to pay for the entire house. I'll put a good down payment on it and you and Mom can pay the mortgage. See, it's going to be your house. He stuffed both hands in his trouser pockets and studied the bathroom floor. I reminded him that Mom always wanted a home of her own. He said he got the message — that he could not give her one. Her people had owned their own home. The way I looked at it, she wasn't going to be around much longer; why not give her the feeling that she was sitting in a place that was hers? He thought about it. He drew some deep breaths. Tell you what, he said. If you want to do this thing, why not put it in the name of your brother and sister? No bank is going to give us a mortgage. It's too late for your mother and me. It's possible we could find a nice two-family place, and John could live upstairs, and we could be downstairs with Adele. Now how does that appeal to you?

It was all right. I left the bathroom and explained it to Elinor on the way home. "Do as you please." she said. "What do I care what you do with your money?" All my money. Checks were coming in from sixteen countries. The television film of the Lincoln book brought a lot more. My lawyer, Harriet Pilpel, who, fortunately, was also my friend, had to advise me how to invest, where, how to defer royalty payments, how much to keep, what records would be required. It was an opium dream. Bank vice-presidents called at the house to make sure I would be in to sign a receipt for the AT&T bonds and the airline stocks. One asked if I wanted to withdraw some money from savings because the government wouldn't guarantee any more than forty thousand. I looked for Barney Finn so that we could laugh together. He and the banker, Frank Weber, would understand the farce of rubbing a magical oil burner until a golden genie emerges.

The Bishops found a house in North Bergen, New Jersey. It was undistinguished, and yet typical of the area. It was a two-family frame house with a gable, a minuscule and mangy lawn, a wrought-iron fence with clanging gate, and no garage. My people looked upon it as a palace. I put a lot of money into it, and guaranteed the mortgage payments. In spite of its age, there would be a natural accretion in value because people who worked in and around New York were forced to find dwellings farther out in New Jersey or on Long Island.

They moved in around the first of June, 1957, and, within a few weeks, there was a dispute. Adele, on the ground floor, said that she had retiled her kitchen walls and that John's kitchen faucet was leaking down on it. John's logic was irrefutable: it's leaking down on her walls, right? Let her get the faucet fixed. It's not leaking upstairs. The great harmony that I had foreseen was not to be. Dad, at age seventy-four, was told that he had arthritis of the neck. He bought a pulley and hoist from a surgical house and rigged up weights and a chin strap. My father's lifetime credo was that nothing is worth doing unless it is worth overdoing. He placed too many weights in the basket on his chest of drawers, adjusted the chin strap, shoved the weights off, and almost hanged himself.

Sea Bright in summer is a nostalgic dream. It's a breeze crossing a strong sun, the thunder of surf against a seawall, tall cool drinks, music, a sandy simplicity, bluefish gasping in a bag, sparrows complaining under eaves, lazy gulls, vacationers, the odor of steamed clams and drawn butter, spear-fishers breaking the surface of the Shrewsbury, and that exotic somnolence that comes with lying in a deep chair and breathing. I had a dock built in back and bought a thirty-five-foot Richardson cabin cruiser. When I wasn't busy being lazy, I studied books on sailing, power boats, charts, how to navigate, the rules at sea, and how to get a license for a ship's radio. It was called *Away We Go*. From my office in the back of the house, it looked like a battleship.

I had Elinor down and we sat on the flying bridge and sailed slowly down the Shrewsbury. I kept the music soft. It was romantic. I made a couple of drinks for her, and some black coffee for me. We sailed down past the Highland Bridge, through Water Witch, past Plum Island, and around Sandy Hook. I detected the tension when the boat rode the first ocean breakers, and we turned back. It was enjoyable, and yet there was something false about it. We were faking admiration, perhaps love. The luxurious setting was far beyond all the earthy things we had meant to each other. I reveled in a new life; she ached to return to an old one.

We talked about my brother, John, and his wife, Anna. They were driving down for a steak dinner. Elinor knew about it. They were no threat. She wished the children had come down for the weekend. I reminded her that it was "we two." The boat sailed upstream slowly. Across the river in Rumson, a Sunday church bell pealed. I asked if she was taking pills, and Elinor said she would rather not discuss it. You must have the confidence of a pharmacist somewhere, I said.

She was in back braving the blue smoke from the steaks when my brother and his wife arrived. Anna seldom drank, but if enough ice cubes were in the glass, she would take one. John and I kidded each other, joshing about things that never happened, when Elinor arrived with the dinner. There were some hellos, but my wife had a grim expression. Perhaps I should have broiled those steaks. Still, it was a cheerful gathering. The sun shadows were deep on the lawn. Elinor didn't sit. She held the empty platter and the big fork, watching John cut into the meat. "How are things?" she said. He nodded.

"What's new?" she said to Anna.

The redhead smiled. "With us, not much," she said.

Then the fury broke. Elinor's eyes did not blaze, they bugged out. She started to scream. "You bum!" she shouted at John. "You think I don't know about the two hundred dollars you borrowed from Jim? You're going to sit there and tell me that nothing is new? John, you're a goddamn moocher, nothing more." The words were coming so fast that I knocked a chair over getting up. The attack was so unexpected that no one responded.

"Elinor," I begged. "They weren't try to keep anything —"

"Ah," she shouted, "you shut up. Take your money and shove it. Listen, these two aren't fooling me for a minute. They thought they were getting away with it." Her lips began to bubble with saliva. "They didn't think I knew."

Anna stood. "Elinor, we knew you knew. Honest."

John stood. He nodded to his wife through the screams. "Let's get out of here," he said. There was a boardinghouse next door. Guests came out on the porch, craning, listening. The sounds were so high-pitched it was as though someone was hurt. Elinor stood inside the screening shouting at the two as they ran to their car.

When it was over, she sat. She was slumped on the small of her back. Breathing was difficult. The lips appeared to be cyanotic. Tears were on her cheeks. I was torn between consoling her and turning my back. Her chest pulsed up and down. Whatever the cause, it was not a fake. It was dangerously real. I poured some coffee and mixed a drink for her. "I don't want it," she said.

I felt that I was breathing rapidly. "Well," I said. "This is the end of the trail, Elinor." She nodded. "I mean the real end. I am not going to try anymore, and I don't want you to try." I thought for a moment. "Twenty-seven years . . ."

"Please," she said.

Toward the end of June, there were no communications from Teaneck. I worried. Phoning achieved nothing. I could speak to Gayle, but she had been primed to say that everything was fine. Elinor was not available. She was taking a nap, or was in the bathroom. Maggy was busy upstairs. A surge of fear was building. It was based on nothing. On a Tuesday evening, I phoned and said: You put Momma on the phone or I'm driving right up there. The ultimatum worked. Elinor got on. Words skated gracefully off her tongue, except that they were not in communion with each other. I asked what was the matter. Nothing, nothing at all. Her voice sounded like someone who is almost awake. I asked how Maggy was. Not so good. She had a lot of trouble breathing. At this point I displayed my gift for saying the wrong thing: the woman is seventy-seven years old. She's five feet tall and weighs a hundred and ninety pounds. What do you expect, Elinor?

This was greeted by silence. I told her I was driving up. They were all coming to the shore with me. That, she said, was impossible. She and Momma hadn't been dressed for days; she wasn't sure how many. Had they eaten? She thought so; she wasn't sure. I told her I was on my way. It's no good, she said. We won't be dressed. On the way to Teaneck, the pity within me went to Gayle. For several years, she had been the willing slave. At a time when she should have been having fun with schoolmates, she was running to buy bottles of gin through the back door of a store because the owner was afraid to have her purchase them in front. She had a cheerful, hoydenish disposition, but no one measured the tension underneath. Virginia Lee once said: "I used to run through the front door after school with a loud, happy 'Hi!' hoping I might hear one in return." The little one had been stuck with the dismal moods, the vague sicknesses, the interchangeable headaches, the exhaustion of two people who shared fears.

The house was reasonably clean. Maggy was in a nightie and a robe. She said she couldn't get dressed. It didn't matter. Elinor was talking — not angry — but it was necessary to listen attentively to understand. Gayle waved her arms, saying, over and over: "I tried to help. Honest I did." The suitcases and schoolbooks went into the trunk. I shut off the services inside the house. We backed out with Maggy trying to be agreeable: "How's the shore, Jim? Nice?" The doctors have a word, *dyspnea.* Maggy had it. In repose on the back seat, she wasn't breathing any easier than when she got in the car. I spent the drive reassuring Elinor. "This will be good for all of us," I said. "My cook makes a great vegetable soup. Chief" — a boyhood friend, John Dundas, who was a permanent houseguest — "will be around all day to help, if I'm not." Glancing to my right now and then, I could see that she was wearing her permanent smile. Helping her into the car, I was shocked at how bony she felt.

There was a corner bedroom upstairs for Maggy. I fixed her summer favorite, a Tom Collins. I kissed her goodnight and tears sprang to her eyes. She and I had been mean sons of bitches and her battle to retain fifty-one percent of her daughter had been unremitting. I would help this woman, but I despised her. "Help me," she said as I switched the light off. I placed a cord in her hand. "It's attached to a bell in the hall," I said. "Ring when you need me. Or the cook."

Elinor and Gayle waited in the master bedroom upstairs. "Mind if I use the bathroom?" Elinor said. I almost smiled. "The house is yours as well as mine," I said. "Use whatever you want." Gayle shifted feet. "Momma," she said, "why don't you sleep up here with Daddy?" Elinor cupped her daughter's face in two hands. "No, doll," she said. "Daddy needs his sleep. I'm sleeping downstairs." I had the feeling, unwarranted perhaps, that Elinor wanted me to say stay with me. I couldn't. It wasn't a matter of sexual symbolism; I was as close as I could be with comfort. It was becoming difficult for me to look at her for more than a moment. It wasn't revulsion. It was the difference between the round flapper of long ago and the edgy, hand-twisting woman who had reached a stage where she couldn't stand noise and couldn't bear silence.

Late in the morning, I phoned Dr. Brenner. I entreated Maggy to see the doctor in his office. "Jim," she said, as though she was imparting a family-held secret, "I can't do it. You see, they want to lay you down on a table. I can't do that. I can't breathe that way. Besides, I told you they laid my sister Bridgie down and she never got up."

Brenner had medical skills, the personality of a hanging judge, and a peremptory way of saying "or else." He examined Elinor, beaming in a Barca-Lounger, and said: "This woman must get to the hospital. Whatever substance she's ingesting is dangerous." My wife began to wave her arms feebly. What came out sounded like "There will be no hospital." That afternoon, amid tears and accusations that I had taken her to the shore under false pretenses, she was driven to Monmouth Memorial Hospital in Long Branch. She was in a state of anxiety. The doctor refused to give her a sedative. Gayle and I sat with her until she dozed.

Brenner examined Maggy upstairs. I felt a surge of pity. This woman, who understood little of life and living except her natural love for children, was dreadfully frightened. The doctor examined, probed, turned her over as though she was a tractable animal, and stood. "I can do nothing with this one," he said later. "Bring her to my office tomorrow. We'll make a few X-rays." The examination would be standing, or we would leave without it. Out in back, Gayle tossed round pebbles onto the flat surface of the river. "Everybody all right, Poppy?" She was trying to turn away from the increase in pain, but she was also afraid not to know.

Within the restrictions imposed by the patient, Maggy was examined. She stood against a wall for the X-rays. When it was over, she smiled and said: "How did I do?" "Terrific," I said. She waited in the reception office as Brenner beckoned me inside. "Know anything about X-rays?" No. He hung the wet plates before a diffused light. He pointed. "See this shadow? That's her heart." I looked. "Don't you see?" he said. "The heart occupies two-thirds of the chest area." He took a small metal ruler. "More than two-thirds. Almost three-quarters. What's keeping that woman alive?" I asked what I should do. Brenner shook his head. "You?" he said. "Don't do anything. There's nothing to be done. How old did you say she is?" Seventy-seven. "Jesus, she's a tribute to something, but I don't know what."

She had been stout all her life. In age, she was so fat that she appeared to be neckless. Brenner had given me some sample tablets. "They're not worth a damn to her," he said, "but if she finds breathing difficult, tell her to put these things under her tongue. Give her a couple of extra pillows and put her in bed." On the way home, I asked Maggy if she would like to stop at the hospital and see Elinor. "No," she said slowly, "I don't think so."

I do not know the recovery rate for drugs and liquor, but Elinor, within two days, not only was sitting in a chair beside her bed, she oozed charm and cheer. She draped herself in a pink peignoir and held court for Ginny and Charley, Gayle and me. The next day she spoke of going home. Brenner said: "Do you know where she's getting the drugs?" I didn't. "I think she found a gold mine somewhere," he said. "She's probably paying a pharmacist who's robbing her blind. Can you stop it?" I said that she could stop it. "I'll keep her one more day," he said. "She's detoxified. Can you find out what's bugging her?"

It was a bright weekend, early in July. Gayle was in the office, keeping Mrs. Walter from work with her chatter. Elinor and I sat in the kitchen, sipping coffee. What was troublesome was finding safe topics, subjects which would not lead to dangerous exchanges. She asked how *The Day Christ Died* was going. I said slowly. In most cases, a book required six months to write because, as a professionally lazy person, I never rewrote, revised, or edited. The slowness had nothing to do with her.

"Momma," she said, pointing to the ceiling. I looked up. We could hear Maggy clumping down the hall to the bathroom. "I hope she stays in bed," I said. "Brenner says she needs rest." Tick-tick had heated some bakery buns. *The New York Times* was open to the sports section. I scratched and yawned. The All-Star baseball game never featured the players I thought should participate. I was still quarreling with the newspaper and some of its coverage when Elinor said: "She's in there a long time." I looked up. Elinor said her mother was still in the bathroom. I asked if she wanted me to go up and see if Maggy was all right. No, she said. She's slow.

There was no clump of feet going back to the bedroom. I folded the paper. I'll take a look, I said. Elinor hung her head. Her hands were clasped on the table. "Oh, stop," I said. I got upstairs and rapped on the bathroom door. There was no response. Of course, she might be back in bed. I turned the knob. Maggy Dunning sat there, the blue eyes wide open. She was looking toward the ceiling. The mouth hung open. The nightgown was draped modestly over both thighs. I wondered why she didn't fall to one side or the other. She was dead. I patted her on the cheek. "Maggy," I said softly. "Maggy." It was a ridiculous gesture. The skin was as warm as in life. I started slowly down the hall, down the narrow stairs. Elinor was staring at me. There is nothing in my recollection to remind me of what I said or what she said. If I could guess, I would say we stared in silence. She knew. Elinor did not go into the frenzy I knew so well. The big brown eyes stared at me and they filled with tears. They were silent too.

I called Brenner. "Get her back to bed," he said. "I'll be there as soon as I can." Gayle and Mrs. Walter had to know. Chief said he would help. The distance from the bathroom to the bedroom was no more than twenty feet, but it seemed a distance to me. I took her under the arms. He lifted the feet. Nothing can be that heavy. I stopped dragging the dead woman several times. Lifting her onto the bed was a task. At last we composed her, smoothed her hair back, adjusted the nightie, fluffed the pillows, and closed the eyelids. "Let's get out of here," Chief said.

Brenner guessed that, in tending to her morning wants, she had strained a little. The heart locked instantaneously. He said she had felt no pain. Elinor shut her ears against any information. It seemed cruel that, having returned from a hospital siege, she should have to stand under what, for her, must have been the world's most crushing burden. The only child and the only mother were apart. Later in the day she asked me to please handle everything. After some thought, she said she would attend her mother's wake, but she couldn't goad herself to go to the cemetery. The girls and I, and Charles Frechette too, followed Elinor's wishes. It was an Irish wake as she planned, with whiskey in the cellar of the funeral home, roast beef sandwiches for those who stayed too long, a solemn gathering of the clan, a priest to recite the rosary, and exaggerated recollections told in the smoking room.

Elinor and I became friends that summer of 1957. She had seizures of sobbing, but it was far less than the hysteria I expected. It was easy to remind her that she had been a devoted daughter, that she had spent most of her life at attention to her mother's wants. The work was over. The job was done. Had her father lived, Maggy would have had to exist on the wages of a bartender who had bad feet and a grouchy disposition. Instead, she had lived with us exactly twenty years. I was not going to state what those years had done to me, or how it had shredded the fabric of marriage; I wanted to remind her that no daughter could have done more.

The book had been completed. Harper felt that it was better than the Lincoln book. I was irritated when I heard that they sent the rough manuscript out to the hierarchies of the many faiths for approval. *The Day Christ Died*, which, under analysis, was no more than a detailed Bible study of one important day, plus some plain and fancy storytelling, won more approval than I anticipated. Some of the leading Protestant figures were willing to be quoted in the advertisements. The archdiocese of New York sifted all the words and stamped it with an imprimatur. Professor Hoenig of Yeshiva University was willing to state that he could find no anti-Semitism in it.

Phyllis phoned. Nothing has happened, she said, I just want to bring you up to date. I offered the book to *Good Housekeeping* for first serial rights and they came up with an offer of fifty thousand dollars. (I was close to a heart attack.) However, she said, I declined. (I was having a heart attack.) I sent it over to *Ladies Home Journal,* and I gave them forty-eight hours to read it and come up with an offer. Timidly, I asked if she had lost her mind. With asperity, she asked if I was going to play literary agent again. No, I said, you're the boss, Phyllis. But if the *Ladies Home Journal* turns it down, I'm dead. If you took the fifty thousand, I'd be far ahead even if the book never sold a copy. She began to "Jim dear" me.

The next day she phoned to say that the *Ladies Home Journal* had offered seventy-five thousand, and she hoped it would teach me a lesson. This, she said, would postpone book publication because the magazine expected to run it in three parts, and Harper would wait. On the other hand, British, French, and Italian editions would be published in September and each of them would like me to be present to give the book a sendoff.

It was a warm day, and I took Elinor to the beach. On top of the seawall was a rickety platform and two park benches. We sat in the warm briny breeze, soaking up sun. I held her hand. The book news shook both of us. One runaway best-seller is rarely followed by another. The week before, while she dozed in Sea Bright, I had gone to New York and bought her a full-length mink coat. This was as thoughtful as buying a ten-speed bicycle for a quadriplegic. She had no use for a mink coat. She seldom dressed; she wouldn't go to the movies or to a restaurant.

I knew that, when we had visitors, she would display the coat on a hanger and listen to the exclamations. It would not be worn. It would be on "loan" to Ginny, or to Agnes. The best I could expect to do would be to get it glazed every summer. In the sun, her skin looked saffron. Would she go to Europe with me? This time she glanced, and smiled. Was there any place she would like to visit? How about a cruise? I was conning my wife, trying to purchase her favor. It was no sale.

She agreed to go to a dinner in my honor at Harriet Pilpel's apartment. My lawyer was a proper lady, addicted to hats in courtrooms, one who did her homework in law and had the support of her attorney-husband, Bob. The dinner would be nothing if I didn't bring my wife. Elinor said she would go — much as she dreaded meeting people. "They're your fans, not mine." It was a lovely evening for five couples. We spent little time talking about books and a lot of time talking about Dwight Eisenhower's second term. There was a spurious fireplace at the far end of the room and Elinor sat near it. Harriet and her husband juggled from chair to chair, dividing time between the guests. The maid came in and said that dinner would be ready in about five minutes.

I saw Elinor start to tilt. She was leaning to the right, and, as I jumped to help, she went to the floor crashing. A lamp was down; so was an end table and a drink. I lifted her up, but there was no response. She was conscious, but not in command of her limbs. People were saying: "What happened?" "Did she hurt herself?" Three cocktails could not have done this. Harriet guessed what it was, and helped Elinor to the bedroom. The shoes were removed, the bedclothes pulled up. "Give her time to rest," Harriet said. I had pushed her too far. She didn't get drunk on the drinks she had at the party. She had insulated herself against strangers before she left Sea Bright. The additional two or three cocktails caused the accident.

The dinner table was animated. The bright speeches covered a dismal event. Harriet glanced at me and looked at a back door. Elinor stood in it, holding onto the jamb. We were in the middle of the entrée, and men moved chairs to make room. She felt her way to the table and plopped. Elinor was not in condition to dine; her black hair was in disarray; the mascara made black teardrops under her eyes. I wished hard that she had remained in bed. The guests tried not to look as something — a bit of potato, perhaps — made it almost to her mouth and fell back on the plate. I made a whispered excuse; I said my wife hadn't been well since the death of her mother. This aroused Elinor. "My mother has nothing to do with anything," she said loudly. "If your friends don't like me, I feel sorry for them."

It is seldom insufferably hot at the shore. But the first few days of August were still under the sun. The sea was quiet, oily. Metal doorknobs were hot. The refrigerator could not keep the beers cold. Up and down the beach we could hear the happy shrieks of young swimmers behind the seawall. Elinor and I had a houseful of guests. This time — on her ground — she seemed confident. She knew that my father's favorite was standing ribs of beef, and she helped the cook roast it.

In the office, Charley Frechette dusted the pool table. Gayle and I were partners against Charley and my father. We played a quarter a rack. Big John and Gayle were poor losers. They paid under protest. Ginny came out and said Grandma felt warm. I said it was a warm day. A bit later she came out and said that Grandma felt faint. I hung the cue and went inside. There was a yellow leather chair near the front door. The women had my mother in it and were fanning her with newspapers. She didn't appear to be faint. She looked tired.

"You all right, Momma?"

"I'm all right. Virginia Lee is taking good care of me." My daughter had been snipping and curling Grandma's hair.

One of the concomitants of diabetes is blindness; another is heart failure. Jenny Bishop had sustained heart attacks and survived them. I'm an optimist by trade, but I began to wonder if we could possibly lose two women in that house within thirty days. An hour later, Ginny was out in the office again: "Grandma's not responding." Dad dropped his cue. He hurried inside and grabbed a newspaper from someone and began to wave it frantically.

I phoned the Volunteer Ambulance Corps. The men, who also served as lifeguards, heard the wailing siren and hurried off the beaches in bathing suits. I phoned Brenner. He said he would meet her at the hospital. I held my mother's hand. "Don't worry, Mom," I said vacantly. "Don't worry." Her cheek felt cooler than the air. I could hear the ambulance siren far off. Four, in bathing suits and bare feet, hopped up the steps. "Your mother?" I nodded. There was something almost amusing in the tender way all those muscles were marshaled to lift her like an infant. They didn't use the stretcher. Someone got a gray blanket, and carried her down and into the open doors in the back.

Ginny began to cry. Gayle looked shocked. My father growled: "Well? What are we waiting for?" We tried to follow them down the beach road but they were too fast. Inside the ambulance, one man propped Momma on two pillows and said: "Now take a look at those estates as we pass by. It'll make you feel better, missus."

In her breathlessness, she had to laugh. "I can't see them," she said. "I'm blind."

The man had prescience. "Okay," he said, "in that case I'll describe them to you, including the scalloped hedges and the flowerbeds."

She was in a room at the end of the hall. Brenner was at her side. It is obvious that doctors have sufficient trouble dealing with emergency cases involving strangers who arrive with no medical history, and dread to deal also with distraught kin. He could not respond to our questions because he was looking at a seventy-three-year-old woman he had never seen. He asked Dad about the A.M. urine test, and Big John said it had been all right. She had also received a shot of insulin in the leg. We sat fidgeting at the end of the hall. My mother looked calm and sleepy.

I suggested that we go home. Dad wasn't sure. "In case anything happens..." "Nothing," I said, "will happen." We were of no assistance sitting in a corridor. Dr. Brenner would phone if he needed us; or if Momma did. Dad was persuaded. We tiptoed into the room. She was not struggling to breathe; she was sleeping. We kissed her and tiptoed out. "She has a doctor in attendance," I said. "I asked for a nurse. She's already there. What can we do?" Big John looked at me as I drove. "Pray?" he said.

Everybody was sitting in thought in the living room. The weekend party was over. At six P.M. the standing ribs were served. Nobody wanted to eat, but everybody told everyone else: "Eat a little." I phoned the hospital twice and the operator said: "Mrs. John M. Bishop? Her condition is fair." There was nothing fair about it. There was a big television set in the living room and we turned it on in the evening. Sight and sound engage part of a mind.

Dad sat alone in the kitchen. At nine o'clock, he came through the swinging door. "Somebody call me?" he said. I shook my head. He smiled apologetically. "I must be hearing things. I distinctly heard somebody calling 'John! John!'" There was no one in that room who would refer to him as John. He returned to the kitchen.

At nine-twenty, Brenner was on the phone. "Jim, I think you ought to get your father and come down here. I don't think your mother is going to make it." The translation was that she was dead. I hurried Dad into the car. This time we spun through all the dirt roads at speed and defied the red lights in Long Branch. We were breathless as we got off the elevator. Both of us passed Brenner in the hall. He was speaking, but I didn't hear him. It was the same white face on the same white pillow. The expression was the same. I bent over and kissed her. The skin was warm. Dad started to cry. He was looking down at her and hollering: "Jenny! Jenny!" His eyes were flame-red and the tears fell off his face onto the blue suit.

A nurse was in the doorway. She was talking to Brenner. She was close to hysteria. "... I had just made her comfortable and I went up the hall for a cup of coffee. It was just nine. I thought I heard some woman screaming "John! John!" so I hurried back. She was choking on a plug of mucus. Doctor, I put my whole fist down there. I'm so sorry I was too late...." Mom had choked to death. It was an adieu I couldn't bear to think about or discuss. All I said to Brenner was: "You don't have much luck with the Bishop women." He looked angry.

The early days of September seemed warmer than summer. The morning of September sixth cradled a bluish haze over the farms behind the

Jersey shore. The entire family left early because the liner *United States* would sail at noon, and these were inquisitive people. This, they had read, was the super ship, a long, graceful steel hull, four gigantic propellers, a big superstructure of lightweight aluminum. It had not been my fortune to enjoy an all-points expense account; now this was the day, the hour. I would return to New York in mid-October aboard the Italian liner *Giulio Cesare*. These would mean more to me, as a dizzying pleasure, than to most because beautiful ships were my love.

The stateroom on the promenade deck was crowded. I had champagne and bottles of booze and buckets of ice. A steward brought canapes. Emil and Kay Herman said they would stow away; Ginny and Charley said no one would dream he was afloat on such magnificence; Betty and Ray Stone helped pour drinks (they had two little girls at this time); Dad sipped a straight rye on ice; John and Anna marveled at the decor, the drapes. Bill Scanlon shook his head and murmured: "Rich bastard. You finally made it." The steward, stiff in a white waistcoat, said he was sorry that he couldn't get tea for me. Elinor declined a drink and kept her arm hooked in my elbow. Gayle was up and down corridors, peering into other rooms and other sailing parties, romping into huge public rooms and, at times, getting lost.

The all-ashore whistle is a basso vibration which, for an instant, freezes the nervous system. I told Elinor I would write. I lifted her chin with my finger and reminded her that since her mother died, she had been unable to go upstairs in the Sea Bright house. I whispered: "It's all in your head. Go up. It's just an empty room except for that little statute of Our Lady of Guadalupe in the hall. She won't bite you. Go up." She said she would try.

At the gangway there were multitudes of kisses and hugs. Passengers were tossing coils of colored paper streamers down the side of the ship. A band was playing. The deep whistle blew again. Below, hundreds of people were hurrying off the gangway looking like cascading confetti. I felt a surge of something — I know not what — a disengagement, a casting off of lines from the family, a disturbing sensation that once we had all been tightly bound like a clutch of arrows. Good fortune had slit the binding and we were in separate places. He of the navy blue suit was far below, waving a pale straw hat. I waved. Then I saw Ginny and blew a kiss. Without a sound, without motion, the great ship began to back out into the Hudson. My eyes frisked the family, and then I saw her. She was under a little white satin hat, waving a handkerchief. I waved; blew kisses; made a comic hug. She was crying. The way Elinor acted, you'd think it was the end of the world.

Outward bound, the seasoned travelers went below to have lunch. I was on deck, drinking in the rare grandeur. When the *United States* dropped the pilot, I wanted to see how long it would take Commodore

Anderson to rack up thirty-one knots. He turned those bronze propellers up to thirty-nine hundred revolutions per minute and, six miles later, still within sight of the beaches of Long Island, the liner trailed a bridal train of white that reached to the horizon. This meant that, in a dead calm, walking forward on an open deck, a passenger would have to lean into a thirty-five-mile-an-hour gale. Near Nantucket Light, she was in a running sea with a tall cross-chop, but the *United States* gave not an inch.

I went below to introduce myself to Commander Gehrig, the purser. All I wanted was a chair at the late lunch and dinner tables. He was a stout man with a moon smile. He took me by the arm into his quarters. On a shelf, he had about everything I had written. "Autograph those for me," he said softly, "and you can have anything you want." The second day, he introduced me to Anderson and the chief engineer. They gave me the freedom of the bridge and the engine room. It was common knowledge that the ship had been built to navy specifications as a troop carrier. Few knew that she had a reserve speed of five knots. Anderson said that she was so true that, if someone dropped a little mooring buoy every 744 nautical miles, his ship would pass each one at the crack of noon.

I made no friends, except for some of the crew. I began to realize that, in traveling alone, women with men enjoy introducing you to women without men. For me, the voyage was too swift. Four and a half days seemed like a weekend. At Southampton, I took the boat train to London and checked into the Savoy Hotel, where most Americans, at that time, stayed. The hotel seemed to me an ugly place in an alley with its back looking at the Thames.

It was my first literary launching of a book. The publisher wore an odd-colored vest over a portable belly. He held a lunch at Brown's Hotel. The critics were, in the main, small Englishmen who smoked pipes and seldom combed their hair. It was important to the publisher, so I answered questions as forthrightly as possible. They seemed agreed that *The Day Christ Died* was an odd choice for an author who had a choice. They wanted to know if I was religious, if I had ever studied for the priesthood, what part of Ireland my forebears had sprung from, would the Pope like the book? Would I call it pietistic or reverential? Had I studied the Dead Sea Scrolls? What was my next book?

At the hotel, a girl was waiting. The Savoy maintains a butler on each floor — he brings tea and biscuits and turns down the bed — and he permitted the girl to wait in the room because, he said, she represented a powerful London newspaper. This one made herself at home. It was understandable that she had to cross her legs as a perch for her note-pad, but not that high. Her attitude was fun-loving. She asked about the book and noted few of the responses. She asked if she might have a whiskey. The domo brought it. When she departed, she asked if I knew London and would like to see it at night. I said the voyage fatigued me; some other time. One of the hoary axioms is: never buck a reporter; they go to press too often. The headline in her paper (two columns wide) stated:

FRIEND OF JESUS
VISITS LONDON

There is a shadow of the incestuous when writers are interviewed by writers. There is a natural resentment on the part of the interviewer toward the interviewed. They are brothers in the same "racket." Nor is condescension a palliative. I learned that the let's-you-and-I-be-boys-together doesn't work. Nor does the spurious I-know-six-rewrite-men-back-there-who-can-do-anything-I'm-doing attitude. There is no comfort in a public condition called fame. Old friends such as Fred Grimsey and Emil Herman and Bill Scanlon — who once had freely shouted "dummy!" — began to back off when I disagreed with them. At lunch, editors conceded that I was profound when I said that a civil rights bill would not be passed in the Eisenhower administration. Rabbis and ministers, who had confided in me for years, began to hedge and murmur: "You won't print this, will you, Jim?" Feature editors phoned and asked: "How about a day in the life of Jim Bishop for a change?" I was invited to racetracks to present a silver cup to a horse; expensive charity dinners at the Waldorf and the Plaza would be less than successful if I didn't grace a table with the single rose in the fluted vase. Radio and television wanted free opinions in parsable sentences. Book-review editors asked if I would write critiques of authors who would be scared shitless waiting for my verdict. Publishers would appreciate ten or twenty words of approbation to be used in promoting a new book. Brokers implored me not to spend it; they would design a profitable portfolio of investments at no charge. Real estate dealers were prepared to give me a house and lot at half-price if they could use my name in the sales brochure. Retired physicians and schoolteachers sent bulky manuscripts for me to read and assess.

Before I departed for Europe, I had signed a contract to address a university — or such unwary students therefrom as could be corralled — at one thousand dollars plus expenses. My father seemed saddened. "They're paying you to speak?" he said, raising the thick white brows and dropping them. I said yes. "Strange," he said. "I wouldn't pay you a nickel to shut up." He was not too far off target.

I wrote two letters to Elinor, posted them, and took the Blue Train to Rome. Before I departed, there was a slight interruption. A writer, Robert Ruark, phoned to ask if I would stop by for a drink. He was "famous." Ruark had been an overseas reporter for Scripps-Howard. It had come to his attention that Major General John "Courthouse" Lee had become an insufferable martinet in Rome. The general forbade all road traffic within two blocks of his headquarters and had engendered a we-the-bosses-you-the-serfs attitude toward Italians. Ruark researched the story, cabled it, and it was published over the masthead on page 1.

It made Ruark and unmade General Lee. Bob was offered a syndicated column and began to write novels. I told him I would bring a suitcase and could spend an hour. "Would you like to meet Ava Gardner?" he said. I said no. He said okay. Just the two of us. I said fine. Ruark had a suite of rooms. He seemed unable to sit. The moment I arrived he asked if he was being personal in asking how much I made from the Lincoln book. I said I would tell if I knew, but that royalty checks were still coming in. To make me feel at home he began to tell me how much he earned from each of his books and "last year I got sixty-five thousand out of the column." Was I into tax-exempt bonds? He had an accountant. I must look into tax shelters. The pacing in the room slowed a little. He had a little place on the sunny coast of Spain. The hell with Rome. I must join him and Ava and we would disport ourselves on the sand.

He perspired and refreshed his drinks from a cut-glass decanter. Ava was down the hall. I sat listening and dredging my mind for what little I knew about this man. It was obvious that he thought we belonged to an esoteric cult which could be charted in dollar signs. My memory told me something else. Ernest Hemingway had spent his life writing about himself as he wished he was — a he-man who flaunted colored capes before bulls and women, a man who, above all, knew how to die. Robert Ruark saw himself as a young Hemingway, sunning himself with beauties, drinking prodigiously, and hunting big game in Africa. I departed thinking that Ruark was a troubled author. No one writes successively better, more worthy, books. The time would come for him and for me when the lead review would state: "... who has written some excellent books in the past, now emerges with a poorly contrived, stilted imitation of his earlier works." I wondered whether Robert Ruark could brace himself for it. Could I?

I had chased success, fame, recognition, riches for many years. Now, in a reasonable measure, I had it. Public figures invited me into their social lives. I appeared on network talk shows. Colleges offered honorary doctorates. Ruark had it too, but when two men face each other in a hotel room, the damning question in two pairs of eyes is: "I know how I did it, but I can't figure out how you made it."

Watching, assessing, I realized that my perpetual questioning of my work could lead to the drunken, sweaty person I observed. In retrospect, I knew that I had drunk my way through the *The Glass Crutch*. The difference between writing the Lincoln book in the cellar and this luxurious voyage to European capitals was nothing more than a transfer of fears. Dreaming beside the explosive oil burner, I wondered if I was truly a cipher, a nothing. These days the hidden fright was that I would write a bad book and fall back into the cellar again.

Rome was as dull as London and Paris. I was lonely. The paradox in this is that I was, and am, a loner as a writer. I work alone, do my own research and writing, and do not seek assistance. And yet, when traveling, I feel depressed when the day's work is done and I must look for a wall table and tilt a newspaper beyond the food. I needed Elinor, and, if not her, then Gayle or Virginia Lee. Ginny would have been ideal because she had what my father called "a good head" and she had an abiding interest in history and shrines. She grew up and married too soon.

I flew to Cannes and checked into the King George and waited to sail home on the *Giulio Cesare* on October fifth. The hotel had the appearance of a white, rich layer cake. Inside the curving harbor, the affluent lounged on anchored steam yachts, the young were towed on skis by speedboats, the rich Americans walked the seaside esplanade in the afternoon to see and be seen. A few congressmen romped in the lobby with French nymphets. I was marking time. The Paris edition of the *Herald Tribune* was submitted to two readings. A letter arrived from Virginia Lee. The envelope alone was so exciting that I ordered tea and kicked off my shoes to read it on the bed.

Dear Daddy:

I'm really sorry I haven't written sooner, but I wanted to wait until I had really good news about Mommy, and now I have. Tonight we arrived home from Westwood and as soon as we got in the door, she announced that she was going upstairs, probably because you had mentioned it in the letter we just finished reading. She asked me to go up and turn on the lights and to please stay with her, which I did. She cried a lot but she did it and so far has been upstairs three more times tonight. She says she can probably go up anytime from now on. So that's one big hurdle she has finally gotten over. She has really been doing well. Gayle Peggy and she came up Tuesday night for Claire's shower. The trip up was fine — Charley drove — she was just a little nervous, but not as bad as usual. She turned out to be the belle of the ball and she was certainly a help to me — she made the punch, fixed the salads, set the table and washed dishes. She must like my cooking, because she even ate well. Honestly, Dad, she's been trying.

She started several letters to you, but her hands shake, so she hasn't completed them. She says she wants to buy a "smart outfit and have me give her a permanent wave" so she'll be a living doll when you come home.... We all send lots of love and kisses and we miss you terribly and wish you would hurry home to us all. Our prayers are always with you and we hope you have a good voyage home.

All our love,

Ginny, Gayle Peggy, Mommy, Charley, Rocky (our black and gold German shepherd, whose proper name was Rocky of Shrewsbury. He was the most innately dignified dog I have known).

Only the crayon of smoke made the *Giulio Cesare* look real. At anchor in the roadstead at Cannes, it looked like a painted ship on a sheet of plate glass. It would sail west, stop for a few hours at Gibraltar, then head across the Atlantic at nineteen knots for New York. The steward, Michael, was a gem of a man, a portly Neapolitan who spoke English better than the Pope. When I think of the numberless times he tapped on the door of cabin U-18 and asked "You all right? I get something?" I felt an empathy far beyond what can be purchased with a generous tip. The feelings he could not translate into English, I could read in his features. I had found two books in English at Cannes, so I had three friends.

After we left Gibraltar, I counted five days to home. The little boy in Saint Patrick's School who had looked longingly at the ships heading for the high seas and incredible adventure was now white-haired, and one month short of fifty. The thrill of travel could be restored if Elinor came along. I wondered how salesmen managed to sit in an automobile all day long and drop into bed in an alien hotel at night. Aft, I stood on deck taking photos of the last land as we passed through the Strait of Gibraltar. Algeciras on the Spanish side was sharp and clear, but Tangier was hazed over at the bottom of the Atlas Mountains.

It was early afternoon and I returned to my cabin. Michael knocked on the door. "Radio room," he said, pointing. I wondered why he hadn't brought the message. I was sure it was King Features, warning me that they had not received the columns mailed from Europe. In that case, they would be forced to tell the subscribing newspapers that I was on vacation, even though I had barely started to write the three-times-a-week piece. The radio operator handed me a telephone. I had forgotten that, in 1957, ship passengers could phone almost anywhere in the world.

To use it, one had to press a button to speak, and release it to listen. For several seconds, I heard nothing but a sound like shrieking wind. Then it was, not King Features, but Ginny. "... Brenner took Mommy to the hospital last week ... didn't want you to worry ... worry ... WORRY! ... said it was pills and liquor ... what? ... wrong. See, the doctor was wrong.... Mommy wasn't on pills ... something broke in her stomach.... Oh, please, Daddy. I wish you wouldn't worry ... they found out yesterday. Hah? Tomorrow. Surgery at ten.... Something broke. Diverticulitis, he says.... Yes, he thought it was tranquilizers.... Hah? What can I do? ... the surgeon examined Mommy yesterday; the operation ... I can't hear you ... Daddy, Mommy loves ... 'Bye."

In U-18, I lost my mind. We had cleared the harbor of Gibraltar a few hours earlier. If I had known that Elinor was in the hospital, I could have flown to London and taken a plane home. I would have been at Monmouth Medical Center in the morning. A punch to the bulkhead wall skinned my knuckles. Michael got some medication from the ship dispensary; my explanation was rerouted in his head so that the word around ship was that a passenger's wife had died. The thought of death became insupportable. This was the thing she had feared all her life. I knew she wouldn't die. Whatever the problem, Dr. Brenner would have it under control. I had a vague notion that a diverticulum was a looped bowel; a few feet of intestine became entangled, or enpouched like an aneurysm, or constricted. I had heard of its being corrected by diet and medication. If this one was severe enough, a surgeon might have to go into the stomach and unloop it or whatever.

No, that was not the cause of my frenzy. It was the knowledge of what this would do to Elinor. This scathing, scornful, spitting woman was in perpetual terror. Twenty-five of her forty-seven years had been spent thinking of herself in a satin-lined box. I also knew that, in spite of our estrangement, she would want me at the bedside to "explain" things. Over the years, I had "explained" toothaches, birth, miscarriages, headaches, abdominal cramps, fears which supported other fears, bad dreams, hot flashes, cigarette cough, hangovers, and excessive bleeding. I had learned to "explain" everything to the irreducible. Now where was I when I knew she needed me? This girl, who had turned in hundreds of false alarms, had a real fire raging and I was on an ocean liner, having fun.

There was a second phone call in the radio shack. This time I ran and prayed at the same time. It was Edward Mahar, city editor of the New York *Journal-American*. This was a joy. Eddie's paper was the New York outlet for my column. He was a small snowy-haired gent who ran the editorial department with a whip and a chair. He had heard that Elinor was sick, and he just wanted me to know that the *Journal-American* was on top of the story. He had asked Guy Richardson, an ace reporter, to contact the doctor. Brenner, assured that the material was not for publication, said that he had signed Elinor in for chronic abuse of liquor and tranquilizers. He thought she was recovering, but she had stomach pains. He found tenderness, but not enough to ring any alarm bells. Today he became convinced of an acute diverticulitis. Rather than take a chance on medication, he had her examined by a surgeon, who would do an exploratory, and possibly corrective, operation Monday morning. When we hear anything, Eddie said, we'll call you at once, Jim. The main thing is not to worry out in the middle of the ocean. Everything was under control.

Late Monday afternoon (ship time) Ginny phoned. Gayle was sick in bed with a high fever. She was in my bed and Brenner was treating the child for pneumonia. He had ordered that no one tell her anything about her mother because "it might upset her." Again I heard the shrieking of the damned wind, or whatever sound permeates a ship telephone. I would not admit to nervousness, but I was pressing the button when I wanted to listen, and releasing it when I wished to speak. The operation had been a success. The surgeon said there had been some complications, but everything was under control.

I didn't get out of the radio room. The operator had a second call. Eddie Mahar said he had good news. I didn't tell him that my daughter had phoned. My wife was down from the surgery, resting comfortably. Some of the reporters — anxious to help — took turns bugging Brenner on the phone. He told one that he was tired of the same old questions, that they should elect one person to maintain contact. Eddie said he would do it. I told him how relieved I felt, how grateful. He said he would have to phone Milt Kaplan at King Features, and Bill Hearst and Frank Conniff at the Hearst Building, in addition to his own editors. I felt an unexpected warmth in being a newspaperman again. These people had time to care; the "famous" author began to feel humbled.

This was a time for relaxation. I graced the second sitting at dinner and bored the ladies and gentlemen with a detailed rundown of my troubles. At ten P.M. Michael brought a tray of cold fruit and a pot of tea. I restrained an impulse to hug him. When he left, I dropped to my knees and said the thank-you prayers. As a Christian, I was aware that I wasn't worth a shit.

Virginia Lee called a bit early on the eighth. I was in the radio room, waiting. Mommy was doing better than expected. She was sitting up, although she said she felt dizzy. Vanity asserted itself: she asked if the scar was ugly. I laughed. Good! That sounded like my true baby. I begged for more and more news. She had asked several times when Daddy was expected home. Ginny told her she had been on the phone with me. I cut in to say that, if her condition improved, I could phone Mommy direct from the ship in the late morning. Perhaps the afternoon would be better. Dr. Brenner thought she might be in the hospital for another five or six days. He didn't want to speculate. I told Ginny to give her mother a big kiss from me, and to tell her I was getting there as fast as I could. Could Charley meet me at the pier? Maybe the *Journal-American* could pull some strings and get me off the ship at the quarantine station. When Mom was strong, I told Ginny, we could go away to the Bahamas for a couple of weeks. I could feel myself edging back to be Elinor's husband again; it was not good thinking, but I was reaching for it.

On the ninth, the phone calls came in threes. The howl of the winds was worse. I had to decipher words, solitary words. The rest seemed to fade into the vastness of the sea, and then float back. Ginny said "Please don't say anything to make me cry, Daddy ... dying ... Charley and I don't know ... peritonitis, that's sure ... yes ... one doctor said fecal matter dropped down inside ... definitely dying, Dad ... we can't tell Gayle. She should be in the hospital. . . . Oh, Daddy, Daddy. What am I going to do?" The second call was from my father. The voice was a fading growl: "It's a crisis, Jim. But don't drink. Whatever you do, don't take a drink. . . ." It had not occurred to me. He may have been thinking of himself when "C" was dying. I tried to get off gracefully. I promised. Eddie Mahar was trying to get me. " . . . news is bad, Jim . . . tragic stuff. . . . We're in touch with Ginny and your father. . . . Say a prayer, kid. The doctors can't do it. . . ."

Between the afternoon of the ninth and the afternoon of the tenth, I have no recollection. Later, I was told that the captain came to my cabin and spent fifteen minutes saying that he understood. I should have recalled part of that visit.

In the afternoon, Virginia Lee called again. The sound seemed to have some clarity. "Mommy died at eight-forty-five this morning, Daddy." Her voice was calm. Instead of sorrow, remorse, a tremendous surge of relief welled in my chest. It was the most reprehensible sensation I have ever experienced. It was as though, in a long dream, the hanging was finally over and someone had cut the rope. "Charley and I knelt at her bed all morning praying. A priest gave her extreme unction. She didn't seem to be in pain. Now and then she mumbled something. Oh, Daddy . . ." Mahar phoned to say that I would be met at Quarantine and taken off in a tugboat. All funeral arrangements would await me on shore. I counted on my fingers: three women in eighty-two days.

Possibly the worst part was Gayle's lack of knowledge. The cheerful slave thought her mother was recovering from an overdose of pills. Ginny walked into the bedroom (as I learned later) and, unthinking, said: "Mommy died this morning." Of course there is no lacy circumlocution which will soften a hammer blow, but the trauma was as distinct as though someone had shot her mother in Gayle's presence. The little girl who had served her grandmother and mother with unremitting devotion had been betrayed. They had died on her without warning. It was unfair to leave the scene forever without a good-bye kiss. For years she had sat, uncomplaining, as they drank themselves into amiable moods, and then to a point of irritation, and finally to shouting accusations and stumbling on the stairs and wetting the beds. Gayle had laughed and joked through scenes of horror, hoping that her "funnies" would be contagious. Her mother had waited until the child was sick, very sick, and, flipping open a magical door, had stepped through and slammed it forever. Of all the family, Gayle was least prepared to allow her mother to go. For a long time, Gayle refused to allow her to go.

If Richard E. Berlin had been a newspaper columnist his name would have been George Sokolsky. As a columnist, George was a hammered-down pedant. He knew everything about everything. We had not met, and there was no reason why we should. His material was so far right that he might have suspected J. Edgar Hoover of communism. Two months after Elinor's funeral, he asked to meet me. I had a feeling that most everything Sokolsky did was sub rosa, au courant, and patriotic. There was a diocesan communion breakfast at the Waldorf-Astoria. He would be present. I had promised someone I would show up. I was surprised to learn that I was seated on the podium; I was expected to sing for my breakfast, too. What the pure-as-snow souls wanted to hear was a description of the Holy Land.

To be succinct, it was dismal. Sokolsky flashed a painfully restrained smile at me as our eyes locked. By the time the speaking was done, I realized that I had killed the chance of anybody's buying *The Day Christ Died* because, in thirty-five minutes, I had told the story. The applause was spirited, but that could have been because I sat down. It could not have been for the crucifixion.

George said he would like to speak to me. He jammed a hand in his trouser pocket, and stood on the lee side. His mouth was adjacent to my good ear. What he wanted, he said, was for me to write the definitive work on the Rosenbergs. The husband-and-wife team of spies had been electrocuted in Sing Sing for stealing the trigger to the atom bomb. Two books had been published. George, I said, why don't you write it? He said he couldn't. He did not have the time or the talent. Sokolsky felt that "pinkos" were peddling books which proclaimed the innocence of Julius and Ethel as upright patriots. George said he could get me in to see Judge Irving Kaufman, who had presided at the trial and sentenced the pair to death. I said I would think about it. As soon as my familly regained its bearings. I would have to think of one more book. There could be little excitement following a trail furrowed by other writers. Rosenberg was not a new subject.

Still, I went to an apartment in upper Manhattan one evening to see Judge Kaufman. Once in a while, I find myself in the presence of a human who, in his attitude, his articulation, his command of his thoughts is so superior to the rest of us that I marvel. Irving Kaufman was a compact, graying man with a lovely wife, two sons, and a den of choice books. He spoke easily of the "all-Jewish trial." The defendants were Jewish; the two defense attorneys were Jewish; the prosecutor was Jewish; the judge was Jewish. When the trial opened, the unspoken aspiration of all was to be as un-Jewish as possible. As the evening progressed, he spun a tale of espionage involving the making of the atom bomb, the Rosenbergs, Mrs. Rosenberg's brother, a mousy professional spy from Philadelphia, a Soviet agent in the consular office in New York — it was like a spy movie with so many small ramifications that, in listening, you wondered how it would come out.

When a New York jury found the Rosenbergs guilty, Judge Kaufman could have imposed a lesser sentence than death. He realized, however, that the Justice Department and the Federal Bureau of Investigation had an overweening desire, to get not the Rosenbergs, but the people who recruited them. The FBI thought it knew the people "upstairs," but would need the testimony of Julius and Ethel to secure the case. Under the law, both deserved death as American spies for a foreign power, but the sentence could also be used as a lever to get that testimony. In the death house, it was Ethel who decided that she and her husband would look better as martyrs than as cringing snitches. It was she who braced the quavering Julius to face death. One of the ironies of the case was that the American communist party said not a word in favor of the Rosenbergs until they had molded themselves for sudden death.

Demonstrations were organized for Julius and Ethel in New York, Paris, Warsaw, Washington, Los Angeles, and Moscow. They became a cause. The two friendless ones were being compared to Sacco and Vanzetti. Lawyers drew fresh briefs. The case escalated all the way to the United States Supreme Court seven times. President Dwight D. Eisenhower was asked for clemency. The liberal noncommunist press was urged to dwell on the possibility that two innocent parents were facing death. Much publicity attended the visits of the Rosenberg children to the death house. The articulate Jewish population was urged to demand clemency from the government, not on the issue of guilt or innocence, but because they were Jews.

Judge Kaufman felt that the book had not yet been written. He had a rare and complete copy of the trial. It was mine. He was interested in me because, he said, he learned that I do all of my own research. "You will get no help from me," he said. Then he amended the statement: "Unless you want an interview about all hell breaking loose in my life between the time the Rosenbergs were found guilty and the time I sentenced them to die. You may find that period of some interest." I was impressed. Phyllis was opposed to the book. She said a new Rosenberg book was about to be published in England by Alan Moorehead. Didn't I say I was tired of coming in second? This time I would be fourth. Evan Thomas restrained his enthusiasm. Harper, he said, wants to publish anything you write. But, unless you have a lot of fresh research about the Rosenbergs, you will be wasting your time.

I asked him to draw a contract and, in spite of Phyllis Jackson's objections, I signed it. The moment of acute danger for the author is when he believes the laudatory press clippings and sees himself as an "important" writer. This is when, removed from the hunger and debt which impelled him to do better than his best, he becomes his own literary agent and his own publisher. He does not seek interviews; he grants them. He is aware that, at social gatherings, he enjoys a special status. Inviting him, hostesses feel important. At universities, hundreds of students sit in respectful silence (perhaps even getting a quarter of a credit for listening to him) as, in glassily smooth sentences, he expatiates on the problems of the world and points a manicured finger at simplistic solutions which, until now, have escaped the secretary of state. His moments of modesty occur only when he is certain that no one subscribes to them. To his family he exhibits less patience. The books of others are digested with less adulation and more criticism. He is inordinately interested in the mystical assortment of words and images which constitute what is called a blockbuster. He is affronted if, on the best-seller list, his lies second to one about a new diet. He has become an all-purpose pain in the ass. Like a growing child, he must try to survive it and see himself as he truly is — a lucky bird who has come to the favorable attention of a lot of people.

The Rosenberg contract was a mistake. I had imposed my whim over the judgment of Phyllis and Evan and the result was years and years of research, scores of notebooks, and no book. It became so exhaustive that Benjamin Pollack, deputy attorney general of the United States, came to Sea Bright to ask if the government could examine my notebooks. I agreed. Mr. Pollack holed up with all the material in the Ship Ahoy Motel. Three days later, he was back in my office. He said that he had been in charge of the Rosenberg case since their arrest and he thought he knew as much about them as anyone. Still, if I would indulge him, he would like to start with book number one and ask some questions. He had thin little interrogation marks in the margins. Where did I learn this? How about that? He was a short, scholarly man with a big nose. At the top of each of the thousands of notes, I had a code mark. A code book would give the source. I told Pollack that, if the source was a public one — i.e., a magazine, a newspaper, a statement — I would reveal it. If it was private, as the result of an interview with, let us say, East Side neighbors of the Rosenbergs, I would not.

Pollack was a flatterer. "I think you know more about it than the government," he said. That wasn't true. The Federal Bureau of Investigation, through Agent-in-Charge Cartha DeLoache, had opened its files to me. Those files formed a skeleton for the remainder of the research. Pollack urged me to write the book. I doubted I would because the immensity of the material was out of hand. Almost every trail I followed out of Alamogordo led to two other trails, or to a split one, and this led to espionage which had nothing to do with the Rosenbergs. The books were returned to a fireproof safe there to dry out, yellow, and curl up — in concert with the author.

The Rosenbergs were guilty beyond doubt. The thousands of pages of terse notes pointed at their heads. I could have summoned enthusiasm for the book if they were innocent. Ethel dominated Julius. The ebullient young mother inspired her husband to seek secrets which could be shared with the Soviet Union. Although she lived only one floor above poverty, payment was not a consideration. Ethel believed that tomorrow's world belonged to the Soviet Republic. It would eliminate the poverty, the tears she saw among immigrants on the East Side of New York. When Julius wavered, Ethel braced him. With the help of her passionate brother, the Rosenbergs stole — not the atom bomb but the implosive device invented by Dr. Kistiakowsky to detonate the bomb. In a process of scientific trial and error, it was felt that the Russians would have discovered it two or three years later. Julius handed it to consul Yakovlev in New York, and he flew at once to Moscow.

Mrs. Rosenberg was a marvel of composure at the trial. When Julius perspired, she patted his hand at the counsel table. The trial attracted world attention and sporadic protests in many capitals. They accepted death in the electric chair as Saint Joan might have accepted the flaming fagots at her feet. They seemed not to notice that Moscow remained silent (as did the sycophantic *Daily Worker* in New York) until it became obvious that the Rosenbergs would not flinch at paying with their lives. Then, and then only, did the communist press adopt them as true heroes of the Soviet Union. Two evenings before they died, the superintendant of federal prisons interviewed them in a concrete room near the death house.

It was not too late, he said, for them to expose the espionage ring and save their lives. Julius looked distraught. His lip quivered as though he wanted to speak. Ethel grabbed his arm, pulled her plump chin up, and said "We don't know what you're talking about."

Visiting graves is flagellation. The footsteps leading to a headstone leave indentations of guilt. I tried it a half-dozen times and quit. The place was Holy Name Cemetery in North Arlington, New Jersey. The stone markers stretched to the horizon. The joke is called perpetual care. The autumn grass was tall and brown. Wax flowers in wire holders shivered in the breeze. Outside the fence, cars honked, trucks ground gears, buses sighed, pedestrians hurried, and colored lights bade the living to stop and go. Little boys with big smiles earned coins running with sprinkler cans for water. Some survivors knelt in damp clay to pray. There was a section of clean granite. In the second row was my mother; two rows behind, Elinor reposed under a rough stone. Her vital statistics were on the left. The right side was blank, awaiting me.

I felt no closeness. It may have been lack of imagination. I studied the grass and knew that, far underneath, she was lying in a beautiful dress with her hands composed over a rosary. Vacantly, I wondered if she came back, might it be different. She could not bear to be away from Maggy, but the old lady was on the opposite side of the cemetery lying over her husband, Frank. This, it seemed to me, is the whimpering end to all stories. One is filed and forgotten. More care is given to the disposal of nuclear fuel rods than humans. It was purposefully ugly. The features of the living looking at grass were depressed. Were they subliminally sorry for themselves — future tenants?

A half-dozen times were enough. Bill Scanlon said it was a mistake to leave the granite blank, that I would not be buried with Elinor. You will fall in love again, he said. That, I knew, was impossible. It had come when I was seventeen and I fell in love with a high-school girl. It wasn't beauty. Nor sexual attraction. It was a magnetism impossible to resist. It came unbidden and could not be stomped to death. Then, Elinor. It became sick, sicker, sickest and I was powerless to walk away from it. Two loves, neither of them ecstatic. Scanlon saw the gray widower as a lure to widows. He reminded me that sizable obituary notices had appeared in *The New York*

Times and the wire services of the Associated Press and the United Press. You think those women don't read? he said. My impulse — unspoken — was to ask what that had to do with love.

Women do read. Flo Walter, in charge of mail, almost choked each morning reading the sympathetic mail. They came from many places, west and south. Almost all of them opened with commiseration; all of them understood bereavement. The second or third page of each letter was salesmanship. Each would like to meet me; just to say hello. They proclaimed themselves to be young and attractive, sometimes afflicted with husbands. Or, I could stop by at their place and say hello; maybe spend a weekend away from the hurly-burly of New York. All of them appreciated true love and true grief.

Many sent photos. It is astonishing how few women submit to the camera unless it is summertime at the beach. One lady, from Midland, Texas, said she knew that I was the father of her baby. She remembered hearing the screen door break one night and, in the darkness, I crept to her bed and placed my finger over her lips. A few anonymous writers said that Elinor was better off dead; they had heard about my philandering. I was known far and wide as a cad who promised Hollywood contracts to innocent girls. Those women weren't fooled. Someday a husband would shoot me.

Freedom was a strange condition. Gayle moved into the house at Sea Bright. I bought her an electric guitar before learning that she was tone-deaf. Virginia Lee gave birth to twin girls — Robin and Pamela. I held the tiny blonds and pondered a new generation. One looks at babies and wonders what a lifetime calendar holds for them. The family seemed like those interminable gothic novels where you read about a growing family and, in a few chapters, it's an old family and they die off, and you follow the next generation through its improbable crises and your eyes are red and dim when a long-dead lover is resurrected or one more generation of youngsters begins to romp on the castle lawns, unaware that their forebears are mad.

I had a luncheon date with Darryl Zanuck. He had read the galleys of *The Day Christ Died*. He wanted to talk of movie rights for Twentieth Century–Fox. Mr. Zanuck, for want of a more appropriate phrase, can be described as intense. He was short and dark, a man with a viable tongue and fatigued ears. He spoke well of polo. He tapped his mouth with his napkin and looked at me as though to reassure himself that what he was looking at was a man who wrote books. It was a terrific drama, he said. It built up and up and up toward the end. He appreciated the fact that it was not an anti-Semitic book. Most of all, Zanuck liked it as an intimate story of Jesus and the Twelve. It was not one of those De Mille movies with a cast of thousands.

I reminded him that the book was nonfiction, that it had followed the words and actions of Jesus and the Jews to the letter of the New Testament. This, he said acidly, he knew. He had read the testimonials of bishops and ministers. "What I mean," I said, "is that if you buy it, the final script must adhere to what we know of what Jesus said and did." He was looking at his watch. Did I ever get to California? Rarely. Had I sold anything there? Well, *The Mark Hellinger Story* to Columbia Pictures and a story about Notre Dame to producer Jerry Wald. Ah, he said in the most neutral tone.

Well, he must be going. He asked for a check. Had I spoken to Phyllis about this luncheon? Only, I said, that I had an appointment with you. Oh, he said, in that case, I'm offering two hundred thousand outright for the motion picture rights and an additional ten thousand for each book club which selects it. As I recall, I burped. What had Phyllis said, I asked. He nodded as he tumbled bills from his wallet to pay the check. Phyllis said it was all right with her, if it was all right with me. Well, Mr. Zanuck, I said, it sure is all right with me. The great man shook hands and hurried to the revolving door. A third of a cigar was jammed between his teeth. I wanted to say that literary whoring is good, but I didn't and I knew I wouldn't. Two hundred thousand is how much? A fifth of a million? And then the book clubs. Mr. Zanuck didn't know it — and neither did I — but six book clubs would pick the book, and that meant sixty thousand dollars more.

It seemed astonishing to me that a book I did not care to write, one I resisted, in truth, was earning three hundred and thirty-five thousand dollars in magazine and movie rights before one copy had been sold. It was then I could see clearly the pit into which Robert Ruark had fallen — think of big sums of money and the hell with how well the work was done. It's a pit softly lined with certified checks. I wouldn't do it. Deep down, I felt humiliated for having written *The Day Christ Died*. These days, ministers from around the nation were writing to say that I inspired them in their work. This is not amusing to a man who has stopped going to church.

The word *hiatus* is pleasant, but *lazy* is accurate. In the first month of 1958, my tax lawyer, Maurice Greenbaum, told me to write a check to the Internal Revenue Bureau for twenty thousand dollars at once. I said it was a lot of money. He said, you earned a lot. Besides, he said, this is merely a first quarterly payment on estimated income. At the time, I had two bank accounts: one-third of income was tax money. The rest was keeping money. The government wanted more than a third. Greenbaum agreed with the government. In the dead of winter, I kicked a snowbank and resolved not to work hard. My ten-dollar tip to a waiter was costing over fourteen dollars in earnings. Like Eisenhower, I had to learn something about the value of a dollar.

There was no work stoppage. No so-called writer's block. I kept to the research on the Rosenberg nonbook. I wrote a book for McGraw-Hill called *Go with God*. This was a cheap effort involving the writing of the same letter to many world personalities, asking for copies of their favorite prayers — assuming that some of them prayed. It is a device for using the brains and words of others. The surprise in what I regard as a dull effort was the response. Letters with prayers came from presidents, cardinals, admirals, generals, rabbis, sports figures, movie actors, statesmen, and editors. I shuffled them and Flo Walter helped type the manuscript. There was a foreword which tried to explain what prayer meant to a backsliding Catholic author. When it was published, *Go with God* looked like a book and hefted like a book. With tortuous index, it came to four hundred pages and, for weeks afterward, I declined to look at *The Times* and the *Saturday Review of Literature*. Fortunately, no one compiled a list of worst-selling books.

My problem with writing bad books was obvious. I was afraid that if two years went by without my writing something, the book-buying public would forget my name. Also, if the little boy doesn't practice the violin every day, he is bound to hit some execrable notes. From day to day, I filtered book ideas through my head. When, at last, I had what I thought was a good one, Phyllis didn't like it. Or, if she did, my current editor didn't.

The book world is a miasma of unverifiable opinions. If, for example, any editor understood the ingredients which constitute a best-seller, it is reasonable to suppose he would publish nothing but best-sellers. The author, on the other hand, has nothing more to offer than talent and enthusiasm. He brings these to bad books on occasion. McGraw-Hill's editors saw *Go with God* as a good book, maybe a fine one. I saw it as a cheap way of getting well-known people to do my work by writing out their personal preferences in prayers.

No one forced me to write the weak ones. I was persuaded by the clock that I had better shake my ass and return to work. When my notions were declined, I listened to editors who thought they knew what I should be writing. The warmth of their enthusiasm to number me among their authors persuaded me that it was therapeutic to be tapping the keys of an old Smith-Corona, dwelling, with pleasure, on the colors and sounds and smells of images which came to life through a black ribbon. All I asked of myself was that the product be better than anyone else could write it. I must confess that, conversely, I was never pleased with a good book either.

More time was spent on the column. I wrote each one with care, honing images and story values within nine hundred words. The remarkable feature of this work was that two hundred newspapers contracted for it, and some of the millions of fans began to buy books. The tide, so far as I know, did not run in the opposite direction. Now and then, Conniff phoned and urged me to do a series of articles. A Jewish temple in Atlanta was bombed. In Florida, four White boys were indicted for the rape of a Black college student. The magnetism of returning to daily newspaper work was irresistible. It was a return to prison as the warden. My ego was soothed by being permitted to write as I please; newspaper trucks raced through the streets of New York with "Don't Miss It!" and "Jim Bishop Says" on the sides. At the out-of-town newsstands, I could see that I made page 1 in San Francisco, in San Antonio, in Boston, Los Angeles, Seattle, and Salt Lake City.

And yet, the recesses of my head told me that I was splitting my work again, just as I had when, as a magazine and book editor, I had written books. Now I was writing books and pandering to newspapers. The spurious modesty of saying that my talent would not permit two types of work did not apply. I could do both adequately. Nor did all of it amount to overwork. I could generate enormous amounts of energy for the typewriter, although the suggestion that I should hammer a picture on a wall could enervate me. The real problem — the true puzzle — was that I never had faith in my work. I never read a book I wrote because I knew that, given one more shot at it, it could be a better book. I seldom read through a newspaper story that I wrote, unless it was to find out where it had been cut. My stuff was good; I knew that. "Faith" tells it bluntly. At no time did I think I wrote a story better than anyone in the world could have told it. The best I could say for myself was "as well as that story can be done." This lack of faith was permanent. That, in turn, led to a premonition that someday the bubble would burst. Younger, fresher writers would be coming into view. They would be lean and hungry and unafraid of hard work.

Now and then, I wrote a magazine article for Father Ralph Gorman. Economically, I caught up with him, even though I realized I would never catch up with him. I wrote some short stuff about Big John, even though Tommy Thompson, editor at King Features, thought it was cheap and silly. The mail which arrived from newspapers proved to the contrary that readers saw my old man as hilarious. It elicited more favorable mail than any other subject. Dad didn't ask me to drop it, but, reaching for his copy of the *Journal-American* he often mumbled to my sister, Adele: "I wonder what the hell he says about me today."

A union leader, James Riddle Hoffa, was in the news. Bill Hearst asked if I would write a series about him. I was interested. The little martinet had one and a half million dues-paying members of the Teamsters Union, and it was growing. He was insolent and cocky. I called Ginny's father-in-law, Dave Frechette, who was an officer of a Teamsters local in Miami. Could he speak to Hoffa? He could. I told Dave that the best I could promise the man was a fair shake. If he was a crook, I would say so. If he couldn't account for Teamster loans, it would be in print. If, in effect, he was unafraid to open the doors to me, I would write the story.

[327]

The other side of this one was the United States Senate. The McClellan Committee had been holding exhaustive hearings involving Hoffa and the Teamsters. The interrogation of witnesses had been acerbic, prosecutorial. The committee, aware that Hoffa's predecessor, Dave Beck, had been convicted of misfeasance, directed its hearings toward proving that the new boss was a thief, or, failing that, could be proved guilty of perjury. I phoned a couple of Senate reporters who advised me that I was wrong. McClellan was not gunning for Hoffa; he would like to have bagged him as a wall trophy, but the senator from Arkansas was anxious to move on to other unions, and possible ties to underworld figures. It was the committee counsel, Robert Kennedy, who wanted to "get" Hoffa to the exclusion of other labor leaders. My contacts insisted that they were right, even when I reminded them that the committee counsel serves on a retainer and his function is to be attuned to the whims of the chairman.

Not so this time, they said. His older brother, Senator John Kennedy, was a member of the committee and supported Bobby. The reporters said that Kennedy, in the most acrimonious exchanges, could do no more than inundate Hoffa with innuendo. The midwestern Teamsters' pension fund had, under Hoffa, lent millions of dollars in questionable ventures, one of which was Toots Shor's restaurant. The committee also proved that Hoffa numbered a surprising assortment of gangsters among his friends. Robert Kennedy, in the libel-free aura of the Senate Hearing Room, had denounced Hoffa as union scum, a man who had grown rich on the dues money of the workers.

I wrote to Robert Kennedy. I explained that the Hoffa articles would be a page-1 story in many newspapers. It was important to me, I said, to get his opinion of Jimmy Hoffa. I would be in Washington the last part of December. If he would kindly name a day and time, I would meet him in a place of his choosing. The letter went out, as I recall, on December 2. In a few days, a bulky package arrived in Sea Bright. It contained four green-bound volumes of Senate testimony. Everything that Hoffa said on the witness stand, and everything that counsel and other witnesses said about him, were in those books. The accompanying letter was not written by Kennedy. It was signed by a committee investigator named Pierre Salinger. It said that I would find what I needed somewhere in the books.

I stayed in a Teamster-owned apartment with Hoffa and Harold Gibbons, vice-president of the International. This was a Mutt and Jeff team. Hoffa was short, stocky, and spoke like an overage truant. Gibbons was six feet four, and had been a schoolteacher. I flew to Detroit with Hoffa. He lived in a modest house; Mrs. Hoffa cooked dinner; Jimmy drove a Chevrolet. "I'm president," he said. "I got a lot of friends. Someday, I won't be president. Nobody is going to know me. So I don't spend it. I sock it away. Now you tell me what you want and I'll tell you what you can have."

I said I would like to spend at least one entire day in his inner office observing and making notes. If possible, I would also like to sit in at a contract negotiation. A full day for an interview, plus a couple of days with vice-presidents and treasurers would add flesh to the material. "All of it," he said. "Okeydokey. I'm a little ahead of you. I set up an extension on my personal phone so that you can pick up and listen to everything I'm hearing." I told him I was a ten A.M. man. He violated this by thumping on my bedroom door every morning at seven and yelling: "Hey, Bishop. Gibbons is up. How do you like your eggs?" He did the cooking.

The Senate books did not present the little boss as a crook. The senators made a lot of charges, but they had no prima facie case against him for anything, except for allowing convicted felons to run Teamster locals. The pension books, according to government auditors, were in order. The senators questioned the wisdom of some of the loans Jimmy granted to friends in New York, Los Angeles, and Las Vegas, but his raucous counterargument was that he could prove that all of them were being repaid.

The story was the antithesis of the sensational document I had envisioned. It was a damp firecracker. I needed some damning material, and I phoned Robert Kennedy, but was told he would not return until after Christmas. I left a message for him to call me. In January, I tired of waiting and wrote the series. The newspapers worked up a bigger display than the material warranted. It made headlines. Toward the end of the series, young Robert realized that he had misgauged the importance of the story to him. He got the name and address of the publisher of every newspaper from coast to coast which had used the Hoffa story, and in a long single-spaced letter, he accused me of seeking a pro-Hoffa story and ignoring the work of the Senate and, in particular, its counsel.

It is difficult, in words, to describe a purpled anger. I read his letter twice and found myself breathing as though I had been running uphill. I wrote a letter to each publisher, explaining what had happened, and how I had given up the notion of getting a story from Senator McClellan in favor of asking for an interview with the committee counsel. I went too far. I reminded the publishers that the young man had flunked law in college and had to be sent to a school where the requirements were not strict. Kennedy, I said, had dragged Hoffa across the Senate floor as many times as the committee could endure it, but, so far, he had proved nothing that would stand in court. His paid investigator, Pierre Salinger, had sent four books. I had read them and strained to find a few credible charges. The opinion of Senate reporters, I said, was that Robert Kennedy was, at best, a pernicious hatchet man. He might bag Hoffa someday, but not in time for my deadlines.

That, I thought, ended that. Ten days later, publishers sent copies of another letter from Kennedy. This one was terse. It said that the rebuttal note from Bishop was merely a journalist's way of "showing off" to his bosses. For a moment, I thought of writing to Senator John F. Kennedy, asking him to explain to Bobby that one of the unforgivables in my profession was to write a complaint over the head of the writer to his boss. In future, if Bobby had a complaint, take it up with the writer. He would have to be rich indeed to afford the enemies he was about to make.

There came a night when the darkness didn't end. It was a Saturday — easily remembered because friends were not invited on any other day. Some were staring out the big picture window at the dark river. A few sat before the yellow and blue flames at the fireplace. Max Lewis crouched over the upright, chording the tones of "Near You." Behind the half-moon Formica bar, Chief mixed drinks. The women were bright and young, well-dressed sparklers who were attuned to a smile from the far side of the room or a whispered word. The busted-nose–breather, Bill, punched tickets at racetracks and had a weakness for slow horses. A few danced slowly, intimately, on the cork floor. D-Honey, so dark that she looked like a pen-and-ink drawing, was in a pet because the man she loved had told her he was a homosexual.

These parties usually moved without effort into Sunday. No one was obliged to sleep with anyone, although few mattresses cushioned but one body. The pianist could play anything, and play well. Someone asked for "Charmaine." Drunk, he played it five ways and a girl sat on his hands to make him stop. There was a fourteen-foot black couch before the fire-place. Behind it was a metal folding tray with cold roast beef, Polish ham, cheeses, sour rye, crackers, and a big thermos of coffee. This room had been built behind the main house, and five steps lower. I was on the top step, absorbing the colors, the noise, and the faces when something inside me jarred loose and fell. It isn't right to say that it was as though my stomach dropped to the peritoneum, but it's close. There was a neurological clunk. I stood there so long that someone hollered; "Hey, is the survey over?" and I went down the steps and locked a casual arm around Emma. She was a tall, thin, compliant brunette who wore her hair like a double-dip ice cream cone. She worked at Abercrombie & Fitch's in guns. Emma, who had never hunted any beast more dangerous than a man, understood rifles and bores and shotguns and ammunition, and was, so to speak, my girl. In the store, she was prissy and humorless; at my house she giggled and drank and followed me around the room with eyes so blue that they were almost royal.

In the moment after that clunk, my friends died. I died. We were chatting in colorless voids. The music became louder; a couple of men started a quartet. Little Imelda, a shapely brunette, was in love with Bill and they proved it by starting an argument over which one drank too much. The groups snapped their conversational tongues at each other and everyone laughed. If this was a depression it was sudden and deep. Another friend wrapped an arm around me and said: "You were more fun, Jimmo, when you drank." His wife had died not long before, but our bonds antedated grief.

Depressed, the human mind does not recollect truly. Elinor had spent time in this room. She enjoyed the view of the quiet river and, in the marsh on the other shore, watching the mother ducks leading babies in single file for their first swim. For a moment, her eyes were amused; she could think of herself later. One baby duck was tossed protesting into the water by its mother's bill, and then, with webbed feet flying and tiny wings outspread, it tried either to fly or walk on the water.

She could see things in a crackling fire. I was cocking my head to listen to Emma, not hearing a word, but nodding at the right time. Elinor and I had spent twenty-seven years in love with each other but not admiring each other, and now that little book had been slammed shut. I tried hard to feel sorry for myself, but I was too cynical to be convincing. Of the two, it was she who had not lived. My life contained a lot of struggle, but it was rewarding. People opened doors, and, with more confidence than talent, I walked through. There were women in my life, some of whom she surmised. I also had the lonely joy of reading.

She had Maggy; the stainless-steel umbilical cord. They had been here — Maggy, Mom, Elinor — and, as if in the third act of an illogical turkey, each had walked offstage to no effect. I had no intention of standing in the middle of my social gathering and asking "Why?" The facts had been shoved to the recesses of the head six months ago. I wept not because I could not. My conscience pinged at such times as I recalled hearing the news aboard ship that Elinor had died — that big chesty surge of relief. Relief? An insoluble problem had been snatched. I no longer had to think of the next reaching out of a hand toward a hand — no more of that.

Unbidden, a stack of memories stood beside me in that room. Oh, how easy to conjure the good times. How selective to see her young, the moon eyes glistening, frying bacon and eggs for dinner because we were over our budget and didn't have the rent. How sweet to see her pirouette in the pale blue dress (seven ninety-eight) with the deep blue sash hugging the side from waist to hem. The first raise, the first car, the first Broadway show — the first, the first. The Gryniak wedding, when Anna's father made pink Polish gin and old relatives actually stiffened on a sofa. The fun in the car, doing sexy things and hoping a tall truck would not draw up beside us. Scores of joyful images; not one bad one.

Success, real success, had come from a group of old notebooks dealing with a dead President. Money was coming to the house in big packages from many parts of the world. She would never have to scrimp again, or write a dishonorable check. We could live in two houses and fly to Las Vegas to gamble with expensive chips. We could afford extensive cruises — by God, we could do almost anything — and she picked a time like that to join her mother. I was dwelling on success in the manner of Robert Ruark, counting the money and the triumphs. She didn't want me to be successful. She said so. She wished I was poor, in debt. Why? Was that a good life? It was an outrageous notion, as though she felt that I was more under her control as a bankrupt.

Leaning on the piano, I was not listening to Max Lewis. He could play and drink straight rye and talk a Jewish stream-of-consciousness and, when I said I didn't understand, he would say: "Tell me what you didn't hear and I'll repeat it." Bill asked if I felt all right. I was fine. Emma suggested a sip of cold white wine to settle the stomach. I walked out the back door to glance at the moorings on the cabin cruiser. There was a slab of cold moon over the empty elms and oaks of Rumson. "Go away," I said to Elinor. Being perverse, she refused. The night breeze was steady and it went through the suit and shirt and undershirt. It was my first experience with what Momma used to call "the blues." I hurried inside, slammed the door, and left Elinor outside.

No field of theater is more difficult than pretending to be of a party when you are not truly there. I sought Emma and we rubbed cheeks and Chief gave her another margarita. Bill was trying to quiet everybody, stating he had an announcement. He was going to marry little Mel. Whenever he made that announcement, we knew he was drunk. He would marry Mel, in time, but he made the announcement at every party. D-Honey had a plan. She said she would knock down the door to her homosexual lover's apartment and screw the ears off him and make him a man. Someone wondered what D-Honey would do if her lover was in bed with a policeman. This for some reason, doubled the party over. Chief was perspiring over roast beef. He would take a bottle of vodka to bed with him in case he awakened alone.

The party broke up like field ice.

Honors are the wax flowers of literature. They look pretty on an end table, but they are useless unless they are drawn unremittingly to the attention of unadmiring relatives and friends. Statuettes, degrees, plaques, proclamations are reminders to the writer that he was a better craftsman in the days when he had two shirts and one pair of shoes. Writers affect contempt for public accolades, but rarely do they refuse them. The ego withers at a typewriter. It craves nourishment. Few comments are greeted with more approval than when the writer is reminded that his is the loneliest job. No one forced him to choose it. He writhes to learn that a good plumber earns more money. What he seeks is universal respect — the reverence European peasants once accorded to silk-hatted physicians.

The cynical side is that those who accord the honor expect a free speech. Some writers are articulate. Some stammer in public. A few, painfully, become masters of equivocation and, without shame, will saddle up and ride four sides of any topical question. It is difficult for any writer to accept an honor, feel that he deserves it, and then mount a platform cloaked in modesty. Those who are prepared to sing for their supper will resolve the European question, the Asiatic question, the Middle East question, and the enigma of the two-party system in thirty-five minutes.

A few came my way. The American Legion, in national convention at Atlantic City, advised me that I had been voted the writer of the year. I asked them to mail the trophy, and did not hear from them again. Syracuse University offered a special and permanent place for my manuscripts, notebooks, and completed works. I declined. A board of editors voted "unanimously" to offer me the Silver Lady award as the "outstanding reporter and columnist" of 1958. I accepted. The heavy and shapely statue is given once a year at a luncheon hosted by Bill Hearst in the main ballroom of the Waldorf-Astoria. I was flattered because the audience consists of two thousand editors.

Saint Bonaventure University offered a doctorate. I accepted and took the entire family to the college at Olean, New York. This too was a morale boost because Bonaventure runs a first-class school of journalism. I might have been more elated if the doctorate had come from Saint Peter's College in Jersey City because, when I was growing up, I touched the stones of those buildings with longing, realizing that I was too poorly educated to attend but knowing that the Jesuits had the kind of schooling I required. Religion aside, they were the best no-nonsense teachers in the East. It was not to be, but at social gatherings, when I was introduced to someone who was called a "Peter's Boy," I hoped to make him look like a jackass.

At Bonaventure I nourished a friendship with Dr. Russell Jandoli, head of the School of Journalism. He was small and dark, a man of lightning reflexes. I proposed arranging a "Mark Hellinger Award" in journalism. We would invite a committee of distinguished journalists to attend an annual luncheon — John Charles Daly; Douglas Edwards; Bob Considine; Frank McLearn, editor of King Features Syndicate; Jimmy Cannon, sports columnist; Louis Sobol — and, of the top five graduates in journalism, they would select the student least able to continue. He or she would be given five hundred dollars and a job. It was one of the few things I planned which worked out.

Fame, which is national recognition of a name, had come to me as it had to Willie Sutton as a bank robber, as Ponzi achieved it with other people's money, as Arthur Fleming did by scraping mold from a dirty plate. Fame is being endlessly asked to join organizations whose philosophies are an abomination to you; to send money to strangers whose mothers have developed brain tumors; to lend your name to politicians who are losers; to assist Negro colleges; to attain status on all the sucker lists in America; to appear on television shows week after week for no other purpose than to promote yourself as a regular guy; to be invited to select black-tie dinners; to be solicited by inventors who have solved the riddle of perpetual motion; to be shown to a front table at Toots Shor's; to get a good table and gifts at the Stork Club; to be told "No check, compliments of the management" at Voisin; to realize that, if you seduce a lovely woman, she may someday write an article about it in *Cosmopolitan* magazine; to be at the mercy of poor relatives who swear that if you will lend a mere five thousand, they will make a mint repairing television sets; to glance at your lather-creamed kisser in the mirror and say: "Baby, you deserve it."

Fame is also charging more for less. Throughout 1959, I cut my work. The cheapest and easiest book to make (with the exception of using the thoughts of other people without attribution) is to compile a list of the author's short stuff and place it between hard covers. Reputable publishers will not consider this type of book unless there is a hook in the contract giving them the right to publish this next work "at terms to be mutually agreed upon." All Saints Press wanted to publish a book of my newspaper columns without the "hook." Among the thousand or so short pieces I had written, there may have been sixty which could be called entertaining. Having made the mistake of allowing this to happen, I compounded it by permitting the editor to select the pieces which should go into the book. Thus, when it was published, my dismay was equal to that of the reader. The only smile in it was when I read the title: *Some of My Very Best.* I did not have the nerve to ask for an accounting of royalties; it may have sold to the number of friends I had who were unemployed.

In a way, this was what I appreciated about my mistakes. The word *minuscule* was not intended for me. The blunders were big; they were ghastly; they were public. Mercifully, some of the better reviewers decided to keep my secret. I gave one copy to my aunt Margaret McCarthy. She used it to prop the fourth leg of a dining room table.

When the weather was good, I was boating. Sometimes I wrote fondly of the sea and the excitement I felt on it. One Sunday a bandleader, Louis Prima, phoned. He was at the Essex House in New York and he asked if I would go up there at once. I said no. He was a hoarse, ugly man who was earning fifteen thousand dollars a week in Las Vegas playing in a lounge. I knew little about him except that he sang something that sounded like "Way, Marie!" and he had a singer wife named Keely Smith. He said please. I reminded Mr. Prima that it was Sunday. I proposed to spend it on my back. He said it was urgent. About what? I said. Boats, he said.

I drove up. The sitting room was a portrait in plates of congealed bacon and eggs and, on the rug, assorted sections of Sunday newspapers. What about boats, I said. He said he had heard that I was a hell of a boatman and, if so, he needed advice. He had been begging Keely Smith to permit him to buy a cabin cruiser. She told him he was crazy because he was living in the middle of a desert. Prima pecked at it. Yesterday, he said, she had surrendered: "Oh, go ahead and buy your old boat. See if I care." The bandleader hurried over to Broadway, where there were a couple of showrooms with cabin cruisers. The biggest one was a Chris-Craft Constellation. It was fifty-five feet long. Louis Prima had a blank check. "If you can move that thing out of the showroom," he said to a salesman, "and truck it down to the river and put it in, I'll buy it for cash right now." They broke the plate-glass window getting the monster out, but nobody cared.

It was tied up at the Columbia Yacht Club. Now, Jim, he said, be serious with me. I want to take Keely and the kids down around Florida and up the Gulf of Mexico to visit my mother in New Orleans. I gotta know two things: how do I get out to the ocean and how do I make the boat go? I choked on a warm cola. He was suggesting a voyage which I would not undertake with a boat twice that size; second, if he didn't know which way to point to get out of New York Bay, how would he navigate the Atlantic coast? I didn't laugh. Louis Prima scared me. Those brown eyes told me that, with or without my assistance, he was going to do it.

I spent the afternoon detailing all the safety checks aboard a well-run boat; I ran a simple lesson in navigation on the dirty tablecloth; and I told him how to start engines, how to engage them forward and reverse. I shook hands. "You," I said, "are not only a certified nut, but I am going to read about you." I did. Ten days later, there was a small Associated Press dispatch which stated that the Atlantic Fleet, engaged in gunnery practice off the Virginia Capes, had spotted a white cabin cruiser wallowing between ships-of-war. A navy tug found Louis Prima and his family aboard and towed them into Norfolk.

An editor of the *American Weekly* asked if I would do a story on Herbert Hoover's eighty-fifth birthday. He lived in the Waldorf Towers alone, except for a secretay and some stenographers. I was interested in this stiff and humorless old man for several reasons. He had been blamed for the deepest of economic depressions; his political party had disowned him; as a lonely widower with few friends, he wrote books which his critics referred to as revisionist history. Yes. Yes indeed, I would write the story. I saw him as the last man in the last raft staring serenely at an empty sea as he adjusted his high stiff collar.

My appointment was for lunch. Most ex-Presidents are called "Mister President." This one was called "Chief." He lived in a large apartment which seemed to be more office than living quarters. There were stacks of gray steel cabinets and the chatter of several typewriters. His security was a cripple, Miss Miller. She was secretary, doorman, screener of visitors and phones, a one-woman canonizer. She carried fifteen pounds of iron on her legs and took each step on the carpet with the rocking motion of one who could not make it to the corner store. She shouted my name and I recalled that Herbert Hoover was deaf.

He had baby skin, a custard smoothness with poached china-blue eyes. He had worn a three-piece suit when he fed the Belgians after World War I; he wore it as secretary of commerce in 1924; he was wearing it on his eighty-fifth birthday. His voice was a baritone growl — the defense of the deaf who fear they are shouting. I wanted to talk politics; his subject was books. He asked what was next on my list. I said *The Day Christ Was Born*, an effort to research the true story of Christmas. He sat behind a desk in the corner of the big room with windows pouring sunlight from his left and his right. The Chief pointed to pads of foolscap and a can of Ticonderoga pencils. "I have contracts for four more books before I die," he said. The implication was that, as a younger writer, I was cowardly. Hoover was unafraid to use the word *die*. He was, by training, an engineer who dealt in absolutes.

His mentality was too exalted for hate, but he came close to it when I got to Franklin D. Roosevelt. FDR was the most arrogant of demagogues, the Chief said. To get elected, he needed a nation cringing on its knees. He was so ignorant that, when he closed the banks, he didn't know that they had been closed. Hoover was so unforgiving that, when Mr. and Mrs. Roosevelt arrived at the White House on Inauguration Day, the Chief refused to sit to coffee and toast with them, standing several feet away, excusing himself on the ground that he had several last-minute bills to sign.

The contempt was still alive. After he lost the 1932 election, Hoover was blamed for the depression. Now, in 1959, we knew that he did not precipitate it and could not resolve it. Hoover's mistake was inside his superpatriotism. As industries grew cold and men sold apples in cities, the Chief believed what he was saying: that the United States of America was economically sound; that it was the most blessed nation in the most blessed century in history. According to Hoover, all America had to do was have faith in itself. He reminded me that, in two terms, Franklin Roosevelt was not able to lift his country out of the depression until he began to build the biggest navy and the biggest air force in the world. It was war, and the imminence of war, that restored prosperity.

I asked if Miss Miller lived in the apartment. He shook his head. She has her own apartment, he said. I asked bluntly who would know if, at age eighty-five, he fell in the bathroom or had a seizure in the bedroom. Nobody, he said. He would not hire a valet, and he tried to hold Miss Miller's assistance to office work. He admitted to being a painful writer. His handwriting was steady, but, as he completed each page of foolscap, he buzzed Miss Miller, who took it to one of three typists. The Chief read it, edited and revised in scrawls all over the page, and had it retyped.

Your party forgave you in 1956, I said. Bluntness seemed not to hurt him. Yes, he said, that was when his onetime subordinate, Major Dwight Eisenhower, had been renominated at the Cow Palace in San Francisco. There was silence. A brief, lightning flash of smile pulled at his lips. What's funny? I said. Hoover chuckled. He said he would remember that event as the day of the autograph. What autograph? I was now President Hoover's straight man.

The Republican party, he said, had invited him as an honored guest to forgive him for an old crime of which he was innocent. Two Secret Service men held him by the arms at the bottom of a concrete ramp. A bright spotlight would illuminate the top of the ramp, the band would play "Hail to the Chief," and the young agents would propel the old man to the top, hopefully to thunderous applause. A young woman approached, a pretty girl, according to the Chief, and asked for his autograph. The Secret Service men tried to wave her aside. No, Hoover said, he had not been asked for his autograph in a long time and he would be glad to give it. He asked the girl for a pen and a piece of paper. She had the pen. Nobody had paper.

I'm sorry, Hoover said, the spotlight is now up there. The girl became frantic. She jammed the pen in the hand of the President. She jammed a slender knee against his hip. Then she yanked her dress high, and said: Will you autograph my slip, sir? The Chief began to chew on a ham and cheese sandwich. I stared at him. He said nothing. Well? I said, irritably. The smile returned. "Did I?" he said mischievously. "Did I autograph that white slip? You bet I did. How many opportunities do you get at my age?"

At four o'clock, I shook hands and left the man to his loneliness. On the street I kicked myself for not remembering to say Happy Birthday.

Gayle was fifteen. I had tried to discuss the mechanics of sex with her. What I got was a flippant "Okay, Daddy-o. What would you like to know?" I was her hero, but there were gray areas of omission. One of the ladies whispered that Gayle, at fourteen, had not begun a menstrual cycle. It seemed gauche to tap the child on the shoulder and ask "Why?" I consulted a physician, who examined Gayle and said she was normal and strong — just slow in the glands. Somehow, when she began to function, Gayle knew what to do. And yet, her physical development was slow. At fifteen, she was still a tree-climbing, basket-shooting tomboy.

She complained of repetitious dreams. She saw her mother in a casket and, as the child stared in horror, Elinor said: "I'm sorry, honey. But this is the way it has to be." I dismissed them. The dreams would fade. I too had dreams about Elinor, but they were jolly good-time dreams. A month would go by without mentioning the dream. I would ask and she would turn solemn. "I still have them. Almost every night. Momma always says: 'I'm sorry, honey. But this is the way it has to be.'"

I began to worry. She said it was all right. Sometimes, in the evening, we went to the Mayfair Theatre in Asbury Park, stocking up on candy bars and dividing them equally. At other times, she walked the two miles to the main part of the village to spend the evening with girlfriends. Gayle was breathlessly alive. Life itself was a raucous laugh. She and Chief argued as equals. I worried more and didn't know what to worry about.

She brought a boy home. His name was Frank Gerace. He was an apprentice jockey at Monmouth Park, a hot-horse walker. He said he would soon be a renowned jockey. I was not appeased. My heart was in my heels. I wondered how long this had been going on, how far, and why I had slept through the early stages. I had a chat with Gayle alone. She would not be dissuaded. "Frank is the only man for me, Dad. I love him." We discussed it — as friends. She burst into tears. A man can lose three women in one way, and a girl in another.

When Frank was due to call, I braced my nervous system. It was not that he was difficult. It was that he was wrong for her, and she for him. I wondered if he realized that he was romancing a fractious filly who, under restraint in a stall, would break the walls. I had chats with him, man-to-man things, but he breezed through them as though he were in a multiple-choice quiz. He loved her. He would love Gayle forever. Both gave the impression that, if I thwarted them, they would run off together. I discussed it with Virginia Lee, who enjoyed a fragile sibling relationship with Gayle. Ginny did not forget that Gayle had been Mommy's favorite. I talked it over with Flo Walter, with Betty Stone, with my sister, Adele. They had little to offer. Women are averse to intruding on affairs of the heart. Especially if the female side of it insists that she is happy. The best communal advice I got was "What will you do if she comes home pregnant?"

Gayle was close to her sixteenth birthday. I drove across the river to see Father Sullivan, small, gray-haired smiler. I discussed a quiet, almost secret wedding. He asked a lot of questions. He would like to talk to Gayle. Later, he phoned. "Make it next Saturday at four," he said, "in the rectory. I'm not sure that boy did his Easter duty." As one who never enjoyed weddings, I attended that one deeply depressed. Some relatives attended. And friends. Gayle looked like a spindly kid who could, if she was dared, leapfrog over the priest. There have been days in my life when I did a bit of dying, but a big chunk went that afternoon.

There was a reception at the house. Gayle was in the kitchen helping the cook to heat something. "This winter," I said to Frank, "I plan to go to Florida. If you two would like to come along —" He grinned. "Go in the kitchen," he said, "and ask my old lady." I folded one fist inside the other and held them in front of me. It became difficult to breathe. He called me "Pops." I said that "Jim" would do. Looking at them, the best I could hope for was that one would not destroy the other.

I had furnished the cellar room and given it to them. Frank worked well. He loved horses. He was especially fond of animals who didn't want to obey his rein. It showed his bosses that he was unafraid, he said. I visited the stables and spoke to a couple of trainers about advancing Frank to the status of jockey. Two said they would think about it. I felt that it wouldn't take long before Gayle was pregnant. Sixty days. The Sea Bright house abounded with secrets which did not reach the ears of men. One which got to me through a steady date was that Frank was very sexy and Gayle was not.

A chronic crisis can rob a man of his skills. When it happens to a writer, his failures become public property. Nine-to-five men can fake a day's work. The writer gulls himself. He sees himself as attaining a mechanical

[338]

and inspirational level of excellence beyond which he cannot rise, below which he dare not fall. In the idiom, this is bullshit. His work is muddied by moods; it leaves a wavy line on a chart. I had completed the slender volume called *The Day Christ Was Born* and had returned to the Middle East to reinvent the town of Nazareth as it was two thousand years ago, and to pace off the trip down the valley of the Jordan to Jericho and up the chalky hills to Jerusalem, then onward five more miles to Bethlehem. As always, the research was the exciting work. In all books, I learned and learned. I didn't know, for example, that so many Jews lived in hollowed-out caves in the sides of hills, that the rabbi directed the father to execute the circumcision of his firstborn, that the tax collectors of Caesar Augustus were frenzied because Jews refused to stay in place long enough to be counted.

And now, a baby would be born at our house. This solitary pleasant thought tore through misery. Once more I would contemplate a beribboned bassinette, hover over a gummy grin, listen to that thin high wail in the middle of the night. Out of what I considered to be the shambles of a girl's life, something blessed would happen. The tomboy looked ridiculous. She had a stomach so far out in front that she leaned backward to keep from falling. There was something different too in the face. The sparkle had died. Gayle was solemn, subdued. She cooked for Frank. She took care of his clothing, his shoes. When he beckoned, she followed. In private, I asked if she was sure she still loved him. She came alive: "Oh yes, Dad. Frank is the only man in the world for me. Honest." Why "honest"? Did she fear I would not believe her? Over and over, mostly in bed, I asked myself how much was my business and how much was theirs.

I asked Frank if he thought I was encroaching. No way, he said. He'd be leaving in a week. The southern tracks were opening and he wanted to work at Hialeah. His wife was going. Where would they stay? Who would look after her health? "Oh, come on," he said. "They have doctors in Florida." Where would they live? "We'll find a place." I lost my temper. I told him that he would be living like a damn gypsy; the pregnancy could be terminated at any time with ugly results. He shrugged. It was his life, his wife. Other couples had to do it on their own. He'd make out. I was close to helpless rage, but, if I alienated Frank, I might not hear from the Geraces. I forced myself to do something I wouldn't for the Pope — truckle, pander. Sure, Frank, I said. Of course. Listen, pal. Let's hear from you once in a while. When you get down there, call me collect. Okay? Sure, Pops. Sure.

The mayor stopped in. The big seawall had cracked in several places. As a Democrat, he had tried to enlist the aid of state and government officials. They made promises. They spoke of applications for federal aid. They did nothing. He was Thomas Farrel, an Irish-American running a village four miles long and a hundred yards wide between sea and river.

Tom thought I might be able to phone somebody. If the wall broke open in the next northeaster, it would sweep homes into the Shrewsbury River and return the village to its original status, a sandbar. I promised to call someone. I knew nothing of seawalls except that they are under the jurisdiction of the U.S. Army Corps of Engineers. One might surmise that the navy would be in charge of keeping the sea out. I didn't know anybody in the army, and wondered why, when people ask favors, I always say that I will get right on it, even when I don't understand the question.

I would make a call and would tell the mayor about it. But who? For no reason whatever, I phoned Senator John F. Kennedy in the Senate Office Building. He was cordial. If he knew anything about my dispute with his brother Bobby, it wasn't mentioned. To the contrary, he had a politician's flair for the right words. He mentioned a few of my books favorably. I told him that the next storm would tear the seawall down and take the village with it. Without being certain of what I was saying, I told him that the Eisenhower administration had turned a deaf ear to a poor fishing village. He said he would get on it right away — those words had a familiar ring.

The mayor could not have been more stunned than I when huge tractors rolled up, cranes appeared on top of the seawall, hundreds of tiny ants of men worked among the huge boulders, and Tom had his picture taken pointing at all the machinery. I had a feeling that I owed Senator Kennedy one. I also had the sensation that, someday, he would call that I.O.U.

Los Angeles was an outdoor smoking room. It is a tedious city, pressing tens of thousands of white-roofed bungalows against the hills. Traffic is in a chronic emergency. There are more beautiful girls serving food to the sides of parked cars than there are beautiful stars in the movies. It's a trick town, conning itself into greatness. The people devise new religions, magnetize dingbats, stock books on shelves as insulation against the cold. The city, which is almost as endless as space, prides itself on the soft music it plays in its cemeteries, its towering office buildings overlooking the concrete footprints of the famous, its trendy restaurants, its fifty-cent maps to the homes of movie stars, its snobbish caste system imposed by producers whose fathers were oppressed and persecuted in Poland, its daily trade papers, enormous studios with enormous budgets reduced to celluloid, its For Rent starlets, columnists, scandals, movie magazines, canyon roads, glittering hotels, and awestricken tourists who return to Iowa and the Carolinas to proclaim: "I saw her in person."

The Democrats held their 1960 convention there. The neurotics chose the asylum. Bill Hearst asked if I would like to cover both conventions for the Hearst Headline Service. I said I'd try one — the Democratic.

I hoped for a brawl. It makes for good imagery. However, the three television networks began to overpower the conventions. They picked up every smirk, every shouted insult. Television also redesigned the order of business. Disputes about party planks were arranged for prime time; no candidate wanted to be nominated after eight P.M. (eleven P.M. Eastern Time). Over forty-five hundred political hams were on the floor. Some — not all — of the spontaneity was gone. The egotistical governor of New Jersey, Robert Meyner, insisted that his name be placed in nomination (with a seconding speech) and froze his state's votes for himself. He had less chance of winning than Speaker Sam Rayburn had of being nominated by acclamation. Stuart Symington, who might have won in an earlier year, was in the race. Lyndon Johnson, as big as Texas and as dusty of speech, was running through the corridors of the Biltmore pleading, stomping, threatening. John F. Kennedy, front runner in the primaries, the dashing charmer, had the damnedest array of volunteer gofers I have ever seen. Adlai Stevenson, the indecisive intellectual, would accept the nomination only if Mrs. Eleanor Roosevelt and the unpledged delegates dragooned him. He wore his insufferable integrity as though he had it copyrighted.

My interest centered on Kennedy. He had six hundred first-ballot votes. The nominee would need about seven hundred sixty. I saw him alone in his suite. "I want to ride along with you in your car the day of the nomination," I said.

He smiled. "Suppose I don't make it."

"I want to ride with the most profound loser in modern times."

"Meet me right here at seven A.M."

"Is it set or will you forget it?"

"Be here." I wondered again if he knew about my fight with his brother. He knew — and I knew — that he could have taken an Associated Press reporter with him in that car and he would have been featured in hundreds more papers than I could muster.

I phoned Senator Henry Jackson of Washington. "The morning after the nomination, I would like to spend some time with you alone."

"What for?"

"I want to cover the reactions of the vice-presidential nominee."

"Where'd you hear that?"

"May I see you alone?"

"I'll be at Washington State headquarters."

Two sources — one at the Kennedy suite in the Biltmore, the other an unimpeachable neighbor in Hyannisport — assured me that if Kennedy was nominated, he was pledged to run with Jackson. I sat back and observed the spasms and wrenchings of the Democratic party over rules, over planks, over the weak keynote speech by Senator Frank Church, over states with two slates of delegates, over state chairmen who, terrified of backing the wrong man, mouthed patriotic platitudes to reporters.

The senator escorted me to a small sedan. A radio reporter sat in back. I stared at Kennedy. He shrugged. A silent chauffeur got in; I sat in the middle; John Kennedy sat next to the door. All day his right hand was on the top of the dashboard, the fingers drumming. All day we went from one state delegation to another, trying to catch it in its ultimate caucus. I followed him all over Los Angeles and, almost by accident, he began that jaunty stride into caucus rooms, just as speakers were shouting and arteries were popping. In every case, Kennedy got a standing ovation. He said a few words, asked candidly for their votes, wore his youth to advantage, and said the nation needed the services of a new generation. Then he got off. He was not above stopping in a restaurant at lunchtime to bend over a congressman, or a senator, and whisper.

His head was firm and masculine. He didn't sweat. The brown suit draped from his body in perfect folds. The tips of the shoes gleamed. He was afraid, and said he was afraid, but he exuded the confidence of a gambler at a fixed race. When he tired of politics, we rode the little sedan and talked of families. Now and then, the radio man in the back would say something like: "Jack, how about Dave Lawrence and Pennsylvania?" Sometimes we stopped so that he could phone Bobby and get the latest vote count. I made notes on everything he said and did and, a little after four, he said to the chauffeur: "Take me home. Then drive Mr. Bishop to the convention." No, I said. No. There were competent men to cover the convention. I wanted to go back to the Biltmore and begin to write this story. On North Rossmore Boulevard, the car stopped. The senator got out. I rolled the window down and he leaned his elbows on the ledge. The radio man thanked him for an interesting day. I said: "You'll make it." Kennedy shook his head. The sailor's wrinkles around the eyes deepened. I'm not so sure, he said. Bobby thinks we have maybe six hundred and ten. They're only pledged for two ballots. "You'll make it on the first. When they get to Tennessee or somewhere, the tide will start to run and chairmen will ask to change their vote." He blinked his eyes. "After two ballots, Jim, they'll fly like birds." He has a firm handshake. (I found out what he did after I left when I sat with Kennedy in the White House in October, 1963. I wish I had known this part of the story on the day of balloting.)

As our car turned away, Kennedy stood in front of a small apartment house. It consisted of a few stories, with apartments front and back, left and right, on each floor. He had rented one on the third floor. Directly beneath his apartment was one rented by a veteran movie actor, William Gargan, and his wife, Mary. As the senator turned to walk through the alley, Gargan mixed an old-fashioned for Mary. She was a stout woman, a devotee of the Catholic Church and John F. Kennedy. She fluffed a few extra pillows on a settee, leaned back in comfort, and said: "Bill, turn the television on." He brought the drink. Some statesman was making a speech on the tube. Mary hoisted the old-fashioned. "I sure hope our boy wins tonight," she said. Gargan fixed a drink for himself and slumped on a chair.

Kennedy waited until our car was out of sight. Then he jogged through the alley, ran toward a fence, and braced his hands on it as his feet went over the top. On the far side were some palm trees, some hibiscus, and, hidden in the greenery, a pale mansion. He loped through the brush and up to the back door. The mansion was owned by Marion Davies. The senator's father, Joseph P. Kennedy, stood in the living room. He was the great liability; the Kennedy politicians had kept him hidden throughout the campaign. Wherever he traveled, he was sneaked to his destination. The Kennedy forces felt that it would be a sufficient problem to combat the fear of the Roman Catholic Church, but there was no way they could overcome the presence of Old Joe. He had been a merciless money manipulator most of his life; he had wrenched a fortune from Wall Street, got himself appointed ambassador to Great Britain, threatened and cajoled scotch-whiskey interests into permitting him to sell their product in the United States when Prohibition was repealed, fought the McCormack forces in Massachusetts until both sides cried "uncle," and bluntly stated that one of his boys was going to be President of the United States even if he had to buy the election.

The boys — John, Bobby, Ted — loved their father for the characteristics which earned national contempt. They knew — otherwise there was no reason to hide him. It was he who infused the win syndrome at all costs — in card playing, sailboat racing, politics, women, touch football. To best others was the quintessential philosophy of life. In factory towns, John Kennedy got to bed at three, was up at five to stand in zero weather shaking hands outside steel mills. "Some mornings," he said, "I shook six hundred hands. If I picked up fifty votes, it was worth it." None of the boys could appreciate a supine adversary, such as Adlai Stevenson. To join battle, to fight tenaciously until you could no longer feel the blows, these were the attributes of the centurions.

He embraced his father. They compared sheets of delegates. The nominee kissed his dad good-bye, ran back, hopped the fence, and hurried to his tiny apartment. He wanted a chilled daiquiri, but he felt he didn't have time to mix it. So he poured scotch on ice, gathered his voting sheets, and switched the television on. There was a bright flash, an effulgence of light, and a small white dot in the center of the screen which refused to die. Kennedy, in effect, was blind. He ran out of the apartment, down the steps, and knocked. "Now," said Mary Gargan angrily, "who the hell is that?" In the sports arena, a voice boomed: "Alabama?" A voice said: "Alabama casts twenty votes for Johnson, Kennedy three and a half. Stevenson one half, Symington three and a half." William Gargan, irritated at the interruption, got to the door, opened it, and glared at a silhouette in the hall "I'm upstairs," the candidate said, "and my set blew out. May I —" Gargan took a long breath. "Mary," he shouted, "it's Jack Kennedy. It's Kennedy himself. Come in and welcome."

Kennedy "made it" on the first ballot. When the switching of ballots was done, Kennedy had 806; Johnson 409; Symington 86; Stevenson 79½; and the rest spread among the petulant Governor Meyners in the hall. I finished the story and filed it for the morning papers, got some sleep, and taxied to Washington State headquarters before breakfast. An aide showed me into a white room with white rug and white walls, a candidate, and a barrel of apples. I pointed to the barrel. Senator Henry Jackson smiled sheepishly. "Oh, come on," he said. "You know we're famous for apples." I asked if the call had come from Kennedy. It had not. A white phone was on a shelf. He pointed to it. "I'm waiting for it to ring." Henry Jackson was an able statesman. He wanted to be President. He could have pitted himself against John Kennedy in the 1960 beauty contest, but he knew he couldn't win, and he believed his friend Jack when Kennedy said: "I want you on the ticket with me. I need you in the West."

We sat by the phone from eight-thirty until noon. Reporters were in the anteroom. They wanted a statement. Aides wanted his attention. He locked the door. When that little white phone rang, he would be ready. The two of us chased dialogue into dark holes. At some point, I began to eat the apples. I wondered if he knew what a poor public speaker he was. In print, Jackson looked good. In person, his nasal voice and hesitant phrases made his audiences itch. I suspected that Jackson saw the vice-presidency as the true path to the White House.

The phone rang. I fumbled for my watch. The precise monologue is lost (even with notes) but it went something like this: "Yeah, Jack. Congratulations. . . . It was great. . . . Uh-huh. . . . No, I knew you'd call. . . . Nothing. Just sitting around. . . . What's that? . . . You know damn well I'm a party man. . . . Sure . . . I don't understand. . . . Ah. Ah. . . . Yes. . . . Of course. . . . I'll see you later in the day. . . ." He hung up softly. Without turning, he said: "I didn't get it. They're giving it to Lyndon Johnson."

Friendship runs in degrees of escalation and few men have enjoyed the hearty confidence of a character as sterling as Tom Ferris. He was short and so fat that his belly made an apron over his knees. He had been born in Belfast, despised the Catholic Church with engaging wit, and drank. He and I grew up in the same county — Hudson — in New Jersey. His goal had been to be a good reporter, but he gave it up early because he had a fear of dying broke. There was money in being a press agent, so he headed for Miami. At the time, Carl Fisher was the highly paid drumbeater on the beach. He hired an Irishman and a Jew — Ferris and an affectionate type named Hank Meyer. In the early days, when beach lots in North Miami were still going for a couple of hundred dollars, Hank and Tom were combing the high schools for girls who would look good tossing a beach ball in the winter tabloids.

I was working twelve hundred miles north, but Hank and Tom became friends of mine. Hank Meyer could make a writer feel important when he wasn't. Tom Ferris was a Gaelic detractor, a man who could say "You're writing over your head" and make you wish to embrace him. Both men, in time, opened their own publicity offices and prospered. In time, the Jew surpassed the Irishman and yet, if life must be short, Ferris drew more joy with every wheezing breath. He worked for the Mackle Brothers,

Florida builders and developers, three men who understood the quality of mercy. They owned the lavish Key Biscayne Hotel and invited me and my troop down for a couple of weeks in late 1959. You don't have to write about the hotel, Ferris said. I said I knew that. Still, he said. . . . I said, don't push me, Tom.

I had a lovely girlfriend, a blond antidepressant, a laugher, one who dressed well. She thought I might marry her, even though I kept pleading that I had been in love twice and could not, would not, fall in love again. Her response was "Who asked you?" I also brought Ray Stone and Betty. The point of the story is not how much fun we had in the warm winter sun, but the opportunities I had to dig deeper under the fat of Ferris and get to know him. He was also a bit crazy, inclined toward the unexpected. One of his clients complained that Ferris had not put the name of his hotel in the newspapers in weeks.

Tom bought a costly and ornate fishbowl. He placed it in the lobby of the hotel and had colored ceiling lights focused on it. The bowl was filled with water. Then he hung a gold-plated sign on the bowl: "See The Invisible Fish." It was a three-day wonder. At a distance, walking, Ferris looked like a mandarin. I told him I had a problem and I wanted to toss it at him in case he might have a solution. Frank Gerace was about to drag my little kid to Hialeah. I proposed to have Tom pretend to employ Frank, and I would slip the wages through Ferris to my son-in-law.

Ferris pointed a finger at his head and said nothing. One of the strange facets of this man was that his wife, Jean, knew that he was drinking himself to death, but he refused all drinks among friends. At poolside, I ordered cocktails with lunch for the group, but Tom would say: "Not me. I like the coffee." Beneath the aplomb, the wit, there was a nameless fear which caused him to sweat a day's work sober, then go home to Jean and drink and drink until he fell on the living room rug. He was too fat for her to move. And, in spite of the friendship, a lecture from me would have been an affront.

Two days later he waddled back to the hotel. "Gerace," he said, "has got a job walking hot horses for Elkam Stables when he gets here with Gayle."

I went home and returned later to occupy a villa at the Key Biscayne Hotel with my father. Gayle was living in a flat across the street from the high hedges of Hialeah racetrack. When I walked up the alley to call, my feet dragged. She looked wan, except for the enormous belly. She prettied her face with a false smile. Frank was ebullient: "We're going to have a real dago dinner — spaghetti. You wanna stay?" I stayed.

The baby was born in Hialeah Hospital, a tiny girl with dark, matted hair who yawned and stretched trembling arms to the world. Gayle had no friends in Florida, no woman whom she might question about the care and feeding of an infant. Whenever I asked about her life, she murmured the monotonous litany: "Frank is the only man in the world for me." I wondered why Elinor had departed so early. There was a word fashionable at the time to indicate the inept: *klutz*. That is how I saw myself. Frank worked steadily and gave his paychecks to his wife. Gayle's culinary ability was confined to large portions of indeterminate Italian dishes. The baby was christened Elinor.

In the winter, Dad and I returned to the Key Biscayne Hotel. He was in his late seventies, addicted to the movement of mouth and bowels. He wore an atrocious jersey shirt with lateral stripes and a pair of ballooning off-white shorts. No one found a way of criticizing him gently. Disagreement induced outrage. He sat on a bench sunning himself and didn't realize that his testicles were hanging out of the shorts. I said that lunch was coming. This got him indoors. I suggested that the sun was strong, that slacks would keep his legs from being burned. He asked what we were having for lunch. I said hamburgers on rolls and a cup of coffee.

When the waiter departed, he asked how much the meal cost. I said seven fifty plus tip. He choked and hammered at his chest. How much? Like a cobra emerging from a basket to the proper notes, he swelled to outrage. For a lousy fifteen-cent hamburger? he shouted. How much tip? I said two fifty. He snarled: "You must be made of money." That afternoon he disappeared. He was a competent man; he wasn't lost; he played fair golf and, in spite of cardiac arrhythmia, he was a good walker. Wherever he had gone, it was purposeful.

Near sundown he was back, carrying a bag, and puffing. He had groceries. "I know you won't let me pay a dime for anything," he said, falling into a kitchen chair, "so I thought I'd help out." He became the cook. He soaked prunes all day, cooked oatmeal, ran ground coffee through a kettle, and fried eggs with fractured retinas. I kept telling him it was great because he expected me to say it. We had spitting, huffing disagreements, but this man was a unique personality. One afternoon he was discussing flight, although he had never been on an airplane. He wanted to talk about a new blind-landing procedure in which a plane, on its terminal leg to an airport, could run down a radio beam in fog and land safely.

I asked why he had never flown. He said when they invent a plane that will let a man keep one foot on the ground, he would fly. Joking, I said: "You've always had a fear of height. If you get on a plane, what can happen? It can crash and kill you. Or you can get a heart attack and die of fright. Honestly, do you want to live forever?" He surprised me. Get two tickets for a short flight, he said; I might as well try it.

It was a giant step, and that is not a joke. Mackey Airlines flew DC-4s out of Miami twenty miles to Fort Lauderdale, then twenty or thirty more to Palm Beach, then seventy miles over the Atlantic to West End at Bahama Island. He wore his gray homburg, the garnet tie, and the gray suit. His teeth were clenched with determination. The blue-veined hands were steady, but the breathing was loud. He walked up the ramp and found a window seat on the left side. I had arranged with the line to bring oxygen if I gave an arm signal. The DC-4 exuded more noise than speed. It thundered down the runway, eastbound, and lifted off. The racket became muted. Below were the sugar-cube roofs of Miami, and then the spangled green of Biscayne Bay. I said nothing.

He didn't turn away from the window. He was the little boy at his first Christmas. "Beautiful," he murmured. "Just beautiful." When I spoke, he did not turn his head. It was as though he had spent years thinking of this moment, and suddenly the fears had dissipated and his eyes were glazed with riotous color. He saw the cars on I-95, the toys of the highway; he saw the fairways and greens of a dozen golf courses, the fair-rimmed horizon, lakes, and, in a moment, Hollywood–Fort Lauderdale Airport.

"Getting off?" I said casually. He turned to look at me. "Off? Is this the last stop?" I said I had two open tickets. Big John couldn't control himself. He got up to go to the lavatory. "Let's stay on all the way," he said. "Let's see the Bahamas." It was my mother who had said, many years earlier: "When your father discovers something, he wants the world to know it." At the villa, the man who had been too frightened to fly sat and wrote expositions about the beauty and grace of flight to his sister, Margaret, his son, John, and others who were afraid to fly. After that day, he spent a lot of his pension checks flying jets up and down the East Coast, finding reasons to go back to my sister, Adele, for a few days, then an excuse to jet back to me. He found Eastern Airline's premiere pilot, Dick Merrill, and made a buddy of him.

Bad news, in our family, is sudden and irrevocable. Ray Stone and Betty were separating. Whatever the cause, the wounds were sufficiently deep that she phoned me and asked if I could find a job for her. I phoned Hank Meyer. He called back. "If she's a real, qualified secretary," he said, "I can put her in the Diplomat Hotel as secretary to our press office." I asked her on the phone if she knew what she was doing. She knew. She said it was already done; she and the two little girls were in a motel in Hollywood, Florida. Also she had a lawyer who, for a low fee, would get her an uncontested divorce.

I asked if she could bring the children to the villa on Sunday. Somebody was going to have to speak to somebody. The day before she arrived, I received a letter from Bill Hearst. It said he had a note from a widow of a famous writer, Joseph Hergesheimer. She lived in Palm Beach and said that a judge in Florida had murdered another judge — or so the charge read — and the trial would begin in St. Lucie courthouse in a week. Would he want to assign someone? Hearst asked me to check into it. The Miami *Herald* published my column, so I drove there to see George Beebe, managing editor. He was a soft drawler, a man with a lot of friends among editors everywhere. I asked about the story. He told me what he could and got the clippings from the morgue.

I phoned Bill Hearst and said that Mrs. Hergesheimer had given him a first-rate tip. Instead of going north, I would move to a motel in Fort Pierce and cover the trial. One of the oddities of journalism is that now and then a story which has "all the elements" does not get national attention because it is assessed as a local yarn. Newspapers in San Francisco and Los Angeles and Boston and San Antonio and New York bought this one as one of the most sensational trials in American jurisprudence.

Dad flew home to my sister. I packed two bags and rented a car. Fort Pierce was a little cracker town which clung to Route 1 for its life. You could buy gasoline if you waited until the man put his toothpick on top of the cash register. The courthouse consisted of round whitewashed pillars, a room with pews and a furled American flag. Behind it was a lovely lawn with curving walkways, benches, and a small stone jail. The judge was an amiable, patient man — D. C. Smith. He knew that the trial was attracting attention, so he told the sheriff to set a basement room aside for the press.

Judge Joseph Peel, on trial for murder, captivated my senses. He was young, a vibrant personality with black wavy hair and a Barrymore profile. He had so much personality that, as he sat in silence at the table of counsel, the shadings of countenance spoke out loud. It was like watching scattered clouds move over a sunny field. Behind him in the second row sat a tall, attractive woman who could wear two-piece suits and shirred white blouses in the manner of a model. Mrs. Peel seldom listened to the evidence. Her eyes were on her husband.

Peel was successful. He was a municipal judge in Palm Beach on his way up. The prosecutor was State Attorney Phil O'Connell, a burly man of middle years, dark and roaringly wrathful. O'Connell and his family were "people of substance" in Florida. They became highly paid, highly stationed public servants who affected the gentility of assured snobs. There was no forgiveness in Philip D. O'Connell.

Perpetual righteousness is a bore. Judge Curtis Chillingworth of Palm Beach might require a half-hour of cogitation if he was offered a choice of a ham sandwich or a cheese sandwich. He would weigh the amount of work in each for Mrs. Chillingworth, moving on to the question of white bread or gluten, to mustard or not to mustard, and, at last, whether to trim the crusts or leave them on. He was a circuit court judge every minute of his life. He looked upon the law as the Jews of Judea saw it, the beginning of life, and the end. He was older than Phil O'Connell, but just as churchy.

It was Chillingworth who had heard stories about Judge Peel. The gossip was as intricately detailed as a spiderweb. It was replete with fine lines which intersected, and some which seemed to go off to a place lost in darkness. There was an anarchic thread to some of them. Palm Beach is two towns separated by the intracoastal waterway. The one on the beach consists of perfumed mansions. West Palm Beach is a sweatbox of small houses and big stores. Judge Chillingworth bridged the water; he had a nice home on the beach at Manalapan. Peel reigned among indolent Blacks, an enclave of Cubans, and the White crackers who wore straw hats over their eyes and tried to think of a way of earning a dollar.

Peel was a lowly judge, but when he sat on the bench in Palm Beach Municipal Court in his black robes he was a genial monarch. Among the swindles of the city was a game called bolita. It was one more numbers game, but it enchanted the poor. Anyone who knew a bolita runner could select a number from one to one hundred and bet a dollar on it. In the late afternoon every day, an anonymous man holding a black plush bag would walk into a neighborhood bar and ask a stranger to dip a hand into the bag and bring up a plastic pill. There was a number on it. That was the winner all over the city. Bolita operators couldn't afford to pay more than sixty dollars to lucky plungers because they had to deduct a percentage for the runner, something for the bolita operator, a little for a rented storefront, and a piece for the law. Judge Curtis Chillingworth heard that Judge Peel was the piece of the law.

If Chillingworth had been a more worldly man, with an appreciation for the excitement of sin, he might have nudged Joe, might even have sent word: "Kid, get out of the rackets before you scandalize the county." The news hit Chillingworth with the same impact as though he had been told that his tie was stained with female secretions. He was outraged. He sought secret assistance from state investigators out of the capital at Tallahassee. They learned that Joe had rounded up all the bolita operators in West Palm Beach and told them that he was their new partner. They would, from that day forward, each pay the judge fifty dollars a week. When any of the runners were arrested by police, they would come before Judge Joseph Peel and he would listen to the evidence and either acquit or fine fifty dollars. If the fine was fifty, Peel said it would come out of the money the operators had already paid him.

It was a nice business. Joe had a small law practice on the side and he was soon driving an air-conditioned Cadillac. His wife drove their little children in a Lincoln Continental. At a second meeting with the bolita operators, the judge said they didn't know how to do business. What would they do if a well-played number hit? They might survive a couple of those, but a half-dozen would bankrupt all of them. He proposed that, when all the numbers were in, they phone each other with the number least played that day. For example, number seventeen. The judge advised them to take number seventeen and place the plastic ball in a home freezer for an hour. Arrange to have a stranger in a bar dip his hand into the plush bag and feel around for the cold one. In that way, they would not only survive, but grow rich.

It was wrong; it was unlawful; and yet it was trifling compared to the crimes of the forebears of those who lived in splendor on the beach. Chillingworth enjoyed inviting his grown daughters and kin to his beach home, there to sit in the breezeway and listen to the ice break in the lemonade pitcher. Peel had a more viable hobby. He enjoyed getting young women to strip in his private office and posing them nude under his diploma from Stetson University. His nudes were so attractive that some of them obscured the framed law degree. This situation, the tainted trivia of a small town, might have endured for years if Chillingworth had learned to keep a secret. He spread the word that he was gunning for Peel, was going to have him disbarred for life and imprisoned for conspiracy to obstruct justice.

Judge Peel heard about it. It depressed him because judges are loath to kill judges. Joe understood that Chillingworth was not the man one could approach with remuneration or remorse. No, Curtis Chillingworth was about to bust Joe and scare the hell out of every other public servant in the sovereign State of Florida.

Peel decided to have Chillingworth killed. Listening to the trial testimony, I surmised that the young judge decided, first, how to murder Chillingworth, and second, who would do it. His contacts with felons were superb. He could choose. The job, he figured, should be expeditious, economically reasonable, and, to coin a poor word, clueless. The assignment was given to George D. Lincoln and Floyd Holtzapfel. Both were minor members of Joe's shakedown rackets. Mr. Lincoln was a mean Black man known to the police as Bobby. He preyed on his people, driving a battered truck through "Colored Towns" west and north of Palm Beach. His habit was to stare unblinking at people who disagreed with him. A few of those are said to reside eternally in the Everglades.

Holtzapfel was a pale Caucasian with a forehead which stopped at the crown of his head. The pale empty eyes matched his intelligence. His nickname, a bit ironic, was Lucky. In the poolrooms of West Palm Beach, hoodlums said that Lucky's virtue was that he could, if necessary, hold a gun to the head of the fairest lady and squeeze the trigger. He thought of murder as a form of predestination; if someone had to be dead at a certain day and hour, Lucky was merely the instrument of something already in the cards. He misunderstood everything on the minimal side. And why not? He had been convicted twice of armed robbery and was pardoned.

Peel put it on the line to Bobby and Lucky: "Chillingworth is trying to ruin *us*. We will have to get rid of the judge." The rest of the conference was devoted to reminding the assassins that all the thinking would be done by Judge Peel. First, Joe explained what a corpus delicti is. If the body cannot be found, how can the state prove murder? Ergo, the judge said, we kidnap Chillingworth, kill him, and make sure the body is never found. People will suspect he ran off somewhere — South America, maybe. Bobby was skeptical, but Lucky was entranced. He could hardly wait to hear how the story came out.

The Chillingworth beach house at Manalapan stood high on the sand. The skinny old judge spent a lot of time there. The married daughters who visited had quarters separated from the main house by a breezeway. Peel said that Holtzapfel and Lincoln should rent a motorboat at one of the marinas. They should run it up on the sand after midnight, go up to the house, rap on the door, and take the judge at gunpoint. Truss him solidly and carry him to the boat. Start the engine, run the boat out into the Gulf Stream about eight miles, weight Chillingworth's body, and ship him over the side.

Did they know anything about the Gulf Stream? Nothing more than that it was out there. The judge explained that it was a river inside the ocean. It flowed north at close to three knots. It ran north to Georgia and the Carolinas, then bent outward to Greenland and Iceland. The Gulf Stream was what produced thick fogs in London. Chillingworth's body would embark on one hell of a voyage. It was a reasonable plot, not a perfect one, but a cut above the time-honored Florida hideaway plan which involved driving the victim into the Everglades and leaving the body to small game.

To Bobby Lincoln, murder was murder, a thing devoid of humor. To Lucky Holtzapfel, it was a play, starring him, and full of make-believe. On the night of June 14, 1955, Lucky wore a yachting cap. Bobby wore a revolver in his belt. They drove to Riviera Beach and rented a motor boat at the Blue Heron Marina. Lucky carried a fishing sack over his shoulder. They wanted the dock boys to know that they were going out for some night spear-fishing. They had glass face masks, heavy cartridge belts, rectangular lead weights, and spears. On the way out, Holtzapfel ran through the details over the roar of the engine. The judge said they should knock on Chillingworth's door and say they had come ashore from a sinking yacht. Could they use the phone? When the job was done, Lucky would phone Peel at home and say "The motor's fixed" and hang up.

A moon came up and silvered the mild sea. The engine overheated. Lucky cursed. He punched the indicator. It wasn't stuck. The marina had rented a defective engine. They cut the engine and drifted. When it cooled, they started south again. Heat stopped them. Lucky had a bottle of bourbon in a brown bag. He of the iron nerve drank deeply. Bobby turned away. An hour later, Lucky stared shoreward, and saw a broad blackness with a single white light. That was on the Chillingworth porch. They swung toward the light and beached the boat.

They jumped out and left the engine idling. The cooling pump began to suck sand. Bobby hid in forsythia bushes near the beach. Holtzapfel was overacting. He bounded up the steps with the sack over his shoulder, prepared to hum a chanty if he could think of one. He knocked. And knocked again. A light went on. A thin man in pajamas adjusted his spectacles. Lucky forgot his line. "Aren't you Judge Chillingworth?" he said. The humorless judge nodded. "I am," he said. The assassin remembered his part and began the story of the sinking yacht. The judge was trying to ask a question. Lucky yanked a gun and said: "This is a holdup. Anybody else in the house? ... Okay. Call them out." Chillingworth, unafraid, shouted: "Margie!" A small woman with dark hair and eyes came out of the bedroom pulling a robe over a nightgown. Lincoln came out of the bushes, startled to find that a White woman was involved. "What are you going to do to these people, Floyd?" he said.

He knew. Both prisoners had their wrists taped behind their backs. Floyd took some quarter-inch manila rope and made two nooses. He slipped these over both necks and ordered Bobby to hold the lines and walk behind them to the boat. Floyd examined the house. No one was inside. He disturbed nothing. The porch light was on. It was extinguished with the butt of a gun. Lucky hurried down the long beach in time to hear a prolonged scream from Mrs. Chillingworth. The butt of his gun put her light out too. He carried her over his shoulder.

Chillingworth concentrated on Bobby Lincoln. "You take care of us and you will never have to work again, boy," he said. It was a mistake to say "boy." Besides, Lincoln knew that if he did not kill this judge, another one would kill Bobby. The only thing that died at this point was the engine. The judge was helped aboard. Mrs. Chillingworth, unconscious and bleeding, was stretched out between seats. Lucky cursed the engine. He cursed the brightened moonlight. He cursed the traffic on A-1A with its headlights probing the beach.

The engine started. The craft headed slowly out to sea. The engine died. Chillingworth said nothing. It was started again. Lucky had no idea where the Gulf Stream might begin. He kept going out. The lights of Palm Beach behind them looked like a rime of foam. He cut the engine. Lucky tried to lift Mrs. Chillingworth. She didn't appear to be unconscious, but the body was limp, yielding. "Help me, Bobby." The canvas belt went around her waist. The weights were heavy. It required both men to lift her over the side. The judge sat up. "Remember," he said, "I love you." She murmured: "I love you too." Mrs. Chillingworth did not protest as she was dropped over the side.

The two turned to the judge. He said nothing, but he squirmed and kicked. He threshed so hard that he fell over the side. In the moonlight, Lucky could see the old man swimming with his hands tied behind him. Bobby tried to hit the judge over the head with a shotgun. The stock broke. The judge, bleeding, was swimming away. They rowed the boat to his side and Bobby Lincoln grabbed the judge by his pajamas and began to hoist him aboard. "No," Lucky said. "Wait a minute." He crouched forward and got the anchor line. It was old frayed rope, but intact. Attached was a pipe embedded in a square block of concrete. Bobby held the judge as Lucky wrapped the rope around the judge's neck and knotted it. Then, without any curtain line, he threw the block of concrete into the sea. Bobby grabbed a heavy-duty flashlight. He turned it downward. The sea was lime-clear. They watched the judge spin downward slowly.

In the St. Lucie County courthouse, the trial moved forward with the precision of a minuet. It had its cadence of motions and objections and voir dires, the things which, like poorly placed parentheses, stop the drama of testimony. In my eyes, Prosecutor O'Connell was the show. His attitude of restrained rage continued for days. His assistant, Eugene Spellman of Miami, turned out to be a legal marvel. He recited the precedents, page and chapter, without consulting books. He wore a boyish smile as he addressed the court, as though the task of sending Judge Peel to the electric chair was not a personal matter; it was a day's work and he would do his best to see that Peel fried.

O'Connell, I felt, was mistaken in his vengeance. Local reporters said that the prosecutor granted immunity from prosecution to Bobby Lincoln, not only for the Chillingworth crime, but for a couple of earlier murders in exchange for his testimony against handsome Joe Peel. White southern juries then looked with amusement on the testimony of Negroes, whether they were confessing or accusing. They gave the words the weight of a feather. Phil O'Connell would need more than Bobby if he expected to nail Peel. So, after a lot of palaver, he got Floyd Holtzapfel. I played golf with Phil and he told me that he promised Lucky nothing. I didn't believe it then or now. Anyone who heard that long-winded whiny witness in the witness chair go all the way back to the early bolita days of Judge Peel and corroborate Bobby's testimony to the letter would have to believe that, if Lucky was not promised leniency or immunity, then all of us were gaping at a nut who was trying to commit suicide through the kindness of Florida's legal system.

On the morning of the verdict, I sat alone with Judge Peel in his cell. He was cheerful. "I'll get a hung jury," he said. No, I said, they're going to send you away forever. Both of us agreed that, if there was a finding of guilt, it was Lucky's testimony that did it. In court that day, both of us were surprised. The jury found Joe guilty, and recommended mercy. Phil O'Connell almost choked. Judge D. C. Smith sentenced Peel to life.

Bobby Lincoln, without a shred of dignity, took the first train out of town. Phil O'Connell prosecuted Lucky and here, ironically, he triumphed. Holtzapfel was found guilty and sentenced to the electric chair. He was on death row a long time, rattling his cage and pleading that he was the penitent one; he had helped the prosecution to get Joe. He did considerable dying before the State of Florida commuted his sentence to life.

When the Hialeah racecourse closed, Frank drove Gayle and the infant Elinor to his mother's house in Cherry Hill, New Jersey. It was a small, neat house, and the welcome sign was out for the Bishops to attend a christening. There is an exaggerating joy in some Latin families, and this was one. The stereo was loud; the food was abundant and steaming; voices babbled unintelligibly; everybody radiated cheer. Except two.

Gayle was lost in a big wing chair, rocking the baby with her knees. In lassitude, her features were fatigued; the hazel eyes stared at a wall. The baby did not smile. When the knees stopped, the whimper started.

Something was wrong. It was chronic. Back in Sea Bright, I asked Floranna Walter and Virginia Lee if Gayle confided in them. They shrugged. All they could think of was that Gayle complained that Frank pressed sex on his wife at his whim. Nothing else. In other things, he was devoted. I decided to have a little talk with Frank. This was wrong, and I knew it was wrong. When we were alone in my bedroom, I asked how he was getting along with his family. The opening gambit is always the same: bright smiles, happy words. I asked if Gayle was content, taking care of a husband and a baby. Sure, sure. Why not? I weaseled my cowardly way down to the subject of sex. I wondered aloud how many husbands realized that, to women, sex is a bit more than fun; that it is as delicate as trying to bag a bird bare-handed in a bramble bush.

No problem, he said. "I'm sexy." I moved a tentative step farther. "She ever say no?" He frowned. I don't recall the precise quotation, but I cannot forget the brutal sense of his remarks: Funny you should ask. When we got married, she was the hottest tomato I ever knew. Honest. Now, when we get in bed, she tries to say no and I'm not going to permit it. After all, I am the husband, Dad. Right? It's the man who calls the shots. My stomach squeezed sharply. I tried to keep the conversation where he wanted it — on a man-to-man basis — but my desire was to lift him under the armpits and bounce his head off the bedroom wall. And yet, and yet, it was none of my business. Within his lights, Frank was right. He didn't realize that this little filly was too young to be broken with a whip.

My confidence dissipated. I was hamstrung. The thought was depressing. Frank had a job working with horses on the Haskins farm. The Geraces had the basement room. In the day, I saw a lot of Gayle and my granddaughter. When I asked how things were going, it was I who choked. She was dull. In an upstairs room were her electric guitar, her Frankie Avalon records, the wall posters, the secret diary, even the yellow dress she wore to see the Pope. The joke books and issues of a magazine called *Mad* were on shelves. Somewhere between that room and the cellar, she had stopped laughing.

A few Sundays later, we attended mass together. As we left, a mighty organ was on vox humana. "Did you hear that?" she said. Hear what? "Mommy's voice." No. When an organ imitates the human voice, listeners perceive it to sound like people they know. What did Mommy say? "She said she was sorry, but this is the way it has to be." The thing I dreaded could no longer be postponed. I would have to find a sympathetic psychiatrist who would help Gayle. It wasn't difficult. Several friends mentioned the same person: Dr. Frank Pignataro of Red Bank. When I asked if she would mind visiting the doctor at his office, she surprised me. The face brightened. No, she said. Not at all. I wondered why anyone would be eager to recite problems which, by their nature, must be secret and private. That evening at dinner, Gayle was bright and bubbly. She fed the baby first, then sat with us. When she told Frank about Pignataro, he frowned. "What for?" he said. "You're not nervous." The question was without malice; he loved her to the fullest of the degree that he understood the emotion.

The next afternoon was one of those sunny ones which almost take the chill from the breeze. I was dated to play golf with Dad; I canceled in order to speak to Pignataro. The office was a small house on Broad Street, standing atop an embankment. He was fortyish, with a kindly Italianate face and errant wisps of gray in thick black hair. He said he was reluctant to see me; he was sure I was going to play the loving father about to paint a portrait of a little angel. I laughed. No, I said, most of what I have read and heard about psychiatry convinces me that it takes an interminable effort on the part of the doctor to get an approximation of truth from the patient.

Well, he said, let us understand each other. The only reason I agreed to see you is that I buy your books and if you are as level-headed as I think you are, maybe you can give me a few items which will help your Gayle. His pen hung over a big pad as I talked. I prattled on and on. Some of what I thought was significant did not move his pen. Other stuff, trivia, induced short scribbles. He was interested, for example, to know that she was late starting a menstrual cycle.. By the time I reached the drunken disputes between Maggy, Elinor, and me the pen was dancing, and I was sweating. I tossed my infidelities into the kitty because I was certain that Elinor had made sure the children knew. About thirty-five minutes into it, he asked if I would like coffee. I would. His secretary brought some and, as I sipped, I thought maybe I was the patient.

When I ran down, Dr. Pignataro dropped another coin into me and we moved on. Why didn't Elinor leave me before she had a successful pregnancy? Why didn't I leave her instead of doing it symbolically by sleeping with other women? There were a lot of questions about Virginia Lee and the sibling relationship. Sometimes he would say: "Never mind how it happened. How did it appear to you?" I was sorry and glad to be there. He was in no hurry, had no appointments. I kept turning damp rocks. By the time I got to the romance of Frank Gerace, his interest was so obviously piqued that I think he was ready to skip dinner.

How many other boys had she dated? Who were her girlfriends? Were they confidantes? Did they share secrets? How did Gayle respond to a group? If she was a slave to her mother and grandmother in their loneliness, how did I account for Gayle's hoydenish attitude, her magnificent sense of humor, her pranks and jokes? Did she cry on occasion? Which occasions? When I related the death of Elinor, Gayle ill and unknowing, Pignataro dropped the pen on the pad. Don't you think Elinor was disloyal, dying while the volunteer slave was sick? Wasn't Elinor running away, sort of? I told him of the recurring dreams and the monotonous phrase from the casket. The voice from the church organ was common to many who husband grief. He got third-hand information about her sex life, the gradual suppression of exuberant emotions toward pallid silence.

"I will see her," he said, "Monday at three." I asked why he couldn't see her tomorrow. This induced the only laugh from his side of the desk. Whatever her problem, an assortment of fears and tension, he said, had been building for years. Gayle had held together this long; a few days would make little difference. One more thing, he said. It is all right for you to tell her that we have met; don't tell anything that was said. Not a word.

The imponderable, to me, was Gayle's eagerness, not only to see Pignataro, but to see the doctor again. She had a half-dozen interviews. The doctor said he would like her to get some solid rest in a sanatarium. I opposed it. What for? I demanded. Is she psychotic? He was surprised, he said, at my attitude. He had assumed that I was enlightened. No, she was not psychotic. How about depressed? he said. Hell, I was depressed lots of times. My mother used to say she had the "blues." I tried to browbeat Pignataro, something I regretted. As a layman, a nonexpert, I had done considerable reading of Freud's speeches in the United States in 1909; I had read the variant positions of Jung and Adler, and, for Pignataro's information, I appreciated Adler. If, I said, one could draw a straight line across a sheet of paper and refer to anything above it as optimistic and anything underneath as pessimistic, I would not like to be the phlegmatic dunce whose emotional life never moved above or below that line.

My analogy, he said, was old. He agreed with it, but I would have to understand that my darling daughter, accustomed to the buoyant life slightly above the line, was now living permanently below it. How about tranquilizers? I said. Fine, he said. He proposed to use them. But I must see such medications as a jack under an automobile. Everything looks fine, including the flat tire, as long as you don't remove the jack. Palliatives had their uses, but wouldn't it be better to find the cause of a depression and root it out? I surrendered. Where? A place in upstate New York. What was it like? Like an old estate, he said. A couple of buildings made of big brownstone, a swimming pool, plenty of lawn cascading toward the river. A colleague of his, a Dr. Nelson, owned the place. It was a good place, nice airy rooms with good food. She could leave if she didn't like it.

Massive guilt began to germinate in my head. Somewhere, I had failed this kid. It couldn't be Elinor and Maggy because she was happily devoted to them. I had given heaping doses of love to Virginia Lee when I was at home, broke, writing articles for *The Sign*. As Gayle began to grow, I became a so-called important writer, at least a high-priced one. When she needed me, I had left home for Sea Bright. If I could no longer endure the antics of the women, what were they doing to warp her head? When they died, and she was mine, I was flying around the nation writing "important" articles; waiting for my name to appear in big advertisements in *The Times Book Review* and slapped onto the sides of newspaper trucks. I made speeches at colleges and at ballroom dinners merely to convince myself that I was a rare bird indeed. I wasn't flogging myself with guilt; I didn't bathe myself with pity. But the analysis was sound. Years before, I promised myself to stick to the marriage to save the children. What I had saved was myself.

I had to speak to Gayle and Frank about the sanatarium. It was as easy as shoving mist uphill. Frank was close to outrage. What for? She's my wife. She's okay. I'll take care of my wife without any help from nuts. Gayle said she was happy to go. Frank's mother would take care of the baby. Little Elinor couldn't be in better hands. Happy to go, happy to go. There was a tinny sound in those words. Who looks forward to life in a sanatarium? No one. Gayle saw it as a vacation. Then, slowly, deliberately, the truth came to me. She wanted to get away from Frank and the baby! She was prepared to leave, even if it meant confinement. I stared across the table at her. "Gayle," I said solemnly, "do you love Frank?" She smiled briefly. "Dad, I told you a hundred times that Frank is the only man in the world for me." It was a lie. A bald-faced lie. She dreaded being near the man. Nor was she prepared to feed and care for a baby.

I phoned Pignataro to tell him. I could sense his smile. "Jim," he said, "for a knowledgeable layman, it took a long time for you to reach a conclusion."

"What do we do?"

"Let her go. Drive her up. Let her look around. She's competent to make her own decisions."

We drove up and headed across the big Tarrytown bridge. We met Dr. Nelson in his office. He was a slender man with white hair, a polite whisperer who, I am sure, could have convinced President Roosevelt in 1942 that World War II was under control. He was a competent psychiatrist with initials behind his name, but I didn't like the place and I didn't trust him to confide in me.

My thinking wasn't orderly. The main building looked like something peeking from the mists on the Scottish moors. It was a movie set in an English mystery. Patients walked the grounds freely. If, as I passed, they smiled and nodded, I marked them as nuts. If they didn't and I nodded, I thought they were withdrawn. Two other doctors were as polite as Nelson. "You sure you want to stay here?" Frank said. Gayle nodded. "I'm very sure," she said. "I wish you and Dad would stop worrying."

Dr. Nelson said no visitors for three weeks. Why? I said. The notion of having her here, he said, is to remove her entirely from her environment.

You're part of that. The staff can do a better assessment if she has no communication with home or friends. I kissed her good-bye as though I was leaving her to the Inquisitors. It's a dreadful sensation. The only way I can describe it is to say that Gayle was helpless and I was helpless to help her.

At home I walked the floors. The typewriter was cold. No work was done. I couldn't respond to mail. The pool table at Jim Sullivan's tavern required concentration and I didn't have it. After two days, I packed a bag and fled to Key Biscayne. I played golf. The nights were empty.

I phoned Betty Stone at the Diplomat. Had she ever been to the jai alai games? No. She asked about Gayle. I said I didn't want to talk about it. Betty said she would try to find a baby-sitter. We had an early dinner at the Dania Fronton. Diners turned to stare at her. I asked if she might go back to Ray. You're behind in family gossip, she said. I'm getting a noncontested Florida divorce. It will be final in a few weeks.

We had box seats. I became more interested in her than the games. Some money was offered for her to bet. She declined to take it. Okay, I said. I'll bet and if I win, you get half for rooting. If I lose, you owe me half. Looking at her smile, I had the impression that I had not seen her before. Maybe her hair was different. It could be that there was something subtle in the glint of diamonds in blue eyes. It could be that she looked so young and I felt so old. When I discussed the players and the odds in the program, I placed an arm loosely around her shoulder. I expected an easy shift away from my hand. It didn't happen.

Jai alai is not an easy game. The players are the only animals who can read the odds board and some had a miserable habit of missing an easy shot. Besides, I could not trust twenty-eight Spaniards who take a bath together. I won two hundred and twenty dollars. It could have been the presence of the beautiful neophyte. On the way back to a little second-floor apartment in Hollywood, I gave her a hundred and ten dollars. She seemed ashamed. You earned it, I said. All that screaming. She was serious. "This is more than I earn in a week," she said.

I asked her to go to the movies the following night. No, she said. She had no baby-sitter. She wouldn't leave Karen and Kathleen. She asked would I like to stop by in the evening. No, I said, I'm fresh out of little girls. The thing I need is a distraction, a game, a movie, a nightclub, a something. Betty seemed to realize that I needed company. Do a favor for me, I said with some urgency. Call an agency and get a baby-sitter for the next week. I'll pay for it and I don't want to hear you refuse. I'll stop by and see the children, but I have to prep myself first. She said she'd try. I shook hands farewell and kissed her on the cheek. Cheeks are noncommittal and almost antiseptic. On the way back to the Key, I wondered why she appeared to be more attractive than before. Not just physically attractive (she looked like a Greek coin in profile with a bun of honey hair on her neck) but bright. I should not have asked her for a week of dates. I was depressed, not lovesick. She couldn't be much more than thirty or thirty-one years of age. I was fifty-two.

The next night we saw a show. The night after that I stopped to see Karen and Kathleen. I was Uncle Jim, and I got ardent hugs and kisses, a complete rundown on the clothes a Barbie Doll needs, and which teacher in the school around the corner the girls liked. We drove to the Carib Motel, where Maxie Lewis was punching a piano. There was a soft scent about her that was not perfume. She wore a small comb sticking up out of the bun. Like most of the Bishop-Stone-Kelly families, she could drink. Not a great amount; the three groups had long been nourished on beer. Driving home, I wanted to reach for Betty's hand, but, if I did, and she withdrew hers, I knew that I would quit whatever game we were playing.

I called off the next appointment because I had spent the afternoon on the phone with Dr. Nelson and Dr. Pignataro. Nelson said it would require more time to evaluate the problem; Pignataro said Gayle was resting. I was sarcastic with Nelson. Could he *surmise* the problem? Just a guess, he said softly, but the symptoms suggest a depression induced by grief. Could a childish marriage have a bearing? We do not know, he said. Anything untoward could have a bearing. Nelson didn't invite me to call next week, or the week after. I understood his position; I don't think he appreciated mine. The lone clue I got from Dr. Pignataro (I cannot understand why psychiatrists dispense information in the form of an interrogation) was: Why do you think Gayle was so eager to spend a few weeks at the sanatarium? Do you think she is running away? If so, Jim, from what? From whom? It could be me, that's whom, but Pignataro was taking dead aim on Frank, although he agreed with me that Gerace was trying to be a good husband. As day followed day, it became obvious that, having made her bed, maritally speaking, she was going to lie in it as her father had done long ago. Abraham Lincoln, who married a hysteric, said: "If you make a bad bargain, hug it the tighter." The aphorism is asinine. Ten days later, Nelson (cautious) phoned to say that Gayle's marriage was the primary depressant; resurrecting her mother was her rebuttal to an agonizing life.

At the same time, I received a note from Gayle. This is one of the few which have been lost, but I can synthesize it because it cheered me with laughter:

> Dear Dad: I'm fine. I hope you are too. I have a room in a small building. An old lady who is bonkers has the one behind me. I made friends with her and we play Old Maid with my marked deck.
>
> I got a note from Frank. He says the baby is fat. Believe me, his mother is the best. She's the kind that doesn't need books with the baby. I wish I could tell you what I do every day, but they don't let you do nuthin'. I'm in with all the tame nuts. Love and kisses, Gayle.

The note did it. I felt better. A call to Betty elicited a weird response: "I figured you stopped seeing me because the neighbors might talk." If the Bishop-Stone-Kelly combine heard that I was dating Betty — except as a peace-making uncle — all three would burst into flames. Was I a graying uncle immersed in self-pity? What happened to the cynic who said he could fall in love but once in his life, and had experienced it twice?

The logical thing was not to become involved. The sensible thing would be to take her *and the children* to dinner. There was a Tahitian restaurant in Hallandale laden with hot pork and pineapple and flame dancers. They had the best Shirley Temple drinks. At least, the most elaborate. The girls were delighted. It didn't please me that Betty thought it was a good idea. Nor did it improve my disposition when one of the waiters recognized me and said: "I read about these people in your column. How nice that you brought Virginia Lee and the little ones." That was enough to macerate all romantic notions. More than enough.

In the morning, I packed and moved to the Diplomat Hotel. The press agent, Don Cuddy, had invited me to play a couple of rounds of golf. We spent the afternoon tramping through woods and dredging lakes for lost balls. I asked how Betty Stone was making out as his secretary. Fine, he said, smacking his lips. What's that mean? Everybody in the place is making passes at her. She's gorgeous. You too? I was irritated to find a world so full of aggressive men and so few beautiful women. Betty had an office in the basement of the hotel. I asked her to stop in my room for a drink. No, she said, the children were home after school alone. Sorry. The cynic within me conceded that she was playing her cards in proper order. I had no intention of assailing her chastity — whatever that means — but she was pretending to be in danger.

There was an impending fight between Ingemar Johansson and Floyd Patterson. I had two tickets; one in the press row, one in the fifth row. The promoter, Chris Dundee, invited me to visit the Swede at a motel south of Palm Beach. I drove up to unscramble his accent into a story for a column. Instead, I was invited to change into boxing trunks and gloves and go one round with him. There is something about the patently insane that magnetizes me. I did it. The photographers outside the ring enjoyed themselves. In one corner was a muscled slugger whose knowledge of boxing barely matched mine. He had a big jaw made of fine crystal. In the other was a short, paunchy Irishman who didn't know to run.

At the bell, Ingemar pawed the air in front of me. He was afraid to hit the little donkey. I'm left-handed, which surprised him because my first shot, coming up from the floor, caught him on the mouth. We were wearing twelve-ounce pillows. The result of the blow was that he lifted his eyebrows. His manager coached me: "Hit him in the belly, Jim. Right in the bonze." I began to dance on my toes. My abdomen rose separately. I lowered my chin, glowered, and hit him with a flurry of nothing. Toward the end of the round, Ingemar miscued and caught me on the side of the head with a short left. He looked frightened and apologized. "Put 'em up," I said. There was no sensation of pain; just an assortment of pins and needles in the legs. There was a clang of a bell; I touched gloves with the Swede and said: "Had enough?" Fortunately, his English was impaired.

The day of the fight, I asked Betty if she would like to go. She didn't think so. She was opposed to violence, dreaded the sight of blood, and couldn't reconcile herself to watching two grown men rendering each other unconscious. I was losing patience, always easy for me. I said I didn't want a recital of how feminine she was; I would take her word for it. Had she ever seen a fight? No. Why not try anything one time? She thought about it. We'll have early dinner, I said. There was a little silence. She would try to get a baby-sitter.

My press seat was almost under the apron. With the exception of the Dempsey-Firpo fight in the Polo Grounds, I doubt that any fight had as many knockdowns in the first two rounds. Good fight fans are hostile. They protest that they pay to see their man win; I don't believe it. They pay to see the other man flattened, maimed, groveling in resin. Ingemar and Floyd, as I recall, came out of their corners to engage in a prairie-hen mating dance. Hitting was unthinkable. They made small gestures like dogs sitting up to beg for food. The crowd, which was scaled from a hundred dollars for a ringside seat, hooted and hollered for blood.

Johansson cocked a right and executed an old-fashioned roundhouse. It caught Patterson on the chin and he was down. He got up as the crowd roared, and caught Ingemar with a left hook. Johansson was on his behind in his own corner. He took an eight count, rose like the stump of a fallen tree, and hit Floyd a shot which set integration back five years. How long this went on my memory refuses to index, but I looked back just in time to find that Betty Stone was the only person in the arena who was standing on her seat, fists swinging, face distorted, shouting: "Kill him! Kill him!"

When the second round began, I realized that we had two men who had no notion of how to defend themselves. Every third punch was solid. The little referee was perspiring from counting over bodies. I looked back. There she was, standing on that chair again, fists swinging. People behind her were shouting: "Down!" "Sit down!" "Down in front!" From my position, Betty seemed to have lost her mind and her breath at the same time. The crowd got to her, and she sat.

Afterward, I took her to Wolfie's for Danish and coffee. She would admit that the battle excited her, but denied that she had stood on the chair, swinging. "I did not. Did not. Did . . . NOT." How long, I said, had she felt this savage lust for blood? It surprised her as much as it did me, she said.

In the morning, Pignataro phoned and said I could bring Gayle home for a weekend within ten days. Nelson would like to have her back the following Monday for more chats. Is she okay? I said. She faces no big problem, he said, except the environment. That environment could include me. Nelson felt that she married Gerace to escape the disciplined environment of her father; too late she found herself in a more confining prison. He wasn't prepared to discuss the future.

There was a surge of relief, like the first breath after a deep dive. Betty, who had known Gayle from early childhood, clapped her hands with joy. We drove to the Mayfair Theatre in downtown Miami to see a foreign movie. It was one of those artistic Scandinavian things in which a sullen woman understands her problems acutely and poignantly, but the man she loves spends a lot of time staring through a cottage window at a damp landscape. The handyman, or maybe it was the local physician, appreciated her problem and had something to fix it. On the way home, I made another tactical error; I asked her to tell me the root of the problem with Ray.

Betty was a mature woman, one of astonishing self-containment. She could live with pain — emotional or physical — without hand-wringing. She could, for short periods, abstain from laughter. But she could not do without tears. She despised them, felt a self-contempt when they sprang to her eyes, but they came at times of distress as well as happiness. My question induced them. My gaze left the road and, glancing at her, I wondered if I could do something right. It was not noisy weeping. It was silent, signaled by a lifting of the head.

She wept and I kissed her. There was a yielding, something like a surreptitious surrender in it, so I kissed her again. The car was parked. She may have felt, with the first one, that I was sympathetic. She was yanked across the seat to the driver's side and I could taste the salt on her lips. All of what the Sisters of Charity used to refer to as my basest instincts were aroused — and welcome. There was an uneasy sensation that I was making a play for a "cousin." Betty broke free. We were speechless. It is not a problem to recall my thoughts. I was scared.

Sex was out of the question because she would expect a commitment. In the hotel, I wondered why I felt "serious" about her. What man would dare to be "serious" after twenty-seven years locked in a mirror maze? Besides, I was beginning to cast a long shadow; she cast none. There is no cuckold like an old cuckold. Her good sense must have told her to seek a younger, less dominating man. The prescription called for an ambitious, intelligent type who could, without strain, fall in love with her children. Eastern Airlines had a late-afternoon flight to New York. I lied to Betty. "Phyllis Jackson phoned. I must be in her office in the morning." She said she understood. I'm afraid she did. That evening I was at the door of her apartment. The girls shouted: "He didn't go! He didn't go!"

I created one impasse after another. It was impossible to speak candidly with Karen and Kathleen on the rug with crayons and drawing books and a television set shouting in the same room. I told the girls to be their own baby-sitters for ten minutes. I took Betty to the car, drove around the corner, and parked under a big ficus tree. Without a word, I took her in my arms. Her fingers clenched my shoulder blades. I was slipping, sliding, skidding when, in truth, I intended to explain how impossible the situation would be for her.

We were there an hour. Maybe more. We talked and clung to each other and whispered. Pedestrians slowed to stare at us. Impossible, I said, when I could catch my breath. I'm fifty-three; you're thirty-two. Her contribution, as I recall, was "I can't go on like this." It sounded like the hackneyed phrase of a woman trying to trap a man. I had heard that one. I had raised two girls, I said; I wasn't going to raise two more. When I mentioned my contempt for PTA meetings, she burst into laughter. Our families would have a fit. Some of my friends would think she was Virginia Lee. Toward the end of the hour, I began to listen to my arguments and I felt sorry for myself. "If," I said, "there was only ten years' difference . . ." Then too, a newly divorced woman, alone for the first time, could be reaching hungrily for the first available man. That one touched a nerve. She pulled free.

I was unhappy in my room; unhappy in the coffee shop; miserable in bed. I tried to congratulate myself on having the good sense to stifle sentiment. Betty was hard to shake. She was in my head in the waking hours. It couldn't be love. Through her, I was reaching for my youth. A young mature woman would be fine if I could hang her in a closet and take her out when I needed her. In any case, I hadn't said: "I love you," and I wouldn't. Two nights later, at dinner in the Diplomat, I studied Betty as she nodded to the music and I felt my throat constrict to the point where each breath produced a whistle. I did not see the show then; I do not recall it now. I took her hand and whispered words which, to me, constitute a one-way contract, a grudging admission of helplessness, a lifetime pledge: "I love you." It was wrong, witless, but I meant the words with every ounce of substance within me. She smiled, patted my hand, and mouthed the soundless words: "I love you too."

I was furious. How dare she be casual? It was like the closing words on a vacation postcard; something said to a cute child. A waiter brought the check. Victor, the maitre d'hotel, said: "Mr. Bishop, the show has just started." I dragged Betty by the hand. In the lobby, I asked sarcastically if she said "I love you too" to all the men who took her out. In anger, my defense is sarcasm. Whatever I said in that lobby may have frightened her; it probably gave her a new look at the man. Her eyes were wide; her lips were apart; she kept shaking her head no.

The throat constriction disappeared. I had sold myself cheaply. An abused phrase is twice abused. If there was any conversation in the car, it is forgotten. At the door, the mood changed once more. I was the heel. What did I expect? Should she have burst into tears and buried her head on my chest? Or perhaps dropped to her knees and said: "Oh, thank you! Thank you!" I had lost perspective; I had copyrighted true love; I was the only person who understood its many levels down to the deepest darkness. I was hitting with ancient pejoratives; I described, with venom, some of her sexy wardrobe.

It isn't often that I go berserk; there is shame in losing control. When the monologue began to stutter in its cadence, she invited me upstairs for a cup of coffee. I sat in silence at a kitchen table. When she lifted her cup, she did it with two trembling hands. I said I was sorry. I apologized. Kindly, she said I ought to go north and think things out. Maybe, I suggested, it was she who needed to sort her thoughts. Stiffly, almost insolently, I repeated the phrase "I love you" as though I despised her. She looked at the cup. I told her I meant it and I was sorry I was messing her life up because she had done a pretty good job of it by herself. Silence. I said I had made up my mind that May would be a good time to get married because I had an overseas assignment and we could fly to Paris, and I kept prattling on and now she was looking at me gravely and I said I could be one heck of a father to Karen and Kathleen because look at all the practice I had and they would hate my guts at first because they would see me as the man who took Mommy away from Daddy, but never mind, I was better with little girls than with big ones and we could all live in that big old wreck of a house at Sea Bright and I would refuse any assignment unless my wife could come with me and she could teach me how to think age thirty-two instead of age fifty-three and I didn't want to rush her but she had thirty seconds to think about it and, either way, we'd be friends.

It went something like that. There was more to it but I ran out of breath. She got up, came around to my side of the table, and kissed me. "I loved you," she said, "before you thought of love." I said something like: What's your full name? "Elizabeth Jane Kelly Stone." I didn't like Betty because it sounded like the old Betty Boop movies; I didn't care for Liz; Jane sounded old hat. Would you mind, I said, if I call you Kelly? She shrugged. If it pleases you, she said.

The portable was packed and I was in Sea Bright the first week of April, 1961. There was a contract with the American Broadcasting Company to narrate the trial of Adolf Eichmann. This is another of the dizzying things in which the affluent author indulges; he scatters himself in air like a windblown weed. Some think they are senators; some run for mayor; a few aspire to professorships; alarmingly, a fair number see themselves as comedians or television personalities.

I was hooked. I would prefer to have been hooked to Kelly, but I reasoned that the trial could not last more than three days; a week at most. Every night the film of the trial was flown to Idlewild Airport. It was placed on a small TV screen and sent to a cellar on the west side of New

York, where I worked. Editors cut it to twenty-four minutes thirty seconds, leaving five and a half minutes for the merchandising of products. The film was shown to me once, at five P.M. The director placed me behind a desk, backed by shelves of fake books. When, in the gloom outside the blinding lights, he dropped his hand, the film began to roll and I told people what I thought they were seeing.

My New York audience was heavily Jewish. The prisoner had been a colonel in charge of the transportation of Jews from Germany to the concentration camps in the east. I opened by stating that the kidnapping of Eichmann in Buenos Aires was in itself a crime. It was also a violation of Argentine sovereignty by Israel. Properly, he could not be tried in Israel because Israel did not exist at the time of commission of the crimes. He should have been sent to Germany for judgment. Having dumped that on the audience, I ridiculed Dr. Servatius, the defense attorney, for not challenging the testimony of death-camp survivors who admitted that they had neither seen nor heard of Eichmann and could connect him to no crime.

One of the comic touches was that the court encased the prisoner in bulletproof glass so that his life might be spared for a proper hanging. I had no sympathy for Eichmann. He had worked for Himmler, and the testimony depicted him as a dapper officer who checked off millions of Jews in cattle cars and knew precisely when the empty cars would return to Munich, Berlin, Düsseldorf, Bremen, and Amsterdam. To him, it was a bookkeeping operation synchronized with railroad trains.

His attitude, from the day he was kidnapped in Buenos Aires, was that he was a dead man. At the trial, he sometimes protested that he was not heartless; some of his best friends were Jews. He not only wore a headset so that he could hear each witness, but was assiduous in holding the device close to his ear. The few days ended, but the trial did not. The prosecutor, Gideon Hausner, had enough evidence to convict his man, but the State of Israel needed Eichmann to resurrect the specter of genocide, and the film kept coming in to New York.

It went on for fourteen weeks at — for me — four hundred dollars a week. I could have spat. There were columns to write, books to research, and there I sat in a cinder-block cellar bleating my scriptless lines on camera, watching the lights dim and die, and seeing the Jerusalem film come up on a monitor. I kept talking, even though a sportscaster, Howard Cosell, threaded through the black cables to his desk, mumbling: "Good evening, Gentleman Jim." One night all the lights went out in New York and I was sure I would get a day off. The inventive producers at ABC had a truck with a noisy generator and I did the program standing in the gutter with a crowd of New Yorkers behind me.

No one agreed with me that the illegal kidnapping and killing of Adolf Eichmann was, in miniature, similar to the kidnapping and killing of 5,900,000 Jews. In spite of the candid character of the program, it won an

Emmy and an award from the Brooklyn chapter of Hadassah. Three months in a cellar generated two pieces of precious metal. It was not the compelling, florid story painted by ABC. The literate world was more interested in Major Yuri Gagarin, a Soviet soldier who became the first man to encircle the globe in a spacecraft. It also wanted to know more about the disastrous invasion of the Bay of Pigs by Cuban exiles. The world of now always takes precedence.

The word was out in Florida that Jim Bishop had "stolen" Ray Stone's wife. Denials have the impact of spitballs against army tanks, so I didn't bother.

In the North the flurry of indictments kept the phones warm. My sister, Adele, broke the news to my father. He shook his head sadly. "Betty Stone?" he said. "She'll kill him in six months." Kelly's brothers, Eugene and James, decided that their sister was a big girl and should know what she was doing. Her younger sister, Janet, was the only person who applauded. She said that marrying Jim Bishop was a great idea. My sister-in-law, Anna, said: "You know what you're doing. What do you care what people say?" A girlfriend whom I respected stopped by to see me. "I heard the rumors," she said. "If you must get married, anybody but that Betty Stone. Anybody." I received some accusatory mail. We were hatless in a hailstorm.

Pignataro phoned to say that we could bring Gayle home for another weekend. The doctor said that Nelson had solid ideas about my daughter. He thought she was faking the marriage, that she was afraid to admit that it had been a childish mistake. The mild depression which followed was endurable, but the baby wasn't. The birth of Elinor seemed, to Gayle, to have sealed off all retreat. The doctors were trying to strengthen Gayle so that she could face her mistakes and make decisions.

On the way home, Gayle was her wisecracking, cynical self. She and Frank sat in the back seat. Kelly and I sat in front. I wondered if it would depress her to know about Kelly and me. In the rearview mirror, she appeared to be happy with Frank. He kept an arm around her shoulder and urged her not to go back to the sanatarium. This time he did not command. Frank told her how well the baby was doing, and he hoped they would have time to drive down to Cherry Hill. The mirror depicted the first crease of pain in Gayle's eyes. She would see, she said. The doctors told her to rest.

At home, when her mood was high, I asked if she thought I should remarry. She assumed one of her arch expressions. "Betty?" she said. She made a pleasant speech built around one of her favorite expressions: "To each his own." Sure, get married. I like Betty, if that's what you want to know. We can get along.

She slept in the basement room with Frank. By Monday morning, she was as depressed as ever. The next time she came home, the same thing happened. She was ebullient driving to Sea Bright, sad and almost speechless on the way back. I asked Dr. Nelson about it. He said not to worry; she would have to admit that certain people, certain situations, depressed her, and, when she did, she would correct them. One weekend she came home and disappeared to have a chat with Frank. When she came back upstairs, she was crying. "It's all over," she said. "It's all over. It's not his fault." She shrugged. "He's going to leave today. He wants his mother to take care of the baby, Dad. She's very good." The tears, I felt, were the first tangible remorse for monumental mistakes rather than sorrow for her losses.

The recovery was magical. The week she shed the responsibilities of wife and mother was the week she stopped taking tranquilizers. She confided in "Aunt" Flo and in Kelly; the best I could get in relayed information was when Kelly said: "Stop worrying about Gayle. She's her old self again." Perhaps.

The wedding day, Friday, May 19, was sunless and chilly. We departed early because the judge said ten A.M. and he would like to have us waiting in his chambers. We didn't do much talking on the way because there was so little left to discuss. Kelly and I had spent the late hours, night after night, discussing love and marriage, the children, the attitudes of our families, the chronic impingement my work would be to our life, the twenty-one-year age differential, and kindred trivia.

The wedding party was small. My sister, Adele, was Kelly's witness; Emil Herman was mine. Janet Hughes beaming; Jim Hughes solemn; Kay Herman laughing at the judge squirming into his black robes and missing an armhole. I stood beside Kelly, who held a pitifully small bouquet, and I clasped my hands before me. The judge had a book and, it seemed, he mumbled at speed and said: "With the power invested in me by the State of New York I pronounce you man and wife." He shook my hand and whirled away, with two aides dogtrotting behind him.

The bride was smiling, eyes glistening. I kissed her. "Missus Bishop," I said. She kissed me back. "My Jim." There was more sensitivity in those words than in the judge's oratorical race against the clock. Adele said: "I hope you both are happy forever." It was legal; it was permanent, but emotionally it didn't get off the ground at once.

We ran into trouble that night at the Stork Club.

Bill Hearst's mother was there, a courageous woman who took a beating in silence when her husband left her for Marion Davies. I sat with her for a few minutes and, without thinking, said I had been married that morning. Mrs. Hearst became excited; I begged her not to mention it, but she signaled for a fat lady to come over. This one was Louella Parsons, movie gossip columnist. I began to perspire as Mrs. Hearst gave Lolly the "scoop." I think Parsons was born with a small pad and pencil in one hand and a shot glass in the other.

I should have paid more attention to Lolly. Whether she was sober or not is unimportant; she wrote an item about a church wedding and referred to Kelly as a "widow." Why, God knows. There was nothing reprehensible in the truth.

There are degrees of happiness. No one could convince me that two humans could reach, and hang onto, a rung of bliss that is dizzying. It was also a form of serenity, but much more. Those hours are to be found only in cheap novels. I asked her to take care of the checkbook and deposits, and not to bother me with it. Also to plan dinners without consultation because I knew little about food beyond steak and potatoes. I would plan where we were going, when and why. She was at liberty to change the furniture, or not. We had one car, and it would have to do for a while. She shopped as I worked. I wrote a book called *The Murder Trial of Judge Peel.* I also hurried to New York and narrated thirty-nine episodes of World War II for television. Now and then, we invited Emil and Kay Herman or Bill Armstrong and Imelda to go boating in the evening. That, and three newspaper columns a week, kept me at top speed.

There was a reason for it. I wanted to drop all work toward the end of July, 1961, and take Kelly on that European honeymoon. First, though, we had to get passports, shots, plane tickets, hotel reservations, and, most important, we were ready to bring Karen and Kathleen to Sea Bright. This event was important. I had won a beautiful woman who had integrity, personality, intelligence — at times I thought God might be squaring things for miseries of the past — but the romance would crack if the little girls were alienated. At naptime, I wondered how Virginia Lee and Gayle would have accepted a new father. When Kelly and I talked about it, I insisted that there would be no problem. I would be me — cross, crotchety, indulgent, impossible — and they would see through the mask and learn to like me.

One afternoon I was on the floor playing with Rock of Shrewsbury. He was a ninety-five-pound German shepherd, dark except for a golden chest and golden feet. Rocky was the epitome of dignity, a nonpanicky, nonbarking dog, who played only to please me. I had a rubber ball which I kept switching from hand to hand behind my back. I wanted him to nuzzle the empty hand. Instead, he straightened, looked at the front door, and growled. I hurried to the window to look. There was a car in the driveway. Then two little girls were on the porch, huddled together, crying. I called Kelly. They're here, I said. Kelly hugged and kissed them and smiled and told them how she had missed them, and then she brought them inside. I saw the way their feet moved inch by slow inch and I knew that I would have to work hard — very hard — to be accepted.

She closed the door. Both saw the dog at the same time. The girls froze, and tried to back up a wall. I wasn't aware that they were afraid of dogs. Rocky pointed his ears up, cocked his head, and listened to the whimpering without moving. It was like an old Mary Pickford–Mabel Normand two-reeler. I said hello and walked out to the office. I couldn't stand the fear. They were eight and six, charming chattels in terror.

In the early days, they were trying to win my approval as I tried to win theirs. It didn't work. At the table, no matter what I said, they nodded gravely and said: "Yes, Uncle Jim." "No, Uncle Jim." At the same time, I permitted license to them that I would not allow my girls. When they were afraid to go upstairs to bed, and afraid to admit it, I went up with them and told stories. Sometimes they were foolish themes and Karen and Kathleen would laugh. I spent considerable time unraveling their obvious fears. Rocky, for example, not only wouldn't bite them but was overjoyed that he had two young people to play with. I put my hand in his mouth and coaxed them to do it. They laughed hysterically when the big teeth did not close down on their fists; he licked their fingers.

They confused acting with reality. Bad men on film scared them. I explained how movies are made, how the bad guy who just shot the lady probably had lunch with her when the director called a break in the shooting. This was difficult to accept. The story had to be told over and over. Both girls were nervous.

I needed time, a lot of time, but there was our European trip. I had contracted to write some stories on Berlin for the Hearst newspapers. Janet and Jim Hughes agreed to take care of the girls and the house.

Some trips are comedic. The captain of our 707 was a small man with the broadest mustache I have seen. He invited me to join him "later" on the flight deck. The Bishops played gin rummy. The clock was running close to an early dawn when Kelly fell asleep. I went to the flight deck and knocked. I knocked twice. Then I opened the door. The jet was averaging close to six hundred miles an hour across the Atlantic and the crew slept. The captain lay head back in his seat, eyes shut. The first officer slept leaning against a window to his right. The engineer slept on folded arms on a small ledge. I tiptoed out.

It was morning when we got into our second-floor room at the Crillon in Paris. The front window looked down on the spot where Marie Antoinette lost her head; the side window had a good view of the American Embassy and a sidelong glance at the lovely trees of the Champs-Elysées. Fatigue was deep. I slept until midafternoon. Softly, I phoned for coffee and toast and marmalade and the Paris *Tribune*. I tickled Kelly awake. One good tickle led to another. This was the first day of a honeymoon. Lovemaking, at times, can be tender and breathless and protracted — like dying in a bed of violets.

That was the situation when I heard a cough. The waiter, I learned, had his own key. He smiled tentatively and, in English, said: "Ah, yes," and then, "Bon jour." I was angry. Kelly yanked the bedclothes over her head. I asked him what was wrong with knocking. Nothing, he said. He assumed that if we wanted coffee and toast, we were prepared for coffee and toast. As a family man, he said, he wouldn't dream of interrupting . . . I had to find a pair of shorts before I could sign the check. "Get," I said.

We gaped; we visited; we bounced over cobbled stones in taxis; we dined at Maxim's; we had good seats at the Folies Bergère — we did all the things American tourists do, including being swindled in the shops. My joy was double; seeing all the places I had read about, and watching the wonder in my bride's eyes. I was learning to read her happiness in Braille. And yet, the purpose of the trip was business. We hurried on to Berlin to research stories about the masses of East Germans who were sneaking into Berlin.

The flight from Paris was short. I looked out the window at the summery forests, the crossroads villages, church spires, the big cities. This was a land soaked in blood. This was the soil over which the Germans and French had fought in three wars from 1870 until 1945. The Meuse, the Somme flowed as peacefully as the Rhine, as though none of them had been witness to the slaughter of handsome young men by the hundreds of thousands. Far below, I could see tides of boys crashing in waves against lovely hills, only to recede and gather a towering strength to crash again.

At Tempelhof I gawked because, in my curious mind, I could see the DC-4s, laden with coal and drugs and flour, coming in low and slow literally between windows of apartment houses to crack the Soviet blockade. No matter where we went, I saw something other than what was showing. Before we got to the hotel, I had to see the hill where Hitler's Reichskanzlei was buried. It was covered with millions of nodding daisies. The Adlon Hotel had been bombed to the ground. The servants' quarters were standing. At the Brandenberger Tor, there were black blast marks and pits on the gray colonnades. At the zoo, a jagged-toothed hippopotamus survived the bombing in spite of the fact that the curator and keepers tried to give the other animals and birds shelter. He snorted water and opened his mouth for chunks of grass.

We stayed at the Berlin Hilton on the Kurfürstendamm. The room was up high. We could see buildings which were still cavities, with saplings growing from the walls. There were hundreds of them. Off to our right the city was building a ski slope more than two hundred feet high with the broken stones and shattered bones they found when peace came. It seemed, somehow, fitting that young Germans would fly downward on immaculate, crunchy snow over what was left of their forebears.

I bent to the floor to open a suitcase and split my pants. It was partly an old herringbone suit and partly a new oversized behind. I said I would throw them out. There was a maid's truck in the corridor. It was laden with sheets, blankets, dust mops, towels. In front was a disposal bucket. I threw the trousers in there.

In the morning, they were resurrected with the breakfast. A waiter had them on his arm. They were pressed and the back had been mended. We discussed the thorough Germans. I said I didn't give a hoot how thorough they were; the pants had seen good days. Kelly was appalled when I threw them out the window and watched them flutter into an empty lot. We went out to visit the receiving centers where West Germans tried to separate East Germans hungering for democracy from East German spies. Our guide, a German who spoke English, gave us lots of material for notes. At six P.M. we were back in the room and so were the pants. I phoned the manager. How, I asked, does one throw something away in Berlin? He was patient. A clerk arrived. I gave him the pants. "*Kaput,*" I said, pointing. He examined the trousers and gave me the tolerant expression the sane reserve for the insane. He said "*Danke*" three times.

The key to the story I hunted was a dining room waiter. He was tall and thin and spoke English with an impediment. He had been a common soldier in the Ukraine. He said his father fought in World War I for the Kaiser, and had fought in World War II "*alʒo.*" The old man had a *Bierstube* in East Berlin. If I paid the old man, would he sneak across the border? Would he sneak? He would sneak with Momma too.

The "in-depth" interview took place in the waiter's apartment. It was, by nominal standards, poor. There was a mohair stuffed settee, a matching chair, a rickety coffee table, a wall lithograph called "Lovers before the Storm" and some weak see-through coffee. The waiter's wife wore what I surmise was her best frock. She was young, had more curves than the road to Moscow, and a friendly smile. I began to appreciate the waiter's speech impediment. Poppa epitomized a cartoonist's notion (Grosz?) of an old German. He was five feet tall, had no neck, and his skull had been shaved to the bone. All except Momma spoke passable English. Momma was a breathless frump in a tight corset. What I looked for was a psychological profile pointing up the reasons why the Germans enjoyed marching off to war.

Rarely, a story will fall apart in the author's hands. This was one. I spent part of the summer trying to nail it down, and the best I could do was to laugh. The old man fought in World War I and World War II because, as he stated, "You play the oom-pah moosic, we march to war." Momma hummed a few bars of "Deutschland über Alles," patting her knees. In Hitler's war, said the old man: "I killed *und* killed *und* killed." He was a Luftwaffe cook and he killed cockroaches. The son had seen service in the snows on the Eastern Front. In battle, he tried to climb the side of a tank to protect himself from the Russians, when, he said: "They shot the basin out. The whole basin."

This required translation. A shell fragment caught him in the buttocks and carried away part of his genitalia. Of course none of the family had joined the Nazi party. We ransacked Berlin for former members. Most of

WHY?

THE QUALITY OF FILIAL KISSES IS ELOQUENT. LITTLE
by little — no pushing, please — Karen and Kathleen came to love me. I suspected it when "Uncle Jim" expired, and "Daddy" came into being. They became my little girls as much as Ginny and Gayle were my big girls. They were such entrancing blonds that Kelly could have wrapped them in burlap and they would still be the cynosure of eyes in the neighborhood. We had long talks about books, God, behavior, money.

I told them stories which I felt were slightly beyond their comprehension, and made them reach high to understand. Two things worried me: one, both girls were timid. The second thing was that Kathleen had heard, many times, that Karen was beautiful; Kathy was pretty. This did little to alter Karen's sweet attitude, but it converted the little one into a climbing, clawing achiever.

In time Kathleen believed that she was as attractive as anyone. At the same time, she began to push hard for her place in the sun. It was good for her to assess her worth, but I wondered if, someday, she would be satisfied with a man she couldn't dominate. Karen, on the other hand, remained timid and retreating, in spite of my urging, until the seventh grade. Then, one afternoon in school she stood, eyes blazing, finger pointing, and shouted: "Mister Schrage! You are wrong in what you just said. If you would please look up the facts, Mister Schrage . . ." Kathleen, two classes away, heard the outburst. It was Karen's first "charge."

My father was at dinner with us, and Kathleen tried to speak. Her mother frowned, and said: "Kathleen, be quiet." Kathleen fell silent. A moment later, she murmured: "But, Grandpa . . ." and again she was ordered to shut up. The third time, braving Mother, she said: "Grandpa is eating with his teeth upside down." His upper plate, reversed, was chewing his gums.

There was a classy gent in Madrid whose work I admired. Samuel Bronston, a small dandy with gray hair and a Rumanian accent, produced motion pictures. He lived in a white jewel of a villa with a gorgeous wife and growing children. Sam was the kind of man who, in conversation, lifts lint from people's clothes. In May, 1962, he was completing a picture called *Fifty-five Days at Peking*. His production people had built an almost full-scale model of the Forbidden City on the plains near the university. Bronston wanted us to see it blown up in the final scene.

My interest was ambivalent. I was willing to witness the explosion, but I really wanted to see Del Valle de los Caídos. When Spain's bloody civil war of the late 1930s was over, Generalissimo Franco, repentant, no doubt, wanted to build a basilica inside a mountain. It would seat fifteen thousand persons and, in the walls, soldiers from both sides of the war would be buried nude, wearing only their dog tags. This indeed was the Valley of the Fallen.

We occupied a suite of rooms on the fifth floor of the Ritz Hotel. It was more Old World bouffant than skyscraperish and had been built by Alfonso XII to accommodate relatives and friends whose presence he couldn't stand in the palace. The ceilings were high, the lighting weak, the furniture antique, and the rugs of that thick embossed style favored by Spaniards who can afford it. Below, in front, was a café-garden, a hedged-in place with immaculate tables, a shaft of spring sunshine, an inoffensive breeze, classical Spanish guitar music, and some of the greatest cheeses and hams ever chased down the human throat with wine.

I said hello to Sam and his Dorothea and hurried off in a chauffeur-driven Cadillac to the Valley of the Fallen. It is a tribute to man's sinful nature that he is impelled to build magnificent structures to God. I had seen some in Westminster, Rome, Reims, Paris, Bangkok, Jerusalem, and New York. This structure was incredible. Franco's thousands of laborers reamed an enormous hole in a granite mountain whose peak jutted above a half-dozen others. Some of the workers died in rock slides; others were exterminated in dynamite explosions. Others grew old and quit.

The interior of the cathedral is fifteen feet longer than Saint Peter's basilica. The walls are severe slabs of gray stone, lightened with huge tapestries and recessed side altars. It is a long walk from the nave to the main altar. Once attained, the altar is simplistic to the point of being anticlimactic. There are three steps leading up to a solid horizontal slab of stone, perhaps thirty feet long. Behind it is a slender sapling, complete with bark, in the shape of a cross. On it is an ordinary statue of Christ. Franco's contribution was that he roamed the mountain searching for a suitable tree, cut it, and made the cross by whittling.

Outside the basilica is a granite plaza as big as an American football stadium. On top of the mountain is a stone cross over two hundred feet tall, across which a sports car could be driven. In the valley behind all of this is a monastery, which was then presided over by a bishop who had eyes for Kelly. His Excellency was a favorite of the fascist government. Each time he approached my wife to guide her to another part of the shrine, his breathing became noisy, almost a whinny. I advised Kelly to ask him to hear her confession. She stopped speaking to me.

If Spain at that time had not been fascist, if the generalissimo had not been seen as a merciless dictator, I am certain that the Valley of the Fallen would have been proclaimed as the ninth wonder of the world. We returned to the Ritz and, in one long night, I wrote a movie short about the cathedral. The plot was pedestrian. It involved a newly ordained priest who waits in his mountain village for orders to serve his first mass. The villagers, who remember him as a tree-climbing, window-breaking youngster, are embarrassed to address him as Father. In his room are photographs of two favorite uncles, men who fought on opposite sides of the civil war. A village girl, who saw the boy as special in her life, hides from him and weeps.

The order comes. He is to serve his first mass at Del Valle de los Caídos. The young priest and his parents are overwhelmed. The honor is beyond comprehension. Poppa borrows a wheezing car in which to make the long journey. At the mass, the camera picks up the sweep, the vastness of the basilica, the cold emptiness, and the congregation of two persons, his mother and father. To them goes his first blessing, his first consecration of the Host; he offers the mass for the souls of his uncles.

It was a poor effort, one designed to capture architectural beauty on color film. Sam Bronston loved it. He asked if I realized that he was a Jew working in an arch-Catholic country. I said it had crossed my mind. He wanted to pay. I told him that the idea wasn't worth a nickel and I wouldn't accept more. And yet, it cost Sam a lot. He had to move seven generator trucks up a mountain to furnish sufficient light for the interior. When it was completed, it was shown to Franco. In competition among the Spanish studios producing pictures in 1962, only Bronston was awarded the Order of Santa Isabella.

At the studio, we had met Ava Gardner and Charlton Heston and Sophia Loren and James Cagney. It was Cagney who touched something atavistic within me. He had retired from making movies, and was on a Mediterranean tour learning how to paint. A slender Russian with an indecipherable accent was teaching him how to mix pigments, how to think of perspective, how to make a landscape come alive.

We slapped each other with Irish stories and departed. Two days later, a studio press agent phoned. "Do you people have a favorite place to eat?" We had. It was a seedy restaurant in Madrid Antigua called Paco's. Why? He wouldn't tell us. A few judicious inquiries revealed the secret. The Bishops had an anniversary coming up and Cagney and his brothers wanted to treat us to dinner. Sam was upset that we chose a dive in a slum. The fop within him cried for elegance and sparkling chandeliers.

It was a memorable dinner. Paco's was at the foot of a cobbled hill. It sported a tattered awning. Inside was a workmen's bar where the bartender lined up a half-dozen glasses and poured *tinto* until it slopped over and ran off the ledge of the bar onto the sawdust floor. The workmen were noisy. Stale wine and an admixture of ammonia emerged from the men's room. To the left was a dark doorway. Inside were a half-dozen white porcelain tables and a wooden stairway.

There was no menu. Paco was a barrel-bellied man with little patience. He served sirloin steaks, potatoes, coffee, homemade bread, and ice cream. His daughter, a melancholy girl of marriageable age, was the waitress. Somewhere beyond the head of the rickety staircase, Momma was the cook. Two seven-passenger Cadillacs drew up, and the sight of them drove the gamins to shrieks and a touching of fenders.

Sam felt hurt. Dorothea, decked in diamonds, was curious. The Russian painter appeared to be relaxed. Cagney and his brothers (retired physicians from Los Angeles) looked the place over and said: Well, this is something. Paco, fatter in a soiled white apron, didn't ask what we wanted. He counted heads. He opened a walk-in freezer a few feet from our table, and began to hack the mold from a side of aged beef. His daughter served glasses of wine as Paco cut thick steaks laterally. The best anyone could say for the wine was that it was last year's.

The steaks went up to Momma. One by one she dropped them into a big cauldron of olive oil. In exactly three minutes, the meat was done. The outside looked like a gleaming black shoe. The interior was red and juicy. We ignored the potatoes. Sam chewed and murmured in awe: "This is the best steak I ever had. The very best." Cagney nodded. The painter laughed and wanted to know how such a memorable piece of meat could be found in a dump. Cagney proposed a toast to the Bishops and Sam stopped picking hairs from my jacket. Dorothea was in awe of the dinner.

Bronston had a conversation with the painter and gushed: 'You don't realize what a plashure it is to speak a beautiful langwidge for a change." Afterward, Paco scaled soup plates at us. Into each went more than a pint of homemade vanilla ice cream. On top he dropped a thousand of the tiniest strawberries to be found anywhere. Dorothea was beyond protesting when Paco passed out tablespoons. Kelly and I thanked Jimmy Cagney for the dinner. He thanked us for finding Paco's.

We returned to the Ritz and Kelly served drinks. At midnight, Santa Isabella Square, below, was drenched with colored lights. Roman candles arced into the night sky; pinwheels whizzed and fizzed; cannon boomed. It was the beginning of the festival of Santa Isabella. I lifted my cup of coffee to Cagney and said: "Jim, you shouldna done it." He shrugged. "Forget it, Jim," he said. "It was nothing."

Cagney, in his field, was what I might have been in mine. I was impressed. He was confident rather than cocky. He worked in Hollywood but was not part of it. He was not the greatest actor, but he was a singular troubadour, playing his own music all the way. He declined sums of money because he felt that the part offered was not in character for him. He did not spit on his profession; he honored it because, a long way back, he had made peace with himself and the fires were banked.

My admiration had nothing to do with our Irish heritage. In our conversations, he confided in me as though we had known each other forever. For a moment, we became instant chums. I wasn't sure of myself as a social animal. He was. Cagney sought no spotlight. At Paco's, at the hotel, he retreated against a wall when someone told a story. It wasn't necessary for that man to prove himself. I had to do it every day.

The city room is noisy at lockup time; the sound is akin to a nest of aggressive insects. The decibels move up and up; humanoids run rather than walk; the final double page of metal is squeezed against a yielding matrix; and sound stops. It is like the final minute of a busy day at the stock exchange. The silence is a form of exhaustion, a breasting of the tape at the end of a marathon; it occurs at most newspapers every day of their life.

This was October 15, 1963, the night Richard E. Berlin slit the throat of the *Daily Mirror* and sold the bones and suet to the *Daily News*. An editor, Selig Adler, held a sheet of copy in his fingers and showed it to Dave Kaufman, assistant makeup editor. "Hold page two for this story," he said casually. "It's a must." Kaufman studied it. "The Hearst Corporation," it read, "announced yesterday that it will cease publication of THE NEW YORK MIRROR with the issue of October 16, 1963. The name, goodwill and other intangible and physical assets of the Mirror have been sold to the NEW YORK NEWS."

City editor Lester Markel slouched behind the big double desk. Once he had been a copyboy hurried to accommodating action by the shouts of rewrite men. He rolled a pencil on a blotter. He had worked his way up to become boss of an empty room. Television crews moved cameras inside and angry reporters yelled: "Get out. What the hell are you doing here?" The news became authentic at exactly six P.M., the tides of incoming nightside reporters meeting the outgoing tide of dayside men and women. They had heard the rumors for months.

The death of a newspaper — any newspaper — humbles the men on living papers. The effect is like the distant and unexpected thunder of cannon and the tremor of earth underfoot. New York had sixteen flourishing newspapers in 1929. Unions were killing them one by one, until, in the latter part of the century, there would be three. None of them was a premeditated felony. As an early member of the Newspaper Guild Assembly, and a member of the Grievance Committee, I had fought for job security. We were also interested in a solid salary structure. The first big Guild strike was against the Brooklyn *Eagle*. The paper collapsed and died.

The lesson nobody wanted to learn was that no newspaper, no matter how profitable, could afford to deal with a strike threat from a different union every few months. Management faced the engravers across the negotiating table for long periods, then, barely rested, faced the printers and their threats to close the paper, then the deliverymen, the Newspaper Guild, the office workers, and so on. It was the printers who had shut the *Mirror* in April, 1963. Neither side assessed the danger of losing habit buyers, which applies to both subscribers and advertisers. A million readers who had been buying both the *News* and the *Mirror* found that they could survive with the *News*. Theaters and department stores, which had advertised in both newspapers, found that the volume of business remained steady with one newspaper. And so, even though the *Mirror* was publishing again, it was losing millions of dollars.

In late summer, the Hearst Corporation began secret negotiations with the *News* management. The *Mirror* was a second-rate competitor, but still a competitor. The *News* offered six million dollars for the Hearst Corporation to kill the *Mirror* and turn over its library of picture and clipping files to the *News*. Richard Berlin was aware that, of this amount, he would have to pay three and a half million dollars in severance pay to employees. This left a taxable profit of two million, five hundred thousand dollars, which is not much, but it stopped the bleeding.

Photographer Emil Herman was at home when the flash reached his television set. He was dying, slowly and doggedly, of cancer of the colon. Pete Barrecchia, assistant night city editor, was in London and read the story in the overseas edition of *The New York Times*. In the city room, somebody needled the silence, shouting: "Come on, you guys. We got a paper to put out." A teetotaler on the copy desk sent a copyboy out for a fifth of whiskey and drank himself into a stupor. Mort Ehrman, night editor, who had helped to put the *Mirror* to bed for forty years and three months, wandered around the room trying to memorize faces.

On the ground floor, the big presses began their high-speed roll. A sheaf of first editions went to the city room for replate corrections. The last paper was typical of all. The headline shrieked: "Family Sees Father Slain." Mrs. John F. Kennedy was resting in Algeria. The rumor in Washington was that Robert F. Kennedy would resign as attorney general in order to become campaign chairman for Jack's second term. The final offering covered fifty-six pages. Walter Winchell's gossip column was in its customary place on page 10. Some of the features — his included — would be picked up by the *Journal-American*. Others would go to the *News*.

The nightside men and women pounded typewriters and edited copy as though the paper would live forever. Jokingly, a rewrite man said to an editor: "And what will you do to me if I refuse the assignment?" By three A.M. they had fallen into whispering groups subconsciously honoring the dead. A little after three, the presses stopped. People who had never listened before heard the final pulse. It was a warm night out and some carried their jackets under their arms. This one time they shook hands with each other; a few scribbled phone numbers. The office loan shark waited in the hall for some who owed a little. The lobster-trick editor, who was paid to work until eight A.M., surveyed the big empty room, the splintered desks, the cold typewriters, the shreds of newspapers. He put his hat on, walked to the exit, took off the hat, and executed a deep bow. To save the final penny, he snapped the lights off.

There are three places around the New York area where the bluefish run well in late July. One is off Shrewsbury Rocks; a second is farther off the Jersey coast at a place called the Acid Bank; and the third is Fire Island inlet. On a handline, a four-pound blue can saw a man's fingers off. Kelly and I anchored the *Away We Go IV* off Fire Island inlet and chummed a three-knot incoming tide.

The boat swung gently in the rip and the fish fought in frenzies. The cabin had a tall refrigerator full of iced drinks and cold cuts. We also had a good stove and, if necessary, places to sleep six. On this day there were just two of us and some soft music. We lifted the hook and sailed for home early because we were tired of the fight. The sea carried a little white feather and it took us two hours to get to Sandy Hook.

By the time we docked, Flo Walter was telling me that the magazine, *Good Housekeeping*, had phoned. Kelly hosed the boat down as I called back. Would I write "A Day in the Life of President Kennedy"? This was a surprise. If *Life* or *Look* had asked the question, it would have been within each one's format. But *Good Housekeeping*? I saw it as a publication for women, replete with recipes, patterns, deodorants, and articles about what to do with your cheating husband, but Kennedy, the White House, the inner politics of an administration seemed out of character. I said I would do it only if the President allowed me the freedom to interview the ushers and maids as well as his staff. The editor chuckled. "No problem," he said; "I will have Pierre Salinger call you in the morning."

That was more forthright than what I had got from Salinger throughout the Jimmy Hoffa series. The jolly cynic was now the President's press secretary. If it was that easy to get him to call me, then the source of the article was Kennedy, not the editors of *Good Housekeeping*. The President had figured a way of using me. I had no way of deciphering what he had in mind. For example: Kennedy had Arthur Schlesinger, Jr., as author-in-residence. This, in itself, was unique because Mr. and Mrs. Kennedy had insisted that everyone who worked in the White House pledge not to write about the Kennedys or their work. Except Schlesinger.

Schlesinger had written a fine work, *The Age of Jackson*, and surely the President expected the author to keep detailed notes on Kennedy so that, after two terms, he would be the "approved" author of a definitive work. Such a book would not be in embryo next year (1964), when Kennedy would be up for reelection. Then too, anyone who understood John F. Kennedy's elaborate appreciation of history would expect that the one-time reporter would write his own book. Besides, he had a word-mole, Theodore Sorensen, in an adjacent office dreaming lofty and poetic phrases. This man, who spoke softly, almost liplessly, had a fine talent for putting excellent words in Kennedy's mouth. Why not Sorensen? The President, in fact, could almost pick the man to write a book, or a number of them to write several books. Most writers who were not hyperpolitical admired Kennedy the man.

Salinger called. He was flattering. I was pleased and worried. Why me? Larry Newman had suggested the idea to the President, and he had said yes. I told Salinger that, if I accepted, it would not be to write a book. *Good Housekeeping* had asked for an in-depth article, no more. Let's go for the article, and, if the research generates sufficient material for a book, we can talk about it later. Salinger agreed. I asked him to please relate the ground rules to the President: (1) I would have access to interviews anywhere in the White House; (2) I would have access to the President and Mrs. Kennedy for interviews at their pleasure; (3) I would be able to see and describe the family quarters; (4) when the manuscript was complete, I would send the original to the editors, a readable carbon copy to the President. He would be permitted — nay, urged — to draw to my attention errors of fact. Pierre Salinger said he would get back to me.

He did. The President agreed. Mrs. Kennedy would be out of the White House for the summer. She had lost a newborn child and would recuperate on a yacht in the Greek Isles. In that event, I said, call me when she gets home. The talk was not that abrupt. It was polite, but I wanted the President to understand that I wanted more than a portrait of a young man in office. To a few in the White House, and to some of the magazine editors, it seemed as though I was purposefully stubborn. This was untrue. I had been broke and depressed, humiliated by writing next to a fitful oil burner. It would not fade — nor would Barney Finn and the personal loan companies. I felt that I knew what kind of story I could write best, and the President didn't.

The summer of 1963 was spent finishing *Honeymoon Diary*, an ugly, gauche, tasteless work. In August, I started writing the Rosenberg spy book, and, in a month, had thirty thousand words on paper. It was poorly organized. The research had been so detailed that I found myself telling the story of the origin of the atom bomb, with anecdotes about Dr. Enrico Fermi and Dr. Niels Bohr, without touching on the characters of Julius and Ethel Rosenberg. I was writing a compendium of atomic discoveries, misadventures, the Manhattan Project, and war. None of it could be salvaged, so it went into the wastebasket.

I was writing the opening chapter when Salinger phoned. He said that President Kennedy and his family would be ready the week of October 20. Kelly and I were at the West Gate at nine A.M. I am not easily awestruck, but I am close to speechless when I see the Executive Mansion. To me, the flag is America. So is the Statue of Liberty, Niagara Falls, a Norman Rockwell drawing, the majesty of the Rocky Mountains, a baseball, the Lincoln Memorial. Collectively, they do not choke my breath as quickly and as chronically as the sight of the White House. On occasion, James Rowley, who was chief of the Secret Service, asked why I walked the corridors on tiptoe. "Maybe," I said, "I think I'm in church."

My newspaper colleagues had a small office inside the West Wing door, a warren bursting with phones and typewriters. They lounged in a big reception hall built around a cracked Indian treaty table and leather couches. At eleven A.M. they would get a press briefing from Pierre Salinger on what the "White House" had been doing in the past twenty-four hours, would do today, or was thinking of doing. Some of these conferences led to acrimonious remarks from the seventy or eighty faces in the room, and sometimes Salinger cut interrogation with a snappish "No comment." There was a daily race to the available phones and then the sitting and waiting, watching distinguished visitors go in, and interviewing them on the way out. It was a Society of Mutual Suspicion, but no man could suggest a way of improving it.

They were eager to know why I was there. I played it down. It's just a magazine article, I said. An assistant press secretary, Malcolm Kilduff, waved us inside. He was short and dark with a grain of gray; an intense man whose do-it-and-be-damned attitude reminded me of Robert F. Kennedy. He had what old-time editors call "savvy," and he walked quickly, a pace ahead, foot and head. He said the President was waiting for us. The Oval Office is enclosed by a curving corridor. There are two main doors. Both are manned by Secret Service agents. As we approached, a tall agent knocked twice and turned the knob. Light and regality seem to flood the room, although both are subdued.

The President was on his feet, a marvel of fashion in brown suit, striped silk tie, and gleaming brown shoes, as he stood and strode around the desk to meet us at the door. It was a vision of a youngish man with square teeth against a background of french windows, small navy paintings on the walls, a pale gray elliptical rug embossed with the seal of the President of the United States, two facing sofas near a fireplace, and a rocker with an antimacasscar which stated: "U.S.S. *Kittyhawk*." He stuck his hand out and called "Jim" as cordially as though this was a reunion. He said "Kelly" before I could introduce her and waved us to chairs beside his desk.

The problem with John Kennedy was that one never knew how much of the warmth was real; he was as effusive with reactionary critics. Some of it was blarney. I didn't want to waste his time and assumed that I would spend a few minutes explaining the material I would need and how I proposed to get it. He interrupted to say that someone told him my people came from County Wexford. Ten feet behind his desk was a table. He called me to it to display a richly bound leather book, a memento with photographs of his visit to Ireland. I noticed that the desk he used was smaller, less ornate, than that used by Eisenhower.

Mrs. Kennedy had selected it. Tucked away in Washington there is a warehouse of White House furnishings, paintings, ornaments, and rugs,

[381]

some dating back to Thomas Jefferson. His wife had ransacked the warehouse and, with a discerning eye for history, had redecorated the mansion. She conferred frequently with the White House architect and with chief usher Bernard West. In the manner of most women, she did not want to move into "furnished rooms," no matter how richly and well the work had been done. She wanted it to be a "Jackie" mansion and had spent a lot of government money buying whatever could not be found in the warehouse.

She'd be around when I was ready, the President said. He said it twice. He spoke of his arthritic spine because I mentioned mine. Steroid injections helped reduce the pain, but he said he was conscious of it all the time. He wore a kidney-shaped brace over his underwear; it kept him from bending forward to ease muscle aches. He spoke of his vertebraical fusion surgery and I got the impression that he was sorry he had had it done.

We agreed that Pierre Salinger should arrange all interviews and, if the President was busy when he was supposed to see me, I should "shoot around" him. I had a preliminary list with me, including Kenneth O'Donnell, David Powers, Salinger, Lawrence O'Brien, Bernard West, Evelyn Lincoln (his secretary), the wire service reporters, the White House chef, the President's valet, Mrs. Kennedy, her assistant Nancy Tuckerman, the chief of the White House Secret Service detail, Ted Sorensen, the President's physician, Mrs. Kennedy's maid Providencia Paredes, and certain advisers who wrote bills in the White House to be presented to the House Speaker.

The President turned the rich smile on my wife. "Kelly," he said, "he ought to get a book out of this — don't you think?" No, sir, I said. My assignment was for a magazine article. "Stretch it a little and you'll have a book," he said. Then, jokingly: "Kelly, you speak to him." He stood. We shook hands and we went to Salinger's office in the West Wing. I was surprised to learn that Kelly had scribbled useful notes in the Oval Office. She wasn't trying to duplicate my work; she had a hunch that she would see things I would not; as I would copy the President's exact words and she would not. It turned out to be a bright piece of work — she noted everything on the President's desk, including photos; she had copied the framed appointment schedule — who and at what time. She also wrote precise descriptions of the drapes, the furniture, and the view of the South Lawn. I urged her to bring pen and pad wherever we went.

The article would, I was certain, be bright and superficial and entertaining. It would not be difficult to chisel a portrait of this young man. The difficulty would be akin to yanking a loose thread from a garment — to stop pulling before a sleeve fell off. The story could become grim. The Federal Bureau of Investigation had tracked a pretty German spy to Savannah in the summer of 1960. They bugged her bed. The noises on the mattress one night indicated that they were made by the Democratic nominee for President. He was attracted to women as a diabetic is to sweets.

To the Kennedy boys, sex was touch football. Winning was all. The

[382]

President's Secret Service driver was sometimes frightened when Kennedy left a well-guarded hotel by the fire escape for an hour's dalliance somewhere in town. The driver told me that, when they sneaked back to the hotel suite, they hadn't been missed. The President seldom carried money; he claimed it marred the drape of his clothing. He borrowed from the Secret Service driver, who kept a book and sometimes dunned the President to get his money back.

The President should have been aware that some of the government departments and bureaus refused to cooperate with each other. James Rowley, head of the United States Secret Service, tried hard to work with J. Edgar Hoover's Federal Bureau of Investigation because some of their work overlapped. Weeks before Kennedy made a trip — to New York, let us say — the Secret Service files turned up all the names of persons in that area who might be dangerous to the life of the President. A copy of the list went to the FBI but a comparable list seldom came back. Hoover insisted that the FBI work alone. He would not share with Rowley, or the Central Intelligence Agency, or military intelligence, his file of psychotics, dangerous aliens, writers of anonymous threats. Frequently, all of them declined to warn any of the others.

Publicly, the President spoke glowingly of J. Edgar Hoover, who had become the haughty, insulated patriot. No one in government dared to bell the old cat. In the office of the attorney general, Robert F. Kennedy drew laughter from his staff when he looked up at a crystal chandelier and shouted: "You bugging, Hoover? Well, listen to this, you old son of a bitch. . . ." The rasp of personalities between those two went out of control when Hoover had an article written about the Valachi papers. It was penned by his third in command, Cartha DeLoache, and taken to the attorney general for an initialed okay. This was pro forma.

Three weeks later, Hoover, who dreaded the threat of confrontation with peers and superiors, sent DeLoache to Robert Kennedy to ask what happened to the Valachi article. The attorney general said he had been too busy to study it. Two months later, the article appeared in *The Saturday Evening Post* under the name of Robert F. Kennedy. There was always a question of whether the Kennedys would permit cooperation from outsiders. They courted subservience, and they trusted none but their own. The clan consisted of the family, boyhood friends, a few educators and writers, and a host of gofers. It was, as Jacqueline Kennedy phrased it, "us" against "them"; the few against the world.

For a few years, George Thomas was an "us." He was the President's Black valet. In a room on the third floor of the White House, he pressed presidential suits tirelessly. Mr. Thomas was one of the few who knew that the President changed his clothing from the skin out four, sometimes five, times a day. There was a lavatory in the Oval Office. Between presidential appointments, Mr. Thomas hurried in and hung a fresh suit of clothing and underwear. Between the next two appointments, Mr. Kennedy would disappear in a brown suit and emerge with a blue one, complete with matching tie, shoes, and fresh shirt. The temperature in Thomas's room was not ideal, and perspiration rivuleted down his chubby cheeks as he guided his hot iron up and down shirts and suits. I asked how he felt about it. He had an engaging smile. "I ain't complaining," he said. He was an "us."

One of the things I recalled from the Eisenhower assignment was attending the National Presbyterian Church with the President and Mrs. Eisenhower. It was not Ike's hymn-singing, which was pleasantly off-key. It was the fact that the entire church had been "sanitized" on Saturday night; the Secret Service had looked for bombs, explosives of any kind; had held Geiger counters to the radiators and the boiler in the furnace room; and, when they were through, told the pastor that the church was off limits to him and everybody else until Eisenhower's arrival.

It was a siege posture and it carried over into the Kennedy administration. Every morning at seven, the President's desk telephones were disassembled. The Secret Service looked for so-called wireless taps. These, as small as a fingernail, can rebroadcast sounds up to one half-mile. If such a bug was in the President's phone, or anywhere in the office, spies could, theoretically, drive a small panel truck around and around the White House all day taping every confidential word. Even the President's gold watch was Geiger-countered every day for high-dosage radiation. The head of the White House Secret Service detail, Gerald Behn, said that an enemy agent working inside the mansion could drill a pin-sized hole in the watch, stick a bit of fissionable uranium in it, and, in a few weeks, the President would become ill.

In some of the interviews with Kennedy, he gave the impression that being President is not the regal position — imperial, perhaps — seen by the rest of the world. He is inhibited in several ways. He can see anybody he chooses "off the record," but the appointments secretary maintains an "off the record" calendar too. To a young, vivacious man who prided himself on the number of "old buddies" he had, the precise cadence of government, the restrictions of formalities, functions, position papers, options, decisions, and politics, kept him from a lot of glorious reunions. He used a toothache as an example, a poor one as it developed because it had no relationship to friendship.

A filling fell out of a decayed tooth. Air touched the nerve. The pain was severe. The President lifted the phone and told Mrs. Lincoln to have a car ready. He was going to his dentist. Gerald Behn heard the news at his office in the East Wing. He phoned the President to explain that he could not visit the dentist at once; the office would have to be "sanitized." Kennedy became irritated. Behn said he would make arrangements right away. A car with five agents hurried out the West Gate and through the streets of Washington to the office of the dentist.

Two men got out and scanned pedestrians, and rooftops on the opposite side of the street. Three went upstairs and, gravely and politely, asked patients in the waiting room to leave. Some didn't want to go. The Secret Service flashed identification and said: "You must. The President needs this office." Some, in pain, were not interested in the President's distress. When the office was cleared, the Secret Service examined the startled dentist and his nurse. The instruments were frisked for radiation.

A signal was flashed to the White House. Kennedy, holding a hand to his jaw, was hurried into a limousine on the South Lawn. A similar car led the way. A third one followed. The dentist, hands shaking, mashed a temporary silver filling into the President's tooth, as the tall, silent men watched. Once or twice, Kennedy said, he left the White House in such a hurry that he almost lost his bag man. This anonymous individual carries the briefcase with its dials for broadcasting to the White House Situation Room and the Pentagon what type of response the President wishes to make to a surprise attack by a foreign power. He can dial anything from an all-out intercontinental ballistic missile retaliation down to a regimental team landing on foreign shores.

If, in the evening, he left the family quarters to pick up a forgotten paper on his office desk, he was watched. Buzzers rang in offices occupied and empty, notifying all concerned that the President was taking the elevator to the main floor. Kennedy appreciated what was done for him. He aged a bit when he stopped smiling and he said he had read my book about Lincoln and he agreed with the sixteenth Chief Executive: "They can't protect you. They do their best, but let me tell you, Jim, if there is someone out there in a high position — you know, where he can look down — nobody can help you." Did he dwell on assassination? Not anymore. When he first assumed the office, it was on his mind much of the time because he was conscious of the protection everywhere. When he became acclimated, it no longer bothered him.

As the days lengthened and the notes grew longer, the President kept asking if I had seen Mrs. Kennedy yet. I said no. The third time he asked that, I felt that Mrs. Kennedy did not want to see me, and that her husband had made an issue of it with her. I made an appointment for late morning. It was a clear gusty day, one which spun leaves into toy tepees. Kelly and I joined her on the second floor in the corridor. Her manner was cordial and folksy. Her son, John-John, was in a nearby room being bathed by his British nanny. Up close, I got the impression of a small body and a huge head. At the time, Mrs. Kennedy wore short skirts, even though her legs were slightly bowed. The big brown eyes were as bright as neon signs. She was willing to listen to my questions, and to respond, but she addressed herself to Kelly. I told the First Lady that I needed a word portrait of the evenings, a closeup of the family in their private quarters.

The smile was fixed, unalterable, but what I wanted was what Jackie did not want to give. Dave Powers and the President had already filled in part of the nighttime story, but Mrs. Kennedy said something about the

President and his "homework" — a briefcase with must-read state papers — and how little they socialized. She told me about a school that she and some Georgetown friends had established in the solarium on the third floor. Caroline and children of comparable age stood at attention two by two in the center hall of the White House every morning at eight-forty-five. The women contributed equally to the salary of the teacher and the pads and pencils. It was an exclusive school; there was no desegregation.

The interview began to stutter. John-John ran out of the bathroom nude. He carried a small American flag on a staff and watched it whip. His mother covered her mouth with her hand and shouted: "John-John. You come back here. Shame on you." The little body glistened with wetness and grace as he made a U-turn and ran back to his room, where Maude waited on her knees with a bath towel. The talk switched to politics. The uniqueness of what Mrs. Kennedy said washed over me without notice. She was about to campaign with her husband. She did not like politics, or politicians. However, there was a bitter dispute among Democrats in Texas, and this time she would be at her husband's side. "Parades and all?" I said, joking. "Parades and chicken banquets," she said. "Texans have outdoor barbecues, don't they?" She showed us through the family quarters.

A little later, Kelly and I were comparing notes on the South Lawn when Mrs. Kennedy and the children came through the Diplomatic Reception Foyer. It was difficult to look at that family, or any part of it, without bursting into applause. Caroline was sweetly feminine, careful of her dress. Mrs. Kennedy, attired for a fall day, sat on a seesaw and chatted with Kelly. John-John, handsome in a white suit, ran headlong into a mound of raked leaves and came out of it stained and damp. The women looked at each other and said: "Boys." We talked trivia for a few minutes and they were gone. Later in the day the President asked twice how the interview had gone. "Did you see Jackie? Was it okay?" It was.

At other times, Kennedy pressed for a book. This became so frequent that I had to ask myself if, indeed, I had sufficient notes for a slender volume. I worked harder getting anecdotes from Powers, waiters, ushers, and what could be wrenched from Kenny O'Donnell, Larry O'Brien, Kilduff, and Sorensen. It was the President who filled in the night hours. A bit of old-fashioned Boston peeked through his habits. He sat on the same cushion of the same settee every night. He lit a big cigar and poured a cold beer. Then, somewhere in the maze of reading and penned annotations, he would ask Mrs. Kennedy to play the same music: a recording of *Camelot*. He was in a pleasant rut: same cigar, same beer, same music, same cushion.

The last interview was with him in the Oval Office. I said I was sure I had enough for a small book. I proposed to fly to Aruba and begin to write it at once. Kelly and I would be alone and, except for a little friendly crapshooting in the hotel casino, I'd be working. The notes were in chronological order, so the task would go quickly. He sat in the *Kitty-hawk* rocker. A photographer was admitted and, as the flashbulbs went off, he seemed irritated. I said that a carbon of the manuscript would go to him as soon as the work was complete. He would have the right to correct any error — in fact, I would appreciate the help — but if any observations of mine hurt him, he should feel free to make a note in the margin of his objection. If I agreed, it would be changed, as I had once changed a description of Francis Cardinal Spellman which he found offensive: "He is a round dumpling of a man, and, in his flaming red robes, he looks like an Easter egg." If I did not agree, my words would stand.

For a reason beyond my divination, he was eager for the little book. "How long will it take? If it gets here before Jackie and I leave for Texas, I'll take it with me and get it back to you." We shook hands and I said: "Next year you come up for reelection and the American people have a habit of giving you guys a second chance."

He laughed. "We'll see," he said. "We'll see."

We were back in Florida on November 20. The book was finished, all thirty-nine thousand words of it. A copy went to *Good Housekeeping*, where the editors were free to publish as little or as much as pleased them. Another went to Random House. What the book did was what it promised to do — give readers an opportunity to see a President up close, at work and with his family. It had no other pretensions and it followed the charter and architecture of other such works. Salinger phoned to say that a carbon had been received, and that President Kennedy had it with him on the trip.

We stayed at the Diplomat Hotel and I played golf with the press agent, Don Cuddy. He was a big fellow, fat and perceptive. We did well together on the golf course because we never counted lost balls or whistling shots which caromed around tennis courts or flipped into lakes. You like Florida? he said. Why don't you move down? I told him I had an old house in Sea Bright and I appreciated every busted beam in it. He said that a developer named Layne had dredged some land on the opposite side of the boulevard and was calling it Golden Isles. There were custom-made houses to be looked at. I declined. After nine holes and lunch, he said he was sure Kelly would like to look.

Don Cuddy is not a real estate salesman. Kelly said she would like to look, but not to buy. Shopping of any kind has never been a joy to me. In the affluent years, I purchased suits of clothing in groups of three, knowing before I entered a store that I wanted one navy blue, one gray, and perhaps a houndstooth-checked jacket with black slacks. I was afflicted with a mild shoe fetish and managed to buy styles which were going out of fashion. Shirts were white on white, a half-dozen, with holes for a gold collar pin. People who saw me frequently assumed that I never bought anything because the finery was always one of three or four assortments. If I don't need merchandise, the notion of stalking windows and racks on foot is reprehensible to me.

The salesman, a leathery-looking diplomat named Leon Yeuell, showed us three houses. They were lovely, new, and empty. I asked my wife if she liked one more than the others. Yes, she said, if she were in the market for a house, it would be the Chinese house with the tiled roof, curved driveway, palm trees and poinsettias, and a big swimming pool behind it. "Sold," I said to Mr. Yeuell. Kelly choked. "Nobody buys a house in ten minutes," she said. I do. A check was written, papers signed, Kelly staggered as though about to faint, and we had a fine fifty-two-thousand-dollar home for less than that. Mr. Yeuell said that we could arrange a mortgage. I wanted one without a punitive provision for prepayment.

Deep down, I knew that Kelly was fascinated with the Gold Coast of Florida. Also, deep down, I knew she saw the house in Sea Bright as Elinor's — though it wasn't. I had worked in and around New York for thirty-five years. Editors rarely care where writers live. Do the best you can; honor the deadlines; be in touch. Besides, jet travel from Miami was two and a half hours to New York. One more thing: sunshine has a therapeutic effect on arthritis, and I wanted to fight mine. It was getting worse. Some mornings, I could lift the head off the pillow, but not the rest of the body. Typically, pain diminished with mobility. I was fifty-six; for two hours each morning I shuffled about bent over like Groucho Marx. I found myself running from doctor to doctor looking for palliatives.

Still, Kelly was almost in tears. It's crazy, she said. In the morning, she wanted to go back to take a longer look at the Chinese house, the terrazzo floors, the elegant marble baths, the pool, the central air conditioning which would cool the premises in summer and warm them in winter. Happiness won. She was thrilled. She walked from room to room, index finger on lips, dreaming of drapes and furniture and a frilly room for Karen and Kathleen. It had three bedrooms and a large garage. We thought that cars are lucky to live in Florida, where they do not need a garage. We would seal it, put two round Oriental windows in the facing, and convert it to an office for me with typewriter, phone, and bookshelves from floor to ceiling.

The *Away We Go III* was docked in Florida. On the twenty-second, we got aboard for a leisurely cruise around the bays and inlets at Fort Lauderdale. We cast off at noon, slow speed, and turned the radio on at the flying bridge. The music was sweet, the sun sparkled on the Intercoastal Waterway, and we sat together dreaming of a dream house. We need fuel, I said. There was a gasoline dock at Fort Lauderdale and, as we turned toward it, the music stopped. There was a gabble of voices, no words. It was a good long-range set; I assumed that we were sailing close to a powerful station which was interfering. The only intelligence Kelly deciphered was a man shouting: "A priest just went into Trauma One."

She went to the bow, tossing a spring line to the boy on the dock. "You hear it?" he said. "The President's shot." I swung the stern in close and idled both engines. He moored the boat. "Where did you hear that?" I shouted down. He shrugged. "Turn your radio up." The best I could get was excited voices. There wasn't a coherent phrase. Kelly came back up. "Kennedy?" she whispered. "Shot?" I shook my head. "Ridiculous," I said. "Maybe a cowboy pegged a shot at him and missed." We listened. Whoever was doing the commentary seemed out of breath. He spoke disjointedly about a parade in Dallas, three shots fired, and said the presidential limousine had taken off at high speed for Parkland Memorial Hospital. "That doesn't mean that he's shot." I said. "Even so, it could probably be a flesh wound." Softly, she reminded me that we had heard about a priest. Who would a priest see? Who would need a priest? The President or his wife. Nobody else. We knew William Greer, the President's driver, but we didn't know his faith — if any. Bill was a gray-haired veteran. I remembered, vaguely, that the Kennedys had spent the night at Fort Worth. Greer would insist on using the bubble-top. Perhaps someone in Lyndon Johnson's car had been hit.

Sometime around one-thirty P.M. or shortly afterward, we heard the bulletin: "President Kennedy is dead. He has been shot by an assassin in Dallas. We are waiting for word when Lyndon Johnson will take the oath of office." It was the longest, most wretched day of the century. The nation spent the next several days staring at television in grief, guilt, and foreboding as Lee Harvey Oswald was shot and John F. Kennedy was buried. To me, it appeared that America had lost its innocence, its spirit of fair play, in one instant. We were not the men in the white hats any longer. We were as vicious as ignorant jungle tribes. It was not the act of Lee Harvey Oswald which altered my thinking. It was the symbol of what he had pulled off so neatly. He had slain, not greatness, because John F. Kennedy didn't have it; he killed confidence and trust; he scarred a national conscience; he proved that anybody can do it if he has a gun and he's a "little higher up."

The early months of 1964 were frustrating. Random House wanted to publish *A Day in the Life of President Kennedy* quickly, before the dark circles of remembrance faded from the eyes of America. Pierre Salinger insisted that Jackie Kennedy wanted to make a few corrections, but couldn't bring herself to read the book. The old house at Sea Bright was a maze of packing crates and sugar barrels. Ginny's father-in-law, David Frechette, secretary of the Teamsters in Miami, saved us thousands of dollars buying rugs and furniture and patio screening. He also arranged for two vacationing Teamsters from New Jersey to drive a truck to Florida with, coincidentally, our furniture in it. He owed me nothing; we seldom saw each other, but Frechette was a big man inside and out. I was impressed because, after the Hoffa series had been published, Attorney

General Robert Kennedy's investigators found that Frechette was my daughter's father-in-law. They badgered him for years and ransacked his office and Teamster books. Finding nothing, they red-lined David Frechette's income tax return (mine too) and audited both every year.

Saying good-bye to Floranna Walter, my long-time secretary, was a heart-wrench because she had been a loyal friend and assistant. Her boys were grown; her husband wanted to retire from government service; the crazy Bishops were her last hearty laugh. As she left, I pecked a farewell kiss and she said: "You better get a second van for the files. Remember, you insisted on keeping carbons of everything." She pointed to tall rows of filing cabinets. "The bank doesn't have this many." My old man studied them briefly and smiled. "Jim has a philosophy," he said. "Anything that's worth doing is worth overdoing."

Jack Paar phoned. He sounded excited; he was stuttering. When will the book be published? In a few weeks. I want you to come on my program and tell us what President Kennedy was really like. The millions who watched television seemed, at that time, to have an overweening curiosity about what public figures were really like. Millions were trying to find out what Paar was really like. And Milton Berle; Lyndon Johnson; Marilyn Monroe; J. Edgar Hoover; God knows who else. The people had become addicted to reading the "inside" story about the famous in the gossip columns of Walter Winchell, Dorothy Kilgallen, Hy Gardner, Louis Sobol, Ed Sullivan, Danton Walker, and the penny-dreadful press, and they wanted "revealations." Few believed that Paar, one of the most popular figures in television, was exactly the same as he appeared to be on camera — as nervous and emotional as the high-school girl who has not been asked to the prom.

To his invitation, I said no. The book wasn't worth it. It was what it pretended to be, but, had I known that Kennedy was about to become an international martyr, I would have started earlier and researched his background, his political decisions, good and bad, and most especially, his defeat in the Cuban missile crisis, which was proclaimed by editors and commentators as a victory. The price of getting the ICBMs out of Cuba was a solemn agreement not to invade Cuba. The President had his triumphs as well as defeats and, above all, he had been a youth-oriented charmer. In contrast, Dwight D. Eisenhower seemed old and sedentary. And yet, nothing Kennedy said or did assured him as solid a place in history as his assassination.

Paar said I owed him the appearance on his program. This was true. I was not one of his "regulars," but close to it. The twenty-five or so guest shots had helped the syndicated columns and the books. He said: "I have five thousand for you." I declined the money. I reminded him that he had been good enough to take me on when I had nothing to promote; this time I would do a favor for him and accept no fee. He refused. "The money isn't mine," he said. "It's in the network budget. This time it is I who need you; everybody wants to know what Kennedy was really like, and you can tell us. The money goes with it whether you want it or not."

The show was on a Friday. The first edition of the book was in the bookshops, but the release was three weeks off. Paar asked a lot of questions; I supplied candid responses. The studio audience seemed to have stopped breathing. When I recited the anecdote about the President's feelings about assassinations, I thought Jack would burst into tears. We talked on and on until I was empty of information. Three days later, *A Day in the Life of President Kennedy* became a best-seller and achieved a place on *The New York Times* best-seller list even though it had not been published. For the first time, I realized the power, the impact, of television. It could assure success for the unworthy; it could insure failure for the worthy by ignoring it. The first royalty check on the book was for one hundred and nine thousand dollars, a tribute, not to the writer, but to Jack Paar and his hundred and forty television stations.

We were in Florida arranging furniture when the first six copies arrived. I asked Kelly if it wouldn't be proper to inscribe one to old Joe and Rose Kennedy and hand-deliver it to Palm Beach. "It's a happy portrait," she said. "It might take their minds off that everlasting funeral." We drove up. Rose Kennedy was a small, perky bird with enormous faith in God and her church. She was the matriarch of a successful Irish family which could sustain successively cruel blows. No group of tragedies could beat this woman to submission, nor cause her to lower her standard of cheerfulness. When Jack was killed, she walked along the beach at Hyannisport, alone. This gave her time to think.

The Kennedys have a Spanish tile mansion on the beach. A stout cook peeled onions and sliced vegetables in the big kitchen. The drawing room was big, with beamed ceilings and artfully arranged clusters of furniture. On the piano and end tables were silver-framed photos of family members, queens and kings and princes. Joseph Kennedy, who was called "Ambassador" by his friends, had sustained a stroke. He sat silently in a wing chair with a nurse in white standing behind him. He was in gray plaid shorts and a sports shirt, the skin as tan as a turkey. The hands, clawed inward, reposed on his thighs. Rose sat a few feet away as straight as a cadet, even though she was too small to sit back in the chair.

I told her that, at the moment, I wasn't sure that what I was doing was right. "Oh yes," she said brightly, "it's right. We've heard about the book and we've been told it's an interesting portrait of the President."

It wasn't Jack anymore. It was "the President." The Ambassador looked up trying to form a word. The face wrinkled in frowns; the eyes seemed helpless. We waited for whatever word it was, running from the will of the brain down the shorted neurological wires to the tongue. At last it came: "Hello!" and it sounded like a cough. The cover of the book showed the President and his wife in their Easter finery leaving a Palm Beach church after mass. The children, both in white, pirouetted in front of their parents.

I was afraid the Ambassador would not be able to hold the book, so I took a chance and set it on one of his bare thighs. His head fell. He studied the rich color, the young family he knew so well, and suddenly I wished I were dead. He was crying. There was no sound. The tears were splatting on the cover.

Kelly said: "Will the family be coming down?" Rose stood. "Oh, yes. Teddy and Joan and Jackie; Bobby if he can get away — here, let me show you the house." They were covering Joe's embarrassment. And mine. We followed Rose on a tour. She was a mass of small bones, tremendous energy. As she described pieces, her hands made little flirtatious motions. At a window on the far south of the building, she pointed to a swimming pool. The water was a bluish cast; the borders were stippled white. She said, simply: "They all grew up there." The pool was as flat as a tin of chilled gelatin. In my mind's eye I could see them, healthy rowdy boys and girls, screaming, jumping, pushing, laughing. Three of those boys would be marked for violent death; one pretty girl would never be able to care for herself. The Ambassador, young and merciless, sitting on a deck chair planning, plotting, not only to exonerate the Boston Irish of being looked upon as immigrant scum, but to hunt, hound, and drive the Pilgrim Yankees from the public sphere. And that prim and proper lady, the rigid spine of the clan, drumming the fear of God into all of them, pretending always to worry more about the dinner menu than the morals of her men.

I hoped to depart on a light note. The Ambassador's knee was bare of book; the tears had dried. I bowed to him. He tried to say "Thanks"; it sounded like "thanks" but it had a woof to it. At the door, I apologized to Rose. "You did the right thing," she said. "That book is going on my night table right now. The Ambassador will want someone to read it to him." Joking, I said that when her son John discussed his trip to Ireland, I had noticed that the concomitant publicity was built around the Kennedy side of the family. There was nothing about her family — the Fitzgeralds. Like a mother warning of an impending spanking, she had said: according to her son: "Yes, and I mean to *talk* to the President about that."

Kelly and I are not addicted to gambling, for one reason. We lose. Not once have we gone to a casino, a racetrack, a dog track, or jai alai games without first debating, in the bedroom, how much we could afford to drop. And yet we relished the atmosphere of gaming. We were enticed by plush casinos, by beautiful tracks, by the sporting crowd. Sometimes we sailed our new Hatteras cabin cruiser to Grand Bahama Island. There, we trolled for big game fish all day, and shot craps part of the night. I wrote columns about it and called them "Fish and Chips." I was afflicted with one kind of luck, hard. At the Lucayan Beach casino, I was chatting with a pit boss before playing. Kelly had been clocking the roulette table and said that the color red had come up six times in a row.

Without breaking the dialogue, I handed her a five-dollar chip. "Put it on black." I was kidding the pit boss because Louis Chesler, who had the Bahamian license for casino gambling, had promised that all the croupiers would be imported from the south of France. They weren't. All the hard, dead faces I saw were out of Las Vegas. They were behind wheels, card tables, and rakes and the nearest they had been to France was buying dirty postcards. Kelly came back. Red had come up again. I gave her ten dollars in chips. "Put it on the black," I said. The pit boss asked what the hell difference it made where they came from; if they were honest, the management wouldn't need pit bosses to watch them, not counting the gnome upstairs who spied through a one-way mirror and camera-taped all the card deals and the payoffs. Kelly said red came up again. "Here," I said, "put fifty on it. How many times for the red?" Eight, she said. "Make it a hundred," I said. It kept coming up red. This was the first time I lost my allowance without ever getting to the table. I wonder if it is possible that Kelly — no, she wouldn't.

We went to Hialeah racetrack. Whoever designed it must have also worked on the Taj Mahal. The avenue of royal palms, the regality of the clubhouse, the aviary, the walls of ivy, the infield lake, the flights of pink flamingos, the august names on the season boxes combined to make Hialeah one of the most beautiful courses in the world. As we turned toward the clubhouse elevator, a uniformed attendant stopped me. "Mr. Bishop," he said, "Tommy Roberts would like you to be his guest today." I looked at Kelly. She shrugged. I looked back at the walking circle. A man with a microphone in his hand was waving to me. One of my many problems is that I was born without warning signals. No red light ever flashes.

Roberts, dark and handsome, was an ambitious kid out of Camden, New Jersey. He had been a radio commentator, a so-called disc jockey; he bought a radio station; he had announced stakes races at Monmouth Park in New Jersey. We had met a few times, and I had shared a microphone with him at a few tracks. So I walked toward him with Kelly, unaware that I was about to hang myself with no rope. Usually, there is time to discuss what we are about to discuss. On this day, a red light was on a camera standing high on a crane. He was on the air.

"This," he was saying, "is a most important day here at beautiful Hialeah. As you know, this is the running of the Seminole Handicap. And — surprise! — as my guest I have that well-known sportsman-author, Mr. Jim Bishop." Turning to me: "Jim, how are you?" I wanted to say sick, but I lied. I wanted to say that I didn't even know that this was Seminole Day. In addition, I didn't know that Mr. Roberts was on a coast-to-coast network. I had not seen a program, and hadn't the remotest idea of what I was about to talk about. "Well," he said kindly, "I see your new book is doing well." Tommy didn't know the name of it, and, at the moment, neither did I.

"Jim, as one of the country's better-known sportsmen, who do you like?" If a man's normal bet is two, two, and two, and that makes him a tout, then I was one of America's finest. I could see Kelly leaning on the rail. Her mouth was hanging open because she could hear the question and realized her husband didn't know the answer. I tried hard to unscramble my senses.

"Tommy," I said, shaking my head, "I must say I don't like the favorite."

"What," he said, "you don't like Admiral Vic?" I now knew the name of one horse in the race. "No, I don't."

"May I ask why?"

"Tommy, this is not precisely his kind of track."

"Jeez, Jim, you know I respect your opinion, but look at the board. The ten horse is going off at one to two, a prohibitive price."

"Tommy, I can only give you my best thinking."

"Okay, who do you like?"

I would like to have been home, that's who I liked. "I think the outsider stands a chance."

"What outsider?"

Now, why did Roberts have to ask it that way? "The far outsider."

Tommy scowled at his program. "Top Gallant?"

I nodded.

"Jim, he said, "that colt is going off at fifty-seven to one."

I was becoming belligerent. "I can't help it, Tommy. I just happen to like Top Gallant." Who the heck was Top Gallant? What was Top Gallant? A few more nonsensical words, and we parted. At the elevator, Kelly said: "You might have the decency to put a few dollars on that horse." I went the limit: four dollars to win and two to place. Admiral Vic and Top Gallant finished in a dead heat, paying fifty-seven to one. Six weeks later, the owner of the track, Eugene Mori, sent a big plaque to my home. It states:

> Presented to Jim Bishop
> in recognition of his extraordinary prowess
> as a horse racing handicapper
> at HIALEAH
> Without benefit of even the Official Track
> Program, Mr. Bishop selected the 57–1
> shot, Top Gallant, for a national television
> audience in the Seminole Handicap, February
> 8th, 1964. Top Gallant finished in a dead-heat
> with Admiral Vic for first.

A few days after the race, I got a phone call from Eddie Mulholland, managing editor of the Boston *Record American*. He was a horse degenerate. "I need advice," he said. "Who do you like in the fourth at Santa Anita?" As politely, as evenly as I could, I explained to Eddie that I had never been to Santa Anita and didn't even know they were running. There was a long sigh. "We run your column, my boy. It isn't always that good. I heard your Hialeah broadcast. I am desperate for a winner in the fourth, Jim, and I don't want any more shit from you. You got ... inside ... information."

Except for moments of low comedy, our new home was a dream. Gayle took some money from her trust fund and bought an apartment nearby. Within the entrance to Golden Isles there was a Catholic church and school — Saint Matthew's. The pastor was a tough old bird who turned the air conditioning off in his curates' rooms when they left the rectory to call on the sick. The teachers were exiled Cuban nuns who were remarkable for two virtues: they could not speak English and couldn't teach Spanish. Linguistically, they were caught in a crack in the sidewalk. Karen and Kathleen were happy in their pale blue uniforms. They despised their saddle shoes but couldn't wear them out. The great gift I had for them was a swimming pool which drank twenty-five thousand gallons of water. They seldom used it. Too late, I understood that growing girls would rather walk a half-mile to a public beach and display their ravishing broomstick figures to growing boys.

Kelly and I enjoyed an ecstasy within those walls. It was the scented dream of a drug addict. We knew that house in Braille. It was ours in far more ways than the economic. The garage-cum-library was isolated for work. The girls' room was lacy, airy, bright, and, inch by literate inch, I was making readers of them. Never would I permit myself — or Kelly — to be in the position of ordering them to read or requesting them to crack a book. The trick was to select one of the four thousand in the library gaited for their ages and tastes, and then tell part of the story at dinner. At an exciting point agreed upon by their mother, I would leave them high and dry. They would become exasperated, asking me to complete the plot. With a sigh, I would arise, fetch the book, and drop it before them. "Read it yourself." It worked.

A nursery lady arrived, and we asked about Florida plantings. What kind? How many? How about shade trees? Flowering shrubs? We created four Oriental gardens within the big patio around the pool. Our plants not only flourished and flowered, they came close to strangling the house. The weather is subtropical at twenty-three degrees north, which implies sudden and violent showers followed by sudden and violent sunshine. The root structures of trees and shrubs do not reach downward for water; they barely hide under the surface and stretch laterally into unlikely places. A native told us: "After a few months, you won't see the palm trees anymore." This was not true. We saw royal blue skies, billowing vanilla clouds, melodramatic sunsets in which the burnt orange and shafts of pink were overdone, a bright moon to read by, and violent thunderstorms which tore palm fronds and scaled them on the wind.

Hallandale had a population of ninety-five hundred and was situated about halfway between Miami and Fort Lauderdale. In midcentury it was run by gangsters. They operated out of a restaurant called the Colony. They were not interested in Hallandale, except as a haven from Dade County police. They were across the line in Broward, and they organized and operated most of the illegal casinos and floating crap games in Miami Beach and Miami. After the war, Harold Conrad, a fellow reporter from New York, got a job with them as press agent. It is difficult to imagine an assortment of hoods paying a press agent, but the don had a chat with Harold and said he could earn a good salary keeping the gangsters out of the newspapers. Conrad sat around the Colony for a few days and said: "The first thing you ought to do is to tell those dopes to stop running to your table to kiss your ring. That tips everybody off who the head man is."

It was a town where, if a citizen wanted a favor from City Hall, he could buy three of the five council votes at two hundred a head. DWI (driving while intoxicated) was as costly. It came to six hundred: two hundred for the policeman making the pinch, two hundred for the officer in charge of the watch, two hundred for the chief. Not all officials could be bought; some were honest mavericks who hurt the game by doing favors free. When illegal gambling tapered off in Miami Beach, the hoodlums departed, but they left one happy man. Just one.

I cannot mention his name because I promised. Driving south to our new home, I stopped to say hello to editors who used my work. It's an inexpensive gesture and it implies gratitude. In one town in a southern state, I paused for lunch and to say hello to the local publisher. He was a big man in his town. He was not only a voice; he was *the* voice. We had lunch. He asked if I was published in the Miami *Herald*. I nodded. You'll love it, he said. Jack Knight and Lee Hills took a weak and shoddy newspaper and built it into one of the richest, most powerful papers in this country. I ought to know; I was the dumb reporter there.

As he discoursed, I sniffed a story I wouldn't be able to use. He wore one of those mobile faces which not only emit sounds, but reflect what he is thinking. The weakness of the Miami *Herald*, he said, was that it was afflicted in those days with pedantic editors with provincial heads. They cared not a fig that an army bomber crashed into the Empire State Building. Or that Harry Truman beat Thomas E. Dewey. They saw themselves as judges who thundered opinions on the editorial pages and who were not above sneering about "outside influences" if an innovator suggested that a great big newspaper ought to seek news from the great big world outside Miami. My publisher friend said that the editors pandered to a large Jewish and Spanish community.

In any case, the editors didn't like my friend. They banished him to Hallandale and ordered him to phone if anything ever happened in the little town. It was a punishment assignment and he should have quit. He stayed on, and soon found himself in the Colony Restaurant brooding over coffee. He had a nodding acquaintance with most of the *capos*, except that he thought they were dealers in olive oil. Now and then, more to assure the city desk that he had not expired, he would phone in a couple of paragraphs. Sometimes, the man on the desk would insult him, calling the man a "dumb reporter."

A year later, at Christmas, two hoodlums spotted him on Federal Highway and whisked him to the restaurant. There, in a back office, a Latin type sat behind a desk nodding agreeably. "Everybody likes you," he said. "You a good reporter, you know?" My friend asked what he had done. "Nuttin. Nuttin. That's exactly it. You done nuttin and everybody's happy. So we brung you a present." He presented my friend with a beautiful alligator briefcase. "It's from the boys," he said. "A little appreciation for all the stories you dint write." My friend said thanks, took the briefcase, and walked down the street to a phone booth. He looked in the case. There, in neat stacks, was twenty-five thousand dollars. He phoned the city desk. "What you got this time?" a voice said.

"Just a question. If a man gives a reporter a Christmas present, should he keep it?"

"Depends, dummy," the voice said. "If he slanted a story, or wrote something to help that person when he shouldn't have, it's a bribe and a disgrace to a great profession."

"Suppose he didn't do anything at all?"

"Then keep the gift. What am I running — a school of ethics?"

My friend hung up. He quit. He took his old car and headed through the southern states until he found a lazy newspaper with a workable Hoe press. He bought it for twenty-five thousand. Today he's the big boy in his little town. And, as he admits, he was a kind of dumb reporter at that.

The days before Christmas, 1963, cast long bleak shadows. Mrs. John F. Kennedy had declined to change the bloodstained dress of Dallas. She wanted "them to see what they had done." On the plane coming home she seemed small, helpless. "They" were probably all of us. The lady's bitterness was understandably deep and bold. The martyrdom was not exclusively the President's. He did not hear the third shot; he was beyond recollection and remembrance. The dread fear, the shattering, never-ending instant, were hers. And when grief, which is as impossible to sustain as ecstasy, paled to moody meditation, Mrs. Kennedy would be transmuted to an iron lady. Call it imperious will, call it venom, call it vengeance, Jacqueline Kennedy found it childishly easy to divide her world into "us and them." Anyone who failed to volunteer to become an "us" automatically became a "them."

Timidly, I asked Pierre Salinger if Mrs. Kennedy might like to read the manuscript of *A Day in the Life of President Kennedy*. Timidly, because I felt certain that she would not want to read anything that would resurrect the bright spirits of happier days; timidly, because she might call it cruel and tasteless of me to ask her to read it; timidly, because the carbon found in the President's briefcase had been read halfway through, judging by the inverted pages; timidly, because I had no agreement with Mrs. Kennedy to read anything. Salinger phoned to say that Mrs. Kennedy would get around to reading it as soon as she felt up to it. She would appreciate it if I would delay publication until she had the time and the disposition.

Before Christmas, I sent a copy of the preface to Salinger, and told him that I had spoken to his secretary, Chris Camp, about writing a book to be called *The Day Kennedy Was Shot*. Editorial instinct warned me that there would be a dozen or more books written about the assassination. The reconstruction of that day was in my métier, even though I had vowed to stop writing such books. This time, it hardly mattered whether my book was first or ninth, so long as I could recreate that day, minute by minute, from the time the President shaved in a green-tiled bathroom in the Fort Worth Hotel to the time, close to four A.M., when Mrs. Kennedy, in the East Room of the White House, ordered the casket to be opened so that she could snip a bit of hair from her husband's head. I reminded Salinger that books about the tragedy "will be done whether we wish it or not."

This drew no response. I wrote a letter to Attorney General Robert F. Kennedy, outlining in detail the book which had just been completed with the President's cooperation, and outlining the assassination book. The new President, Lyndon Johnson, had appointed the Warren Commission with subpoena powers to accept depositions and to interrogate witnesses to the tragedy. Several writers, according to *Editor and Publisher*, were already in Dallas. I reminded Robert Kennedy (knowing he had a long memory) that he and I were not friends, but: "I do not think it lies within your power to stop these people — even if you feel so inclined — but it certainly does lie within your power to slow the sensational writers by having Mrs. Kennedy select a writer with whom the family is willing to work. The writer, of course, does not have to be me; it can be anyone in whom the family reposes confidence."

Later I learned that those two sentences created considerable excitement at Hickory Hill, the home of the attorney general. Bobby and Jackie and others of the clan were moved to find a worthy author. They agreed at once that it would not be Jim Bishop. I was seen as a brassy Irishman, one who stubbornly insisted on doing things his way. Bobby didn't like that one all the way back to the Hoffa series. Jackie despised him on several levels: "He wants to know what you have for breakfast and what you wear to bed; you should read some of the third-rate clichés."

In spite of a good literacy level, they could not come up with a well-known author whom they might trust. Someone brought up the name of William Manchester, a Connecticut writer who had once interviewed Jack for a piece to be published in *Holiday* magazine. At the interview, the President and the author discovered that they had fought in the same theaters of the Pacific war, even though they had not met. The President insisted that Manchester stay beyond the appointed time to discuss their experiences. The final family vote was "The President liked Manchester; let's get in touch with him." The President had been cordial to me, too, but it counted for nothing. Manchester turned out to be a fine, sensitive writer who seemed to have been waiting in the wings to be asked to write *The Death of a President.* Sensitivity is not among the traits admired by Kennedys. In retrospect, it is just to concede that they selected the right man for the glowing, gladiatorial type of tragedy they had in mind. Jackie wanted poetry and incense, and William Manchester may have been the only author in the country, with the exception of Robert Frost, who could have pleased her.

No Kennedy told me that I had been eliminated. In late February, Senator Edward Kennedy sent a personal thank-you for the newly minted book on his brother. Bobby also thanked me, with a degree of circumlocution.

One of my now-and-then fans was Janet Auchincloss, Jackie's mother. On the first day of spring, 1964, she thanked me for a copy of the book. Although it made her very sad, she wrote, she felt that over the years it would be interesting to see what a day in a President's life was like.

Baseball and forsythia arrived at the same time that year and the Kennedys announced that William Manchester would write the "authorized" assassination. I congratulated Jackie on selecting a writer, and told her that I was sorry that I had not survived family scrutiny. "Your action has reduced the field to one family-endorsed book," I wrote. "One hundred years from now, that is the one historians are going to have to study." It would be deceitful, I thought, if I gave her the impression that I had dropped the notion of writing about the assassination. "Even though my book will carry no such endorsement, I do hope that you and other members of the family will permit interviews by me," et cetera, et cetera. This infuriated the lady. Kenneth O'Donnell, who had been one of John F. Kennedy's Boston Bully Boys in the White House, was a good pipeline for information. Jackie, he said, was very angry because I had not dropped my book. He said she had some sort of contract with Manchester which would siphon a large part of his royalties, such monies to go to the building of a John F. Kennedy Memorial Library.

And yet the Kennedy correspondence rolled on and on. In June, Jackie wrote a letter thanking me for a newspaper column I wrote about the Kennedy Library. The Library was the cause closest to her heart, and she appreciated my thoughtfulness in telling people how much it had meant to her late husband. It didn't surprise me to learn that Jack, in office only about a thousand days, had planned a literary monument to himself. His predecessors had home-town libraries full of state as well as personal documents. With the exception of Franklin D. Roosevelt, I think that Jack Kennedy had a keener appreciation of history, and the nuances of history as it affected him, than any other Chief Executive. Kennedy, for the sake of history, altered the admonition of an old headmaster: "Ask not what your school can do for you, ask what you can do for your school," and made of it a patriotic cry for the nation.

There was an element of deceit and fakery in the Kennedy correspondence. The sweet words soured. I felt that I was being jollied to inactivity. They wanted their boy to get a good head start. If this were so, Jackie and Bobby would goad Manchester to the limits of endurance with threats. Their book contract was negotiated with Harper, in fact with Evan Thomas, my longtime editor. Thomas was a tall, dark, forward-leaning man with an innate elegance and a flair for editorial daring. The Manchester-Kennedy contract placed me — or Thomas — in an awkward position. I had taken *A Day in the Life of President Kennedy* away from Harper because Evan said he saw it as a magazine article rather than a book. It had been edited by Robert Loomis at Random House. I told Thomas he'd be sorry, but, in any case, I was leaving Harper for one book and, like Douglas MacArthur, I would return. Earlier, Harper had published John Kennedy's *Profiles in Courage* and I felt that Jackie and Bobby would return to the same publishing house in order to make money for the memorial library.

Thomas, it seems, was caught in an ethical puzzlement. He could hardly publish two competitive books on the same event. He could not ignore a steady bread-and-butter author such as I was, and he dared not turn away from the tear-streaked face of the martyr's widow. Neither Thomas nor Manchester was in a position for hard negotiations with the Kennedys about a contract. The Kennedys knew that they could take their business to any publishing house, and to almost any nonfiction author in America, and be greeted with hosannahs. In the summer of 1964, *the book* was touted in the press as a precisely orchestrated act of patriotism.

The former First Family had a truckling respect for the Catholic priesthood. Getting close to God was so important that most of the Kennedys cultivated a ranking priest, Richard Cardinal Cushing. He was a big, lean, hardworking prelate, who, at least once a year, donned an apron and knelt to wash the feet of the poor. My wife and I knew him. Why not write to Cushing and find out if the Kennedys, while assisting Manchester, would block Bishop's efforts? All I had to do was to tell His Eminence that I was writing a book about the assassination and would, in time, visit him for an interview about the President. I knew he would phone Hyannisport to clear it.

On July 24, I got a reply.

The cardinal said he had contacted the Kennedy family. He regretted to tell me that the Kennedys had engaged a writer by the name of Manchester to write the authorized version of the tragedy. He said he was sorry that he could not obtain permission for me to write a similar work. Cushing's inquiry aroused the Kennedys. He had been a "fan" of my work and he may have innocently put in a strong bid for me before the family had an opportunity to tell him that Jackie did not entertain the thought of Jim Bishop's writing anything about the assassination.

Her irritation with me dated back to the time when I told the President that I could not write a portrait of him unless it involved his family life in the White House as well as his work in the Oval Office. This explains why, on several occasions, he asked, "Have you seen Jackie yet? Have you interviewed her in the family rooms?" She had been gracious to Kelly and to me, but it was obvious that she would not forget that I had used the President to force the issue. I could hear doors being slammed in Washington, Dallas, Boston, and New York.

The first man I interviewed — President Kennedy's valet — had been cordial when I spoke to him at the White House. Now he just shook his head. "I'm sorry," he mumbled. "I cannot tell you anything, Mr. Bishop." He was not an important figure, and I knew if they had already silenced him, I could expect mute stares the rest of the way. Other authors were writing books about the tragedy — some of them superficial and trashy — but no one apparently barred the door to them. The first of the legion of "conspiracy" books was already in the works in England.

When Bobby Kennedy learned that I had signed a contract with Bennett Cerf at Random House to write *The Day Kennedy Was Shot*, the attorney general ordered an assistant to find out the particulars. This Kennedy had a flair for going a step too far. He phoned Joe Fox at Random and demanded to know why Random would publish a Bishop book on the assassination when Manchester had the concurrence of the whole Kennedy family. Fox reported this to Random partner Bernstein. Bernstein related it to Bennett Cerf. In August, 1964, the publisher wrote a letter to the attorney general. In it he tried to convince Bobby that, while it was good for the Kennedys to endorse the work of one author, other books would be written about the assassination. Cerf tempered his anger in the face of Kennedy power and "urged" the attorney general to broaden the cooperation to include a successful and respected person such as Jim Bishop.

Of course I had no notion that Cerf had written such a letter until he sent a carbon copy. More doors, if possible, were being slammed. Cerf tried to soften Bobby toward my work by reminding him that I had been the first to popularize books based on the minuscule events of a single day. The thing that truly angered Cerf was not mentioned in the letter. He told me that Kennedy was using the letterhead of the attorney general of the United States in asking people not to speak to me. Bennett couldn't countenance the truth that the Kennedys were almost equally fervent in trying to get one book published while suppressing another.

To compound the confusion, *A Day in the Life of President Kennedy* was on the best-seller lists. At the same time, I met Cardinal Cushing and he told me that William Manchester had stopped by for an interview and told the cardinal that he had already seen the Warren Commission report, even though it had not been published. President Lyndon Johnson had pushed and shoved the commission to hurry its work to a conclusion. A national election was imminent. The President knew that the torrent of evidence pointed to Lee Harvey Oswald as the sole assassin, and he wanted all twenty-four volumes of testimony in the public domain before ballots were cast. The national bleeding had not stopped. It was incomprehensible to millions of citizens that a handsome young President could be shot to death by a lone misfit, a rejected defector to the Soviet Union. Few were prepared to believe that a man who didn't even know the parade would pass the building where he worked until the day before it happened could crouch in an upper window with a $24.50 Italian rifle whose sights were four degrees off true and, in three shots, blow one-third of the president's skull off.

I refused to quit. I tested two more closed doors. One was the Federal Bureau of Investigation, which nominally was under the control of the attorney general. Cartha DeLoache was the perennial number three man at the FBI. It was he, rather than J. Edgar Hoover and Clyde Tolson, who directed the day-to-day activities of the bureau. The FBI was a monastery, and "Deke" DeLoache was its abbot. He was the coolest man under stress I had ever seen. He had opened doors for me in earlier research — would he slam it this time? The phone call from Sea Bright was tense on my end.

He pretended not to know that the attorney general — his attorney general — was feverishly opposed to any assistance for me. I leveled with him. Deke listened and said: "When you're ready to go to Dallas, see me first." That was it; that was all. A huge door was wide open. In time, the extensive body of reports would be open to me; the special agent in charge at Dallas, Gordon Shanklin, and his agents would help me with a minute-by-minute reconstruction of what happened on November 22, 1963; eight inspectors of the FBI, each with his sectional report of the work of his department, would sit at FBI headquarters with Kelly and me, giving almost endlessly of the assassination investigation.

There was a second door, a possible door. The key was held by James J. Rowley, chief of the United States Secret Service. He was a short, unassuming smiler. Years earlier, he had read *The Day Lincoln Was Shot* and was profoundly impressed by the fifty or so assorted acts, which, if they had not occurred in direct sequence, would have spared the President's life. At that time, Rowley was chief of the White House detail of the Secret Service. He ordered his agents to read the book.

Rowley, in time, had been promoted to chief. It was his custom, after hours, to drive to the White House and park at the back of a row of automobiles, sitting alone in the dusk, watching. When I had business at the White House, I sometimes saw him there and asked why. "No reason," he would say. "Just looking at the faces going in and out." His chronic worry was that someday he might lose a President. Inside the White House, the head of the detail was Gerald Behn. He didn't appreciate his chief's worrying inside the gate.

Weeks before the trip to Dallas, the Secret Service and the FBI had sifted the files for lists of men and women who might be dangerous to President Kennedy. DeLoache and Rowley had exchanged information. Had they been beside Kennedy in the limousine, they could not have saved his life. Rowley had worked for several Presidents. At the end of his career, he lost one. Those who loved Kennedy could hardly have suffered more than the chief of the Secret Service. It was with this knowledge that I phoned to ask about a door. "Jim," he said softly, "a number of our personnel appeared before the Warren Commission. Of course their testimony will be made public in the report. When you finish the testimony, any questions you wish to raise can be handled in my office."

A second door was open. A big one. I told Jim that a White House secretary told me that President Lyndon Johnson had expressed appreciation of some things I had writtten. I was no longer in a mood to race Manchester to a publication date. Speaker of the House John McCormack had told me that Johnson would, in time, become the most productive President the United States ever had. If Johnson was receptive, I could do a book on him. I had been told that he was a big boisterous Texan, an earthy man who had pledged himself to enact into law the noble program devised by Kennedy.

Rowley said he would ask the President's press secretary, George Reedy. A few days later, Jim phoned to say, "The President says he'll be glad to see you. Call Reedy for an appointment." I began to feel optimistic about the assassination book. Johnson could reopen a lot of closed doors. As far as publication was concerned, I might come in tenth or twentieth, but I felt that I had the tools with which to reassemble that day in Dallas minute by minute.

On September 17, 1964, I received a handwritten note from Jacqueline Kennedy. The first page was partly smudged. She asked me not to write the book. The subject was distressing to her. The whole year had been a struggle. Sometimes, when she took her children to a news shop, there was a picture of Lee Harvey Oswald staring from a wall. As I read, I had an image of a grieving widow trying to explain to two little ones why their daddy had not returned from Texas.

She seemed to dread the Warren Commission report, which was still pending, and she would try not to read the newspapers. Mrs. Kennedy knew that the Manchester book was public knowledge, and she had to think of a reason why that one should be published while mine was stopped. The letter began to limp a bit. She hired Manchester to protect the President and the truth. If, she said, she decided that the book should not be published, Manchester would be reimbursed for his time. On the other hand, she might permit it to be published at a future time, when the agony of that day was not so fresh.

I had the proper reaction; I felt like an arrogant heel. Then, I felt, Mrs. Kennedy made a mistake. She said that all those who had talked with

Manchester had been requested not to discuss the assassination with anyone else. So, she added, that left nothing for an author like me except the Warren report. The letter closed pleasantly, reminding me that I had once been sensitive to her feelings.

In writing a letter like that, Jackie proved that it was important, for some reason, to stop me. She didn't address other writers who were trying to unravel the minutiae of that day in Dallas. Why me? I sat with her letter in my hand wondering why, if she wanted a so-called official version of the tragedy, she hadn't asked Arthur Schlesinger, Jr. He had served as Kennedy's historian-in-residence. But then, the question echoed its proper response. The balding, bow-tied Schlesinger could not be controlled. Then too, he might be disinclined to write it. His primary interest centered around the politics of politics. To him, perhaps, the shooting merely closed the Kennedy book. He was hardly the man to permit the First Lady to tell him what could be published and what could not, and when it might be screened by friends of the President, and how much of the royalties would go toward the building of a Kennedy library.

Her White House was the first to exact a promise from employees and intimate friends not to write books about their experiences with the Kennedys. Whatever material came from the White House was to be given to Arthur Schlesinger, Jr. Everybody promised; in time, most everybody wrote a book, including the British nanny who took care of the children. Less than a month after Mrs. Kennedy's letter arrived, Bantam Books clipped, pasted, and hammered together the first book on the assassination. Pierre Salinger and Sander Vanocur had another on *The Times* best-seller list the last week of September. Putnam mailed an announcement that they had the American rights to a British best-seller entitled *Who Killed Kennedy?* This was the first of the mystery books.

The Warren Commission report was a joy and a disappointment. I paid for two sets because, in clipping and annotating, a writer often uses both sides of a page. It was a joy because the commission, and especially the bright team of attorneys who worked for it, did a handsome job of locating and questioning every available witness. The material was rich, but the makeup was inexcusable. If the President had not badgered the commission to complete its work and publish its findings within ten months of the assassination, the exhibits might have been published chronologically. Instead, many of the events of the afternoon (the killing of Officer Tippit is an example) are in the early volumes, and prenoon observations by witnesses are in the late volumes.

As always, I bought an assortment of black notebooks and began to paste everything under the proper hour and minute. It was a chore, and at times a bore, but I never trusted anyone to know what I might want to preserve. Before the spring of 1965, I wrote to Evan Thomas at Harper and asked, bluntly, why he had chosen the Manchester book instead of mine.

In his reply, Thomas mentioned that he had turned down *A Day in the Life of President Kennedy* because he couldn't see publishing campaign magazine pieces as books. Then, after the assassination, he had ruled that there was to be no profit-making on the Kennedy tragedy, that all the profits on the memorial edition of Kennedy's *Profiles in Courage* would be given to a memorial award, and that the profit on any other Kennedy publications would go to the Kennedy Library. He went on to point out that the family wanted nothing to be published in the near future but that they might permit a book by Manchester to be published through Harper, even though Manchester was another publisher's author. Thomas signed an agreement with the family to the effect that when they permitted publication of the Manchester book, Harper would make no profit on it.

Evan was speaking the truth as he saw it, but it didn't come close to the way in which I saw the Kennedy threats. Evan thought I would be happier, and the Kennedys too, if I dropped the notion of writing a book "until some number of years have passed." This was too gratuitous. Jackie and Bobby were afraid of my book — for whatever reason — and my hunch was that they would goad and shove Manchester to complete his work as quickly as possible. The thought, expressed by Jacqueline and by Evan, that the Manchester book was far, far beyond the horizon was, at best, deceitful. They wanted me to think that the Manchester book might never be published. Evan was donating company funds to the Kennedy Library, declining a profit on the old *Profiles in Courage* by Jack Kennedy, declining future earnings on *The Death of a President*, prepared to turn a fortune over to the Kennedys while hinting that the book might never see the light of day.

This was incomprehensible. In the history of publishing, I could not recall an instance in which one person held an author and a publishing house in the palm of her little hand. Harper had, literally, been "hired" without hope of profit perhaps to publish a book by a "hired" writer, who would be paid for his "time" if his book was not published. Over a span of years, newspaper stories gave me the impression that the author too had signed over a percentage of his royalties to the library. I did not know Manchester or his work, but I knew that no one could properly assess the worth of his intellect, his time, his fidelity to accuracy, his skill with words, and the wrenching of integrity which accrues when he performs under the threats of "laymen." I should have spared myself such expressions of understanding. Somewhere along the line, Mr. Manchester stood up on his hind legs and metaphorically told Bobby to go to hell.

The heresy caused whitecaps in the Kennedy pool at McLean, Virginia. He may have begun the assignment feeling awed and honored to have been selected. There came a moment in the progress of *The Death of a President* when, no matter how outrageous Manchester's rebellion, they could no longer dispense with his services. *The New York Times* said that Robert Kennedy threatened to take authorship away from Manchester and turn to Jim Bishop. It was too late to court me. I was deep in my own book. Besides, they had word that President Johnson had been reopening a lot of doors for me. They reasoned that I must be close to publication date. I was far from it, because, at the time of the Kennedy-Manchester showdown, I was working on a book about Johnson.

Evan Thomas wrote that my name, and the names of other writers, had been used to nudge the Kennedys toward granting permission to publish *The Death of a President.* The explosion occurred on a hot day when sickly poplars were trying to spawn leaves. It was one of those nothing days when editors leave the office at noon with bulging briefcases, pretending that it is easier to read at home than in the office. The flash on radio said that Jacqueline Kennedy was filing suit against William Manchester in federal court. It was a loud noise. *The New York Times* published in-depth stories which had little depth. The reason was that the plaintiffs were willing to be quoted about anything but the truth. The Kennedy lawyer hinted at passages which were offensive to Jackie. The author seemed tired of being manipulated. Harper and Row, which is to say executive vice-president Evan Thomas, played the part of the neutral pacifier, tilting toward the Kennedys.

The suit was the literary sensation of midcentury. It did not come to trial. Few expected it to get beyond chambers. Mrs. Kennedy could hardly be expected to take the witness stand as an accuser and face cross-examination about the specifics of the contract and her knowledge of literary merit. The story which ran up and down Madison and Park avenues (all the editors were guessing) was that, although William Manchester and Harper did not have permission to publish the book, the author was allowed to take his manuscript to magazines and peddle first serial rights. Jackie, severely uncertain in many areas, had deputized a newspaper editor, John Siegenthaler, to read the manuscript for her and to trim sections which might be offensive, untrue, or in poor taste. A completed manuscript, to an author, is almost always his best. It represents thousands of approximations of truth filtered through the head of the writer emerging from his fingertips as orderly words, sentences, thoughts, and sometimes judgments. Manchester's work had to pass the critical scrutiny of the Kennedys' friendly connoisseurs of the written word, and editors at Harper.

When Siegenthaler told Manchester that he was free to take his work to magazines, but not to publish the book, *Look* magazine bid six hundred thousand dollars. It is my surmise — and that's all it is — that, in dictating the contract, Bobby Kennedy forgot to ask for a big percentage of first serial rights. How else can one rationalize the fact that Jackie, in Europe, flew home in a fury and filed suit? She complained of certain passages which she found offensive, but, on the other hand, insisted that she could not bear to read the book. Six hundred thousand dollars represented 10 percent of the projected cost of the Kennedy Library. The public furor was good for the book, although all the parties deplored it. It was now one of those properties which invite publishers of yellow journals to bribe a printer with five thousand dollars to smuggle a complete set of galleys prior to publication.

The offensive paragraphs were redrafted to the sullen satisfaction of all. Evan decided to send out a publicity release. Once more, he decided to mention the author as the third party: "Mrs. John F. Kennedy, Harper & Row and William Manchester have resolved the differences which led to legal action. Certain personal passages of concern to Mrs. Kennedy have been deleted or modified by mutual agreement of all the parties. Therefore, Mrs. Kennedy has terminated her lawsuit. All parties agree that the historical record has not been censored in any way. . . ."

When, at last, the book was published, I thought that Manchester would inscribe a copy and send it to me. I played Mephistopheles to his Doctor Faust while Marguerite played with her jewel box. I bought a copy and enjoyed the scented poetry, the lively images of Camelot, the dark thread of unspeakable tragedy.

Lyndon Johnson was a fresh experience to anyone who met him. He was a caricature of a Texan, a cartoon of a big man in a big cowboy hat squinting at herds of Santa Gertrudis cattle murmuring "Sheee-it." He was at once the earthiest and most productive President in American history. The President was a little better than six feet four inches tall with a nose less than a foot long. I saw him take some beautiful blue worsted suits and ruin them by putting them on. The White House kitchen had a big sign over the stoves: "Please Don't Ask the President to Have Seconds. Lady Bird."

He invited me to write a book about him, and, although I was not his fan, he was bound to be good copy. I was white-haired, fifty-seven, prepared to snap if I heard snarling. It was the summer of 1965 and Mr. President assigned Kelly and me to Room 313. We were down the hall from where Kennedy's valet had steam-pressed suits all day.

The President treated me like an ugly relative. He was pleased to look down to the top of my five feet seven inches, the small brown eyes trying to hide behind his nose, and ask: "They takin' care of ya? Y'all right, Mistuh Bishop?" I was all right. My attitude toward the President underwent a metamorphosis. The more I saw of him the better I liked him. He was all surface. What you saw was all there was. Even his deviousness was apparent. He was the first President to assess the hammerlike power of television news and he had three sets recessed in the lower wall of the Oval Office. He could, with a remote switch, watch three networks while listening to one. He cultivated the esteem of reporters and commentators on a one-to-one basis. It was said that he warmed the hell out of some of the prettier ones, the most amusing being a bedroom scene in which he is alleged to have edged into a bed, whispering: "Move over, honey. This is your President."

Kelly and I were in the office of Mrs. Roberts, his secretary, one morning when I saw him striding mightily out of the mansion, followed by a comet's tail of Secret Service men. When he reached Mrs. Roberts's office, he paused close to me, looked down, pointed his finger at my head, and said: "How come you rate so good with the servants and the ushers?" I said: "Mr. President, that's probably because they remember me from other administrations. May I ask you a question? How come the President of the United States polled the servants about a writer?" It was the first time I had seen Johnson laugh. It was an explosion and a buckling of the San Andreas Fault. He wrapped a heavy arm around me and was my friend for the rest of his life. Whatever I needed, it was granted. A lot of things not needed were offered aggressively.

He staged an evening cruise on the presidential yacht. He ate ribs and licked his fingers and asked why I spent so much time with his foreign adviser, Walt Rostow. We turned upstream at Mount Vernon and a shore cannon boomed spears of blue smoke. The President could not find out whether they were doing it for him or for George Washington. I appreciated the candid quality of his responses so much that I feared he might say something involving American security. "Don't you worry about that," he said. "Don't you ever worry about that."

He invited the Bishops to attend a cabinet meeting and we declined with thanks. Outsiders seldom attend because, in the United States, it involves the highest personages in the government and, no matter what the presidential agenda may decree, a secretary may bring up a subject which should be off the record. Johnson glared at me. "You goin', Jee-im. You see Mizz Roberts at ten in the morning. She has chairs for you."

That night in our room I scanned his record as President. To study an array of deeds at a glance sometimes reveals a pattern. Johnson was implementing many of Jack Kennedy's impossible dreams — his entire program including civil rights legislation, Medicare, Medicaid. A torch had truly been passed. He admired his predecessor even though he was aware of the cruel jokes around the White House: "Where'd you send Lyndon this week? India? Not far enough." His hates were "the effete Eastern establishment," "Bobby," "Independent Democrats," playboy congressmen who were seldom seen in their offices at midnight, as he was. He referred to it as "contempt for men who don't do their homework."

There were three interviews with Mrs. Johnson. My memory conjures up a small, practical woman in a brown kickpleat skirt. She loved Lyndon and she understood her man far better than he did her. She wasn't surprised, the day he married her, to learn that he forgot to buy a wedding ring. He sent his best man across the street from the chapel to get one in Sears for two dollars and ninety-eight cents. Later, he would buy

"Bird" flashy ones encrusted with diamonds, but she hid those in bank vaults. The one she exhibited to queens and prime ministers was the Sears ring.

The President told me, as solemn fact, that he never made a statement to Congress or a speech to the nation without first reading it aloud to Lady Bird in the bedroom. She sat. He stood. I asked why. "I thought you knew," he said sonorously. "Bird has a degree in journalism." When they first moved into the White House, Mrs. Johnson hurried out the front door and down the walk headed for a taxicab and a sale on blouses and skirts. She was startled to see Secret Service men pop from behind hedges and trees. They told her — rather, they apologized — the First Lady could not jump into a cab or go downtown to buy attire from racks. On the South Lawn there were limousines. One would precede her; she would ride in the second; the third would — "I know. I know," she said sadly. "I forgot. I'm sorry, gentlemen."

Several times, Mrs. Johnson dropped the same bomb. "You will never know Lyndon unless you see him at home on the ranch." I didn't want to go to Texas. I had sufficient notes for the book, and I wanted to write it and get back to those newly opened doors. A big mistake, she said. He's quite another man at home. They were leaving for a weekend at the ranch. Kelly said she trusted Lady Bird's judgment. We stayed over. Perhaps it is worth the extra time to see how a President travels. I recalled Franklin D. Roosevelt's special railroad car with the roll-away ramps for his wheelchair, and the extra steel sheathing underneath and on the sides to absorb the impact of bombs. The attention span is longer and more acute at the side of a Chief Executive. Lyndon Johnson didn't notice the two-inch-thick bullet-proof windows along the front of the White House, but I did. They were new and frightening. He assumed that the windows had always been like that.

We waited in the Diplomatic Foyer for the President. It was stacked with wedding presents for Luci. She and her pretty sister, Lynda, peeked into cartons, giggling. Mother said: "Have you started writing the thank-yous yet?" Luci shook her head. Lady Bird assumed her severe expression. "I want you to start now. Today. You're a lucky girl and I expect proper gratitude." Luci nodded. Her mother wasn't assuaged. "On the plane. Start it." As the father of girls, I saw Lyndon's daughters as normal feminine types. Lady Bird impressed on them that their father didn't own the White House; he was a tenant. Whenever one of them wanted to change her room, redesign it, for instance, Mrs. Johnson returned to the "tenant" story and said the place must be left pretty much as they found it.

Lynda adored reading poetry and playing records and dating George Hamilton, a movie actor. She asked me not to mention Hamilton in the story. I said I was sorry; it had been in gossip columns. "All right, Mr. Bishop," she said, "but please don't overemphasize it." The President came

[409]

flailing through the hall followed by men. He smiled at Kelly. I was given a curt nod. We followed him out on the lawn. A big green helicopter crouched like a dead insect. The President taught me, at a visit to the Tomb of the Unknown Soldier, to walk a pace behind him. He didn't have to teach Mrs. Johnson. The moment he boarded the helicopter, it became Air Force One. The President motioned me to sit beside him. The family, along with Kelly and Secret Service agents, occupied seats behind Johnson.

Before we were airborne for Andrews Air Force Base, the pilot was given an altitude, speed, and a safe corridor across the Potomac. Planes coming into, or departing from, National Airport, Andrews, Dulles, and Anacostia were vectored away from the helicopter. My presidential guide pointed to the White House, receding like a lump of sugar on a pool table. His eyes lingered on the majesty of the capitol as though he had thoughts he could not share. Whatever great and terrible things Lyndon Johnson had done were done under that dome. A long time ago, the young hillbilly had waited for a certain train at a crossing in Texas. He had jumped aboard when it slowed; strong men tried to shove him off. Franklin D. Roosevelt, watching with amusement, with the jaunty cigarette-holder clenched, said: "Let him be. Let him be. Who are you, son?" And Lyndon Johnson mumbled his name, said he was a Democrat running for Congress for the first time, and he wanted to be photographed with the President of the United States. He got his photo. And he got an issue to preach in the hill country: rural electrification.

He had gone to Washington to sit in a rear seat under the great dome and had became an outrageous boozer and braggart. He had no friends, so he didn't lose any. Party leaders such as Sam Rayburn and John McCormack told him he was going to be a notable ex-congressman. Johnson cut the drinking, the parties, and the heroic stories. He remained in his office late every night because he was a slow learner and he wanted to understand the aspects of every bill before the house. It was "homework."

Now he was much older, impatient, with two heart attacks in the records, and a great elective sweep to the highest office. The night he returned from Dallas he had gone home with Lady Bird and she did something rare. She made a stiff drink for him. He sat in a small den-bar and looked up mournfully at a portrait of Rayburn as he raised his glass. "I wish to hell you were here," he mumbled and downed the bourbon.

The helicopter swung onto the concrete at Andrews in a slow waltz. The big white jet was waiting, whining like something trying not to cry. Johnson shook hands with a group of men who followed us aboard. They went to the rear of the plane, which buttoned up at once and fled down the runway. The men were congressmen who lived in Texas and Oklahoma. Johnson liked to do favors for votes. He was not above personally phoning congressmen in the late hours and asking for a yes vote, not because of reasoning or calculation, but as an act of friendship. On a Friday I saw him working with pad and pencil and look up smiling. "Medicare comes up in the Senate Tuesday," he said. "We win by one vote." I asked how he could be sure that the vote would remain steadfast over the weekend. "It will," he said. "We win by one." Kelly was in Kenny O'Donnell's office that Tuesday when someone phoned with the Senate roll call. Medicare, and Lyndon Johnson, won by one vote.

The presidential party occupied the center of the plane. Lyndon Johnson sat behind a gleaming curved desk. His chair could be raised or lowered pneumatically. Mrs. Johnson and the girls were on wall couches. Kelly and I were against the opposite bulkhead. The President spoke softly and played with a television set. At cruising altitude, Air Force One was ripping through thin air at close to six hundred miles per hour. He wanted to watch the Saturday morning cartoons. He had a pretty good picture of Donald Duck at Charleston, West Virginia, but the fowl began to quack unintelligibly as we receded from the signal. He was telling me that he had not forgotten my question about U.S.–Soviet relations and I must be patient. It was complex, he said, involving angles, options, and attitudes, some of which would be altered as we spoke of them.

Between Louisville and Nashville, he had good reception on something called the Road Runner, a small feathered creature who had as much speed as a Minuteman missile. The President forgot the Russians, and me, as he watched the Road Runner escape the clutches of a long-tongued animal which set snares for the feathery one. Every time a huge boulder was about to fall on the Road Runner, the President would slam his big fist on the desk and roar "Go!" and the little thing would take off in time. That too faded and Johnson turned the switches and tried to coax the picture back. Between Little Rock and Shreveport he had Bugs Bunny and Daffy Duck, but he seemed to lose interest. He left the swivel chair and went to his cabin. Someone said he had been advised to take frequent naps, but he was too impatient for that. He left standing orders with the Situation Room in the cellar of the White House that he was to be awakened by a bedside phone "if anything happens anywhere at any hour." Like most Presidents, he felt a subliminal resentment of sleep. He did not want to read it in the newspapers or hear it on television.

We landed at Bergstrom Air Force Base. The President descended the steps as a military band played "Hail to the Chief." A crowd of several thousand base employees and families crushed against a tall fence to get a look at the most powerful man in the free world. They waved. They shouted. He nodded at the ranking officers, who saluted. To most Presidents, the music of "Hail to the Chief" is an irritant. The first few dozen times it is balm for the ego; it is being played solely to announce your august presence. People stop talking. They come to attention. Then the time comes when a President sees the band and braces himself for the first notes of "Hail to the Chief." Later in his administration, if he can ask a favor ahead of schedule, he will ask that the band play "America" or any other patriotic tune except "Hail to the Chief" and the vocally difficult "Star-Spangled Banner."

He saw me linger with pad and pen, and motioned to close ranks. He boarded a small executive jet. The local congressmen waved farewell to him. In a moment, we were airborne. The band below was silently sliding those gleaming trombones, fingering the valves of cornets, whacking bass drums. The government had built a tarmac landing strip behind Lyndon Johnson's ranch house. We landed there and I noticed that the President had changed to a wild flowering yellow sports shirt and tan slacks. "You bring slacks?" he asked. "Too bad. Give ya a pair a mine, but my ass uhd make three a yours." A white golf cart stood beside the jet. He motioned me to sit beside him. Kelly and the Johnson ladies sat in back.

He pointed to wild peacocks on a rail fence. "Ain't them birds purty?" he said. I realized at once what Mrs. Johnson had in mind. At home he would drop the mask of the presidency. Down home he would speak in down-home patois. I had listened to him many times in the White House and, though the tone and pitch had an edge of hill country Texas, all the sentences were parsable and the words well ordered. This was going to be a sentimental relapse to boyhood. His aunt had owned this house on the edge of the shallow, stony Pedernales. Lyndon bought it. No matter how lofty the triumphs in Washington, he wanted to return to this old clapboard house with its two farm stoves in the kitchen, its primitive hardwood furniture, and the old fire engines he kept in an open barn.

This, then, is where the heart was. To the left of the house, he had built a small swimming pool, a touch of elegance. A navy Filipino messman was trying to escort the Bishops to their room upstairs, but I followed the President. He clumped through the dining room to the kitchen, studied the backs of two Negro cooks engulfed in blue smoke at the stoves, and sat in a kitchen chair tilted against the wall. He waited a moment and then pulled rank. "Okay, you two," he said like a cop interrogating felons, "I want to hear every bit of dirt that happened on the ranch since Bird and me went to Washington. I want to hear every bit of dirt out of Johnson City. Come on, you two. Ah'm waitin'." I stood in the doorway. The two women, who must have heard the speech many times, broke down in laughter. They didn't even turn to look at him. One had been with the family nineteen years; the other, twenty-two.

They shrieked and stomped their feet. He listened. They told about a Mexican boy who was dating a local girl. "Ah know about that," he said, interrupting. "He's been doggin' that poor girl a year. What's he going to do about it?" Well, he had proposed marriage, but he wasn't earning enough pushing Lyndon Johnson's cows to support a wife. "Okay," he said, "we'll jack his salary a little. Think they'd like that empty cabin on the hill?" The women turned and gave him a big smile. "Okay," he said. "That's the one that Bird can always see James Arness in. We'll give it to them as a wedding present. Come on, you two. You're holding out. . . ."

We walked to the low stone wall. The graves were shaded by leafy cottonwoods. Johnson removed his cowboy hat and held it over his heart. No tear misted his eye, but I wondered if he knew how much of himself he was revealing. "It ain't much," he said, "but I like to keep it nice. We all came from around here and it's right we should rest here. On the ranch, I mean. Now that one on the left" — he pointed to a row of polished sandstone headstones etched with the customary statistics — "that's my daddy. He served in the Texas legislature and he made money a couple of times and went bust. Now that next one, that's my momma. She's right next to my daddy; she belongs there. You notice there's a space next to my momma?" I nodded. "I go there. See, I'm entitled to go next to my momma because I'm the oldest. The others, they died early, or they was cousins, and they are further down the row. But that empty space is mine." He glanced at his mother's headstone. All she ever asked of him was to be a good boy. He felt he owed her. A lot of the good things he did, Lyndon did to win approval from his mother. She wasn't known for saying "Well done."

We walked slowly and talked. He had not mentioned a space for Lady Bird. It could not be an oversight. Perhaps he expected Bird to share the same grave. We got into a Lincoln which had real horns on the radiator and a noisemaker that made a sound like a steer. The corral gates were fashioned so that he could edge his car against them and they would open without scratching the paint. He drove over a rocky rise, the springs screeching, and he stopped at an auction. Black calves were being sold. He mixed with the buyers and auctioneers, needling, kidding, slapping his thigh and bursting into laughter, demanding to know who, in mock severity, was stealing his baby calves at rock-bottom prices.

Dinner was at a shining oval table with the President at the head and the rest of us spread out within reach of plates and conversation. He reminded Bird that his favorite food in the whole world was tapioca pudding and he couldn't understand why he had to come all the way home from Washington to find that no one made the pudding. Because, Mrs. Johnson said, when we have it, Lyndon, you eat a soup-bowlful. He asked what was wrong with a bowl of tapioca. Mrs. Johnson allowed the topic to wither in terse responses and questions directed to Luci.

Going to church with the President, like almost everything else, was a unique adventure. The road from the ranch to Johnson City is macadam and empty, except for thousands of small birds who sat on telephone wires to watch the great man go by. He went fast. The Secret Service car ahead had trouble remaining in front. Kelly and I sat in the back seat and he talked to us through the rearview mirror. It lifts the heart toward God, like being on the maiden voyage of the *Titanic*. His heavy foot depressed farther and farther. At some point, Mrs. Johnson would turn and glance at the side of his face. She said nothing. You could feel the car slow. The foot — dear God! — was lifting.

He said: "Ah built this road." I squeezed Kelly's hand, a silent signal that he was bragging again. "What bill was that, Mr. President?" I said, not caring. The President snorted. "Ah said ah built it. These hands built it." He wasn't being boastful. At one time he had been a day laborer. He had been a big, well-muscled boy and his mother couldn't afford the tuition at Southwest Texas State Teachers College. Lyndon Johnson spent an entire summer with pick and shovel hacking this black scar. He pointed to a brook. "Momma gave me a can of peaches for lunch." He tied a string around it at sunup and left it in the cool swirling water. At eleven-thirty A.M. he was hacking the top from the can, gulping the sugary syrup and tasting the salt of his sweat. He didn't regret it. Growing boys should have one summer like that. "No matter how hard you swing that pick, you look up and see how much road is still left to go."

Johnson City is a painted splinter hugging a highway. The shops are built along boardwalks a foot above the road. There was a house in that town where he was born. It is a Texas shrine. A lady caretaker will show the chairs and beds and tables of a President's nativity. He refused to show it to me. I could see it on my own time, he said. He wanted me to see a barbershop with a striped pole. The car slowed, almost stopped. "Out front Ah had a shoeshine stand," he said. I was about to say, "And I used to scale newspapers on porches — so what?" He shook his head. "Five cents a shine. Five-cent tip for a good job. You ever shine cowboy boots, Jee-im?" I shook my head. "First you take a putty knife and scale the cowshit off." Mrs. Johnson glared at him. "Then you dig between the soles and the uppers to get the caked mud out. Then you wash them boots down with a damp rag. You dry them. After that, you can start applying polish and a brush."

In front of the Christian Church, parishioners tried not to notice Lyndon Johnson. The Secret Service had sanitized the place the night before. The President turned on the deep wrinkles of his smile and nodded. The people nodded and said, "Howdy" and "Good morning, Mr. President." There was an unwritten ethic that those who wanted autographs or snapshots did not approach Johnson on his way into church. They nailed him on the way out, when, presumably, his soul was drenched in Christian forgiveness.

He didn't have a pew of his own, as George Washington did at the church on lower Broadway. We occupied the fourth pew on the right side. Behind the altar rail were little children who would lead the congregation in singing hymns. They wore scrubbed faces and neat brushing. I recognized the starched frocks, white socks, and Mary Janes. It was obvious that they had been warned not to stare at the President of the United States. All the little blue and brown eyes were fixed on a stained-glass window on the opposite side of the church. Except one little blond girl.

She was born to villainy. Without turning her head, she swung her eyes all the way across her nose, stared at the big man, dropped her lids modestly, and smiled at her hymnbook. The President was game. He caught the smile and executed a slow-motion wink. The choir and the congregation were singing something which testified to their love of Jesus. I don't think anyone else noticed the byplay. The little girl pretended to flick her hair into place. It was an excuse to turn and look directly at him. He was singing as loudly, and as off-key, as Dwight D. Eisenhower (a remarkable achievement), but his attention was on the hummingbird. She smiled right at him and showed the darkness of a missing tooth. The flirt in the fourth pew winked rapidly, and lowered his eyes modestly to his hymnbook.

When we left, the parishioners flexed their shutters and the President posed this way and that. When flashbulbs didn't work, he had the patience to wait until fresh ones were inserted. A few men tried to exchange bluff man-to-man greetings, but the presidential presence made them sound inchoate. He posed behind the wheel of the car. Then we hurried back down that road, a car flying a quarter of a mile ahead, one directly behind. He pulled the car into a little breezeway metal frame behind the house and said: "Make yourself at home."

Mrs. Johnson removed her Sunday hat before she left the car. In the kitchen, the cooks were boiling greens and potatoes. A roast was in an oven; a big ladle scooped juices from the pan and drenched the top of the meat. The odors of a Sunday farm kitchen should be bottled. We walked out front. There was a young man, scholarly in glasses, sitting on a stiff lawn chair. "I think I'll go in and ask the President about the Russians," I said. The young man stood. "Not right now," he said. "He's inside talking to General Westmoreland. Excuse me." He held his hand out. "I'm Bill Moyers."

We chatted awhile. To Lyndon Johnson, Vietnam was his cancer. It might have been excised early, before it metastasized. The President had told me that it was costing thirty billion a year, in addition to thousands of flag-draped caskets. Publicly, he talked tough about Nam. Privately, he was sickened. In the Situation Room, he no longer listened to the body counts. I was present in the Oval Office when he asked an articulate critic, Senator Fulbright, to come over and talk to him.

Adjacent to the Oval Office is a tiny alcove with a couch, a chair, an end table, and a lamp. Some of the weighty decisions are made there. He excused himself and went to the cubbyhole to talk to Fulbright. When he returned, he was angry. "He's a son of a bitch," he shouted. "I told him we had only three courses of action in Vitenam — either put more men and weapons in and win it; stand fast and let the Viet Cong come to us; or take our men and weapons and just get the hell out. I told him that, con-

[415]

sidering all the criticizing he was doing all the time, maybe he'd tell me what I ought to do. You know what he said? You know what he told me? He said he didn't care which course of action this administration follows — he's going to feel free to criticize me whatever I do."

I remembered. And now he was in there with Westmoreland, the handsome urbane general who knew that Lyndon Johnson had little understanding of strategy and tactics. I could almost guess what the general would ask: "Mr. President, give me three more infantry divisions and I'll mop up this operation in ninety days." Maybe not. But it was that kind of counsel which got Eisenhower to send the first military "advisers"; Kennedy to send ammunition, guns, and regiments; and Johnson to send tractors, divisions, defoliants, and napalm. It was like swatting sand flies; you kill after they have bitten.

It was morning and we were sleeping upstairs when the Filipino knocked. He said the President wanted to see me "now." I was crouching behind the door in a T-shirt. "As soon as I shave," I said. The young man shook his head. "Now." I had wretched carpet slippers which had fought my feet for years and lost. The navy blue bathrobe had epaulets of shaving cream. "Later," I begged. "This minute," the servant said. Kelly sat up in bed, looked at the bathrobe, the disorderly white hair, the slept-in face, and said: "Have you lost your mind?" I went.

He was alone in bed, playing with his television switches. The three sets on the upper right-hand wall flashed A.M. game shows. He saw the pad and pen. "Follow me," he said. He got out of bed in shorts and walked into a small bathroom. He was still using the pleasant-sounding down-home speech, which, to me, remained remarkable because it was so unpresidential. "Now," he said, lifting a huge bathtowel, "about the day-em Russians." He cinched the towel around his waist, and, from the inside, dropped his shorts. He motioned for me to sit on the john. I wanted to be funny, and say: "With the lid up or down, Mr. President?" but then, neither of us was a comic.

I was fascinated by the concealment. In Johnson's relations with men, he was country-club casual. Golfers know that nudity in the locker room and shower area is as common as grass stains on spiked shoes. The ugly distortions which accrue to the human frame, the balcony bellies which overlook kneecaps, the sunken chests and alligator asses, cause the observer to wonder what anatomical blindness God inflicts on the world of females to cause them to look with hope and hunger on these wretches. Lyndon Johnson will not be remembered for modesty. Nor, let it be said, was he immodest if ladies were present. He was careful in speech and decorum, although he enjoyed assuming a presidential prerogative as a flirt. He could grin, roll his eyes knowingly, and stare at a shapely stranger. He said he figured that he was harmless — that most women would enjoy a mild flirtation with him, and, at an East Room reception, at least one dance, although he could not dance.

He turned the shower on until it hissed with warmth. His eyes were on my pen, skating airily across the pad. His monologue was loud enough to triumph over the sound of water, but there was little substance. The President opened the chased glass door and slid into the shower stall with the towel. A big hairy arm emerged, felt around the outside of the door for a metal rung, found it, and hung the towel. This was indeed a surprise. I assumed that, in genitalia, he had equipment similar to millions of other men. Surely no one, not even a President, had optional equipment. Without thinking, I reached across and slid the towel farther from retrieval.

Under the torrent of water, his voice boomed like a hollow log. He said he had leveled with me since he met me. He seldom had time to read books, but his assistants had assured him that I had a following. That's why he agreed to the book. If I was on the level with him, my book, published a year before he ran for a second term in 1968, would be a vote-getter. "Mah administration is going to do everything it can to sell yo' book, Jee-im. Moyers says one of yo' books got him out of college. Now, about the Soviets. This involves mah defense people and Ah spoke to my defense people and asked how much I could say." He was scrubbing his hair with vigorous fingers. A pink distortion of his big frame could be seen through the chased glass.

"Ain't much. One thing is sure — there will be no Summit unless they tell my people they got something to bring to the table. Gonna be no sittin' around a big table makin' up press releases. They wanna cut down Warsaw Pact tanks and field artillery, we ready to chop tanks and infantry divisions from NATO. They inclined to stop building missiles, we stop the same day. They want to act détente instead of talking détente, we are friendly people. They want to bug our embassy, we gonna fill them with a load of shit they ain't never gonna decipher."

Vaguely, I could see that he was trying to stand on one foot while soaping the other. "Let me put it to you this way. They enjoy saying threatening things. It's good for home consumption. Makes 'em sound big and tough. You understand? Under the table, they ain't half as tough. Never were. This man Gromyko has been hangin' around us so many years he's more American than Dick Nixon. Ever see him smile? Gromyko, I mean? It hurts his face. Pretends like he speaks no English so he'll look good at home. That man knows every idiom, every cussword, that I know in American."

He shut the water off. "Point is, foreign relations with the Soviets is almost always a little better than it looks. Truth is, I think they're more afraid than we are. Russians like to think big, Jee-im. At Stalingrad they had sixteen miles of field artillery hubcap to hubcap. You remember when Khrushchev had his missile test in the Arctic?" I said yes. "He said he fired a missile with the equivalent of sixty million tons of TNT. Who knows? Maybe yes, Maybe no. It was a blockbuster, that's for sure. It's part of their character that bigger is better. You ever see a group of Russian mommas. Lordeee!"

The hand emerged. Then the arm. He couldn't find the towel on the rack. I had engineered a childish trick. He kept speaking, but, enchanted, I stopped taking notes for a couple of moments. The arm reached farther and farther. He did not ask for help. I shrank inside my robe. At last he had it between the tips of two fingers and drew it inside. It was obvious that the President had no intention of emerging bare-assed. He remained inside the shower, drying himself from crown of head to the area between the toes. He might have been saying something of importance to the book, but my pen was supine on the pad. He wrapped the towel around his waist, tucked an edge inside, and emerged looking no better than when he disappeared.

The white shorts were draped on the edge of the bathtub. Getting them on, while dropping the towel, was bound to be a feat of engineering beyond his capabilities. The towel could not remain in place as he hauled the shorts up because the towel was too wet. Any "simultaneous" move would wet the shorts and render them unserviceable. I pretended to continue to take notes, but I had to watch the drama-cum-pratfall. He asked how much more material I would need. "I have more than I need, Mr. President." He held the shorts in one hand and glanced at the towel. "Ain't rushing you, Jee-im. You need anything, you tell me." His broad back was toward me. "You can open some doors that Jackie has shut," I said. He looked at me and, for a moment, the brown eyes looked melancholy.

"Bobby's been doin' a lot of that shuttin'. Deke DeLoache says you been in touch with the FBI. He and the old man are going to help you a lot. When you're ready, start with me. I was a couple of cars behind the President, but I can give you a good idea of what we had been talking about in Texas, what the party fight was all about, and how he hoped to resolve it. I want you to see Secret Service men like Rufus Youngblood, who dumped me down on the back seat and fell on me when the shots were fired." I was taking notes again. I noticed that the down-home patois was gone. In midthought, he was again speaking like a President. "In that little clinic where they hid me, I was scared. They were telling me that it could be a massive plot to kill the whole structure of government. I have a lot to tell you when you're ready. If anybody turns you down, you call Mizz Roberts at once and tell her who it is. We'll take care of everything from the White House."

He grunted. The mood had changed. I wanted to leave the bathroom. But that would give him notice that I knew that he would like to conceal his body from me. It would have resulted in two-way embarrassment. I sat, squirming, looking toward the window. This too was witless because it too was chased. President Johnson was busy trying to figure a way of dropping the towel and raising the shorts in one electrifying instant. I wished that I knew him well enough to say that it could not be done, under pain of a possible fractured leg.

Obviously, his hopes were beyond his competence. With one hand, he flipped the towel loose. As it started to flutter downward, the other hand was reaching toward the shorts on the bathroom floor. It was a painful moment. He nearly carried it off. The big pink towel made it safely to the cold tile. For an instant, the huge Johnsonian behind was exposed. There was room, I thought, for three miniatures of the Mount Rushmore Memorial. Savagely, he yanked the shorts upward. There was a tearing sound. His foot was caught in the crotch. He was almost breathless as it came up to his waist. The underwear covered the structure of his body except that the entire crotch was gone. As he left the room, he appeared to be wearing a half-slip.

Kelly invited my father to live with us. He was eighty-two years old, the snowy hair thinning in a monk's cowl, the frame leaner with the exception of a basketball belly, a man of fourteen-karat dignity and an over-assessment of his intelligence and knowledge. We gave him a room with a sign on the door that said "Opium Den." He drew his police pension and his Social Security and, as a longtime barroom sport, was humiliated to find no place to spend the money. One evening Rocky Marciano, retired heavyweight champion, came to the house and sat beside Big John and showed movies of all his fights accompanied by a fluent commentary. Dad said it was one of the greatest nights of his life. And yet, in hearing him say it, I gathered that it was no more than he deserved.

Dr. Louis Bennett became the new doctor. Bennett was a dedicated internist, a small dark man who tracked clues inside an old body. He advised my father to have a glass of wine at dinner. This was akin to handing a book of matches to a pyromaniac. He called his son, John: "Johnno, my boy. Buy a couple of gallons of good wine for me and get one for yourself." Within a short time, his mood became optimistic and he was unsteady on his feet.

He spent time dwelling on his death, more in a practical way with a tinge of sorrow than in a maudlin manner. Frequently, he beckoned me to the Opium Den with a crooked index finger and prefaced a lofty speech with "Now when I go . . ." One of the more repetitive dirges was: "I have a little green box in that drawer. It's metal. Inside you will find three hundred smackers which I want you to spend on masses for the repose of my soul. Jim, I'm going to need all of them. There's another three hundred in there, and that's for you to buy dinner for whoever shows up at my wake."

He teased and tortured a duodenal ulcer to death. He ingested food and drink which must have gone over that ulcer like spinning nailfiles. One night he took us to dinner and, after we had ordered various fancy Italian foods, he told the waiter: "Bring me a bowl of Corn Flakes." The waiter glanced at me. "This is a dinner place," he said. "We don't have Corn Flakes." The owner, who looked like a hairy bowling ball, came over and asked the problem. I told him. He nodded to the waiter. "Run down to the store and buy some Corn Flakes." My father rubbed his stomach. "It's my ulcer, Joe," he said, grimacing. The waiter got the Corn Flakes and a pint of milk. "Okay, Mr. Bishop," he said, with poised pencil. "What'll you have to go with it?" My father looked up. "Let me have a double rye on ice," he said.

Once a month, he expected a priest to stop by and hear his confession and give him Holy Communion. He computed that he could keep his soul reasonably well scrubbed for thirty days. Beyond that, neither he nor God could guarantee it. The priest was young and dark, one who rarely smiled. Each month, he tiptoed into the Opium Den, closed the door, heard the confession, gave the absolution, and administered the Eucharist. I suspected that my father gave the priest two dollars, which Big John thought to be a considerable gift to one who had taken a vow of poverty. Once, just once, the priest was in that room overtime.

When he departed, my father crooked his finger and told me to close the door. His cheeks were red; his eyes glittered with anger. "Let me tell you something in confidence," he said. "I had only one sin to confess, and would you believe it, when the priest asked what it was, I forgot. I said to give me a little time. Then it came to me: I told him I had been glancing through one of your big medical books and there was a figure of a woman in it — in color — and I had an evil thought. He asked how many times and I said once, what do you take me for? Then he said: 'Okay, John, say a good Act of Contrition.' Now Jim, I've been saying that one for seventy-five years. I started it and he started the Latin absolution and in the middle, I forgot the next line and he kept right on, but he was glaring at me. When he finished, he said: 'I'm surprised at a man your age not knowing the Act of Contrition.' Well, I fixed him good. I said: 'Father, when you get my age, I'd like to hear you say it.'"

He slept half-upright in a Barca-Lounger, and muttered interminable prayers for the dead among his family and his friends. When he was eighty-three, we had a party and he made a little speech. I should recall the exact words, but I don't. It was after three shots of Schenley. He said he wanted to thank everyone for coming to his party. Jim, he said, was a good son but thought he was a person of consequence because he had written some books. It so happened that a lot of writers wrote better books than Jim. No, the best move Jim ever made was in marrying Kelly. She is not only a dandy cook, he said, but a first-class looker and a lady.

Now, he said, I know most of you here think that eighty-three is a nice ripe age and something to brag about. Well, so did I a century or two ago. It's untrue. Old age and good health is a swindle. I have outlived all the people I love. They are all gone. If I want to speak to Jim, I must remember that he is a generation behind me. Kelly is two generations back — harder for her to understand what I'm thinking. Karen and Kathleen and Gayle and Virginia Lee — hell, I gave that up long ago. John arose silently to get his father another drink in case he blubbered. He didn't. The point I'm trying to make, he said, sitting down, is that when you become the last man, it isn't a victory at all. It's a resounding defeat. Now let's have some music and see what the boys in the back room will have.

He enjoyed life in Florida and sometimes looked at the sunny waters and said: "You know, this is about the nearest to heaven I'm going to get." I took him with me to the golf course as frequently as possible. He said he was too old to play, but he rode the cart. The ancient eyes drank the trees and shrubs, the flowers and the onyx lakes with a sort of longing and intoxication as though this was the last time. He felt the same way when Kelly and I had to travel. We took a trip around the world with our friends Gene and Sophie Kroll. Big John stood on the lawn waving bye-bye as though we would never see him again.

In Boston there is a broad swath of tenements and saloons and churches where the belligerent citizens refer to themselves as "Southies." Mostly they are the offspring of immigrants from Ireland, Italy, and Poland, and you might find one — a rare bird — who will deny his heritage but you will never find one who is ashamed of being a Southie. The men are loaders, dockers, truckers, policemen, bartenders, bookies, and thieves.

The Irish have dominated South Boston for a hundred and thirty years culturally, politically, and economically. The measure of a man is assessed by the size of his funeral. The women are stout and hearty, churchgoing gossips, ladies who are consumed by envy when a neighbor buys a piano on the time-payment plan. At night, a quiet tavern can frighten an entire neighborhood. When Southies drink, they want noise: someone to sing a heartbreaking ballad; two men willing to take their fists out into the alley; an assortment of the latest dirty jokes; a soft-shoe jig; a torrent of abuse for the government; a wild shot at the British; a savage snarl for the local pastor who thinks of nothing but money; and the boisterous levity which leavens all these things.

Jocko was a Southie. He was a skinny giant with a cavernous face, huge feet, hands which looked like standing ribs of beef, and a voice a few decibels lower than a freight train passing through the living room. The only time anyone called him John McCormack was when he was in trouble. When I met him, Jocko was an official of the Canteen Corporation, an organization which peddles food to stadiums, racetracks, dog tracks, and so on. His uncle was then the Speaker of the House of Representatives; his brother Edward had been attorney general of the state of Massachusetts. His father, the fat Knocko, was dead and, as a saloon-keeper-cum-politician, had enjoyed one of the longest funeral processions in Southie.

I didn't meet Jocko until I was old — close to sixty — and it seems strange, in retrospect, to state that we became friends almost overnight. We never saw each other more than three times a year, and we blew a lot of dimes on phone calls, but the friendship was as enduring as brotherhood. Jocko was what I wasn't. He could rattle off four hundred jokes without losing his place; he was in and out of the halls of Congress with that stooping, rolling sailor's gait; he was addicted to dog races and bet large sums on animals that betrayed him; he was on a permanent wagon (when he married the attractive Lorna one of the stipulations was that he never touch a drink again. Once, absentmindedly, I said I'd make a drink for him while I dressed. He said: "Do that, Jim, and I'll make a parking lot out of your house in ten minutes"); a bartender told me that Jocko was the best alley fighter "in Boston."

He read a lot of spy books and sports books. He was sentimental, a part-time bookie, a roistering man who laughed at his own jokes, a dead-loyal friend who was ashamed to kiss a buddy on greeting him, but couldn't stop doing it. He was well scarred by the kicks life gave him, but he was the kind who kicked life back. He had but three loves in his life: Lorna; his only child, Sean; his mother, May. As his losings at the track were monumental, so were his winnings, and chunks of it went to Lorna, Sean, and May.

After Pearl Harbor, Jocko bucked a long line of outraged youngsters at the Federal Building. He enlisted at once, in the navy. For him, it was a rapid war. He was shipped out to Tulagi and Espíritu Santo and had four cruisers sunk under him before he appreciated night battle stations. They sent him back to Pearl, probably figuring that he was a beacon for Japanese torpedoes and shell fire. Navy doctors should have discerned that anyone that big and that zestful was bound to get into trouble.

He was becoming a good gunner's mate when the navy shipped him to Norfolk, Virginia. Elements of two task forces were in port for repairs. So was a British aircraft carrier. It was damaged, and was given priority over American vessels in the repair yards. It should be noted that one of the U.S. Navy's cardinal mistakes was in granting Jocko shore leave. On shipboard, he seldom got into trouble except for finding a way of distilling potato skins into liquor.

He was on shore in a bar listening to a limey who was demeaning the American war effort. "Great Britain did all the fighting against the Nazis," boasted the limey. "The Americans always move in after it's practically won. They have everything that money can buy — except guts. You see those Yankee carriers out in the roads? The most action they've seen is when the skipper gets a nosebleed."

The saloon was becoming quiet. Three of McCormack's buddies wanted to jump the Briton. They fell on him in a scramble of uniforms and caps. Jocko stood back and yelled: "Give the lad a break. Give the lad a break." What he wanted was a little room so that he could kill the Englishman.

When his friends stepped away, Jocko picked the sailor off the floor, straightened his uniform, and told the bartender: "Give this man a triple on me." The sailor was grateful. Jocko made it two triples. Then a third. The British sailor started to slide into a brass cuspidor. "Get his feet," Jocko said.

They carried him next door to a tattoo parlor. Jocko paid for the artistry. In the morning, the situation became serious. The British admiral asked permission to confer with his American counterpart. He was accustomed, he said, to black eyes, hangovers, and bloody cheeks after shore leave. One of his sailors had a big American flag waving across his chest. "This man is married," the admiral said to the admiral. "His wife will be looking at that flag for the rest of her life." A shore party was put to work finding out what ship the Americans came from. By elimination they targetted McCormack's heavy cruiser. All sailors and ratings had to stand to attention on the quarterdeck. The abused Briton was brought over from his ship to see if he could identify four sailors. He paced up and down the lines and picked four. McCormack and his buddies were hustled off to the brig.

The court-martial, like most navy disciplines, was short, terse in testimony, and deadly in punishment. The three who tried to beat him up acknowledged their guilt. A four-striper pointed at McCormack. "How about this one, son?"

"Oh, him," the Briton said. "I'd have been killed if it hadn't been for him. He's the chap who shouted, 'Give the lad a break.' I think this one saved my life." Three men were sent to Portsmouth Prison.

Jocko stood at the head of the companionway as they passed on their way to doom. The three glared at him grimly. "My mother told me," he simpered, "always to stay away from ruffians and hoodlums. I always listen to my mother."

When the big war ended, Jocko's small ones with life didn't. He still drank, fought, loved, and laughed. He hadn't met Lorna, his tamer, yet. He couldn't find a job in Southie, so he reverted to his old trade of booking bets. Well, not precisely. He and a partner named Louie booked horse bets, but they also sold a tip sheet and picked up the bets from bartenders from whom, of course, it was considered honorable to buy a drink. Fifteen or twenty saloons made the partners jolly indeed. One day they lost the first three races and a man with the Jocko tip sheet had the temerity to ask McCormack why he didn't bet on the horses he selected. "Because," Jocko shouted, "that tip sheet is for suckers."

If it is true that, in time, even the best horse players will go broke, it is equally true that sometime, someday, a chronic horse player will have a beautiful, blazing day on which he can do no wrong.

A good day. A phenomenal one. He and Louie made the rounds of the taverns, picking up bets. They took their customers' money and parlayed it into fourteen thousand dollars. As they won, they doubled on the next race. And redoubled. Suddenly, the whole game became easy. They paid busted buddies to sign the I.R.S. card for big winnings. When they left the track, the two men were glazed of eye with granite smiles. "What'll we do?" Jocko asked. Then, fearful that Louie might say something sensible, Jocko said: "Let's go to that hotel in Providence. We can rent the whole bridal suite if it's empty. We can afford a good party. We'll get half a dozen call girls and the biggest steaks in the kitchen. How about some twelve-year-old scotch and some music?"

They did it. And did it well. They wolfed steaks and fine liquor. They paid a pianist and violinist to play dance music. Drunk, they fell into beds with girls who were more durable than they. When Jocko awakened, his hair hurt. His eyes were like dozing frogs'. Sips of ice water brought jets of steam to his mouth. Somehow, vaguely, he recalled that his girl was particularly athletic; at one point she had twirled him so that his head was caught in the venetian blinds.

"Honey," he said solicitously, "have you ever been to the races?" She shook her head no. "You can come with us," he said. On the street, they studied Louie's four-hundred-dollar bomb, the one with the tail pipe dragging in sparks. "We ain't et since last night," Jocko said. "How about it, Louie?"

"Wait a minute," Louie said. He took the fat roll out of his pocket, held it next to his good ear, and riffled the pile of bills. "Sorry, Jocko," he said. "We can't eat. I got an even twelve thousand."

At the track, McCormack ditched the girl. He gave her a hundred and put her in a good seat. "Bet whatever you want," he said. "Have fun." Jocko and Louie went off to their favorite corner to dope the horses intelligently. They lost the first four. As sports, they doubled and redoubled the bets as they picked slow horses. The great McCormack was attacked by his conscience. He went back to the girl. "How you doin', honey?"

She smiled. "This is terrific," she said. "I won three out of the first four. Look. I have over two hundred and sixty. Believe me, this beats working the suckers."

McCormack was surprised. "How'd you do it?" he said.

"Hell," she said, "I don't know one horse from another, Jocko. So I kept betting on any horse wearing blue and white — the Blessed Mother's colors."

He had been chastened and reformed by the time I met him. He never drank, wouldn't glance a second time at any woman except Lorna, and such dog-betting as he did was with his own money — after the family budget was deducted. The old spirit was still viable — the zest for life, the fine appreciation for laughter; he became a businessman nudging sixty years of age who didn't rue a day of his life and loved to tell the anecdotes which accompanied his youthful sins. Sometimes, on a cold, blustery afternoon, you could see him in the street before the house he owns in Framingham, tossing a football back and forth with little boys.

[424]

At home I had completed *A Day in the Life of President Johnson* and it went off to the publisher. I had spent a lot of time in Washington researching the final hours of *The Day Kennedy Was Shot*. The world of book publishing was being pummeled with stories which seemed to be filled with questions never to be answered. The authors insisted that (1) Lee Harvey Oswald didn't do it; he was a "fall guy"; (2) Lee Harvey Oswald shot Kennedy, but the plot was hatched by a rich homosexual; (3) Castro's Cubans shot the President; (4) the Central Intelligence Agency shot him; (5) the Soviet KGB ordered local Texas communists to shoot the President; (6) two mysterious assassins fired shots from a grassy knoll, and were later killed and their bodies disposed of by the cartel which hired them.

I read most of them because there was always a chance that an author might have a fact, or many of them, which had escaped my notice. The nonfiction writer carries his cross by choice, or because he lacks sufficient talent to write fiction. There has been but one other time when editors were as careless in confusing speculation with truth, and that was in the American Civil War. In the era 1964–1968 the publishers reached, one and all, for an analgesic to soothe the pain of the people. The drive for sensational royalties was so acute that novelists changed fiction titles to include words such as *President, Dallas, Assassination, Jackie,* although the contents may have had nothing to do with the event. For a time, Mrs. Kennedy was the martyr queen. She married Aristotle Onassis, and fell off the pedestal. Photographers and gossip columnists harried her days. Women writers did their research among backstairs maids and in bedrooms. The sacred became sacrilegious. Jacqueline the insecure little girl was doing what she always did — insuring the future. I marveled that she had the will to remain at sea on the yacht *Christina* for such an interminable time. Assuming that she loved the bridegroom, she had to summon an indomitable will to remain confined within a steel hull every day, to wonder about the fashions among the couturiers of Paris, to disavow the dim roseate lights of exclusive nightclubs and the company of her cadre of adoring authors and fashionable men-about-town, not to mention the horsy set and the secretive Kennedy councils inside the compound at Hyannisport. It seemed to me — the outsider — that this was her time of trial. She survived; she won. To some of us, addicted to dirty jokes at Toots Shor's bar, Onassis was hardly a romantic. Most of us felt he married the widow of the President of the United States in the manner of one who has just bought a fleet of tankers.

My work moved fast, but, after the third year of research, I felt it would never be complete. Each hourly notebook was fat to bursting. Kelly and I flew to Dallas and rented an open car at the airport. She drove the parade route four times — starting at the moment when the President's motorcade moved out. She hugged the curbs as we loafed at eleven miles per hour. I stood, aiming a Nikon left and right to catch every building, every sign to the Texas School Book Depository and beyond to Parkland Hospital. The boardinghouse woman who rented a room to Lee Harvey Oswald and his rifle the night before the shooting got twenty dollars to show us the room, to let us photograph it and to interview her. Roy Truly, the manager of the School Book Depository, was a hard-boiled Texan who seemed surprised that I wanted to use the freight elevator to get to the sixth floor and crouch in the window to see what Harvey saw below.

A judge who wanted to be mentioned in the book took us to the jail cell where the assassin had sulked until he was shot leaving the building. The prisoners — Black and White — remembered bits and pieces about Lee. The short priest who administered the last rites to the President was stunned when he read that Mrs. Kennedy faulted him for not kneeling in the blood which dripped from the hospital stretcher onto the tile floor. He pointed out that the stretcher was so high, and he was so small, that he could not have anointed Kennedy while kneeling. Witnesses who lined the edge of the sod at Dealey Plaza that day were willing to tell what they saw and heard. I was astonished at how many had noticed the barrel of the rifle sticking from a sixth-floor window. They assumed — almost universally — that the rifle was held by a Secret Service man. In Parkland Hospital, two doctors admitted that they did not know the President was dead when he arrived in Trauma Number One. A doctor hopped astride John Kennedy and leaned rhythmically on the chest cavity until he noticed that, with each press, brain matter was escaping from the occipital cavity in the back of the head.

The Secret Service sneaked Lyndon Johnson to a curtained clinic and some of the agents frightened him with speculation that it could be a massive plot to kill high government officials. For a half-hour, nobody could find the bag man, who carried the coded responses to a nuclear attack by an enemy. Mrs. Kennedy wanted the death to be "official" at one-fifteen P.M. because she feared that Catholic extreme unction might not be valid if her husband expired before the priest arrived. The sacrament was indeed valid, although Kennedy died instantly when he was hit in the head by the third shot of an erratic rifle. The slug caused a five-and-a-quarter-inch section of skull to fly outward and backward.

The only person who refused to be interviewed was Captain Will Fritz of the Dallas Homicide Division. It was he who interrogated Oswald after the shooting of Officer Tippit and the arrest of the assassin inside the Texas Theatre. Fritz took no notes. Police headquarters was choked with fat black cables leading to television cameras and a mob of reporters who tried to get to the captain's office. Motorcycle policemen, two of whom had been showered with cranial matter, spoke calmly about what they had seen and heard, and explained the difference between channels two and one on their headquarters radios.

For a moment, I thought what a runaway best-seller I would have if I could prove that the assassination was indeed a conspiracy. The opposite was true. The more I positioned each minute of November 22, 1963, the more apparent it became that the shooting was a cry for attention from a sullen cipher. There was no one else; there was no room to sneak anyone else in it. The more I studied the early life of Oswald (especially the testimony of his buddies in the Marine Corps), the more it became apparent that this young man would find it impossible to share his moment of "glory" with anyone. The Warren Commission, which, besides having distinguished membership, enjoyed a stunning array of tenacious counsel and investigators, subpoenaed everyone who thought he heard or saw something pertinent. This was carried out to the absurd.

Kelly and I occupied the suite of rooms at the Hotel Texas in Fort Worth where the Kennedys had slept the night before Dallas. It was, at best, adequate. The rooms were in the form of a capital L at the end of a corridor. Kennedy slept in a double bed (he asked for a board under his mattress). There was a small center hall and a living room with a television in a green Chinese cabinet between his room and hers. Mrs. Kennedy was in a small room at the top of the L with a tiny brassy bedstead and a thin mattress. The President called the night manager and complained that he couldn't find the air conditioning switch. It was behind an open door.

He wanted a window "one-third up." The manager said the President would not be able to sleep because, a few blocks away, there was a railroad yard with freight cars being coupled and uncoupled all night. Mr. Kennedy said he would chance the noise; he could not sleep with a working air conditioner. In the morning, I interviewed employees, and shaved in the green-tiled bathroom where John F. Kennedy had a final look at his handsome face.

Gordon Shanklin was in charge of the Dallas office of the Federal Bureau of Investigation. Cartha DeLoache, in the Washington office, told Mr. Shanklin that the "old man" (J. Edgar Hoover) expected him to help in any way he could to achieve accuracy in the book. Shanklin's Dallas bureau caulked gaps in my notes and granted interviews with Vincent Drain, who was the agent at police headquarters throughout that dismal day. The test of cooperation occurred when I mentioned James Hosty. This agent had aroused the hot wrath of Hoover and had been sent off in silence to a station in Montana.

The FBI had been aware of Lee Harvey Oswald when he defected to the Soviet Union. The case file was slender and succinct. In the Marine Corps, he had worked as an airport radar operator. In barracks, he had studied Karl Marx and his *Manifesto*. He became a communist, but not a member of the American Communist party. His party politics were closer to the Chinese doctrine or the Albanian. American Reds, he seemed to feel, were the mendicants of socialism, meeting in secret to gabble like little boys bleeding into each other's wrists. Nor was he adulatory of the Soviet type of communism; however, Russia was the motherland and the most powerful.

It was a crushing humiliation when Oswald, the defecting U.S. Marine, arrived in Moscow prepared to denounce imperialism in his native land. Everywhere he went, officials refused his invitations to talk. He said he wanted to divulge U.S. radar secrets, but the Muscovites felt that their radar was as sophisticated as any in America. He became a bit feverish in his desire to impress third-rank officials. He gave freely of his counsel, explaining that they were doing a lot of things wrong in both military affairs and in politics. The Russians thought Oswald was insane, and took him off to a psychiatric hospital. Confinement in a ward was the ultimate defeat.

The Russians wanted him to go home. He said he couldn't. It was agreed that he could remain on Soviet soil if he would leave Moscow and accept a factory job in a city like, say, Minsk. There he was given a small apartment. There he learned to speak idiomatic Russian. There he fell in love with a girl named Marina. Still, the nagging problem remained constant: no one in the greatest democracy or the greatest socialist nation paid attention to him. He applied at Spaso House in Moscow for a State Department loan to bring him and his wife to Texas. He also wrote a note to Secretary of the Navy John Connally demanding an honorable discharge from the Marine Corps.

In Dallas, FBI agent James Hosty had a case load. One of his files was marked: "Oswald, Lee Harvey." At random times, it was Hosty's duty to check on the defector. He had an address. Hosty knocked on the door and spoke to Marina. He identified himself and asked the whereabouts of her husband, whether he was working, and where. Marina's English was not much more than a mumble because Lee forbade her to learn it. He wandered from unemployment to menial jobs and back to unemployment. One time he walked into the Dallas office of the FBI and announced that if the bureau didn't stop harassing his wife he was going to punch somebody. That was the only note of threatened violence in the case history.

Weeks before the President's trip to Dallas, the Secret Service examined its revolving file to find out who might be dangerous to the life of Kennedy. Some names flipped out. The Secret Service asked the FBI if they knew of any dangerous characters in the Dallas area. J. Edgar Hoover asked Gordon Shanklin to take care of it. He came up with a few names. James Hosty didn't put the name of Oswald forward because, so far as anyone knew, he had never committed an act of violence. The bureau had a couple of informers inside the Texas communist party, and Lee Harvey Oswald had been too haughty to join. He saw himself as a pure idealist far above the maneuvering of practical politics. Oswald even managed to alienate the small group of Russian émigrés around Dallas.

That is why, when Oswald aimed his rifle out of the window at the

President, James Hosty was having a sandwich and coffee in a fast-food restaurant a few blocks away. It was a ten-million-to-one shot but it crippled Hosty's career. He would be transferred without a hearing, just as another agent whose little son released the brakes on Daddy's car, which slammed into a parked car, was sent to Butte. The director felt that FBI agents should know better than to have careless children.

The Day Kennedy Was Shot finished itself and I was chagrined to find that it came to three hundred fifty thousand words. My notion was to recreate the happenings of one day minute by minute, but not to drench the reader in trivia. The editor insisted that there was little trivia — at least none that he proposed to cut. He was later supported by some critics who felt that the ominous tick of the clock toward the first shot, fired at twelve-thirty, was unbearable. In any case, the book ran up and down the best-seller lists, but it was beaten by the earlier publication of *The Death of a President*. It was translated into many tongues, but readers preferred the one endorsed by Jacqueline Kennedy. A Kennedy friend said she had taken my earlier work about the President — the one inscribed to her — and held it between thumb and forefinger, with her other hand pinching her nose, and dropped it into a wastebasket. This, quite possibly, was the beginning of the lady's education as a book editor.

One of the joys of that Chinese house was having my father there. It required no retrospection to realize that he was the most important person in my life. I loved my mother more — loved in the emotional sense of huggability with a smidgen of sainthood. I loved Big John as a father, a buddy, a mentor, a mortal enemy, one to debate with fury, a man who could tell stories on himself, an egotist who did not forget that the politicians had promised to promote him to captain and failed to do it; one who took volume one of the *Encyclopaedia Britannica* into his Opium Den and leafed through it, sponging a bit of knowledge here and there, moving on to volume two, always leaving it on the settee next to his Barca-Lounger open to the proper page, emerging sometimes in the morning to observe: "Did you know that the Iranians speak Parsee? Now what the hell is Parsee? They were Persian once. Isn't there a Persian language?" Or: "Now you take logarithms. I went to night school and we couldn't even spell logarithms, but I was surprised to find that a mathematician in a prison cell was trying to stave off lunacy and he wrote logarithmic tables all over his cell wall. Did you know that, Jim?"

He was a joy, even when he whispered that he knew that Kelly no longer loved him because, lately, he was getting four prunes for breakfast instead of the customary five. I used him as a character in the column, and old ladies from Kennebunkport to Seattle addressed modest, scented notes to him. Sneak that he was, he didn't tell me about this "fan" mail, and, in that entrancing script he had, he responded with outrageous lies: "... as you know, I am living with my oldest son, Jim, and, thank God, enjoy good health. The doctor says I have the blood pressure of a growing boy. Jim golfs about five times a week at the Diplomat Country Club and takes me along for the sun. I'm eighty-five now, but people tell me I look sixty-five. I still think of women as God's fairest creation, and my wife, Jenny, lived to celebrate her golden anniversary with me before she passed on. Jim keeps me busy, of course. There are social events and lavish restaurants and nightclubs; he trades his big cabin cruiser in every year for a new one. Strangely, there never was a writer in my side of the family, although some insist that he gets his talent from me. He signs contracts for a speaking engagement and earns more money in thirty minutes than I did as a lieutenant of police in thirty years. On the other hand . . ."

On January 9, 1969, at five-five P.M., he died in Hollywood Memorial Hospital. He wasn't sick; like his mother in 1941, he was tired. He complained of no pain. Big John was propped up in bed. Brother John and his Anna sat at the foot, visiting. My father's mouth hung open; the eyes were two-thirds closed. He had looked at a television set in the wall and murmured: "Are those the men coming to take me home?" My brother didn't answer because Dad seemed to be dozing. They watched the Adam's apple move up, hold its place, then drop. They saw it stop. Fearful, they told each other to get a doctor.

I knew he would want to be buried where he came from. I was surprised that *The New York Times* gave him considerable space. The Miami *Herald* ran the story across the bottom of page 1. He was what he aspired to be — important. There was one more thing due him by right of intelligence and service. In death, he was going to be a police captain. Deputy Chief Frank Moran of the Jersey City Police Department phoned and asked what he could do. I told him. "Consider it done," he said. The distance between Routh's Funeral Home and Saint Paul's Church is about three hundred feet. Six police captains in uniform carried that casket every step of the way.

Inside the church, I was reminded of something Big John had said. When he was a little boy, he had served as altar boy. Father Scharken had offered a funeral mass for a rich old gaffer. My father, nine, splendid in black cassock and white surplice, had yawned through the blessing over the casket. Father Scharken dressed him down for it. I spent this mass watching a red-haired boy preparing cruets of wine and water. He almost made it to the end. Then the palm of his hand came up to his mouth. He yawned.

One of the dangers of a biographer is a burgeoning admiration for the subject. Unless this is checked, sublimated, the book will be published with lacy edges of adoration around the pages that work to the detriment of the hero and, at the same time, scar the author. Sometimes it is so offensive that the portrait emerges blindingly white, with no shadows at all. The antithesis of this is start a work with an appreciation of the subject and see him diminish as the research digs deeper and deeper. Neither is a rarity in literature. On two occasions, my heroes shrank in stature and nobility. The first was Mark Hellinger, a Broadway sport to whom I owed much. He used me a great deal to do his work, and I was flattered. When he was getting a thousand a week, he paid me ten dollars. His facade was the most genial, the most ingratiating I have known, and yet, when he saw that his work as a movie producer might be terminated, he beat Warner Brothers and Twentieth Century–Fox to the draw by using his excellent contacts with the press to make extravagant and unsubstantiated charges against the studio and resigned publicly.

The second was Martin Luther King, Jr. When he was shot on the porch of the Lorraine Motel in Memphis, I thought I saw a vague analogy to Jesus' laying down his life for the brotherhood of man. Phyllis Jackson was opposed to a biography: "The drugstores will be full of soft-cover quickies before you have time to organize your notebooks." I disagreed. She didn't say, "Jim dear." An appointment was made with John Dodds, editor at G. P. Putnam's Sons. He had a great asset: he was a tall, rather more friendly than imposing man, who could sit back, fold his arms, and listen to an author talk a book for an hour without interrupting or losing attention. I talked the book from front to back. The Black prophet had been with us a short time and I proposed to present an accurate picture of King behind the scenes as well as in front. His childhood, his growth in his father's church would be dealt with briefly. John Dodds liked the idea.

The signing of a contract, to me, is like unsnapping the leash on a hound dog. He will run at top speed in many directions before stopping to sniff at small bushes and hummocks of trees and groundhog holes. The wind will pin his ears back and he will bark and bay, alarming most of the game in the area. I spent eight days in the main library of New York City reading newspaper and magazine accounts of the many places the minister had been and the many viewpoints he expressed. Getting the pertinent notes in the proper places in books required two more weeks at home. There is a frenzy of excitement inside the hunt for facts. The game bag is filled every day and the hunter becomes obsessed with his marksmanship. He cannot miss. No matter how many books he writes of biography and history he forgets that his success leads eventually to a scarcity of quarry. In time, he will have a bag full of unsupported "facts," and the frenzy of excitement will become despair as he searches for corroborative witnesses. I was in several of those empty fields before *The Days of Martin Luther King, Jr.* was complete.

We were at a party at Harold Conrad's apartment in New York and Norman Mailer said it was idiocy or bravery for any writer to look for material in the Black ghettos of the South. He hooked an arm around another writer (it may have been Budd Schulberg) and said: "You wouldn't catch two nice Jewish boys from Brooklyn doing that!" It was a joke, but he was right. Finding the printed word about King was easy. Locating honest witnesses to the aspects of his life was difficult. The witnesses were divided between the Blacks who canonized him and the Whites who despised him. J. Edgar Hoover could barely mention the name without bubbling at the lips. The old man saw the preacher as a buffoon who lusted after White women and cunnilingus in motel rooms. (He had photos snapped through a one-way mirror.) The Kennedys honored King publicly as a leader of his people, but denounced him in private as a cracker preacher who could be bought with an invitation to the White House. The Black race seemed to be divided; the average apolitical citizen regarded Martin Luther King, Jr., as a savior, one who could free them from the bondage of bigotry. Militant Blacks told me King was an "Uncle Tom," one whose nonviolence had stagnated the movement. He was "safe"; he would turn the other cheek.

Reporters at the Montgomery *Advertiser* — men who were assigned to the preacher day after day — thought King thought of himself as an American Gandhi, ready to topple the giant establishment with meekness and love. Each one I spoke to said he was a physical coward, ready to run at the crack of a bullwhip or the sound of a shotgun. One and all insisted that the little preacher did not march with his Negroes from Selma to Montgomery. He arranged with Alabama state troopers that he would lead his people across the Pettigrew Bridge over the Alabama River, and would turn back before he reached the wooden carpenter's horses across the highway on the far side. The reporters stated that he marched in the front ranks as long as the television truck was immediately ahead of the line of march, but when the truck rolled away, he got into a sedan and was driven back to his parish house in Montgomery. The marchers slept at Black farms under the stars.

My hero was diminishing. Inside Selma, I interviewed White merchants up and down Broad Street and then went into the ghetto to find preachers. A few told me, with some embarrassment, that King had used their churches and their pulpits to exhort Black Baptists to brave Sheriff Jim Clark's horses and flying bullwhips. Some of the poor were shamed into forming ranks and marching. They felt humiliated when their hero concluded his bellicose statements to the press and was "dragged off" by his silk-suited apostles. In some small towns he nerved himself up to being arrested, but the humiliations to which he was subjected by White officers in city jails depressed him. After two days — three days — Martin Luther King, Jr., figured that he had established his point and expected to be bailed out.

The interviews in Atlanta were numerous, but the most revealing was with Martin Luther King, Sr. He was a bull of an old man with the steady stare of an infant. The red-brick Ebenezer Baptist Church was his — more his than the Garden of Gethsemane was owned by that Irish priest — and the old man made it plain that he had offered an associate pastorship in the Ebenezer Baptist Church to his "Martin." The son was intelligent, studious, motivated, but, for a reason beyond "Daddy" King's ken, Martin felt compelled to go away, to establish himself as a pastor somewhere else. The father tried to understand this, and at times he seemed ready to accept that sons of successful fathers might wish to go out and lock horns with an alien world. It pained this man to know that his son was buried beside the church. I asked a number of questions, but I couldn't stare him down to the point of asking: "If you had it to do all over again, would you be willing to trade all the honors a nation accorded to your son, and the Nobel Prize for Peace too, to have your son back here as your associate?" The old man sat in his little office off a corridor to the church, rolling his thumbs against each other, a courageous man who would prefer that I ask: "Would you rather have been the target on that porch in Memphis, instead of Martin?"

Nearby was a small building where young King's legacy, the Southern Christian Leadership Conference, survived. Some of the Blacks lounging in the corridor were, I was told, ministers. Behind a desk on a swivel chair sat the Reverend Ralph Abernathy. The evidence is clear that King loved this man and this man loved King, but the dissimilarities were comical. Abernathy was a fat Black man who spoke in muffled woofs. He was an arm-waving man enamored of multisyllabled words, quite close to the White supremacist's vision of an interlocutor in a ministrel show. The Montgomery *Advertiser* reminded me that Abernathy had once been chased down dark streets by the husband of a choir singer. The husband was swinging an ax. Abernathy, as heir to King, applied himself to hold the organization and its motivation together, but it was slipping away. This was not his fault; King had been losing power and credibility among Blacks and empathizing Whites for a year before his death.

He was still shouting and waving his arms and making good use of repetitive phrases, but he jumped a step beyond moral challenge, as when he said: "There are good laws and there are bad laws. I will not obey the bad laws." He lost the indulgence of the White House and the protection of the Justice Department as he lost the polite obeisance of the Student Nonviolent Coordinating Committee, which tried to wrench the torch from his hand.

In the final days, Dr. King alienated Memphis followers when a newspaper revealed that he was staying at a White motel. He moved to the Lorraine, but the story damaged him. He was in the front rank of a parade, grinning and waving, when a follower told King that young men, eleven rows behind him, were breaking ranks to smash store windows and loot. Those who marched close to him thought he was suffering a heart attack. He staggered and clutched his chest. Two men grabbed him by the arms and propelled him out of the line of march and saw a slow-moving car with two middle-aged White women in it. "Quick," they begged. "This is Dr. King. Please take us to the motel."

The research depicted the assassin, James Earl Ray, as an inept recidivist. The record was detailed and comical. Surely this man spent more time trying to get into jail than out. He was caught in air conditioning vents, hanging on to prison drainpipes, trying to climb stone walls. He was born to be caught. In his plan to hold up a grocery store, he retained the services of an ex-convict who was deaf. The deaf one was to hold a gun on the customers. As women shouted and wept, he kept yelling: "Hah? Hah? What's that?" Ray found the manager on the opposite side of a row of canned peaches and had to aim his gun through a hole in the row. The manager studied the gun and said: "Can't you see I'm busy?" Patience paid, and he and his partner went out to their waiting car, drove up a cobbled hill at top speed, and, at the summit, watched a squad car hurry downhill. It seems incredible, but James Earl Ray made a hundred-and-eighty-degree turn and followed the police back to the scene of the robbery.

I spent time in the roominghouse where Ray rented a room. I stood in the bathtub where he stood, and saw the porch of the Lorraine Motel four hundred and fifty feet away. With a four-power scope, the preacher appeared to be so close that Ray might have felt he could almost touch him. The jacketed shell sped across the backyard to that porch at a half-mile per second. It hit Dr. King a half-inch below the right side of his lip, shattered the jaw, and drilled between two vertebrae, severing the spinal cord and slamming the preacher five feet across the porch to a sitting position against the wall.

Everything I saw in the notes made me certain that, in spite of Ray's bigotry, he would have had to be paid for the work. At the Birmingham airport, he bought the wrong kind of gun and was back in an hour with the correct name and number and scope. In California, he paid for a course in bartending because someone told him that this was a trade he could use in any country. His formal education was meager, and it is doubtful that he knew on which continent Rhodesia reposed. And yet, that was one of the few countries with which the United States had no extradition treaty. His airline tickets took him from Canada to Great Britain on the first leg of that journey.

Few believed his yarn about being employed by someone he knew only as Raoul. I believed it. The man or men who paid for the assassination hired someone to act as their ambassador to Ray. Raoul pretested James Earl Ray with ridiculous trips for idiotic purposes. Ray turned out to be obedient as long as the money was fluid. When the killing was done, he had his airline tickets and money. He was an almost ideal imbecile. When he was apprehended, he had no road of identification back to Raoul. He confessed that he knew no last name, no address. Raoul was lost among two hundred million people. Assuming that Raoul was smarter than Ray, he too would have been paid sufficient money to make it worthwhile, and he too would have flown to a far-off place.

The contempt in which some Whites hold Blacks was exemplified at

[434]

the Lewis Funeral Home. It was Ernest Merriwether, Black funeral director, who picked up Dr. King's body at the John Gaston Hospital after the autopsy. When he got it into the tiled room where the dead are made to appear to be in slumbrous repose, he yanked the sheet back and shook his head in disbelief. The White doctors had not returned the organs to the stomach, which caved toward the spine. The brain had been removed and the calvarium (the bony top of the head) had not been replaced so that King's head stopped at his eyebrows. I asked one of the funeral workers why the top of the skull had not been replaced. "I don't know," he said. "Maybe some White doc wants King's head for an ashtray."

It was in the 1970s that I began to question my judgment. My calendar age was sixty-three years. I felt them not. The hair was snowy, but there was lots of it. Spinal arthritis asserted itself in the morning and surrendered to a golf swing later in the day. A series of complete examinations portrayed a short, deeply tanned man who, in spite of smoking three packages of Carltons every day, appeared to be destined to continue blustering and bluffing his way for a few more years.

The question of judgment was disturbing. A socially acceptable madness permeated America, the Colossus of the West. Distrust, even hate, was directed at "the establishment" — a euphemism for the government. In such diverse places as Park Avenue parties and ghettos and the offices and plants between, there were strong currents of anti-American feelings among Americans. The unending war in Vietnam became a never-ending feature of despair on television. The high courts tilted the scales against the police in favor of the accused. A congressman tried to impeach a Supreme Court Justice. Students at Kent State taunted frightened National Guardsmen and four were killed. The stock market became a seismograph; prices trembled at public utterances anywhere. The great democracy became hypochondriacal; it acted sick. Young reporters became prosecutors. Some of the published interviews seemed like police interrogations. On television, news reporters who had to vie for thirty or forty seconds of network time empurpled their prose and speculated bravely, not so much on what happened, but what might happen because of what happened. The book publishers, staid and sedentary heretofore, discovered sex. Those who protested that it was an old subject were shouted down.

They were wrong. The people wanted sex. They would buy it without the customary plain brown wrapper, and they wanted it to be told in lip-smacking detail. The sexual aggression by females was sudden and volatile, triggered by the Pill. Feminists denied it and said that it was all part of an Equal Rights Amendment. In the consciousness of millions of people around the globe, the orgasm became more important than God — assuming that there was a God.

My judgment was faulty. I saw America as an unwashed man scratching his crotch. I would not write about him; *could not* is a better phrase. I was pro-sex to the outer limits of my capabilities, but I could not entertain the thought of writing a book about sex in a home for wayward girls; or drawing on psychiatrist friends for juicy case histories. In restaurants, men refused to don a tie. Boys grew ugly beards. Girls lived in worn denim slacks and faded blouses; they were opposed to lipstick and powder and, while demanding that males stop treating them as sexual objects, decided not to wear brassieres anymore. Salaries and the price of merchandise swept by on a tandem bicycle; blue-collar workers were taking their wives to romantic Hawaii for holidays.

It was the beginning of an incredible decade, a time of instant gratification. To the romantic writers, it was synonymous with the decline of the Roman Empire. To others, it was time to face ourselves honestly and practically. Young girls began to share apartments with young men, and the criticism was muted. Music was loud or it wasn't music. The jails were jammed. Muggings, rapes, armed robbies became more fashionable than swindling and forgery. *The New York Times* was prepared to face the wrath of the Justice Department by publishing government documents marked "Secret." The greatest crowd-pleasers became rock concerts, where a hundred thousand young people could exalt their spirits with narcotics and enjoy the din, leaving wreckage and carnage over thirty acres of pastureland. Millions of youngsters were proclaiming that they were searching for an identity; other millions protested: "I have to be me."

There was a psychological credo: "If it feels good, do it," which might be a simplistic way of defining the decade. It is too pat, too superficial. To me, standing aside, watching, listening, it seemed more like an unexpected natural phenomenon — a cold and dead volcano rumbling, a tidal wave racing across a flat sea as humans watch from the shore, the ear-busting explosion of old pack ice when it cracks, a heavy squall lasting for years. Whatever it was, the worlds of science and politics in tandem were not strong enough to stop it.

On the other hand, it was easy to convince myself that old rheumy eyes enjoy viewing with alarm. In the midst of joy, I found time to worry. Karen and Kathleen, in the spring of 1971, were pretty adolescents, and this led to grumpy decisions about boys, movie dates, and pajama parties with concomitant pillow fights. It is the father who uses the checkrein on daughters. He also asks profound questions, such as "Why are the fellows and girls holding the swim party at night? Whatever happened to sunshine?" Far to the north, the Charles Frechettes were celebrating the birth of their eighth child, a daughter. It had been assumed in the family that Ginny paid a great compliment to her stepmother when she began to send Mother's Day cards. The affection between the two was deeper. The new baby was christened Kelly Elizabeth. My wife radiated joy. The effect on me was to choke my breathing. Little Kelly made a total of nine grandchildren. Elinor Gerace was attending grade school, prettier day by day, something which accrues to budding females while growing boys are blessed with acne and big feet. At the same time, I was blessed with a faulty memory, thicker spectacles, expensive bridgework, and a temper which I managed to lose now and then.

Fortunately, I seldom saw myself except at ablutions. I was on the good side of my eyeballs, looking out at a world which consisted of my wife and sundry impedimenta. She was forever young and vibrant, and, like Will Durant's wife, Ariel, she had learned something of the trade and frequently knew what I was searching for before I had decided. In addition, I began to congratulate myself on the long-range plans I had implemented for our daughters. Percentages of the royalties of each book went to Ginny and Charley, on the one hand, and Gayle, on the other. Both had started so young that I was sure that a house and a bank account would serve them best.

Karen and Kathleen, on the other hand, were assiduous students. They worked for good marks. I decided to try to push, as gently as possible, for first-class educations for them — to arm them against the world. It is not a cheap ambition, but it is to their credit rather than mine that, in time, they would achieve high marks in college and earn master's degrees — Kathleen in social work, Karen in teaching learning-disabled children. Their mother fashioned the ladies; I molded the inquisitive, inquiring minds. In later years, unknown to anyone, I would go into the bedroom, lock the door, stand in front of a big wall mirror, applaud myself, and take a deep, solemn bow. After all, I was the ignoramus who never got to high school.

The sheen had worn off authoring. There was no thrill in the prospect of writing one more book. All the old ones had been specially bound in russet leather and sat in cases on the piano. On a Saturday morning, Karen was dusting them. There aren't many writers who have written this many, she said. "When I die, I said, "and somebody asks what your father did for a living, you tell him that he wrote three feet of books."

The older, experienced writer is difficult to please. At night, Kelly and I would remain at the dining room table, cutting through a variety of subjects. She said I was the man who could make her laugh. And yet, no matter how silly the subjects, sooner or later we returned to books. In non-fiction, sex and diets were still selling, and I could do neither. Besides, I was unable to think a book, or work on one, unless I felt the excitement, the tickling thrill of wanting to learn, that irresistible motivation which some mistakenly call inspiration. It had to be something I *had* to know all about.

We found it. I had written an article for Jack O'Connell at the *American Weekly* about the death of Franklin D. Roosevelt. Why not write a book about the last year of this man's life? It could be a good final book for me for several reasons: I saw him as a gallant cripple in a wheelchair, a statesman who had been at the helm at the bottom of the depression, a gifted person who had broken with tradition to help the laborer, the elderly, the less fortunate; one who had been elected by the people to the highest office four times; one who had waged war successfully on opposite sides of the world; a man with an inventive mind who devised a national pacifier called the "Fireside Chat"; an executive in love with a woman other than his wife; and, quite possibly, a President who was dying when he ran for the fourth term.

I phoned Phyllis. The notion excited her. Of course, no book is ever perfect in its conception or its execution. Roosevelt had been dead twenty-six years. Finding original sources would be a race with death because all of the President's young people were old. They would be dying as I hurried from place to place. Howard Cady of William Morrow became the editor who helped, hurried, and harried. His buzz of excitement matched mine, even though we realized that Roosevelt, in a way, had already been relegated to History 4-A, worth one-quarter of a credit to a college freshman. None of us believed that hosts of readers would buy a book which concerned itself with the most dangerous year of the twentieth century — March, 1944–April, 1945 — a span when World War II reached the high point of fury, a time when the splitting of the first atom would be decisive, a year when a tired old man would travel to Yalta to help decide the form of the world to come.

The weakness in the work would be my admiration for Roosevelt. Behind the pince-nez, the tilted cigarette holder, the square, stained teeth, he was a father-teacher, one with a talent for explaining, in the simplest terms, why "we" had to sacrifice meat and gasoline, new automobiles and paper. Of all the Presidents, he was the consummate politician; he played upon the sentiments and convictions of the American people as though, in concert, they were his instrument and only he could coax harmony from it. Those who were not in accord with FDR despised him. Never have I seen so many lips curl with disdain as when he announced that he would run for a third term. He was called a "traitor to his class"; powerful publishers carved phrases of contempt they wouldn't use against a felon.

In private life, Roosevelt was a practiced flirt. He spent scores of hours at Hyde Park, in good weather, sitting over afternoon tea enchanting exiled queens and princesses. He was in love with a woman, Lucy Mercer. He was parsimonious to the pinching point. He wore an old gray suit so many years that, near the end, it flapped on his bones and Eleanor begged him to buy a new one. In his wallet pocket he kept an account of the firs he grew at Hyde Park, how much the seeds cost, the time spent on growth, and how much he had been paid by neighbors for his "Christmas trees." At a polling place, when he was asked his occupation, the most powerful man in the world said "Me? I sell Christmas trees."

The first fact I confirmed at Warm Springs, Georgia, was that the White House had been divided between Franklin people and Eleanor people. The traffic between the East Wing and the West Wing was minimal and coldly cordial. Mrs. Roosevelt, perhaps the only First Lady who might have been a competent statesman in her own right, gathered all the feminists and the radicals to her bosom. In the West Wing, the men and women appeared to be in love with the President and appointed themselves as protectors of his time. He seldom gave as much love as he got. When his secretary and confidante, Marguerite LeHand died, the President acted as though someone had hung up a phone. Grace Tully stepped into the empty slippers with ease. Dorothy Brady, the youngest and most buoyant of the private secretaries, was "borrowed" from a government agency and remained at the White House for the rest of FDR's life.

At Warm Springs, Mayor Frank Allcorn was still alive. So was Ruth Stevens, who stirred a steamy Brunswick stew for FDR the day he died. At Augusta, Georgia, I found the rusted spur of tracks where the presidential special reposed for as long as three days while he was the houseguest of Lucy Mercer Rutherfurd and her husband, Winthrop. I saw the firm indentations in the cork floor left by Mr. Rutherfurd's cane, and I wondered how much the old man knew about the love affair between his wife and the President of the United States, a situation which endured the Washington whispers of scandal from 1915 to 1945. The last vision FDR saw, when he felt the terrible headache which preceded unconsciousness and death and turned away from a portrait painter, was the lovely face of Lucy. She was sitting near the french doors at Warm Springs, almost silhouetted in noon sunlight. There were stories within stories; there were political absolutes and war decisions which made it appear that the President was gingerly walking a tightwire with most of the world on his shoulders.

There were retired Secret Service men who were willing to give freely of their recollections so long as I could prove I wasn't "Eleanor people." These men were almost as close to him as his skin. It was they who lifted him into the bathroom and placed him on a board straddling the tub so that he could bathe himself. I tracked Anna Roosevelt to a lonely R.F.D. mailbox in New York State. As her mother's daughter she served as her father's hostess when he invited Lucy to dinner while Eleanor was away. Some say it would have made a difference to the marriage if Mrs. Roosevelt was at her husband's side. I don't think so. She had borne six children quickly and was crushed when she learned about Lucy. Elliott was eight years old, in the room, as his mother confronted his father with the secret correspondence and swore she would never sleep with him again. Each had a secret life to live while holding hands and radiating confidence to the nation.

I hurried to Madison, Wisconsin. My man died before I got there. Admiral Leahy's son granted special permission to study secret war diaries. It was a race, a chase, and the faces were becoming older as I traveled. Mine was one of them. The gold mine is discovered, quite often, where it is least expected. Mine was uncovered, glistening a blindingly bright yellow, at the roof restaurant of the Hotel Washington. I had interviewed House Speaker John McCormack, getting information about his private chats with FDR after Yalta, when someone mentioned a name: Lieutenant William Rigdon. He lived in Bethesda and had served as FDR's overseas secretary. When the President traveled to Hawaii in war, or Africa, or Yalta, or Cairo, he never took Grace Tully or Dorothy Brady along, although he was not above begging Anna to accompany him.

Rigdon came to dinner. He carried a satchel. The lieutenant was about seventy years of age, dim of vision and whispery. He had served the appropriate hitches in the navy and been pensioned. He said nothing about his private life. A long time ago, someone in the Bureau of Personnel had recommended this inordinately quiet man to do some work for the President, and, like Dorothy Brady, he never got home again. One can also envision FDR assessing this man as the perfect automaton — a man whose stenography was swift and flawless, one who never questioned or commented, one who responded when called and disappeared at the flick of a finger.

If this was President Roosevelt's appraisal, he was wrong. Rigdon had the inquisitive mind of a friendly spy. He had a neurotic compulsion to take notes on everything and everyone. He wasn't critical; he was a fact hunter. He made notes about gunnery mounts; the officers' mess; the President's soft cough; the speed of a heavy cruiser; how the Washington mail was dropped by bombers at sea and scooped up by trailing destroyers; what FDR really thought about Joseph Stalin, Winston Churchill, legislation signed and unsigned, Alger Hiss, Admiral Leahy, the United Nations — Rigdon even made notes of how much of FDR's breakfast was uneaten. He loved the President, and said the reason he accepted our invitation to dinner was because the word was being passed that I was not "Eleanor people."

I disabused the lieutenant. I admitted that I admired FDR, but it didn't follow that I disliked Mrs. Roosevelt. History would depict her as a great humanitarian of the twentieth century. In a man's world, she would have been ideal as the first secretary-general of the United Nations. If my book quarreled with Eleanor, it was on these grounds: (1) she was to the left of her husband politically; (2) whether she slept with him or not, her place was at his side and she was seldom at the White House; (3) she was not above bursting in on a cabinet meeting with a "Franklin, you must do something about this boy at once. He writes that he has been overseas two years. His officers refuse to give him leave. I wish you would do something about this today. . . ."

Rigdon nodded. He had the grin of a Huckleberry Finn. He said he understood, because he had been chasing facts most of his life. After the war, he had allowed a few years to lapse, then had read some of his scores of thousands of notes. He dallied and danced with the notion of writing a book — especially where the President's public pronouncements were contravened by his private expressions, as for example, when he was on a bed undergoing a passive rubdown. Historians, Rigdon said, assumed that FDR was so sick at Yalta that he was gulled by the Russians, especially as it pertained to the future of Poland and the inauguration of the United Nations. Roosevelt knew that he was being euchred out of Poland, but the option was, after meeting Russian divisions on the Elbe, to take up arms against them and dispossess them to some nebulous area behind the Vistula. It would not only be expensive in lives and treasure; the United States would have to remain on the ground to keep the Soviets from returning. FDR continued to protest the occupation of Poland, but was willing to trade it off for membership of the Soviet Union in his United Nations.

Rigdon brought his suitcase to the tablecloth. The notebooks were infinite in number and, thankfully, they had been typewritten. I swallowed. Lieutenant, I said, I cannot accept these. Kelly seemed about to faint. I can't, I said, because I can see that what you have here is a complete and perhaps fine book. It hurts to admit this, but I think you have more of a confidential nature in these notes than I have in mine. He shook his head no. I had my chance, he said. His eyesight was almost gone. "I get free treatment by a navy ophthalmologist at Bethesda, and I will never get to write the book. It's yours." I offered to pay. Rigdon sat up straight. You shouldn't have said that, he said. At home I have a couple of your books and I think these notes will be in good hands. Okay, okay, I said. I am grateful. Suppose Kelly and I Xerox these tonight. We can have the notes back to you in the morning.

It was agreed. We rented a copying machine at twice the cost per hour to stand most of the night copying, copying, copying. At four A.M. the work was done. The treasure was returned to Lieutenant Rigdon. Many critics become sensitive when a writer of nonfiction states that a certain character "thought." Rigdon's notes put me inside the President's head, but when the book was reviewed, some of the reviewers skipped the preface, which explained Rigdon's peculiar position. Some of Roosevelt's original "Brain Trust" were interviewed in Washington. In 1933–1936, they were young and dashing. They turned out to be old and garrulous, less interested in Roosevelt than in their personal positions in history. With one exception, they trod deep rugs in gleaming shoes extolling their roles in momentous legislation. As Edwin Stanton believed that he made a good President of Abraham Lincoln, so too did the once-young men feel that, with their help, FDR became an American hero. The exception was Ben Cohen, an old man walled by books, who threw a rubber bone to a wire-haired terrier, as he explained how Roosevelt had dragooned the special men for his first team and how he had molded them into an undammable stream of liberal advisers. "The President," Cohen said solemnly, "fashioned us. We were very young, rather quick-witted lawyers. He pointed us and we ran as fast as we could." The dog crouched on the rug, waiting for the next toss. "There will be a lot of revisionist history," he said. "In a way, you're lucky. You may be the last person to get to the original sources."

Ben Cohen loved the President. In the spring of 1944, Oval Office friends advised him that FDR would run for a fourth term. Mr. Cohen found himself caught between personal admiration and practical politics. He was the only one on the Roosevelt team who wrote a letter (eight pages) to the President advising him not to run. It insured Cohen's political death, but this man, who might have graced the Supreme Court of the United States, thought that FDR's usefulness would be over after military victory. He saw a certain courage in champions stepping down as champions. The most cogent part of his argument appeared in one paragraph on page 3:

> There is danger which cannot be wholly ignored that a fourth term would be an anticlimax. There is danger that Rooseveltian ideas, like Wilsonian ideas, may be discredited for a considerable period, not because they are basically unsound but because political conditions will not permit them to be accepted or even fairly understood. There is a question whether the influence of Roosevelt and his ideas may not be greater in the period following the war if there is no fourth term. If there is no fourth term, the people will always remember that in no crisis or emergency did Roosevelt let them down. Whoever succeeds the President, the common people will always be asking whether the new President is fighting for and watching out for their interests as did Roosevelt.

Roosevelt was irritated. He had tossed James A. Farley overboard as ballast when the ship of state sailed safely to a third term. It was Ben V. Cohen's turn: "Dear Ben: That is a tremendously interesting analysis — and I think a very just one. You have only left out one matter — and that is the matter of my own feelings! I am feeling plaintive. As ever yours, F.D.R."

His will had stiffened. He had to die, but first he had to win the war, restore prosperity, and guide the future of countries through the fiery hoops of the United Nations. His legacy was to be a sort of economic and political charter insuring that if its bylaws were followed to the letter, man would never again be a bankrupt and irrational animal. The dying was in his mind, a now-and-then thing which intrudes on men who are intelligent, helpless, and aging. His physician, Vice Admiral Ross T. McIntire, inaugurated a conspiracy of silence in March, 1944. At Bethesda Hospital, a young and conscientious cardiologist, Howard Bruenn, was pressed into examining the President in a suite in which the dominant theme was secrecy. Bruenn was outranked by almost everyone at the hospital. He was a lieutenant commander who, with an hour of warning, was ordered to clear out patients and personnel and prepare himself to examine someone "important."

The doctor was surprised when he saw the wheelchair, the gray fedora, the congenial smile. He was impressed. However, immediately after mutual introduction, Bruenn became the professional doctor. If, for the moment, the President of the United States was his patient, then that man was about to undergo an examination such as he had not undergone for years. As Bruenn chatted and readied his instruments, Roosevelt decided not to volunteer information. He would be jocular. The doctor noted the trembling of the fingers, the flaccidity of buttocks and leg muscles. FDR could hold his breath for thirty-five seconds — fair capacity. Bruenn heard the soft cough. He phoned McIntire and demanded the patient's medical records. When they arrived, his hazel eyes ran down the pertinent numbers; he was studying a man whose physical condition had declined from 1941.

Blood pouring through the atrium of the left ventricle was meeting resistance. Blood pressure was 186/108. His patient was hypertensive. Any physical effort, such as turning over on a hospital table, induced open-mouthed breathlessness. The heart was enlarged. Bruenn made a note that he could hear a "blowing sound," which indicated that a mitral valve was not closing properly. The liver was normal in size. For fluoroscopy, two men were summoned to hold the President erect. When Roosevelt left, he shook hands with Bruenn. "Thanks, Doc," he said. The doctor nodded. The physician spent the rest of the afternoon and the evening preparing notes about Roosevelt. McIntire phoned in the morning. At the White House, Bruenn went over his findings, line by line. He was surprised to note that the admiral wasn't surprised. It was as though he was hearing a remembered litany.

How would Bruenn like to serve "under" the admiral as physician-in-attendance? The young man agreed. He might have felt flattered, but he wasn't. The admiral was stuck with a dying president — not dying at once — but one on an irreversible road to death. McIntire said that Bruenn would report all findings to him; he, Bruenn, would not be permitted to divulge medical truth to the President or the First Family. Did the lieutenant commander understand? He understood. McIntire phoned Bethesda. He spoke to Captain John Harper, medical superintendent. Within a few minutes, Bruenn found himself on detached service at the White House.

The conspiracy of silence began. Bruenn sought no miracle. He could not restore health. The patient, he knew, could expire at any time, but, with the hope of youth, he felt that certain measures could keep Roosevelt alive and functioning — for how long? Six months? A year? Maybe two? There was the weighty question of how much the patient surmised about his condition. Dr. Bruenn had to suspect that the President was part of the conspiracy. They would be in intimate contact every day for the next year, and not once would FDR ask: "How am I doin', Doc?" Never would he say: "Why do I need a cardiologist?" When medication was administered, the President never asked "What is this for?" Each morning, he was agreeable to Bruenn; within limits, he tried to obey medical orders. But always, the President spoke of nonmedical matters — the weather, sports, D-Day, New York, the campaign. It was as though the genial, witty head was not attached to the decrepit body. In spite of the daily proximity of the young man and the old man, the doctor could see the continuing recession of eyes into dark oyster patches, the graying of skin tone, the increasing palsy, the unendurable affliction of twelve pounds of steel on the legs.

At some point in 1944, the President surrendered to the inevitable. He wrote his burial wishes "if I die in office." It was addressed to his eldest son, James, and asked for a service of "utmost simplicity"; "no lying in state anywhere"; the sailor asked that the navy be in charge of the final service at Hyde Park and the burial. In the hands of Bruenn, the President lived for twelve and a half months. It was a tribute to the skills of the young man and to the indomitable spirit of the old man. Near the end, he insisted on driving his special automobile down a valley from Warm Springs into leafy glens smelling of bruised sassafras to meet Lucy, his love, to drive her back to the Little White House, to whisper of the memories of 1915 stirred anew in mist, and to frisk her for news about the young lady he loved secretly, her daughter Barbara.

Now and then the syndicated column touched on politics. I found, unhappily, that I was taking frequent shots at President Richard Nixon. It was not a personal animosity. In the early summer of 1968, playing golf, I told Gene Kroll and Milton Goldstandt that, if the Republican party nominated Richard M. Nixon, we would all hear the word *impeachment* for the first time. My reason for such a dolorous prediction was not that Nixon would be a bad President if elected. On the contrary, few aspirants were so thoroughly trained to grace the Oval Office. But he had two character flaws which usually are considered minor: a notable lack of a sense of humor and an inability to forgive.

When he lost to John F. Kennedy in 1960, Richard Nixon and I spent hours overturning the litter of the campaign looking for clues, messages. He was not a conversationalist. He asked a lot of questions; he contributed little. If I search my memory for a synthesis of Nixon predictions, it would be this: "I've got a good offer from a New York law firm, two hundred fifty thousand plus.... I will run against Ed Brown for governor of California in 1962 and beat him. This will give me a national platform, a new one. I will spend my term visiting every county leader of every state because that's where the power is. I will not run against Jack in 1964, because it's an American habit to give the President a second term. I'll be ready, and more than ready, in 1968."

Nixon didn't laugh. He opened his mouth, squinted his eyes, and said, "Ha, ha." I asked among his friends if Nixon had ever laughed heartily. Sammy Walsh, a comedian, said "once." The vice-president was in a restaurant with his friend Bebe Rebozo. The Latin said: "Sammy, say hello to Dick Nixon. Tell him a joke." Walsh said: "Mr. Nixon, let me tell you the three most famous lies ever uttered. Number one: 'It's in the mail.' Number two: 'If I get you pregnant, I'll marry you.' Number three: 'I didn't vote for the son of a bitch.' " Witnesses said that Nixon tossed his head back and really laughed. He called Walsh back to the table, and said: "How does that joke go again?"

If he had been a teenager in our set, we'd have called Richard Nixon a get-even guy. Slights, rebuffs, effronteries, defeats — each was graven indelibly on the mind. Some said he was paranoid, but I suggest, without qualifying as an expert, that he wasn't. He was a schemer, a plotter. In the small span when I knew him, Nixon didn't utter a word of criticism against Dwight D. Eisenhower, but I had a feeling that he had to bite his tongue to keep from shredding his President. Nixon and Sherman Adams spoke caustically of trying to make Ike a "Republican." Eisenhower felt no indebtedness to the party for putting him in office. The GOP, he felt, needed him. He also had a snappish way of decapitating party members. Ike assured himself of first place on Nixon's hate list when he put his running mate on trial in the "Checkers" speech. It was a political move designed to throw young Nixon to the wolves for accepting eighteen thousand dollars a year from California businessmen.

The maudlin, meandering speech did not endear Nixon to the public, but the young man exonerated himself when he sobbed about his little girls, his hard work, his menial salary, and his wife's good Republican cloth coat. Eisenhower wasn't sure he wanted to run on a ticket with Nixon until he heard the verdict. Then he met Dick at the plane, hugged him, murmuring: "My boy! My boy!" Eisenhower tossed Sherman Adams out without a hearing after the gift of a vicuña coat became public property. The distance between their two offices was forty-five feet, but the President refused to speak to him. Nixon knew that his President was not stocking that Gettysburg farm with his own money. The tractors, threshers, Land Rovers, jeeps, the cattle, even the elaborate fence were said to be gifts from grateful Americans. The victorious general didn't have many friends in the army, but he cultivated heads of corporations after he became President and drank nothing but twelve-year-old Chivas Regal.

Nixon became the White House horse. In the manner of Lyndon Johnson, he arrived early and left late. At a press conference, when Ike was asked what Nixon did as vice-president, he said: "Give me a week or two and I'll think of something." Nothing that I saw in the dour, unforgiving aspects of Dick's character would lead me to believe that he would shrug that remark to oblivion. He would contain himself, refuse to respond, and go into a room alone and shriek justifiable venom. Whatever true sentiment he felt was reserved for Julie, Tricia, and his wife — possibly in that order. To be known as a private man is not a fault, but few men among his associates could decipher which Nixon they were facing at any given time.

As I recall, he was trying to get "peace with honor" out of Vietnam when my phone rang one morning. It was Herb Klein, White House director of communications. Klein had, for many years, been a buffer between Nixon and the press. Of all the White House personnel, only Herb went back to the distant, dirty days when a man named Murray Chotiner was advising Nixon how to campaign for office. The tactic used against Helen Gahagan Douglas in a fight for the United States Senate became standard operating procedure for the rest of Dick's life: "Accuse your adversary of the most reprehensible attitude, and when he denies it, crouch as though you are being attacked by overwhelming forces."

Herb said the President felt hurt about a newspaper column I had written. It was early; I had a head which had been slept in. "Tell him I'm sorry, Herb," I said, "but that's the way it goes."

"Just a minute," he said, "don't you want to hear what the President didn't like?" I said something; I forget what. Klein said that the President had underscored in red the sentences he thought were in error. "Shall I read them?"

"Please."

Klein did his work patiently. I thanked him. He said something about correcting the material.

"Oh, no," I said. "What he underscored are my opinions. I believe those things." I could hear a long breath.

"The President said to tell you that this is not the Jim Bishop he used to know." I thanked him and hung up. It seemed amusing, at first, that a President who was trying desperately to disengage from a losing war would have time to read columnists and underscore sections be believed to be untrue.

In June, 1973, the President was bogged in a scandal dubbed "Watergate" and, it appeared to me, sinking deeper with each effort to extricate himself. The word *impeachment* was heard. I felt no surge of triumph for my prescience. He was not a favorite of mine, but I felt that it was in the national interest for him to survive. It is demeaning, humiliating to hear a Chief Executive protest: "I am not a crook." The crush of public hearings, investigations, revelations, dismissals, writs, executive orders, snitches, grants of immunity had a cosmic tumbling effect, as though the globe was falling in on itself.

Then, on June 28, I picked up *The New York Times* and there I was. It was one name among many, and it stated: "Jim Bishop, author, columnist, King Features Syndicate." I had made the White House Enemies list. It could hardly be viewed as a medal, an award. Within a month, I received several letters from persons who wished to organize a select fraternity of "White House Enemies." From the tone of the appeal, I knew that some people thought of us as an elite group. I didn't respond. I drew no pleasure from being cited as untrustworthy by my Chief Executive. I studied the list, then I said to myself: "Fuck you, Nixon!" and tossed the paper on the floor.

[446]

The sixty-seventh birthday was upon me in November, 1974, and, for a moment, I stopped running to study the scenery. If love is the business of two, death is the province of one. A little time was allocated to meditation. It wasn't morbid; the little pump inside the chest had pulsed and contracted two and a half billion times without flagging; the lungs had fought the smoke of cigarettes and carbon monoxide for a half-century and survived. There was a small open field of pink scalp at the top of my head. The metamorphosis from Sunny Jim (assuming there ever was one) to a wounded bull was complete. While shaving, I surrendered the face to something I would describe as "pinched Irish," a vertical erosion. Dr. Louis Bennett gave me a passing grade. My attention span had shortened; I excused this on the ground that too many people were talking nonsense. My stride was as strong as ever, up to and including two hundred feet.

My meditations were inconclusive. Death is a direct consequence of birth, but I pondered paradise, penance, purgatory — the promises of organized religion. These, singularly and collectively, could be inventions, the result of a fear of nothingness. If it turned out to be nothing, I feared not, because I would float off into an unremembered blackness and could not fault myself for being a fool. Religion helped me to be a reasonably good citizen. My natural skills involved research and planning, and I could have been an inventive bank robber, or a confidence man at large with rich ladies. If there was a hereafter, with the judgment I expected, I would be punished for cumulative wrongs and — who knows? — perhaps meet my father in purgatory. No theologian professed to understand the substance of heaven, but I could not subscribe to lolling on fleecy clouds listening to harp music. The more I tortured my head the more inconclusive death became. My faith in all the gorgeous tomorrows had not been impaired. Nor did I ever believe that one had to be a practicing Roman Catholic or an Orthodox Jew or a Moslem to attain those gates which are not pearly. I felt that a bona fide atheist would be as welcome as a Pope.

The act of dying held no interest for me. No fear. It would probably be an event which engages the medical art, a momentary defiance of the will of the Almighty. The doctors would lace me with green plastic tubes; machines would drip, pump, and ooze. I hoped to have sufficient strength to punch the first doctor who walked into my room burbling: "And how are *we* feeling this morning?" At the final moment, my loved ones might lean over the bed to catch the final words of the genius. Dying would not trouble me. The state of being dead, of missing all the action, of not being paid to observe that most wonderful of all disoriented creatures — man — would hurt. Not to hear the old music, not to see the mares' tails in a summer sky, or the misjudgment of one nation by another, the future of flight, the quantum leaps of science in diverse directions, the maturing of great-grandchildren; not to have the chance to sit back and watch the aggressive young talents find a toehold on success, or savor the night scent of a Caribbean cruise, or cherish being married to Kelly — oh, thousands of joys and appreciations great and small.

Not to know, not to be aware, is the ultimate punishment. And yet, at age sixty-seven, I could manage a little smile, remembering the words of Big John: "Dying is something I reserve as the last thing I want to do." My women lied gallantly, saying that I looked forty-seven. There is a stage of growth in girls when awe is supplanted by a maternal instinct. Virginia Lee was thirty-seven, her energies diverted from raising a big family to selling real estate; Gayle was assisting at autopsies at age thirty-one; Karen, at twenty-one, qualified as a teacher of learning-disabled children and was studying for a master's degree; Kathleen, at nineteen, was bucking for a bachelor's degree at Florida Atlantic University in social work.

The accomplishments and the numbers are prosaic, but, to me, it represented a steady running of fine sand to the bottom of the glass. The younger girls were grown. Physically, they were a bit more than pretty. Through nonpaternal eyes, Karen and Kathleen were gorgeous creatures. It hurt when they used the artifices of lesser humans — blue eye shadow, glistening wet lipstick, rouge. They would have attracted attention if they had scrubbed their hands and faces, brushed their hair, and worn paratrooper coveralls. To my sorrow, I learned that it would not do for me to tell them how ravishingly attractive they were just once — it was an assessment to be verbalized every day. They had dates with young men, but not the inundation I had expected. They chose carefully, in the manner of women who carry a shopping list. Young men of several sizes and personalities sat in our living room waiting, testing my patience with elaborate circumlocution. At times the family discussed love, and the best I could do was to say: "Never look for it; it will come looking for you."

I wondered if any of the young men knew, or cared, that these were intelligent girls with integrity. Most, I surmised, didn't want to explore beyond skin. Kelly said I should observe and remain silent. A lot of time and affection and treasure goes into the upbringing of any child and I choked when Kathleen brought a young man in who asked me about my karma. He was an expert on transcendental meditation and I suspect that he wished to have our Kathleen join him somewhere among clouds of galactic gases.

The personalities diverged, as they should. It is remarkable that two persons, brought up in the same bedroom and at the same table, appear to be similar (even though antagonistic) in their likes. And yet two full flowers on the same stem are not only different from each other, but not nearly as similar as when they were buds. Karen became the sentimental soul of the Bishop family; it was she who worried if anyone was hurt, or rebuffed. It was she who lingered over the news photo of the crippled child, the plight of the Blacks and the elderly. She was a string-saver, a photo-snatcher, one who hid old letters, one who would hold an old lady's hand and counsel the woman about her rights.

Kathleen was easily as attractive, but she was all intellect, all probing. At nineteen she was a female Sammy Glick, shrieking at a blank wall: "How dare he give me an A minus! How dare he, that woman-hating apology of a man!" She worked fast and well as though immersed in viscous fluid hungering for air. Her weakness was a fear of trying anything new — the first day of school, the first date, the first time behind the wheel of a car, the first time in high heels. At the sign of innovation, she paused, tossed awake all night, and then plunged ahead. Like Karen, she was an old lady before she was a young one, advising college chums in the devious passages of their love affairs before she had her first one. I appreciate Kathleen, because, to her, none of it was easy. And, like Virginia Lee, she was indomitable in her ambition to carve a niche for herself. If I were to run a business, I would not feel at ease if either of them was my second in command.

The younger girls were in college when *FDR's Last Year* was published in the autumn of 1974. There was a feeling of accomplishment about this book, and I didn't want to celebrate it by appearing on "The Mike Douglas Show." He had been a warm friend and a generous host, but I needed a smaller, more select audience for this one. Kelly and I drove up to Saint Bonaventure University, where I had friends on the faculty and on the *Times Herald*. There was a weak sun and a cold wind which raked the branches of trees in the woods. Some students and Olean citizens were in a long queue as I curled fingers around a pen and began the ritual of autographing. It is a small scene, but it was as important as though I were being knighted. It was my favorite book, which is an oblique way of saying that it came closer to the shadings of meanings locked inside my head than any of the other books. My only fear was that knowledgeable reviewers might refer to me as "Franklin people" or "Eleanor people."

The *Saturday Review* gave the book a full-page review. A good one. I was flattered. Had I the echo chamber of a memory left, I should have memorized it, boring friends to death with adroit superlatives. The lyrics escaped me, but I knew the tune. The last half of the last paragraph was a cooling unguent to an old bruise. "Jim Bishop says rightly that Mr. Roosevelt neglected his body 'in exchange for a firm seat in the chair of power.' This assessment is unquestionably true of a president completely aware of his unique place in U.S. and world history. One somehow understands it all better because of this thorough and fascinating volume, which will, I suspect, find a wider audience than any of Jim Bishop's other 17 books, because it is probably the best of them."

It was, in all aspects, a happy book for me. It sold well, and clung to the best-seller lists at a time when the nation was transfixed at television sets watching and listening to a seriocomic play called Watergate. Many of us hoped it would never end, that it would unreel itself, an episode at a time, arousing us to lofty incredulousness as we listened to the brassy trumpets coming from the capitol, followed by the bass horn counterpoint from the White House. I cannot recall buying any books at that time, unless they were the hysterical preludes to the exposés we would read in the years following Nixon's tearful flight to his expensive refuge. Watergate, like a masterfully told novel, is not something one wants to conclude; toward the end the reader teases himself with a paragraph at a sitting, or maybe two.

Karen met Paul Sayrs, a young teacher, and fell in love. They were married in July, 1975. I was almost as pleased as Karen because Paul, a bright young man with a slightly mad sense of humor, was a teacher of emotionally retarded children, as Karen was. We staged a wedding reception, the cost of which would have served as a down payment on a house. Sayrs, broke, bought a house in Palm Beach County. Kathleen returned to college, sorting term papers and men in her head. I was a pallbearer at the funeral of Bob Considine, and I cite it because his death, which occurred months after a balloon accident, shocked his friends. Considine was the jazz pianist of the written word. He could write anything from sandlot baseball to a series on the Kremlin versus détente and whatever miasma of realities lies between. This is to say that, somewhere, there is an unknown writer who can do a better story on sandlot baseball than Considine, but he can't do anything else; and that goes for the Kremlin story too. Always he was a gracious, generous moose, one who believed in you as well as in himself. I saw him write drunk and I saw him write sober; between the two I'll take drunk. He loved his wife and children; he chuckled through life and, it seemed to me, was always in debt. His syndicated column was well received by feature editors because, while it was street-wise and sophisticated, it was also modest, and only a jazz pianist can hit those diminished sevenths.

Few human situations are as aboriginal as being a pallbearer. The slow, solemn toll of deep bells, the craning of the curious, the unctuous whispers of the funeral directors, the on-cue sobbing of the next of kin, the richly ornamented ministers of God who stand, kneel, sit, and bow as they consign the soul of the deceased — the only part of him not present at the funeral — to Almighty God. I feel about funerals as I do about weddings: expensive shows designed to impress strangers. I saw Toots Shor, gray, solemn, tired. Jack Dempsey, eighty-one, limped along the sidewalk before Saint Patrick's Cathedral on a cane, glancing up under furry brows to gauge how much further the torture. He, above the host of others, epitomized to me what time does to the best. I watched him try to negotiate the steps and saw him accept help from a young woman, and I remembered the blooded fury of this man in Boyle's Thirty Acres as he cut through Georges Carpentier in the fourth round of a championship fight. It seemed then as though nothing could diminish those enormous muscles, those canallike arteries. I remembered when a trusted chauffeur picked up Eleanor Roosevelt at her town house to take her to Hyde Park to die. Her dress was disordered; her slip was cockeyed; her hair had been slept in; if the great humanitarian eyes showed anything it was the fear of a child facing the unknown.

Once — just once — I sat with John Wayne in a small hotel in Carson City and watched him smoke, and drink tequila. He had survived cancer of the lung and, as we chatted, he talked of the movie he was making in the fields outside of town. It was called *The Shootist* and the hero was an old cowboy with terminal cancer who faces his final gunfight. Mr. Wayne walked pigeon-toed, held his arms away from his body as a balance, and croaked his sentences. "Ever feel old, Mr. Bishop?" I said I had no inclination to dump my bullshit philosophy on him, but old, like twilight, is not an instantaneous thing. At forty one can feel old and incompetent for a day, and feel fine for the next ten. I thought it was when the sensations of being old are more prevalent than the optimistic days that the patient must either fight harder or surrender gracefully.

He lifted the left side of his upper lip as he spoke. "Are you old?"

I nodded, "Yes, sir. There was a day in November, 1975 — I think it was the last day — when I felt mildly depressed. This isn't unusual. It isn't worth a tranquilizer, but I felt as though I had been playing some sort of phony role — you know, act young, think young, be young, jump over the tennis net — and I resolved to play the old man." He was grinning. The tape machine was almost silent. "It's a greedy, grubby part in which the subject substitutes insolence and calls it candor; an old man is forgiven bad manners and crudities denied to the young. Everyone who shakes hands with him says, 'You look terrific,' and he learns to accept homage which he hasn't earned — am I boring you?"

He slapped his knee hard. "Keep on, by Christ. You *are* terrific."

He invited us to his home at Newport Beach, California. I could see that, in a manner of speaking, John Wayne was me if I had been a mediocre, overpaid actor. He had a big squarish house facing an inlet on the sunny bay. The furniture was early leather with bronzes of cowboys rearing on horses and twirling tiny copper lariats. He had bought an overage navy minesweeper and had sailed her to Europe, nearly drowning everybody on board. He was a first-class dreamer. He loved Latin women and cigarettes and tequila and children. As he matured, he saw that his place was at the side of the insufferable rich, preaching lower taxes, less government, saluting the flag, more soldiers and missiles and less welfare, a patriot who was happy to be identified with Richard Nixon.

I watched him stand in a cold, dead field outside Carson City waiting for the cameras and the lights. Technicians were building a twenty-foot railway so that, in the next shot, they would have a closeup of the Duke as he showed a growing boy how to draw a gun swiftly and fire. His head was down; he studied one of his dusty boots tracing something in dirt.

Kelly was blowing on her hands and stomping her heels. The Duke's cowboy jacket was open; the plaid cotton shirt was buttoned to the neck. He waited a long time. Wayne was a superstar; he was automatic front money; his frozen face guaranteed box-office profits — but he didn't complain. He had been doing this for many years in many movies. He knew that if the director managed to film three pages of the script in one day everyone would feel good.

When the little railroad was ready, groups of men began to move lights. The rocks and unseen culverts made them uneven. Time was spent testing them for shadows. When it was all ready, the director said: "How about a little run-through?" The Duke shrugged. "If you say so." Someone ran to find the boy, who was warm in the farmhouse. They ran through it twice, including the speech Wayne would make about drawing a gun. He took aim at a slender beech sixty feet away. When everyone was ready, voices as far away as the road began to shout: "Quiet on the set." The star said the only noise he worried about was an overhead jet from Reno. The Western antedates flight. "We have speed." The film was rolling; the boy asked how to fire a gun in a showdown. Wayne made his little speech; the camera picked up his whimsical grin; it backed away and got behind him as he bent both knees suddenly, drew the revolver, and fired. I saw a piece of the tree bark fly off. "That," I said later, "is some shooting." John Wayne laughed. "We always fire blanks. Always. The bit of bark is pasted on the tree. A tiny wire leads to a man crouching in the grass. When he hears my gun, he yanks." I said if you can't believe John Wayne, who can you believe?

Curiosity, a perennial seducer, caused me to sign one more book contract with William Morrow Company. In the latter part of 1975, the United States began to gear up to celebrate its two hundredth birthday with an overlay of whooping and tall ships and the Boston Pops and garish colors streaking across a night sky and the Statue of Liberty, bandstand picnics, sonorous speeches, and What So Proudly We Hailed and the confetti of freshly minted books. Mine was one. It was called *The Birth of the United States* and confined itself modestly to a reexploration of the first four days of July, 1776. Through the generosity of reviewers, it is called a book, but it is in actuality a smooth rewrite job.

It was an enjoyable task, because, one more time, I was being paid to fit and solder and plane bits and chips of history together. The difficult aspect was in locating first-class biographies of many of the members of the Second Continental Congress, and, while drawing from them material applicable to early July, 1776, encapsulating each character with a suitable anecdote, one which revealed his true nature. An example is John Hancock, who announced that he had signed his name large so that the king would not have to wonder whose head he was after. The British had convicted John Hancock of smuggling and had been trying to hang him for some time. There were phrases, noble words, which I suspected Thomas Jefferson had purloined from an earlier document drawn up by the Virginia House of Burgesses. Although slavery was being denounced around the rim of the North Atlantic, not a word of this sentiment was permitted to creep into the American Declaration of Independence.

There was a world apart from books, a cacophony in which I played the inquisitive pedestrian. I digested news magazines, newspapers, *Harper's*, *Atlantic*, *Playboy*, the Miami *Herald*, *The New York Times*, the telephone with its daily dose of gossip, mail from readers of two hundred newspapers and television. I was never one of those authors who nurture library dust. Kelly and I enjoyed Caribbean cruises, four-day trips to the craps tables at Las Vegas, flights to New Jersey to re-count nine grandchildren, dining out and sipping white wine until both of us began to rephrase how terrific I looked, sitting with a handsome man like John Monaghan to listen to genuine Irish blarney, worrying as my wife sought out a Roman Catholic annulment of her first marriage so that we might be buried in consecrated ground.

I still used a manual portable Smith-Corona typewriter, and it was of some solace to learn that the machine had grown so old that the company had trouble finding parts. Not every writer outlives the machine which made his living. Then, on April 26, 1977, Kelly got a phone call from our oldest daughter, Virginia Lee. She had become a grandmother. One of the twins (Pamela) had given birth to a girl whom they had named Farrah Rizzo. I felt no spasm of joy. I felt solemn, like a drunk who has staggered up a stone step. Was all of this — all of this that happened — that long ago? That far away? Elinor was nineteen when I met her, an overrouged flapper. Not much more than a willful child, surely. Look how long we had waited for Virginia Lee. For Christ sake, seven years! And then she had grown up and married Charles Frechette and had eight children and *they* had grown up and now one of the twins was married to Joel Rizzo and they had a baby who would grow up and — I had a headache.

Audiences give standing ovations to survivors. The hero of these pages, he who scorned plaques and awards, began to accept a few. He cringed with his hand out. I was given the President's Gold Medal at the University of Detroit; I hurried to Chicago to grab the "Journalist of the Year Award, 1979" from the *Encyclopaedia Britannica*. I was becoming shameless. Some of the newspaper photos showed a wizened character in cap and gown grinning as he held a scroll which he couldn't decipher. The best, though — the very best of all — was an event staged by Mayor Francis X. Smith of Jersey City. June 14 was Flag Day everywhere in America except Jersey City. There, from dawn to midnight, it was Jim Bishop Day.

Jersey City is far from the richest town in America, but it can generate a million dollars' worth of enthusiasm. The sheriff and his deputies met us at the hotel. We swept through city streets with sirens open, squad cars racing ahead to clear cross streets, baritone voices squawking through official radios, lights flashing red and orange. We pulled up in front of Saint Patrick's School, where, not long ago, I had perspired over the eight-times table. The place was now part of the inner city and the students were Black, scrubbed and healthy. The schoolrooms were the same. I knew the desks with the splintered edges. The stone stairways had long since been grooved by little feet marching two by two.

At the rectory, the burly cops punched a doorbell and scared the hell out of a young bearded priest. He looked down the flight of steps where Father Edward A. Kelly had once frowned on a schoolyard full of idiots, and the young priest said: "Excuse me? What's the occasion? Who are you?" I told him and he took me on a tour of the big old stone barn. "We don't use the main church anymore," he said softly. "Not enough Catholics. We use the little chapel. Do you remember it?" I remembered. "I read about you in the paper," he said. "They're having some sort of a day or something."

The motorcade made a lot of noise and we hurried off, down past where the Eagle Oil Refinery used to be and a railroad yard called Black Tom. On this day it was a sweep of attractive green sod called Liberty Park. It was a summery day with a breeze coming off New York Bay. There may have been four or five hundred people in the park, most of them wearing identifiable faces and unidentifiable names. Kelly and I kissed and hugged and shouted at the faces; sheriff's deputies pretended to clear a path through the "enormous crowd." I noticed that the park was situated behind the Statue of Liberty. Her bronze-gowned back seemed gigantic with a little expanse of bay between the lady and the park. Mayor Smith, to whom I owed so much, was a black-haired Irish type with a shingle of hair fluttering on his forehead.

We lounged with our friends as the mayor yanked a ribbon from a scroll, tapped a loudspeaker with his hand, and announced that this was Jim Bishop Day in Jersey City. There was polite applause. In the background, police were clearing little boys from an acre of sod. A bright blue helicopter was descending. Out of it stepped Governor Brendan Byrne, a white-haired patrician who got to the stand and announced that this was Jim Bishop Day everywhere in the State of New Jersey. I was impressed, even though such days do not speed the wheels of production or slow them. Most of all, I felt excited that, at last, I was somebody in my old hometown. In my family, and all its ramifications, pejoratives were administered "for your own good." There were some wage-earners who looked with honest suspicion at anyone who was paid for what he scribbled. When the *Jersey Journal* began to publish my syndicated column, no relative called or wrote to advise me, and not one admitted, in a local pub, that I was a cousin or a nephew or an uncle.

Kelly got to the speaker's stand first. She leaned down to help me. Toward the middle, aligned on chairs which gave the appearance of so many sparrows on a phone wire, were a priest and a nun. The priest, no doubt, would deliver an invocation or a benediction. Jersey City is more arrogantly Catholic than the University of Notre Dame. But why the nun? She was short and plump; I could see part of a pink laughing face inside the white corrugation. Then I knew. It was Sister Maria Alacoque (Horan), the one who had taught me in the third grade of elementary school. I embraced her and then remembered that I'm not supposed to do that. "Jimmy," she said, "we're so proud of you. You know, the gentlemen drove all the way out to Convent Station to pick me up and they're going to drive me home."

I could barely digest the thought. It was a miracle, the Resurrection, the Second Coming, impossible. To her, I was one of hundreds of boys who staggered through her class on the way to harsher shadows. To me, she was the one teacher who approached my failures with sympathy, who told me to be patient with myself, who proved to me that I could not entertain fear and fresh knowledge at the same time. She is also the teacher who executed such an interminable blackboard drill that I wet the entire aisle before she gave me permission to leave the room. Amid all the music and shouting, she said she would have a birthday tomorrow. I took a long chance and kissed her on the side of her habit. "How old will you be?" She smiled coyly. "Eighty, Jimmy. Eighty." It was impossible to resist. I took the microphone, told the crowd about the birthday, and announced that if Sister Maria Alacoque was eighty years old tomorrow, then she was ten when she taught me.

The priest, a short dark man, stood. He said he was Victor R. Yanitelli, a Jesuit. He had served as president of Saint Peter's College and this would be his last official act. He presented to me a doctorate in humane letters. The effect on me is secret because I do not know the proper words to describe it. It was a big document, frozen forever in plastic on grained walnut. It was a surprise of such proportions that it ruined my day. I had made a lot of public appearances and had developed a glib, amusing style which can be substituted for talent. I looked at the doctorate, glanced at Yanitelli, said something, and tried to shake his hand.

I would like to have said: "This should have been my alma mater fifty years ago. It was I, the copyboy, who rubbed the red stones of the old college building when it was downtown; it was I who needed the discipline and the philosophy of the Jesuits; it was I who chose to hustle sauerkraut juice for hungover reporters at twelve dollars a week. It wasn't that bad a trade, Father Yanitelli. In passing, I think I should admit that I lied. When journalists said: 'What school, Jim?' I said, 'Saint Peter's, Jersey City' to counter their claims on Dartmouth and Princeton and Cornell and Missouri."

Words were spoken into the microphone and I was mouthing them. I could see faces laughing — Jack O'Connell, Roger Donald, Gene Kelly — but I didn't know what they were laughing at. I tried to get away without saying anything, and almost made it. My chin was quivering. My hands barely embraced the doctorate. A friend, Father Joseph Kerr, stood up and took it away. The doctorate should have been hammered to a wall with the others. Kelly put them in my closet with the shoes. I didn't protest because she had spent the good years as a boudoir press agent, telling me that my best writing was yet to come, that I imagined I was tired, that, physically and mentally, I was about forty-five years old.

I had a dinner date with a girl who, without conscious effort, was bound to make me feel ninety-five. In Hollywood, Florida, there is a restaurant called "Top O' The Home." My date was with Miss Elinor Gerace. She arrived with Frank Gerace's sister, Frances. I kissed a tall, dark young lady in a white party frock. It looked like a prom dress. The hair was carefully curled upward on the ends and bounced as she walked with exaggerated dignity to a table. Her friends, she told me, called her "Missy." This was the ninth — the unknown grandchild. I had seen her in pink hat and dress, sucking her thumb while sleeping on her mother's lap. I gathered several impressions almost at once. She was pretty; she had big eyes and was vibrant with life; she dated boys and wanted to be a veterinarian; she liked me and called me "Grandpa." Through all those years, this child had been nurtured with care by Grandma Gerace. She showed snapshots of her German shepherd; we spoke of school and grades and she hinted that Cherry Hill is "just a little bit" away from Philadelphia airport.

Her affection was so unaffected that she managed to drench me in guilt. I loved her, but I never did anything for her. I saved all the Christmas cards from the days of the big X kisses, but I never sent one. Gayle had been firm in stating that she wanted to forget that part of her life; she refused to touch foot in any part of New Jersey; she asked me not to show photos of Frank or Missy. I respect trauma but I do not understand it. Now we sat at dinner in a restaurant which, in the glitter of saffron lights below, lit Gayle's house three miles to the west. This child was going to ask, "When can I visit my mother?" and I had no words for her. She told me how she had asked Grandma Gerace for permission to fly to Florida with Frances and spend ten days at Eastertime. Such permission is customarily granted to females after Grandma audits her checklist of things ladies never do.

It was a good dinner. Twice, fumbling, I tried to make Missy understand that I truly loved her, that I thought we should get to know each other. It sounded specious. I told her that her mother loved her. She started to bounce up and down happily. "When can I see her?" Ah, well. Sure. I mean, she'd be proud. Medically, well, she's in perfect condition. See, I didn't tell her that you were here. I could have. It wasn't a secret or anything. Your mother had a couple of problems growing up, and now they're all behind her. "For many years," she said slowly. Yes, sir. For many years. That's the point. You and I have to work this out carefully. It wouldn't be right to just bust in. I mean ... Her eyes widened. She said it slowly. "She . . . doesn't . . . want . . . to . . . see . . . me." No, I said. That isn't it. It's more as though you were once caught in a stalled car on a railroad track. You'd be terribly careful about crossing gates, wouldn't you? She nodded. She grinned and put an arm around me and kissed my ear. "Let's talk about you," she said.

The year 1979 was slipping away. Almost every day at three, Kelly sat at the dining room table reading mail. She enjoyed this task because much of it came from readers of two hundred newspapers. She valued their opinions, even though some of the names they called her husband were untrue and unnatural. She had passed her fiftieth birthday; makeup barely concealed the steel-point etchings around the mouth and eyes. Now and then she forgot the arthritis in the right hip and stood too quickly, limping on one foot. The beautiful honey-bun coiffure was gone because her arms no longer had the power to brush long tresses. The lady who had always done her own hair now visited a lady who knew how to trim wild locks, how to rinse the right hue, how to shampoo and wave so that more than a semblance of the original was displayed.

It is unremarkable to state that Kelly was still the most engaging, the most captivating woman for me. In frosty ballrooms, I have seen her encode a half-dozen types of smiles which could be decoded only by me. At parties, I was surprised to find that women admired this woman. Men liked her, too, but a woman with a good figure and carriage should attract smiles of appreciation. Kelly had women friends, I think, because she knew how to smooth the harsh edges of life and living. She would never concede, for example, that any woman was ugly. She was "plain." A woman was never ignorant; she may have been "a bit too intuitive for her own good." Kelly had a special glue for mending chipped and broken dreams.

In all the years we were together, I seldom sat in bed in the morning without looking at the face on the other pillow and muttering: "Holy mackerel! It's mine!" And when, in late 1979, she was fifty and I was seventy-two, I realized that it was she who was going to need the courage now. Writing in the office, I could remember everything but the name — the man, his history, his achievements, the story down to the dullest dangling participle — but no name. Several times a day I walked back into the kitchen, gave a fatigued description of a cocky statesman, let us say, in bowler and cigar, and, without turning, she would say: "Sir Winston Churchill." There were hundreds and hundreds of these.

It was names and more than names which seemed to be stepping on me with hobnailed boots. Kathleen had attained her master's degree in social work and was living near St. Petersburg, Florida. I thought she treated men like a spoiled brat fingering a box of bonbons. Then she met a social worker named Christopher Curtler, a young man who came of a line of Virginia teachers. I realized that, for Kathleen, it was serious because she brought him home for the family scan, which now included Gayle, Paul, and Karen. He sat quietly, politely, a fairly tall young man with thinning hair, a rich smile, and a chuckle which he confined to the bottom of his throat. Within the first hour I realized that the Bishops were not scanning Curtler; he was scanning us, tapping us for bits of information; I put him down as a first-class psychologist or a second-class confidence man.

Within a few weeks, Kathleen sent a note that she was in love. She was a girl such as will play the feminine mystique as an interesting ploy, but, if she is ready to surrender to marriage, then the game ends without a winner because, when Kathleen loses her balance, she usually falls from the top of the stairs. They set a date. Kelly called the caterer. The reception was held out by the swimming pool. The combo played a lot of effervescent jazz, and one male guest danced his way through the guardrail of a bridge over the pool and out into space.

She was the last of the kittens. Kelly said: "We ought to move." The Chinese house was big for two aging people and a dog named Chang. A dog, by the way, who had no notion of his proper duties and who snored through the night. The utility bill for a month was three hundred fifty-four dollars. No one disturbed the flat blue face of the swimming pool. There was a dock on the lagoon but no boat. The sorrow of leaving that place for the final time was that it contained all of the ecstatic memories, all of the truly hard work, some of the heartaches, practically all of the hilarity, and it was the place where, without regret, we shed our maturity and traded it for age.

We bought a house, a nice place on the edge of a golf course, at Delray Beach. Kelly looked at it three times before we both said: "I like it." I wrote a check to hold the sale until the bankers had an opportunity to agonize over the mortgage. Then we went back to the Chinese house and asked ourselves what terrible thing we had done. Sixteen years is not a long time to spend in one house; many spend their lives in but one. She flipped the mail over, looking for the names of senders. Then she got excited and ripped an envelope. It was a notice from the archdiocese of Miami granting Kelly an annulment of her first marriage.

She wept. The blond head flipped upward, as I had seen it do so long ago, and the tears floated within the lids. The document meant more to her than it did to me, because, while I had not lost faith in God or in the Church, I could live comfortably in a world of daily prayer. Kelly could not. Now she cried and I had to find a way to stop it. So I said, I haven't agreed to any marriage ceremony, you know. Now that you're free to marry, maybe I'll have to think about it. This brought a little laughter in the tears. You're funny, she said. No I'm not, I said. You want me this time, you propose to me. The tears dried in a grimace of laughter. Kelly refused to propose. I refused to marry her.

Kelly dropped to one knee and said "Will you marry me — please?"

"I'll have to speak to my mother," I said. The giddiness passed and we phoned the news. Virginia Lee said: "It's about time you made us legitimate." Karen had similar feelings. Kathleen asked if Mom was going to wear a short dress or a long one (I could never comprehend why plumage enjoys a high priority), and Gayle asked who was going to give Mom away. They were happy for us — all of them. The grandchildren, who were not invited to the ceremony, saw the whole thing as "high camp."

As a Jew feels comfortable in a temple even though he may criticize the communicants and the rabbi; as a Moslem feels a relaxation of tension when he hears the melancholy call to prayer; so too I felt as though I were sitting in God's reception room when I was in church. I never enjoyed attendance at mass as far back as memory totters; it was a chore, like school attendance. In age, when life becomes dicey, many men turn to religion. Some do it without reasoning. Others compute the odds and decide to play the probabilities. My faith had not flagged, at least not to the point where I was confident that I could negotiate the rest of the voyage alone.

Saint Matthew's Church is a few hundred yards from our house. Kelly had conferences with Father Ronald Brohammer, the bearded young pastor. He was cordial, and turned the ceremony over to his associate, Father Michael Tabit. Kelly set a date and a time; the dress would be flowered, simple, attractive. I began to hate this wedding as I had the others. Nothing on the head (whatever that means). No flowers. I was reminded that I would have to go to confession and receive communion first. Nobody cared what I might wear; they expected my soul to be scrubbed.

There was a time, long ago, when I would hunt for an Italian priest who understood little English, or a Yugoslavian on a two-week visa, or even a Cuban. Sins accumulate alarmingly, like paper clips. Part of me was saying not to worry, that the priests had heard all the sins many times. The other half smirked and reminded me of some exotic ones which might not occur to an enraged orangutan. My soul shuddered. This business of confession is worthless unless it is full, complete, laden with remorse and a solemn promise never to commit those sins again. So, after judicious thought, I drove to another town on a Saturday afternoon, found a Roman Catholic church, knelt in a pew, and ransacked my mind for crimes. It wasn't easy. At times, I was alarmed at some of the memories which popped up. Is it possible, I wondered, that I am about to brag myself into a caustic dressing-down by a strange priest? It wasn't. He listened, hand shading his face, restrained himself from murmuring, and asked me to say an Act of Contrition. It was easy.

The wedding was a week away when Kelly decided to invite some people. Of course. There should be guests. Most of our families were in New Jersey. They would not be finessed into paying the air fare. There were others, book publishers, editors, writers. It would be demeaning, I thought, to invite them to give up their work in New York for twenty minutes in a Florida church. There didn't seem to be much contrast between the sacred and the ludicrous. There was no hope of filling the church unless we featured topless ushers.

So we invited some neighborhood friends. These were the people — mostly couples — who had survived sixteen years of social sifting. If they shared a trait, it was that they were serious people who didn't take themselves seriously; persons who, over a couple of scotches and cheese bits, could condemn or exalt statesmen and nations. Those who couldn't tell a terse joke could laugh at one. They were the little flecks of gold which boiled to the top of that steamy, swampy soup called Florida.

So Kelly phoned invitations to Dorrie Goldstandt, Dr. Lester Keiser and Phyllis, Hank and Helen Waldman, Mildred and Paul Frehm, Sid and Ollie Schulman, and I yelled, "For God's sake, Kelly. Invite a Christian." So she invited Gayle, and Karen and Paul, honeymooners Kathleen and Chris, Marilyn and Bill Kofoed, Kay Herman, and Gene Riggio. There was one extra invitation, but we knew it would be declined for business reasons: "Jocko" McCormack and his Lorna. They are dear friends, but they're the kind who fight extradition from Framingham, Massachusetts.

My brother, John, was best man, which is like asking assistance of a cigar-store Indian. His wife, Anna, was, what do they call it, "matron of honor." Then, of course, everything went wrong because, although Kelly had all day until seven P.M. in which to prepare herself, the dress didn't hang right, the slip was crooked, the beautician sent a substitute coiffeur, the fingernails would not dry in time, she wanted to use her old wedding ring and had trouble getting it off, the phone rang like a betting parlor, the caterer arrived early with platters and tableware, somebody left the front door open, and the dog ran up the block.

We drove to the church. John and I entered by a side entrance. The bride walked down the center aisle past a lot of empty pews. Father Tabit, properly vested, waited at the gates of the altar. "I hate these things," I whispered to John. He nodded and spoke out of the side of his mouth: "You picked a good time for it." The bride was trembling, a cogent clue to the fakery in these ceremonies. The edifice is bright and modern, an almost intimate church, unlike the old Catholic churches, which are shaped like caskets and suitably lighted within.

Father Michael was a joy. Before he began the ceremony, he nodded to the organist, who responded with peals of thunder. A tall, burly priest, Father Edward Olszewski, burst into song. He sang, not a hymn, but a popular number called "There's a Time for Us." He was good — loud and on key. John gave me the ring. Kelly held the hand out. The ring would not go on. I took it and spit on it. This caused my brother to bend over with laughter. The ring, barred by a second knuckle, went on. Father Tabit said all the solemn words. Then he said he pronounced us man and wife and I could kiss the bride. Strange, Kelly and I were the same height the night before; now she was two inches taller. I had to get on my toes to kiss her.

The wedding party returned to a pew and knelt. Father Tabit, with a little clearing of the throat, began a hesitant homily. I turned my dead-fish expression on him. He was speaking of love. Slowly, but with increasing speed, I found myself interested in the words. What he said, in fifteen minutes, I couldn't duplicate in fifteen years. It was his notion of the philosophy of true love. It wasn't pretty, as wax flowers can be; it had a growth, like dozens of tea roses on a vine. It was a symphony in color only, the most important being the giving of love, the innate desire, not to be pleased but to please; the compartmentalization of a young mother's heart in love with husband, mother, children, siblings; the timeless wear of love, which, in some instances, is more enduring at the end than at the beginning; the adding of one to one, making, not two, but many in strength and fortitude.

It was a tiny masterpiece of thought by a man who had not experienced any of it. We hurried home with our guests to chilled wine, roast beef, some cheeses, and Karen's three-layer heart-shaped chocolate cake. Two priests stopped by for the jollity. Some of the Jews wanted to ordain Father Tabit an honorary rabbi. Somebody played the piano. Father Ed sang. At midnight, Chang was in the center hall, head on paws, meditating on ankles and feet outward bound.

The dishes had been washed and stacked. Kelly waited for me to walk her to the bedroom. I checked the locks and doors and windows (the perennial son of the policeman), extinguished the lawn lights, and retired. "A lovely day," she said, undressing in her closet. I couldn't get my shoes off without sitting on a bench. I put on a white T-shirt, which keeps the chill from my shoulders and gives me the appearance of an old cherub.

The radio was turned on to schmaltzy jazz. I found a book, which constitutes heresy on a honeymoon. Kelly sat on her side of the bed in a billowy nightgown, romantic in fresh makeup with diamonds glittering coldly in ears and around the throat. "My love," I said, "I am now seventy-two years of age and I am going to read. We have now been married twice and this is positively the last time." She fell asleep giggling.

The book was not for reading; it was a springboard for thought. My father used to say that two hookers of whiskey could bring a man's youth into focus and make it appear to be better than it was. I lay there, propped up on an elbow, doing it without the whiskey. In sum, I was pleased. It is a long way back to Bramhall Avenue in Jersey City, but only a step or two around the corner to the Clinton Avenue Library, where many of my books repose. I had achieved practically everything I set out to do and had lived a couple of lives as well.

Sleep came slowly. My eyes were blinking with sand when it occurred to me that most women and men live through the full four seasons. A cogent memory showed me that I had experienced but two. There was that interminably bitter winter of numb fingers and chattering teeth, and then a verdant spring of tulips and forsythia and azalea and sparkling brooks, which endured year after year after year. The hot summer, the crisp amber of autumn never arrived.

I turned out the light. Under the sheets, my foot sneaked across the bed until it touched hers. It was a most remarkable season.